EXPERIMENTAL
SOCIAL
PSYCHOLOGY

EXPERIMENTAL
SOCIAL
PSYCHOLOGY

Edited by

Charles Graham McClintock

Published for

The Society for the Psychological Study of Social Issues

HOLT, RINEHART AND WINSTON, INC.   New York
Chicago San Francisco Atlanta Dallas Montreal Toronto London Sydney

TO DANIEL KATZ

Who as a scholar has made major contributions to social psychology in all its aspects, and as a man enjoys the love and respect of his students and colleagues.

FOREWORD

As Chairman of SPSSI's Publications Committee for over ten years, I have reviewed quite a number of proposals for books to be sponsored by SPSSI. Many were unacceptable, but not because they were unworthy of publication. The essential criterion used by the Committee expressed a basic policy laid down by SPSSI Council many years back: SPSSI should endorse and indeed sponsor the publication of books that were innovative in the sense of filling a gap or meeting the felt needs of those who taught or did research in social psychology, or even those who were more directly involved in attempts at social change in real life settings. Thus, one need only think of Newcomb and Hartley's *Readings in Social Psychology*, published in 1947, or Jahoda, Deutsch, and Cook's two-volume *Research Methods in Social Relations,* published in 1951, to see this policy put into practice. Both of these books "caught on" because indeed they met the felt needs of those who taught, did research, or were simply concerned about social psychological problems and questions.

When Charles McClintock's proposal for a "different kind" of experimental social psychology text first came across my desk, I knew immediately that this was a publishing venture SPSSI should undertake. My colleagues on the Publications Committee agreed with my own assessment that he had indeed discovered an unusual and significant way of presenting some of the basic conceptual and experimental paradigms of social psychology to students and researchers alike. In the Preface that follows, McClintock refers to the volume as an "in depth analysis" of such paradigms. But for me the uniqueness of his approach was not in the level of analysis but rather in who was to do it and how it was to be done. The conceptual and methodological development of the research model was to be given first hand; namely, by the researcher who formulated it, nurtured it, tested it, suffered through its trials and tribulations, and indeed who, because of the requirements imposed by McClintock for writing a chapter in the proposed volume, had to face up to its weaknesses and limitations as well as its strengths and assets.

The value of all this, as McClintock suggests, lies in the fact that the reader can learn in simple and direct terms how experimental research models in social psychology begin, evolve, are used, and consequently contribute to the accumulation of scientific knowledge in the field. But for me there is something even more compelling in the approach of the present volume. In a sense it represents at least a partial "blueprint" of the status of the field of experimental social psychology. It tells us not only where we have been and how we got there, but also what we can expect from renewed attacks upon complex problems in social psychology using such experimental paradigms. Ostensibly McClintock himself must have been aware of the "stark revelations" that would follow from an approach that asked researchers to present a direct, ingenuous, and self-conscious analysis of their attempts to study a particular conceptual issue. In the first three chapters of the book, particularly in Chapter 3, the basic dilemmas, issues, and obstacles involved in the use of the experimental social psychological approach are very sharply drawn.

If the "blueprint" character of this volume was appealing to me when Mc-Clintock first proposed the book some four or five years back, I find it even more so right before publication. The fact is that for a variety of reasons the field of social psychology—and particularly its underlying primary research strategy, the experimental paradigm—is at important crossroads. It is being asked by students, government officials, and community administrators alike to prove itself, to demonstrate that its accumulated knowledge not only provides understanding but also solutions to complex social problems. It should be evident that the hue and cry for "relevance" in teaching and research is really a demand for knowledge that—to use Lewin's terms—is socially useful as well as theoretically meaningful.

Research that is not theoretically meaningful cannot be socially useful in any significant sense, and the fact is that experimental social psychology has provided us with very little theoretically meaningful knowledge. Daniel Katz's appraisal of the field in the final chapter of the book is an extraordinarily perceptive analysis. Like his colleagues who wrote the first three chapters of this book, he also is straightforward when he states:

> Of the thousands of experimental studies published in social psychology in the past 20 years, the number that supplies new information to a cumulative body of knowledge is surprisingly small. A great deal of the experimental effort has been without impact not because of poor method but because of the lack of ideas behind the work. The development of experimental social psychology has been costly if the energy input is compared to the significant output [p. 557].

Does this mean we should discard the experimental paradigm in social psychology? Absolutely not. What is at fault is not the model but the way in which it has been used. According to Daniel Katz what has been lacking is "ideas," and we would add that the lack of ideas reflects the almost obsessive desire to achieve scientific respectability by the use of the experimental model in the narrowly defined context of the college laboratory. Thus, it is evident that not only must the field of experimental social psychology evolve new and more potent theoretical conceptions, but it must be willing to use its basic research paradigm with greater flexibility in a variety of data collection contexts. The model must be adapted to the nature of the phenomena being studied and not the obverse. It is time to risk being somewhat less respectable scientifically in the hope of eventually being more productive in the accumulation of scientific knowledge.

How to proceed and in what directions to move at this point in the development of experimental social psychology are, of course, very difficult questions to answer. Yet to begin even thinking about them, one must know what has happened, and just where, how, and with what results the experimental paradigm has been applied. The McClintock volume is by no means complete but it indeed includes most of the significant areas of investigation undertaken with respect to individual function and group process. The key and indeed most influential concepts of the last twenty years are covered: cognitive dissonance, attitude change, person perception, social facilitation, conformity, group decision, bargaining, game behavior, and others. The student and interested researcher, as we already suggested, are directly immersed in the research process not only by being given a simple and direct account by those who formulated and tested their own experimental paradigms, but more importantly by the authors' reflection upon the dilemmas, limitations, and even doubts that often attend the research process. In a sense then—particularly if he uses the first three chapters and the last chapter of the book as a guiding framework—the reader may learn and understand not only what to do in the formulation and development of experimental paradigms in social psychology but also what not to do.

But there is much more that the perceptive younger reader may get from this volume. If, as Daniel Katz suggests, the development of social psychology during the last twenty years has been costly because there was relatively little return from our considerable investment of energy, then today's crop of new young researchers must be ready to think twice before continuing this investment pattern. Clearly there are indications in the volume of where particular research paradigms paid off and where they did not. It provides both implicitly and explicitly a frank and critical appraisal of our research efforts in experimental social psychology, and in this sense it *challenges* the researchers to break away from established modes of thinking both theoretically and methodologically. If Daniel Katz's final chapter does anything, it unquestionably precludes an air of acceptance or complacency on the part of either the young or experienced researcher insofar as the status of the field of experimental social psychology is concerned. Because social psychology like other behavioral science fields is at important crossroads at this point in its history, Charles McClintock's volume is both timely and significant. We had better know where we have been and what we have done to get there if we expect to make a sagacious choice in the direction that experimental social psychology should go in the next twenty-year period.

Harold M. Proshansky
Graduate Center
The City University of New York

PREFACE

This volume was undertaken to meet the frequently expressed need for a book that would provide the reader with an in-depth analysis of some of the fundamental conceptual and experimental paradigms employed in social psychology. There are, to be sure, numerous textbooks, handbooks, annual reviews, collected readings, and journal articles devoted to describing, reviewing, and summarizing conceptual and empirical efforts in social psychology from both a psychological and a sociological perspective. However, at the time this volume was initiated, there were few, if any, textbooks or references that described the conceptual and methodological development of a representative group of major research paradigms in experimental social psychology in nontechnical terms. It was this editor's belief that a book could be written in which a number of paradigms would be presented with sufficient simplicity and detail that readers, with or without strong behavioral or social science backgrounds, would be able to perceive the manner in which theory and method develop and interact in the process of accumulating scientific knowledge. And, perhaps the reader might even feel himself a part of the scientific process wherein prior work is reviewed, assumptions are made, hypotheses are formulated, measures are developed, experiments are designed, methodological problems are encountered and resolved, results are analyzed and interpreted, hypotheses are reformulated, and the whole complex and fascinating process is reiterated in the hope of achieving a greater understanding of man's social behavior.

In order to complete such a volume, it was necessary to enlist the aid of eminent scientists working with given paradigms in particular research areas. Only such individuals, drawn from both the psychological and sociological traditions of social psychology, would possess the requisite knowledge and experience necessary to describe and evaluate a given research paradigm in detail. This, of course, implied that the volume would be multi-authored, and, indeed, twenty-five authors and co-authors finally participated in its preparation.

In undertaking a volume of this magnitude, it also seemed appropriate to ask SPSSI, the *Society for the Psychological Study of Social Issues*, to act as a sponsor for the project, since it would require the coordinated efforts of a number of social psychologists, and because SPSSI had sponsored a number of multi-authored volumes in the past to promote the development of theory, research, and application in various areas of social psychology. The organization agreed to undertake this role, and appointed Professor Harold Proshansky to act as liaison between SPSSI, the editor, and the publisher. In addition, SPSSI recommended an appropriate editorial advisory committee for the project. Happily all those nominated agreed and served in this capacity: Professors Donald Campbell, Harold Gerard, Daniel Katz, Harold Kelley, William McGuire, David Messick, Jozef M. Nuttin, Jr., Harold Proshansky, and Robert Zajonc.

The next major task was to decide which experimental paradigms in social psychology should be represented in the book. After soliciting a number of recommendations, a group of research areas was chosen which seemed to fairly represent the field. The editorial advisory committee then recommended a list of potential contributors who had developed or were developing conceptual and empirical paradigms in each of these areas. These scholars were then contacted and all but two agreed to participate; the two who declined recommended alternative authors, who in turn agreed. Subsequently, two from the original list of contributors withdrew for personal or professional reasons. As a result, a chapter in Section I on computer applications in social psychology was replaced by the chapter entitled "Problems and Anxieties in Research," and an intended original chapter on dissonance was replaced by the present chapter by Sherwood, Barron, and Fitch, which, although it had appeared elsewhere, clearly met the goals of the project.

As noted previously, the principal purpose of the present volume is to provide a description and intensive analysis of a representative group of experimental paradigms in social psychology. In meeting this goal, it was decided that the initial section of the book should include a general discussion of the role of theory, a review of the principal research designs, and an analysis of the major methodological problems in the experimental study of social behavior at the individual, interindividual, and group levels. Following this section, the subsequent four sections include thirteen chapters (Chapters 4–16) each of which reviews one major experimental paradigm. The authors of individual chapters are, in most instances, scholars who have been deeply involved in research utilizing the paradigm under discussion. As one would anticipate, those with a sociological orientation are more strongly represented within those sections that focus upon paradigms for investigating social interaction and group structure and membership, whereas those with a psychological orientation are more strongly represented in sections concerned with the social psychology of the individual and group influence upon individual behavior. The final section of the book considers the relationship between experimental social psychology and the field of social psychology as a whole. The author, Daniel Katz, is eminently qualified for this task, since he has been actively involved in the major areas of social psychology—in basic and applied research in laboratory and field settings.

This book has been organized to serve several potential readerships. Chapters can be sampled to fit the needs of the audience, since each paradigm is described independently of the others. In general, the contributors have assumed an elementary knowledge of statistics, although readers without any statistical background will be able to follow most of the discussions in the book. An appendix appears at the end of the book, in which are defined most of the statistical terms that appear in the various chapters. The author, David Messick, is both a social psychologist and a statistician, and the reader who is unfamiliar with or has forgotten a particular statistical or mathematical term should find this section helpful.

The book was prepared with the following possible audiences in mind:

1. Students in a first course in social psychology where the instructor wishes to focus strongly upon an experimental approach to social behavior.
2. Students in upper-division courses in experimental social psychology which may or may not have accompanying laboratories.
3. Students in first-year graduate survey courses in various departments in the behavioral sciences.
4. Students in more applied programs in the social sciences, including education, social work, and management science, who can use this book as an introduction to experimental studies of social behavior and to the role of theory and methodology in such efforts.
5. Professionals in the social and behavioral sciences interested in theory and methods in the social sciences and in an in-depth review of a number of contemporary conceptual and experimental paradigms in social psychology.

In concluding, it should be noted that the present volume reflects the efforts of many persons. The editorial advisory committee has contributed time, energy, and wisdom in advising this editor, and in reviewing and commenting on the various chapters. It is, of course, the chapter contributors themselves who have carried the major work load of the project. Each of them is highly involved in the development of theory and research, and must also meet the other responsibilities that attend an academic career. Furthermore, the years in which the chapters were being written placed even heavier demands than usual upon members of most academic communities, since they were a time of confrontation and turmoil. The editor and SPSSI are indeed grateful to the authors for the extra work they assumed without remuneration in preparing the various chapters. This editor would also like to express his appreciation to Hal Proshansky, SPSSI's representative to the project, for his guidance and encouragement. The publisher's representatives, Tom Davies and Deborah Doty, have contributed technical advice and have shown remarkable patience in the face of the delays that invariably accompany a project of this sort.

In addition, the editor would like to thank those unsung heroes of the academic world who contribute much to the development of a professor, his graduate students. Many of the more compelling criticisms and astute suggestions for revision of manuscripts, including the editor's, have come from the following group, most of whom will be developing under the guidance of their own graduate students when this book appears: Steve McNeel, Dan Williams, Mike Kuhlman, Frank Stech, Rusty Campos, and Jim Livingston. For two of the years during which the editor was coordinating the project, he was in a visiting status at two of Europe's most distinguished psychological research institutes. Both Dr. George Vassiliou, Director of the Athenian Institute of Anthropos, Greece, and Professor Jozef M. Nuttin, Jr., Director of the Laboratory for Experimental Social Psychology at the University of Louvain, Belgium, have created in their institutes environments supportive of research and other professional activities on the part of visitors and nonvisitors alike. Finally, the editor would like to acknowledge his debt to his harshest and most constructive critic, Evie.

Charles G. McClintock
Editor

ACKNOWLEDGMENTS

Chapter 1

Excerpt from Thibaut & Kelley (1959) used with the permission of John Wiley & Sons, Inc.
Excerpt from Katz & Kahn (1966) used with the permission of John Wiley & Sons, Inc.
Excerpt from McGuire (1960) used with the permission of Yale University Press.

Chapter 2

Table 2.1 from Campbell & Stanley (1963) used with the permission of the publisher.
  Copyright by the American Educational Research Association, Washington, D.C.

Chapter 4

Excerpts from R. B. Zajonc (1960) used with the permission of the author and *Public
  Opinion Quarterly*.

Chapter 7

Figure 7.1 from data in Bergum & Lehr (1963) used with the permission of the author
  and the *Journal of Applied Psychology*. Copyright 1963 by the American Psychological
  Association.
Figure 7.2 from data in Harlow (1932) used with the permission of the author and
  The Journal of Genetic Psychology. Copyright 1932 by The Journal Press.
Figure 7.4 from Gates & Allee (1933) used with the permission of the author and the
  Journal of Comparative Psychology. Copyright 1933 by the American Psychological
  Association.
Figure 7.6 from Horenstein (1951) used with the permission of the author and the
  Journal of Comparative and Physiological Psychology. Copyright 1951 by the American
  Psychological Association.
Figure 7.8 from data in Lee (1961) used with the permission of the author and the *Journal
  of Experimental Psychology*. Copyright 1961 by the American Psychological Association.
Figure 7.9 from data in Zajonc & Nieuwenhuyse (1964) used with the permission of the
  author and the *Journal of Experimental Psychology*. Copyright 1964 by the American
  Psychological Association.
Figure 7.10 from Cottrell et al. (1968) used with the permission of the author and the
  the *Journal of Personality and Social Psychology*. Copyright 1968 by the American
  Psychological Association.
Figure 7.11 from data in Zajonc et al. (1970) used with the permission of the author and
  Experimental Social Psychology. Copyright 1970 by Academic Press, Inc.

Figure 7.12 from data in Cottrell et al. (1967) used with the permission of the author and the *Journal of Personality*. Copyright 1967 by Duke University Press.

Figure 7.13 from data in Matlin & Zajonc (1968) used with the permission of the author and the *Journal of Personality and Social Psychology*. Copyright 1968 by the American Psychological Association.

Figure 7.14 and *Tables 7.3* and *7.4* from Zajonc et al. (1969) used with the permission of the author and the *Journal of Personality and Social Psychology*. Copyright 1969 by the American Psychological Association.

Figure 7.15 from Tolman (1968b) used with the permission of the author.

Table 7.5 from Paulus & Murdoch (1971) used with the permission of the author and the *Journal of Experimental Social Psychology*. Copyright 1971 by Academic Press, Inc.

Chapter 8

Excerpt from Edward E. Jones & Harold B. Gerard, *Foundations of Social Psychology*. Copyright © 1967 by John Wiley & Sons, Inc. Reprinted by permission.

Excerpt and *Table 8.1* from Gerard et al. (1968) used with the permission of the author and the *Journal of Personality and Social Psychology*. Copyright 1968 by the American Psychological Association.

Chapter 10

Excerpt from *Bargaining and Group Decision Making*, by S. Siegel & L. E. Fouraker. Copyright 1960 by McGraw-Hill. Used with the permission of McGraw-Hill Book Company.

Figure 10.2 from "Interaction Process and the Attainment of Maximum Joint Profit," by H. H. Kelley in S. Messick & A. H. Brayfield (Eds.), *Decision and Choice*. Copyright 1964 by McGraw-Hill. Used with the permission of McGraw-Hill Book Company.

Chapter 11

Excerpt from Caplow (1956) used with the permission of the author and the *American Sociological Review*. Copyright 1956 by the American Sociological Association.

Table 11.1 from Stryker & Psathas (1960) used with the permission of the author and *Sociometry*. Copyright 1960 by the American Sociological Association.

Tables 11.2–11.4 from Vinacke & Arkoff (1957) used with the permission of the author and *American Sociological Review*. Copyright 1957 by the American Sociological Association.

Tables 11.5–11.8 from Psathas & Stryker (1965) used with the permission of the author and *Sociometry*. Copyright 1965 by the American Sociological Association.

Table 11.9 from Gamson (1961a) used with the permission of the author and *American Sociological Review*. Copyright 1961 by the American Sociological Association.

Chapter 12

Tables 12.1–12.3 from Hoffman (1959) used with the permission of the *Journal of Abnormal and Social Psychology*. Copyright 1959 by the American Psychological Association.

Tables 12.4–12.5 from Hoffman & Maier (1961) used with the permission of the *Journal of Abnormal and Social Psychology*. Copyright 1961 by the American Psychological Association.

Table 12.6 from Levy (1964) used with the permission of the *Journal of Abnormal and Social Psychology*. Copyright 1964 by the American Psychological Association.

Chapter 13

Figure 13.1 from Burnstein & Zajonc (1965b) used with the permission of the author and *Sociometry*. Copyright 1965 by the American Sociological Association.

Tables 13.1, 13.2, and *13.4* from Burnstein & Zajonc (1965a) used with the permission of the author and *Sociometry.* Copyright 1965 by the American Sociological Association.

Excerpt, *Tables 13.5–13.7,* and *Figures 13.2–13.4* from Burnstein & Wolosin (1968) used with the permission of the author and the *Journal of Experimental Social Psychology.* Copyright 1968 by Academic Press, Inc.

Chapter 14

Table 14.1 from Torrance (1955) used with permission.

Chapter 16

Tables 16.4–16.6 from Slater (1955) used with the permission of the author and *American Sociological Review.* Copyright 1955 by the American Sociological Association.

Table 16.10 from Burke (1967) used with the permission of the author and *Sociometry.* Copyright 1967 by the American Sociological Association.

Excerpts and *Tables 16.12* and *16.13* from Burke (1968) used with the permission of the author and *Sociometry.* Copyright 1968 by the American Sociological Association.

CONTRIBUTORS

Elliot Aronson *Department of Psychology, University of Texas at Austin*

James W. Barron *Graduate School of Business Administration, University of California at Los Angeles*

Gordon Becker *Department of Psychology, University of Nebraska at Omaha*

Linda Bell *Department of Psychology, Duke University*

Joseph Berger *Department of Sociology, Stanford University*

Peter J. Burke *Department of Sociology, Indiana University*

Eugene Burnstein *Department of Psychology, University of Michigan*

Donald Campbell *Department of Psychology, Northwestern University*

Bernard P. Cohen *Department of Sociology, Stanford University*

Edward S. Conolley *Department of Psychology, University of Southern California at Los Angeles*

Nickolas B. Cottrell *Department of Psychology, University of Iowa*

H. Gordon Fitch *School of Business, University of Kansas*

Harold B. Gerard *Department of Psychology, University of California at Los Angeles*

Edward E. Jones *Department of Psychology, Duke University*

Daniel Katz *Department of Psychology, University of Michigan*

Stuart Katz *Department of Psychology, University of Michigan*

Harold H. Kelley *Department of Psychology, University of California at Los Angeles*

Charles G. McClintock *Department of Psychology, University of California at Santa Barbara*

William J. McGuire *Department of Psychology, Yale University*

David M. Messick *Department of Psychology, University of California at Santa Barbara*

Norman Miller *Department of Psychology, University of Minnesota at Minneapolis*

Jozef M. Nuttin, Jr. *Psychologisch Instituut, University of Louvain, Louvain, Belgium*

Harold Proshansky *Graduate Center, City University of New York*

Paul C. Rosenblatt *Division of Family Social Science, University of Minnesota at St. Paul*

Dietmar P. Schenitzki *Department of Psychology, State University of New York at Geneseo*

John J. Sherwood *Department of Psychology, Purdue University*

Sheldon Stryker *Department of Sociology, Indiana University*

Robert Zajonc *Department of Psychology, University of Michigan*

Morris Zelditch, Jr. *Department of Sociology, Stanford University*

Robert C. Ziller *Department of Psychology, University of Oregon*

CONTENTS

EXPERIMENTAL
SOCIAL
PSYCHOLOGY

section one
THEORY AND METHODS

The first three chapters of this book review the principal theoretical and methodological goals of the field of experimental social psychology, the major strategies for and obstacles to reaching these goals, and the current status of the field relative to attaining these objectives. It is intended that these initial chapters will aid the reader in developing his own set of criteria for understanding and evaluating the more specific conceptual and experimental paradigms presented in Chapters 4 through 16. One could argue that a more effective didactic approach would be to confront the reader immediately with a series of specific paradigms, and then conclude with a more abstract consideration of theory and method. In a limited way the present book utilizes both strategies. The last chapter, Chapter 17, of the present contains a summary critical review of the field in terms of both its history and its relationship to related disciplines.

In Chapter 1 by Becker and McClintock, the proposition is advanced that theory plays a number of essential functions in man's continuous effort to order and to understand the nature of his environment and those who inhabit it. Formal theory is viewed as both a pragmatic vehicle for the development and evaluation of social and psychological knowledge, and as an ideal towards which the scientific community strives. At the same time, the limitations of theory are recognized insofar as it is a human product, and, as such, it is subject to the uncertainties and biases of any man-constructed view of the world.

It is immediately apparent that judged against the stringent requirements established in the natural sciences, social psychological theory is lacking in scope, formalization, and precision. What the reader will indeed discover as he reviews the multitude of relatively limited conceptual systems introduced in the various chapters of this volume is that the field contains a number of rather narrowly circumscribed conceptual systems for dealing with a small number of variables, and a limited number of experimental paradigms that have been developed to evaluate each of these conceptual schemes. This, in part, reflects our theoretical and methodological inability to consider within one system the total complexity of social behavior and the multitude of interacting processes that serve as its determinants.

There are those who would argue that conducting studies utilizing limited sets of variables impedes the scientific process insofar as the most that one will discover is a diverse collection of findings which hold only under very limited conditions. Rather than enter this argument, it is sufficient to note that the present conceptual and methodological status of the field necessarily leads to the utilization of relatively restricted conceptual and empirical paradigms. Whether the findings thus obtained will contribute to substantial increases in our knowledge remains an empirical question for which only the future can provide an answer.

Chapters 2 and 3 by Rosenblatt and Miller focus primarily on the principal research designs that can be employed to test hypotheses in social psychology, and on the major obstacles to obtaining valid findings. More specifically, Chapter 2 describes various types of experimental and quasi-experimental designs that can be used to assess whether a relationship exists between two or more social psychological processes or events. These designs are systematically evaluated in terms of the major classes of uncontrolled variables that can confound one's observation and thereby reduce the internal or external validity of one's findings; for example, the nonequivalence of experimental and control groups, the effects of the measurement process itself, and possible sources of interaction between selection of subjects and the treatment they receive.

Chapter 3 outlines other major problems in social psychological investigations. The reader should be forewarned that the chapter reads somewhat like "The Perils of Pauline" insofar as the authors indeed identify a number of major problems that can befall any investigator who utilizes humans as subjects. One of the major pitfalls is the investigator's ability to influence unintentionally, yet systematically, the subjects' behavior, as well as certain unconscious predispositions which may lead an observer to be selective in recording and interpreting another's behavior. The preceding represent two of a number of sources of experimenter bias in social psychological research. One is also confronted with the fact that an individual who knowingly participates in an experiment may experience certain demands upon him which result in behaviors that cannot be generalized outside of the specific experimental setting in which they were obtained. There is indeed a real danger that experimental social psychology cannot produce valid theories of the social behavior of humans when its investigations are restricted to laboratory settings. This problem is receiving considerable attention by social psychologists. The reader who is interested in various ways in which one can reduce or eliminate such experimental demand characteristics will find a recent book by Webb, Campbell, Schwartz, and Sechrest entitled *Unobtrusive Measures: Nonreactive Research in the Social Sciences* (1966) to be of great interest. An excellent example of nonreactive research, which in effect implies that the observed is unaware that his behavior is being observed, is contained in the work on status reported by Zelditch in Chapter 15 of this volume.

Chapter 3 also considers the fundamental question of whether identical instructions or manipulations are psychologically equivalent across subjects. The problem of stimulus equivalence is not unique to experimental social psychology, and is but one example of a fundamental requirement in the development of any science. In effect, it relates directly to the fact that in order to define or assess differences in the behavior of any object, physical or social, one must first achieve standardization in one's constructs, one's manipulations, and one's measures. Osgood (1964) succinctly summarizes the range of problems which this question of identity raises with three simple questions, "When is the same really the same?" "When is the same really different?" "When is different really the same?" Precise responses to these questions are necessary in the development of valid theories and rigorous methodologies.

Finally, Rosenblatt and Miller confront the two ethical problems which all experimental social psychologists must consider, namely, "What are the ethical implications of deceiving human subjects?" "Does collecting data about an individual's attitudes or behavior represent an invasion of his privacy?" These indeed are serious questions, and to date the profession has put forth somewhat equivocal sets of standards regarding ethical conduct in these areas. Webb et al. (1966) observe that we need, not only a general ethical code, but also more specific criteria for evaluating, for any given project, the possible costs and rewards for those "multiple interests potentially threatened by social science research: the privacy of the individual, his freedom from manipulation, the protection of the aura of trust on which the society depends, and, by no means least important, the good reputation of the social sciences [p. vii]."

In concluding this introduction to Section I, it should be pointed out that many of the theoretical and methodological issues raised in these initial chapters will be discussed repeatedly throughout this book within the context of specific conceptual and experimental paradigms. It is to be hoped that this redundancy will provide the reader with a more specific understanding of the many points raised in Section I, and thereby precisely demonstrate the relevance of these issues in any attempt to understand the social determinants of human behavior.

And, finally, we would call to the reader's attention the appendix of statistical terms and definitions which appears at the end of this book. Although a concerted attempt has been made to minimize the amount of statistical knowledge required to understand the following chapters, concepts may be introduced with which the reader is unfamiliar or whose meaning he has forgotten. Should the reader encounter statistical or methodological terms which require explanation (such as analysis of variance, correlation, mean, reliability, or validity) he may consult the appendix.

REFERENCES

Osgood, C. Semantic differential techniques in the comparative study of cultures. *American Anthropologist,* 1964, **66,** 171–200.

Webb, E., Campbell, D., Schwartz, R., & Sechrest, L. *Unobtrusive measures: Nonreactive research in the social sciences.* Chicago: Rand McNally, 1966.

SCIENTIFIC THEORY
AND SOCIAL PSYCHOLOGY

Gordon Becker
Charles G. McClintock[1]

Every scientist, regardless of his specialty, is involved in the search for order in the physical, biological, and social world. The art of science and its methods of inquiry represent a single subsystem among many human enterprises. This scientific subculture (McCain & Segal, 1969), like other cultures, has distinguishing features. These features are the primary foci of the present chapter, especially those that characterize social psychology.

A subculture can perhaps best be described as a grouping of individuals who are part of a larger culture, and who can be distinguished by their behavior, which follows a more or less common set of norms or rules, their ideology, which reflects a common value system, and their language, which permits them to transmit and to share norms, rules, and values. The scientists' norms include rules for generating, evaluating, and disseminating knowledge. Scientific values stress "truth," "reliability" (the ability to replicate and duplicate experiments and observations), and precision in word and deed. The language of science is highly stylized and formal, with considerable emphasis on clarity and conciseness.

The present book in a very fundamental sense is designed to help indoctrinate the reader into the scientific subculture of social psychology. The reader will be exposed in these pages to the norms, the value system, and the language of this discipline. It is only through such exposure that one can understand, evaluate, and participate in the work that goes on within a given field of scientific inquiry. This process involves learning the explicitly stated aspects of the subculture, and obtaining an intuitive grasp of the many facts, assumptions, and most cherished values which are not explicitly recognized by its members.

The present chapter attempts to characterize the role of theory in social psychology as well as in the scientific enterprise in general. In the sciences,

[1] The preparation of this chapter was supported in part by Grant R01 HD03258, National Institute of Child Health and Human Development.

social psychology can be identified as a special branch aligned with both psychology and sociology. At one time, the latter were special branches of philosophy. All three major parent disciplines continue to exert a strong theoretical influence on their offspring. In recent years social psychology has often attempted to disown or ignore its philosophical roots, and to minimize the importance of theory within social psychology. However, the science continues to be influenced by its heritage, and there remain social psychologists engaged in theory construction.

In considering the role of theory in social psychology, we will discuss how theory functions across disciplines within the scientific subculture. To illustrate some of our points, we will draw upon an existing social psychological model, namely, a syllogistic analysis of cognitive relations advanced by McGuire (1960). The reader will recall that a syllogism represents a logical form of analysis in which a major and a minor premise are stated, and that if both are true, there follows a conclusion which also must be true. The following statements are of this form: (a) *Minor premise*: Theory organizes knowledge; (b) *Major premise*: Organizing knowledge is valuable; (c) *Conclusion*: Therefore, theory is valuable. McGuire employs such a syllogistic model to evaluate whether an individual's beliefs can be characterized as "logical" or "wishful," and as a basis for understanding the social psychological forces giving rise to changes in beliefs.

Defining Science

Although it is difficult to define science, most scientists would probably accept Albert Einstein's statement (1953) that:

> Science is the century-old endeavor to bring together by means of systematic thought the perceptible phenomena of this world into as thoroughgoing an association as possible. To put it boldly, it is the attempt at the posterior reconstruction of existence by the process of conceptualization. . . . It is the aim of science to establish general rules which determine the reciprocal connection of objects and events in time and space. For these rules, or laws of nature, absolutely general validity is required—not proven. It is mainly a program, and faith in the possibility of its accomplishment in principle is only founded on partial success. . . . Although it is true that it is the goal of science to discover rules which permit the association and foretelling of facts, this is not its only aim. It also seeks to reduce the connections discovered to the smallest possible number of mutually independent conceptual elements. It is in this striving after the rational unification of the manifold that it encounters its greatest success, even though it is precisely this attempt which causes it in turn to run the greatest risk of falling prey to illusions. But whoever has undergone the intense experience of successful advances made in this domain, is moved by profound reverence for the rationality made manifest in existence [p. 601–606].

In this chapter we equate any scientific theory in social psychology with an attempt to state a rational unification of concepts, laws, and connections that pertain to social behavior. Such a theory not only represents an attempt at a "rational unification of the manifold," but also predisposes the observer to view the world in a particular fashion, to collect only certain data on which subsequent laws and connections are built. The views of the experimentalist and of the theorist, their search for and construction of reality, are a product of their own prior knowledge, experience, and concerns. They reflect and express the existing scientific subculture of a particular discipline. New theories are always a product of older theories and cultures since the data for the new theory is a result of observation based on the older theories and cultures. Hence, theory, like all knowledge, is relative, not absolute, and the scientist, like all members of any subculture, is subject to "falling prey to illusions" of his historical antecedents. There exists no certain path to escape one's heritage (P. Frank, 1953).

Theories serve many purposes, one of which is filling the void in man's ability to answer questions about himself and his world. Most people, including many scientists, find it difficult to endure uncertainty, or to admit that they are unable to answer any question, or to conceive of a world in which there are events that no one can explain. Theories not only provide comfort to such people, they also organize old answers and generate new ones by providing a framework for known facts. This framework permits men to store knowledge in a way that facilitates the comparing of new facts with old, makes it easier to retrieve facts relevant to current problems, and accentuates any inconsistencies or gaps in the body of accumulated facts.

The inconsistencies and gaps disclosed by a theory serve to motivate research within those areas and to encourage scientists to resolve the inconsistencies. A theory also serves to generate new knowledge by providing a system for deducing new relationships and facts from existing ones. However, a poor theory can lead to wasted effort by encouraging logicians to deduce false facts from false premises in the theory, and by inducing experimentalists to follow erroneous leads and fictitious problems. The amount of research, the number of studies generated by a theory, and the number of resulting publications should be distinguished from the amount of new or useful information that a theory produces. A false theory may generate mountains of useless data and a wealth of experiments that lead nowhere.

THE ELEMENTS OF THEORY

Since in essence theory is a framework that dictates what to observe, how to record the observations, how to transform observations into data, and how to draw conclusions from data, a theory can be described as a set of rules. These rules must be stated in some language, a set of sentences. Such sentences are asserted to provide a true description of the real world. Some of the sentences must be accepted on faith—others must be proven to be true before they are accepted.

Axioms

Those sentences accepted without proof are called the axioms of the theory. Sentences that are proven to be logical consequences of the axioms are called theorems. Those sentences that are proven to be consistent with observation and axioms are called laws. Most scientific theories include as part of their axioms, the theories from other branches of science. Logic and mathematics are always adopted implicitly in social psychological theory without reference to the particular arithmetical, physical, or logical systems that are to be included.

For example, in McGuire's theory of beliefs, he postulates that an individual's beliefs are "logical" to the degree that these beliefs or expectations on related issues meet the formal logical requirements of syllogistic analysis. In effect, this formulation uses a logical-theoretical model to evaluate the logic of human behavior in the empirical world.[2] Most social psychologists also accept current physical theories as part of the axiom system, especially those aspects related to the description and measurement of physical attributes in time and space. Kurt Lewin (1943, 1951), another social psychologist, borrowed a number of terms from physics (e.g., vector, valence, and energy) in his attempt to construct a field theory that would account for the dynamic as well as the structural basis of human social behavior.[3] Such theoretical interrelationships unite the various sciences and make every scientist reluctant to accept any theory that contradicts facts established in any other branch of science.

Primitives

Some of the words or forms that comprise the language of a theory are defined in terms of other words that are not defined within the language. If every word had to be defined in terms of other words, it would lead to an infinite regress with an infinite number of words in the language. In order to avoid such a condition, without in turn creating a vicious circle in which words appear in their own definitions, some words in the language are accepted as meaningful without definition. These words are called primitive or undefined words. Often these primitive words refer to things at which one can point, or to qualities and relationships that can be demonstrated.

McGuire's definition (1960) of the term *cognition* provides an example of the use of primitives:

> By a "cognition" we mean a response by which a person indicates his assent to the assignment of an event to a given position on a dimension of variability. "Event" here refers to any object of judgment, whether a physical entity, a be-

---

[2] McGuire maintains that logical thinking can be defined by the following expression: "$((a \text{ n } b) \text{ u } k) \rightarrow c$, namely, if a person assents to both a and b, or if he assents to k, then to be logical he must also assent to c [p. 68]."

[3] A more extensive exposition of Lewinian theory can be found in Cartwright (1959); Deutsch (1968); Deutsch and Krauss (1965); and Leeper (1943).

havior, an occurrence, a contingency or a combination thereof (e.g., El Greco's "Toledo," my voting in the next election, man's reaching the moon, or the probation of swimming at public beaches) [p. 67].

The primitives in his definition are those forms which he defines by pointing to examples: a "physical entity" (El Greco's *Toledo*); a "behavior" (my voting in the next election); or an "occurrence" (man's reaching the moon).

Data or Facts

Some of the axioms in a theory describe the rules for translating observations into the words and concepts used in the theory, that is, for translating from the scientists' raw sense experiences to sentences in the theory language. The sentences formed from applying these rules to experience (observation) are called data or facts. A fact is expressed by a sentence which purports to describe something actually experienced. The sentence itself is a translation from sensations to words.

The facts or sentences constructed in accordance with the axioms of a theory are accepted as true within the theory. For example, to obtain data to test his theory of beliefs, McGuire scattered a number of propositions from various syllogisms within a questionnaire. Subjects were then asked to rate the "truth" probability of each proposition on a scale from 0 to 100. In his theoretical statement, McGuire explicitly postulates that the answers of subjects on this scale can be given numerical values consistent with the axioms of probability theory. By applying the rules of formal logic to these ratings, an estimate of "logicality" is obtained from subjects, and these numbers are considered as facts or data sentences for that theory.

It should be noted that if the axioms for translating experience into sentences differ for two theories, the facts and data based on the same experience may differ for the two theories. Thus, sentences called facts or data in one theory need not be accepted as fact or data by another theory (Turner, 1965; Maslow, 1965). Nothing is sacred when one changes from theory to theory.

For example, in an experiment on attitudes towards marijuana, the data collected would depend on the theory being tested. Some theorists might require recording subjects' words, mannerisms, and physiological responses; others might require more or less or different observations. Consider a situation in which 100 students are asked to indicate whether they are for or against smoking marijuana. Suppose that 50 indicate they are against smoking pot. Some theorists might consider it a "fact" that 50 of the 100 are against smoking pot. However, some theories that include consideration of the effects of conformity pressures would not accept such a conclusion from the above description, but would require that additional data regarding the biases of the data collectors and the method under which the responses were elicited also be included. If it were not possible to measure the biases of the data collectors, some theorists would consider the experiment and the results meaningless and uninterpretable, whereas others would consider these features irrelevant and completely ignore them. In this example, the "facts" of the different theories involved merely the modification of one set of observations by the addition of another set. Sometimes, however, the differences between two conflicting theories may be so complex that reconciliation of the "facts" is impossible, and, in these cases, completely different aspects of the situation may need to be observed.

Theorems and Models

In addition to axioms for translating experience into sentences, every theory contains axioms that are assumed to describe the empirical world. These axioms and the theorems which are logical consequences of the axioms, combine to form a model of the real world (Lachman, 1960; Turner, 1965). In order to determine whether or not a theory is valid, the model or the theorem is compared with observed facts. Thus the facts, that is, sentences generated both from experience and from some of the axioms of the theory, are compared with other sentences generated from other axioms and theorems of one's model. If the sentences obtained from these different parts of the theory do not correspond, the model, and hence the theory, is said to be invalid. A single exception proves the theory wrong. Scientific theories can be proven false by a single instance. However, a theory can never be proven to be true: empirical evidence can at best support a theory (Popper, 1963). In order to prove a theory true, it would be necessary to prove every sentence in the theory to be true for all times—an impossible requirement.

Let us again use the attitudinal theory of McGuire as an example. It postulates that one of two conditions obtains in the real world: (a) an individual's beliefs are logical (follow the syllogistical model); or (b) they are "wishful," that is, they are desirable regardless of truth or likelihood. Given these assumptions, plus several that are unstated in the theory, the following theorems are derived: (a) initial levels of belief in logically related propositions contain a compromise between logical and wishful thinking; and (b) inconsistency-reducing changes brought about by authoritative messages arguing for the truth of a premise are more persistent than inconsistency-increasing changes. It is this model of the real world that McGuire tests empirically by evaluating and attempting to manipulate the subject's ratings of the truth value and desirability of outcomes of the various propositions of syllogisms. And, in fact, his data support the first, but not the second, of these theorems.

Hypotheses and Laws

Some of the sentences that can be formed in the language of the theory are of the form, "If . . ., then . . .," where the two parts "If . . .," and "then. . . ." are both statements that would be called facts if certain observations occurred. Sentences of this type are called hypotheses and are used to test the validity of the theory. If a hypothesis is logically consistent with the axioms and the facts, the theory is supported. If the facts are inconsistent with such a hypothesis, the theory is proven wrong.

McGuire conducts a number of empirical studies to test various hypotheses deriving from his theoretical statement. For purposes of example, let us examine one. He hypothesizes that a first elicitation of beliefs (including rating the truth value and the desirability of syllogistic propositions) would sensitize the subjects to (logical) inconsistencies, so that an adjustment away from the wishful thinking distortion (and towards logical thinking) would be found in the second session. Stated in an "If . . ., then. . . ." form, his hypothesis might read: "If subjects are sensitized to logical inconsistency in the first presentation of a set of syllogistic propositions, then they will tend to be more logical in their thinking in a second presentation." In this instance, the hypothesis was indeed supported by the data obtained from subjects.

A hypothesis may be qualified by such phrases as: "For any x, if x . . ., then. . . ." "For some x, if x . . ., then. . . ." "If and only if . . ., then. . . ." The conditions described in the qualifying phrase serve to limit the generality of the hypothesis. Some scientists consider the conditions described in the "If . . ." phrase as the "cause" of the condition described in the "Then . . ." phrase. However, many philosophers and scientists do not accept such correlations as cause-effect relationships. They require proof that the cause *precedes* the effect in time, and that the effect never fails to follow the occurrence of the cause.

Hypotheses that are shown both to be empirically valid and logically consistent with the axioms and theorems are called laws. Every law contains a theory that has passed the empirical test. The hypothesis provides the basis for such tests and thus for the discovery of laws. All laws, like all hypotheses, may not be stated in the "If . . ., then. . . ." form described above. However, any hypothesis or law can be translated into such a form.

There may be sentences of the "If . . ., then. . . ." form that cannot be shown to be either consistent or inconsistent with the theory. Such sentences are not called hypotheses within that theory, and thus they cannot be used to test the theory or to generate laws. In such instances, the sentences are considered as "meaningless" and there is no way to establish their validity.

REDUCTIONISM

A theory at any level can be used to generate theories at higher levels. Thus, physiological theories at the cell level can be used to generate behavior theories at the person level, and theories at the person level can be used to generate social theories at the group level. Some scientists and philosophers believe that the lower the level of the theory, the better the theory. The attempt to reduce the elements of theory to the finest details in nature is called Reductionism. There are a number of difficulties involved in such a position. For example, in order to generate a theory at the person level from a physiological theory at the cell level, the physiological theory would have to include axioms, theorems, and laws that describe the behaviors of all or most of the cell configurations found at the whole person level. Not only would it be difficult, if not impossible, to discover such a complete and valid physiological theory, but the problems involved in aggregating lower level relationships to the whole person level would require the solution of many difficult and unsolved mathematical problems. Moreover, it would probably require more information processing and integrating capacity than is possible given present technology.

The aggregation of lower level sentences into high level sentences might also amplify the errors at the lower level, thereby resulting in either gross errors at the higher level or very crude descriptions. Of course, it sometimes happens that aggregation cancels errors, and thus produces a higher level theory more accurate than the lower ones. Such a fortunate state should not be expected to occur simply by chance. When the aggregations are statistical averages of lower level measurements, the aggregated theory may be in less error than the lower level theory; but if the higher level theory involves sums or products of the lower level measures, the higher level theory may contain considerably more error than the lower level theory.

Since the difficulties involved in aggregating lower level theories can be avoided by constructing theories at the level of one's ultimate interest, many psychologists construct theories at the person level. However, social psychologists who are primarily interested in group behavior, such as that of teams or nations, also tend to build theories at the lower level of the individual person. Social psychologists are themselves human beings and are so aware of feelings and behavior at the person level that they find it difficult to construct or accept theories that do not describe the personal phenomena with which they are so familiar. The concern for the fine details of individual behavior force many social psychological theorists to construct very complex theories many levels below the group phenomenon which they are investigating. In contrast, the physical sciences were very fortunate that they did not have access to spectroscopes and atomic microscopes in their early years. Their inability to see the fine fluctuations and details of the physical world enabled them to construct higher level Newtonian theories before embarking on explaining the details of atomic and sub-atomic matter. Social psychological theory may be seriously hampered by the attempts to develop fine grain theories that account for all the human idiosyncrasies that human beings observe in themselves and in others.

EVALUATION OF A THEORY

Theories, like most human products, are evaluated on the dimensions of good and bad. Scientists, like most people, are seldom unanimous in their evaluations of a human creation, especially when it comes to judging a particular theory. The disagreements stem in part from differences in the importance they attach to the various criteria that scientists employ in judging theory, and in part from differences in their knowledge about the available evidence relating to the theories. This section discusses some of the criteria that are actually used to judge theories.

Validity

Most scientists agree that a good theory is one that is valid—one that tells it as it really is. But how do we know what it really is without some theory to determine how it is or what it is. A meta-theory is needed to determine such validity. The meta-theory comes before the theory to be judged, and dictates how to create a theory and how to judge its validity. A meta-theory is necessarily accepted without test. In general, most scientists include as part of such a meta-theory two types of validity: logical consistency and empirical consistency.

Logical Consistency

Logical consistency refers to the way in which various sentences in the theory relate to each other. If two sentences contradict one another, or if one sentence can be broken into two or more contradictory sentences, then there exists a logical inconsistency. If a theory contains even one such inconsistency, the theory fails to satisfy the criteria of logical consistency. One such inconsistency is sufficient to permit the user of such a theory to deduce all kinds of contradictions and to prove any sentences in the theory both true and false. Logical inconsistencies are, for example, sometimes created by experimentalists when they analyze empirical results. A common mistake is to use mathematical techniques that contradict the theory or that make contradictory assumptions about the world. For example, it is not unusual for social psychologists to use statistical tests to determine the validity of a theory that assumes behavior to be nonstatistical. The theory and the statistics assume two contradictory states of nature.

The transformation of observation sentences into mathematical measures may also be performed in a manner that is inconsistent with the underlying psychological theory. Every measurement procedure, every rating scale, every statistical test, every transformation of the data, every translation of raw experience into records makes assumptions about the world and about people. Measurement and social psychological theory are not independent; they are in fact often the same thing. Every measurement theory used by social psychologists is actually a social psychological theory, and every social psychological theory, if it is to be tested, must include a theory of measurement. The experimenter is therefore not free to choose any measurement technique or any data collection method, but must select those that are consistent with each other, and with the theory or theories under investigation. Failure to assure such consistency leads to serious logical errors that mislead the investigator and unfortunately are often never noticed by others. Such errors impede the development of a science.

Empirical Consistency

The second type of consistency, empirical consistency, refers to the agreement between theory and observation, that is, between those sentences which derive from translating observations in the real world into the data of theory, and those predictions about such observations which derive from other rules of the theory.

It involves the agreement between hypotheses and facts. This strong reliance upon empirical validity differentiates science from some of the older branches of philosophy and other more humanistic fields of inquiry. However, every theory, except a valid and a complete theory, will be inconsistent with some "facts" in some area. When such inconsistencies are discovered, the theory, according to the meta-theory, should be, but generally is not, rejected. Scientists are generally unhappy with such inconsistencies, and search for a new theory that revises the old one and that is consistent with the disputed facts. But generally the old theory continues to be used until a new theory is proven better (Kuhn, 1962).

Breadth and Level

The breadth of coverage of a theory is another important characteristic of a theory. Since all scientists are specialists, each generally considers coverage within his own area more important than coverage of other areas. However, few scientists consider any area unimportant. Social psychologists, for example, are concerned not only with how much of social psychology a particular social psychological theory embraces, but also with how much and how consistent it is with theories in other specialties of psychology, sociology, and even physiology, chemistry, and economics.

Theories differ in the depth or level of detail that they embrace as well as in their breadth of coverage. Those that deal primarily with the grosser aspects of the highest levels of aggregation are called molar theories. Those that deal with the more elemental or finer details are called molecular or atomic theories. Naturally these terms are relative. A molar theory in physics would be a sub-atomic psychological theory. Most theories are used at several levels. The names molar and molecular are thus often interchangeable depending upon which use of the theory is denoted. The validity of a theory will often differ from level to level. As noted previously, some scientists and philosophers believe that the lower the level to which a theory can be applied, the better the theory. However, as also discussed previously, accuracy at a low level does not guarantee accuracy at higher levels. The relevance attached to the various levels reflects in part the particular scientist's notion of what he considers to be the more critical issues within his field. The importance of the problems a theory addresses and resolves, and the impact the theory has on other theories and other areas of investigation are additional criteria for judging the worth of a theory. Various subcultures and interest groups will naturally differ in such judgments, these differences reflecting their own values, traditions, and aspirations.

Clarity

The clarity with which the concepts of the theory are understood is also a criteria used to judge the value of a theory. Many scientists insist that the concepts are clear only when they are defined in terms of a set of rigorous operations to be performed (Bridgman, 1954). Thus, for example, an inch defined according to operations using a straight wooden ruler is considered different from an inch measured with a sophisticated timing device. The insistence on precise operational definitions arose in physics (Bridgman, 1927) and was at one time widely proclaimed in psychology (Skinner, 1953; Turner, 1965). Recently, however, some psychologists have argued against strict operational definitions (Campbell, 1969; Campbell & Fiske, 1959; Webb et al., 1966). There are also pleas today to return to the less "mechanical" and more "humanistic" or intuitive use of language. Although the humanistic pleas and the anti-operationalism arguments may sometimes disregard the need for clarity in scientific endeavors, they help to make explicit many of the shortcomings of strict operationalism.

The concern for clarity also has led to a distinction between (a) those concepts that refer to "things" that have not yet been observed, and (b) those concepts that refer to relations that bridge the gap between things but which are assumed not to have any physical existence themselves. The "things" in a theory, if they never have been observed, are called hypothetical constructs. The electron and the atom are such hypothetical constructs in physics; attitudes and social motives are often treated as hypothetical constructs in social psychology. The relations that bridge the gap between things are called intervening variables, and are not presumed to have any real existence. Intervening variables are introduced in a theory merely to make the mathematical equations relating events in the "real world" produce numbers that correspond to those actually observed. Thus, a constant of proportionality is an intervening variable. One does not ask what an intervening variable means, from whence it came, or how it effects anything. It's merely there to serve a mathematical function. Such variables have found limited usage in social psychological theories to date since they imply marked mathematical precision in the statement of relationships (MacCorquodale & Meehl, 1948).

The clarity criterion also refers to the precision and completeness of the categories used in the theory. A clear definition permits the user to classify everything accurately, to classify the same thing the same way he did before, and the same way that anyone else would classify it. Ambiguous concepts lead to unreliable classifications. Naturally, there are doubtful classifications when one measures or observes different dimensions or uses a different measure than the ones described in the theory. The errors from such misuse do not reflect discrepancies in the theory but rather indicate errors on the part of the user. The dimensions and the precision of the theory must be followed precisely if one is to judge the clarity of the theory. The more dimensions and the more precision the theory employs, the more categories will be possible. It is desirable to have only as many categories as are necessary to distinguish things worth distinguishing. Theories differ in what they consider to be a difference worth considering as a difference.

Practicality and Appeal

Theories are also judged by such pragmatic considerations as: How difficult is it to teach others to use the theory; how difficult is it to learn; how easy is it to apply the theory to "real" problems; how much does it cost in time, money, and/or personnel to revise the training programs, materials, research programs now in progress? The complexity of the language and the laws of the theory affect these judgments. Most scientists prefer the simple to the complex, the compact to the voluminous. Parsimony is highly valued in science.

The aesthetic, pragmatic, and other criteria mentioned above are not the only considerations that influence the evaluator. The motivational appeal of the theory also affects its acceptance. Allegiance to a given theorist, the amount of time consumed and the conditions under which the theory was orginally examined, the manner in which the theory was presented, and sometimes even the threat the theory poses to one's own work can all affect the acceptance of a theory. Although scientists try to disregard these irrelevant considerations, the human qualities of the scientist sometimes prevent his being as completely objective as he would like to be.[4] Moreover, the theory that a social psychologist builds is likely to reflect those very social forces he is attempting to explain in his theory. No man is completely independent of those historical and societal forces which have shaped his attitudes and his behavior.

CURRENT SOCIAL PSYCHOLOGICAL THEORY

In the preceding sections of this chapter we have attempted to describe the elements of theory, and to consider how a theory might be evaluated. Contemporary social psychological theory generally falls considerably short of the enumerated requirements. It is not possible within the limits of a single chapter to review in detail the strengths and weaknesses of specific contemporary theoretical efforts in the field. However, in this section we shall discuss several general characteristics of current social psychological theory.

In reviewing the theoretical efforts in social psychology one is struck by the fact that there exists no general theory of social behavior that has stimulated an extensive and ordered set of empirical studies. We do not even have a general theoretical model that can serve to initiate the basic reiterative process of science, namely, hypothesis derivation, observation in the real world, confirmation or reformulation of theory, hypothesis derivation, observation, etc. There have been some relatively general theoretical statements, for example, Lewin's field theory (1943; 1951) and Thibaut and Kelley's (1959) theory of dyadic (two-person) interaction; but these have seldom been stated with sufficient precision of definition or relationship to be systematically validated against observation in the real world.

Contemporary social psychological theories tend to fall between comprehensive and mathematically rigorous theoretical statements, and pragmatic, empirical, and often unconnected statements of relationship. The theories currently employed to direct empirical investigations in the field approximate what

---

[4] For an excellent discussion of many of these points see S. M. Lamb (1966). For the reader who wishes more depth on many of the theoretical issues raised in this chapter, see Becker (1963), Braithwaite (1953), Kuhn (1962), Tarski (1965), and Turner (1965).

Merton (1957) has aptly described as middle-range theories. These formulations can be characterized as employing a loosely related set of assumptions and a limited set of hypotheses which are more or less rigorously derived deductively from the assumptions, for example, Festinger's theory of social comparison (1954), McGuire's syllogistic model of cognition (1960), Zajonc's theory of social facilitation (1965), and Deutsch's theory of cooperative and competitive behavior (1949, 1962). Such middle-range theories have served a valuable function in organizing previous findings in the field, and as a heuristic device for directing future experimentation; however, they remain more informal than formal in their internal logical structure, and generally pertain to some more or less limited aspect of social behavior. Substantively, they rely heavily upon the variables, relationships, and measurement techniques developed in the neighboring fields of psychology and sociology.

As is true in all fields in the behavioral sciences, there has been an increasing tendency in recent years to introduce formal mathematical models into social psychology. In one sense, Lewin (1935, 1938) anticipated this trend towards more rigorous and potentially powerful theoretical statements 30 years ago. But today's formal models are generally restricted to particular aspects of social behavior (e.g., decision theory, game theory, and communication theory), and have enjoyed limited success when attempts have been made to validate them against observations from the real world. We can anticipate, however, that theory will continue to be formalized through advances in those areas of mathematics that can describe the dynamics of social interaction and social behavior. The growth of more sophisticated measurement and computer techniques will accelerate this process.

The organization of this book reflects, in part, an ordering of levels of analysis among the various theoretical and empirical orientations in contemporary social psychology. From a historical standpoint, the major focus in the field has been upon how a single individual is influenced by other persons in his environment, especially how others affect his attitudes, beliefs, motives, and behavior. This historical emphasis derived in large part from the strong influence the field of psychology has had upon social psychology. In the former, most conceptual formations follow the traditional stimulus-response paradigm, namely, variations in behavior are seen to be some function of variations in the stimuli perceived by the organism. In the social psychology of the individual, these stimuli are generally viewed to be the behavior or the behavioral products of other organisms.

A second theoretical focus or level in contemporary social psychology is of more recent origin partly because the theoretical and methodological problems it poses seem intrinsically more complex and difficult to analyze than the above orientation. This focus is concerned with social interaction, particularly as it occurs between members of a dyad or within a small group. In essence, one is concerned about simultaneous and sequential patterns of behavioral interdependence or reciprocity between individuals. Here, the stimulus situation for a given actor at a given point in time is in part the prior response pattern of the other(s), and in part the set of internalized expectations some of which the actor brings to the situation and others that grow from modifications during the course of interaction. The same condition obtains for the other actor or actors in the situation. The complexity of the analysis required to investigate such social interaction is noted by Thibaut and Kelley (1959):

> We now merely note that methodologically the complexity that is added by reciprocal control (between individuals) may be denoted by the loss of a clear separation between independent and dependent variables. Each subject's behavior is at the same time a response to a past behavior of the other and a stimulus to a future behavior of the other; each behavior is in part a dependent variable and in part an independent variable; in no clear sense is it properly either of them [p. 2].

A final theoretical focus in contemporary social psychology is upon group structure and group process. The historical roots of this area are embedded more in the neighboring field of sociology than psychology. In essence, the area is concerned with the norms, products, and organization of social interaction in large groups such as corporations, societies, or neighborhood communities. The theoretical emphasis is not placed upon the psychological attributes of the individual, but rather upon how organizations shape human interaction according to certain structural and functional demands. Recent conceptual developments in this area include the utilization of general systems theory as a model for describing organizational development and functioning in living agents ranging from unicellular animals to complex technological societies. The utilization of systems theory in the social psychological study of social organizations is reflected in a recent theoretical statement made by Katz and Kahn (1966) which emphasizes the centrality of human actors in an organizational context:

> Open-system theory with its entropy assumption emphasizes the close relationship between a structure and its supporting environment, in that without continued inputs the system would soon run down. Thus one critical basis for identifying social systems is through their relationships with energic sources for their maintenance. And human effort and motivation is the major maintenance source of almost all social structures. Hence, though the theoretical approach deals with relationships, these relationships embrace human beings. If we are concerned with the specifics of the maintenance function in terms of human behavior we are at the social psychological level. In open-system theory the carriers of the system cannot be ignored because they furnish the sustaining input [p. 9].

Thus, one can identify three major orientations or levels of analysis in contemporary social psychological theory and research: the social individual who responds to external and internalized social stimuli; actors who interact in situations of social interdependence where both can affect their own and other's outcomes simultaneously; and actors behaving in organizational settings where the norms and values of a given organization impose certain rules of relationship upon participants and where, in turn, participants serve as "carriers of the system." In Sections II, III, and IV of this book we will examine some of the conceptual and empirical paradigms that are employed to investigate behavior at each of these three levels of analysis. In the subsequent two chapters, various methods for experimentally investigating one's theoretical propositions will be discussed as well as a number of the methodological problems that confront the experimental social psychologist.

REFERENCES

BECKER, G. M. *On the organization of psychological knowledge. SP-250.* Santa Barbara, Calif.: *Tempo*, General Electric Co., 1963.

BRAITHWAITE, R. B. *Scientific explanation: A study of the function of theory, probability and law in science.* London: Cambridge University Press, 1953.

BRIDGMAN, P. W. *The logic of modern physics.* New York: Macmillan, 1927.

BRIDGMAN, P. W. Remarks on the present state of operationalism. *Scientific Monthly,* 1954, **79,** 224–226.

CAMPBELL, D. T. Definitional versus multiple operationism. *Et al.,* 1969, **2,** 14–17.

CAMPBELL, D. T., & FISKE, D. W. Convergent and discriminant validation by the multitrait-multimethod matrix. *Psychological Bulletin,* 1959, **56**(2), 81–105.

CARTWRIGHT, D. Lewinian theory as a contemporary systematic framework. In S. Koch (Ed.), *Psychology: A study of science.* Vol. 2. New York: McGraw-Hill, 1959. Pp. 7–91.

DEUTSCH, M. A theory of co-operation and competition. *Human Relations,* 1949, **2,** 129–152.

DEUTSCH, M. *Cooperation and trust: Some theoretical notes.* In M. R. Jones (Ed.), *Nebraska Symposium on Motivation.* Lincoln, Nebr.: University of Nebraska Press, 1962. Pp. 275–318.

DEUTSCH, M. Field theory in social psychology. In G. Lindzey (Ed.), *Handbook of social psychology.* (Rev. ed.) Vol. 1. Cambridge, Mass.: Addison-Wesley, 1968. Pp. 412–487.

DEUTSCH, M., & KRAUSS, R. *Theories in social psychology.* New York: Basic Books, 1965.

EINSTEIN, A. Science, philosophy and religion. In P. Wiener (Ed.), *Readings in the philosophy of science.* New York: Scribner, 1953. Pp. 601–606.

FESTINGER, L. A theory of social comparison processes. *Human Relations,* 1954, **1,** 154–181.

FRANK, P. Modern science and its philosophy. In P. Wiener (Ed.), *Readings in the philosophy of science.* New York: Scribner, 1953. Pp. 473–479.

KATZ, D., & KAHN, R. L. *The social psychology of organizations.* New York: Wiley, 1966.

KUHN, T. S. *The structure of scientific revolutions.* Chicago: University of Chicago Press, 1962.

LACHMAN, R. The model in theory construction. *Psychological Review,* 1960, **67,** 113–129.

LAMB, S. M. Epilegomena to a theory of language. *Romance Philology,* 1966, **19,** 531–573.

LEEPER, R. W. *Lewin's topological and vector psychology.* Eugene, Ore.: University of Oregon Press, 1943.

LEWIN, L. *A dynamic theory of personality.* New York: McGraw-Hill, 1935.

LEWIN, L. The conceptual representation and measurement of psychological forces. *Contributions to Psychological Theory,* 1938, **1**(4), 1–247.

LEWIN, L. Defining the field at a given time. *Psychological Review,* 1943, **50,** 292–310.

LEWIN, L. *Field theory in social science.* New York: Harper Torchbook, 1951.

MACCORQUODALE, K., & MEEHL, P. E. On a distinction between hypothetical constructs and intervening variables. *Psychological Review,* 1948, **55,** 95–107.

MARX, M. H. *Theories in contemporary psychology.* New York: Macmillan, 1963.

MASLOW, A. H. A philosophy of psychology: The need for a mature science of human nature. In F. Severin (Ed.), *Humanistic viewpoints in psychology.* New York: McGraw-Hill, 1965. Pp. 17–33.

MCCAIN, G., & SEGAL, G. M. *The game of science.* Belmont, Calif.: Wadsworth, 1969.

MCGUIRE, W. J. A syllogistic analysis of cognitive relationships. In M. J. Rosenberg & C. I. Hovland (Eds.), *Attitude organization and change.* New Haven, Conn.: Yale University Press, 1960. Pp. 65–111.

MERTON, R. K. *Social theory and social structure.* (Rev. ed.) Glencoe, Ill.: Free Press, 1957.

POPPER, K. R. *Conjectures & refutations: The growth of scientific knowledge.* London: Routledge, 1963.

SKINNER, B. The operational analysis of psychological terms. In H. Feigl & M. Brodbeck (Eds.), *Readings in the philosophy of science.* New York: Appleton, 1953. Pp. 585–595.

TARSKI, A. *Introduction to logic and to the methodology of deductive sciences.* New York: Oxford University Press, 1965.

THIBAUT, J. W., & KELLEY, H. H. *The social psychology of groups.* New York: Wiley, 1959.

TURNER, M. B. *Philosophy and the science of behavior.* New York: Appleton, 1965.

WEBB, E. J., CAMPBELL, D. T., SCHWARTZ, R. D., & SECHREST, L. B. *Unobstrusive measures: Nonreactive research in the social sciences.* Chicago: Rand McNally, 1966.

ZAJONC, R. B. Social facilitation. *Science,* 1965, **149,** 269–274.

2

EXPERIMENTAL METHODS

Paul C. Rosenblatt
Norman Miller

Any chapter concerned with methodological issues is likely to discourage the beginning student (and perhaps the advanced student too). A methodology chapter must inevitably focus on the problems one might encounter in attempting to perform research. It is not our intent to be discouraging, rather we think that an enormous number of fascinating social psychological questions await scientific attack and are presently amenable to competent research design. The keys to coping adequately with research design problems are an understanding of the kinds of trouble that can arise and a knowledge of how best to cope with them. We hope that this chapter will raise many of the methodological issues that deserve concern and provide some clues for evaluating and dealing with them.

SCIENTIFIC IDEAS

Sophisticated methodology is worth little to a researcher if he lacks good ideas about a researchable bit of reality. What is a good idea and where to find one are not easy to learn and are partly a matter of taste, but it might be useful to mention some of the criteria that contemporary social psychologists use in deciding whether an idea is worth developing into research plans.

First of all, we must consider the aim of anyone interested in scientific research, namely, discovering a relation between phenomena. The basic form of scientific laws—If a, then b—provides the first criterion for evaluating an idea. A good idea must relate two (or more) classes of phenomena.[1] Thus, an idea such as "the back of the planet Pluto is pink" would be of little scientific value in itself. It is merely a descriptive statement rather than a statement of relation-

---

[1] Of course, a more ambitious and scientific goal is to develop a theory, that is, to discover and organize a set of laws all of which are concerned with similar or related events and the variables that control their occurrence. The degree of similarity among the events defines the scope or breadth of the theory. If the events were quite dissimilar one would have a theory of considerable breadth or generality.

ship between categories of phenomena. If, however, one also had some speculations about why Pluto might have a pink backside, the picture would change completely. Now one could relate "pinkness" to some other events or circumstances.

Second, good ideas are capable of being refuted. Suppose a psychologist suspects that people avoid information that raises tension or dissonance, for example, information that implies that one has made a bad decision. It would be impossible to test this suspicion if the psychologist's implicit definition of "information avoidance" were so broad that he interpreted any behavior of people he thought were experiencing tension or dissonance as a symptom of "information avoidance." Since there would be no possible way for him to disconfirm his suspicion, conducting research to test it would simply waste his time. This example may appear utterly naive, silly, and trivial when stated in this direct manner and, therefore, not even worth considering. Yet the "problem" does arise. The researcher who is anxious to confirm his suspicion can easily slip into the position of accepting an increasing variety of outcomes as an attestation of its truth—not realizing that he has implicitly taken the position that *all* or *any* behavior constitutes "information avoidance." In short, an experiment which cannot, no matter what the outcome, disconfirm our suspicions is a waste of time.[2]

Thus the logical restrictions regarding what is or is not testable partly define the quality of an idea. Related to the question of testability are restrictions stemming not from logic but from technological, methodological, or ethical limitations. An idea that qualifies as scientifically good because of its logical testability may nevertheless remain untestable because we lack sophisticated measuring instruments, effective ways of inducing a given psychological state, or because ethical considerations do not allow us to use certain procedures. For instance, it would not be feasible within our present society to experimentally study what effect depriving a child of motherly love might have on fantasy and neural activity during intercourse in adulthood. Ethical considerations probably preclude the independent manipulation and the two dependent measures, and additionally, the dependent measures are fraught with technological and methodological problems.

Third, good ideas have some general applicability. Unique, esoteric, bizarre, or rare groups of people or events may have fascination for us, but it is presumably more valuable to find laws that might tell us something about human nature in general. Perhaps another way of saying the same thing is that most contemporary social psychology deals with theoretical problems rather than with specific, applied problems. Likewise, it deals with problems that have implications for many situations and people rather than with problems only relevant to some unique state of affairs or group of people.

Somewhat related to this point about general applicability is the notion of

---

[2] As a matter of fact, the hypothesis that people selectively expose themselves only to information that is not dissonance-arousing is one hypothesis that has been frequently disconfirmed in social psychological research (Freedman & Sears, 1965).

"impetus for systematic research." An idea that generates a set of related experimental tests, that triggers off other related hypotheses that can be subjected to experimental verification, is more powerful. The issue here is one of "scope" (Bergmann, 1957). Theories, laws, and hypotheses that possess greater scope or breadth are in a sense more powerful; they comment on a bigger slice of the total pie.

Some social psychologists feel that ideas stated with a little bit of imprecision possess a certain heuristic advantage (e.g., Zajonc, 1968). When they take this position they are probably considering this question of scope. The ambiguity in the statement of the idea may lead to a greater variety of specific experimental tests of it—the different tests stemming from each researcher's idiosyncratic interpretation of the precise measure or the best experimental operationalization of the terms in the idea.[3] The preceding remarks notwithstanding, for the beginning researcher we advocate modesty, precision, and narrowness in the formulation and statement of research ideas. Translating ideas into specific experimental procedures to test their veracity often looms as the biggest problem faced by the beginning researcher. Vague ideas clearly intensify the problem.

A final common criterion for judging the value of a research idea is whether it is nonobvious. It is true that obvious ideas are sometimes wrong or only of limited relevance to the real world and thus deserve disconfirmation. But an experiment that demonstrates something nonobvious adds immeasurably more to our suspicions about human nature than one that confirms what even the lady across the street suspected. (Some of the preceding comments bear on a discussion of theory. A fuller discussion of theory is presented in the first chapter of this book.)

Where ideas come from is easier to say than how bright researchers get them. Of course, ideas come from theories and from the implications of research already done. Research ideas also come from common sense, from insights into what happens around us or to us, and from recognizing alternative interpretations of research already done. But there are many who feel that most of the potential subject matter of behavioral science has not yet been well explored (e.g., Chomsky, 1968, p. v). Some examples of social psychological issues that fall into this category are: (a) the consequences of physical attractiveness; (b) the psychology of secrets; (c) the effects of different types of educational systems; (d) long-term friendships; (e) the psychological effects of crowding; what are the consequences of being surrounded (without choice) by many people throughout one's daily life; (f) sexual attraction; (g) why people hunt; (h) hope and despair; (i) why men (and not women) corner the market of political authority; (i) what are the psychological functions of our beliefs and customs regarding death; (k) what determines people's preference for different modes of social control; (l) love; (m) do spouses tend to discuss their most personal concerns with others and not one another, and if so, why; and (n) why

---

[3] A comparison between two cognitive consistency theories, dissonance theory and congruity theory, illustrates some of these theories. The nature of these theories is spelled out in Chapter 4 of the present volume.

does the content of so much human communication consist of things that most of us would judge dull, inane, or pointless had we not said it ourselves or heard it from someone toward whom we have positive feelings! This list is of course not exhaustive nor do we mean to imply that these topics necessarily constitute the most important problems. Some of these issues have only begun to receive attention, others have been explored extensively but the quality of research has been poor. Only trivial aspects of others have been attacked, and some still await exploration.

WHY DO SOCIAL PSYCHOLOGISTS LOVE EXPERIMENTS SO?

In much of contemporary social psychological research, a researcher manipulates something and then notes its effects. In the most common alternative to a manipulation study—a correlational study—one assesses the relation between variables without manipulating them. Typically, the label experiment is reserved for those studies in which the experimenter *manipulates* one or several variables. A critical feature is that the experimenter himself determines whether or not (or when) a subject will be exposed to a given event (treatment) and subsequently measures the effect of this exposure on some other aspect of the subject's behavior. Social psychologists commonly believe that experiments more powerfully probe into the causes of behavior than correlational studies. In an experiment, manipulation eliminates many plausible rival explanations of a relationship between the variables being studied. In a correlational relationship, it is often more difficult to be sure of what caused what; furthermore, two things might correlate with one another as a consequence of any number of third factors.

Difficulties in a Hypothetical Correlational Study

To be concrete, suppose one asks a group of people to listen to a speaker advocate a controversial position. Afterwards one might find that those who indicate that they like the speaker a lot agree more closely with the position he advocated in his speech than they initially did. One might erroneously interpret this positive correlation between liking of the communicator and persuasion as an effect of liking on persuasion. But alternatively, it might represent an effect of persuasion on liking. The persuaded subject might, for example, tell himself: "I would be a fool to be persuaded by somebody I didn't like. I think he influenced me. Therefore, I must like him."[4] On the other hand, the unpersuaded subject would not have any need to "adjust" the degree to which he likes the speaker.

---

[4] Of course, the same causal sequence could occur even if the persuaded subject did not have such a well-articulated awareness of his cognitions. In other words, this causal sequence might actually occur even if the subject lacked insight or was unable to give us a self-report of the thought processes described above.

Also, as already indicated, correlation could be an effect of any number of third factors. In a correlational study such as the one on liking and persuasion, when all subjects are exposed to the same stimuli, many of the potential third factors are dimensions of individual difference. Two individual difference variables that commonly concern social psychologists are the need for social approval and intellectual ability. Subjects might differ in how much they want to appear as helpful, reasonable persons, how much they have a "need for social approval" (Crowne & Marlowe, 1964). Assuming the communicator was not unattractive and the communication was inoffensive, those more strongly motivated to seek approval or to make the socially acceptable response might be more willing to be persuaded (or to give liking-of-the-communicator responses) than those less motivated to obtain social approval. Similarly, more intelligent subjects might be more offended by a communicator and less persuaded by him if, for example, his communication contained logical fallacies.

Both of these individual difference variables could produce a correlation between "liking for the communicator" and "persuasion" when no intrinsic relation exists between them. In the first case, subjects intent on always giving helpful or "correct" responses in any situation might tend to say, "Yes, I like the communicator," and, similarly, "Yes, I like to agree with people, whatever the position they advocate" more than those less concerned with social approval, thereby producing a positive correlation between the two variables. In the second case, illogical arguments might incline intelligent subjects toward greater anger at the communicator and his communication than less intelligent subjects. This, too, might lead to the appearance of a positive correlation between liking and persuasion. The reader might join us in the alternative interpretation game by thinking of other individual difference factors that in conjunction with some specific characteristic of the speaker or his communication might produce a correlation between liking of the communicator and persuasion that would be absent if this third factor were not present. For example, what if subjects differed in fear of being hoodwinked and the speaker had been an ex-convict?

If instead of correlating liking of the communicator and persuasion, an experimenter had manipulated liking (e.g., for half of the subjects the communicator is made to smell bad, look messy, speak affectedly, while for the other half he is perfectly presentable), the effects of most if not all of these third factors could be ruled out. When manipulations are employed, subjects can be randomly assigned to conditions (assigned in such a way that all subjects are equally likely to be assigned to any one condition). Such random assignment is the best protection against systematic initial differences between the subjects in the various conditions. With substantial numbers of subjects in each condition, the innumerable individual difference factors are ordinarily distributed comparably in all conditions, making it possible to discount them as explanations of a relationship between the experimental variables. Thus, in the case of need for approval, the possibility that those high on this trait might report or display more persuasion and like the communicator more should make no difference since random assignment makes it likely that in each experimental treatment group there would be similar distributions of scores on need for approval.

It is important to note, however, that manipulating liking does not necessarily mean that individual differences no longer matter. It could still be the case that a given manipulation of liking could interact with individual differences to produce whatever persuasion effect we observe. For instance, one interpretation of the effects of high need for approval argues that it reflects a greater sensitivity to cues that might enable one to obtain the experimenter's approval or do what one thinks the experimenter would like (Miller, Doob, Butler, & Marlowe, 1965). Thus, in our illustrative experiment on liking and persuasion, those high in need for approval might attend more closely to the communicator's characteristics and more readily infer whether the experimenter wants them to show agreement or disagreement with his speech. Those low in the trait might not attend to these cues. As depicted in Figure 2.1, the effect of liking on persuasion could be entirely attributable to those subjects high on the individual

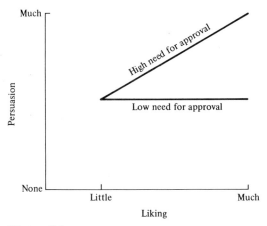

Figure 2.1
Interactive effect of need for approval and liking on permission.

difference variable. And, if the experimenter never measured subjects on this trait, this qualification of the relation between the two variables would remain undetected. We would mistakenly think that there was a main effect when in fact there was an interaction.[5]

---

[5] This example gives a good illustration of what is meant by an interaction—an instance where the relation between two variables depends on the level of a third. In this case the third variable is the individual difference variable "need for approval." If liking had the same statistically significant effect on persuasion, regardless of whether subjects were high or low in need for approval, the outcome is called a main effect. Sometimes a study might yield a main effect as well as an interaction; for example, there is greater persuasion when the communicator is liked, but the strength of the effect of liking is greater for subjects who have a greater need for approval. To make usage clearer, a main effect refers to a more general outcome; that is, it is obtained despite the effect of other variables. Where there is an interaction, the direction or strength of an effect depends on the particular level of some other variable(s).

How might we ascertain the relation between these two variables, liking and persuasion, less ambiguously? The manipulation of likeability could be altered so that subjects are induced to like or dislike the communicator but at the same time have no reason to believe that the experimenter knows of their feelings toward the communicator. For instance, a confederate of the experimenter could "accidentally" interact pleasantly or unpleasantly with the subject in an elevator or on a picket line. The following day this same person could appear for the same experimental session as the subject. The experimenter could pretend to flip a coin to determine which subject will be assigned the role of delivering a speech and which the role of audience in such a way that the confederate is always assigned the role of speaker. With this manipulation of likeability, even if the subject with high need for approval is intent on pleasing the experimenter, he lacks reason to believe that the experimenter wishes him to agree with the speaker. Of course, even this experiment might not do the trick. Further analysis may always reveal additional interpretations of what appeared at first to be an unambiguous contribution to human knowledge.

While experiments are preferred because they most effectively eliminate plausible rival explanations of a finding, other ways to eliminate plausible rival explanations do exist. For instance, one could take additional measurements. In the case of a correlational study of liking for the communicator and persuasion, one could measure need for social approval and intellectual ability. With luck, one might discover that no relation exists between either of these personality traits and persuasion or liking for the communicator.[6] In addition, a variety of statistical techniques supposedly remove the effects of third variables from correlations, but their epistemological respectability is as yet unclear.

Another procedure for eliminating alternative explanations is to arrange or attend to the temporal ordering of events. One could establish liking for a communicator before his message is delivered. For example, one could artificially impose a ten or fifteen minute delay in the start of the speech ("The slide projector hasn't arrived yet"), and instruct the speaker to chat casually about things within earshot of all the subjects before delivering his communication. Presumably, the chat might produce different degrees of liking among the subjects. One could then take measurements of liking before the delivery of the communication and measure amount of persuasion at the end of the speech. If a positive correlation was found under these circumstances, it could not be explained as an effect of persuasion on liking since the degree of liking was established prior to the presentation of the communication.

It may now be apparent to the reader that eliminating alternative interpretations is more easily accomplished in an experiment. One doesn't have to measure

---

[6] Of course, all the usual precautions about interpreting a no-difference effect are applicable here. The fact that our procedures fail to detect a relation does not necessarily mean that one does not exist. The more reliable our measures of intellectual ability and need for social approval and the larger our sample size, the greater our faith that in fact there is no relation between either of the individual difference variables and persuasion or liking. But, one can never be sure.

individual difference variables and do considerable statistical analysis after-wards, plagued with the fear that one failed to measure subjects on one or more crucial individual difference variables. And one doesn't have to make an additional measurement (e.g., of liking), which might sensitize subjects to the purpose of the experiment. That is, if we tried to assess liking (by question-naire or interview), the subject might easily determine that we were studying the relation of liking to persuasion. As a consequence, we might only discover how subjects behave when they know the question that our research asks.

Potential Problems in the Experiment

Although we have more faith in experiments than in other methods, we must confess that experimental social psychologists have not begun to consider sys-tematically factors that may covary with manipulations and may contribute to or be responsible for findings. Indeed correlated artifacts may contaminate our experimental manipulations as frequently as they intrude into the most naive correlational studies. Taking our communicator likeability manipulation as an example, it may not in fact be responsible for our observed persuasion effect. As we have already observed, in attempting to manipulate likeability, we may instead effectively manipulate subjects' suspicions about what occurs and what the experimenter expects them to do. Subjects with the unpleasant communica-tor might say, "Aha, the experimenter doesn't want me to like this guy. Why? Maybe because he doesn't want me to believe the guy. Well, I won't ruin his experiment by being persuaded." This reaction may characterize subjects both high and low on need for approval. Alternatively, an effect attributed to the manipulation of liking might actually stem from the artifactual manipulation of the subject's attention to the communication, of distraction, of liking for the experimenter, of judgments concerning the communicator's expertise (e.g., "No guy who is that sloppy could be knowledgeable"), of perceived similarity of communicator to subject, of understandability of material (it may be harder to understand somebody who speaks affectedly), or of something else. It should be confessed that considerable subjectivity enters our evaluation of experiments. What looks like a clear manipulation to one social psychologist looks like a very complicated and undoubtedly confounded manipulation (vary-ing more things than intended) to another. For example, experimental research on cognitive dissonance, which some people feel has been one of the substantial contributions made to human knowledge by experimental social psychology, has been accused of using manipulations so complex that valid conclusions can rarely be drawn from the obtained data (Chapanis & Chapanis, 1964). Yet some manipulations of theoretical variables have been implemented in different experiments with a diverse set of actual experimental operations and still yield consistent outcomes. When this occurs, we can have substantial faith that most of the alternative explanations for any single experiment in the group can be ruled out. But even so, some of these manipulations may be more complicated and confounded than we suspect.

Another matter for subjective judgment is determining the appropriateness of manipulations for testing hypotheses. What manipulation seems properly relevant to testing a given hypothesis is a matter of judgment. For example, manipulating messiness, smelliness, and affectedness of the communicator in order to manipulate likeability probably would be inappropriate if subjects serving in the experiment are messy, smelly, and affected themselves. Furthermore, odor may have little effect when the speaker speaks in a well-ventilated room; messiness may have little effect in a dimly lighted room or when subjects do not attend to the speaker. Affectedness may have little effect if the sound system masks the affectation. What at first strikes us as an adequate manipulation may lose its appropriateness in a particular context.

More clearcut blunders than these do occur. The operations designed to represent some variable may plainly be wrong. A misguided person might attempt to manipulate likeability by manipulating the alleged expertise of a speaker, the position he advocates, or the size of the room he is in (to take progressively more ludicrous examples).[7] Furthermore, social psychologists disagree among themselves regarding what theoretical variable a given experimental procedure manipulates. It has been waggishly suggested (Kiesler, Collins, & Miller, 1969, Ch. 2) that even sophisticated researchers reviewing filmed versions of a dozen experimental manipulations of the same variable might vary considerably in their identifications of what variable was supposedly being manipulated.

A casual glance through any current social psychology journal shows that cleanliness and appropriateness of manipulations is a substantial problem in that numerous experiments examine alternative interpretations of previous studies or attempt to demonstrate the appropriateness or inappropriateness of some set of manipulations for testing some hypotheses. Many people argue that the current state of experimental social psychology requires that we always check our manipulations by making additional measurements of either the experimental subject or additional control subjects. Others, however, argue that such checks waste time or incur risk. The opponents of checks (e.g., of asking subjects in experimental conditions designed to produce different degrees of liking for the communicator how much they do in fact like him) argue among other things that the checks may sensitize subjects if they antecede dependent measures. Alternatively, or in addition, they may not represent a subject's feelings at the time he responds on the crucial measures. They might argue that if a check indicates that the manipulation produces no effect, one might just as well blame the lack of effect on the check (the measurement lacked sensitivity) as on the manipulation. And if the check indicates that the manipulation was valid but one still gets no effect, one knows little more than one would without a check.

[7] Of course, in the final analysis, the extent to which these are manipulations of three distinct theoretical variables or contrariwise, three different operationalizations of a single theoretical variable, remains an empirical question. If by some unexpected chance the relation between each of these three manipulations and all other variables were indeed identical, we would be forced to conclude that the latter was in fact the case.

Despite the problems created by checks on manipulation, social psychology has much more to gain than to lose from additional information about the effects of manipulations in an experiment. In addition to checks on manipulation effects included within the experimental design, manipulations may be evaluated by using pilot subjects or by administering postexperimental interviews to experimental subjects. As Becker and McClintock's discussion in Chapter 1 indicates, there are many criteria for the evaluation of assertions. Should a research finding support a theory that seems sound by such criteria as parsimony and logical consistency, we might discount evidence from the manipulation check that seems to indicate that the manipulation failed. Of course even in this case the researcher should report the outcome on the manipulation check.

In concluding our introductory discussion of the relative merits of correlational and experimental studies, it is important to emphasize that even though we advocate experimental studies for most situations amenable to either experimental or correlational research, there are situations in which correlational studies are preferable. In some situations a correlational study is more practical than an experimental one. In others, manipulations create problems so severe that a correlational study is actually easier to interpret than a manipulative study. For example, if one is interested in the effects of number of brothers and sisters, father absence, long-term illness, marriage, or death of a loved one, it would obviously not be practical or ethical to do a manipulative study. The experimental studies that could be done to test a given hypothesis may take far more time and be far more expensive than the correlational alternatives, or the manipulations needed to test a given hypothesis may invariably distort subject responses or risk injury to subjects. In these cases, a correlational study may be the only reasonable alternative.

THE DESIGN OF EXPERIMENTS

In what follows, 11 of the most commonly used experimental designs and 11 of the most frequently observed sources of experimental invalidity are discussed. The discussion draws heavily on the work of Donald T. Campbell (Campbell, 1957; Campbell & Stanley, 1963). Table 2.1, which can be found at the end of the chapter, summarizes the discussion. Some readers will be surprised to find minimal use of statistics here. Although space limitations are partly responsible for the absence of statistical guff, the crucial reason is that statistics should play a very small and perhaps semiautomatic part in the inference process in comparison to the considerations discussed in the following pages.

If our discussion succeeds, careful readers will more capably design experiments to test ideas and more readily recognize sources of invalidity in their own work and in the work of others. The good experimental design minimizes the number of plausible rival explanations of obtained data. Perhaps no experiment can eliminate all alternative interpretations, but the good one eliminates those judged as likely candidates in terms of present knowledge and scientific custom.

Design 1: The One-Shot Case Study

The first design is the simple One-Shot Case Study, which may be diagrammed as follows:

$$X \quad O$$

An X represents an experimental manipulation—the independent variable, and an O represents an observation—the dependent variable. The left-to-right ordering of the symbols represents the temporal order of treatments and measurements. In this instance the manipulation X precedes the observation O.

If one were to yawn in the face of one or more persons and then observe whether they yawned, whatever else might be said of one, it could also be said that one was conducting a One-Shot Case Study. Observations made in One-Shot Case Studies may appear no worse than some of the illustrative experiments discussed in the preceding pages in that, like those, they are subject to numerous alternative interpretations. In fact, however, they are distinctly worse in that they are altogether uninterpretable. Without any observations other than the postmeasure, one cannot know what effect has been obtained. Lacking a comparison or control group not yawned at, a One-Shot Case Study omits the basic feature of an experiment. If all the people one yawns at yawn back, it may reflect the fact that people yawn continually, or they always yawn when they see you, or that they always yawn when you look at them the way you did when you were observing their reactions.

If these alternative interpretations seem bizarre, it is partly because we really have some implicit expectations concerning the outcomes obtained in a typical Design 1. We make such inferences because we *think* we know something else, namely, how a comparison group *would* behave if we had not yawned. And, in fact, when people report Design 1 studies they talk as though they have bases of comparison in mind. However, if they do not make these explicit, anyone wishing to evaluate what the study found, if anything, would find it difficult to do so. Furthermore, even if the researcher explicitly describes the comparison group in mind, any so-called comparison remains largely meaningless. One can never be certain that the people in the One-Shot Case Study and the people in the "in-mind" comparison group were initially similar.

An example of a One-Shot Case Study that could be called social psychological would be investigation of the effect of a human relations training program on the ethnic attitudes of teachers. Having made a postmeasure of teacher attitudes one again remains in the position of not knowing what the data mean. Are the attitudes different than before the training program or not? If they are, and we can only speculate about this in a Design 1 study, are we justified in attributing the differences to the training program?

The following 10 designs use explicit bases of comparison and resemble more closely than Design 1 what social psychologists have in mind when planning experiments. In discussing the remaining designs, common sources of invalidity are considered.[8]

Design 2: The One-Group Pretest-Posttest Design

Adding a pretest to a Design 1 study produces what may be called a One-Group Pretest-Posttest Design:

$$O_1 \quad X \quad O_2$$

It introduces a basic feature of an experiment—the possibility of comparison. Instead of merely guessing about the characteristics of the comparison group we now know; the subjects have been measured before the treatment. Let's assume that one finds a difference between pretest and posttest scores: people yawned more during the minute following your yawn than during the minute before, or the teachers showed more tolerant ethnic attitudes following the human relations training program than preceding it. This design is clearly superior to the preceding one, but it still contains many faults. While one hopes that the experimental treatment had an effect, many other possible interpretations of a pretest-posttest difference arise. Five of the common sources of invalidity can be conveniently discussed in an evaluation of Design 2. Moreover, additional sources of invalidity that will be discussed in conjuction with other designs may also apply.

History. Any events that occurred between the two measurements, O_1 and O_2, that are not part of the manipulation could be responsible for the observed change. Typically, the greater the elapsed time between observations, the more likely an uncontrolled event will produce changes. In a short-term study, such as our apocryphal experiment on yawning, historical artifacts, such as an odd thing one says while introducing the experimental manipulation or sensitizing remarks made before the second measurement, may be responsible for the obtained effect. History effects, even in studies of short duration, may be more or less beyond the control of the experimenter (e.g., a distracting noise, another person snickering, and the like). For a long-term experiment in which subjects are often outside the experimental situation, such as the study of the effect of a human relations course, the many other events outside the experiment—a politician's speech, an assassination, a moving television program—become even greater threats to an experiment's validity. Although experimenters differ in the extent to which they seem able to eliminate history effects from their experi-

---

[8] By experimental validity we refer to the extent to which the effect of an experimental manipulation on some dependent measure can only be attributed to the experimental manipulation.

ments, we doubt that even the best of them can do a Design 2 study on most social psychological topics unthreatened by history effects. More importantly, without additional observations on the same subjects or on appropriate control subjects, there is no way to assess whether one adequately protected the experiment from history effects.

Maturation. Biological and psychological processes that change systematically over time—fatigue, growth, boredom, etc.—may produce any observed changes between pre- and postexperimental observations. The simple Design 2 does not effectively protect us from such sources of invalidity. Here again, the greater the passage of time between observations, the greater the threat to validity. A yawning study in which the premeasurement occurred hours before postmeasurement would almost certainly be affected by ordinary fatigue (and consequent yawning) more than a study in which the premeasure and postmeasure were separated by a few minutes. A study using physiological measures (which are often desirable because they are harder for subjects to fake) may show systematic changes in observation over time that resemble treatment effects but which, in fact, stem from increases in subjects' boredom, fatigue, hunger, or the like.

Testing. Design 2 does not measure or control the effect of participating in a pretest (O_1) upon performance on a subsequent test (O_2). For example, in a study of attitudes, the pretest may instigate thought processes that either facilitate or reduce attitude change. The pretest may change subjects' conceptions of what is proper for a reasonable person to believe or may commit them to their initial position and reduce the likelihood of change in response to a given manipulation. If ability is being measured, practice acquired on a pretest may produce apparent, but artifactual, improvement on a second testing. However, pretests or other initial observations differ in the degree to which they might produce testing effects, that is, in their reactivity. If we covertly observe subjects with a hidden observer, or in an every day situation in which the subject doesn't suspect an assessment, the likelihood of testing effects diminishes. Webb, Campbell, Schwartz, and Sechrest (1966), and Sechrest (1967) discuss a number of clever ways in which initial testing can be disguised. For example, instead of employing standard attitude questionnaires to measure the effects of our hypothetical human relations course, it would be preferable to measure ethnic attitudes indirectly, for example, by covertly observing teacher interactions with children of different ethnic backgrounds before and after the course.

Instrumentation. Changes in the measuring instrument from one measurement to the next may be responsible for apparent but invalid effects. Once again we are talking about systematic changes that occur over time. Design 2 experiments provide no protection from instrument errors. If we use human observers as the measuring instruments, such effects are particularly likely. Numerous systematic changes in human judgments occur over time due to fatigue, boredom, or changes in standards. Although human judges are generally less trustworthy than other instruments, all instruments should be suspected: electrodes may pull loose or corrode, historical events that occur between pre- and posttesting may change the meaning of key questions, etc.[9]

Statistical regression.   When one selects from a distribution of scores those persons with either the high scores or the low scores, the mean of this group will typically shift toward a more middling score when one remeasures them. This is due to statistical regression. Consequently, any study that uses a sample of subjects atypical of the population from which it was selected is vulnerable to the effects of regression. If the experimental treatment applied to the group is designed or hypothesized to make them less extreme, regression constitutes an alternative explanation of any observed shift. If instead, the researcher predicts that the treatment will increase their extremity, regression will tend to counteract the treatment effects. In this case, if the comparison of pre- and postmeasurement shows no treatment effect, the conclusion of "no effect" may be erroneous.

No measurement or score perfectly measures a trait or response. Measurement theory assumes that the magnitudes of errors are normally distributed around a mean of no error at all and that errors are independent. Thus, there would be no way to predict either the direction or magnitude of error in a person's score by knowing the size or direction of error in his score on a previous administration of the test. If the size of errors is normally distributed, large errors will occur less frequently than small errors. For illustrative purposes, consider a person whose true score is middling (and therefore more common). If he obtains an extreme score because of a large error component, he is less likely to have that same magnitude of error on a second measurement. Some of the people who were selected for inclusion in the extreme group precisely because of their extreme scores will not have true scores that are extreme. Consequently, when measured again they are more likely to have a middling score. Hence, the inclusion of people like this in the extreme group will automatically insure that remeasurement of the group will show an average shift toward a more middling score.

Of course it is a simple matter to assess the extent to which such a shift is due to regression and not the experimental treatment (e.g., the human relations training course). For instance, one can split the group in half, apply the treatment to only one half, and postmeasure both groups. Regression should shift mean scores toward a more middling score. The change measured in the treated half should be evaluated against the shift shown by the untreated half. But obviously this is a different experimental design. Design 2 simply does not afford us this protection.

Design 3: The Static-Group Comparison

Adding a nonequivalent control group to Design 1 produces what Campbell calls the Static-Group Comparison. The X_1 for the upper group represents the experimental treatment: The X_0 for the lower group symbolizes that the groups

---

[9] Additional anxieties about instrumentation are discussed under the heading "Interaction of Treatment and Testing" in the discussion of Design 4.

experience identical events except for the experimental treatment. The dashed line symbolizes the nonequivalence of the groups, that is, they represent teachers from different school districts, people with different scores on some measure, people who served in the experiment at different times of the year, etc.

$$X_1 \quad O$$
$$- - - - -$$
$$X_0 \quad O$$

The important point is that subjects are not selected from a common pool and then randomly assigned to the conditions.

Selection Differences. Nonequivalence of groups potentially threatens the validity of any experiment, but with random assignment of subjects to conditions, the hazard is remote. Design 3 is particularly vulnerable to nonequivalence. For example, if teachers at one school receive a human relations training course and teachers at another school do not, for any number of reasons the teachers of these two schools might differ in bigotry at the outset. For instance, more minority children may attend one school and, therefore, bigoted teachers may avoid appointments in that school. As we have stressed, *only* by randomly assigning subjects to conditions can we create equivalence between experimental and control groups. Even showing that two nonequivalent groups have equal mean scores on 2 or 3 or 847 critical premeasures never assures us that they do not differ significantly on some other critical trait or ability. In other words, matching subjects from nonequivalent groups on all the variables one thinks might be relevant—even if it were practical to do so, which may not often be the case—is clearly inferior to working with equivalent groups.

As indicated, the obvious weakness of Design 3 is that we have no reason to expect initial equivalence between the groups, and since the design does not include a pretest we cannot even assess the preexperimental comparability of the two groups. Consider another example. Perhaps, in fact, the experimental group that received the human relations training course was highly favorable to ethnic group members before the course and less so afterwards. If the control group consists of ethnically prejudiced people, the training course might seem to be of value in making people more tolerant when it actually makes them less tolerant. Having no pretest measurement makes the experiment vulnerable to that possibility. Contrariwise, if the researcher premeasured the subjects in the two groups, their initial nonequivalence would be apparent from the start and would (or should) lead him to abandon the study right then.

One important point needs reemphasis. The preceding point may erroneously imply that if the design included a premeasure and the mean premeasure scores of the two groups were identical, one need no longer worry about their nonequivalence. Wrong! As indicated earlier, they may still differ on some other (unmeasured) critical variable that in interaction with the treatment, produces postmeasure differences. Only random assignment can guard against this possibility.

Mortality. Sometimes different numbers of subjects in each experimental condition drop out or refuse to be measured. The production of differences between measurements due to differential loss of certain kinds of persons from conditions cannot be detected in Design 3. Without knowing the preexperimental positions of subjects, for example, a human relations training course may appear to be effective when it may only be losing more bigots than another group. Even if an equal number of subjects are lost in both groups, there may still be a problem. If the subjects the experimental group loses are the most prejudiced members of the group, while those lost by the control group are not the most prejudiced members of that group, the apparent treatment effect will be mistakenly interpreted as an attitude change effect when it is really an effect of differential changes in the membership of the groups studied. Mortality is always something to be concerned about if substantial numbers of subjects are lost, and always a threat to validity in such instances unless there are pre-measures or other data to show that between-group differences do not reflect differential mortality.

In some cases, experimenters have created mortality artifacts by discarding subjects. Discarding subjects from one's analysis is not necessarily illegitimate. For example, subjects who obviously misunderstand instructions may reasonably be discarded. But, it is illegitimate to discard subjects because they have atypical scores on the dependent variable or to discard subjects on some grounds that might represent an effect of the experimental manipulation. For example, if communicator credibility were manipulated it would be wrong to discard data from subjects (a) merely because they believed a communicator low in credibility, or (b) because they failed to listen to a low credibility communicator (assuming more subjects in a low credibility condition showed such inattention). In the first case, one may be ignoring data that disconfirm the hypothesis merely because they do disconfirm the hypothesis. In the second case, one may be ignoring data that represent the operation of the process being studied; inattention may be one effect of low credibility.

The following three experimental designs constitute the strongest of the designs used in experimental social psychology.

Design 4: The Pretest-Posttest Control Group Design

In this design subjects are randomly assigned to conditions. The letter R designates random assignment. Such assignment is likely to establish the equivalence of groups.

$$R \quad O \quad X_1 \quad O$$
$$R \quad O \quad X_0 \quad O$$

Although Designs 3, 4, 5, 6, and 10 are depicted here as using only two groups —an experimental group and a control group—the logic of our analysis can be applied to such designs when they contain more experimental treatment levels $(X_1, X_2, \ldots X_n)$.

Design 4 copes adequately with history, maturation, regression, selection, and mortality effects by providing equivalent groups with concurrently comparable experiences (except for the experimental manipulation). Additionally, since it provides premeasures, it permits assessment of the initial comparability of groups and evaluation of mortality effects. History effects—occurrences unique to the individual sessions—may not be adequately controlled if the two conditions are studied by running two large groups of subjects, one of which receives the experimental treatment and the other of which does not. It is always possible that one uncontrolled event, an audible yawn, a passing airplane, a garbled instruction, an interruption by the janitor, or the like, may produce a large history effect in one group. Because of this, replicating the same condition numerous times or running subjects in all conditions simultaneously in the same setting are preferable alternatives to running conditions separately and only once or a very few times. With many replications, odd bits of history may be randomized between experimental and control groups.[10]

Design 4 controls for testing effects by providing a comparison group with equivalent testing experience. It controls instrumentation providing that the instruments are used in the same way at the same time. Instrumentation effects would be risked in Design 4 if, for example, measurements involving some subjectivity were made by a different observer for each of the two groups or if the same observer made measurements (e.g., scoring tape recordings of interactions, scoring TAT protocols, rating movies of the distance between subject and stooge, recording the number or types of gestures used by subjects when extemporaneously delivering a speech) on the two groups sequentially.

The Interaction of Treatment and Testing. The interaction of testing and experimental treatment is a potential source of invalidity in Design 4. It is possible for the pretest to sensitize experimental subjects. For example, assessing people's attitudes on a topic may make them more interested in a communication on the topic or quick to suspect that you are trying to persuade them when you expose them to a communication on that topic after a pretest. Thus, the experimental manipulation could seem in itself to have an effect when the effect can only be obtained from pretested (sensitized) subjects.[11]

The Interaction of Selection and Treatment. The possibility that an effect only exists for the specific population studied is another problem in Design 4. In experimental social psychology, a piece of folklore that may be more true than we would like to admit is that many effects may be obtained more easily

[10] Even then, if subjects are not run individually, statistical analyses representing the nonindependence of individual subjects (random blocks designs) are preferable to conventional statistics (Campbell & Stanley, 1963, p. 193).

[11] It must be admitted that the typical study that attempts to assess interaction effects between pretest and treatment finds little or no such effect. But most of these studies are Design 10 studies, the vulnerabilities of which are described in subsequent pages of this chapter. Moreover, in these studies the research typically did little to mask the intent of the experiment. In other words, in some sense all subjects may have been behaving as though pretested. Therefore, even though some have concluded that we may have been overly cautious in worrying about the sensitizing or commitment effects of pretesting (Campbell, 1969; Lana, 1969), we remain suspicious of designs that omit control for these effects.

from female subjects than from male subjects (Stricker, Messick, & Jackson, 1967). Additionally, most of us worry about the implications of investigating college students most of the time. We don't mean to imply that college students are not human, but they may differ from most people by being more rationalistic (hence less able to live with dissonant cognitions), more flexible (hence more willing to adjust to odd social situations), more open-minded (hence more willing to listen to persuasive communications), and in other ways. If so, the treatment effects we observe may be different for them than for other populations. Since most subjects occupy more humble positions than most experimenters, we have the status difference as another possible source of effects unique to the subject populations we study. As you can see, the list of reasons to suspect results could be quite long. At this point all that can be said is that we must be cautious in generalizing our results until we know more about population differences and population treatment interactions.

Compared to the first three designs, Design 4 is relatively free from potential alternative interpretations; but it may be useful to emphasize at this point that Design 4, or any other design, may produce a perfectly replicable effect—that is, the effect may appear again and again in the situation—and yet not be generalizable. The effect obtained in any experiment may be present only in that specific setting, only with the measuring devices used, only when the material is presented in the way it is presented, and so on. There is little doubt that the future of social psychology will be filled with effects and theories that subsequently turn out to have very limited applicability. For this reason, testing the odd application of an idea, working in novel settings, and using unusual materials, will always be of value in social psychology as a check on this generality of its theories and observations.[12]

Confounding of Other Nontreatment Effects with Treatment Effects. Confounding is a danger in any study. However, many control group experiments are needlessly weakened because by the design of the experiment the control group differs from the experimental group in more respects than just the receipt of the experimental manipulation. Frequently occurring, designed-in, nontreatment differences between experimental groups and control groups, any of which might produce an effect in itself, include the following: the experimenter interacts more with one group than with the other; the amount of time between pretest and posttest differs between groups; subjects in one group have more to do than subjects in the other; subjects in one group have more reason to think the experiment silly than subjects in the other (this happens, for example, when control subjects in a communication study receive a communication irrelevant to the attitude measured); the experimental subjects do not perform the control task (making it possible that the difference between groups reflects the control group's experiences rather than the experimental group's); or subjects in the control group receive a different rationale for the experiment than subjects in the experimental group.

---

[12] This point does not contradict an earlier admonition against studying unique groups or esoteric variables. Here we argue for the importance of testing theoretically important relations in new circumstances, not unimportant ones in whatever circumstances.

Design 5: The Solomon (1949) Four-Group Design

Solomon and Lessac (1968) give a detailed discussion of this design. The design includes a pair of control groups (X_0) that make it possible to assess both the effect of testing and the interaction of testing with treatment.

$$
\begin{array}{cccc}
R & O & X_1 & O \\
R & O & X_0 & O \\
R & & X_1 & O \\
R & & X_0 & O
\end{array}
$$

If the two pretested groups differ from the two groups that were not pretested, or if there is an effect only in the pretested group receiving the experimental treatment (X_1), one is justified in concluding that the pretest has in some way sensitized subjects.

Design 6: The Posttest Only Control Group Design

This is a relatively economical design in terms of expenditure of subject time and eliminates the effect of testing by eliminating the pretest.

$$
\begin{array}{ccc}
R & X_1 & O \\
R & X_0 & O
\end{array}
$$

Design 6 makes it almost impossible to evaluate the degree to which randomization establishes equivalent groups, but with large numbers of cases per condition this is not very likely to be a serious problem. For whatever it's worth, current custom in social psychology treats approximately 15 to 40 subjects per condition as the appropriately large number.

Design 6 also makes the interpretation of direction of effect open to question if the study employs only two conditions. For example, if two groups of children differ in the amount of pressure applied to them not to play with a toy, cognitive dissonance theory predicts that for those children who complied with the pressure, those who do so with less pressure will subsequently devalue the toy more. However, even if such a result were obtained, one could argue in the absence of premeasures that the difference between groups really stems from the high pressure condition. For example, stronger pressure not to play with a toy may lead children to attribute a higher value to the toy, or stronger pressure may create more negativism in children—more inclination to resist the pressure by valuing what they are being pressured to avoid. Thus, rather than cognitive dissonance producing devaluing among children complying with minimal pressure, some entirely different mechanism may enhance the value among children complying under high pressure. This problem is lessened to the degree that we do not have two experimental groups but instead have an experimental group and a true "control" group—a group which when measured reflects the pretreatment status of the experimental group. One could, in the present example, include an additional group that experiences the same amount of interaction with the experimenter and the same exposure to and contact with the crucial toy as the other groups, but receives no pressure to avoid playing with the toy.

The last five designs to be discussed in this chapter are quasi-experimental; they provide some protection against sources of invalidity while not meeting the high standards for control met by true experimental designs (Designs 4, 5, and 6). They are discussed because they are commonly used and because, in many situations, they appear more convenient to use than the true experimental designs.

Design 7: The Time Series Experiment

This design relies on the making of many observations on the same persons in order to evaluate the effect of an experimental manipulation on subsequent observations.

$$O \quad O \quad O \quad O \quad O \quad O \: X \: O \quad O \quad O \quad O \quad \text{etc.}$$

The number of observations may vary, but the lower the variability of scores among preexperimental observations and the greater their number, the more impressive is an effect that shows up in the expected place on one or more posttreatment observations. Studies resembling a time series design have been done on conformity, except that typically there has been a substantial sequence of treatment-observation pairings following an initial series of observations. In these cases the design has been something like:

$$O \quad O \quad O \quad O \quad O \: X_1 \: O \: X_1 \: O \: X_1 \: O \quad O \quad O \quad O$$

In experimental social psychology the time series could be used for studying many things, such as the effect of a single persuasive communication on communication-relevant behaviors. For example, smokers or people with other observable vices could be observed over a long period of time during which they have been exposed to a communication opposing their observed vice.

One major threat to the validity of a time series experiment is the possible co-occurrence with the treatment of some extraneous event that might effect one or more postmeasures. Temporally placing the observations close together and replicating the design on different subjects at different occasions minimizes threats from history. Instrumentation problems develop when measurements involve an observer or even a scorer of objective items who knows precisely at what point in the sequence of observations the experimental treatment occurred. If the observer or scorer knows where in the sequence of observation the experimenter placed the experimental treatment, he may intentionally or unintentionally bias the measurement. Interaction of the treatment with testing also strongly threatens the validity of time series designs. If assessing something sensitizes subjects, then a frequent assessment of that thing in a time series design will surely maximize the chances for such sensitization. This consideration argues particularly strongly for the use of indirect, disguised, or unobtrusive measures in time series designs.

Although not as powerful as the true experimental designs, Design 7 is often quite useful. The numerous assessments provide protection against maturation, mortality, and testing effects. Regression effects are unlikely to lead one to a false inference. Likewise, there is no danger from selection differences or from the interaction of selection with maturation or other things since the comparisons are within-group. For these latter effects to occur, one, of course, needs more than one group.

Design 8: The Equivalent Time Samples Design

This is a typical Skinnerian (operant conditioning) design for within-subject experiments, though there is no reason why it cannot be done with replications across many subjects.

$$X_1O \quad X_0O \quad X_1O \quad X_0O \quad \text{etc.}$$

In fact, because subjects in social psychological experiments rarely are as isolated as rats in Skinner boxes, replication may be useful in Design 8 in order to cope with variability problems; that is, replication is especially useful in making the operation of some process clear when there are many possible sources of uncontrolled random intrusions into the process being studied. Hence, a design using a single animal in a tightly controlled setting probably should be replicated if done on people because people cannot be caged individually, fed and watered on a tightly controlled schedule, etc. Design 8 has many of the virtues of a time series design but lacks some of the vices, since the frequent within-subject replication of the experimental treatment precludes odd history effects and reduces the chances of instrumentation effects occurring.

Multiple Treatment Interaction. The production of an effect that can only occur when the same subject is exposed to more than one treatment is a possible source of invalidity in Design 8 and in any other design that exposes subjects to more than one treatment. Premack (1968) shows how these problems may exist in the ordinary operant conditioning paradigm, and his discussion has implications for social psychology. The problem with multiple treatments is that they may sensitize, fatigue, or otherwise affect responding so that the phenomena we observe are not generalizable to situations that lack multiple treatments. One could, for example, risk contrast effects wherever treatments vary markedly on aesthetic dimensions (rude people seem more rude if one has just interacted with polite people; graceless rhetoric seems more clumsy if one has just heard polished oratory; supportive people are more comforting if one has recently experienced a series of distressing failure experiences, and so on).

Perhaps the safest way to avoid multiple treatment interaction in experimental social psychology is to work with stimuli that are familiar to subjects and behavior that is well learned. One form of social behavior that could be neatly studied with Design 8 and that would be unlikely to be influenced by multiple treatment interactions is one's response to common social situations. For example, one might, in the spirit of Argyle and Kendon (1967), study postural and gestural responses to variations in the conversation of another. One could manipulate the intimacy of the topic discussed, its threateningness, its friendliness, and so forth.

Another potentially strong danger in Design 8 is the development of an awareness by the subject that (a) he is in an experiment, and (b) that the sequence of events he has been experiencing constitute an experimental variation. Any time a human subject is exposed to a sequence of variations, especially when the cycle is repeated, the observed effects may arise from the subject's knowledge of the comparisons the experimenter wishes to make (Miller, Doob, Butler, & Marlowe, 1965). No experimenter would deem it wise in, say, a Design 4 experiment to inform subjects beforehand of the other conditions of the study.

Design 9: The Equivalent Materials Samples Design

This design resembles Design 8 closely, but it varies the material with which the subject works. In the following paradigm, M represents a set of materials.

$$M_a X_1 O \quad M_b X_0 O \quad M_c X_1 O \quad M_d X_0 O \quad \text{etc.}$$

Often it makes little sense to use the same materials several times in an experiment—each instance of presentation occurring in conjunction with a different experimental treatment. This would be true, for example, when learning or retention is being measured or when one is studying reactions to strangers. Moreover, it sometimes is valuable to shift the materials in that such shifts may reduce the likelihood that the subject will recognize what the experimental manipulations are. One must, of course, assume that the materials are equivalent and that their use in a Design 8 study does not destroy the equivalence (through warm-up effects, learning-to-learn effects, etc.). If the materials are equivalent then the data from all the instances of a treatment ($M_a X_1$, $M_c X_1$, $M_e X_1$, etc.) may be pooled in data analyses.

Design 10: The Nonequivalent Control Group Design

This design is one of the most common designs in experimental social psychology:

$$O \quad X_1 \quad O$$
$$\text{-------}$$
$$O \quad X_0 \quad O$$

A Design 10 arises whenever subjects in different treatment conditions come from different populations (e.g., different schools or classrooms), or are otherwise not randomly assigned as individuals to the experimental conditions. The nonequivalence may not be intended by the investigator or may seem unimportant to him. However, differences between experimental conditions in pre-existing characteristics of subjects could account for posttreatment differences between the groups. These differences could be mistakenly attributed to the experimental manipulation.

Regression effects are always a possibility if groups are selected in such a way that the treatment and the regression effect both operate in the same direction. However, the pretest provides some protection against regression effects by allowing an assessment of pretreatment equivalence on the trait being measured. For this reason, Design 10 is more powerful than Design 3.

The possible interaction of selection with other things—regression, maturation, mortality, treatment, and so on—constitutes the greatest problem with Design 10. Even apparent equivalence on the premeasure does not protect against this possibility. To take an example of interaction of selection and treatment (or selection and regression), if the experimental treatment is an antiprejudice film and its audience consists of people who voluntarily attended the film, even a group of nonvolunteers apparently from the same population and possessing identical prefilm attitudes might be nonequivalent. The true underlying attitudes of nonvolunteers may be more prejudiced than the attitudes of volunteers, or the treatment may only work on the kind of person who would volunteer for it.

Studies of the relationship between personality and social behavior ordinarily use Design 10. Many evaluate response to some social event among people who differ in personality. For example, one might study the effect of aggressive communications on the opinions of people who differ in aggressiveness. Unfortunately, personality is almost always correlated with pretest differences on the communication topic. Aggressive people will generally have more hostile, nasty attitudes toward anything, including the content or communicator of the persuasive communication they are to receive. This form of pretest nonequivalence makes any treatment effect difficult to interpret. First, personality will be confounded with the amount of opinion change being advocated (e.g., more aggressive persons may be faced with a more discrepant communication if a communication advocates light prison sentences for wealthy tax evaders). Second, personality may also be confounded with perceived characteristics of the communicator (e.g., with apparent similarity to the subject and consequent trustworthiness). If one only has posttest scores in such a study, as one does in Design 3, they are uninterpretable. One needs to know where the subjects started. (One would be foolish to conclude that nonaggressive people were more persuaded by a communication advocating tolerance of tax evaders if all he had were posttest data. Perhaps nobody was persuaded, or perhaps aggressive people were more persuaded but the persuasion failed to overcome an enormous pretest difference).

However, the change scores that might ordinarily be used by someone who recognizes the danger of using only posttest scores and hence looks at differences between pretest and posttest are also difficult to interpret. First, the confoundings with personality variables have not been removed from the situation. Second, the change scores may represent differential end effects—one

Table 2.1
Sources of Invalidity

Design	HISTORY	MATURATION	TESTING	INSTRUMENTATION	REGRESSION	SELECTION	MORTALITY	INTERACTION OF TESTING AND X	INTERACTION OF SELECTION AND X	MULTIPLE-X INTERFERENCE
Preexperimental Designs										
1. One-Shot Case Study $\quad$ X $\quad$ O	−	−				−	−		−	
2. One-Group Pretest-Posttest Design $\quad$ O$_1$ X O$_2$	−	−	−	−	?	+	+	−	−	
3. Static-Group Comparison $\quad$ X$_1$ O $\quad$ - - - - $\quad$ X$_0$ O	+	?	+	+	+	−	−		−	
True Experimental Designs										
4. Pretest-Posttest Control Group Design $\quad$ R O X$_1$ O $\quad$ R O X$_0$ O	+	+	+	+	+	+	+	−	?	
5. Solomon Four-Group Design $\quad$ R O X$_1$ O $\quad$ R O X$_0$ O $\quad$ R $\quad$ X$_1$ O $\quad$ R $\quad$ X$_0$ O	+	+	+	+	+	+	+	+	?	

Table 2.1—continued

Design												
6. Posttest-Only Control Group Design R X_1 O R X_0 O	+	+	+	+	+	+	+	+		+	+	?
Quasi-Experimental Designs												
7. Time Series O O O O X O O O O	−	+	+	?	+	+	+	+		+	−	?
8. Equivalent Time Samples Design X_1O X_0O X_1O X_0O, etc.	+	+	+	+	+	+	+	+		−	?	−
9. Equivalent Materials Samples Design $M_a$$X_1$O $M_b$$X_0$O $M_c$$X_1$O, etc.	+	+	+	+	+	+	+	+		−	?	−
10. Nonequivalent Control Group Design O X_1 O - - - O X_0 O	+	+	+	+	?	+	+	−		+	?	?
11. Counterbalanced Designs X_1O X_2O X_3O X_4O - - - - - - - - - - - - X_2O X_4O X_1O X_3O - - - - - - - - - - - - X_3O X_1O X_4O X_2O - - - - - - - - - - - - X_4O X_3O X_2O X_1O	+	+	+	+	+	+	+	?		?	?	?

NOTE. This table is derived from Donald T. Campbell and Julian C. Stanley, Experimental and quasi-experimental designs for research on teaching, in N. L. Gage (Ed.), *Handbook of Research on Teaching* (Chicago: Rand-McNally, 1963), pp. 178, 210. Copyright by the American Education Research Association and reproduced by permission. In the tables, a minus indicates a definite weakness, a plus indicates that the factor is controlled, a question mark indicates a possible source of concern, and a blank indicates that the factor is not relevant. It is with extreme reluctance that this summary table is presented because it is apt to be "too helpful," and to be depended upon in place of the more complex and qualified presentation in the text. No + or − indicator should be respected unless the reader comprehends why it is placed there. It is against the spirit of this presentation to create uncomprehended fears of, or confidence in, specific designs.

kind of subject was closer to the end of the measurement scale than the other, and this limits the amount of change he can show. It should be emphasized that end effects may arise short of the actual end of the scale, for example, subjects may typically be more reluctant to make a more extreme response. Worse still, we hardly ever know the size of intervals beween adjacent points on the scales we use. Consequently, any time we move people through different regions of scale scores it is difficult to interpret their changes.

The obvious experimental alternative to individual difference studies of the relation between personality and social behavior has been to manipulate personality rather than to select groups on the basis of personality. For example, in a study of aggressiveness, one might manipulate aggressiveness by angering a randomly chosen proportion of subjects. The gravest problem with such a procedure is that the experimental manipulation of a disposition may in fact produce the same problems that exist when the disposition is studied as an individual difference variable. For example, even if people are randomly assigned to conditions and the different groups of subjects are equivalent on aggressiveness before the experiment begins, when aggressiveness is manipulated their pretest attitudes may be manipulated. Hence, the attempt to control pretest attitudes through random assignment of subjects may be stymied by the unintended effect of the manipulation of aggressiveness.

Possibly the most daring and creative attempts to cope with confounding problems, such as those of Design 10, in the study of personality and social behavior have been those by Blum and his associates (Blum, Geiwitz, & Stewart, 1967), by Rosenberg (1960), and by Zimbardo (1966) to manipulate dispositions by hypnotism in a way intended to remove selection confoundings. For example, subjects may be given a posthypnotic suggestion that they are more or less aggressive and also that their pretest attitude is a certain value. If the posthypnotic suggestions work, pretest equivalence of attitudes plus differences in aggressiveness are both established. There are skeptics who suggest that hypnotism does nothing more than tell the subjects to behave cooperatively, no matter what the experimenter's hypothesis. However, a still more serious conceptual problem that must eventually be faced in studies using hypnotism is the extent to which the induced disposition resembles the pure theoretical concept with confoundings removed, or, instead, is a different genre of disposition.

Design 11: The Counterbalanced Design

This design exposes all subjects to all treatments.

Group A	X_1O	X_2O	X_3O	X_4O
Group B	X_2O	X_4O	X_1O	X_3O
Group C	X_3O	X_1O	X_4O	X_2O
Group D	X_4O	X_3O	X_2O	X_1O

Inspection reveals that all treatments appear at all positions in the ordering of treatments an equal number of times, and no treatment antecedes any given treatment more frequently than any other treatment does. The greatest threat to the validity of Design 11 is the possibility of multiple treatment interactions. Such confusion is especially great when the treatments, applied to equivalent materials, are given in sequence before any observations are made. Subjects may become confused about which instructions apply at any point in time, or they may become suspicious of the variations they are experiencing. In addition, treatments may have an effect only when they are placed adjacent to some other particular treatment.

Of course, it is always possible in a study with nonequivalent groups for selection to interact with other things. That is not such a grave problem in the various Counterbalanced Designs because comparisons may be made within subjects as well as pooling across subjects.

CONCLUSION

The student who has read this difficult chapter carefully and has mastered its contents is now equipped to do a modestly competent job of criticizing published social psychological research. However, he is not much more prepared to do his own experiments than a person who knows some neuroanatomy is to do neurosurgery. There are several important design problems yet to be discussed; we have not touched on most of the central concepts and issues in measurement and statistics; and the actual doing of experiments requires imagination and a sensitivity to what is affecting people—a sensitivity that cannot be learned from reading our words, or Freud's, or anyone else's. Table 2.1 summarizes some of this chapter's discussions of experimental designs and their vulnerabilities. In the next chapter we introduce the reader to some less rudimental design considerations, to some ethical issues that are of concern in social psychological research, and to some important ideas and issues in measurement and statistics.

REFERENCES

ARGYLE, M., & KENDON, A. The experimental analysis of social performance. In L. Berkowitz (Ed.), *Advances in experimental social psychology.* Vol. 3. New York: Academic Press, 1967. Pp. 55–98.

BERGMANN, G. *Philosophy of science.* Madison, Wis.: University of Wisconsin Press, 1957.

BLUM, G. S., GEIWITZ, P. J., & STEWART, C. G. Cognitive arousal: The evolution of a model. *Journal of Personality and Social Psychology,* 1967, **5,** 138–151.

CAMPBELL, D. T. Factors relevant to the validity of experiments in social settings. *Psychological Bulletin,* 1957, **54,** 297–312.

CAMPBELL, D. T. Prospective: Artifact and control. In R. Rosenthal & R. L. Rosnow (Eds.), *Artifact in behavioral research.* New York: Academic Press, 1969. Pp. 351–382.

CAMPBELL, D. T., & STANLEY, J. S. Experimental and quasi-experimental designs for research on teaching. In N. L. Gage (Ed.), *Handbook of research on teaching.* Chicago: Rand McNally, 1963. Pp. 171–246. (Reprinted: *Experimental and quasi-experimental design for research.* Chicago: Rand McNally, 1966.)

CHAPANIS, N. P., & CHAPANIS, A. Cognitive dissonance: Five years later. *Psychological Bulletin,* 1964, **61,** 1–22.

CHOMSKY, N. *Language and mind.* New York: Harcourt, 1968.

CROWNE, D. P., & MARLOWE, D. *The approval motive: Studies in evaluative dependence.* New York: Wiley, 1964.

FREEDMAN, J. L., & SEARS, D. O. Selective exposure. In L. Berkowitz (Ed.), *Advances in experimental social psychology.* Vol. 2. New York: Academic Press, 1965. Pp. 58–97.

KIESLER, C., COLLINS, B. E., & MILLER, N. *Attitude change: A critical analysis of theoretical approaches.* New York: Wiley, 1969.

LANA, R. E. Pretest sensitization. In R. Rosenthal & R. L. Rosnow (Eds.), *Artifact in behavioral research.* New York: Academic Press, 1969. Pp. 119–141.

MILLER, N., DOOB, A. N., BUTLER, D. C., & MARLOWE, D. The tendency to agree: Situational determinants and social desirability. *Journal of Experimental Research in Personality,* 1965, **1,** 78–83.

PREMACK, D. On some boundary conditions of contrast. In J. T. Tapp (Ed.), *Reinforcement and behavior.* New York: Academic Press, 1969. Pp. 122–145.

ROSENBERG, M. J. Cognitive reorganization in response to the hypnotic reversal of attitudinal affect. *Journal of Personality,* 1960, **28,** 39–63.

SECHREST, L. J. Naturalistic methods in the study of social attitudes. *Human Development,* 1967, **10**(34), 199–211.

SOLOMON, R. L. An extension of control group design. *Psychological Bulletin,* 1949, **46,** 137–150.

SOLOMON, R. L., & LESSAC, M. S. A control group design for experimental studies of developmental processes. *Psychological Bulletin,* 1968, **70,** 145–150.

STRICKER, L. J., MESSICK, S., & JACKSON, D. N. Suspicion of deception: Implications for conformity research. *Journal of Personality and Social Psychology,* 1967, **5,** 379–389.

WEBB, E. J., CAMPBELL, D. T., SCHWARTZ, R. D., & SECHREST, L. *Unobtrusive measures: Nonreactive research in the social sciences.* Chicago: Rand McNally, 1966.

ZAJONC, R. B. Cognitive theories in social psychology. In G. Lindzey & E. Aronson (Eds.), *Handbook of social psychology.* Vol. 1. Reading, Mass.: Addison-Wesley, 1968. Pp. 320–411.

ZIMBARDO, P. G. The cognitive control of motivation. *Transactions of the New York Academy of Sciences,* Series 2, 1966, **28,** 902–922.

3

PROBLEMS AND ANXIETIES IN RESEARCH DESIGN AND ANALYSIS

Paul C. Rosenblatt
Norman Miller

The preceding chapter constitutes the required epistemic scaffold for a person who wants to do research in social psychology or to evaluate the research of others intelligently. In the present chapter, we discuss two serious design problems that can arise in most laboratory research on people, introduce the student to some considerations dealing with the maximizing of research effects, discuss some problems that give most social psychologists nightmares, and consider some rudimentary issues in measurement and statistics. This chapter and the preceding one are separated because they represent different levels of sophistication in social psychological research methodology. Chapter 2 might bring the student to the level of an advanced undergraduate in psychology. This second chapter might bring the student to the level of a graduate student in the midst of his first year in a social psychology graduate program. Research in social psychology can, like a lot of other intellectual endeavors, produce deep gratification and also pain and anger. By the time the student finishes reading this chapter, he will probably feel exhausted from pondering various strategic and tactical problems in research design and analysis, and even then he will be far from being an expert. But what can one expect when the object of the game is to understand something as complex and resistant to superficial analysis as human social behavior?

TWO THREATS TO THE VALIDITY OF ANY LABORATORY STUDY

Laboratory settings, as we have declaimed in the preceding chapter, are often quite useful. They allow precise control over what happens to the experimental subject, elimination of extraneous stimuli, and the use of complicated equipment. In addition, they are less threatening for the experimenter and are usually easy for volunteer subjects to find. Unfortunately, a laboratory setting also has disadvantages, for instance, it restricts the generality of findings to laboratory or laboratorylike situations. Also, apart from questions of generality, there are two problems that often arise in laboratory research and severely threaten the validity of its outcomes: *experimenter bias* and *demand character- istics.* However, these problems are not restricted to laboratory experiments; their muddling effects may appear just as readily in field experiments and in correlational studies.

Experimenter Bias

Experimenter bias is a term usually reserved for the intentional or unintentional influencing of the subject by behaviors of the experimenter that are not intended to be part of the experimental manipulation. Before Robert Rosen- thal (1964, 1967) started using the term in this way, the term might also have applied to instrumentation errors where the instruments are humans. However, the discussion here will be limited to experimenter behaviors that may inap- propriately influence the subject. When an experimenter knows what effect he wants from a given subject and especially when he has a strong ego investment in obtaining the effect, he may inadvertently communicate his expectations to subjects by a variety of behaviors: by showing tension or relief at appropriate times, by subtle ways in which he reads instructions, by nodding his head, or by other gestures and cues. (There is also an occasional experimenter who inten- tionally biases his result, for example, the bored rat runner who gives the slow running rat a push or who enters a fictional datum because he failed to start a timer. Such practice is so obviously objectionable that there is no need to dis- cuss it here.)

At this time it is still unclear to what extent unintentional experimenter bias threatens our faith in research outcomes. Although Rosenthal and his colleagues published some dramatic illustrations of experimenter bias, most of them do not examine the behavior of experimenters across two or more experimental conditions (Aronson & Carlsmith, 1968). For example, Rosenthal, Persinger, Vikan-Kline, and Fode (1963) found that when each of twelve experimenters running subjects on the same task received biased data from their first two subjects (who were accomplices of Rosenthal and his colleagues), these early returns somehow influenced the data they collected from subsequent true subjects. The four experimenters who received hypothesis-confirming data from their first two subjects obtained the strongest confirming data from naive subjects who served after the two planted subjects. The four experimenters who received disconfirming data from their first two subjects obtained the most disconfirming data from the naive subjects who served after the plants. The control group of experimenters, who ran only naive subjects, obtained data with values between those obtained by the experimenters whose initial data tended to confirm the hypothesis and those whose initial data tended to dis- confirm the hypothesis. Thus, early returns seemed to bias subsequently obtained data.

However, one could argue that the results from this and other studies of experimenter bias could not be obtained if the same experimenter worked with subjects in all "conditions." Would bias appear if each of the twelve experimenters ran subjects in all three conditions? One could argue that the pressures for standardization of interaction with subjects would eliminate bias where experimenters work with subjects in each condition.

Barber and Silver (1968a, 1968b) argue that the importance of Rosenthal's findings on experimenter bias has been markedly exaggerated. They assert that the use of relatively untrained students as the experimenters studied, the use of statistics that obscure the degree to which chance factors could be operating, and the exertion of strong pressures on the experimenters studied to obtain biased effects (e.g., a higher rate of pay for hypotheses-supporting results) are among factors in Rosenthal's research that make the generality of unintended experimenter bias in social psychological research open to question. The data on experimenter bias effects are not all in, and one could currently rationalize a decision to ignore anxieties about bias effects. However, the wiser policy might be to minimize the possibility of their occurrence in one's own research and to respect the research of others more when the possibility of experimenter bias has been minimized.

There are various means of minimizing the possible occurrence of unintentional experimenter bias effects. One can eliminate communication of expectations by using automated procedures, such as tape recorders or TV cameras, or by otherwise minimizing interaction of the experimenter with the subject. If subjects have less reason to be motivated to please the experimenter (e.g., if the experimenter is not of higher status than the subjects, if subjects remain anonymous, or if the subjects don't know they are in an experiment) bias effects may be minimized. Bias effects have also been handled through use of experimenters with differing expectations regarding the outcome of the study. Thus, one might merely include experimenters with different hypotheses in all experimental conditions. In one interesting study (Carlsmith, Collins, & Helmreich, 1966), experimenters with different hypotheses about the effects of the manipulated variables were included as one of the variables in the experimental design. In this instance, the researchers assessed whether their own differing expectations produced different outcomes. There have also been studies (e.g., Miller & Levy, 1967) conducted by presumably unbiased experimenters that have included experimenters as a factor in the data analysis. When dependent variables show no systematic effects due to different experimenters on crucial comparisons, as was the case in the Carlsmith et al. and the Miller and Levy studies, the effects obtained are more impressive. Likewise, if a researcher obtains similar effects across several individual experimenters who each collect data for all conditions, the results have greater generality. They are no longer specific to an experimenter with a specific set of characteristics.

Conducting an experiment like the Carlsmith, Collins, and Helmreich one in which experimenters interact considerably with subjects and in which bias is a possibility is an expensive way to find out whether or not there is indeed a bias effect. Setting up and doing an experiment often takes much time and money.

Including procedures to minimize bias might be more sensible than attempting to assess it. Some additional means of minimizing bias effects include running subjects in all conditions simultaneously (so that the experimenter interacts identically with subjects in all conditions), training experimenters well, or keeping the experimenter in ignorance of the experimental conditions of the subject (e.g., by having crucial events happening to the subject outside of the awareness of the experimenter). To the extent that the experimenter is a standard stimulus or no stimulus at all, the possibility of obtaining effects due to experimenter bias is minimized.

Demand Characteristics

Demand characteristics is the phrase used to describe aspects of the experimental situation (other than those intentionally manipulated) that cue the subject to respond in a fashion that appears to him as consistent with the hypothesis of the experiment (Orne, 1962). Campbell (1957) has called both demand characteristics and experimenter bias *reactive arrangements*: aspects of an experimental setting that may obscure the phenomena of interest, but may produce (alone or in interaction with intended manipulations) effects that could be confused with the phenomena of interest. As an example of a design producing demand characteristics, consider a study of attitudes in which a communication is sandwiched between a pretest and a posttest of an attitude. Many of the subjects may infer that the experimenter is concerned with attitude change. If there were an experimental group that received the communication and a control group that received no communication, the implied demand characteristics in the experimental group might produce attitude change even if the communication were a silly one. The experimental subjects might think "I'm supposed to be influenced," whereas the control subjects who receive no communication but whose attitudes are measured twice might think, "Maybe the consistency of my attitudes is being measured." Demand characteristics, of course, may emerge from the physical characteristics of a laboratory setting. For example, expensive electronic equipment with flashing lights may intimidate subjects and make it more likely that they will be anxious not to ruin an experiment by failing to respond to any subtle influences they perceive in the situation.

Demand characteristics are as yet little studied and little understood. First, we do not know under what conditions subjects perceive them. In the past, social psychologists rarely attempted to assess subject suspicion (Stricker, 1967). This neglect is puzzling, since it would be unfortunate if psychologists only obtained effects because their subjects understood what the experimenter's hypotheses were and behaved in order to be helpful. Questioning intended to measure subject suspicion produces some reports of suspicion but also creates new problems. For example, it is possible that the probe of suspicion itself produces suspicion. It is also possible that demands may have effects without subjects being able to verbalize an awareness of demands. Subjects may also withhold suspicion, expecting that the experimenter's feelings would be hurt or something more embarrassing might happen if suspicions were revealed.

In two studies, most subjects given information by a subject who had served previously about the true nature of an experiment, withheld reports of suspicion when probed for suspicion by the experimenter (Freedman, Wallington, & Bless, 1967, Experiment 1; Levy, 1967). A third study reported that among subjects with a preexperimental tip-off from a subject who had served earlier, those encouraged strongly to report prior information about the experiment in a postexperimental interview did so (Golding & Lichtenstein, 1970). Finally, in a study of classical conditioning of eyelid blinking, subjects given conventional suspicion probes reported no suspicions; but when strongly questioned, and upon being told that their data would be discarded unless they could describe the purpose of the experiment, subjects did an excellent job of describing the purpose of the experiment (Goodrich, 1966, p. 5).

A second problem in coping with demand characteristics is that we don't understand what type of influence they may have. It is by no means obvious that demand characteristics will always produce the desired experimental effect. Sometimes the effect of demands may compete with the hypotheses tested, and it may well be that subject attitude is an important aspect of responsiveness to reactive arrangements. If subjects are inclined to be uncooperative, they may respond in opposition to demand characteristics. One may thus have to find out what the demands are and whether the subjects are either cooperative or uncooperative. Recently social psychologists have begun to respond to the potential seriousness of the problem by attempting to assess the effects of subject suspicion whether aroused with an experiment (Cook, Bean, Calder, Frey, Krovetz, & Reisman, 1970; Sigall, Aronson, & Van Hoose, 1969) or derived from past experience in other experiments (Cook, Bean, Calder, Frey, Krovetz, & Reisman, 1970; Fillenbaum, 1966; Holmes, 1967; Holmes & Appelbaum, 1970). It may turn out in the long run that demand characteristic problems are not serious in laboratory experiments, (Cook, Bean, Calder, Frey, Krovetz, & Reisman, 1970), but it would seem preferable to avoid risking them as much as possible by working with subjects who do not recognize that they are in experiments, whose alertness to demands are minimal, or who are given no cues at all that suggest what is being measured.

MAXIMIZING THE CHANCES OF FINDING SOMETHING

It has been an article of faith among social psychologists that increasing an experiment's realism and impact for subjects will create bigger differences between conditions on dependent measures and decrease the likelihood that subjects will respond to the epiphenomena of demand characteristics and experimental bias. Aronson and Carlsmith (1968) discuss at length devices for augmenting experimental realism. In general, these require that the subject involved find the experiment engaging and all events, including measurements, plausible. Subjects should be unaware of the hypothesis, but as we have indicated in discussing demand characteristics, this is difficult to verify. The usual device for keeping the subject unaware of the experimenter's hypothesis is to provide him with an alternative hypothesis in a so-called cover story. Unfortunately, the alternative hypothesis, though it might indeed be diverting, nevertheless provides a contextual effect that (a) is hard to evaluate, and (b) may be necessary for producing the obtained treatment effects, thus limiting the generalizability of findings.

We concur with the principle of manipulating independent variables as strongly as possible. Increasing the involvement of subjects may not only reduce the hazards of experimenter bias and demand characteristics, but, additionally, it may increase the likelihood that the effect sought will appear. Furthermore, it probably reduces the number of subjects needed to reach an adequate level of experimental sensitivity. Of course, the strength of any stressful manipulation must be limited by consideration of how much discomfort it causes subjects.

Psychological Equivalence and Actual Equivalence

One issue that arises from discussion of the impact of manipulation is the actual equivalence versus psychological equivalence of experimental instructions and events for subjects within a given experimental condition (Aronson & Carlsmith, 1968). Should all subjects for a condition receive identical treatment or should they all be brought to the same desired internal state? Whenever a subject feels that he doesn't fully comprehend the instructions, it is customary in psychology to give him a chance to hear them again, perhaps reworded, perhaps not. Yet whenever the experimenter knows what responses he desires from the subject to support his hypothesis, even this customary practice may increase the risk of experimenter bias (however unaware the experimenter may be of such bias).

Aronson and Carlsmith recommend, though with reservations, that one consider achieving psychological equivalence for subjects within treatment groups by varying the treatment. We see real danger in this approach. To illustrate, we will present a somewhat extreme example that undoubtedly exceeds the amount of nonequivalence any researcher would advocate. Consider an experiment studying the effect of the extremity of a communicator's position and its relation to persuasion. To implement great extremity for subjects in the high extremity condition, we would want to be certain—taking the psychological equivalence approach—that all the subjects in this condition experience the communication as very extreme. If we have premeasure scores on each subject, we might tailor the stand taken by the communicator to this premeasure score. In other words, each subject would receive a communication of a different degree of extremity depending on where the subject himself initially stood on the issue. To carry the principle further, if we suspected or knew that a communicator taking a more extreme stand is generally believed to be less credible, more of a crackpot, or otherwise odd, we might change his credentials in the high extremity condition (e.g., attribute higher status to him, describe him as more expert, imply that he and the subject have some dimensions of coorientation in life, etc.) to ensure that the effect of the communication on persuasion is not due to differences in perceived credibility of the communicator but rather to extremity of the position advocated. Furthermore, if we had a measure on each subject that indicated the extent to which the extremity of a communicator's position made him less credible, we might apply different additions to or subtractions from the communicator's credibility for each subject within a particular experimental condition. While this procedure is appealing on the surface, as previously indicated, it has clear dangers and we strongly recommend against it. It is difficult to assess equivalence of involvement, of orientation, or of the meaning of any given experience. It is even more difficult to assess these matters without changing them in the process. Any question assessing equivalence will intrude into subjects' thought processes and might affect other relevant aspects of their behavior.

Another basis for rejecting the notion of psychological equivalence stems from a basic philosophical issue. Is social psychology working toward a catalog of input-response relations (S-R or stimulus-response laws) or toward one of internal state-response relations (R-R or response-response laws)? Actual equivalence of experience for subjects in a given condition means that the experimenter determines in advance the exact stimulus condition for each experimental group within the design. He uniformly applies that stimulus (treatment) to all subjects within the cell. In contrast, psychological equivalence requires that the experimenter first know some response of the subject before he knows what magnitude of stimulus to apply to that subject in a given experimental condition. In other words, in the latter case the experimenter's behavior toward the subjects within an experimental treatment lacks uniformity. His behavior must always depend on some prior aspect of subject behavior.

It is not hard to trace the historical origins of a preference for psychological equivalence. At the top of this ancestral tree are Lewin, the Gestaltists, and other phenomenological psychologists. Lewin adopted an essentially ahistorical position on psychological processes. His approach emphasized the meanings that a subject carries around with him and the extent to which he interprets each new stimulus setting in terms of these previously acquired meanings. The Lewinian position is principally concerned with discovering the relation between one's present interpretation of a situation and how one will respond to it in the next instant in time.

We believe that a catalog of input-response relations (S-R laws) is preferable. Such a catalog is more elegant, less complicated, and easier to apply. In contrast, a catalog of relations between indices of internal states and other responses (R-R laws) is in a sense a catalog of individual difference correlations (with inherent interpretation complications created by third variables). In terms of the increasing interest in applying social psychological laws to real world problems, R-R laws almost completely lack value. The person interested in applying known information would indeed know how people in a given psychological state might respond in the next instant (an R-R relation), but he still would lack knowledge about how to get them into that psychological state in the first place. Thus, even if the Lewinian program were complete (all the social psychological laws he ever wished to discover were indeed discovered), the practicing social engineer would still have to discover for himself an entire science of S-R relations—the relation between antecedent stimulus conditions and the current internal state or meanings.[1]

Perhaps the most valuable anxieties created by the question of actual versus psychological equivalence are those concerning the validity of two common pretenses in social psychology: (a) that there is a clear and simple relation between stimulus events and internal states (doing X to people makes them think, feel, believe Y), and (b) that people's basic responses to events are generally homogeneous. In order to build a science, pretenses of simplicity are necessary. However, which pretenses profit us must necessarily be judged by a standard of accumulation of consistent findings. Thus we must eventually drop our pretense that we can easily manipulate internal states or that people are homogeneous if social psychology cannot produce a body of mutually consistent, replicable effects by use of these pretenses.

Manipulation Complexity

Another issue that warrants consideration is whether adequate and proper impact of the treatment on a subject requires complex manipulations (Aronson & Carlsmith, 1968). What is the consequence of complexity? Complexity refers to a compounding of instructions, extensive and consistent cover stories for all events, and perhaps a complicated series of events in order to create the proper state (belief, motivation, set, etc.,) within a subject. We recognize that there may often be no simple way to produce a desired disposition or state in a subject. But each complication contributes additional possibilities for alternative interpretations of obtained effects. In general, the simpler the manipulation sufficient to constitute a treatment, the better. Perhaps in the long run we will find that only the studies employing simple manipulations produce replicable effects.

Given that many of our studies use complicated treatments and design or

---

[1] Of course, the expert sensitive researcher in the "psychological equivalence" tradition may in fact know such S-R laws. In order to effectively produce psychological equivalence, he must be able to correctly diagnose and alter psychological states in the right direction and to the appropriate level. The problem is that at best the possession of this skill can only be inferred from a favorable outcome in the experiment—confirmation of the hypothesis. Even if we assume that the skill exists, it may operate unconsciously and thus remain irretrievable for teaching and application purposes. Furthermore, even if thoroughly conscious, which would be optimal, it remains an uncodified clinical skill— knowledge that still remains unavailable to our hapless social engineer.

measurement quirks that engender alternative interpretations (any of our good graduate students can propose additional interpretations for almost any published experiment in social psychology), it seems necessary to be cautious about placing confidence in the finding of any single study. The better studies in the field suggest a minimal number of alternative interpretations and make these conceivable alternative interpretations seem of minimum plausibility. But even these studies require a number of replications with design changes to take into account alternative interpretations. One antidote to the increase in the number of alternative explanations that goes along with the added complexity of manipulations is modified replication. When the same theoretical variable is manipulated with an entirely different set of complicated experimental procedures, we can more confidently accept the researcher's own explanation of the finding. Of course, with complex experimental inductions, it is always possible that some subtle critical artifact common to the two superficially different manipulations of the particular theoretical variable is truly responsible for a consistent outcome.

Failures to Replicate

What if a given finding is not replicated? Our current ignorance about research methods traps us into being unsure about what to believe when a study yields negative results. Negative results can always be obtained by an incompetent experimenter, so a negative result in itself does not disconfirm a hypothesis. Negative results can always be blamed on botched instructions, offended subjects, and the like. Nonetheless, it is disquieting that people who do not belong to the ingroup doing research designed to support (test) a specific theoretical position more often report negative results than those in the ingroup. One suspects that the methods sections of papers reporting results often fail to mention crucial factors necessary for getting an effect of a certain kind. So when an outgroup member performs a study that uses a procedure designed to parallel one in a methods section of a paper published by ingroup members, he makes crucial errors. Certain required characteristics of the setting or implicit assumptions about the specific conditions under which the hypothesis applies, which appeared obvious to the original experimenter and therefore unnecessary to report, may not occur to all (e.g., that the confederate of the experimenter with whom the subject interacts is perceived by the subject to possess equal status or a similar value system).

This problem is not necessarily proof of a need to chastise researchers for writing poor or incomplete descriptions of their methods. Limited journal space requires an abbreviated terse style of reporting, and a report of every detail of the research setting could take thousands of pages. It may always remain true that experienced researchers with extensive first-hand familiarity with a particular content area may possess an astuteness in choosing a particular set of experimental materials or in deciding on a particular way of inducing a motivational state that less experienced researchers lack. And there are simply many subtle decisions for which extensive justification and explanation can't be expected in a standard procedure section of a journal article.

A rash "solution" to this problem is to reject or ignore the negative results of "untrusted" or naive outgroup researchers. This seems like a poor solution that may create more problems than it solves. A better solution, which even those inclined to discard the negative findings of "untrusted" researchers might find agreeable, might be to encourage researchers to send a very detailed procedure section (including materials and measuring instruments) to an expert in that particular area. The expert would then decide whether the induction and manipulations adequately engaged the relevant theoretical variables. Subsequent negative results could no longer be readily dismissable if the expert had decided in advance that the materials represented an adequate test of his hypothesis (as previously confirmed in published research). This may place an undue burden on more experienced researchers in the field, but perhaps the incentive of joint authorship and the feeling of responsibility by all who publish research of theoretical significance would balance things somewhat. Although this procedure seems tedious and effortful, it would provide considerable help toward solving the problem.

The need for apprenticeship when trying to master subtle techniques for performing research in a given area is indirectly realized by many sophisticated psychologists who visit laboratories where others actively work in the area. They observe the research process rather than use published material as their sole guide. Perhaps one thing we may have to work on soon in social psychology is how to make explicit exactly what it is that successful researchers accomplish when they decide to do one thing or another about the myriad apparent irrelevancies of a study that may in fact influence obtained results (i.e., the way the experimenter dresses, the time of day the study is done, arrangement of seating, precisely how subjects are recruited, as well as the more potent considerations such as the manner in which the experimenter interacts with the subjects and the choice of materials for the particular experiment).

The preceding paragraphs may seem incongruous in an introduction to research method, but we include them as a warning to the novice researcher of possible frustrations and as a suggestion that he will probably be in a much better position to produce and study some phenomenon if he receives advice from people who previously produced it. In this respect, social psychology is no worse off than the "hard" sciences. Natural scientists know they usually must apprentice themselves to experts in an area in order to learn to do a particular kind of research. Chemists have a journal that publishes, along with the report of an effect, the results obtained when two members of the journal's editorial board try to replicate the procedure specified in the initial report. And a distinguished biologist we know of had to bring a former assistant of his back from her honeymoon because his other assistants, following procedures in the assistant's laboratory reports, could not replicate the effect she obtained. A crucial factor, as it turned out, was that she added a pair of reagents to some biological materials in a different order than the other assistants had.

Field Studies

Returning to an earlier point, we noted that experimental realism is surely preferable to a transparent and uninvolving state of affairs. But, as indicated, some of the recommendations for implementing it—psychological versus stimulus control and maximal complexity in experimental inductions—introduce other problems. However, these are not the only solutions to the problem. We have tried throughout these chapters to present the kinds of artifacts that commonly plague social psychological research as it is performed in the laboratory along with some careful consideration of their sources and effects. The most complete way to rule out many of these artifacts and to handle the problems of lack of experimental realism, impact, and subjective involvement, is to perform thoroughly disguised experiments in which subjects have no idea that they are participating in an experiment. Moving from laboratory settings to nonlaboratory or other disguised settings, namely, performing experiments in the field, seems to be the obvious solution.

There are now several dozen interesting examples of social psychological experiments done in field settings. In the Miller and Levy (1967) study mentioned previously, the subjects were women in shopping centers who were led to believe that they were being interviewed for a radio program. In a study of the effect of modeling on assistance giving, Bryan and Test (1967) report four experiments. In one, the measure was of drivers stopping to give assistance to a girl standing by a car with a flat tire, and the manipulation was the presence or absence of a girl two blocks up the street watching a man change a flat tire. In two others, the dependent measure was dropping money in a Salvation Army kettle and the independent manipulation was the presence or absence of a model performing the same behavior; and in the fourth, the dependent measures were the percentage of people dropping money into the Salvation Army kettle and the amount of money collected, and the independent variable was the race of the Salvation Army bellringer.

In a study of the effect of insult on persuasion, Abelson and Miller (1967) reported the results of interviews of people sitting on benches in Washington Square Park in New York. While the experimenter interviewed the subject on a controversial topic, a confederate of the experimenter, sitting on the same bench as the subject, either made insulting or nonoffensive remarks while disagreeing with the subject. Also manipulated were (a) the presence or absence of a crowd that supported the subject, and (b) whether or not the confederate left before the interviewer obtained the final opinion measures. Lefkowitz, Blake, and Mouton (1955) manipulated the apparent status of a conferderate by dressing him neatly or shabbily and studied the inclination of people to follow him across the street in the face of a red light. These field experiments not only circumvent many of the problems peculiar to laboratory experiments in social psychology, but one also suspects that because of their field setting, the results are more generalizable (McGuire, 1967).

DECEPTION AND ITS ALTERNATIVES

While the field setting may be the most ideal one for thoroughly disguising the fact that the subject is in an experiment, some of the deceptions perpetrated in laboratory research are sufficiently disarming and convincing that the subjects' conceptions of what has occurred or what is being studied are as far from the truth as are the conceptions of subjects in many field studies. Of course, many researchers feel compelled in either setting to set the record straight by debriefing subjects when they complete their participation (telling the subject the purpose of the study, what lies were told to him, and explaining the necessity for the deception).

Deception and Morality

As indicated social psychologists often use deception. The deception may be *active* in that it misleads subjects about what is going on. They may be told that comprehension is being studied, when it is actually attitude change that is being studied. They may be told that taste thresholds are being studied, when actually what is being studied is how monetary incentives to participate in the study affect pleasantness ratings of bitter solutions. The number of different active deceptions that have been used in social psychological research must be in the thousands.

Deceptions may also be *passive* in that no lies are told. Instead, subjects are merely being studied without their awareness. One may, for example, be watching what ordinary pedestrians do when an experimenter's accomplice jaywalks, or one may be studying the effect of sitting immediately adjacent to someone in an otherwise empty library reading room. The question to be asked of both active and passive deception is one of ethics. Can one justify lies? Can one justify studying people without their awareness and, consequently, their consent? In either case, deceit is dishonest and deprives the subject of his freedom. It is also capable of permanently hurting people. For example, what if you convince the subjects that they're incapable of thinking consistently? Perhaps, too, it is bad for public relations and thereby jeopardizes other worthwhile work performed by psychologists. Some of the undesirable, potentially damaging effects of manipulations may persist even following careful debriefing (Walster, Berscheid, Abrahams, & Aronson, 1967). In the final analysis these questions, like all ethical questions, cannot be answered for you. Nevertheless, we include some of our thinking about the issues in the following paragraphs, and try to show that they are indeed complex.

While most of us prefer to think that our answers to ethical questions are absolute—that our values are not relativistic or subject to the sway of forces around us, the tides of history, or custom—it nevertheless seems appropriate to judge the ethical quality of any act both in terms of other contemporaneous cultural-historical events and in terms of the full consequences of the particular act. More simply put, we must consider the moral virtues as well as the hazards of any act and consider them against the general cultural standards of ethical behavior. Passive, innocuous, or apparently harmless lies are better in some sense than those falling at opposite ends of these dimensions. Added tolerance for them can be justified in terms of the goal of developing a dependable social science. This is not to argue in some dogmatic way that ends justify means, but more properly, to look for the perspective against which to make sane and moral judgments.

Are experiments in which we temporarily induce states like anxiety necessarily bad? If for humanitarian reasons we strongly oppose inducing high anxiety states in students in the laboratory, perhaps we could more profitably turn our attention to other areas in which we may have control and in which the balancing "social good" of developing a social science is absent. For example, there is the ordinary testing and examination ritual characteristic of most undergraduate and graduate programs. It seems clear to us that the level of anxiety induced by assessment in these programs is often substantially greater and more pervasive than that produced in our experimental laboratories.

The ethical standards recommended for psychologists by a committee of the American Psychological Association in 1959 include the following injunction: "Only when a problem is significant and can be investigated in no other way is the psychologist justified in giving misinformation to research subjects or exposing research subjects to physical or emotional stress [p. 282]." Apparently, because of disagreement on how to decide the value of research, this committee avoided saying one can do research that may be harmful to subjects only when it has overwhelming value. Instead, they asserted, "the psychologist believes that society will be best served when he investigates where his judgment indicates investigation is needed [p. 279]." As far as we know, most social psychologists worry about the value of their research and balance the judged value against possible harm to subjects. But there can always be disagreement about whether a problem can be investigated in no other way, whether there is substantial stress involved in being a subject in some given experimental condition, and whether a problem is worth working on. It is difficult to adjudicate disagreement. Can a person be objective about the value of his own research? Can a psychologist working in a different area or a nonpsychologist know enough to judge the importance of a research problem or the possibility of studying the problem with alternative procedures? For that matter, how does one measure the value of any research or the benefit to be obtained from one set of procedures as opposed to the benefit to be obtained from some alternative? What has research on the atom done for us? Are we better off with the National Aeronautics and Space Administration programs than we would be with space programs that spent no money on transporting men from this planet?

The alternative to a deception experiment (with or without a subsequent debriefing) may elicit greater psychological pain. For instance, consider a researcher who wishes to study unethical behavior. He might arrange various conditions that lead subjects to engage in an unethical act and unbeknownst to them observe the degree of their infraction under different conditions. As an alternative method for obtaining information, another researcher might interview people and elicit detailed accounts of previous occasions in which they behaved unethically along with descriptions of the circumstances under which the infraction occurred. The probing by the interviewer may be fairly intense in order to penetrate rationalizations, misperceptions, and general defensiveness. Who is to say which of the two approaches might arouse greater psychological pain or produce long-term damage? In addition, the alternative to deception may yield more ambiguous results.

In the face-to-face interactions of personal life—the one segment of life for which the moral man might consider ethical infractions most intolerable—we often engage in deceptions and fail to disclose publicly our motives and intentions to other persons. Obviously people can tolerate some deception. Perhaps we can conclude that real life often differs little from a deception experiment with the exception perhaps that debriefing (revealing what deceptions have been perpetrated and why they were needed) in real life is often either completely omitted or substantially delayed.

Debriefing.   Whereas many researchers feel compelled to debrief subjects after an experiment, it is not clear that the debriefing necessarily relieves subjects (Walster, et al., 1967). It may leave them more suspicious of future research in which they participate (Brock & Becker, 1966); and it often provides the direct experience of witnessing a prestigious model such as a college professor lie (Campbell, 1969). Furthermore, as Campbell notes, public exposure and confrontation of one's own naivete, gullibility, cruelty, bias, lack of independence, etc., may be more damaging to a subject than helpful, and in many instances the debriefing may in reality do more for the experimenter's guilt than for the subject's supposedly damaged psyche. Furthermore, eliciting the promise not to tell, which is the standard request after debriefing a subject, may not protect the research from actual disclosures to other potential subjects (Wuebben, 1967).

The point here is that perhaps we have been too rigid in automatically debriefing subjects. Debriefing should be reserved perhaps for those situations in which the potentially harmful effects of the experimental treatment can truly be alleviated.

Informed Consent.   Another issue is whether subjects should know what they are getting into when they agree to participate in an experiment. This question of informed consent is a difficult one. That many psychology departments require students to participate in research as an adjunct to the introductory course complicates matters. In an effort to deal with the problem of informed consent, students are sometimes allowed to volunteer and by doing so to earn extra credit toward a final grade. But this may not reduce the coercive aspect of the procedure. Those who do participate may feel that they really need the extra credit and consequently may feel little freedom in their choice to volunteer.

From the standpoint of valid experimentation, the issue is critical. With informed consent, subjects know the nature of the manipulations in advance, and we may no longer know what the results mean. All the previously mentioned potential artifacts stemming from experimental demand and motives to present a proper image offer strong alternative interpretations to any outcome.

The problem of informed consent is obviously not restricted to social psychoogical (or behavioral science) research. Clearly, for all the instances of institutionalized deception that pervade the culture there is little if any informed consent.

Role Playing Experiments.   To the extent that we question the possibility of constructing a mature social science out of the laboratory lie-pen in which we tether our sophomores, we can move to the field setting where our respect is less tarnished and treachery is closer to social custom and more readily taken for granted. Campbell (1969) has ably and forcibly shown a variety of ways in which good research can be conducted in the field setting without subsequent moral remorse. Kelman (1967, 1968) has also considered these issues at length and takes a somewhat harder position on contemporary social psychology. One alternative he advocates for the study of social behavior of others is role playing.

In a role playing experiment, the researcher asks the subject to behave *as if* something is true. He may be asked to give a persuasive speech on a topic as if he really believed it (Janis & King, 1954; Festinger & Carlsmith, 1959); to act as if he controlled the national resources of country X in an international conflict situation (Guetzkow, et al., 1963); to act as if he was a department store owner who had different affective feelings toward three things, namely, high sales volume, modern art, and Mr. Fenwick, the manager of the rug department (Abelson & Rosenberg, 1958); to make a decision between different job situations that vary in terms of facets of equity (Weick and Nesset, 1968); or to respond in the way he thinks he would if he were going to receive a strong electric shock (Kelman, 1968; Greenberg, 1967). The crucial thing for Kelman is that the subject be made aware from the outset of the make-believe situation in which he is embedded. There need be no surprises at the end.

There are two slightly different types of role playing instructions that the subject can be given: (a) he can be asked to respond as he thinks he would if he were in that particular situation, or (b) he can be asked to respond as he thinks others typically would respond in that situation. The first stresses, or with proper instructions can be made to stress, subjects' own idiosyncratic reactions to the situation. The second asks subjects to give their judgment or provide information about normative behavior for that situation—how most people would act.

The virtues of role playing can be quickly enumerated. For Kelman, its first and major virtue is that it eliminates the ethical problems that characterize much of other behavioral science research. Second, when instructions are carefully given and the setting is "right," it seems that subjects can get involved in the particular situation—that their true feelings do get engaged. Furthermore, the results obtained with role playing procedures do sometimes partially replicate prior results obtained with deceit procedures (Greenberg, 1967; Bem, 1967). Lastly, there is some *a priori* validity to the role playing technique as a research procedure in that there are numerous real life situations that are in fact role playing situations. In considering a job change, one must imagine what the new situation would be like if one were in it; one must imagine how one would feel about the job with only incomplete information (e.g., a description by others of what the job is like) about the situation. The consequences of such preliminary role playing might determine whether or not one tries to obtain a particular job.

When is role playing most likely to be effective as an experimental technique? So far little is known about the comparabilities of results obtained with role playing procedures and ordinary experimental procedures. Ultimately, the usefulness of role playing is an empirical question, and Kelman's enthusiasm for it as a solution may turn out to be unwarranted. In the absence of specific knowledge, we can only speculate intelligently about the circumstances under which role playing is most likely to yield the same results as the analogous deception procedure. First, it seems likely that results will generalize to non-role playing situations when the role playing induction is specific, engaging, and less hypothetical. Role playing should be more effective when it consists of behavior that the subject considers important, that he really cares about. Second, subjects should serve in only a single role playing condition (or if they do serve in multiple conditions, the results for the repeated measures portion of the experiment should be examined separately from those obtained from each subject's first role playing condition), and, certainly, if the design contains multiple treatments for each subject, subjects should not be alerted to this fact in advance. Third, since the role playing procedure leaves the crucial response measure so vulnerable to the response biasing effects of personality traits such as need for social approval, or acquiescence, it seems particularly important to search for unobtrusive response measures that can be used in the role playing situation. Fourth, since the role playing procedure does appear to be particularly vulnerable to demand effects, extra precautions should be taken to prevent them and/or assess them. Lastly, individual difference variables may be relevant to the generalizability of role playing results. Conceivably, certain types of persons may yield results more comparable to those obtained from non-role playing experiments, for example empathetic people.

To the extent that the details of the make-believe situation are not clearly spelled out, the subject must add them himself. This may create greater variability in behavior among subjects than is characteristic of a comparable "real experimental situation." Consequently, roie playing experiments may more often yield negative results (no relation between the variables hypothesized to be related to one another). Particularly in situations where the experimenter is asking "what is normative of people in general" (rather than "what are your own idiosyncratic reactions"), it is important that the experimenter spell out for the subject the people whom he, the experimenter, wants to know about: what social class, race, sex, age, educational level, intelligence level, etc.

The problems of generalizability have already been stressed. The great vulnerability of the role playing situation to presentational motives ("How can I behave to make the experimenter think I'm really a neat or great person?" has been indicated. Likewise, the highly cognitive role playing situation (subjects are pretending rather than responding spontaneously to a realistic situation) may not generalize to more behavioral situations. If we followed Kelman's advice, we might develop a complete science about role playing, but one that tells us nothing about how people actually behave when faced with these "as if" dilemmas. Indeed, some studies point to differences between cognitive or verbal responses and gross behavioral responses (DeFleur & Westie, 1958; Festinger, 1964). Other studies that do not directly examine the consistency among different types of human responses, but instead attempt to "replicate" some prior finding using a role playing technique, often do not confirm the outcome of the original experiment in detail (Greenberg, 1967; Jones, Linder, Kiesler, Zanna, & Brehm, 1968). It remains to be seen whether these discrepancies in "replication" are of a larger magnitude than the discrepancies that occur when any study is replicated directly.

In conclusion, what can we say about role playing? All we can say at present is that there is no substantial evidence that it is or is not the panacea for our ethical qualms. Clearly we need more information. And certainly the role playing situation is worthy of further study, both for ethical reasons and in its own right.

MEASUREMENT

Measurement of the subject's response is a crucial part of the research process. It is not merely that we need some formal way to assess what subjects are doing. Often the effect on an experimental treatment is very subtle; when it is, precise sensitive measurement is needed for an effect to be detected. By measurement we mean any assessment of behavior or behavioral disposition: self-report (a subject's recall or report of his own feelings, attitudes, behavior); observations in free responding or structured situations; responses on paper-and-pencil tests; recording of physiological reaction; response on a projective test; etc.

Reliability. The most basic and minimal requirement of any measure is that it be reliable. Reliability has been defined as the ratio of true variance to error variance plus true variance. Put less technically, we can imagine that at a particular point in time there is one score on a test or measure that truly represents a particular subject's level on the trait or disposition under consideration. To the extent that a measure is reliable, had we measured the subject at that instance an infinite number of times, he would have obtained an identical score on each measurement. In other words, reliability reflects the consistency of a measure. As Cronbach (1960, p. 138) has pointed out, however, when we actually compute reliability of a measure, our typical techniques include different amounts of error in our estimate, some of which add to and others of which subtract from the true reliability of the measure.

The correlation coefficient is the typical index of reliability. Consider a set of items designed to measure attitudes toward unions. Reliability can be estimated by correlating measures obtained at two different points in time, *test-retest reliability*; by correlating the score on one half of the items with that on the other half, *split-half reliability*; or by constructing two different sets of items (or dividing the items in half), and administering them on two separate occasions, *alternate form reliability*. From our earlier discussion of designs, you should now be in a position to think of the kinds of error factors that, although unrelated to attitudes towards unions, might artifactually inflate or lower the reliability estimate obtained from any of these procedures.

Most practicing researchers in social psychology pay little attention to the reliability of their measures. In other words, although they may report an estimate of reliability (after completing the experiment), they spend little time refining and improving their measures in advance of their experiment. This may seem patently foolish, in that any experiment that uses unreliable measures is doomed to failure. In defense, the researchers would argue that their time is better spent refining experimental procedure—developing a strong and theoretically unambiguous experimental treatment. This amounts to a hunch or bet that a manipulation with strong impact makes up for a weak measure. There seems to be substantial appeal to this argument, and we are inclined to go along with it. Even a measure of attitude toward unions consisting of three or five items written in a few minutes typically will possess some minimal level of reliability, whereas a thoughtless experimental treatment may have no effect whatsoever.

The social psychologist might protect himself from unreliability by using many items to measure the same thing. Researchers can most easily add to the reliability of a measure by increasing its length—by adding items to an attitude scale, increasing the length of an observation period, using more cards on the TAT, applying the physiological measure several times instead of just once, etc. Unfortunately, although in theory added length increases reliability, in actual experimental settings the added length may have mixed value. It may, for example, lower reliability by adding the effects of fatigue and boredom to subjects' responses to end items whereas these elements are absent in responses to earlier items; the same may be said for repeated observers' ratings or repeated physiological measures.

Alternatively, increasing the length of a measure may increase reliability in an undesirable way—by adding to the scale the effect of other characteristics that are peripheral to our actual concern, for example, perseverance. In other words, we may achieve a more reliable measure by adding to the factorial complexity of the measure when we only want to measure attitudes toward the union. If so, what do we suggest? We certainly don't believe in using single items, extremely short observations, etc. Especially when paper-and-pencil measures are used, multiple items cost little researcher effort. At the very least, one's measuring instrument should be long enough to give variability a chance to emerge. (Without variability it is impossible to detect differences between treatment conditions.) At the other extreme, one's measuring instrument should not be so long that it produces distortions by altering subject's fatigue, boredom, and the like. For any particular measurement problem, many other practical problems arise to affect what one does—cost in time and experimenter effort, longevity of the psychological state under study, availability of measures used in other studies, etc.

Lastly, if one plans to use a measuring instrument with multiple items (pooling several responses to produce a single score for each subject), he must remain committed to using that pooled score. There are temptations to attend to specific items if the analyses of pooled scores are disappointing. However, this allows one to capitalize on chance variations that probably have nothing to do with actual psychological processes. Under no circumstances should the one or two or few items that worked be reported while no mention is made of the others.

Validity. Aside from reliability considerations and the design problems created by measuring, a principal concern in measurement is one of validity. Although there is an impressive literature in the field of testing on validity (Scott, 1968, deals with applications to social psychology), the typical social psychology experiment settles for measures that have only face validity according to the intuitions of the researcher. By "face validity" we mean that the measure looks to the researcher as though it measures what he wants measured. One could argue that reliance on face validity is not entirely without merit. More elaborate validation procedures are costly in terms of both the researcher's and the subjects' time, and low validity suffices when experimental treatments have strong effects and there is an adequate number of subjects. Of course, if a researcher fails to obtain validity data, he may be measuring something different from that which he thinks or says he is measuring. Some people argue that results in support of a hypothesis simultaneously provide support for the hypothesis and validate the measures. However, the alternative interpretation, in the absence of validity data on measures and checks on manipulations, is that the results simply represent a compounding of errors.

In validating a measure, one question to be answered is whether the measure assesses the appropriate disposition more than it assesses some other disposition (Campbell & Fiske, 1959). This question is inextricably bound with the question of the *construct* validity of the disposition, the question of whether there really is such a disposition. Failure to find data that validate a measure may indicate either that the disposition doesn't exist (that there is no construct) or that it does exist but one's measure is poor.

In validating a measure one must correlate scores on the measure with scores on other measures and show that the measure correlates with what it should and fails to correlate with what it shouldn't. The greatest threat to validity probably comes from measures of other things obtained by the same method (Campbell & Fiske, 1959); for example one's paper-and-pencil measures of anxiety are probably most likely to correlate too strongly with one's other paper-and-pencil measures (e.g., of happiness, of mental health, etc.).

The studies designed to assess validity across several kinds of measures and several dispositions address questions of generalizability of effects. That is, are effects obtained from paper-and-pencil measures comparable to effects obtained from less symbolic behavior? While the literature on intermeasure correlations in social psychology suggests that correlations between measures of the same thing are substantially less than perfect and that dispositions are often multidimensional, there is fortunately some consistency (Campbell, 1963). Other indices of measure adequacy that may be desirable to obtain, which are discussed at length by Scott (1968), include convenience of use and insensitivity to effects of extraneous variables. Furthermore, measures that deal with important theoretical concepts and that have several parts (e.g., paper-and-pencil tests with many items that are supposed to measure aggressiveness) should be homogeneous (and generate similar subject responding to all parts) in order to support the theoretical conception.

One of the temptations for people concerned with the validity of their measures is to use "canned measures"—measures that are already available, that have been studied in other situations on other subjects, that were standardized and validated beforehand for some other purpose. There is nothing sinful in using such measures, but there is a risk. The risk is that the measure may not be valid on the subject population to be studied or in the experiment one intends to do. The best protection against that possibility is to build validation procedures into the actual experiment. In effect, this means making multiple measurements of the dispositions to be measured. Unfortunately, making the multiple measurements may alter the dispositions, especially if the measurements are not well disguised. For example, multiple measurements may add demand characteristics to the situation. Moreover, earlier responses may differ from later responses because making the earlier ones may change the subject's dispositions, for example, reduce his need to express some feeling. Alternatively or additionally the strength of a disposition may change over time. Still another possibility is that earlier responses may build an artificial stability into dispositions by creating a set in the subject to appear consistent.

Other Measurement Problems. Measuring the dispositions of subjects is not independent of experimental design problems. As we previously stated, measurement procedures may create additional interpretations of the obtained data by giving subjects additional ideas about what is going on, by constituting a treatment in itself (e.g., measuring an opinion may moderate extreme opinions by showing subjects that less extreme opinions may exist), by giving the subject a chance to present himself in a favorable light, etc. Because of this, disguised measures are to be preferred to measures made with the subject's knowledge that he is being studied (Campbell, 1950; Webb et al., 1966). Even if treatments are applied in the laboratory, measures may be disguised by being taken in a different setting from the laboratory (e.g., Leventhal, 1965) or by presenting an effective cover story.

A problem related to that of using standardized dependent measures is the use of standardized experimental materials. It is always possible that experimental materials perceived in a certain way in one population will be perceived in a different way in another population. For example, it is customary in studies of impression formation to ask subjects to evaluate persons by using a set of adjectives whose value on a goodness-badness dimension has been assessed in the past. For some studies, it is crucial that the researcher know whether each adjective used is on the good or bad side of neutral; use of standardized adjective lists without a check of the particular evaluative set of subjects under study may produce findings that artifactually reflect temporal or geographic differences in the favorability of adjectives.

There is yet another reason for avoiding the use of identical experimental materials if possible. Although it does add to the generality of our results if they can be confirmed with a different population, the generality of the relation gains even more substantial increment when the replication uses different experimental materials. Then we can assert more assuredly that nothing intrinsic or specific to the materials produced the outcome.

STATISTICS

It is assumed that the reader of this chapter has enough statistical sophistication to decide what to do with his observations in order to evaluate the effects in his experiments. A good rule to follow is to avoid starting an experiment unless you know precisely what statistical procedure you are going to follow to evaluate your experimental effects. What observations will be used in what data analyses employing what statistics?

Some people think psychologists do odd things with statistics. Many experts describe the function of statistics as enabling one to make inferences about the characteristics of a universe from results obtained on a random sample drawn from that universe. Yet social psychologists rarely sample randomly and rarely are clear about what universe they are interested in, although one suspects that the interest is in people in general. If social psychologists are not using their statistics to generalize about the universe of people—when this is typically the universe that truly concerns them—what are they doing? Apparently statistics are used to provide an indicator of whether a treatment effect is large enough so that it would likely be obtained again if the study were done again in a similar way on a similar sample (Winch & Campbell, 1969). Whether replications do in fact work most of the time is impossible to say. Negative results don't usually get published, nor do studies that replicate positive results but report nothing new. Hence, we are in no position to evaluate confidently the trustworthiness of our findings or to judge whether the customary way in which social psychologists use statistics has the value we think it does. Furthermore, some common practices in social psychological research probably increase the likelihood that published effects are unreplicable (Walster & Cleary, 1969).

Frequently social psychologists must do pilot studies. Manipulations must be perfected and measures evaluated. Many consider pilot studies to be legitimate and desirable, although one could argue that theoretical concepts are weak when operations that appear on the surface to represent them fail to represent them as demonstrated in a pilot study. Unfortunately, some uses of pilot studies undesirably affect the results of the typical statistical analyses of social psychologists. In a pilot study, one sets up manipulations and measures, runs subjects, examines results, and revises manipulations and measures. This process of check and revision is the purpose of pilot studies. Once one develops a pattern of manipulations and measures that seems to work, the temptation is to include the final pilot data with the data gathered during subsequent formal experimenting. This inclusion of pilot data, data gathered tentatively without precommitment to use them, increases the probability of concluding that there is an effect when there really isn't one. (We argue that more than 50% of the time, the final pilot data provide stronger direction of effect than the subsequent data.) In effect, one has selected the most favorable data yet obtained as part of the data for use in the final analyses. This practice is illegitimate and increases the likelihood that nonsense findings will be taken seriously. Statistical inference processes exist that could make use of data such as pilot data and that help to avoid other problems (Edwards, Lindman, & Savage, 1963), but these are rarely used or taught in psychology departments.

Another related common practice that artificially elevates alpha levels is sequential sampling. The alpha level is the probability or chance that what appears to be a difference due to treatments is in actuality a chance variation. Usually we attempt to set the alpha level at 5 percent (.05), which means that if our obtained difference would occur by chance less than 5 percent of the time, we will consider this difference as due to the treatment(s). In sequential sampling, one runs a group of subjects and examines the data; if the obtained difference hasn't reached the 5 percent level, he runs an additional group of subjects, examines the pooled data, and so on, stopping when the 5 percent level is reached. This practice capitalizes on chance variations in treatment differences by selecting the best data obtainable as the last block of data of the experiment. It elevates alpha above the 5 percent level in that it makes it likely that much more often than once in twenty times on the average, one treats a chance variation in treatment effects in the last block of data as though they were not identical. It is far preferable to predetermine sample size. And if one has no idea of what sample size will be needed in a novel research area, it is better to overestimate the size and stick to that commitment even if subsequent analyses reveal that it was unnecessary to run that many subjects.

There are many other practices that raise alpha levels and, as a consequence, are illegitimate. These practices include reserving the decision about whether some subjects should be discarded on a given ground until all the data are examined. If one only decides to discard some data after discovering that the treatment effect in his experiment has not reached the 5 percent (.05) level of statistical significance, he really is using some level higher than the 5 percent (.05) level. This is quite different from developing some *a priori* rules for discarding data that apply to all studies in a given problem area and necessarily require inspection of the data to determine whether the rule about discarding subjects does apply. The important difference is that this latter procedure does not allow (or at least is less likely to allow) the development of subtle contingencies between the direction of effect and the decision to retain or discard a subject's data. Ideally, data inspection and decisions regarding discarding data would be made by someone ignorant of the experimenter's hypothesis.

Another undesirable practice is the failure to mention studies that yield negative results. Negative results admittedly resist explanation and may simply reflect a variety of methodological inadequacies, but mentioning only studies that work effectively also changes one's alpha level. For example, the researcher who finds support for his theory only half the time but never reports his failures is really using some less rigorous level of significance to decide what to think about his theory. One good argument for manipulation checks is that in conjunction with good judgment they could enable the compulsively honest researcher (who somewhere mentions his failures in print even if he doesn't describe them in thorough detail) to legitimately exclude as "true failures" those studies in which the manipulations apparently failed. These studies are excludable in that with inadequate manipulation they do not really constitute a test of the hypothesis or theory.

Still another illegitimate practice is to search (after the data are gathered) for the one statistical test or method of organizing the data that best supports one's viewpoint. This practice also elevates alpha levels and should be replaced by preexperimental commitment to a specific mode of data analysis and organization of the data. It is usually known well in advance of the execution of a study which statistical techniques are more powerful (sensitive to any subtle difference in means) for analyzing a particular type of data. The use of different statistical tests within a single study for analyzing similar or equivalent types of response measures is particularly suspect. Although the problem is less blatant, one has the same doubts and suspicions when different statistical techniques are used across similar types of studies or studies that use similar types of response measures. That is, it is undesirable to use certain justifiable criteria in one study as reasons for turning to another mode of statistical analysis (e.g., citing heterogeneity of variance as the reason for abandoning analysis of variance and instead using chi-square), but not using the same criteria in another study that exhibits the very same problem.

There are other undesirable practices that could be mentioned but the important thing to emphasize is that the statistical procedures ordinarily used in social psychology require preexperimental commitment to all procedures to be used in dealing with and reporting the data, to unbiased procedures, and to a willingness to abide with results that fall short of proving one omniscient.

CONCLUSION

This chapter provides the beginning of the input that must be potentially available to a researcher in social psychology. Many methodological problems can currently barely be coped with, but these lead to interesting problems for methodological research in social psychology. The importance of the topic and the fascinating ideas developed so far in the field should encourage even the most pessimistic student to take on the difficult problem of doing good research in social psychology. Surely almost all the good work and brilliant innovations in social psychology are yet to come.

REFERENCES

ABELSON, R. P., & MILLER, J. C. Negative persuasion via personal insult. *Journal of Experimental Social Psychology,* 1967, **3,** 321–333.

ABELSON, R. P., & ROSENBERG, M. J. Symbolic psycho-logic: A model of attitudinal cognition. *Behavioral Science,* 1958, **3,** 1–13.

AMERICAN PSYCHOLOGICAL ASSOCIATION, COUNCIL OF EDITORS. Ethical standards of psychologists. *American Psychologist,* 1959, **14,** 279–282.

ARONSON, E., & CARLSMITH, J. M. Experimentation in social psychology. In G. Lindzey & E. Aronson (Eds.), *Handbook of social psychology.* Vol. 2. Reading, Mass.: Addison-Wesley, 1968. Pp. 1–79.

BARBER, T. X., & SILVER, M. J. Fact, fiction, and the experimenter bias effect. *Psychological Bulletin Monograph,* 1968, **70**(6, Pt. 2), 1–29. (a)

BARBER, T. X., & SILVER, M. J. Pitfalls in data analysis and interpretation: A reply to Rosenthal. *Psychological Bulletin Monograph,* 1968, **70**(6, Pt. 2), 48–62. (b)

BEM, D. J. Self-perception: An alternative interpretation of cognitive dissonance phenomena. *Psychological Review,* 1967, **74,** 183–200.

BROCK, T. C., & BECKER, L. A. "Debriefing" and susceptibility to subsequent experimental manipulation. *Journal of Experimental Social Psychology,* 1966, **2,** 227–236.

BRYAN, J. H., & TEST, M. A. Models and helping: Naturalistic studies in aiding behavior. *Journal of Personality and Social Psychology,* 1967, **6,** 400–407.

CAMPBELL, D. T. The indirect assessment of social attitudes. *Psychological Bulletin,* 1950, **47,** 15–38.

CAMPBELL, D. T. Factors relevant to the validity of experiments in social settings. *Psychological Bulletin,* 1957, **54,** 297–312.

CAMPBELL, D. T. Social attitudes and other acquired behavioral dispositions. In S. Koch (Ed.), *Psychology: A study of a science.* Vol. 6. New York: McGraw-Hill, 1963. Pp. 94–172.

CAMPBELL, D. T. Prospective: Artifact and control. In R. Rosenthal & R. L. Rosnow (Eds.), *Artifact in behavioral research.* New York: Academic Press, 1969. Pp. 351–382.

CAMPBELL, D. T., & FISKE, D. W. Convergent and discriminant validation by the multitrait-multimethod matrix. *Psychological Bulletin,* 1959, **56,** 81–105.

CARLSMITH, J. M., COLLINS, B. E., & HELMREICH, R. K. Studies in forced compliance: I. The effect of pressure for compliance on attitude change produced by face-to-face role playing and anonymous essay writing. *Journal of Personality and Social Psychology,* 1966, **4,** 1–13.

COOK, T. D., BEAN, J. R., CALDER, B. J., FREY, R., KROVETZ, M. L., & REISMAN, S. R. Demand characteristics and three conceptions of the frequently deceived subject. *Journal of Personality and Social Psychology,* 1970, **14,** 185–194.

CRONBACH, L. J. *Essentials of psychological testing.* (2nd ed.) New York: Harper & Row, 1960.

DEFLEUR, M. L., & WESTIE, F. R. Verbal attitudes and overt acts: An experiment on the salience of attitude. *American Sociological Review,* 1958, **23**, 667–673.

EDWARDS, W., LINDMAN, H., & SAVAGE, L. J. Bayesian statistical inference for psychological research. *Psychological Review,* 1963, **70**, 193–202.

FESTINGER, L. Behavioral support for opinion change. *Public Opinion Quarterly,* 1964, **28**, 404–417.

FESTINGER, L., & CARLSMITH, J. M. Cognitive consequences of forced compliance. *Journal of Abnormal and Social Psychology,* 1959, **58**, 203–210.

FILLENBAUM, S. Prior deception and subsequent experimental performance: The "faithful" subject. *Journal of Personality and Social Psychology,* 1966, **4**, 532–553.

FREEDMAN, J. L., WALLINGTON, S. A., & BLESS, E. Compliance without pressure: The effect of guilt. *Journal of Personality and Social Psychology,* 1967, **7**, 117–124.

GOLDING, S. L., & LICHTENSTEIN, E. Confessing of awareness and prior knowledge of deception as a function of interview set and approval motive. *Journal of Personality and Social Psychology,* 1970, **14**, 213–223.

GOODRICH, K. P. Experimental analysis of response slope and latency as criteria for characterizing voluntary and nonvoluntary responses in eyeblink conditioning. *Psychological Monographs,* 1966, **80**(14, Whole No. 622).

GREENBERG, M. S. Role playing: An alternative to deception? *Journal of Personality and Social Psychology,* 1967, **7**, 152–157.

GUETZKOW, H., ALGER, C. F., BRODY, R. A., NOEL, R. C., & SNYDER, R. C. *Simulation in international relations.* Englewood Cliffs, N.J.: Prentice-Hall, 1963.

HOLMES, D. S. Amount of experience in experiments as a determinant of performance in later experiments. *Journal of Personality and Social Psychology,* 1967, **7**, 403–407.

HOLMES, D. S., & APPELBAUM, A. S. Nature of prior experimental experience as a determinant of performance in a subsequent experiment. *Journal .of Personality and Social Psychology,* 1970, **14**, 195–202.

JANIS, I. L., & KING, B. The influence of role-playing on opinion change. *Journal of Abnormal and Social Psychology,* 1954, **49**, 211–218.

JONES, R. A., LINDER, D. E., KIESLER, C. A., ZANNA, M., & BREHM, J. W. Internal states or external stimuli: Observers' attitude judgments and the dissonance-theory-self-persuasion controversy. *Journal of Experimental Social Psychology,* 1968, **4**, 247–269.

KELMAN, H. C. Human use of human subjects: The problem of deception in social psychological experiments. *Psychological Bulletin,* 1967, **67**, 1–11.

KELMAN, H. C. *A time to speak,* San Francisco: Jossey-Bass, Inc., 1968.

LEFKOWITZ, M., BLAKE, R. R., & MOUTON, J. S. Status factors in pedestrian violation of traffic signals. *Journal of Abnormal and Social Psychology,* 1955, **51**, 704–706.

LEVENTHAL, H. Fear communications in the acceptance of preventive health practices. *Bulletin of the New York Academy of Medicine,* Series 2, 1965, **41**, 1144–1168.

LEVY, L. H. Awareness, learning, and the beneficent subject as expert witness. *Journal of Personality and Social Psychology,* 1967, **6**, 365–370.

McGUIRE, W. J. Some impending reorientations in social psychology: Some thoughts provoked by Kenneth Ring. *Journal of Experimental Social Psychology,* 1967, **3,** 124–139.

MILLER, N., & LEVY, B. H. Defaming and agreeing with the communicator as a function of emotional arousal, communication extremity, and evaluative set. *Sociometry,* 1967, **30,** 158–175.

ORNE, M. T. On the social psychology of the psychological experiment: With particular reference to demand characteristics and their implications. *American Psychologist,* 1962, **17,** 776–783.

ROSENTHAL, R. Experimenter outcome-orientation and the results of psychological research. *Psychological Bulletin,* 1964, **61,** 405–412.

ROSENTHAL, R. Covert communication in the psychological experiment. *Psychological Bulletin,* 1967, **67,** 356–367.

ROSENTHAL, R., PERSINGER, G. W., VIKAN-KLINE, L., & FODE, K. L. The effect of early data returns on data subsequently obtained by outcome-biased experimenters. *Sociometry,* 1963, **26,** 487–498.

SCOTT, W. A. Attitude measurement. In G. Lindzey & E. Aronson (Eds.), *Handbook of social psychology.* Vol. 2, Reading, Mass.: Addison-Wesley, 1968. Pp. 204–273.

SIGALL, H., ARONSON, E., & VAN HOOSE, T. The cooperative subject: Myth or reality? *Journal of Experimental Social Psychology,* 1970, **6,** 1–10.

STRICKER, L. J. The true deceiver. *Psychological Bulletin,* 1967, **68,** 13–20.

WALSTER, E., BERSCHEID, E., ABRAHAMS, D., & ARONSON, V. Effectiveness of debriefing following deception experiments. *Journal of Personality and Social Psychology,* 1967, **6,** 371–380.

WALSTER, G. W., & CLEARY, T. A. Current editorial policy: A type I error. Unpublished manuscript, 1969.

WEBB, E. J., CAMPBELL, D. T., SCHWARTZ, R. D., SECHREST, L. *Unobtrusive measures: Nonreactive research in the social sciences.* Chicago: Rand McNally, 1966.

WEICK, K. E., & NESSET, B. Preferences among forms of equity. *Organizational Behavior and Human Performance,* 1968, **3,** 400–416.

WINCH, R. F., & CAMPBELL, D. T. Proof? No! Evidence? Yes! The significance of tests of significance. *American Sociologist,* 1969, **4,** 140–143.

WUEBBEN, P. L. Honesty of subjects and birth order. *Journal of Personality and Social Psychology,* 1967, **5,** 350–352.

SOCIAL PSYCHOLOGY OF THE INDIVIDUAL

As noted in the first chapter, the major historical orientation of the field of social psychology has been towards the goals of describing the orientations of individuals toward their social milieu, and determining how these orientations (e.g., attitudes, beliefs, percepts, and motives) are socially acquired and modified. In general, the fundamental model of behavior employed by social psychologists derives from the traditional approach where one is concerned with how various stimuli affect changes in the predispositions of an organism to behave in certain ways towards various objects, social and nonsocial, in its environment.

In this section, three kinds of predispositions are considered: cognitive, attitudinal, and perceptual. Chapter 4, which is the only chapter not specifically written for the present volume, presents a concise review of one of the most influential conceptual paradigms in contemporary social psychology—cognitive dissonance. In effect, the paradigm concerns the amount of conflict an individual experiences and how he resolves it when he holds cognitions (ideas) that are inconsistent with one another. As the authors of the chapter observe, the major reason that dissonance theory, which is fundamentally concerned with cognition as a psychological process, is treated as a major topic in social rather than cognitive psychology is because it was formulated by Leon Festinger, for long one of the leading theorists in experimental social psychology. In addition, it has been employed as a conceptual model for investigating processes which have been traditional subject matter in social psychology (e.g., opinion change, social influence, and conformity).

As the reader will observe in reading the chapter, dissonance theory is a highly abstract theory with a very limited and perhaps insufficient set of definitions. It is imprecise in specifying the particular conditions which give rise to dissonance or what forms of behavior will ensue. Its major contribution to date has been to stimulate a wide range of empirical studies, and to provide a highly abstract framework within which a wide range of phenomena can be integrated. But until the variables in the theory are more explicitly stated, it will continue to function primarily as a heuristic framework for, as it is stated, one cannot systematically derive hypotheses to test its validity in the "real" world.

Chapter 5 by McGuire begins with the observation that the concept of attitude has historically been the central variable in social psychological inquiry. Although in recent years the range of phenomena the field considers has diversified considerably, theories of attitude formation and change and the relationship of attitudes to behavior remain the principal preoccupations of social psychologists concerned with the psychology of the individual. McGuire next notes the variety of ways in which the construct attitude has been theoretically employed as both an independent and dependent variable, and briefly outlines four major conceptual paradigms that have served as the bases for most attitude change research: information processing, consistency, functional and perceptual theories. Dissonance theory, as outlined in Chapter 4, provides an example of a consistency orientation. Chapter 6 by Jones, Bell, and Aronson can be considered, in part, an example of perceptual orientation. The reader interested in a more detailed review of the functional approach may wish to examine the theoretical and empirical work of Katz and others (1956, 1959). McGuire spends the major portion of his chapter outlining in detail an information processing orientation towards attitude change which assumes six major stages through which a message must go prior to its producing a behavioral effect: *presenting, attending,* and *comprehending* the stimulus, *yielding* or changing one's attitude, *retaining* the attitudinal change, and *behaving* consistently with the change. He then considers how the personality of the target might affect each of these stages, and how the arousal of fear in the target person might affect the attitudinal change process. He concludes with an evaluation of the present status of the information processing paradigm.

As noted, Chapter 6 is concerned with the general phenomena of social perception and, more specifically, with the area of person perception. Within the latter area, the authors focus principally upon a set of propositions and prior empirical studies concerning the relationship between one's similarity with and one's attraction to another person. After reviewing these, the authors outline in some detail an experimental paradigm that they have employed in several studies to determine the relationship between perceived mutuality of attraction (liking), attitudinal similarity, and subsequent liking.

We will not attempt to review the findings of their investigations here. One major value that attends reading the authors' detailed account of their research is the insight it provides into the tortuous path the process of discovery and evaluation generally takes in social psychological investigations. Such insight is generally not available in the carefully abstracted and ordered research reports in professional journal articles. In effect, the researchers clearly demonstrate that the process of investigating what might seem to be a simple and obvious proposition, such as, "similarity in attitudes between individuals leads to mutual attraction," may indeed turn out to be a complex and difficult scientific challenge.

These three chapters provide several examples of conceptual and experimental research paradigms employed in the investigation of the social psychology of the individual. It is obvious that we have presented only a few of the paradigms constructed to investigate cognition, attitudes, and social perception. Furthermore, other problem areas remain unrepresented although they fall within the orientation of this section, for example, those of social learning and social motivation. The work of Bem (1967) on the use of learning theory as a basis for interpreting dissonance theory results is an excellent example of using learning concepts as a basis for understanding social behavior. Other examples of learning theory approaches include Zajonc's theory of social facilitation (See Chapter 7), and Byrne and Rhamey's (1965) conceptualization of the similarity-attraction relationship based upon reinforcement principles which is discussed in Chapter 6. Finally, an example of a conceptual paradigm focusing on social motivation is discussed in Chapter 9 of this volume where the writer reviews various motives that underly cooperative and competitive forms of behavior.

REFERENCES

BEM, D. Self-perception: An alternative interpretation of cognitive dissonance phenomena. *Psychological Review,* 1967, **74,** 183–200.

BYRNE, D., & RHAMEY, R. Magnitude of positive and negative reinforcements as a determinant of attraction. *Journal of Personality and Social Psychology,* 1965, **2,** 884–889.

KATZ, D., SARMOFF, I., & McCLINTOCK, C. Ego-defense and attitude change. *Human Relations,* 1956, **9,** 27–45.

KATZ, D., & STOTLAND, E. A preliminary statement of attitude structure and change. In Koch, S. (Ed.), *Psychology: A study of science.* Vol. 3. New York: McGraw-Hill, 1959. Pp. 423–475.

4

COGNITIVE DISSONANCE: THEORY AND RESEARCH[1]

John J. Sherwood
James W. Barron
H. Gordon Fitch

In 1957, Leon Festinger put forth a little, but fascinating, theory in his book A Theory of Cognitive Dissonance. *The book created an immediate sensation and has produced a decade of feverish research activity. It is a little theory because it is based upon a single principle and because it uses only a few concepts. Furthermore, it does not pretend to be a big theory; that is, it does not pretend to be a theory of behavior or personality. Yet at the same time, it is an important theory in that it is apparently useful in a wide variety of behavioral contexts—from studies of social problems and morality to the swimming of rats, from studies of attitude change and social influence to defense mechanisms. Finally, it is a fascinating theory because researchers have used it to make some "surprising" predictions that do not easily follow from common sense or from other psychological theories.*

The theory of cognitive dissonance is frequently referred to as a social psychological theory. That is probably because Festinger is best known as a social psychologist and because the theory has proved to be particularly useful in areas of social psychological concern, such as attitude change, social influence, and conformity. More accurately, however, the theory of cognitive dissonance is a cognitive theory of motivation. The term "cognitive" comes from the Latin word for "knowing" and refers to processes of thought and perception.

INTRODUCTION TO THE THEORY

The basic assumption underlying dissonance theory is that an individual *strives for consistency among his opinions, attitudes, and values.* Festinger replaced the word "consistency" with the more neutral term *consonance.* Similarly, "incon-

---

[1] This chapter originally appeared as Chapter 4 in R. V. Wagner and J. J. Sherwood (Eds.), *The Study of Attitude Change* (Belmont, Calif.: Brooks/Cole, 1969), pp. 56–86, and is reprinted with the permission of the authors and the publisher.

sistency" was replaced with a term having a less logical connotation—*dissonance*. So a restatement of the basic proposition is that there is "pressure to produce consonant relations among cognitions and to avoid dissonance" (Festinger, 1957, p. 9).

The existence of dissonance is assumed to be psychologically uncomfortable. It is an aversive motivational state that impels a person to try to reduce the dissonance and to achieve consonance. In addition to being motivated to reduce dissonance, the person actively avoids situations that are likely to increase the dissonance in his cognitive world.

A state of dissonance exists when a person holds, at the same time, two cognitions that are inconsistent with each other according to his psychological expectations. The two cognitions are said to be dissonant with each other if—for the person—the obverse of one cognition would follow from the other. Thus, if cognition A implies cognition B, then holding A and the obverse of B—that is, not-B—is dissonant. For example, "viewing oneself as an honest person" (A) and "behaving honestly" (B) are consonant, because B follows from A. On the other hand, "viewing oneself as an honest person" and the *obverse* of "behaving honestly"—such as "stealing from the poor box"—are dissonant conditions.

A cognition is any knowledge, belief, attitude, or value that a person holds about himself, about his behavior, or about his environment. Expectations about what cognitive relationships are consonant—that is, what follows from what—are acquired through an individual's experience, the mores of his culture, and his notions about logical relations between events. If a person were to stand in the rain and yet not get wet, the cognitions representing these two facts would be dissonant with each other because people usually learn from experience that getting wet follows from standing in the rain.

The amount or level of dissonance aroused is (1) a function of the ratio of dissonant to consonant cognitions, and (2) a function of the importance of each cognition to the person. Although the precise nature of these functions is an empirical question that is not yet fully understood, the basic relations between amount of dissonance and the cognitions held by an individual are represented by the following:

$$\text{Dissonance} = \frac{\text{Importance} \times \text{Number of Dissonant Cognitions}}{\text{Importance} \times \text{Number of Consonant Cognitions}}$$

This heuristic expression is not meant to be precise in terms of specific numbers or measurements but to suggest a number of relationships—for example, that dissonance will be reduced if the number or importance of consonant cognitions in a given situation is increased.

The meaning of "importance" is not clearly explicated in the original theory. A definition that seems to fit the theory is that "importance" refers to the instrumentality of the cognition for the satisfaction of the individual's needs and values, particularly those central to his wider value system. However, at times, situations may become so salient as to attach temporary importance to otherwise peripheral cognitions.

The initial observational basis for Festinger's notion that people actively seek to avoid and reduce dissonance among cognitions came from trying to understand some bizarre rumors that started after a major earthquake in India in 1934. The rumors were recorded in an area where people felt severe and prolonged tremors but did not suffer any injury or witness any damage. These are samples of the rumors: "There will be a severe cyclone in the next few days," "There will be a severe earthquake on the lunar eclipse day," "A flood is rushing toward the province," and "In five days the fatal day will arrive . . . unforeseeable calamities will arise." These observations seem to contradict the widely accepted hedonistic assumption that people avoid unpleasant things, such as anxiety and the prospect of pain.

Some comparable data from people who were actually in an area of death and destruction in another natural disaster show a complete absence of rumors predicting further disaster. The data from the two communities do not agree with so-called common sense. Why should the occurrence of an earthquake—in the absence of death and destruction—be correlated with such frightening and exaggerated rumors, while people who were actually in an area of disaster did not invent such rumors? For Festinger, the rumors fell into place when viewed in terms of relations between cognitions. In the community that experienced only the shock of the earthquake but no suffering and destruction, Festinger assumed that the residents had a strong and persistent fear reaction yet could see nothing to fear. The *feeling* of fear in the absence of an adequate *reason* for fear was dissonant. The rumors predicting future disaster, if believed, provided the residents with cognitions that were consonant with being afraid. The rumors were, according to the theory, "fear justifying" rumors and thus a shared mechanism for dissonance reduction.

Examples of Dissonance Reduction

It is assumed that if a person holds two cognitions that are inconsistent with each other, he will experience dissonance—an aversive motivational state—and he will then try to reduce the dissonance and achieve consonance. Dissonance can be reduced in several ways, including increasing the number and/or importance of consonant cognitions. The fear justifying rumors, an example of the first method, served to reduce dissonance by adding new elements that were consonant with being afraid. An example of changing the importance of consonant cognitions is in the person who—rather than stop smoking in the face of its danger to health—increases the feeling of enjoyment he receives from smoking. He might also add new consonant elements, such as "Smoking is not so deadly as this publicity suggests; I run a far greater risk whenever I drive a car."

The smoker, instead of seeking to enhance the consonant aspects of his behavior, could act to remove the dissonant elements; he could give up smoking and thereby remove one major dissonance-producing cognition. Or he could attempt to minimize the other by distorting or ignoring the claims of medical research on the relation between smoking and health, perhaps by carefully avoiding exposure to articles or arguments discussing the ill effects of smoking.

According to the theory, the individual will choose one or more of all these possible ways to reduce dissonance. As might be expected, there is no unambiguous way of predicting which he will select. However, the general rule for determining the mode of dissonance reduction is that of least effort; that is, the cognition least resistant to change will be changed. Resistance is in part determined by (1) the number of presently irrelevant cognitions with which the changed cognition will become dissonant, thereby creating new dissonance, and by (2) the importance of these newly relevant cognitions in terms of the person's system of values.

Moreover, although dissonance can be reduced by decreasing the number of dissonant cognitions, the theory is not clear on how that can be done. The ease with which reality can be changed (or distorted) depends, among other things, on the concreteness or abstractness of the cognition, the extent to which it is private or public, and the relative ambiguity or clarity of the reality that it represents.

Anyone doubting the efficacy of consistency as a principle of behavior might remember having seen some person suddenly reverse his direction of travel on a crowded sidewalk and then remember having noticed his public attempt to make this seemingly inconsistent behavior seem consistent—for example, he might have consulted his watch with an amazed expression, or he might have made some utterance like "I forgot my briefcase."

Although dissonance theory is undeniably useful in a great many situations, problems are encountered if we attempt to extend the theory beyond the limits originally intended for it. One of these problems stems from the theory's incompleteness, which Festinger acknowledged when he said that "there are generally so many other cognitive elements relevant to any given element that some dissonance is the usual state of affairs" (1957, p. 17). He also states that dissonance is not always reduced—that it sometimes cannot be. A person, for example, might invest a great deal of money in a company that declares bankruptcy soon afterward. The action is irreversible, and the elements are so important to the person that all of the dissonance cannot be eliminated, at least for some time. It would seem, then, that people either (1) *constantly* experience the psychological discomfort or tension that accompanies cognitive inconsistencies and are constantly motivated to dispel it or (2) have some tolerance for a certain level of dissonance, further reduction of which is unnecessary or not particularly satisfying.

If we accept the first alternative above, the goal of the organism would be to reduce *all* dissonance, and the logical end-point of this process would be a completely quiescent state. In other words, the organism would be striving for a condition that contains no imbalance or incongruity. Several other motivational theories have this characteristic, and all of these are challenged by evidence showing that organisms do *not* pursue a quiescent state in which all motivational tensions have been reduced but in fact often seek out higher levels of stimulation, tension, or dissonance. Mild stimulation, tension, or dissonance may actually be pleasurable.

This line of argument would seem to favor Alternative (2). Indeed, the development of various "optimal level of arousal" theories (for example, Berlyne, 1960) clearly indicates that a position advocating the maintenance of a certain amount of dissonance or imbalance is at least tenable. Dissonance theory in its original form did not deal with this problem but assumed that any inconsistency between cognitions would lead to attempts to reconcile it or to restore balance.

Commitment and Volition

The most extensive modification of dissonance theory as originally stated by Festinger has been that of Brehm and Cohen in their book *Explorations in Cognitive Dissonance* (1962). In their summary of the research literature on dissonance theory at that time, they demonstrated the predictive value of the theory in these situations: (1) the period after a free choice among *attractive alternatives* (decision making in which dissonance is a function of the relative number of favorable cognitions of the unchosen alternatives); (2) instances of forced compliance, in which a person is induced to *behave* in a manner inconsistent with his attitudes; and (3) situations in which a person is exposed to *information* inconsistent with his attitudes.

Brehm and Cohen's primary contribution, however, was in their demonstration of the importance of commitment and volition to the predictions of dissonance theory. According to Brehm and Cohen, "Commitment provides a specification of the conditions under which one cognition follows from the obverse of another. . . . A central kernel of dissonance theory . . . is the notion that *a person will try to justify a commitment to the extent that there is information discrepant with that commitment*" (p. 300). They define "commitment" very simply as a decision (to do or not to do something) or a choice (and thereby a rejection of unchosen alternatives) or active engagement in a given behavior.

Presumably, when a person engages in a course of action discrepant from an attitude that he holds about this action, he will experience dissonance. He may reduce the dissonance by bringing his attitude into consonance or agreement with his behavior; that is, he might change his attitude about the behavior. An example is a high school student who praises ivy league schools and denigrates state universities and afterward discovers he cannot get into an ivy league school. If he then chooses to enter a state university, dissonance theory would predict his attitude toward state universities would become more favorable and, possibly, his attitude toward the ivy league more negative. By his actions he is now committed to a state university, and his actions are dissonant with his formerly critical attitude toward state universities. Of course, one's attitudes toward a state university might change for many other reasons, but in this example the student's entry into the state university is crucial. His entry is contrary to his attitude toward state universities, and it is likely that his attitude will become more favorable in order to be more consonant with the fact that he is now attending the state university.

The crucial variable in commitment is *volition*, which refers to the degree of free choice involved in the decision to behave in an attitude-discrepant way. Thus, to the extent that the student in the example saw himself as being *forced* to attend a state university, the theory predicts he would experience less dissonance and, therefore, less pressure to change his attitudes about state universities than he would if he saw himself as making a *free* and uncoerced choice. A frequent, and non-obvious, finding in research on dissonance theory is the *less* the reward for engaging in an attitude-discrepant behavior, the greater the resultant attitude change is likely to be. Similarly, it has usually been found that the *less* the coercion used to force compliance or commitment, the greater the likelihood of attitude change. Presumably, a person finding himself committed to doing something contrary to his attitudes for a large reward or from coercion can deny responsibility for his behavior. He can externalize the reason he is doing what he is doing; that is, he can say to himself: "I don't really believe in this, but I really had no choice because I cannot afford to refuse such a large reward; therefore, I am justified in doing this even though I believe it is not what I should be doing." On the other hand, a person who receives a minimal reward or very slight coercion cannot justify his attitude-discrepant actions so easily. He is more likely to conclude: "I got myself into this situation, and because I don't normally do things in which I don't believe, there must really be something to the position I am advocating."

An Example of Research: The Effects of Temptation

Consider a person who is tempted by anticipation of reward to do something he thinks is immoral. If he performs such an act, dissonance will ensue between his knowledge that the act is immoral and his knowledge that he has done it. One way to reduce this dissonance would be to change his attitude—to decide, "It's not really so very bad."

As with other attitude-discrepant behavior that is a consequence of forced compliance, the amount of dissonance created decreases as the strength of the inducing force (temptation) increases. Therefore, one would expect, the *greater* the reward for performing an immoral act, the *less* the dissonance. The cognitions about the large reward received are consonant with performing the act; that is, the immoral act can be in some sense "justified" by the large reward.

How about the person who is tempted but resists? For him giving up the reward induces dissonance. He can reduce this dissonance by increasing the number and/or the importance of cognitions that are consonant with his behavior. If he has refrained from doing something he thinks is wrong—in spite of a reward—he can then convince himself the act is extremely immoral, thus justifying the behavior to which he has committed himself.

Whereas the person who *succumbs* to temptation and commits an act he considers immoral has less dissonance the greater the reward he gains, the person who *resists* temptation has more dissonance the greater the reward he forsakes. These hypotheses were tested by Mills (1958) in an experiment with sixth graders. They were first given a questionnaire to measure the severity of their attitudes toward cheating. Then they participated in a contest in which they worked individually at a task involving eye-hand coordination. Three experimental conditions were created: (1) high temptation to cheat (offer of a large prize for outstanding performance on the task) together with low restraints against cheating (the students were given the opportunity to cheat while scoring their own performance); (2) low temptation (small prize) together with low restraint; and (3) high temptation together with high restraint (little opportunity to cheat). Cheating could be secretly detected by the experimenter. Some students cheated, some did not. One day later, the students were again asked about their attitudes toward cheating.

The findings generally supported dissonance theory. Attitude change scores showed on the average that those children who cheated tended to become more lenient toward cheating and that those who did not cheat became more critical of cheating. Students who cheated for a small prize became more lenient toward cheating than did those who cheated for a big prize. For the students who did not cheat, those giving up a large prize became more severe in their condemnation of cheating than did those who gave up only a small prize.

Finally, Mills' study showed that the effects of dissonance arousal are limited to cognitions directly relevant to the decision involved. Attitudes were also measured about other aggressive actions unrelated to cheating, but these attitudes were unaffected by the experiment.

The following sections of this chapter will review research that has been generated by dissonance theory. At the outset, it is probably safe to say that this theory has produced more research in the period from 1957 to the present than any other single theory in social psychology. A systematic literature survey (Fitch, 1967) revealed almost 400 separate studies dealing with various derivations and implications of dissonance theory.

The discussion immediately following examines both predispositional and situational factors that influence the arousal or induction of cognitive dissonance and the magnitude of dissonance experienced. We next look at various modes of dissonance reduction and attempt to determine whether or not the experimental evidence supports a particular mechanism of dissonance reduction.

Dissonance theory is then examined in the context of some other psychological theories. Finally, criticisms of dissonance theory are reviewed, and the current status of the theory is examined.

THE AROUSAL OF COGNITIVE DISSONANCE

Individual Differences

One would expect to find individual difference, or personality, variables related to the amount of dissonance induced in a given situation. It is an empirical fact that individuals engage in different amounts of dissonance reducing behavior, but the research conducted so far on this question has by no means clearly defined the realtionships or even specified the variables that are most directly involved. Investigation of this issue seems to be very promising and seems likely to lead to further development of dissonance theory and related theories of cognitive motivation. The problems inherent in the issue, however, make the research challenging, as can be inferred from the difficulties encountered by investigators in the studies conducted to date.

In one of the earliest attempts to develop a measure of individual tolerance for dissonance, Aronson and Festinger (1958) found that none of five tests developed for this purpose effectively discriminated between subjects showing a high amount of dissonance reducing behavior and those showing a low amount. Taking a different approach, they looked at students who changed their major during their junior year in college and reasoned that they must possess an unusually high tolerance for dissonance. The researchers found substantial differences in six areas of a personality inventory administered to these students.

In an exploratory study of individual differences, Stack (1964) studied prospective college students. The subjects rated various colleges both before and after their decision on which college to attend. A measure of the relative amount of dissonance reduction was obtained by measuring the changes in the ratings of the various colleges rated by each student after his own decision had been made. Of the 13 personality variables studied, only 3 correlated with the measure of amount of dissonance reduction. For females, Rosenzweig's measure of "extrapunitiveness" (the extent to which people blame others for their own feelings of frustration) and their grade point average while in high school were inversely related to amount of dissonance reduction. For males, a measure of risk taking propensity was inversely related to one type of dissonance reducing activity.

In another exploratory effort, Brewster (1966) found no significant association between dissonance and the personality variable known as "field dependence-independence." Gallimore (1965), in a study primarily concerned with discovering dissonance-associated autonomic activity, administered several personality scales in an attempt to discover personality-associated differences in modes of dissonance reduction. None of the personality scales discriminated a preferred mode of dissonance reduction.

Although exploration of the predictive value of traditional personality scales for amount of dissonance has shown them to be largely unsuitable, more success has been achieved with a number of special variables that have some intuitive connection with dissonance induction.

Fillenbaum (1964) studied the relationship between dissonance and degree of open-mindedness as measured by Rokeach's dogmatism questionnaire and found a significant correlation. The more dogmatic subjects experienced higher dissonance. However, he found a comparable correlation in the relevant control condition, so that his results are inconclusive and must simply be considered a stimulus to further research on the question.

Rosen (1961) studied the relationship between dissonance and the variable "category width," which refers to a measure of individual differences in the widths of the cognitive categories people employ when they judge things. Some people regard rather diverse events as equivalent, whereas other people do not. Rosen found that narrow categorizers showed a more extreme preference for supportive, consonant reading material, a preference suggesting that a higher level of dissonance had been induced in these subjects. This finding held for males but not for females.

Harvey (1965) studied the relationship between the cognitive variable "concreteness-abstractness" and dissonance reduction. He found that when subjects argued against their own beliefs about philosophy, the more "concrete" subjects engaged in more dissonance reducing activity. This increase was evidenced by greater attitude change when measured both immediately following and one week after their arguments.

Harvey's theory assumes that the more "concrete" individual thinks in black and white terms and is less able to tolerate contradiction or incongruity between cognitions. It may be that Harvey's measure of "concreteness" contains or approaches in some way a measure of an individual's tolerance for dissonance. The precise relationship between the two variables is presently unclear, but it is worthy of further consideration.

Brasfield and Papageorgis (1965), hoping to discover some relationship between anxiety and dissonance, administered the Taylor Manifest Anxiety Scale (MAS) to 30 subjects and then measured their reaction to a dissonant self-relevant communication. The communication, which was allegedly based on the Holtzman Inkblot Technique, gave (disguised as a test result) a threatening but false profile. As predicted, only the high anxiety subjects accepted the communication, presumably because they experienced more dissonance upon being confronted by the discrediting communication.

Suinn (1965) investigated the same hypothesis in a different fashion. He administered the MAS and two "measures" of dissonance. The expected relationship, that people high in manifest anxiety experience greater dissonance, was found to hold with one of the measures but not the other. In general, the findings of studies on anxiety and dissonance are in line with dissonance theory because dissonance is alleged to have characteristics of psychological tension. Thus, presumably, a person experiencing dissonance would experience an increase in anxiety.

In conclusion, an individual's tolerance for dissonance is not easily predicted from standard personality scales. However, variables such as dogmatism, concreteness-abstractness, and category width seem to be related to differences in the amount of dissonance experienced by different subjects in the same situation. The conceptual relation between these variables and tolerance for dissonance is still confused and requires further research. Finally, anxiety is a variable that may be useful as a measure of the *level* of experienced dissonance, and differences in susceptibility to anxiety could be related to individual tolerances for dissonance. But here again, this is a speculative comment; only additional research will help us determine any relationship between personality factors and dissonance arousal, tolerance, and reduction.

Situational Factors

The Brehm and Cohen review makes it abundantly clear that commitment plays a critical role in the arousal or induction of cognitive dissonance. According to their definition, commitment follows a *decision* among alternatives. The crucial variable in producing commitment is *choice* or *volition*, so that the person feels responsible for and, in general, bound to the decision or the act. When the act is at odds with his private beliefs, dissonance is created.

It seems evident that the experience of dissonance should be higher if the actor sees his decision as voluntary—as his own decision—than would be the case if he is forced or required to engage in behavior discrepant with his private beliefs. In the latter case, dissonance can be avoided or reduced very simply: "I am being forced to do this; I really didn't have any choice. Therefore, it doesn't change my own beliefs about the matter at all." The research provided and reviewed by Brehm and Cohen indicates that people do in fact experience more dissonance under the condition of commitment than they do when they can satisfactorily externalize the responsibility for their discrepant behavior. A reasonable modification of the "formula" given previously suggests the relationship of commitment to the amount of dissonance induced:

$$\text{Dissonance} = \frac{\text{Degree of}}{\text{Commitment}} \times \frac{\text{Importance} \times \text{Number of Consonant Cognitions}}{\text{Importance} \times \text{Number of Dissonant Cognitions}}$$

We have a theoretical definition of commitment, but we still need to know how the concept has been defined operationally. Two techniques have received frequent experimental use. The first method of inducing commitment is to vary the degree of influence or persuasion utilized by the experimenter in getting the subject to engage in the attitude-discrepant behavior. For example, in order to produce a feeling of free choice and consequently high commitment, the experimenter might say to the subject, "I realize you are against issue X, but we are short of subjects and we really need someone to argue *for* issue X. Would you mind doing that?" Usually the experimenter takes care *not* to appear overfriendly or overly in need of the subject's help; in fact, the experimenter may behave in an especially brusque fashion in order to prevent the subject from reducing dissonance by justifying his attitude-discrepant behavior with a cognition such as "I really don't believe what I am about to say, but he needs help, and anything to help science."

The second technique commonly used to induce commitment is differential reward. Paying some subjects a large amount of money for behaving in a particular way presumably reduces their choice in engaging in the attitude-discrepant behavior, whereas paying other subjects a small amount for the same behavior presumably induces high commitment. In the latter case, it would seem that the subjects value their integrity more than their small payment and might say to themselves: "I am responsible for this reprehensible act, and this isn't enough payment to justify what I am doing."

An example of the use of this technique is the classic Festinger-Carlsmith study (1959) using forced compliance with differential reward. They first had college students perform a boring experimental task. A third of the subjects (the control group) was then asked how they felt about the task, and they frankly described it as an unpleasant one. The two other groups had one duty to perform before they rated the task: They were paid to assist the experimenter by introducing the next subject, who was waiting outside, to the task by describing it as interesting and enjoyable. The required behavior was obviously discrepant with the subjects' own cognitions about the pleasantness of the task. The members of one group were paid $1 for this attitude-discrepant behavior, and the others were paid $20.

Dissonance theory predicts that one way to reduce the dissonance aroused would be to change one's attitudes about the task to coincide with what he had just said about it—or decide that the task really wasn't so unpleasant. In addition, high reward for the behavior should lower the likelihood of attitude change because commitment to the expressed point of view is less than when one is paid very little.

The results of the experiment were that the group of subjects receiving $20 rated the original task neutrally; in fact, their ratings were not significantly different from those of the control group. The subjects who made the same discrepant statements but were paid only $1 rated the task as more pleasant and enjoyable than the other two groups did. These findings confirm the dissonance predictions that (1) making a statement discrepant with one's true evaluation tends to produce change in evaluation toward the position in the statement and that (2) the amount of change *decreases* as the amount of reward for making the statement *increases*.

One consequence of adding the commitment variable as an important one in the production of a state of cognitive dissonance has been that a new question has been raised: Is it necessary for the person actually to *perform* the discrepant behavior once he has committed himself to it in order to produce attitude change, or is commitment alone sufficient to produce attitude change in the direction of the position to which the person is publicly committed but privately opposed? Brehm and Cohen report a number of experiments in which commitment alone was sufficient to produce some attitude change. The question has, therefore, become the relative *amount* of attitude change produced by commitment alone, commitment with subsequent dissonant behavior, and dissonant behavior alone (for example, improvisation of arguments against private attitude) without choice or commitment in performing this behavior. Specification of the conditions under which one of these techniques for inducing dissonance and subsequent attitude change is more effective than others has not yet been systematically undertaken but is another area for continued research.

At least two conclusions on the commitment variable have emerged. First, this addition to dissonance theory has made the theory more explicit and has been instrumental in generating further research. Second, the variable of commitment seems to separate clearly dissonance theory from a host of other currently popular cognitive consistency theories. It is clear that other consistency theories do not account for this variable and that it is a crucial one in dissonance theory in both extending it and indicating a limitation in terms of attitude change techniques.

The Scope of Research Generated by the Theory: Factors in Dissonance Arousal

The following selection from the excellent review and summary by Brehm and Cohen (1962) condenses some of the major findings of research attempting to isolate the factors affecting the magnitude of induced dissonance. The extent of the list—and the fact that it is only a partial one—indicate the wide range of research stemming from just this one dissonance problem.

1. Dissonance arousal is greater the more attractive is the rejected alternative when the person chooses between attractive alternatives (college students chose between appliances and other consumer goods [Brehm, 1956]).
2. Dissonance arousal is greater the more negative are the characteristics of the chosen alternative (college students who decided to become engaged [Cohen in Brehm & Cohen, 1962]).
3. Dissonance arousal is greater the larger is the number of rejected alternatives when the person chooses between attractive alternatives (purchasers of cars in a Midwest city [Ehrlich et al., 1957]).
4. Dissonance arousal is greater the more important are the relevant cognitions surrounding a decision (clerks in an office indicated their preferences for various jams [Deutsch, Krauss, & Rosenau, 1962]).
5. Dissonance arousal is greater the lower is the amount of positive inducement for commitment to the discrepant behavior:
    a. the smaller the financial incentive for commitment (college students who agreed to go without food for a long period of time [Brehm in Brehm & Cohen, 1962]).
    b. the less the justification for commitment (college students who wrote essays against their own positions on a salient issue [Cohen, Brehm, & Fleming, 1958]).
    c. the more negative the characteristics of the inducing agent (Army reservists who agreed to eat grasshoppers [Smith, 1961]).
6. Dissonance arousal is greater the more there is choice in commitment to the discrepant behavior (college students who delivered electric shocks to another person [Brock & Buss, 1962]).
7. Dissonance arousal is greater the less coercion that is applied in order to induce the discrepant behavior (nursery school children who gave up an attractive toy [Aronson & Carlsmith, 1963]).
8. Dissonance arousal is greater the less the person's ability or self-esteem

would lead him to perform such a discrepant act (college students judged the homosexual arousal of others in an interpersonal assessment situation [Bramel, 1962]).

9. Dissonance arousal is greater the more the person has to actually engage in the negative behavior (junior high school students ate disliked foods [Brehm, 1960a, b]).

10. Dissonance arousal is greater the more negative information the person has about the discrepant situation to which he is committed (college students spent three hours copying tables of random numbers and learned that someone else, not themselves, was to be paid for the work [Brehm & Cohen, 1959a]).

DISSONANCE REDUCTION

Once dissonance has been aroused, theoretically, the person will be motivated to reduce it by using one or more of the various modes of dissonance reduction that may be available. In a discussion of dissonance reduction, two main questions should be considered. First, how may the person reduce his dissonance? Second, what determines the preferred or chosen mode of resolution?

To answer the first question, we shall outline three ways an individual may reduce the dissonance in a given situation: (1) revision of a dissonance producing *attitude*, (2) *selective exposure* to dissonant information, and (3) changing *behaviors* that produce dissonant cognitions.

Attitude Change

One of the most common forms dissonance research has taken requires that the subject find himself in a situation that contains dissonance for him because of some attitude he holds; that is, the subject's attitude toward some issue must be inconsistent with his behavior. A change in the attitude, as measured before and after performance of the behavior, is then said to be evidence for the psychological discomfort resulting from the inconsistency. Thus, the attitude change is theoretically motivated by and reduces the experience of dissonance. The discrepancy between a subject's attitudes and his behavior is often made salient by using either of two procedures termed "inadequate justification" and "effort expenditure."

The Festinger-Carlsmith study described previously, in which subjects were paid $1 or $20 for misrepresenting an experimental task by telling other subjects that it was enjoyable, is an illustration of the "inadequate justification" technique. Here it is assumed that a low reward is insufficient reason for the subject to express an attitude discrepant with one he privately holds; that this behavior is dissonant with his attitude; and that, because the behavior cannot be changed, the attitude will be changed. Subjects paid $20, on the other hand, had adequate justification for their behavior, and dissonance was thus not so strongly aroused.

The special significance of this design is in its implication that both high reward and strong coercion provide justification for attitude-discrepant behavior. Consequently, if one is interested in changing another's *attitude*, it is most effective to use as little reward or coercion as possible above some minimum amount in producing the necessary *behavior*. Note, however, that this behavior (or a commitment to behave in this way) must nevertheless occur.

The second experimental procedure for introducing a discrepancy between attitudes and behavior is "effort expenditure." This procedure focuses on the amount of effort the subject puts into an attitude-discrepant task. The more effort he expends (unpleasantness?), the more dissonance is aroused between the behavior on the task and the attitude toward the task. And one way to reduce the resulting discomfort is to change the attitude to fit more closely the behavior on the task (for example, to like the task more).

Yaryan and Festinger (1961) designed an experiment to examine this hypothesis. In order to show the effect of "preparatory effort" on one's belief in a future event, they asked subjects to prepare for an IQ test by studying an information sheet on which there were definitions essential to the test. The subjects were told that they were participants in a "techniques of study" experiment that was supposed to investigate the techniques, hunches, and hypotheses that students use to study for exams. The experimenter said that only half of them would later actually take the IQ test.

In the "high effort" condition, the subjects were asked to study the sheet and memorize the definitions; in the "low effort" condition, they were asked simply to glance over the definitions briefly and were told that they would have access to the sheet later if they were actually to take the test. After studying the material, the subjects gave their estimates of the probability that they were part of the group that would be taking the IQ test. The results showed that the high effort group considered themselves more likely to take the test.

The authors' interpretation of these results is that the more effort expended in preparation for a future event, the more dissonant is the cognition that the event may not occur. Thus, subjects in the high effort condition should believe more strongly in the likelihood of the occurrence of the event. This should be the case regardless of whether one is apprehensive about the event (considers it unpleasant) or whether one looks forward to it.

Selective Exposure

If a person holds two cognitions that are inconsistent with each other, it is theorized that he will try to find ways to reduce the feeling of dissonance caused by them. Searching for new cognitions that support the favored side of the dissonant pair would be one possibility; avoiding new cognitions that would increase the dissonance would be another. In situations in which a person has some control over the kind of information to which he is exposed, according to the principle of selective exposure, he will (1) seek out dissonance reducing information and/or (2) actively avoid dissonance increasing information.

One of the earliest dissonance studies is related to this hypothesis. Ehrlich, Guttman, Schonbach, and Mills (1957) looked at the selective reading of automobile advertisements by people who had just purchased a new car and by others who owned older cars. The researchers guessed that someone who had recently made an important decision in favor of one make of automobile would be more likely to read material favoring that make than would people who had either bought another make or not made a recent decision in favor of any automobile. They also expected new car owners to avoid reading materials that favored a brand other than the one they chose.

The first prediction, that owners of new cars read advertisements of their own car more often than of cars they considered but did not buy and more often than other cars not involved in the choice, was supported by the evidence. However, this experiment as well as several others, such as Mills, Aronson, and Robinson (1959), Rosen (1961), and Adams (1961), did not yield evidence confirming the proposition that dissonant information will be avoided in proportion to the amount of dissonance produced. It seems, then, that people tend to seek out dissonance *reducing* information, but they do not necessarily *avoid* dissonance *increasing* information.

Perhaps this rather consistent finding, which conflicts with a direct prediction of the theory, can suggest a direction in which attempts to modify the theory might proceed. We know that people seek consonant information but can also tolerate dissonant information. In fact, there is some more recent evidence (Feather, 1963) that not only do smokers not avoid information linking lung cancer and smoking but, if anything, show a slight preference for it. This finding has been replicated in an unpublished work by Brock in 1965. Canon (1964) has shown that even though information increases dissonance, it may also be *useful* to the individual. The utility of information may often be more important than the dissonance it arouses, in which case it will be carefully studied. Canon's data also suggest that people may expose themselves to dissonant information largely because it is dissonant—they can in this way develop counterarguments to refute the dissonant position (Weick, 1965, p. 1268).

An expansion of the basic dissonance idea in order to incorporate these findings could use the concept of "information processing." When people develop arguments and attitudes, they seem to require a certain amount of information on both sides of the question in order to feel justified in holding them. This means an individual may purposefully introduce dissonant cognitions. Dissonant and consonant information may be *processed* differently by the individual, but to assume that the latter is sought for the comfortable feeling it provides and that the former is unpleasant and therefore to be avoided, denied, or distorted is far too simple for a theory of human behavior.

Behavioral Changes

If behaving in a certain way produces cognitions that are inconsistent with some attitude, dissonance theory predicts that either the attitudes or the behavior will change. In order to demonstrate this concept experimentally, Weick

(1964) devised a situation in which the subject could reduce dissonance only by changing the level of a behavior; other ways of reducing dissonance were blocked. Weick was able to show significant attitude change *and* behavioral change in the form of enhancement of and working harder at an experimental task in which subjects were provided insufficient justification for engaging in that task.

In this experiment, the subjects were first assembled in a group. The experimenter then came into the room and in a rather discouraged manner informed the subjects that he had just been told by the head of the psychology department that he would not be allowed to offer class credit to participants in the experiment as originally promised because he was not a member of the psychology department staff. The experimenter then said rather brusquely that anyone who wanted to leave could at that time but that they might as well stay and participate in the experiment. (A few subjects did get up and leave at this point.) The subjects who stayed then worked at a concept attainment task. The startling finding was that these subjects worked harder at the task and liked it better than did subjects in control groups, who initially thought that they would get experimental credit. (Actually, at the end of the experiment, all subjects were informed of the ruse and were given equal credit for participating.)

The surprising aspect of this outcome is that Weick was able to demonstrate an increase in productivity with a reduction in the reward offered—an outcome exactly opposite to what traditional incentive theory would predict. This outcome may be seen by comparing the experimental and control conditions. In the experimental group, the subjects thought they were *not* going to receive class credit, and they were staying for an experimenter who was anything but warm-hearted. The latter aspect hopefully eliminated the dissonance reducing cognition that one is really staying to help out a warm, deserving person. The experimental subjects worked harder and performed better than those who received the expected reward of class credit. The manipulation, moreover, produced behavioral change in the form of increased productivity—not merely attitudinal change.

Choosing between Various Modes of Dissonance Reduction

Three ways of reducing dissonance have just been discussed, and these are by no means exhaustive. Changing the importance of relevant cognitions, or the importance of the entire set of cognitions, selective recall of dissonant information, perceptual distortion, and denial of commitment or volition are all possibilities. What, then, determines which of these alternatives will be used by a given individual in preference to others?

We mentioned earlier that Festinger's original conception was that an individual would prefer to reduce dissonance by making the least effortful change he could make. The cognition least resistant to change would be selected, in other words. Research on this hypothesis has raised a number of questions indicating that the picture may be more complicated; indeed, the principle may eventually need to be replaced by a better one.

Dissonance theory itself is not equipped to predict which means of reducing dissonance will be chosen. Dissonance theorists, however, have made attempts in this direction. For example, Weick (1964) has conducted research leading him to believe that people sometimes choose the method of dissonance reduction that affords the most *stable* resolution. If one has two inconsistent attitudes about some issue, it might be easiest simply to change one's attitudes on one side of that issue and thus reduce dissonance. But if one *behaves* in a way that is consistent with one attitude but not the other (thus producing a behavioral commitment to the first), then one's position is solidified, less resistant to change, and more stable. Weick's research on behavioral change reinforces this notion; he feels that behavior can be used to *validate* a cognitive realignment.

Other research has "sharpened the kinds of issues that must be resolved to gain greater accuracy in predicting how dissonance will be reduced" (Weick, 1965, p. 1266). Weick includes these: (1) Are attitudes easier to change than behavior? (2) Do people not under experimental constraints typically use more than one mode of dissonance reduction simultaneously? (3) Are denial mechanisms more likely to be used than acceptance mechanisms? (4) Is dissonance reduced in the least effortful manner or by the method that yields the greatest gain?

McGuire reviews the work of such people as Abelson, McGuire, Newcomb, Rosenberg, and Tannenbaum on the question of alternative modes of dissonance reduction and concludes that "despite (or because of) all this work, the issue remains conceptually confused and cries for further, less haphazard study" (McGuire, 1966b, p. 27).

Summary of the Dependent Variables in Dissonance Reduction

To complement our summary of research on dissonance arousal, the following outline, again from Brehm and Cohen (1962), indicates the range of experimental contexts used to investigate this segment of the theory.

1. Attitude change: Changes in opinion (acceptance of a compulsory religious requirement or abolition of all intercollegiate athletics at Yale University)
2. Attitude change: Changes in evaluation
   a. liking for people (for example, one's fiancee)
   b. attraction to groups (for example, a sexual discussion group)
   c. preference for objects (for example, toys, appliances)
   d. evaluation of activities (for example, a boring and time consuming task)
   e. food preferences (for example, jam, grasshoppers, disliked vegetables)
   f. sensory characteristics (for example, preference for colors, judgment of weights)
   g. subjective experiences (for example, pain, hunger, thirst)
3. Exposure to information (selective exposure to and avoidance of infor-

formation on child rearing practices, car advertisements, probabilities of winning or losing in a gambling situation)

4. Recall of information (selective recall of ratings about oneself or about one's favorite TV personalities)
5. Perceptual distortion (projection of one's own experience of homosexual arousal onto another person)
6. Change in overt behavior (job productivity, drinking water, conforming to a group norm)

DISSONANCE THEORY IN THE CONTEXT OF OTHER PSYCHOLOGICAL THEORIES

Festinger's theory can be considered the third major phase in the development of consistency theories in general. Consistency theories focus on those aspects of man's behavior, thoughts, attitudes, and beliefs that are organized in meaningful and sensible ways. These theories are concerned with man's apparent need to believe himself rational, even if he has to distort or ignore reality to preserve this belief. They reinforce the psychoanalytic notion of rationalization, which holds that man strives to understand and justify painful experiences and to make them sensible and rational but sometimes employs completely irrational methods to achieve this end.

Zajonc (1960a) has provided an excellent historical review of the development of consistency theories, from Heider's balance theory, to Osgood and Tannenbaum's principle of congruity, to Festinger's theory of cognitive dissonance. Zajonc's review will be briefly sketched here.

Balance Theory

In 1946, Heider formulated a system for looking at one particular set of relationships—those involving a person (P) who is the focus of analysis, some other person (O), and one impersonal entity (X), which could be a physical object, an idea, an event, or the like. These three elements form a triad, among which are three possible relationships: the relation between P and O, between P and X, and between O and X. Heider's inquiry was to discover how relations among P, O, and X are organized in P's cognitive structure and whether there exist recurrent and systematic tendencies in the way these relations are experienced.

P's cognitive structure representing these relations is either what Heider called balanced or unbalanced. In particular, he proposed that a balanced state exists if (1) all three relations are positive or (2) two are negative and one is positive. All other configurations would be unbalanced, unstable, and likely to change to a more balanced state. For example, if one person likes another (P likes O) and also likes a certain activity (P likes X), but O does not like X, there is only one negative relation, and the system is unbalanced. If P decides to dislike O or to dislike X, balance would be restored. Similarly, if O decides to like X, the system would again be in balance.

Heider's contribution was a significant one and has stimulated much of the thought on the subject of consistency. However, there are some shortcomings. The theory does not concern cognitive structures including more than three elements. In addition, it does not specify the rules governing which elements would change in the case of an unbalanced structure; nor does it allow for P's beliefs about himself, which could conceivably be negative—for example, P could have very low self-esteem. Third, the theory does not allow for degrees of liking; according to this theory, a relation is either positive or negative.

The first of these objections was dealt with by Cartwright and Harary (1956), who constructed a more general definition of balance by using digraph theory. Their formulation covers any number of cognitive elements and also treats balance as a matter of degree, ranging from 0 to 1.

The balance notion is, of course, testable, but its apparent simplicity is misleading. It is easy to demonstrate that certain "balanced" situations are preferred to their "unbalanced" counterparts, but it is equally easy to think of examples that do not seem to fit. For example, when two attractions exist but are very dissimilar in nature and origin, do the predictions of balance theory still hold? Zajonc recalls an inquiry that Festinger once offered in a jocular mood: Would it follow from balance theory that, because he likes chicken and chickens like chicken feed, he must also like chicken feed or experience the tension of imbalance (Zajonc, 1960a, p. 285)?

The Principle of Congruity

Osgood and Tannenbaum (1955) advanced the principle of congruity, which is a special case of balance. It deals specifically with the *direction* of attitude change.

> The authors assume that "judgmental frames of reference tend toward maximal simplicity." Thus, since extreme "black-and-white," "all-or-nothing" judgments are simpler than refined ones, valuations tend to move toward extremes or, . . . there is "a continuing pressure toward polarization." Together with the notion of maximization of simplicity is the assumption of identity as being less complex than the discrimination of fine differences. Therefore, related "concepts" will tend to be evaluated in a similar manner. Given these assumptions, the principle of congruity holds that when change in evaluation or attitude occurs it always occurs in the direction of increased congruity with the prevailing frame of reference (Zajonc, 1960a, pp. 286–287).

Typically, a person (P) has attitudes, either positive or negative, toward both a *source* (S) and an *object* (O). Moreover, person S is said to make assertions, either positive or negative, about the object O. Thus, for example, if one originally has positive attitudes about S and O, and S makes a positive assertion about O, the assertion is *congruent*. If S makes a negative assertion, then, as was the case with balance theory, the single negative element is *incongruent.* Congruity theory would predict that *P* will discredit either the source or the object but not both. The one chosen will depend on which of the two is more polarized—that is, extreme—in his attitude system.

The great advantage of the congruity principle over earlier attempts is in its precision. Congruity theorists can make predictions of the extent and direction of attitude change—predictions that their studies confirmed fairly well. Refined measurements have been made using Osgood's (1952) method of the "semantic differential" that are significant improvements over the positive-negative dichotomy to which balance theory is limited.

Dissonance Theory

Festinger has used the same basic assumptions as those in the consistency theories just mentioned, but his dissonance principle has been found useful in a wider range of situations. Of the three formulations, dissonance theory has been associated with the largest systematic program of research. This theory has organized a diverse body of empirical knowledge by means of a limited number of fairly reasonable assumptions.

Before assailing a theory so firmly entrenched as this one with the criticisms that come in the next section, perhaps it is wise—and only fair—at this point to compliment its special achievements. Weick (1965), in a critical review of the theory, calls attention to several issues in social psychology that have, intentionally or not, come into sharper focus as a result of work related to dissonance theory.

First, dissonance theory has emphasized that "rewards" are not always attractive. More accurately, inadequate extrinsic rewards do not always produce cessation of activities or dislike of them. "Instead, low rewards seem to prod individuals to look more closely at what they are doing and to discover satisfying features that had gone unnoticed" (Weick, 1965, p. 1271). Moreover, increasing reward may increase the feeling of coercion as well, thus producing a more stubborn unwillingness to perform the task.

> What these findings suggest is that high rewards have their drawbacks. Frequently, they constrain actions. Furthermore, when extrinsic rewards are diminished, persons may substitute their *own* rewards which are often more appropriate and satisfying. It seems clear that any social psychological research should take careful note of the fact that *cognitions* about rewards exert a significant effect on their *impact* (Weick, 1965, p. 1272, italics added).

Dissonance theory has been successful in clarifying another issue in social psychology—that of the discrepancy between public and private beliefs. Attention has been directed to the finding that these discrepancies generate more tension than was suspected. In addition, evidence has been collected to support the idea that private beliefs may change so that they furnish more support for the public actions. It was generally assumed before that an individual could maintain discrepancies with few costs and no changes.

In their efforts to find theories to oppose dissonance theory, persons have found that few exist. This is not because dissonance theory is necessarily robust, but rather because there just are not many useful theories of social behavior available. The interest generated by dissonance theory may be due more to the lack of theories than to its unique characteristics and predictive power (Weick, 1965, p. 1271).

CRITICISMS OF THE THEORY AND ITS EVIDENCE

Several facts associated with the theory of cognitive dissonance cannot be disputed and provide reasons for giving it so much attention. One of these facts is that a great deal of research on the theory has been done in the last 10 years, most of which confirms the theory's predictions. Another is that many researchers have used the theory to explain a wide array of events and phenomena, and the explanations usually seem reasonable. These facts suggest, more than anything else, that the theory has been surprisingly fashionable, although this trend is beginning to decline.

Chapanis and Chapanis (1964) provided one of the first extended criticisms of dissonance theory and also offered a reason for its popularity. In their words, the theory is engagingly simple:

> Its magic . . . seems to lie in the ease with which imponderably complex social situations are reduced to simple statements, most often just two such statements. This having been done, a simple inspection for rational consistency is enough to predict whether or not change will occur. Such uncomplicated rationality seems especially welcome after having been told for years that our attitudes and behavior are strongly dependent on motivational, emotional, affective, and perceptual processes (p. 2).

Theoretical Problems with the Theory

This engaging simplicity of dissonance theory is a problem that theorists have been hard-pressed to solve. In any situation, including the laboratory setting, an individual will entertain an impossibly large number of cognitions. Even if we could know what all of these are, how do we decide which pairs or sets are dissonant? To say that dissonance is culturally determined merely bypasses the difficulty; the responsibility for specifying the dissonant aspects of a situation must eventually fall on the personal judgment of the observer. This responsibility gives the researcher the tempting possibility of creating situations that have predictable (intuitive) outcomes, then generating the cognitions to which it would be reasonable to attribute dissonance, and finally offering the results as support for the theory.

Given these considerations, it is surprising to realize that no special effort has been made to determine whether a subject has *experienced* the tension called dissonance; or whether the "salient" cognitions were actually salient to him; or the extent to which contaminating cognitions were present. It would not seem unreasonable to *ask* the subject after an experiment if he saw the problem the way the experimenter did, even though this procedure admittedly calls attention to a certain vagueness in the theory.

A related problem is that of "confounding" the relationships between cognitions. The more complex a social setting, the greater the number of inter-related cognitions. One can *assume* that a particular pair of this large set of cognitions will arouse dissonance and will in turn change some dependent variable. But it is inevitable that other pairs will be dissonant, either more or less so, and, because all the other possible pairs cannot be tested, they are commonly ignored. Thus, the experimental "effect" is attributed, say, to the dissonance created by cognitions *a* and *b*. Yet in fact, some other pair, *a* and *e*, or *e* and *f*, might be responsible for the effect—in other words, they might be confounding the main effects of *a* and *b*. There is no way to control this problem completely, but Chapanis and Chapanis feel that it will be minimized if dissonance researchers will restrict themselves to less complex social situations. In those experiments where discrepant internal cognitions are said to follow the presentation of relatively simple contradictory statements, syllogisms, or opinions, the results are more consistent and clear-cut.

Weick (1965, p. 1263) cites the work of Adams and Jacobsen (1964) as an example of an "uncomplicated" dissonance study, one not so "needlessly complex" as many dissonance experiments. These researchers explored what happened to the quality and quantity of output on a proofreading task when there was a marked discrepancy between a person's input and the salary he received. Here it is relatively easy to isolate the cognitions that will be most salient for the subject and to infer the amount of dissonance he will experience in the situation.

But even though this study involves relationships between dissonance and expenditure of effort, "a problem that seems easier to simplify than problems of attitude change, decision-making, or interpersonal perception," Weick himself later offers an alternative set of cognitions that may be operating in the Adams and Jacobsen experiment. In their study,

> a person takes a test of proofreading ability, fails it, and then is hired "reluctantly" by an employer to be a professional proofreader. This manipulation is intended to create a discrepancy between what a person contributes to a job and what he receives. [The subject] may not be bothered as much by this discrepancy as by the discrepancy between the initial test data and his beliefs about his capabilities. He may believe that he is qualified to detect typographical errors only to discover that tests show he is not. An easy way to resolve the discrepancy between self-concept and test data is to discredit the test. If this occurs, [the experimenter] has created dissonance, but not where he intended (Weick, 1965, pp. 1264–1265).

The ambiguity in the locus of dissonance, or even of the "major" or "important" cognitions in a situation, is subject to interpretation. This ambiguity too often leads to more than one "reasonable" interpretation and thus to a misleading ability to "explain" nearly anything.

It is to this flaw that Bem (1967) refers when he argues that dissonance theory has attempted to bypass a functional analysis, which will eventually have to be performed to eliminate the ambiguity in the definition of dissonance. He offers a theoretical alternative to dissonance and explains much of the same data given in its support.

Methodological Problems with Dissonance Research

The five years following the appearance of Festinger's first statement of the theory saw the rapid growth of experimental work testing its propositions. The empirical evidence supporting dissonance theory was impressive and, to many critics, convincing. It was at this point, however, that Chapanis and Chapanis (1964) discussed in a lengthy critique some aspects of dissonance research that, taken together, left them unconvinced about the theory's generality. Their controversial paper dealt largely with two major flaws in the methodology typically applied to dissonance research. The first was concerned with the extremely complex manipulations used to create a dissonant situation in the laboratory— that is, with "whether an experimenter really did what he said he did." The second involved what Chapanis and Chapanis considered technically questionable methods of treating the experimental data—"whether the experimenter really got the results he said he did."

To illustrate the first argument, let us look again at Yaryan and Festinger's (1961) study using the "effort expenditure" paradigm. The experiment was designed to show that high effort on a task (preparing to take an IQ test) would lead to a stronger belief that the event the task prepared for (the test) would occur. The high effort group was told to study their list carefully, whereas the low effort group merely glanced over the list without studying it. The former group thought it was more probable that they would take the test.

Yaryan and Festinger explain these results by *inferring* that the high effort subjects held the cognition that they had exerted "a great deal of effort" and that this cognition is inconsistent with not taking the test. There is no way to observe any *direct* evidence that the subjects actually held these cognitions or thought in these terms. Moreover, Chapanis and Chapanis offer an alternative explanation of the results that seems equally reasonable:

> In this experiment the variable of effort is confounded with the presence of other predictors for the event. All subjects had been told that this was an experiment on the techniques of study, but the only group which *did* any studying was the high-effort group. In addition, the studying that was done was highly relevant for the IQ test. Under the circumstances, it does not seem at all surprising that subjects in this group took these additional cues to mean that they were assigned to the complete experiment and to the IQ test. As it stands now, the Yaryan and Festinger experiment does not separate the effect of effort from that of additional cues (Chapanis & Chapanis, 1964, p. 9).

For such reasons, it is not at all clear that an experimenter always sets up the conditions or the controls that he thought he did.

Another study described earlier, that of Ehrlich et al. (1957) on the selective exposure of automobile buyers to information about different brands, was among those criticized for committing a different kind of error common to many dissonance experiments. A technique used many times in these studies is to discard the data from certain subjects because those data are "unreliable" or "inappropriate." In the Ehrlich et al. study, "as much as 82 percent of the original sample was discarded in certain categories!" (Chapanis & Chapanis, 1964, p. 15).

Under some conditions, this procedure is justifiable; however, under other conditions, it can lead to a definite bias in the results. The above example was criticized because the *reasons* for rejecting parts of the data were not made clear in the presentation of the study. But in some cases, selecting the data can "*violate the whole concept of controlled experimentation.*" Chapanis and Chapanis outline the faulty reasoning used by some dissonance researchers:

> If some subjects do not follow the specific predictions in a particular experiment (for instance, if they fail to show any opinion change) then those subjects are probably reducing their dissonance through some other channel or else they had little dissonance to begin with. If either of these conditions holds it is legitimate to exclude these subjects from the analysis since they could not possibly be used to test the particular hypothesis in the experiment. An inspection of results is considered sufficient to determine whether subjects are, or are not, to be excluded. Unfortunately, this line of reasoning contains one fundamental flaw: *it does not allow the possibility that the null hypothesis may be correct.* The experimenter, in effect, is asserting that his dissonance prediction is correct and that subjects who do not conform to the prediction should be excluded from the analysis. This is a foolproof method of guaranteeing positive results (Chapanis & Chapanis, 1964, p. 17).

Perhaps, then, experimenters do not always get the results they thought (or said) they did.

These criticisms, of course, do not apply equally to all of the experiments in the dissonance context—many of them are relatively unassailable. Chapanis and Chapanis call attention to only a segment of the evidence and ask that it not be taken so unequivocally as the evidence obtained with more care and logic.

One of the classic dissonance experiments (Festinger & Carlsmith, 1959), the forced compliance design using $1 and $20 conditions to produce attitude change, has been criticized by Rosenberg (1965) for containing a confounding influence he calls "evaluation apprehension." This is essentially a suspicion on the part of the subject that he is being evaluated by the experimenter. Rosenberg's replication of the former study obtained results directly opposite to those of Festinger and Carlsmith.

Rosenberg's study was, in turn, replicated and expanded by Linder, Cooper, and Jones (1967), and a variable accounting for the discrepancy between the two experiments was reportedly isolated. The entire issue is too lengthy to be included here, but is recommended to the reader as an excellent example of the use of experimentation to test the conflicting predictions of two theories.

CURRENT STATUS AND SOME PREDICTIONS ABOUT THE FUTURE

The Role of Dissonance—The Beginning of a Theory?

Zajonc (1960a) has drawn an interesting parallel between dissonance as an explanatory principle and another principle that is important in the history of science. He suggests that the role of these two principles may be comparable and that making the comparison can help us understand their common context and bring both the faults and the contributions of the dissonance formulation into perspective.

For centuries, a number of related phenomena were accounted for by a commonly accepted principle. The principle was used to "explain" such facts as (1) pumps can lift a column of water by removing the air from the top of a tube; (2) two hemispheric vessels, placed together with the air removed from between them, are held to each other; and (3) a suction (force) can be established by drawing air from a vessel. Each of these phenomena involves the absence of air, and all were accounted for by the principle "Nature abhors a vacuum." The evidence for this principle was so overwhelming that it was seldom questioned.

Then people noticed an exception. Pumps can only draw water to a height of 34 feet. The principle had to be modified to deal with this observation. This state of affairs was satisfactory until Torricelli discovered that mercury can only be lifted 30 inches. It was becoming uncomfortable to employ a principle that had to include so many exceptions—it now read: "Nature abhors a vacuum but only below 34 feet when we deal with water and below 30 inches with mercury." Torricelli was therefore led to formulate the more general notion that it is atmospheric pressure that forces air into a vacuum and that this force can sustain the weight of 34 feet of water or 30 inches of mercury. This was a revolutionary concept, and its consequences had a drastic impact on physics.

Similarly, human nature is said to abhor dissonance. But there are many exceptions to the consistency principle—people enjoy watching a magician, whose task it is to produce dissonance. In a magical act, the obverse of what you see follows from what you know. People spend a good portion of their income on insurance, and many at the same time are willing to gamble at casinos. The first action is intended to protect against risks; the second implies an enjoyment of taking risks. The dissonance principle as it stands does not seem to be universally or unequivocally true, and yet it serves a useful function. Returning to Zajonc's parallel:

> . . . *Horror vacui* served an important purpose besides explaining and organizing some aspects of physical knowledge. Without it the discomfort of "exceptions to the rule" would never have been felt, and the important developments in theory might have been delayed considerably. If a formulation has then a virtue in being wrong, the theories of consistency do have this virtue. They do organize a large body of knowledge. Also, they point out exceptions, and thereby they demand

a new formulation. It will not suffice simply to reformulate them so as to accommodate the exceptions. I doubt if Festinger would be satisfied with a modification of his dissonance principle which would read that dissonance, being psychologically uncomfortable, leads a person to actively avoid situations and information which would be likely to increase the dissonance, except when there is an opportunity to watch a magician.

Also simply to disprove the theories by counterexamples would not in itself constitute an important contribution. We would merely lose explanations of phenomena which had been explained. And it is doubtful that the theories of consistency could be rejected simply *because* of counterexamples. Only a theory which accounts for all the data that the consistency principles now account for, for all the exceptions to those principles, and for all the phenomena which these principles should now but do not consider, is capable of replacing them. It is only a matter of time until such a development takes place (Zajonc, 1960a, p. 296).

On this optimistic note, let us look at a theoretical trend that may eventually assimilate the principle of dissonance and fit it into a more comprehensive framework.

Future Directions: Consistency Theory versus Complexity Theory

In Feldman's (1966) book entitled *Cognitive Consistency*, McGuire contributes an excellent account of "the place of consistency theory in the larger psychological scene." He, too, assumes that the theory will eventually come to be considered a part of some larger, more inclusive formulation. One possibility is that dissonance, or, more generally, consistency, will be fitted into psychological thinking as a *motive*, thereby joining the ever increasing number of new motives proposed by psychologists (for example, the achievement motive, the affiliation motive, and the approval motive). Another possibility is to consider consistency from a *functional* point of view:

> Attitudes have been analyzed as serving many functions: utility, expression, meaning, ego-defensiveness, etc. It seems likely that maintenance of consistency plays an important role in all of these functions; certainly, in the last two. We feel that an integration into the functional approach is another avenue by which consistency theories, to the mutual benefit of both kinds of approach, could be brought into heuristically provocative interaction with other approaches (McGuire, 1966b, p. 35).

A less cautious prediction, but one with which we tend to agree, is McGuire's extension of what he considers a new, corrective trend in psychology—one antithetical to the consistency approach but able to integrate some of its concepts. He cites Berlyne (1960), Fiske and Maddi (1961), and Fowler (1965) as representative of approaches he subsumes under the "unsatisfactory rubric of 'complexity theories.' " Contrasting the "classical" view of an organism as having a "penchant for stability, redundancy, familiarity, confirmation of expectance, avoidance of the new, the unpredictable," complexity theory's "romantic organism works on a quite different economy. It has a stimulus hunger, an exploratory drive, a need curiosity. It takes pleasure in the *unexpected*, at least in intermediate levels of unpredictability. It wants to experience everything; it shows alternation behavior; it finds novelty rewarding" (McGuire, 1966b, p. 37).

Complexity notions, although not logically contradictory to consistency theory, seem to have the reverse psychological flavor. McGuire feels that the two approaches are interrelated and that, in the swing he sees in psychology from a classical to a romantic phase, complexity theories may be expanded to encompass both points of view. Perhaps then several "principles" of social psychology can be integrated into a realistic theory. Nonetheless, one thing remains clear. Whatever the future directions of the theoretical work in this area, dissonance research has contributed a wealth of experimental data that will continue to support, challenge, and contradict the attempts of later workers to find a way of systematizing it.

REFERENCES

ADAMS, J. S. Reduction of cognitive dissonance by seeking consonant information. *Journal of Abnormal and Social Psychology,* 1961, **62,** 74–78.

ADAMS, J. S. Inequity in social exchange. In L. Berkowitz (Ed.), *Advances in experimental social psychology.* Vol. 2. New York: Academic Press, 1965. Pp. 267–300.

ADAMS, J. S., & JACOBSEN, P. R. Effects of wage inequities on work quality. *Journal of Abnormal and Social Psychology,* 1964, **69,** 19–25.

ARONSON, E., & CARLSMITH, J. Effect of the severity of threat on the devaluation of forbidden behavior. *Journal of Abnormal and Social Psychology,* 1963, **66,** 584–588.

ARONSON, E., & FESTINGER, L. Some attempts to measure tolerance for dissonance. USAF WADC Technical Report, 1958, No. 58–492.

ASCH, S. E. Review of L. Festinger, *A theory of cognitive dissonance. Contemporary Psychology,* 1958, **3,** 194–195.

BEM, D. J. Self-perception: An alternative interpretation of cognitive dissonance phenomena. *Psychological Review,* 1967, **74,** 183–200.

BERLYNE, D. *Conflict, arousal, and curiosity.* New York: McGraw-Hill, 1960.

BRAMEL, D. A dissonance theory approach to defensive projection. *Journal of Abnormal and Social Psychology,* 1962, **64,** 121–129.

BRASFIELD, C., & PAPAGEORGIS, D. Manifest anxiety and the effects of a dissonant self-relevant communication on self-perception. *Proceedings of the 73rd Annual Convention of the American Psychological Association,* 1965, 193–194.

BREHM, J. W. Postdecision changes in the desirability of alternatives. *Journal of Abnormal and Social Psychology,* 1956, **52,** 384–389.

BREHM, J. W. Attitudinal consequences of commitment to unpleasant behavior. *Journal of Abnormal and Social Psychology,* 1960, **60,** 379–383. (a)

BREHM, J. W. A dissonance analysis of attitude-discrepant behavior. In C. I. Hovland & M. J. Rosenberg (Eds.), *Attitude organization and change*. New Haven, Conn.: Yale University Press, 1960. Pp. 164–197. (b)

BREHM, J. W., & COHEN, A. R. Choice and chance relative deprivation as determinants of cognitive dissonance. *Journal of Abnormal and Social Psychology*, 1959, **58**, 383–387. (a)

BREHM, J. W., & COHEN, A. R. Re-evaluation of choice alternatives as a function of their number and qualitative similarity. *Journal of Abnormal and Social Psychology*, 1959, **58**, 373–378. (b)

BREHM, J. W., & COHEN, A. R. *Exploration in cognitive dissonance*. New York: Wiley, 1962.

BREWSTER, G. W. Attitude change as a function of cognitive dissonance due to attitude ambivalence, field independence, resolving ambivalence, and discrepant compliance. *Dissertation Abstracts*, 1966, **27**, 248–249.

BROCK, T. C. Cognitive restructuring and attitude change. *Journal of Abnormal and Social Psychology*, 1962, **64**, 264–271.

BROCK, T. C., & BUSS, A. H. Dissonance, aggression, and evaluation of pain. *Journal of Abnormal and Social Psychology*, 1962, **65**, 197–202.

CANON, L. K. Self-confidence and selective exposure to information. In L. Festinger (Ed.), *Conflict, decision, and dissonance*. Stanford, Calif.: Stanford University Press, 1964. Pp. 83–95.

CARTWRIGHT, D., HARARY, F. Structural balance: A generalization of Heider's theory. *Psychological Review*, 1956, **63**, 277–293.

CHAPANIS, N. P., & CHAPANIS, A. Cognitive dissonance. *Psychological Bulletin*, 1964, **61**, 1–22.

COHEN, A. R., BREHM, J. W., & FLEMING, W. H. Attitude change and justification for compliance. *Journal of Abnormal and Social Psychology*, 1958, **56**, 276–278.

DEUTSCH, M., KRAUSS, R. M., & ROSENAU, N. Dissonance or defensiveness? *Journal of Personality*, 1962, **30**, 16–28.

EHRLICH, D., GUTTMAN, I., SCHONBACH, P., & MILLS, J. Postdecision exposure to relevant information. *Journal of Abnormal and Social Psychology*, 1957, **54**, 98–112.

FEATHER, N. T. Cognitive dissonance, sensitivity, and evaluation. *Journal of Abnormal and Social Psychology*, 1963, **66**, 157–163.

FELDMAN, S. (Ed.), *Cognitive consistency*. New York: Academic Press, 1966.

FESTINGER, L. *A theory of cognitive dissonance*. Evanston, Ill.: Row, Peterson, 1957.

FESTINGER, L., & CARLSMITH, J. M. Cognitive consequences of forced compliance. *Journal of Abnormal and Social Psychology*, 1959, **58**, 203–210.

FILLENBAUM, S. Dogmatism and individual differences in reduction of dissonance. *Psychological Reports*, 1964, **14**, 47–50.

FISKE, D., & MADDI, S. *Functions of varied experience*. Homewood, Ill.: Dorsey, 1961.

FITCH, H. G. Dissonance theory and research: A complete bibliography. Unpublished manuscript, Purdue University, 1967.

FOWLER, H. *Curiosity and exploratory behavior*. New York: Macmillan, 1965.

GALLIMORE, R. G. Reduction styles and dissonance-associated autonomic activity. *Dissertation Abstracts*, 1965, **25**, 6759.

HARVEY, O. J. Some situational and cognitive determinants of dissonance resolution. *Journal of Personality and Social Psychology*, 1965, **1**, 349–355.

HEIDER, F. Attitudes and cognitive organization. *Journal of Psychology,* 1946, **21,** 107–112.

LINDER, D., COOPER, J., & JONES, E. E. Decision freedom as a determinant of the role of incentive magnitude in attitude change. *Journal of Personality and Social Psychology,* 1967, **6,** 245–254.

MCGUIRE, W. J. Attitudes and opinions. *Annual Review of Psychology,* 1966, **17,** 475–514. (a)

MCGUIRE, W. J. The current status of cognitive consistency theories. In S. Feldman (Ed.), *Cognitive consistency.* New York: Academic Press, 1966. Pp. 1–46. (b)

MILLS, J. Changes in moral attitudes following temptation. *Journal of Personality,* 1958, **26,** 517–531.

MILLS, J., ARONSON, E., & ROBINSON, H. Selectivity in exposure to information. *Journal of Abnormal and Social Psychology,* 1959, **59,** 250–253.

OSGOOD, C. E. The nature and measurement of meaning. *Psychological Bulletin,* 1952, **49,** 197–237.

OSGOOD, C. E., & TANNENBAUM, P. H. The principle of congruity in attitude change. *Psychological Review,* 1955, **62,** 42–55.

ROSEN, S. Postdecision affinity for incompatible information. *Journal of Abnormal and Social Psychology,* 1961, **63,** 188–190.

ROSENBERG, M. J. When dissonance fails: On eliminating evaluation apprehension from attitude measurement. *Journal of Personality and Social Psychology,* 1965, **1,** 28–42.

SMITH, E. E. The power of dissonance techniques to change attitudes. *Public Opinion Quarterly,* 1961, **25,** 626–639.

STACK, J. J. Individual differences in the reduction of cognitive dissonance: An exploratory study. *Dissertation Abstracts,* 1964, **24,** 4806–4807.

SUINN, R. M. Anxiety and cognitive dissonance. *Journal of General Psychology,* 1965, **73,** 113–116.

WEICK, K. E. Reduction of cognitive dissonance through task enhancement and effort expenditure. *Journal of Abnormal and Social Psychology,* 1964, **68,** 533–539.

WEICK, K. E. When prophecy pales: The fate of dissonance theory. *Psychological Reports,* 1965, **16,** 1261–1275.

YARYAN, R. B., & FESTINGER, L. Preparatory action and belief in the probable occurrence of future events. *Journal of Abnormal and Social Psychology,* 1961, **63,** 603–606.

ZAJONC, R. B. The concepts of balance, congruity, and dissonance. *Public Opinion Quarterly,* 1960, **24,** 280–296. (a)

ZAJONC, R. B. The process of cognitive tuning in communication. *Journal of Abnormal and Social Psychology,* 1960, **61,** 159–167. (b)

5

ATTITUDE CHANGE: THE INFORMATION- PROCESSING PARADIGM

William J. McGuire

The study of attitudes has always been a central focus of social psychology. Indeed, when social psychology emerged as a recognized field of study a half century ago, prominent theorists as varied as the sociologists W. I. Thomas and F. Znaniecki (1918) and the behavioral psychologist J. B. Watson (1925) agreed that attitude was the core concept of the field and even equated social psychology with the study of attitudes. During the quarter century that followed these pioneering formulations, attitude research largely concentrated on measuring attitudes and identifying their structure and correlates. In the more recent quarter century, ever since the mid-1940s, this study of attitude as a static construct has given way to the more dynamic study of attitude change. The conceptual and empirical work in the area is now directed primarily toward developing theoretical formulations to account for the development of attitudes, the efficacy of variables in producing attitude change, and the interrelations between attitudinal and behavioral change.

HISTORICAL TRENDS

Attitude change, in its broader usage, refers to the general area of social influence processes, that is, how a person's feelings, beliefs, or behaviors are influenced by stimuli received from other people. This broad use includes a variety of social influence situations, such as suggestion and hypnosis, conformity, group discussion, mass media communication, and total institutions. Because other chapters of this volume, particularly those in Sections III, IV, and V, focus on some of these types of social influence situations, we shall here consider "attitude change" in the narrower sense of social influence exerted through verbal communication, usually in the form of written or spoken messages arguing for a point of view on some issue.

Even this narrow sense includes a substantial body of research. About 25 percent of recent social psychological textbooks was devoted to the area of attitude change (McGuire, 1966a). The 1967 volumes of the *Psychological Abstracts* show that about 17,000 psychological studies were published during that year. Of these, well over 1000 were in the area of social psychology and about a quarter of these latter abstracts dealt with attitude change research. Hence, the amount of research that focuses on attitude change, even when it is defined in a fairly narrow sense, is formidable both relatively and absolutely.

The dominant single factor to which this flourishing of the attitude change area can be traced is the research by Carl Hovland and his colleagues during World War II in the Army Information and Education Division and during the next decade at Yale University. At the time the Hovland group began its work, the study of attitudes was at a relatively low ebb in social psychology, as the earlier work of the static aspects of attitudes mentioned above had lost much of its interest for active researchers. During the early years of revived interest in the dynamic aspects of attitudes, the work of the Hovland group was overshadowed within social psychology by the flourishing research on group processes under the impetus of the followers of Kurt Lewin at the University of Michigan and elsewhere. But by the late 1950s, interest in the study of group processes temporarily ebbed (just as interest in the static study of attitudes had two decades previously) and some of the most active researchers in the group area followed the Hovland group at Yale and elsewhere in taking up the study of attitude change.

Since the late 1950s, the area of attitude change has been the most active focus of research in social psychology. This writer feels that the current wave of interest in the area has reached its peak. Recently, social psychological research on attitude change has been growing at a less rapid rate than that of other areas, such as the study of nonverbal communication, social aggression, interpersonal liking, and prosocial behavior. It seems likely that the percentage of all social psychological research devoted to attitude change will decline somewhat during the 1970s. However, while there will continue to be ebbs and flows in social psychological interest in areas like attitudes, group processes, social perception, etc., it is likely that there will be an appreciable amount of research in such areas even during their most quiet years.

CURRENT CONCEPTUALIZATIONS OF THE ATTITUDE CHANGE PROCESS

The paradigms that develop in an area of inquiry are represented in the questions that are asked and the answers that are tried out. One current strategy for questioning in scientific psychology involves starting with a dependent variable (in this case, attitude change), which is one's focus of interest, and then identifying certain domains of independent variables that one suspects to be functionally related to this dependent variable. One's theoretical preconceptions are used to derive, usually quite informally, hypotheses about relationships between various independent variables and attitude change. We might call this strategy the "convergent" approach, since it begins with a dependent variable focus of interest (attitude change) and converges on it from all directions, to account for its variations in terms of many antecedents.

An alternative strategy of comparable popularity, which might be called the "divergent" approach to heighten the contrast, starts with a theoretical position that focuses interest on certain antecedent factors that affect a variety of dependent variables. Those who resonate better with this style of hypothesis generation make predictions about how the independent variables of their theoretical interest relate to attitude change as one type of dependent variable among many. Each of these styles of hypothesis generation has been conducive to creative thinking about attitude change so we shall report here the yield of both styles where they have clarified the attitude change process.

When the researcher has generated a hypothesis by his preferred style of thinking, he typically tries to put it to an empirical test by some generally approved procedure. At the present time, the preferred testing procedure has almost invariably taken the form of a laboratory manipulational experiment. There are, however, some signs (See McGuire, 1967, 1969b) that other testing paradigms are beginning to come back into social psychological fashion, including the manipulational experiment in natural settings and even correlational approaches that utilize information about actual social events preserved in archives and social data banks.

The Variables in Attitude Change Research

Dependent Variable: Attitude Change. Our discussion of attitude change should begin with mention of the current conceptualization of attitudes. In general, attitudes are considered to be behavioral predispositions that describe a person's tendency to perform certain classes of responses (usually locatable on a favorable-unfavorable dimension) toward a specifiable class of stimuli, such as events, institutions, individuals, or groups of people that have social significance. In attitude change research, these behavioral predispositions have typically been defined operationally in terms of responses on a self-report inventory or "opinionnaire." The items on such inventories ask the person to make a response which assigns an object of judgment (e.g., an institution or a group of people) to some evaluative dimension of variability. The person might be asked whether he agrees, disagrees, or is neutral as regards the proposition "free public education should be made available to all qualified students through the college years," or "abortion laws should be repealed, leaving it a medical procedure to be determined by the woman and her physician." Often the scale on which the person makes his response allows more gradations of assent than the three mentioned in this example; also, the attitude on an issue is usually measured by more than one item, so that the distribution of attitudes on an issue can be more finely graded than this example might indicate. Whereas the statement on the attitude scale usually involves judgments that have an explicit social desirability value, occasionally the judgments regard dimensions that are, at least superficially, affectively neutral (e.g., judgments regarding the probability of occurrence of some event). Some commentators prefer to reserve the term "attitudes" for dimensions that are clearly evaluative and to use "opinion," "beliefs," etc. when other dimensions are involved. In the present chapter "attitudes" will be used in the broader sense. (See McGuire, 1969a, for a fuller discussion of this point.)

Attitude change is typically measured by the movement of the person's response on such an opinionnaire from an administration before he is exposed to some social influence induction to an administration after the induction. Alternative to this "before-after" design is the "after-only" design which uses the logically equivalent procedure of measuring attitude change in terms of difference in post-induction opinions among groups exposed to one or another message treatment, where the persons in the several groups are assumed (on the basis of random or matched assignment to the several groups) to have been equivalent as regards premessage beliefs.

Independent Variables.   The researcher's theoretical predilections suggest to him the kinds of independent variables among which he searches for functional correlates of the process under study. As regards the study of attitude change through persuasive communication, there is a categorization of the relevant independent variables which is highly inclusive and suggestive. It appears in the guise of various terminologies, one popular example being that proposed by Lasswell (1948) who said that communication is a matter of who says what, via what media, to whom, and with what effect. The same set of categories is identified within the communication engineer's vocabulary as: source, message, channel, receiver, and destination. The current body of knowledge on attitude change has recently been summarized (McGuire, 1969a) in terms of independent variables falling into these five classes and the interested reader can pursue the details in that reveiw. Table 5.1 outlines many of the variables; here it will suffice to mention some frequently studied variables within each of the five classes.

As regards *source*, popular variables include the extent to which the credibility, attractiveness, and power of the person to whom the message is attributed affect its persuasive impact. Credibility is frequently investigated in terms of the source's social status, educational level, general or specific expertise, sex, perceived objectivity, etc. Attractiveness factors include the source's familiarity, similarity, etc., to the receiver, the legitimacy of his being in the communicator's role, the receiver's liking for him, need to identify with him, etc. Power variables that have received some research attention include the source's control of means to sanction the receiver, his concern whether the receiver conforms or not, and his capacity to scrutinize the receiver's conformity.

Message factors affecting attitude change have probably received more attention than any other class of independent variables. Included here are such variables as message style, content, and organization. Stylistic dimensions include the clarity and dynamic quality of the message and the use of humor, etc., in the message. Content factors include appeal variables (such as relevance

Table 5.1

The Five Components of Persuasive Communication, Each Illustrated by Heavily Researched Variables

---

I. Source variables
  A. Credibility
    1. Expertise
    2. Trustworthiness
  B. Attractiveness
    1. Similarity
    2. Familiarity
    3. Liking
  C. Power
    1. Control over means and ends
    2. Concern about compliance
    3. Scrutiny over compliance

II. Message variables
  A. Type of appeal
    1. Ethos, pathos, logos
    2. Positive vs. negative (fear) appeals
    3. Reinforcements within the communication
    4. Message style, humor, etc.
  B. Inclusions and omissions
    1. Implicit vs. explicit conclusions
    2. Refuting vs. ignoring opposition arguments
    3. Repetition of the message
  C. Order of presentation
    1. Conclusion first or last
    2. Ordering with respect to desirability and agreement
    3. Climax vs. anticlimax (strongest arguments last or first)
    4. Refuting opposition before or after own supporting arguments
  D. Discrepancy from receiver's initial position
    1. Selective exposure
    2. Perceptual distortion; differential recall
    3. Discrepancy and attitude change

III. Channel variables
  A. Direct experience with object vs. communication about it
  B. Modality (eye vs. ear, etc.)
  C. Mass media vs. face-to-face personal influence
  D. Relative efficacy of the different mass media

IV. Receiver variables
  A. Active vs. passive role
  B. Generality of susceptibility
  C. Demographic variables (sex, age, socioeconomic class, etc.)
  D. Ability factors
  E. Personality factors

V. Destination variables
  A. General effects beyond specific target issue
  B. Immediate vs. delayed impact
  C. Direct impact vs. immunization against counterarguments
  D. Verbal attitude change vs. gross behavioral change

---

to the receiver, positive versus negative appeals, etc.), the amount of repetition, whether the conclusion is explicitly drawn or left to the receiver to draw for himself, whether opposition arguments are refuted or ignored, etc. Message organization variables include whether the stronger arguments are presented early or late in the message, and whether refutations of opposition arguments are more effectively done before or after presentation of supportive arguments, etc.

Much less psychological research has been done on the third class of communication variables, the *channel* through which it is transmitted. Some attention has been paid to the relative persuasive efficacy of different sensory modalities, such as the printed versus the spoken word; and to the persuasiveness of a given message when it is communicated directly to the receiver as compared with when it is communicated indirectly via one of the mass media.

The popularity of the fourth class of communication variables, those having to do with *receiver* characteristics, is second only to message variables among attitude change researchers. Such research has included both transient and stable individual differences among receivers, for example, abilities, personality, emotional state, and demographic characteristics. Also included are such variables as the recipient's physiological state, the degree of his active participation in the communication process, the extremity of his initial position, his stand on related issues, etc.

The fifth (somewhat peculiarly named) class, *destination* variables, has to do with the characteristics of the target of the persuasive communication. Included are variables having to do with the type of issue (e.g., matters of fact versus taste) in terms of which the persuasive impact is being measured, the time of the effect (e.g., immediate versus long-term effect), etc.

This typology is useful in organizing our knowledge of the persuasion process and identifying areas of ignorance. It does not, however, constitute a theory of persuasive communication, if by "theory" we have in mind a heuristic tool used by researchers in the creative task of generating hypotheses. An attitude change researcher, even if he were aware of a list such as this one, would rarely run through it to come up with some plausible independent variable to investigate in connection with some puzzling attitude change phenomenon. Hence, whereas this classificatory system shows the scope within which the paradigm operates, it does not itself constitute the dynamic force that supplies the paradigm with its creative provocativeness. This latter is found in the theoretical orientations that guide attitude change researchers in their formulation of the problem and search for solutions. It is to these conceptual orientations that we now turn.

Theoretical Paradigms for Attitude Change

Four general conceptualizations have been put forward as underlying most of the thinking in the attitude change area (Smith, 1968; McGuire, 1968b, 1969a). These might be called information-processing theories, consistency theories, functional theories, and perceptual theories, in order of descending frequency of use. It is these four approaches that might most appropriately be termed the paradigms that provoke, guide, and limit current thinking about attitude change and persuasion. We shall concentrate in this chapter on the first of these approaches, since we feel it has the greatest potential and actual productiveness. But before employing and evaluating the information-processing paradigm through detailed illustrations, we shall present a brief synopsis of all four theoretical approaches.

The Consistency Theory Approaches. The general conception of the person that underlies the consistency approach to the study of attitude change is that each person tends to maintain a considerable amount of connectedness and coherence among his beliefs, feelings, and actions, as well as within each of these domains. The person is viewed as an honest broker striving for a solution among all of these contending forces that minimizes the extent to which any one will get out of line from the others.

A number of theories regarding attitude change fall within this consistency approach family. There are several thorough and convenient reviews of such theories (Abelson et al., 1968; McGuire, 1966b). One of the oldest such theories, which still attracts active research interest, is the "p-o-x" formulation proposed by Heider (1946, 1958). Originally, it dealt with the tendency to maintain coherence between one's own view of other persons and their views of objects of common concern. The original theory dealt with three-component systems but has been generalized to n-component systems by Cartwright and Harary (1956) and by Abelson and Rosenberg (1958). Another venerable and still provocative theory is the "congruity" approach originally proposed by Osgood and Tannenbaum (1953). McGuire's (1960, 1968d) "probabilogic" formulation is still another such theory. Undoubtedly Festinger's (1957) dissonance theory approach has been the most fertile of all the conceptualizations in the consistency family. (The preceding chapter reviews dissonance theory in detail, and comments on its relationship to the approaches of Heider and Osgood.)

The critical condition for attitude change posited by the consistency approach is the introduction of discrepancies between the given attitude and other attitudes, feelings, or behaviors that are already in the believer's repertory. As contrasted with the information-processing approach that will be stressed in this chapter, the distinguishing characteristic of the consistency approaches is that they do not require the introduction of any new information into the cognitive system in order to produce attitude change. The person's belief on a given issue can be changed by sensitizing him to already held beliefs that are discrepant from the given one and related to it, as in the "Socratic approach" method suggested by McGuire (1960). Or, as in many of the dissonance studies, the person's beliefs are changed by having him engage in discrepant behavior, so that the person, in order to justify his actions, will under appropriate circumstances alter his beliefs to conform to the behavior. The dissonance approach has called our attention to the notion that, while there is probably some truth in the common sense conception that actions flow from beliefs, there is also much to be said for the contrary order of causality—that we develop our beliefs to rationalize our actions.

The Perceptual Theory Approaches. The basic concept underlying the perceptual approaches to attitude change is that adjustment involves not only the person changing himself to conform to the demands of the environment, but also changing his perception of environmental demands to conform to his own needs. The altered perception may involve denial and pathological distortion, but more typically takes the form of selective attention and reinterpretation that lies within the normal range. For example, a person who has rated a series of political mottoes and is then told that a motto he rated as dreadful was given a top rating by an authority whom he reveres, tends to change his own rating in an upward direction. But when confronted by the change in his judgment of the motto from before to after he learned of the authority's endorsement, his explanation suggests that what he has changed is not his evaluation of the motto, but rather his perception of the task. For example, he explains that he first gave the motto a low rating under the impression that he was supposed to rate how true and noble the sentiment was; but after being told about the high rating the motto had obtained from his hero, he realized that he was supposed to be ranking it for its diabolical cleverness and effectiveness as propaganda. To paraphrase Asch's apt distinction, what has changed is not the person's attitude regarding the object, but rather his perception of the object about which he is giving his attitude.

While this perceptual approach is an old and enduring one, it has provoked far less empirical work than the consistency approach. However, while workers in this area have been few, they have had an influence disproportionate to their number. Empirical workers within this conceptual framework include Sherif (1935); Sherif and Hovland (1961); Sherif, Sherif, and Nebergall (1965); Luchins (1945); Luchins and Luchins (1959); Asch (1946, 1952, 1956); and to some extent Helson (1964), although the application of his work to the attitude area has been only implicit. Work stemming from the perceptual approach has dealt with the availability of preexisting categories and labels as determinants of one's attitudinal response to stimuli. Even more attention has been given to the discrepancy variable, that is, how the size of the discrepancy between one's initial opinion and the opinion being urged in the persuasive message affects the person's opinion and his perception of the message. Perceptual issues also arise in predicting the relative utilization of the various modes of response to a persuasive message, such as changing one's opinion, distorting the message position, downrating the source, etc.

The perceptual approach to understanding attitude change emphasizes a preexisting set of categories (or labels, frames of reference, schema, etc.), and the relative availability of these categories as provided by the person's culture, ability, personality, etc. The attitude process itself is conceptualized as involving an alteration in the cognitive coding of the situation. Hence, the person is left more or less with his original set of ideological principles but has reinterpreted the task so that a different principle is operative from the one to which he was previously responding.

Functional Theory Approaches. The gist of the functional approaches to attitude change is that the origins of attitudes and their change lie in the satisfactions they provide for the person's basic needs. As compared to the other approaches, the functionalist's position emphasizes that a given attitude may be based on factors that have very little to do with the object toward which it is expressed. To illustrate this point by the classical example of the authoritarian personality (Adorno et al., 1950), a person's prejudice against a racial or religious minority (or various deviant groups in a society, such as criminals or artists) may derive hardly at all from any specific information or misinformation about the nature of the group in question. Rather, the hostile attitude might be a defense mechanism that aids the person in his repression of some unacceptable hostility toward his father, acquired quite early in life, via a reaction formation that involves idealizing the father and other authority figures in the society, and bolstering this with hostility and dislike toward groups that lie outside the society's main power structure.

The main insight regarding attitude change offered by the functionalists is that when one deals with such ego-defensive attitudes, it is rather ineffective to provide the believer with favorable information about the outgroup or to enlist his sense of justice or charity on their behalf. Rather than try to change the person's relation to the outgroup itself, it is best to try to change his relation to his father, or at least the relation of these feelings to his outgroup hostility. As the example suggests, most of the conceptual and empirical work stemming from the functional approach has made creative use of psychoanalytic concepts such as repressed drives and defense mechanisms (Adorno et al., 1950; Bettelheim & Janowitz, 1950; Smith, Bruner, & White, 1956; etc.). In broader statements of the approach, particularly those formulated by Katz and his Michigan group (Katz, Sarnoff, & McClintock, 1956; Katz & Stotland, 1959; Katz, 1960) it has been pointed out that besides these interesting ego-defensive functions of attitudes, they may serve other functions, an analysis of which offers some interesting implications for the attitude change process.

The Information-Processing Approaches. The central notion of this fourth general approach is that persuasion is a problem in communication rather than in overcoming active resistance to change. Attitude change is regarded as involving a successive series of steps, each of which has only a certain probability of occurring, but all of which must occur for the production of attitude change. Specifically, for a communication to produce a persuasive effect, it is necessary that the person attend to it, comprehend the arguments, and yield to what he has comprehended. We might test the process up to any one of these steps by an appropriate measure (e.g., content analysis, an attention test, a learning test, or an attitude change test). For attitude change to occur, it is necessary that the person yield to what he has learned; but the contribution of the information-processing approach is to emphasize that attitude change also requires that he has attended to and learned the message. Hence, to understand how any independent variable affects the attitude change impact of a message, it is necessary to consider the variable's effect, not only on tendency to yield, but also on attention and learning of message content. Indeed, an adumbration of this conceptualization of the attitude change processes is called the "learning theory" approach, since it calls attention to the learning mediator that the other approaches tend to neglect. But to avoid an overemphasis in the opposite direction, it should be understood that the information-processing approach deals not only with the mediational role of learning, but also gives equal stress to the mediational role of yielding, attention, etc.

Among the empirical workers who have drawn inspiration from this information-processing approach to attitude change are Hovland (Hovland et al., 1949, 1953, 1957, etc.); Campbell (1963); Anderson (1965); Janis (1959); and McGuire (1957, 1968a). The approach has proved provocative and useful in the study of a wide variety of attitude change problems, such as the effect of source credibility, the ordering of material within the persuasive message, the uses of fear appeals, the role of personality factors, time trends, etc. The quantity and quality of the empirical work on attitude change that has stemmed from the information-processing conceptualization exceed that of the work derived from any of the other approaches. In the remaining sections of this chapter we shall concentrate exclusively on this popular paradigm and describe several cumulative lines of research that illustrate its utility, limitation, and current empirical status.

Interrelations among the Approaches. These four theoretical orientations constitute different points of departure from which problems in attitude change have been approached, and different viewpoints from which the problems have been regarded. They are not at all mutually exclusive or contradictory, in the sense that if one is right the others are necessarily wrong. Each of the four approaches has proponents who often struggle more vehemently among themselves than with advocates of the other approaches. Some theorists have attempted to make one approach subsume another as a special case. At other times, the approaches are used to supplement one another by accounting for some of the attitude change variance left unexplained by the variables suggested by another approach. In other cases, the relationship is one of supplanting, where one approach is used to assign a relationship, discovered by another approach, to a quite different underlying mechanism. Occasionally there is a relationship of outright opposition, where two of the approaches seem to make opposite predictions regarding an attitude change effect. Numerous examples can be given of each of these relationships (McGuire, 1968b, 1969a).

When these paradigmatic approaches confront one another empirically for any length of time, a tendency toward mutual accommodation and convergence ensues. Even where two of the approaches seem to be in direct conflict in that they make opposite predictions regarding a relationship, continued work usually reveals that each of the approaches makes a valid prediction, depending on other variables in the situation. Such has been the case, for example, with the controversy between the consistency approach and the information-

processing approach as regards how the size of the reward for publicly supporting a position discrepant from one's private belief affects one's own position.
Or when two of the approaches interpret a given relationship as being due to
different mediators, it has frequently turned out that there is room for the
operation of both. An example of this tendency towards peaceful coexistence
of mechanism is provided by the work on why the first side in a debate often
has an advantage. The information-processing approach has argued that primacy effects are due to this earlier learned material's interference with reception
of the later material; while the perceptual approach has attributed effect of
the earlier material to a distorted perception of the later material. It appears
that each of the mechanisms may play some part.

Even though there is only a limited amount of inherent conflict among the
paradigms as regards what they predict, and although such initial differences
as there are tend to be resolved with continued empirical work, the existence of
different approaches is useful in the progress of the field. There is utility to
having different theories, even though it is true that once a relationship has been
firmly established each of the theories usually can be adjusted adequately to
subsume it. There is much more to scientific theories than accounting for what is
already known. An even more useful function is in generating new hypotheses.
A given paradigm tends to be useful in that it generates predictions that might
never have been thought of by use of the other paradigms, although once the
prediction is confirmed, the other paradigms can adequately account for it. The
separate theories may have great utility for this heuristic, provocative side of
the scientific enterprise, even though they all seem to be saying the same thing
once we know what has to be said.

THE INFORMATION-PROCESSING PARADIGM

The foregoing brief description of the four alternative theoretical paradigms
for attitude change research does not provide an adequate description of any
one of them. It does, however, help to put into perspective the more detailed
presentation of the information-processing paradigm to which the remainder of
this chapter will be devoted. We shall first give a general description of the
paradigm, and then illustrate its usefulness by applying it to two successive
areas, personality correlates of attitude change and the effectiveness of fear
appeals in attitude change. A final section will discuss limitations of the paradigm.

General Description

As mentioned in our capsule description in the previous section, the heart of
this conceptualization is, first, to analyze the attitude change process into a
series of information-processing behavioral steps, and second, to predict the
relationship between any independent variable and attitude change by considering that variable's effect on each of the behavioral steps.

Behavioral Steps in Persuasion.   We consider here the common sense behavioral steps by which the information contained in the persuasive message must be progressively converted into the desired attitudinal or behavioral change, if the communication is to be effective. (In cases where the target attitude or behavioral change is not produced, the failure can have occurred at any one of the mediating behavioral steps.) Six successive behavioral steps, as shown in Figure 5.1, can be considered as occurring in the persuasion process. For the message to be effective in producing attitude change it is necessary first that it be *presented* to the target person. Given that it has been presented, the person must pay *attention* to it. Given that it has received attention, the effectiveness of the message next requires that the person *comprehend* the conclusions being urged and, to some extent, the arguments being martialed in favor of them. It is necessary further that he *yield* to this comprehended content if any immediately detectable attitude change is to be produced. If we are interested in persistent attitude change over any period of time, the person must *retain* his yielding to this new position. And if there is interest, further, in whether he carries out some overt action on the basis of the new urged position, then it is necessary that he *behave* on the basis of his new belief.

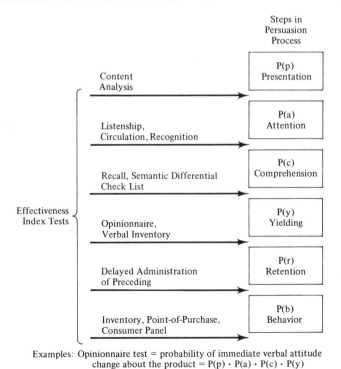

Examples: Opinionnaire test = probability of immediate verbal attitude
           change about the product = P(p) · P(a) · P(c) · P(y)
Behavioral test = probability of actual purchase = P(p) ·
           P(a) · P(c) · P(y) · P(r) · P(b)

Figure 5.1
Indices of communication effectiveness related to the behavioral steps in being persuaded.

Each one of these steps occurs with a probability that seldom approaches unity. If any given step fails to occur, then the chain is broken at this point and the subsequent steps cannot occur. For example, if the person does not yield to the position being urged, it is vacuous to ask whether he retains that yielding until a subsequent point in time. In general, the probability that any later step will be taken is proportional to the joint probability that all of the previous steps will occur. Thus, if the probability of step 1 is .80, step 2, .50, and step 3, .30, then the probability that step 4 will occur is some proportion of their product (.80 $\times$ .50 $\times$ .30) or .12. That is, the probability of step 4 has an upper limit of .12.

Consider a straightforward situation where the persuasive effectiveness of an advertising campaign urging that the public buy a certain brand of tooth-paste is measured by the change in the actual sales of the brand from before to after the campaign in a set of communities where the campaign was launched, as compared with a matched set of communities in which the campaign was not conducted. The probability that a sizable difference in sales will be found is proportional to the joint probability that all of the six behavioral steps discussed above occur. Assuming that these events are independent, then the probability of a sales difference equals the product of the probabilities of the six successive steps. This equation gives good insight into how difficult it is to run an effective advertising campaign. Even if each of the successive steps had a good chance of occurring, there would be a low probability of any appreciable change in ultimate sales. For example, even if each of the six steps has an even (.50) chance of occurring, the likelihood of any sizable effect on sales would be quite low, namely, $.5^6$ or less than two chances in a hundred. (And it is likely that advertising campaigns, whether directed at selling toothpaste, a political candi-date, or an annual medical checkup, seldom achieve anything like a .5 probabil-ity of eliciting any of the steps, much less all of them.) In the light of this analysis, the wonder is not that advertising campaigns have so little effect but that they have any discernible effect at all.

The above formulation also suggests why we should expect more verbalized attitude change effect than change in the actual behavior. An immediate attitude change is picked up by an opinionnaire filled out immediately after the persua-sive communication is presented, and so it depends on only the first four steps in the process to occur; while for the person actually to behave in accord with the new attitude requires two additional probabilistic steps to occur.

Multiple Foci of the Independent Variable's Impact.   The second general pro-cedure in applying the information-processing approach is to consider how a given independent variable affects attitude change via its impact on each of the six mediating steps described above. (Independent variables might include the many aspects of the communication process outlined in Table 5.1.) For exam-ple, we might wish to predict whether a persuasive communication will be more effective if it comes from an expert authority figure or from a close friend of the receiver who is no more expert than himself. Using the approach under discussion, we would ask how this variable would affect each of these six successive steps in the behavioral process. We might hypothesize regarding the first step of being presented with the message that the target person's ever-present friend would have greater likelihood of satisfying this step than would the relatively remote authority figure. As regards the second step, the likelihood that any presented message will be attended to, we might predict that the expert will receive more attention since his novelty, authoritative status, etc., have more attention-provoking potential than would the comments of a familiar equal. With the third step of comprehension, the peer might have the advantage, since his way of presenting the material would be more familiar to the recipient and in his own idiom, so that it would be easier to understand. On the other hand, the expert might have the advantage for the next step of evoking yielding, since his high prestige status and perceived knowledgeability should constitute a more compelling force on the recipient to agree with such material as he has understood. (With matters of taste, where expertise may be less important than common background and familiarity, the peer may evoke more yielding.)

With this source variable as an example, a typical complexity results even on the basis of our quite informal and incomplete analysis. Namely, the variable of expert-versus-peer source is positively related to persuasive impact via some of the mediating steps and negatively related by others. Hence, the net relationship between this variable and attitude change can be either positive or negative, depending on whether the particular social influence situation with which we are dealing allows for more variance in one mediator or the other. For example, if the message is a very simple and repetitious one that most normal people would understand regardless of the source to which it is attributed, then we could assume that the comprehension mediator would play little role in determining the net relationship between the source variable and attitude change. In other situations, where the message is much more complicated, and hence there is considerable variance among the recipients in the extent to which they understand the message, then the comprehension mediator will be more important in determining the net relationship between the source variable and the amount of attitude change produced.

In summary, there are two phases in the information-processing approach for predicting how a given independent variable in the persuasive communication will affect its attitude change impact. First, one estimates how the independent variable in question will affect each of the six behavioral steps into which the persuasion process has been analyzed. Second, one analyzes the given social influence situation to estimate how much variance in each of the behavioral steps is likely to occur in that situation. On the basis of these two considerations, it is possible to estimate the net relationship in any given communication situation between an independent variable and its attitude change impact (McGuire, 1968b). Also, it is possible to make further predictions regarding complex effects among several independent variables in producing attitude change. In addition to these two considerations, the information-processing paradigm typically uses additional auxiliary hypotheses regarding the psychodynamics of social influence. These auxiliary hypotheses enrich the heuristic potential of the paradigm. Since a consideration of them complicates exposition, we shall introduce them in connection with the specific examples taken up in the next two sections.

Illustration 1: Personality Correlates of Attitude Change

The information-processing approach is useful in predicting how personality and ability characteristics are related to susceptibility to persuasion. A discussion of this application will be useful in clarifying the approach itself, as well as in providing a grasp of the complicated empirical results in this subject area. In the present section we shall first consider the confusing findings regarding personality correlates of persuasibility; then we shall apply the information-processing approach to the topic in order to clarify existing findings and yield new predictions; finally, we shall consider how the predictions that stem from this theoretical paradigm have fared when put to empirical tests.

The need for a theoretical paradigm that makes sense of the very complex and seemingly contradictory findings in the attitude change area is nowhere more apparent than with this topic of personality correlates. Experiments often produce outcomes that are opposed to intuitive common sense or, even more embarrassing, to the findings of previous experiments. We have described elsewhere (McGuire, 1968a) the confusing set of findings in the personality-persuasibility area even with regard to the single personality characteristic of self-esteem, a variable that has received a great deal of research attention. For example, two typical studies done in the mid-1950s on the relationship between self-esteem and susceptibility to social influence yielded quite opposite results. Janis (1954) found that the higher the person's self-esteem the harder it was to persuade him; while McGuire and Ryan (1955) found the reverse, that the higher the person's self-esteem the more susceptible he was to being influenced. A decade later, in the mid-1960s, the situation had become, if anything, more complex and ambiguous. Cox and Bauer (1964) found that the relationship between self-esteem and persuasibility was nonmonotonic, describing an inverted U-shaped function, with maximum susceptibility at an intermediate level of self-esteem. On the other hand, Silverman (1964) found a nonmonotonic relationship, but in the opposite direction—a right-side-up U with people at the middle levels of self-esteem being the least susceptible to persuasion. Lest we seem to be picking out aberrant cases that can be found in any heavily researched area, it should be noted that each of these findings (except possibly the last one) has been replicated a number of times. We can expect that any paradigm powerful enough to save the appearances when they constitute so complex a set of findings as these will also be fertile enough to generate new predictions for testing.

The Information-Processing Paradigm Applied to the Personality Persuasibility Area. On this confusing topic of how personality and other individual difference variables are related to persuasive communication impacts on attitude change, the information-processing approach accounts for already obtained results so that they make better sense, and also generates a variety of additional predictions that can be experimentally tested. Use of the approach in this area involves the two stages already discussed in general terms above. In addition, when the approach is applied to any given area, auxiliary hypotheses are added to make the approach more relevant and powerful in the given area.

The first stage involves considering how the specific individual difference characteristic in which we are interested is likely to affect each of the mediating steps into which being persuaded has been analyzed. While this stage might seem obvious to the point of embarrassment, it is surprising how often we are led into false expectations regarding personality-persuasibility relationships through failure to engage in this common sense procedure. For example, when the layman is asked to conjecture how intelligence is related to persuasibility, he typically predicts a negative relationship. He conjectures that the more intelligent a person is, the harder it will be to persuade him, because the more intelligent person will have more arguments in support of his beliefs, will be better able to see the flaws in the opposition's arguments, will have more confidence in himself, and will thus be able to endure a discrepancy between his own beliefs and those of the message source, etc. All of these conjectures may well be true, but they focus on the yielding step in the process and ignore the other five steps.

When we consider the likely effect of this intelligence variable on other steps in the persuasion process, we see that the situation is more complex. The more intelligent person will more adequately attend to and comprehend the message. Since he usually has a wider range of interests and concerns, a greater variety of message topics will attract his attention and he will usually have a longer attention span, etc. Even more obvious, the more intelligent the person, the greater the likelihood that he will adequately and correctly comprehend the point of the persuasive message and the arguments used. This positive relationship of intelligence with attention and comprehension-mediating steps tends to enhance the more intelligent person's susceptibility to persuasion.

Restricting our analysis even to these three steps of attention, comprehension, and yielding already shows that the relationships between intelligence and persuasibility are complexly mediated, so that predictions about the net relationship must be made carefully and with reference to the particular circumstances. Several implications follow from this situation where intelligence tends to make the person more susceptible to persuasion as far as the attention and comprehension mediators are concerned, and less susceptible as far as the yielding mediator is concerned. For one thing, when we have a "compensation" situation such as this one, where two variables are related in opposite directions via the operation of separate mediators, then it follows under a wide range of conditions that the overall relationship between the two will be nonmonotonic in the form of an inverted-U. That is, persons with medium levels of intelligence are most susceptible to attitude change, whereas people with higher or lower intelligence than this optimal intermediate level will be less persuasible.

The above reasoning is illustrated in Figure 5.2. Reception is represented as a positive function of intelligence, that is, receptivity increases as intelligence

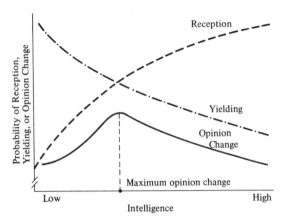

Figure 5.2
Nonmonotonic relationship between intelligence and opinion change as a function of intelligence having opposite effects on the two mediators, reception and yielding.

increases. Yielding is represented as a negative function, that is, yielding decreases as intelligence increases. Assuming that increased reception and increased yielding are both conducive to opinion change, a multiplicative combination of these two functions produces the nonmonotonic (inverted-U) curve of opinion change illustrated in Figure 5.2. This curve indicates that maximum opinion change will occur at an intermediate level of intelligence. A detailed elaboration of the algebraic computations on which these three functions are based can be found elsewhere (McGuire, 1968b).

Applying the information-processing approach to any specific question, such as this personality-persuasibility relationship, involves analyzing the particular communication situation to estimate the amount of interpersonal variability that the situation allows in each of the mediating steps. Social influence situations vary greatly in the room they leave for individual differences in message comprehension. If the persuasive campaign involves a very simple, repetitive message (e.g., the type used in hypnotic inductions or in political or marketing campaigns based on repeated presentations of a slogan), almost everyone who attends to the message will comprehend it completely. Under these circumstances there would be little individual difference in message comprehension, and so the positive relationship between intelligence and persuasibility that derives from better comprehension that goes with intelligence would be largely eliminated from the equation. On the other hand, where the campaign involves a quite abstruse argument (e.g., an argument for a new economic policy as a means of combating inflation or a recession), there is likely to be considerable variability among the listeners' comprehension of the arguments. In this latter case, the tendency for a positive relationship between intelligence and persuasibility due to the comprehension mediator would loom relatively large.

Likewise, situations vary greatly in the room they leave for individual differences in yielding. Some persuasion situations are so compelling that anyone who fully comprehends the message would be almost certain to yield; for example, where a mathematician is trying to prove to a student that his initial answer in incorrect, it seems likely that, to the extent the student understands the demonstration, he will yield to the arguments and admit the correctness of the teacher's answer. In such a case, the tendency for a negative relationship between intelligence and persuasibility due to the yielding mediator would be largely washed out, since yielding would contribute little to the covariance between intelligence and persuasibility. On the other hand, in situations dealing with matters of taste or involving less rational arguments, there might be considerable individual difference in the amount of yielding to message comprehension. In these cases, the tendency for intelligence to be negatively related to persuasibility via the yielding mediator would loom large in determining the net relationship between the two.

The first stage of the application of the information-processing model has led us to the conclusion that in any one social influence situation, the overall relationship between intelligence and persuasibility is likely to be nonmonotonic, with those at intermediate levels of intelligence the most susceptible to persuasion. The second stage in the application has led us to the further complexity that, within any segment of the total range of intelligence, the relationship between it and persuasibility can be either positive or negative, depending on whether the situation leaves more room for individual variation in the comprehension step or in the yielding step of processing the information in the message.

Success of the Approach in Personality-Persuasibility Relations. So far in this discussion of the applicability of the information-processing approach to personality-persuasibility relations, we demonstrated the current state of confusion in the field by the case of how self-esteem relates to persuasibility. Then, for pedagogic purposes, we switched to intelligence as our individual difference variable, since the new issues raised are more immediately obvious in terms of an abilities dimension like intelligence than a more dynamic trait like self-esteem. However, the whole discussion of the realtionships between intelligence and persuasibility and the mediating steps can be applied fairly directly to the relationships of self-esteem to these other variables. For example, the higher the person's self-esteem, the more susceptible to persuasion he tends to be through enhanced attention and comprehension, and the less susceptible via the yielding mediator. For one thing, self-esteem tends to be positively related to intelligence; in addition, the psychodynamic aspects of self-esteem tend to produce such a relationship to the mediating steps. Some reflection will probably suggest the plausibility, if not the incontrovertibleness, of these assertions. More detailed discussions can be found elsewhere (McGuire, 1968a).

Insofar as the above assumptions and the information-processing approach are valid, it would follow that the confusing set of findings already reported in the literature (as mentioned above) regarding how self-esteem relates to susceptibility to attitude change can all be understood in terms of this analysis. In addition, if the approach is to be fruitful, it must give rise to additional hypotheses of interest that predict new relationships not yet reported. On both of these scores, the information-processing model has stood up fairly well. Previously reported findings make better sense when put within the theoretical housing provided by this approach (McGuire, 1968b). More important, the model itself has given rise to new predictions that have been tested in a number of recent studies conducted by our students and others (e.g., Millman, 1968; Nisbett & Gordon, 1967; Zellner, 1970; Lehmann, 1970; and Johnson & Izzett, 1970). In general, derivations regarding nonmonotonic relationships and reversals of the direction of relationships with situational differences in how much variance is contributed by the several mediating steps, have received a good deal of support from empirical work. On the other hand, the confirmation score falls far short of perfection and the empirical work has caused some revisions in the model and has left a residual set of questions regarding the validity of the model far from answered. We will return to these questions in the final section of the present chapter.

Illustration 2: Fear Appeals and Attitude Change

As a second application, we shall bring the information-processing model to bear on the problem of fear appeals in persuasive communication. When a source presents a persuasive message urging the recipient to adopt some new attitude or behavior, he can use either positive or negative appeals. A positive appeal stresses the benefits to be gained from adopting the new attitude, whereas negative appeal focuses on the undersirable consequences of failing to adopt it. The present discussion is concerned mainly with the effectiveness of these anxiety-arousing negative appeals, and especially with the relationship between the level of threat used and the persuasive effectiveness of the message. We shall first describe the nature of the problem regarding the effectiveness of threat appeals; then we shall apply the information-processing approach to bring comprehension to the confusion of findings in the area and to yield new predictions.

Positive versus Negative Appeals. In most attitude change campaigns in the natural environment, the source has the option of using either positive or negative appeals. Such is the case whether the campaign is to sell merchandise, solicit votes for a political candidate, or get the public to have periodical medical checkups as part of a public health campaign. For example, if one is trying to sell toothpaste, one can use the positive appeal of stressing the benefits to be derived therefrom or, conversely, the negative appeal of stressing the dire effects of failing to use the product. To be sure, some campaigns lend themselves more obviously to the use of one type of appeal rather than the other. For example, if one is trying to sell chocolate bars, it is easier to think of positive appeals (most obviously, the taste enjoyment to be obtained from using the product) than it is to think of negative appeals that point out the horrors that might eventuate if one does not eat these chocolate bars. Conversely, if one is trying to induce the public to get annual checkups to detect any cancer symptoms at an early stage, it is easier to think of negative appeals (namely, the terrible consequences of allowing the disease to develop undetected) than it is to think of positive appeals that would stress the pleasant aspects of the examination. However, although some campaigns lend themselves more to one or the other type of appeal, a little ingenuity allows some use of the alternative. For example, the benefits of the cancer checkup can be stressed in a positive way by pointing out that most people do not have cancer and that the medical examination will reduce one's anxiety by providing reassurance that one does not have the disease.

The information-processing paradigm stresses that there is an asymmetry in the operation of positive versus negative appeals. The notions here are analogous to those applied to the roles of reward versus punishment in learning, a discussion that goes back to the 1920s work of Thorndike on the "Law of Effect" and research on avoidance conditioning. It has been stressed in this reward versus punishment learning research that the two work in different ways so that they are not symmetrically equivalent. That is, producing learning by punishing errors is not a simple inverse function of producing learning by rewarding correct responses. The asymmetry can be grasped if we think of learning as involving strengthening correct habits and weakening incorrect ones, that is, training the person so that when he is in a given situation he gives the correct rather than the incorrect response. Reward increases the likelihood of the desired response in two ways: first, it makes the situation in which he has been rewarded an attractive one for the learner so that he seeks it out; second, when he is in such a situation it increases the probability that he will make the previously rewarded response. Punishment weakens the likelihood that the person will make the incorrect response in two ways: first, by training him to avoid the situation in which he has been punished; second, by making it less likely that he will make the punished response in the same situation. However, punishment does not increase the likelihood of a correct response via both mechanisms. The first mechanism has the quite different effect of training the person to avoid the situation in which learning occurs rather than to make the desired response.

The use of positive versus negative appeals in attitude change is analogous to the use of reward versus punishment in learning situations. If we use positive appeals to get the person to perform the desired action (such as eating more chocolate bars or getting checkups for cancer), we increase the likelihood he will think about the topic and make the desired response. On the other hand, when in urging the person to adopt the desired attitude or behavior, we use a negative appeal that stresses the dangers of noncompliance, we get a double effect, one beneficial and one detrimental to the desired response. The beneficial effect is that the threat appeal increases the likelihood that the person will take the preventive action being urged when the topic occurs to him; the detrimental effect is that the threat inclines him to repress the whole topic because the appeal has attached so much anxiety to it. Via this latter mechanism of avoidance or repression, the threat actually tends to reduce the likelihood of the desired attitude or behavior.

A large body of research has been done on this type of analysis ever since the provocative study by Janis and Feshbach (1953). It has concentrated largely on the question of what level of fear arousal is most effective in producing attitude change when one does use negative appeals. A number of detailed up-to-date analyses of the resulting research are available (Janis, 1967; McGuire, 1966a, 1969a; Sears & Abelson, 1969), so we shall not attempt an extensive review of this body of research here. We shall discuss rather how the information-processing paradigm bears on this fear appeal issue.

The Two-Factor Theory of Anxiety. The gist of applying the information-processing paradigm to the use of fear appeals in producing attitude change involves taking into consideration how the level of fear used in the message will affect each of the six behavioral steps in the persuasion process. The effect of a fear appeal on any of those steps is best understood in current psychological theorizing as a manipulation of the recipient's anxiety, which is regarded as a two-factor state. Anxiety is conceptualized as having both dynamic and directive impact on behavior or, using behavioristic terminology, as having both drive and cue value. As a drive, anxiety is a motivating force that tends to arouse the individual to a higher level of activity and serves as a multiplier of behavioral inclinations that are operative at the moment. In this way, anxiety operates like other drive states such as hunger. As a cue, anxiety is regarded as a distinctive state with its own characteristic stimulus quality, to which specific responses tend to become attached. From its drive component, anxiety tends to increase the likelihood of preexisting response tendencies; from its cue aspect, anxiety tends to evoke distinctive response tendencies. We shall consider each of these aspects in turn.

Anxiety as a Cue. Because of anxiety's cue aspect, the attitude change impact of a persuasive message will vary complexly with the level of fear appeal that it uses. Anxiety is a distinctive stimulus state that evokes a particular set of responses, including responses innately linked to that stimulus state through the phylogenetic experience of the species and acquired responses that have become attached to that stimulus state through the ontogenetic experience of the individual. The psychodynamics involved in the innate and acquired cases are not very different. Anxiety is a noxious state, perhaps best thought of as a signal warning the organism to terminate a present condition that threatens his well-being. A number of response classes will serve this end, most obvious of which is flight from the present situation and other avoidance responses. Responses such as hostile reactions to certain aspects of the current situation might also serve this end. Insofar as such responses have been effective in the past in terminating the threat that produces the anxiety, to that extent the individual will tend to respond by such flight or fight behavior when subsequently threatened in similar situations.

How would the characteristic response elicited by anxiety in its cue aspect affect each of the behavioral steps in the persuasion process? In general, the characteristic responses anxiety tends to evoke are likely to interfere with both attention and comprehension of the persuasive message. Reactions like flight (whether literally removing one's self from the situation or doing so metaphorically by repression and avoidance of thinking) tend to interfere with the person's ability to concentrate on the topic at issue and to assimilate rationally the contents of the persuasive message. Somewhat similar effects, detrimental to attitude change impact, result as regards the steps of retention and of subsequent overt behavior in line with the message conclusion. In general, to the extent that a high level of fear is aroused in the message, for example, by stressing the dangers of cancer in order to encourage periodic medical checkups, it becomes increasingly likely that when the topic of cancer arises, the recipient will respond, not so much by rushing out to get a checkup, but by repressing the whole matter.

Creative applications of the information-processing paradigm to this area of fear appeals in attitude change stem from the above analysis. Here we have been saying that in its cue aspect, anxiety has a detrimental effect on attitude change via the attention, comprehension, retention, and overt behavior steps. The analysis allows us to make still further predictions of other circumstances that intensify or mitigate this detrimental effect. For example, to the extent that the person is already worried, any additional anxiety arousal is increasingly likely to have a detrimental effect. Also, to the extent that he is already in a high arousal state through other needs (e.g., to the extent that he is hungry, fatigued, or sexually frustrated), these detrimental effects will become more pronounced. Likewise, to the extent that the message is very complex and hard to understand, or to the extent that the overt behavior being urged is particularly onerous, distant, or difficult to carry out, then the use of high threat appeals will become increasingly detrimental as compared with low threat appeals. The predictions mentioned here are illustrative rather than exhaustive. Some of them have been tested in studies, but most of these predictions remain to be tested.

In this discussion of anxiety in its cue aspect we have not yet mentioned its possible effect on the yielding mediator. While anxiety would have a detrimental effect on the other steps, it is likely to have a facilitating effect on the yielding mediator. Among the characteristic responses attached to anxiety through previous drive-reducing reinforcement is a tendency to be subservient, to reduce one's self-esteem, self-confidence, etc. By evoking these response tendencies, the higher fear arousal should make the individual more compliant and yielding. Hence, the cue aspects of anxiety will tend, through this mediator, to facilitate attitude change, as opposed to its attitude change inhibiting effects via the role of the other mediators.

Once again the information-processing paradigm has led us to see that a relatively familiar and simple variable will be rather complex in its relationships to attitude change. Even considered solely as a cue (and we have not yet considered additional complications arising from its drive component), anxiety has opposite effects on attitude change via the several information-processing steps in persuasion. Via the yielding step, it facilitates attitude change, and via the other steps it interferes with attitude change. We can therefore expect an overall nonmonotonic inverted U-shaped relationship, with an intermediate level of fear appeal producing maximum opinion change. This optimal level will shift upward or downward depending on other aspects of the situation, such as message complexity,.fatigue of the recipient, difficulty of the behavior urged in the message, etc. Hence, the information-processing paradigm guides our understanding of the complex relationships found between the level of fear arousal in a persuasive communication and its attitude change impact, as well as leads to additional predictions involving interaction effects between the level of fear arousal and other aspects of the communication situation.

Anxiety in its Motivational Aspects. The complexities discussed above concern anxiety in its cue aspects. Further complications arise when we recognize that anxiety also has energizing or drive properties that tend to increase the general activity level of the organism and to multiply ongoing response tendencies in a manner comparable to that resulting from increasing the animal's drive state in other ways such as by food deprivation or pain. We shall consider here the impact of anxiety in this drive aspect on each of the behavioral steps involved in the persuasion process.

We saw above that anxiety in its cue aspect tends to be detrimental to attitude change (with the one exception of its effect on the yielding mediator), although its drive component tends to facilitate persuasion (again, with some secondary detrimental effects). Given that there is some initial tendency in any communication situation for the normal person to pay some attention, comprehend the message as well as he can, etc., anxiety as a drive would tend to multiply all of these initial tendencies and make them more likely to occur. For this reason, the drive component of anxiety tends to enhance the persuasive impact of the message, so that the higher the fear appeal the greater the attitude change.

The relationship between the drive aspect of anxiety and the yielding step is more complex than in the case of the other steps. In many situations there will be some initial tendency to respond to a persuasive message in a compliant way; hence, to the extent that the yielding tendency is the dominant response, increasing the level of fear appeal should enchance the amount of attitude change. On the other hand, there will be some situations in which the dominant initial inclination will be to resist the urgings of the message and to maintain one's own initial attitude. Hence, whether anxiety's drive aspect is detrimental or conducive to attitude change via the yielding mediator depends on whether the dominant initial tendency is resistance or compliance. Insofar as the yielding step in the persuasion process is an important contributor to attitude change variance, increasing the level of fear appeal in the message would be predictably detrimental or conducive to attitude change, depending on the extent to which the person is highly involved in his initial belief, the extent to which he dislikes the source of the message, etc. This area of research on fear appeals in attitude change has been relatively neglected in the abundant experimental literature.

Composite Predictions. Still more complications arise when we consider both the cue and drive determinants of how fear appeals affect attitude change.

Even considering each of the aspects separately, we are led to conclude that the overall relationship between level of fear appeal and attitude change would be nonmonotonic in the form of an inverted-U. Combining the two should produce a nonmonotonic effect of an even more complex, multimodal form, perhaps an M-shaped one.

Trying to capture so complex a relationship in any one experimental design is a demanding enterprise. Since the paradigm makes such complex predictions when its full implications are used creatively, we are faced with an embarrassment of riches. That is, almost any obtained outcome can be accounted for by so complex a theory, depending on the segment of the overall M-shaped relationship that we are investigating—just as the proverbial blind men who explored different parts of the elephant came up with conflicting conclusions about the nature of the beast, based on their partial truths. This prowess in being able to accommodate conflicting findings calls the scientific status of the paradigm into doubt, since a criterion of scientific theory is that there must be some specifiable outcome that would tend to disconfirm it.

Actually, the situation is not so harrowing. To be sure, our primitive psychological scaling generally makes our theorizing of a nonparametric type, and hence it is difficult, if not impossible, at this time to specify the exact levels of anxiety arousal at which the maximum or minimum amounts of attitude change will occur. If we simply use only a two- or three-level manipulation of the independent variable of fear arousal, almost any outcome can be interpreted as in conformity with the theory. However, as we use wider ranges of fear arousal with many intermediate points, it becomes increasingly possible to test the theory adequately in terms of how fully the complex predicted relationship is revealed by the data. More practically, the theory makes further predictions about interactions with other variables. Whereas, because of the absence of specification of exact parametric values, the theory cannot predict at just what point inflections will occur, it does at least say how the inflection points should move as certain other independent variables are varied orthogonally. For example, while we cannot specify for any given level of message complexity exactly what level of fear arousal will be optimal in producing attitude change, we can specify that as message complexity increases, the maximal point will move to the left, so that with increasing message complexity lower and lower levels of anxiety will be optimal in producing maximum attitude change. Similar interaction predictions can be made for the many other independent variables mentioned in this section.

CRITIQUE OF THE INFORMATION-PROCESSING PARADIGM

In our exposition of the information-processing paradigm as a theoretical and methodological guide to the study of attitude change we have, up to this point, been accentuating the positive. We have been stressing the paradigm's power in bringing order to the very complex findings already reported in the literature, and its more important value as a heuristic device that leads us creatively to the derivation of new hypotheses regarding the attitude change process that can subsequently be put to empirical test. In this section we shall adopt a more critical stance regarding the paradigm and raise questions about its initial assumptions, its empirical status, and its adequacies in accounting for the whole range of findings.

Inadequacies of the Initial Assumptions

The basic assumption of the paradigm is that attitude change involves the successive behavioral steps discussed above. The success of a persuasive communication is assumed to depend upon the occurrence of each of a series of probabilistic steps including: being presented with the persuasive message, attending to it, comprehending its contents, yielding to these contents so as to adopt a new attitude, retaining this newly acquired attitude, and subsequently behaving on the basis of this attitude in the way urged in the message. This analysis has a common sense obviousness about it that provides some immediate aura of plausibility but also betrays an overly rationalistic view of the persuasion process. People do not always behave in this neat, orderly way and under some circumstances later steps may occur in the absence of earlier ones or the order of some of the steps may be reversed.

Omissions of Earlier Steps.   There are a number of possible cases where later steps can occur in the absence of earlier ones. For example, if the phenomena of subception (unconscious perception) and learning without awareness are valid, then it would be possible to yield to a subliminally presented message without attention or comprehension. The empirical status of subception is by no means strong, but its possibility should at least be mentioned in passing.

There is more solid empirical evidence for another case of omission of earlier steps without a detrimental effect on the later ones in the phenomenon of post-hypnotic suggestion. It has been demonstrated frequently that a person will overtly behave on the basis of a suggestion made to him while he was in a hypnotic state, even though, due to suggested post-hypnotic amnesia, he may not be able to recall any such suggestion and, in a sense, never attended to or comprehended the suggestion in his normal state. The hypnotic state is a peculiar one, but it cannot be discarded altogether on this basis. Moreover, there is some question about the extent to which any meaningful "retention" of an initially induced attitude change is necessary in order for the subsequent overt behavior to occur on the basis of the new attitude. Watts and McGuire (1964) raised the possibility that, whether or not attention and comprehension may be necessary to produce the initial yielding, persistence over time of the new attitude might become functionally autonomous of the retention of the material that initially produced the attitude change.

Reversals in Order of Steps.   Even more exotic exceptions to the basic assumption of the information-processing model are cases where not only do the later steps occur in the absence of the earlier ones, but the order of the steps is actually reversed. One such case is the phenomenon of selective attention, which involves an almost self-contradictory state of affairs. We refer to a person who guides his exposure to information on the basis of his preconceptions, so that he strengthens his initial attitudes by seeking out and attending to information in agreement with them and avoiding belief-discrepant material. The previously described sequence of steps is here reversed in that yielding, in a sense, precedes attention. The reversal involves a paradox in that selective avoidance seems to require that the individual somehow knows that the material is opposed to his preconception and therefore avoids attending to it, when it would seem that he must first attend to it in order to know this. It now appears (See McGuire, 1968c) that this selective avoidance mode of information-processing is not so pervasive as once thought, but it does seem to occur under some circumstances (Katz, 1968; Mills, 1968). A similar case of reversal occurs in perceptual distortion and selective retention, where the steps of yielding precedes that of comprehension, in that the person distorts what he learns so that it agrees that what he has already adopted in the way of attitudes.

Another example of reversal in the steps (and one that has attracted a great deal of attention lately due to the influence of dissonance theory) is the case where overt behavior precedes the yielding. The common sense analysis embodied in the information-processing approach implies that the person is influenced by the communication first by adopting the new attitude, and then by changing his behavior on the basis of this new attitude. The reversed direction stressed by dissonance theorists is that after the person's behavior is changed, he then changes his attitude post factum in order to justify his new behavior. While this reversal has proved somewhat elusive empirically, there is ample evidence that it occurs under some circumstances (although exactly what these circumstances are remains to be specified). The current state of this "counter-attitudinal advocacy" issue has been conveniently summarized elsewhere (McGuire, 1966a; Sears & Abelson, 1969).

Proximal and Distal Variables: An Empirical Paradox

In the earlier discussion of the information-processing paradigm we stated that a great number of its implications for the attitude change area have already been empirically tested, and that it has passed many of these tests but failed others. We have not attempted to detail this scorecard either in our general discussion or in connection with the two illustrative applications (to personality-persuasibility relations and to the effect of fear appeals), because detailed and up-to-date reviews are available elsewhere (see McGuire, 1969a). Here we shall advert to only one empirical inadequacy that has developed with respect to the information-processing paradigm, choosing this one because it is a fairly pervasive one and has a peculiar interest.

Nature of the Paradox.   A fairly general and paradoxical empirical failure of the paradigm has to do with its proximal, as contrasted with distal, predictions. It was stressed above that we use the paradigm to predict how any independent variable in the communication process will be related to attitude change by considering how the independent variable in question will affect each of the mediating processes. For example, the relationship between an independent variable like anxiety level and attitude change is derived by considering the effect of anxiety on the successive steps of attention, comprehension, yielding, etc. By considering how anxiety affects a proximal variable like, for example, message comprehension, it is possible to derive its more distal effect on attitude change. It has been found with respect to a number of independent variables (including both the personality and fear arousal cases in the previous section) that the independent variable often has the effect on the distal dependent variable of attitude change that one would predict on the basis of the paradigm. But paradoxically, the independent variable turns out not to have the predicted effect on the more proximal dependent variable of message comprehension. And yet, this assumed proximal effect on comprehension was the main reason for predicting the more distal one on attitude change. The paradigm thus seems puzzlingly to have led us to make the right prediction for the wrong reason.

Resolutions of the Paradox.   A number of possibilities are at hand to explain this apparent paradox. For example, the measures of message comprehension used in most research in attitude change are rather poor, being added as an afterthought to check on the assumption regarding the independent variable's effect on comprehension. Since this proximal relationship appeared to be almost a truism, the measure of comprehension was often developed rather carelessly. However, this excuse no longer seems tenable, because lately, although more and more sophisticated measures of comprehension have been used, it is still common to find that the independent variable has the predicted effect on the distal variable of attitude change, while not showing the proximal effect on comprehension that the model assumes.

Another possible explanation is that our comprehension tests frequently do not measure the right thing. That is to say, it may be inappropriate to test the information-processing model by measuring the comprehension step in terms of recall of any testable material within the message. We have to ask more carefully not just how much is comprehended, but what is comprehended. For example, in the work on fear appeals, the comprehension test often measures how well the person remembers the threatening content and not just how well he remembers the urged new attitude and behavior, although it is only the latter that the paradigm would say is related to attitude change. Perhaps if more care were taken in teasing out the pertinent aspects of the message for the comprehension test (rather than just measuring comprehension for such contents of the message as are easy to measure), the apparent paradox would at least partially dissolve.

Other possibilities for the paradox become increasingly speculative. For example, some theorists might say that the comprehension step and the yielding step are co-effects of the independent variable, rather than that the comprehension mediates the yielding or vice versa. If so, the correlation between the two would tend to be small. It is also possible that the direction of causality is here reversed, and that yielding precedes comprehension in the sense that the person first adopts the new attitude and then reorganizes his memory of the content in order to conform to it. However, even where this kind of reversal might occur, it would still imply a closer correlation between comprehension and yielding effects than is usually found in the literature. Still another possibility is that learning the message content and yielding to the content are alternative modes of handling the new information. This is a more radical suggestion than that the two are co-effects, since if comprehension and yielding are alternative modes, then one would expect an appreciable negative relationship between the two. That is to say, in this hydraulic model, a variable that tends to produce high yielding would tend to produce low comprehension and vice versa.

The paradox that we have been discussing here, where the paradigm is often successful in predicting the independent variable's distal effect on attitude change while failing to predict its proximal effect on comprehension, remains something of a mystery. It almost seems a possibility for a sixth proof for the existence of God, Who is shown here to work His mysterious way, leading us to the truth even when we are blinded by our inadequate theories. Those who cling tenaciously to the classical theological paradigm might feel that the evidence is more in accord with it than with the information-processing paradigm in the case of this particular finding.

Insufficiencies of the Information-Processing Paradigm

In our earlier discussion of two applications of the information-processing paradigm, we pointed out that the basic notions of the paradigm do not by themselves allow us to make predictions about how a specific independent variable will affect attitude change, except in a rather general way. As we attempted to deal with the intricacies of the process and to account for seemingly contradictory findings that arise from experiment to experiment, it became necessary to take into account other variables in the situation. To do this, we had to keep adding to the paradigm additional auxiliary postulates which had very little to do with its initial inspiration.

For example, in making our first application of the paradigm (to the personality-persuasibility area) we found it necessary to assume a "compensatory" postulate, such that any personality or ability characteristic that tended to make a person vulnerable to attitude change via one of the mediators would tend to protect him via other mediators. This assumption was completely unrelated to the initial inspiration of the paradigm and was grafted onto the analysis because of a number of theoretical and empirical considerations (see McGuire, 1968b for a fuller discussion of the origin of this compensatory postulate). Equally arbitrary and independent of the information-processing formulation, per se, was the important additional assumption (made in our discussion of fear appeals in attitude change) of the two-factor concept of anxiety. As with any other theoretical paradigm, this one has insufficient specific applicability and explanatory power unless we use it in conjunction with additional auxiliary assumptions. To emphasize this inadequacy it will suffice to mention two more examples, one in the personality-persuasibility area and another in the fear appeal area, the two areas already used for illustration.

Further conceptual and empirical work on personality-persuasibility relationships has led us to make an additional auxiliary assumption that there tends to be a structuring among personality variables that facilitates the individual's coping with his environment. We have elsewhere (McGuire, 1968b) argued that an intermediate level of susceptibility to social influence is probably optimal for survival in the human environment, in the sense that if the person were completely closed to social influence or yielded completely to it, he would probably be at a disadvantage compared with the person who was somewhat, but not completely, open to persuasive communication. Hence, any chronic personality trait that tends to make the person extremely resistant or extremely receptive to social influence probably becomes embedded over time in a matrix of other traits that serve as correctives in moving the person towards an intermediate level of openness. For example, if the person has extremely low self-esteem so that he yields abjectly to all social influence attempts, this symptom probably becomes embedded in a syndrome that includes the tendency to withdraw from social situations. This withdrawal tendency would protect him from attitude change via reduced message presentation, attention, and comprehension, and compensate for his too great susceptibility via excessive yielding.

Elsewhere (McGuire, 1968b) we have illustrated how this tendency for a chronic personality trait to become adaptively embedded in a set of corrective traits also leads to a methodological danger. Specifically, this embeddedness is likely to cause the relationship between a personality variable and attitude change to vary depending on whether we are considering the person's natural chronic personality trait or his acute state induced by an experimental manipulation. Hence a correlational study that uses the natural level of the person is likely to lead to different results from those obtained in a manipulational study. These additional considerations affect how the information-processing model should be applied to the attitude change area, although they do not derive from the fundamental inspiration of the paradigm.

A final example of how auxiliary hypotheses are necessary for adequate use of the information-processing paradigm can be cited in the second area of application that we have been considering in this chapter. If the paradigm is correct in its prediction that the overall relationship between level of fear arousal and attitude change is nonmonotonic, then it would tend to follow that if a person is chronically anxious, further arousing his anxiety by a fear appeal would be less beneficial than if he is initially a relaxed and calm individual. However, when one tests this interaction prediction in a complex experimental design in which both chronic and acute anxiety levels are varied orthogonally, conflicting evidence is obtained. It is likely that the auxiliary "embeddedness" hypothesis mentioned in the previous paragraph clarifies these results. Specifically, the straightforward interaction prediction assumes that chronic and acute manipulations of anxiety are equivalent, whereas the embeddedness assumption suggests that people who are chronically at different levels of anxiety have acquired different modes of coping with threat, so that they are qualitatively and not just quantitatively different in their response to the fear arousal in the message. If so, a situational increase in the anxiety level will move the person not to different degrees of response, but also to different types of response, depending on whether he is chronically high or low in anxiety.

To say that any simple paradigm is insufficient by itself to account adequately for the whole range of obtained and potential empirical relationships is not a criticism of this paradigm relative to other paradigms. This insufficiency of the information-processing paradigm is typical of that which obtains for all other equally parsimonious formulations. We have mentioned these limitations only to call attention to the general necessity of using any paradigm in conjunction with one's creative imagination, mastery of the empirical findings in the field, and personal grasp of the realities, if the paradigm is to be exploited adequately. This consideration does become a basis for the comparative evaluation of paradigms, in that some are more suitable than others in terms of the availability of the needed auxiliary hypotheses and in the heuristic power of the given paradigm in suggesting what auxiliary hypotheses are necessary.

CONCLUSION

In the previous section we stressed the information-processing paradigm's shortcomings as a theoretical and methodological guide to the attitude change area. We should point out in closing that the inadequacies, invalidities, and insufficiencies of the paradigm have not yet sufficed to cause its being discarded and are unlikely to have this effect in the near future. This tenacious adherence to the paradigm even in the face of a variety of shortcomings might seem to be inappropriate stubbornness in an empirical science. However, we believe that this high threshold for rejection of a general paradigm is as it should be. We regard it as functional rather than unfortunate that paradigms tend to persist even in the face of contradictory evidence until a better paradigm becomes available to supplant it.

The danger of a paradigm lies not so much in its persisting in the face of some contradictory evidence as in the possibility that it will blind workers in the field to the implications and even existence of discordant evidence. Fortunately this danger is somewhat lessened in the attitude change area by the coexistence (not always peacefully) of alternative paradigms of contrasting inspirations that guide the research of workers who do not resonate with the information-processing formulation. There are, for example, the three alternative paradigms mentioned in the opening section of this chapter: the consistency, functional, and perceptual approaches. Like the man of one book, the researcher of one paradigm who learns it to the exclusion of others tends to be a bore and a limited contributor in the long run. A researcher who works in the attitude change area should learn any one paradigm thoroughly and master it so that he can use it creatively, but not think of it in such exclusive terms that it blinds him to the usefulness of the other paradigms.

When there is not exclusive preoccupation with one paradigm that blinds the researcher to the contrary evidence and creative value of the other approaches, we see no danger in continuing to use it for the derivation of predictions and the understanding of the findings, even though it has numerous shortcomings. We think that even poor theories are useful and are certainly better than none. Scientific progress tends to be a cumulative process in a given direction, rather than just one experiment after another. Hence we should guide our steps by general theoretical approaches such as the information-processing paradigm, and proceed through experiments in a sustained direction.

We feel that an appropriate analogy for the use of an imperfect paradigm can be found in the image of a Boy Scout lost in the woods. If the boy strikes out in any one direction and keeps making progress in that direction, it is likely that he will eventually find his way out of the woods. It might be that if he had pursued a different line of progress he would have gotten out even sooner, but almost any line of advance will suffice if pursued sufficiently long. The only real danger is that one will not persist in any one direction but will wander around at random and never get out of the woods. Analogously, if the empirical scientist is lost in a complex area, his pursuing the implications of any reasonable paradigm in a steady direction will probably lead him to some ultimate clarification of the area. If instead he drops each theory as soon as the slightest negative evidence crops up, there results the danger that he will wander around in circles and not obtain any clarification. The researcher who keeps the faith and pursues his paradigm to ultimate enlightenment may find that there is a much better theory he could have chosen initially. But his persistence will also have demonstrated the truth of Blake's proverb that "if the fool would persist in his folly, he would become wise."

REFERENCES

ABELSON, R. P., ARONSON, E., McGUIRE, W. J., NEWCOMB, T. M., ROSENBERG, M. J., & TANNENBAUM, P. H. (Eds.), *Theories of cognitive consistency*. Chicago: Rand McNally, 1968.

ABELSON, R. P., & ROSENBERG, M. J. Symbolic psycho-logic: A model of attitudinal cognition. *Behavioral Science,* 1958, **3,** 1–13.

ADORNO, T. W., FRENKEL-BRUNSWICK, E., LEVINSON, D. J., & STANFORD, R. N. *The authoritarian personailty.* New York: Harper & Row, 1950.

ANDERSON, N. H. Primary effects in personality impression formation using a generalized order effect paradigm. *Journal of Abnormal and Social Psychology,* 1965, **2,** 1–9.

ASCH, S. E. Forming impressions of personailty. *Journal of Abnormal and Social Psychology,* 1946, **41,** 258–290.

ASCH, S. E. *Social psychology.* Englewood Cliffs, N.J.: Prentice-Hall, 1952.

ASCH, S. E. Studies of independence and conformity: A minority of one against a unanimous majority. *Psychological Monographs,* 1959, **20**(9, Whole No. 416).

BETTELHEIM, B., & JANOWITZ, M. *Dynamics of prejudice: a psychological and socio-logical study of veterans.* New York: Harper & Row, 1950.

CAMPBELL, D. T. Social attitudes and other acquired behavioral dispositions. In S. Koch (Ed.), *Psychology: A study of a science.* Vol. 6. New York: McGraw-Hill, 1963. Pp. 94–172.

CARTWRIGHT, D., & HARARY, F. Structural balance: A generalization of Heider's theory. *Psychological Review,* 1956, **63,** 277–293.

COX, D. F., & BAUER, R. A. Self-confidence and persuasibility in women. *Public Opinion Quarterly,* 1964, **28,** 453–466.

FESTINGER, L. *A theory of cognitive dissonance.* Stanford, Calif.: Stanford University Press, 1957.

HEIDER, F. Attitudes and cognitive organization. *Journal of Psychology,* 1946, **21,** 107–112.

HEIDER, F. *The psychology of interpersonal relations.* New York: Wiley, 1958.

HELSON, H. *Adaptation-level theory.* New York: Harper & Row, 1964.

HOVLAND, C. I., LUMSDAINE, A. A., & SHEFFIELD, F. D. *Experiments on mass com-munications.* Princeton, N.J.: Princeton University Press, 1949.

HOVLAND, C. I., JANIS, I. L., & KELLEY, H. H. *Communication and persuasion.* New Haven, Conn.: Yale University Press, 1953.

HOVLAND, C. I. (Ed.), *Order of presentation in persuasion.* New Haven, Conn. Yale University Press, 1957.

JANIS, I. L. Personality correlates of susceptibility to persuasion. *Journal of Person-ality,* 1954, **22,** 504–518.

JANIS, I. L. Motivational factors in the resolution of decisional conflicts. In M. R. Jones (Ed.), *Nebraska symposium on motivation.* Vol. 7. Lincoln, Nebr.: University of Nebraska Press, 1959. Pp. 198–231.

JANIS, I. L. Effects of fear arousal on attitude change: Recent developments in theory and experimental research. In L. Berkowitz (Ed.), *Advances in Experimental Social Psychology.* New York: Academic Press, 1967. Pp. 167–224.

JANIS, I. L., & FESHBACH, S. Effects of fear arousing communications. *Journal of Abnormal and Social Psychology,* 1953, **48,** 78–92.

JOHNSON, H. H., & IZZETT, R. R. The relationship between authoritarianism and attitude change as a function of source credibility and type of communication. *Journal of Personality and Social Psychology,* 1968, **13,** 317–321.

KATZ, D. The functional approach to the study of attitudes. *Public Opinion Quar-terly,* 1960, **24,** 163–204.

KATZ, D., SARNOFF, I., & MCCLINTOCK, C. Ego-defense and attitude change. *Human Relations,* 1956, **9,** 27–45.

KATZ, D., & STOTLAND, E. A preliminary statement of a theory of attitude structure and change. In S. Koch (Ed.), *Psychology: A study of a science.* Vol. 3. New York: McGraw-Hill, 1959. Pp. 423–475.

KATZ, E. On reopening the question of selectivity in exposure to mass communica-tions. In R. P. Abelson, et al. (Eds.), *Theories of cognitive consistency.* Chicago: Rand McNally, 1968. Pp. 788–796.

LASSWELL, H. D. The structure and function of communication in society. In L. Bryson (Ed.), *Communication of Ideas.* New York: Harper & Row, 1948. Pp. 178–190.

LEHMANN, S. Self-esteem and anxiety in persuasion and conformity. *Journal of Personality and Social Psychology*, 1970, **15**, 76–86.

LUCHINS, A. S. Social influences on perception of complex drawings. *Journal of Social Psychology*, 1945, **21**, 257–273.

LUCHINS, A. S., & LUCHINS, E. H. *Rigidity of behavior.* Eugene, Ore.: University of Oregon Books, 1959.

McGUIRE, W. J. Order of presentation as a factor in "conditioning" persuasiveness. In C. I. Hovland (Ed.), *Order of presentation in persuasion.* New Haven, Conn.: Yale University Press, 1957. Pp. 98–114.

McGUIRE, W. J. A syllogistic analysis of cognitive relationships. In M. J. Rosenberg, & C. I. Hovland (Eds.), *Attitude organization and attitude change.* New Haven, Conn.: Yale University Press, 1960. Pp. 65–111.

McGUIRE, W. J. Attitudes and opinions. In P. Farnsworth (Ed.), *Annual Review of Psychology.* Palo Alto, Calif.: Annual Review Press, 1966, **17**. Pp. 475–514. (a)

McGUIRE, W. J. The current status of cognitive consistency theories. In S. Feldman (Ed.), *Cognitive consistency.* New York: Academic Press, 1966. Pp. 1–46. (b)

McGUIRE, W. J. Some impending reorientations in social psychology. *Journal of Experimental Social Psychology,* 1967, **3**, 124–139.

McGUIRE, W. J. Personality and attitude change: An information-processing theory. In A. G. Greenwald, et al. (Eds.), *Psychological foundations of attitudes.* New York: Academic Press, 1968. Pp. 171–196. (a)

McGUIRE, W. J. Personality and susceptibility to social influence. In E. F. Borgatta, & W. W. Lambert (Eds.), *Handbook of personality theory and research.* Chicago: Rand-McNally, 1968. Pp. 140–162. (b)

McGUIRE, W. J. Selective exposure: A summing up. In R. P. Abelson, et al. (Eds.), *Theories of cognitive consistency.* Chicago: Rand-McNally, 1968. Pp. 797–800. (c)

McGUIRE, W. J. Theory of the structure of human thought. In R. P. Abelson, et al. (Eds.), *Theories of cognitive consistency.* Chicago: Rand-McNally, 1968. Pp. 140–162. (d)

McGUIRE, W. J. Nature of attitudes and attitude change. In G. Lindzey, & E. Aronson (Eds.), *Handbook of social psychology.* (2nd ed.) Cambridge, Mass.: Addison-Wesley, 1969. Pp. 136–314. (a)

McGUIRE, W. J. Theory-oriented research in natural settings. In M. Sherif, & C. W. Sherif (Eds.), *Interdisciplinary relationships in the social sciences.* Chicago: Aldine, 1969. Pp. 21–51. (b)

McGUIRE, W. J., & RYAN, J. Receptivity as a mediator of personality-persuasibility relationships. University of Minnesota, LRSR, 1955, 20 pp.

MILLMAN, S. Anxiety, comprehension and susceptibility to social influence. *Journal of Personality and Social Psychology,* 1968, **9**, 251–256.

MILLS, J. Interest in supporting and discrepant information. In R. P. Abelson, et al. (Eds.), *Theories of cognitive consistency.* Chicago: Rand-McNally, 1968. Pp. 771–776.

NISBETT, R. E., & GORDON, A. Self-esteem and susceptibility to social influence. *Journal of Personality and Social Psychology,* 1967, **5**, 268–276.

OSGOOD, C. E., & TANNENBAUM, P. H. The principle of congruity in the prediction of attitude change. *Psychological Review,* 1955, **62**, 42–55.

SEARS, D. O., & ABELES, R. P. Attitudes and opinions. In P. H. Mussen, & M. R. Rosenzweig (Eds.), *Annual Review of Psychology,* Palo Alto, Calif.: Annual Review Press, 1969, **20**, 253–288.

SHERIF, C. W., SHERIF, M., & NEBERGALL, R. E. *Attitude and attitude change*. Philadelphia, Pa.: Saunders, 1965.

SHERIF, M. A study of social factors in perception. *Archives of Psychology,* New York, 1935, No. 187.

SHERIF, M., & HOVLAND, C. I. *Social judgment.* New Haven, Conn.: Yale University Press, 1961.

SILVERMAN, I. Differential effects of ego threat upon persuasibility for high and low self-esteem subject. *Journal of Abnormal and Social Psychology,* 1964, **69,** 567–572.

SMITH, M. B. Attitude change. In D. L. Sills (Ed.), *International encyclopedia of the social sciences.* Vol. 1. New York: Macmillan, 1968. Pp. 459–467.

SMITH, M. B., BRUNER, J. S., & WHITE, R. W. *Opinions and personality.* New York: Wiley, 1956.

THOMAS, W. I., & ZNANIECKI, F. *The Polish peasant in Europe and America.* Boston: Badger, 1918.

WATSON, J. B. *Behaviorism.* New York: Norton, 1925.

WATTS, W. A., & McGUIRE, W. J. Persistence of induced opinion change and retention of inducing message contents. *Journal of Abnormal and Social Psychology,* 1964, **68,** 233–241.

ZELLNER, M. Self-esteem, reception and influencibility. *Journal of Personality and Social Psychology,* 1970, **15,** 87–93.

6

THE RECIPROCATION OF ATTRACTION FROM SIMILAR AND DISSIMILAR OTHERS: A STUDY IN PERSON PERCEPTION AND EVALUATION[1]

Edward E. Jones
Linda Bell
Elliot Aronson

Many contemporary social psychology experiments are undertaken because of an investigator's interest in challenging a truism. Whereas the field of social psychology is characterized by widely varying research approaches, a prominent strategy has been to consider a generally accepted "common sense" proposition and to think of conditions under which the proposition would not be likely to hold or might even be reversed. It is intriguing to find the conditions under which people seek out painful stimuli, are moved in the opposite direction by a persuasive communication, or like someone who has been nasty to them. Interest in the paradox, the "nonobvious finding," may be carried to absurd and unprofitable extremes, but the confirmation of a surprising hypothesis can be an important step in the discovery of a larger truth, a more fundamental generalization that explains both the obvious finding and the surprise. If properly controlled, the pursuit of the nonobvious finding is a reasonable development in a science that seeks to supplement common sense and to penetrate beneath the surface of social events.

This chapter discusses one attempt to confirm the paradoxical hypothesis that, under certain conditions, a person will like someone who is dissimilar to himself better than he will like a similar other. We shall first examine some of the underlying issues involved in the relations between similarity and attrac-

[1] This chapter was prepared with the support of a National Science Foundation grant to the first author.

tion, and then describe the procedures and results of two closely related experiments designed to clarify the *joint* effects of similarity (dissimilarity) and being liked (disliked) on reciprocated attraction.

It hardly needs to be argued that the study of interpersonal relations crucially depends on our ability to specify the determinants of attraction and dislike. Whether a person forms an initially favorable or negative impression of another determines in an important way the course of their subsequent interaction. Often, of course, an initial impression would be radically changed if persons could readily gain access to more information about each other. But the very fact that one's initial impression of another is negative tends to create physical or psychological avoidance, and to interfere with communications that would otherwise ameliorate the situation (Newcomb, 1947). Such communication breakdowns can more easily be overcome as we gain a clearer understanding of those initial forms of evidence that push impressions in approaching or avoiding directions.

SIMILARITY AND ATTRACTION

Two of the best established propositions about the determinants of interpersonal attraction are that people tend to like those who like them and those who share similar values and beliefs. The results of many studies (reviewed by Jones & Gerard, 1967; Berscheid & Walster, 1969; Bramel, 1969) offer general support for these propositions in a variety of experimental situations, but a moment's reflection suggests several qualifications to each proposition.

Turning first to the proposition that similarity begets attraction, this is much more likely to be true of certain kinds of personal characteristics than of others. Such personal attributes as the need to dominate, the need to nurture, and the need to be controlled seem to be out of phase with the similarity proposition. In fact, Winch (1958) has championed the importance of need complementarity rather than similarity as a major basis for attraction in mate selection. Kerckhoff and Davis (1962) present data on "seriously attached" college student couples that suggest that similarity of interests may be initially important in sustaining a relationship but that need complementarity may be more important in the long run.

However, it seems clear both from theory and evidence that people who share the same interests, values, beliefs, or attitudes, are likely to be attracted to each other under a wide variety of conditions. We know of no research evidence, in fact, establishing the conditions under which people are more attracted to those with dissimilar than with similar attitudes. But there are conditions under which people prefer to *affiliate* with dissimilar others. Each of us knows people who are so confident about their beliefs that they are attracted to those who believe the opposite. This gives them the opportunity to express their views against a meaningful opponent and perhaps to enjoy the fruits of social influence. Likewise, Gordon (1966) showed that those who were certain of the correctness of their opinion preferred to affiliate with those holding radically different opinions. Walster and Walster (1963) found that subjects would rather interact with dissimilar than similar others *if* they were assured that the others would like them. This suggests that much of the natural gravitation toward similar others is prompted by the greater likelihood of acceptance by them; when one is assured that he will not be rejected by dissimilar others, the thought of associating with them may become positively attractive—perhaps because dissimilar people can provide new information, more surprises, and give the person new perspectives on his ideas and abilities. To what extent affiliation implies attraction, however, is not clear in these examples. In conclusion, data suggesting a preference for dissimilar versus similar people are sparse and difficult to interpret.

And what of the proposition that we like those who like us? In the vast majority of cases and for a variety of reasons we would certainly expect attraction to be reciprocated. Those who like us can be counted on to help or at least not to hinder us in our attainment of desirable objectives. In addition, the mere fact of being liked typically adds to our sense of worth as a person. A person who likes us represents a "safe" sector of the environment; he does not threaten rejection or humiliation. And yet there may be some exceptions to the robust proposition that we like those who like us. A number of psychologists (e.g., Heider, 1958) have suggested that this may depend on how much we like ourselves. To the extent that we have unfavorable attitudes toward our own personal qualities, we are in disagreement with those who hold us in high favor. Thus any positive effects of being liked are pitted against the negative effects of opinion dissimilarity, the self being the object of the dissimilar opinions. Since most people do place a positive value on the self, it is not surprising that the proposition of reciprocated attraction is usually confirmed. In fact, while self-esteem may play a role in the evaluation of others (Deutsch & Solomon, 1959; Walster, 1965) we know of no findings that show greater attraction toward someone who dislikes, than toward someone who likes, the subject.

There is considerable evidence, on the other hand, suggesting the importance of the context and manner in which liking is expressed in determining the extent to which attraction will be reciprocated. Aronson and Linder (1965) have shown that the amount of liking received (the number of reinforcements) is less important than sequences of gaining versus losing attraction. In their experiment subjects were more attracted to those who grew to like them than to those who liked them all along. Other features of the context may suggest that ulterior motives are involved in expressing complimentary evaluations. To the extent that expressed liking may be interpreted as flattery, the amount of attraction reciprocated tends to be lowered (Jones, 1964).

Various characteristics of the liking person, such as his discernment or physical attractiveness may also affect the magnitude of reciprocated attraction. Landy and Aronson (1968) found that discerning positive and negative evaluators were both liked better than their nondiscerning counterparts. They had expected to find that the discerning *negative* evaluator was especially disliked.

Sigall and Aronson (1969) found that a physically attractive female confederate was liked better when she evaluated the subject positively than was the same confederate appearing in an unattractive wig and tasteless makeup. When she evaluated the subject negatively, the confederate was liked less when she was attractive than when she was unattractive. We shall return to this finding in discussing the results of the present experiments.

We are now in a position to deal with the focal problem of this chapter: how do similarity and liking combine in affecting one person's impression of another? How do we feel when we find out that a person who is very similar to us likes or dislikes us? How about our response to being liked or disliked by a dissimilar person? There are several ways to approach these questions. Perhaps the most explicitly elaborated approach is that of Byrne (lucidly summarized in his 1969 chapter).

Byrne's Paradigm

In a series of studies over the past several years, Byrne and his colleagues have developed an increasingly refined picture of the relationship between similarity and attraction. Most of Byrne's studies have involved the same basic procedure: subjects are given an attitude scale that has been allegedly filled out by a "stranger." Unbeknownst to the subjects, they have been handed a predetermined set of responses designed to vary the similarity between the stranger's attitude ratings and their own, the latter being determined by their responses to the same questionnaire in an earlier classroom administration. After examining the bogus questionnaire the subjects are asked to convey an accurate impression of the "stranger" by filling out a six-item Interpersonal Judgment Scale, the last two items of which are intended to be measures of attraction. The first of these two items asks the subjects to rate their degree of liking for the stranger on a seven-point scale, and the second asks whether they would enjoy working with him.

Proceeding in this way, Byrne and his colleagues have found highly consistent relations between attraction and similarity. Not only do subjects in general prefer a similar stranger to a dissimilar one, but the degree of attraction is closely related to the proportion of similar to dissimilar opinions. In fact, Byrne proposes that the two are related in an empirical law by the formula Y (attraction) $= 5.44$ X (proportion of similar attitudes) $+ 6.62$.

The generality of the similarity-attraction relationship within Byrne's paradigm is indicated by the following results. (a) Byrne and Clore (1966) found it did not make any difference whether the stranger's attitudes were expressed on a mimeographed scale, a tape recording, or on the sound track of a movie. McWhirter and Jecker (1967) extended this finding to a face-to-face interaction in which a confederate followed the subject in responding orally to the attitude items. Such variations in the *mode of presenting* the similarity-dissimilarity data thus were shown not to affect the similarity-attraction relationship. (b) The relationship was shown to hold with high consistency among such *different popu-*

lations as female clerical workers, job corpsmen, primary and secondary school children, hospitalized schizophrenics, alcoholics, and, of course, male and female college students. (c) At least some *generality of response* has been demonstrated. The Interpersonal Judgment Scale has been shown by Schwartz (1966) to correlate .68 with a 10-item social distance scale, and the same general similarity-attraction relationship was obtained when subjects responded to the two crucial attraction items by dropping an indicator into an appropriate wooden slot in a specially constructed rating box rather than expressing themselves by paper and pencil ratings.

Byrne prefers to theorize about the similarity-attraction relationship in terms of reinforcement concepts. Exposure to similar attitude statements is rewarding because such statements satisfy the learned drive to be logical and to interpret correctly one's stimulus world. Beyond this, Byrne feels that it is convenient to treat the reinforcement potential of attitude statements in quantitative terms. Thus in his formula relating proportion of similar opinions to degree of expressed attraction, the particular attitude statements are considered as interchangeable and treated as equivalent units of reinforcement. The important thing for our purposes is that Byrne follows this logic in dealing with combined information about similarity and being liked or disliked.

In order to extend the model, Byrne and Rhamey (1965) informed each subject not only concerning the degree to which a stranger was similar to himself but also provided information regarding how the stranger had evaluated him after having read the subject's own attitude responses. They found that both the stranger's opinion similarity and the direction of his evaluation of the subject affected the latter's reciprocated attraction. The two effects were additive—the similar, liking person being liked most and the dissimilar, disliking person least—leading Byrne to conclude that personal evaluations operate in the same manner as attitude statements. Such evaluations are, it might be contended, simply attitude statements about a person who happens to be the subject. By making the further assumption that personal evaluation involves reinforcements of greater magnitude than attitude statements about other issues, Byrne and Rhamey were again able to describe their experimental data by their linear formula relating similarity to attraction.

It should be noted that the personal evaluations in the study just reviewed were based solely on the stranger's *alleged* exposure to the subject's own attitude statements. Thus in the high similarity, positive evaluation condition, for example, the subject knows that he is similar to the stranger in a variety of attitudes and he further knows that the stranger, also having been apprised of this similarity, thinks that the subject is intelligent, likeable, etc. Thus the information about attitude similarity and personal evaluation is actually not independent—the evaluation is based on no other information than the attitudes themselves. Although personal evaluations seem to operate in the same manner as miscellaneous attitude statements (if somewhat more powerfully), this similarity may well be a function of the fact that the former are contingent upon the latter in the subject's mind.

The situation with which we are primarily concerned in this chapter is one in which evidence about being liked or disliked is based on personal contact *in addition to* information about attitudes. Our hunch is that such a situation may give rise to quite different results. Aronson and Worchel (1966) designed an experiment to determine whether attitude similarity and information about personal evaluation have independent and additive effects on attraction in a face-to-face situation. Each male subject met with an experimental confederate who had been carefully trained to play the role of another subject. The "subjects" responded to a seven-item attitude questionnaire and then discussed their responses and the reasons for them. The naive subject always responded first so that the confederate could by his responses appear to be similar or dissimilar. Following this, the subjects were instructed to write down their comments about the experiment and these were exchanged between subject and confederate as a "source of additional information." The confederate's written comments indicated either that he enjoyed working with the naive subject and found him a profound and interesting person, or that he did not enjoy working with him and found him shallow and uninteresting. The subjects were then asked to evaluate each other on Byrne's Interpersonal Judgment Scale. Aronson and Worchel found that the personal evaluation messages had a clear impact on the subject's reciprocated attraction, but the effects of the similarity variable were considerably less pronounced. This led them to surmise that the similarity-attraction relationship may be mediated by the subject's assumption that he will be liked by a similar person. The perception of being liked, not the perception of similarity, may be the crucial determinant of attraction.

Byrne and Griffitt (1966) replicated the Aronson and Worchel experiment but increased the attitudinal difference between the similar and the dissimilar confederate. They found highly significant effects both of the similarity variable and the being liked variable, and attributed the Aronson and Worchel findings to their restricted range of attitudinal agreement or disagreement on the similarity-dissimilarity dimension.

But in these two studies there again is strong emphasis on the attitude statements themselves and, in spite of the face-to-face quality of the interchange about the subjects' mutual positions, the personal evaluation is closely linked to the attitude statements endorsed. Indeed, the particular messages used to convey personal evaluation appear to emphasize this linkage. The similar-like message says, "We agreed on many things. I enjoyed working with him in the experiment. . . ." The dissimilar-like message says, "Although we disagreed on most things, I enjoyed working with him in the experiment. . . ." Each message, in its own way, seems to reinforce the notion that similarity and attraction *should* be, and usually are, related. Furthermore, the context in which the personal evaluation messages are received is a rather unconvincing and peculiar one. What is a subject to make of the confederate's gratuitous remarks about him in a note supposedly commenting on the experiment? In the positive evaluation conditions he may decide that the confederate is something of a flatterer, but there is no point in punishing him for this in his own evaluative ratings. In the negative evaluation condition, it is quite possible that the subject is just as angered by the gratuitous quality of the negative comments as by their content alone. It is one thing to be disliked; it is quite another when the one who dislikes you goes out of his way to tell you about it.

The Present Study.   The experiments to be reported below were designed to provide a more realistic test of the similarity-attraction proposition under conditions where female subjects also learn whether they are liked or disliked. An attempt was made to convey the liked-disliked information in a manner that fit naturally into the experimental cover story. In addition, the subject was clearly being liked or disliked for something besides her expressed attitudes.

In brief outline, with a more detailed account to follow, each subject was interviewed under the presumption that the interview was being video taped for replay in the next room where another subject was supposedly waiting. She then filled out an opinion questionnaire and learned that she was either similar or dissimilar to the other "subject" in her opinions. She next observed a closed-circuit showing of the other "subject" (the confederate) presumably monitoring the tape she had just made. This "closed-circuit showing" was actually a video tape through which the subject learned that she was either liked or disliked. The subject was informed that the other "subject" (the confederate) had been hooked up to a machine which allegedly could measure her emotional reaction to other people. The measure of her reaction to the actual subject was displayed on the video tape so that the subject could not only watch the other "subject" presumably watching her, but she could observe the direction and intensity of the other "subject's" feelings about her.

On top of the similarity-dissimilarity information that she had already received and begun to digest, then, the subject learned that the other "subject's" emotional reaction to her was either predominantly positive or negative, that is, that the other "subject" *really* liked or disliked her. The subject was then shown, while she was hooked up to the emotional reaction machine, a video tape of an interview between the experimenter and the other "subject," similar in form to the tape she herself had made. Since she was prevented from seeing any readings from this machine, it was appropriate to ask her afterwards to estimate the average reading of her liking or disliking of the other "subject" on the machine during her observation of the taped interview. This provided our main measure of the subject's attraction toward the other "subject." She then filled out a number of evaluation scales to provide further information about her feelings and impressions. Before reviewing the theoretical issues involved, and our predictions concerning the outcome of the experiment, it is necessary to back off for a moment and to consider the problems associated with trying to measure attraction.

Measuring Interpersonal Attraction: A Digression

One person's perceptions of another can only be inferred from his responses to or about that other. These responses are typically a verbal mixture of description and evaluation. Indeed it is difficult to find terms relevant to the perception of persons that are affectively neutral and have no evaluative overtones. Perhaps our judgments of others are typically cast in evaluative terms because people are so important in our lives. In everyday social interaction we are always confronting decisions with respect to approaching or avoiding others—whether to smile or frown, to agree or disagree, to accept or reject, to be involved or indifferent. When a person meets another and is asked to form an impression of him, he will ask himself such questions as: Is he sincere? Does he believe in the right things? Is he intelligent? Can I trust him? Sincerity, insight, intelligence, trust—all are clearly evaluative dimensions and lie at the heart of freely formed impressions.

It is common knowledge, well verified by research data, that one's general positive or negative impression of another does influence his ratings of specific traits or attributes. This tendency, termed *halo effect*, has been an annoying source of concern to those trying to increase judgmental accuracy. Since our own primary interest lies in the measurement of attraction, we are in a position to exploit the natural contamination of description by evaluation and to try to find indices that are especially sensitive to the evaluative tone of a global impression.

Not surprisingly, then, many studies of interpersonal attraction summarize the ratings of evaluative traits as the main dependent variable measure. If most trait dimensions are suffused with global evaluation, it should be possible to measure variations in evaluation by combining the ratings of several traits. Even if one accepts this as a reasonable procedure for measuring gross variations in attraction, many questions remain. Are some traits more sensitive indicators of attraction than others? Are there distinct advantages to the technique of summarizing trait ratings over more direct questions about liking? We know surprisingly little about the answers to such questions. Individual investigators who conduct research on the determinants of attraction generally choose a dependent variable measure that seems appropriate for a particular setting, subject sample, etc. Certain investigators characteristically use direct measures of liking, others prefer more subtle and indirect indices. The point is that there is no solid knowledge to inform the investigator whether he would be better off using a direct question about liking, various kinds of attribute rating scales, or perhaps some form of overt behavior implying attraction.

Let us briefly consider some of the problems posed by different kinds of attraction measures. Why not simply ask the subject to indicate how much he likes or dislikes the target person? Such a measure has often been used as the main measure of attraction in a particular study and it has obvious advantages of directness and face validity. But there are problems as well. It is very hard for many of us to admit that we dislike another person. In our culture, tolerance for diverse views—and sometimes even for obnoxiousness—is a prized virtue. No matter how hostile a subject feels inside,. he may be quite reluctant to acknowledge this hostility to an experimenter. Similarly, at the other extreme, it may be difficult for subjects to acknowledge intense liking for another subject whom they have known for a very short time. The safest response is one that lands the subject somewhere near the midpoint of the scale, or perhaps closer to the "like" end to demonstrate his tolerance and forbearance.

The main measure of attraction used in the present study is a novel variation of this direct approach designed to minimize bland safe ratings. Subjects may be reluctant to concede the extent of their negative feelings about another subject to an experimenter, but this reluctance should be minimized if the subject believes that the experimenter has some other way of knowing how negative these feelings really are. If that could be arranged, the subject would quite probably try harder to portray his feelings accurately.

Toward this end, we decided to measure attraction by hooking each subject to a machine that allegedly measured her emotions, arranged to have her observe the target person while attached to this machine, and finally asked her to estimate the average "like-dislike" reading of the machine—her true emotional reaction to the other person. The basic assumption of this technique is that subjects believe they have insight into their own emotions and have no desire to be second-guessed by a machine. They should therefore be motivated to be as accurate as possible in their estimates, even at the risk of presenting themselves as hostile and intolerant or as overly affectionate and gullible.

Since this was an untried technique, it was necessary to check its validity against additional measures of a conventional sort. This led us to consider a number of trait dimensions that could be combined into indices of evaluation. Almost without exception, attraction experiments are disguised as something else when presented to the subject. This is because subjects alerted to the experimenter's interest in their attraction to another subject might be overly cautious in their reactions or try to meet what they judge to be the experimenter's expectations about how they *should* feel in the situation. As in the case of many other studies of attraction, then, the present study was thinly disguised as a study in first impression formation. Presumably, each subject expected to record her impression of another subject, but she did not realize the experimenter's primary interest in using her evaluative ratings as a measure of liking.

But how does one decide which traits to use as indices of attraction in an experiment of this type? There are many potential problems associated with the choice of trait dimensions. An obvious problem is that some of the dimensions may be especially sensitive to particular information conveyed by or about the target person. For example, if the experiment were to involve a search for the conditions under which people dislike those who behave in an overly friendly manner, one would hardly choose "friendly-unfriendly" as a trait dimension to measure attraction. Ratings of this trait should obviously be directly affected by the information about friendliness built into the experiment.

A related problem is that each evaluative rating refers to a specific characteristic as well as reflects the subject's global, good-bad impression. If one wishes to use a summary index of various evaluative traits, then, it is important to insure that a variety of characteristics are being evaluated so that some particular dimension is not overrepresented. On a priori grounds, furthermore, there would seem to be two basic content areas of evaluation that merit separate examination. On the one hand, there are those trait dimensions that tap evaluations of warmth, sociability, sincerity, that is, qualities of *social attractiveness*. On the other hand, there are ratings of *personal competence*: intelligence, discernment, and maturity. It is an interesting question whether different clusters of traits, such as these two, behave differently in attraction experiments. Intuitively, it would seem that social attractiveness traits should behave more like the machine reading estimates (the global measure of attraction) than the competence traits should. It seems more plausible that one could dislike a competent person than a warm and sympathetic one. Traits of each type were therefore included in the first impression rating questionnaire of the present experiment.

Unfortunately, we are still at the stage in experimental studies of interpersonal attraction where each investigator must fall back on his own intuition, to some unknown extent, in choosing his measure of liking. The measure should be relatively uncontaminated by obvious nonevaluative factors; the measure and the manner in which it is administered should be a natural part of the experimental setting; finally, it should be appropriate to the independent variables being studied without being exclusively tied to them. These considerations suggest that there are two conflicting pressures on the investigator as he designs his experiment. In the interests of generating cumulative knowledge about the determinants of a particular attraction indicator, he can settle on a general all-purpose measure of interpersonal evaluation. Osgood's semantic differential technique has been widely used in this way (Osgood, Suci, & Tannenbaum, 1957). Or he can choose a measure that might be unique because it is particularly relevant to the hypothesis being tested and the setting for the test.

The former approach hopefully leads to empirical generality—different experiments may be more easily compared and be seen to build on each other. This strategy has undeniable advantages in stimulating research continuity, but they may be earned at the cost of variations in the relevance of the all-purpose measure to the subtleties of a particular experiment. The latter approach is risky, intuitive, and raises clear problems of comparison across experiments. But it has the advantage of giving the theoretical hypothesis a fair and relevant test. Those who pursue this strategy seem willing to give up the possibilities of empirical generality for the more important long-range goal of conceptual generality. If one's theory keeps getting confirmed with a variety of measures in a variety of situations, this makes the theory seem even more powerful than if predictions were restricted to effects on only one kind of response measure. In this latter case, one is left to wonder if some artifact associated with the measure itself is responsible for the result.

Is there any way to capitalize on the advantages of both strategies? Cannot the investigator single out one measure that reflects the most precise test of his hypothesis and use this along with other measures that may be more generally used? This, in fact, is the compromise strategy we recommend, although caution is required in its implementation. Since the use of more than one dependent variable measure raises problems of sequence effects, the most relevant and crucial measure should be administered first. It should then be kept fully in mind that all subsequent measures may be contaminated by the subject's response to the first one. Especially if the measures are closely related in form and content, the subject will be trying to make his later responses consistent with his earlier ones. The multiple measure strategy also raises problems in the event that some measures show significant effects of the experimental variables and some do not. There should be a prior commitment to the dependent variable that is considered primary in testing the hypothesis. The other (subsequently administered) variables should be viewed as providing further information about underlying processes or perhaps facilitating comparison across different experiments.

In the experiments to be reported below, we have followed this strategy rather closely in that the primary machine reading estimate was followed by more conventional trait-rating measures of the subjects' first impressions. As it turned out, much was learned by the inclusion of these "secondary measures." Close examination of their patterning helped us to understand the judgmental and evaluative processes at work, but if we had included only these conventional measures we would have missed an important aspect of the subjects' reaction to the experiment. We would, then, have been misled by concentrating on any single measure of attraction in the experiment to be reported below. Finally, in cases where several dependent variables each confirm the theoretical hypothesis, the investigator gains some assurance that his results have general significance— they are detachable from a particular way of phrasing the rating scale or inter- view question and apparently reflect inner psychological processes.

One of our interests in this chapter is to explore the impact of conditions designed to influence attraction on a direct measure of liking as well as on more indirect ratings of positive and negative personal qualities. Our primary purpose in conducting the experiments, however, was to test a particular hypothesis about the responses of subjects to the information that they are either liked or disliked by another person who is either similar or dissimilar to them. Before examining the details of experimental procedure, let us return to the question of similarity and attraction and consider the various theoretical alternatives involved.

Similarity and Being Liked: Some Theoretical Alternatives

How might attitude similarity and the news of being liked or disliked combine to affect attraction on the measures we have just discussed? One theoretical alternative might be called the *violated expectancy hypothesis*. This hypothesis assumes that a subject who finds he is similar to the confederate will expect to be liked by him whereas subjects in the dissimilar condition will expect to be disliked. Because of these expectations, subjects in the similar-liked and dis- similar-disliked conditions will be relatively unaffected by the information about the confederate's evaluation of them. These evaluations are consonant with their expectations and not very informative about the impressions created through the video-taped interview. By comparison, subjects in the dissimilar-liked con- dition have been treated to a pleasant surprise and those in the similar-disliked condition have been stunned by nasty news indeed. In the first case the subject has managed to win the affection of a stranger in spite of their disagreement on a variety of opinion issues; we might imagine the subject concluding, "she must like me for some essential quality that came out during the interview, and not just because we happen to agree on a few things." In the similar-disliked case, the subject expects to be liked, but finds that she has created a negative impression. This impression cannot be explained away as a natural reaction to dissimilarity, and the subject's major option is simply to respond in kind with negative feelings of her own. In effect, the violated expectation hypothesis predicts that within each condition of evaluation (being liked or disliked), subjects will like a person who is dissimilar to themselves better than a similar person.

On the face of it, this contrasts sharply with the *additive hypothesis* of Byrne. If similar attitude statements and indications of liking are both construed as positive reinforcements, differing in their magnitude perhaps but not in their basic psychological significance, subjects in our experiment should respond most positively to a combination of similarity and being liked and most negatively to dissimilarity and dislike. We call this the additive hypothesis because the positive effects of liking are merely added to the positive effects of similarity to produce a highly positive resultant impression, just as the negative effects of dissimilarity and dislike summate to produce a very negative impression.

The third alternative might be called the *balance hypothesis*. It assumes that people are most comfortable when events are consistent with their expectations and that they should respond positively to those who are, in a sense, agents of expectancy confirmation. Operating on these assumptions, the subjects in our experiment should respond more positively to the confederate who is both similar to the subject and likes him than to the dissimilar-liking confederate. When the confederate indicates dislike for the subject, however, the confederate should be better liked when they are dissimilar than in the similar case. It.can be seen that the balance hypothesis carries the same prediction as the expectancy violation hypothesis when the subject finds she is disliked, but predicts the opposite result when the subject finds she is liked. The additive hypothesis is simply the opposite of the expectancy violation hypothesis, but agrees with the balance hypothesis in the being liked conditions.

It should be pointed out that nothing we have said is intended to rule out a sizable direct effect of being liked versus disliked. To be liked is almost always better than to be disliked, and none of the hypotheses predicts that any of the conditions where the subject is disliked will elicit more reciprocated attraction than any of the liked conditions.

How might the subject respond if she had no information about being liked or disliked, but did learn that she was either similar or dissimilar to the other "subject" in the experiment? It is not enough merely to assume that because Byrne consistently finds his subjects more attracted to similar than to dissimilar others, there is no need to demonstrate this preference in the present experiment. The existence and extent of such a preference is crucial to any interpretation of results when information about being liked is combined with information about similarity. To provide a link with studies within the Byrne paradigm, control conditions were included as part of the experimental design. These conditions were identical to those already described except that control subjects received no information concerning the other "subject's" liking for them after the evidence about similarity or dissimilarity was introduced. The additive hypothesis would clearly predict a preference for the similar versus the dissimilar "other subject," since a basic assumption of this hypothesis is that similarity is positively reinforcing and dissimilarity is negatively reinforcing. The other two theoretical positions have nothing to contribute regarding the control conditions, since there is no confirmation or violation of an expectancy.

The alternative hypotheses can be summarized in the following diagram, where $+$ and $++$ signify degree of attraction and $-$ and $--$ dislike of other:

Attraction	Attitudes	Expectancy Violation Hypothesis	Additive Hypothesis	Balance Hypothesis
Being Liked	Similar	$+$	$++$	$++$
	Dissimilar	$++$	$+$	$+$
Being Disliked	Similar	$--$	$-$	$--$
	Dissimilar	$-$	$--$	$-$
Control	Similar	$+$	$+$	$+$
	Dissimilar	$-$	$-$	$-$

Our own preference, reflecting our interest in the paradoxical, is for the expectancy violation hypothesis. The reasoning behind such a hypothesis comes closest to a conception of the subject as a concerned, emotionally involved participant in a social episode having implications for her self-esteem. It was our intent to construct such an episode by our experimental design. Assuming our success in gaining the involvement of the subject, the violated expectancy hypothesis seems more closely tied than the other two to a playing out of the subject's fears and hopes for herself in a setting of mutual evaluation. Whereas in one sense it is paradoxical to predict greater attraction toward a dissimilar other, in another sense the hypothesis derives logically from an attempt to appreciate the situation from the subject's point of view. By comparison, the additive hypothesis seems to us to be overly mechanistic and to ignore the personal dynamics of the subject as she attempts to come to terms with a consequential situation. The balance hypothesis seems to place too great an emphasis on the affective consequences of cognitive inconsistency to the exclusion of other factors. To the extent that subjects are genuinely involved in what happens to them during the experiment, they should prefer to be pleasantly surprised than to have an unpleasant expectancy confirmed. While the human preference for balance or consistency is undoubtedly a pervasive principle, the balance hypothesis in the present context does not take sufficient account of the particular informational value of the positive disconfirmation for the subject. In the dissimilar-liked condition, the fact that she is liked conveys information about crucial personal qualities that must have shown through in the interview. In the similar-liked condition, on the other hand, information about the other "subject's" response to these qualities is highly ambiguous. The subject is in a poor position to determine whether she is liked merely because she is similar or for some other reasons as well.

EXPERIMENT I

As described in the preceding overview, the experiment included the following sequence of events: (a) subject is briefly interviewed in front of video camera; (b) subject exchanges an attitude questionnaire with other "subject" (the confederate) and finds that they have quite similar or dissimilar attitudes; (c) subject's video-taped interview presumably played back to other "subject" while true subject observes her reaction on closed-circuit monitor, during which time she learns that she is liked, disliked, or receives no information about liking; (d) subject is then hooked up to emotional reaction machine while she observes video tape of other "subject" being interviewed; (e) subject is asked to estimate average machine reading of her attraction to other and fills out impression questionnaire. The experimental conditions thus fell into a design in which information about attitude similarity-dissimilarity was combined with information about being liked (or disliked, or no information), making a total of six cells or conditions.

Subjects

A total of 78 female undergraduates participated as subjects in the experiment as a requirement in the introductory psychology course. Four of these subjects did not complete the experiment because they knew the accomplice who served as the second subject. Two others were excluded because they were suspicious of the procedures. Each of the remaining 72 subjects was randomly assigned to one of the six conditions. The experimenter was a female graduate student.

Procedure

We wanted to accomplish a number of objectives in the present experiment, and many of these could not be attained without deceiving the subjects as to the true nature of the situation confronting them. In order to introduce effective experimental control, it was very important that each subject in a particular condition be exposed to the same carefully constructed sequence of experiences. And yet it was equally important that the experiences seem real and therefore emotionally involving to the subjects. These dual objectives of control and impact were sought by trying to convince the subjects that another subject was in a nearby room, and that she was responding honestly and directly to the first subject. In fact, the subject's actual contacts with her fellow subject were restricted to video tape exposures that were exactly the same (standard) for each subject and whose place in the sequence of events fit reasonably into the cover story. The other "subject" was an accomplice of the experimenter; she made the video tapes before the first real subject was run and was never present thereafter. Other more specific experimental objectives will be noted as we now describe the procedure in some detail.

The Cover Story.   Each subject was initially told that the experiment was a study of "the impression formation process"—how people form impressions of other people in a brief social interaction. She was then given a plausible but fictitious overview of the experimental design into which her own participation would fit. She was told that two subjects were signed up for each hour and that they met each other in one of four different ways. Either they exchanged notes about themselves, made and exchanged audio tape recordings, made and exchanged video tape recordings, or talked together face-to-face for 15 minutes. At the end of whichever kind of experiment they underwent, all subjects were to give their impressions of each other. The purpose of this research program was allegedly to find out what kinds of cues (visual, auditory, etc.) people paid most attention to and were most influenced by in forming an impression. Each subject was then informed that she and her partner were in the condition where each would make a video tape to be exchanged. Hopefully, this description of research objectives would serve to divert the subject from recognizing our true interest in her degree of attraction for the accomplice.

The Emotional Reaction Machine.   The experimenter then pointed out that, after making the tape, all subjects would get a chance to exchange opinions on a variety of issues. Then they would have a chance to observe each other on video tape. Their reactions to the other's video tape would, the experimenter continued, be measured by "a new kind of Galvanic Skin Response—you know, GSR—machine." The machine allegedly was able not only to measure the magnitude of emotional arousal but to distinguish between positive and negative emotional states, between like and dislike. Each subject was then shown a standard GSR machine and her attention was drawn to the summarizing dial that reflected an integration of the subject's feelings at a given point in time on a scale ranging from -3000 to $+3000$.

In fact, such a refined measure of the intensity and direction of one's feelings is well beyond the capacity of any known machine. The GSR was introduced to the subject in this manner to serve two basic purposes. First, if the subject could be convinced of the validity of the machine readings, she would take quite seriously the subsequent evidence presented on the summarizing dial displayed during the televised interview that she was liked or disliked by the accomplice. The subject could not easily assume, in the liked condition, that the accomplice was just being nice or was withholding her negative feelings. Second, the machine provided a plausible way to measure the subject's own attraction toward the accomplice. As she observed the accomplice being interviewed, the subject would be attached to the machine herself. Although she could not see her own dial readings, it was reasonable to ask her to estimate what the average of these readings had been while she was observing (and presumably thinking about) the accomplice. As we have already noted in the introductory section, in using these estimates as a major measure of attraction, we were making the assumption that most people would not want to be second-guessed by a machine—that it would be embarrassing for a person to claim he liked or disliked someone if it turned out he "really" did not.

In the liked and disliked conditions, each subject was told that she would be allowed to observe on her TV monitor the actual dial fluctuations of the other person as she observed the subject being interviewed. This was tossed off rather casually as having been "interesting and educational for previous subjects." In the control, or uncertain, condition, each subject was simply told that she would be able to see the other subject watching her tape, but not her meter reactions. The reactions were considered to be "confidential information."

Making the Video Tape.   The experimenter then proceeded to make a video (TV) tape of samples of the subject's behavior. Actually, although the video camera was ostentatiously adjusted and focused for the event, only an audio tape recording was made. As the camera presumably began to "roll," the subject was asked to describe a moment when she was very proud about something and a moment when she was quite embarrassed. Finally, the subject was asked to read aloud from a classic American novel enough material to insure that each tape would be the same length. When the interview and reading session had lasted for about two and a half minutes, the subject was asked to stop and the camera was "turned off."

Exchange of Attitude Ratings.   As part of the getting acquainted process, the two subjects next filled out and exchanged a 15-item attitude questionnaire. The items were selected from a list of items used by Byrne in many of his similarity-attraction studies. They covered a wide range of content from premarital sex relations to the admission of Red China to the UN. Each item was represented by six statements ranging from extreme pro to extreme con. After the subject completed her questionnaire, the experimenter took it and left the room to complete the exchange. Actually, the experimenter hastily completed a questionnaire with responses that were either very similar or dissimilar to the subject's. Subjects in the similar conditions then received a questionnaire whose ratings were identical on two items, differed from their own by one point on 11 items, and by three points on two. Those in the dissimilar conditions received an exchange questionnaire differing from their own by three points on 13 items and one point on the other two.

After having a chance to examine the exchange questionnaire, the subject was asked to fill out a second, five-item attitude questionnaire, indicating her own attitudes and predicting how the other subject would answer the same items. The purpose of this step was to check on the extent to which the subjects perceived themselves to be generally similar or dissimilar to the accomplice.

Watching the Accomplice Watch Her.   After the subject completed this second questionnaire, the experimenter left announcing that she was going to play the subject's video tape for the other subject and that she would be able to watch the other subject's reactions "live" over her own TV monitor. The subject was actually then exposed to a standard video tape of the accomplice. This tape began with the experimenter attaching GSR electrodes to the accomplice's arm and explaining the machine to her. Depending on the condition to which the subject had been assigned, the video tape either included a view of the summarizing dial or it did not. Having secured the electrodes, the experimenter then asked the accomplice to think of her best friend. If the dial was in view, the needle moved toward the extreme positive side of the dial face. (Movement of the needle during the taping of this standard presentation was remotely controlled by a rheostat.) The accomplice was then asked to think of someone she did not like, and after protesting at first that she could not think of anyone, she apparently did hit upon someone she did not like and the needle began to move toward the negative side of the dial face. In the conditions where the dial was not in view, the experimenter asked the accomplice to think of the same kinds of persons and commented to her on the value of the dial readings. The purpose of these preliminaries was to give the subject confidence that the machine did pick up variations in liking and disliking and to reinforce the cover story about its amazing capacities.

Following this, the accomplice was instructed to concentrate on her monitor where the subject's video tape would shortly appear. The remainder of the tape showed the accomplice staring intently at something across the room while the audio version of the subject's own interview was replayed through a speaker in the subject's room. In conditions where the dial was visible, the indicator needle started at the neutral point and moved either toward the positive or negative side of the dial face as the accomplice continued to "watch" the subject on the monitor. In this way the variable of being liked or disliked was introduced. It is important to note that the accomplice in the liked and disliked conditions initially felt neutral about the subject. The subsequent positive or negative needle excursion must logically reflect her impression of the subject gained from watching her perform on the video tape and must be relatively unaffected by her supposed knowledge of attitude similarity-dissimilarity. This feature separates the present study rather sharply from the experiments of Aronson and Worchel (1966) and of Byrne and Griffitt (1966) described in the introduction.

Reacting to the Accomplice. Returning to the subject's room once again, the experimenter attached electrodes to her arm and proceeded to review with her the capacities and function of the machine. The subject was informed that the accomplice was very accurate in guessing her own meter readings and the experimenter suggested that the subject ought to be able to make quite accurate estimates herself. She was then asked to think about her best friend and about someone she disliked or was mad at. The experimenter apparently recorded the meter readings at this point and told the subject, who could not see the meter, that the machine seemed to be working properly. Once these preliminaries were concluded, the subject was exposed to a standard video tape showing the accomplice being interviewed by the experimenter, describing a prideful and shameful moment, and reading a brief passage from the same book that had been given to the subject. Throughout this observational period, the meter was presumably reflecting the subject's emotional reactions to the accomplice, although the dial face was turned away from her and the meter was actually inoperative.

Measuring Attraction. Immediately after observing the tape of the accomplice, the subject was asked to estimate her average meter reading, being reminded that the scale ran from -3000 to $+3000$. This was to serve as the primary and initial measure of attraction, under the rationale outlined above. The subject then filled out an impression formation questionnaire the major portion of which consisted of 12 15-point trait rating scales, each expressed in antonym form (intelligent—unintelligent, friendly—unfriendly, etc.). For each of these the subject was to circle a number ranging from one extreme (-7) through neutral (0) to the other $(+7)$. The subject then evaluated herself on the same dimensions. Additional questions were included to explore the subject's perceptions of the experiment. The content of the rating dimensions, as well as the additional exploratory questions, are discussed in some detail in the next section.

Results

The first question usually asked when an experimenter turns to his results is whether his intentions in conducting the experiment were effectively carried out. In the case of the present experiment this breaks down into three separate questions. First, were the intended differences in attitude similarity correctly perceived? Second, did the subjects correctly note whether the accomplice's meter showed liking or disliking? And third, did they believe that the meter readings were an accurate reflection of the accomplice's true feelings?

Perceived Similarity. Immediately after exchanging her "survey of attitudes" with the accomplice, each subject was asked to record her own opinions on five additional opinion items and also to predict the most probable response of the accomplice. By summing the resulting subject-accomplice differences across the five items, we could obtain a self-other discrepancy score for each subject. This score should tell us not only whether the rigged attitude similarities and dissimilarities were correctly perceived, but also whether the subjects took this to mean that the similarity-dissimilarity was rather basic, extending beyond the particular fifteen items on the survey. The results show clearly that the subjects in the similar attitude conditions predicted a smaller discrepancy on the five new items than did those in the dissimilar attitude conditions. These results appear in Table 6.1, where it may readily be seen that the intent to manipulate perceived similarity was effectively carried out. It is extremely improbable that the size of the differences observed could have occurred by chance, the probability that differences this great would occur by chance being less than 1 in 1,000 ($p < .001$). A glance at Table 6.1 also makes clear that there were no significant differences in the discrepancy index as a function of being liked. Of course, we would have expected no differences here because the similarity manipulation *and* the measure of its effectiveness occurred before the subject learned that she was liked or disliked.

Table 6.1

Mean Discrepancies Between Own Attitudes and Those Predicted for Accomplice: Experiment I

		Being Liked			
		YES	NO	UNCERTAIN	TOTAL
Attitudes					
	Similar	3.83	3.83	4.33	4.00
	Dissimilar	11.17	9.00	9.83	10.00
	$P_{diff.} <$	.001	.001	.001	.001

Perceptions of Being Liked.   Each subject was asked two questions to determine whether she had correctly perceived the meter fluctuations on the video tape and whether she considered the meter to be an accurate reflection of the accomplice's true feelings about her. When asked, "According to the machine reading, how did the other subject react to you?" subjects in the liked condition responded with a mean score of 12.13 on a 15-point scale; disliked condition subjects averaged 3.17. This difference was, of course, highly significant ($F = 523.37$, $p < .001$); attitude similarity did not affect these perceived liking scores.

When subjects were asked, "Do you personally feel that the machine gave an accurate description of the other subject's feelings toward you?" the average response was 10.5 toward the "very accurate" end of a 15-point scale. An analysis of the condition means did not reveal any significant overall effects of similarity or being liked, but as one might expect, subjects in the similar-disliked condition were the most skeptical. In fact, the mean perceived accuracy score was significantly lower in this condition (8.6) than in the other conditions combined ($F = 4.23$, $p < .05$). We shall return later to the implications of this finding.

Measures of Attraction and Regard

As described in the introductory and procedure sections, the subject could indicate various feelings and reactions toward the accomplice on several response measures that we expected to be generally but imperfectly related to one another. Immediately after observing the video tape of the accomplice, each subject was asked to estimate the average value of the attraction meter attached to her, which allegedly had provided for the experimental record an accurate tracing of her true feelings about the accomplice. Since to our knowledge this is the first time such a measure of attraction has been used, there is no prior evidence to support its validity. One source of internal evidence is the correlation between meter estimates and subsequent ratings in response to the direct question, "How much do you like this person?" These correlations averaged .66 in the first experiment and .81 in the second closely related experiment to be described. These coefficients are large enough to suggest that the subjects treated the meter estimate and personal liking questions as roughly equivalent. (This equivalence may have been artificially increased, of course, because all subjects made their meter estimates first and may have felt committed to these estimates when subsequently confronting the liking question.)

It is common knowledge in social psychology that people tend to attribute positive characteristics to those they like. Nevertheless, as we have already argued, expressed liking and positive attribution are not precisely equivalent measures of one's attraction for another. After all, one can like another person in spite of certain serious shortcomings, and one can dislike a virtuous paragon. In view of our special interest in tapping the quality as well as the intensity of the subject's feeling for the accomplice, we included a number of different attribute rating scales in the booklet of measures to be filled out by the subject. For purposes of scoring and analysis, these scales were combined into two clusters each containing five attributes judged by the investigators to be related. The first cluster we shall call *social attraction*. It includes ratings on 15-point scales defined by the following questions or antonyms: "How much would you enjoy meeting this person socially?" "How interesting do you find this person?" "Where would she be rated between the antonyms Unfriendly—Friendly, Insincere—Sincere, Cold—Warm?" The second cluster we shall call *competence* and includes ratings (again on 15-point scales) of Unintelligent—Intelligent, Not Discerning—Discerning, Insensitive—Sensitive, Not Perceptive—Perceptive, and Maladjusted—Well Adjusted.

Table 6.2

Estimates of Own GSR Attraction Reading: Experiment I

		Being Liked			
		YES	NO	UNCERTAIN	TOTAL
Attitudes					
	Similar	+1396	−642	+1392	+715
	Dissimilar	+1852	−38	+981	+932
	Total	+1624	−340	+1187	

NOTE. The meter dial on which estimates were to be based ran from −3000 to +3000.

The results of each of these three evaluative measures are presented in Tables 6.2, 6.3, and 6.4.[2] Table 6.2 presents the meter estimation data, chosen to reflect global evaluation and to provide the most direct measure for evaluating the main experimental hypothesis. The condition means are clearly ordered in line with prediction: when information about being liked or disliked follows information about similarity or dissimilarity, the dissimilar accomplice is liked more than the similar accomplice. When specific information about being liked

[2] Analysis of variance summaries of the results presented in Tables 6.1 through 6.8 are presented in a "statistical appendix" at the end of this chapter.

is lacking, however, the similar accomplice is liked more than the dissimilar accomplice. This is what is referred to in the jargon of analysis of variance statistics as an *interaction effect* because the contribution of the similarity variable differs as a function of the being liked variable. Unfortunately, the variability of scores within each experimental condition is great and the statistical interaction falls short of the conventionally acceptable .05 significance level ($F = 2.77$, $p = .07$). The effect of being liked is extremely powerful ($F = 19.98$, $p < .001$), dwarfing the effect of attitude similarity. Subsidiary comparisons show that when there is no clear information about being liked, the preference for the similar over the dissimilar accomplice is not significant. This is surprising in view of the clear evidence that the similarity differences were perceived and in view of the strong evidence from Byrne's research relating degree of similarity— even on a few peripheral issues—to magnitude of attraction.

Table 6.3 presents the means for each condition for the social attraction cluster. The items contained in this cluster refer to the approachability of the accomplice, her openness to friendly overtures. We would expect this cluster to measure much the same thing as the meter estimation scores except they should be somewhat more intellectualized—less a matter of "gut" reactions than of how one *should* feel when considering the qualities of another. As Table 6.3 shows, once again there are negligible, nonsignificant effects of attitude similarity ($F < 1.00$), and the similar accomplice is now slightly preferred, on the average, to the dissimilar accomplice. The effect of being liked is again highly significant ($F = 19.39$, $p < .001$). The main difference between the social attraction cluster data and the meter estimation results is that the trend toward the hypothesized finding of greater liking for the dissimilar accomplice completely washes out.

Table 6.3

Social Attraction Cluster Ratings: Experiment I

		Being Liked			
		YES	NO	UNCERTAIN	TOTAL
Attitudes					
	Similar	58.4	32.5	47.3	46.1
	Dissimilar	52.4	32.9	40.4	41.9
	Total	55.4	32.7	43.8	

NOTE. The higher the score, the more favorable the evaluation. Scores could range from a possible minimum of 5 to a maximum of 75.

Data on the competence cluster, the final measure of evaluation in the experiment, appear in Table 6.4. Although the being liked variable is again highly significant ($F = 7.69$, $p < .01$), the effects of the similarity variable are complex and differ from both of the previously presented patterns of results (see Tables 6.2 and 6.3). There is a significant overall interaction between

Table 6.4

Competence Cluster Ratings: Experiment I

		Being Liked			
		YES	NO	UNCERTAIN	TOTAL
Attitudes					
	Similar	60.1	42.6	55.7	53.1
	Dissimilar	54.8	49.7	49.3	51.2
	Total	57.8	46.1	52.5	

NOTE. The higher the score, the more favorable the evaluation. Scores could range from a possible minimum of 5 to a maximum of 75.

similarity and being liked ($F = 3.32$, $p < .05$), but the biggest contribution to the overall interaction occurs in the conditions where information about being liked is conveyed. Here, the means in Table 6.4 reveal that the similar accomplice is seen as more competent than the dissimilar accomplice when she likes the subject, but the dissimilar accomplice is seen as more competent when she *dis*likes the subject. This particular interaction (ignoring the uncertain liking conditions) is significant ($F = 4.91$, $p < .05$). These competence results provide support for the balance hypothesis, which is another way of saying that they support the additive hypothesis in the being liked condition and the violated expectancy hypothesis in the disliked condition.

Discussion of Experiment I

What can we make of these results? The most striking finding, of course, is the great importance of being liked or disliked as a determinant of reciprocated attraction. The effect itself is not surprising, but the results on all three measures of evaluation establish the potency of conveying evidence of being liked, by a meter which is allegedly tuned to another person's basic emotions.

The contributions of attitudinal similarity-dissimilarity to the results are less consistent and more confusing. The first surprise to contend with is the absence of a clear, statistically significant preference for the similar accomplice when no specific information about being liked is conveyed. While the similar-dissimilar difference was consistently in the expected direction, it was never large enough to approach statistical significance. Our failure to obtain this difference raises some serious questions about the importance of attitudinal similarity when additional information about the person is also presented. In Byrne's basic studies, indications of attitudinal similarity-dissimilarity were presented in an informational vacuum—this was the only information available for making a judgment about liking. In other studies in which Byrne and his colleagues attached photographs of the alleged respondent to the contrived questionnaire answers (e.g., Byrne, London, & Reeves, 1968) or added information about the respondent's occupational status (Byrne, Griffitt, & Golightly, 1966), only the extremes of attitude similarity-dissimilarity between subject and other were compared. Similarity was found to be a significant determinant of liking in these "enriched information" experiments, but this is hardly surprising considering the extremes employed.

In the present experimental setting, the subject does receive additional information, even in the uncertain conditions, as she watches the video-taped performance of the accomplice. Perhaps this minimal information about physical appearance, plus gestural cues and a few comments about prideful and embarrassing moments, is enough to push the attitudinal information into the background as a determinant of attraction and positive evaluation. This still does not explain why Byrne and Rhamey (1965) and Byrne and Griffitt (1966) find results supporting the similarity-attraction hypothesis in a face-to-face situation. However, it may be important that similarity-dissimilarity of attitudes was emphasized in these studies since the behavior of the face-to-face confederate featured a recital of his opinions and little else.

Our main *a priori* measure of attraction was the meter estimation score. Here we came very close to confirming the primary hypothesis of the study at the conventionally accepted .05 significance level. Relative to their modest preference for the similar accomplice under the uncertain liking conditions, subjects are basically more attracted to the dissimilar accomplice who clearly likes or dislikes them than to the similar accomplice. When we shift from basic attraction to ratings of competence (intelligence, perceptiveness, etc.), the preference for the dissimilar disliking accomplice is maintained, but the similar liking accomplice is seen as most competent of all. Let us see if we can understand why this might be so, and why the competence ratings give a different pattern than the meter estimation scores.

We assume, first of all, that the meter estimation scores are candid judgments of experienced emotion, unmediated by considerations or calculations about how one *should* feel under the circumstances. There is no reason to dislike someone who is both similar in attitudes and obviously likes you, but this is hardly an exciting development. When you are led to expect a rather negative evaluation, because of information about attitude dissimilarity, and the evaluation is instead very positive, this should generate considerable positive emotion in return. You have been liked for what you are, for some essence that has come across the video tape, and not simply because you share the same attitudes. Similar reasoning may be applied to the cases in which the subject learns that the accomplice dislikes her. The sting of this news should be soothed by the prior expectation that because of clear attitudinal dissimilarity the person is not likely to like the subject. When liking is expected and disliking is received, on the other hand, the impact of this should be rather devastating. This much is merely a restatement of our expectancy violation hypothesis and the reasoning behind it.

When the subject is asked to evaluate the accomplice's intelligence, perceptiveness, discernment, etc., a slightly different set of considerations are involved. Such judgments are bound to be influenced by the subject's basic disposition to like or dislike the accomplice, but there should be a rational component to the judgment as well—a greater concern for consistency than when there is a meter there to "keep you honest" regardless of consistency or logic. If we examine Table 6.4 once again, we see that within both the first and the second column, it is the consistent conditions that give rise to the highest competence ratings. That is, if a person who is similar likes you or who is dissimilar dislikes you, that person is demonstrating her discernment, if nothing else. Of course, it is a better state of affairs overall if she likes you, but you cannot take away from the dissimilar disliker the fact that she is responding consistently and intelligently under the circumstances. Perhaps this is why the balance hypothesis is supported by the competence cluster data.

A comparable pattern may also be observed with the social attraction cluster, although the critical statistical interaction is not significant. This pattern is not too difficult to understand, since the various social attraction ratings should be more affected by emotional considerations than the competence ratings and more affected by rational considerations than the meter estimation scores.

EXPERIMENT II

Although we were encouraged by the results of Experiment I, they obviously could not be considered conclusive. We realized that there were certain accidental factors and errors of procedure that might have reduced the significance of our main hypothesis. We were well aware that the accomplice was an extremely attractive girl, but we had not anticipated that she would be elected Campus Sweetheart in the middle of our experiment, with about a third of the experimental subjects still to be run. Fortunately, very few subjects properly identified her after her election, but the very fact that she was so pretty and so clearly considered attractive by a wide range of fellow students prompted us to speculate on the role of the accomplice's physical appearance in the experiment. Perhaps our results were weak because her physical beauty simply dominated all other considerations, even washing out the attitude similarity effect repeatedly obtained in other experiments. Perhaps those subjects who had psychological reasons for disliking the accomplice inhibited their feelings in deference to her physical attractiveness.

There was also evidence from the first experiment that some subjects escaped the implications of being disliked by a similar person by questioning the accuracy of the machine. Subjects in the similar-dislike condition were significantly more skeptical about the accuracy of the machine than subjects in the remaining conditions. This is psychologically interesting although not terribly surprising: this is the one condition where there not only is a violation of expectancy, but the departure is in an unpleasant direction. If the subject could avoid the implications of being disliked under such circumstances by questioning the machine, this would operate against the confirmation of our main hypothesis. An underlying assumption of that hypothesis is that subjects in the similar-disliked condition would accept this information as painfully valid and then retaliate with strong negative feelings of their own.

A third problem with the first experiment was that inadvertently, the experimenter did not clearly establish for the subject the most likely end points for her own meter readings. Thus it was possible for some subjects to reason that their own meter would never drop much below neutral, whereas others might make quite different assumptions about their own particular negative excursion. This may have contributed in an important way to the sizeable variances noted in all measures.

Method

A second experiment was planned to see if the results of the first experiment could be strengthened by attention to these difficulties. It was essentially a replication of the first experiment with three major changes:

1. A different accomplice made a new set of video tapes. She was by no means an unattractive person, but she was not the striking beauty our first accomplice was. Because she wore glasses, no makeup, and a very plain blouse, her appearance on the tape was of a rather ordinary and physically undistinguished undergraduate. We also slightly altered her script to make her seem like a less exciting, less popular person. For example, whereas the first accomplice described an embarrassing moment in which she met a boy at the show after telling him she had to baby sit and could not go out with him that night, the second accomplice described an episode in which she was talking about a girl she did not like and then noticed that the girl's roommate was overhearing her remarks.

2. In an effort to increase the perceived validity of the emotional reaction machine, and to motivate the subject to be even more candid in reporting her affective response, the experimenter placed greater emphasis on the importance of the "breakthrough" that led to the machine: "The reason psychologists are so excited about this machine right now is that they have been studying emotions for a long time, but up until now all they could really do was to ask people how they felt. And, human beings have an unfortunate habit of trying to be reasonable or logical. Sometimes, even if people are really trying to be honest, if they can't think of a single reason *why* they should dislike someone, they probably will not *say* they dislike him. And this machine just cuts through all that and gets a really basic emotional feeling. As a result you get readings that are very surprising sometimes, but very accurate." When the subject was later asked to estimate her own meter reading, the experimenter added (only in the second experiment), "It's my pet hypothesis in this study that people are perfectly capable of [guessing their own emotional reaction]. . . . People may not want to tell you their emotions, but usually they know them. So please be as accurate as possible when you guess."

3. The final change was that each subject was given the same clear information about the meter readings during the validation period—when she was thinking of her best friend and then of someone she did not like. She was told

that the meter reached a maximum of +2500 when she was thinking of her best friend and dropped down to a minimum of −2000 when she thought about a person she did not like.

Subjects

Female subjects were recruited later in the same semester in which the first experiment was run, and they participated to fulfill the same course requirement. A total of 74 subjects were run, but 5 of these were dropped from the sample because they questioned whether another naive subject was actually present in the next room. An additional subject was the victim of an experimental error: the bogus attitude questionnaire was incorrectly doctored and conformed neither to the similar nor to the dissimilar pattern. The remaining 68 students were distributed so that there were 12 subjects in each of the four conditions in which information about being liked or disliked was provided and 10 subjects in each of the two uncertain conditions.

Results

The same measures used in the first experiment were examined to evaluate the success of our attempt to vary perceived similarity of attitude, belief in the accuracy of the machine readings, and the perception of being liked or disliked. In addition, the two experiments could be compared with respect to the perceived attractiveness of the accomplice.

Perceived Similarity. Averages of the discrepancy between the subject's own recorded opinions and those estimated for the accomplice appear in Table 6.5. These values can be compared directly with those in Table 6.1. They show, once again, that the intended differences in perceived attitude similarity were clearly picked up by the subjects. Not only are the discrepancy scores lower in the similar than in the dissimilar conditions ($F = 52.03$, $p < .001$), but there are no unexpected variations across the various conditions of being liked by the accomplice.

Table 6.5

Mean Discrepancies Between Own Attitudes and Those Predicted for Accomplice: Experiment II

		Being Liked			
		YES	NO	UNCERTAIN	TOTAL
Attitudes					
	Similar	3.92	3.92	5.40	4.11
	Dissimilar	11.25	9.67	9.10	9.50
	$P_{diff.} <$	.001	.001	.001	.001

Perceptions of Being Liked.   The average subject correctly perceived that she was liked by the accomplice when the meter reading portrayed on the video tape was positive and disliked when the reading was negative. Subjects in the liked condition responded with a mean score of 11.13 on a 15-point scale, about a point below the value reported for Experiment I, and subjects in the disliked condition averaged 3.89 as compared with the mean of 3.17 noted in Experiment I. The difference between liked and disliked conditions was highly significant ($F = 45.23$, $p < .001$). The differences between respective conditions in the two experiments did not approach statistical significance.

Subjects also attributed a high level of accuracy to the machine, with condition means ranging from 10.91 to 11.83 on a 15-point scale. The differences between conditions were well within the limits of chance variations and, in contrast with the first experiment, there was no special skepticism concerning the meter in the similar-disliked condition. In fact, the average subject attributed slightly greater accuracy in this condition than in the other conditions. Since there were no overall differences in judged accuracy between the two experiments, it is not clear whether the observed difference in this particular condition stems from our efforts to place greater stress on the validity of the machine in the second experiment, or reflects some other more subtle difference between the two experiments. We shall return to this issue in a later discussion where the two experiments will be directly compared.

Differences in Judged "Attractiveness": I versus II.   A deliberate attempt was made to make the accomplice in the second experiment less attractive than our beauty queen accomplice in the first experiment. Our attempt to reduce the perceived attractiveness of the accomplice was quite successful. Subjects in both experiments were asked to rate the other person on a 15-point scale ranging from unattractive to attractive. There was hardly any overlap between the rating distributions of the two experiments. The first accomplice received an average attractiveness score of 12.90, the second accomplice received a score of 8.07. In the eyes of our subjects, then, the first accomplice was judged to be extremely attractive and the second was judged to be slightly more attractive than average. This overall difference in attractiveness was, of course, highly significant ($F = 125.80$, $p < .001$).

Measures of Attraction and Regard

As in the first experiment, scores were derived from each subject on each of three measures of evaluation: a meter estimation score, reflecting the subject's global emotional reaction to the accomplice; ratings combined into a social attraction cluster; and ratings combined into a competence cluster. The results of each of these measures are presented in Tables 6.6, 6.7, and 6.8. These may be compared directly with Tables 6.2, 6.3, and 6.4 respectively.

It is certainly no surprise that the second accomplice is less positively evaluated than the first in most conditions and on most measures of attraction. This greater preference for the first accomplice reflects our intent to make the second appear somewhat less attractive. What is of much greater interest, and of greater surprise value, is that the pattern of results is quite different from the pattern of the first experiment. There it will be recalled the dissimilar other was better liked than the similar other on the basic meter estimation measure; in the second experiment, the similar other was liked better regardless of variations in infor-

Table 6.6

Estimates of Own GSR Attraction Reading: Experiment II

		Being Liked			
		YES	NO	UNCERTAIN	TOTAL
Attitudes					
	Similar	+821	−383	+740	+393
	Dissimilar	+810	−625	+300	+162
	Total	+816	−504	+520	

NOTE. The meter dial on which estimates were to be based ran from −3000 to +3000.

Table 6.7

Social Attraction Cluster Ratings: Experiment II

		Being Liked			
		YES	NO	UNCERTAIN	TOTAL
Attitudes					
	Similar	51.50	39.83	46.90	46.03
	Dissimilar	45.00	30.92	41.90	39.12
	Total	48.25	35.38	44.40	

NOTE. The higher the score, the more favorable the evaluation. Scores could range from a possible minimum of 5 to a maximum of 75.

Table 6.8

Competence Cluster Ratings: Experiment II

		Being Liked			
		YES	NO	UNCERTAIN	TOTAL
Attitudes					
	Similar	51.00	48.33	52.00	50.44
	Dissimilar	47.75	40.92	45.60	44.76
	Total	49.88	44.63	48.80	

NOTE. The higher the score, the more favorable the evaluation. Scores could range from a possible minimum of 5 to a maximum of 75.

mation about being liked. On this measure (See Table 6.6) the effect of liking is again highly significant ($F = 7.01$, $p < .01$) and much larger than the overall effect of attitude similarity ($F < 1.00$). However, on the social attraction cluster (Table 6.7), the effects of being liked and of attitude similarity are both statistically significant. When the other person's meter shows liking for the subject, the accomplice is judged more socially attractive than when the meter reads "dislike," with the uncertain (no-information) condition falling in the middle ($F = 8.88$, $p < .001$). Regardless of condition, the similar other is judged to be more socially attractive than the dissimilar other ($F = 7.01$, $p < .01$).

Finally, turning to the competence cluster, the being liked variable is no longer significant ($F = 1.60$) but the attitudinal similarity variable is ($F = 5.91$, $p < .05$). Thus, as we shift from the most direct measure of emotional liking (the meter reading) through a mixture of liking and regard (social attraction cluster) to the most direct measure of regard or respect (competence cluster), the effects of being liked become less prominent and the effects of attitude similarity grow in relative importance. We shall try to account for this shift in emphasis across the different measures in the forthcoming discussion of the two experiments. In spite of the shift, the basic pattern of results is actually quite comparable across the three measures. In each case, at least, the effects of attitude similarity and being liked appear to be additive; that is, it is as if the accomplice received a certain amount of credit for liking the subject. The size of the credits involved appears to depend on the particular measure of attraction or regard being examined. That the two variables perform in an additive way is confirmed by the fact that on each measure the similar-liking accomplice is viewed most positively (with one very slight reversal involving the uncertain condition) and the dissimilar-disliking accomplice is viewed least positively. This finding is not without precedent since it fits with Byrne's additive theory and the data from the Byrne and Griffitt (1966) experiment. It does conflict, however, with our initial hypothesis and runs counter to the results of the first experiment. It is incumbent on us to try to discover why the second experiment gives so much more support than the first to the additive hypothesis.

DISCUSSION OF BOTH EXPERIMENTS

In our attempt to replicate and strengthen the findings of Experiment I, we succeeded in producing an entirely new pattern of results. And this was not because we failed to achieve our concrete objectives of making the accomplice less attractive and the meter validity more salient. We were clearly successful in achieving the first of these objectives and the evidence is consistent with success on the second. What could have happened to change the results in this particular manner?

The major procedural difference, of course, is that a different and less attractive person was employed as the accomplice. By choosing a different person, getting her to dress very plainly, and having her give bland answers to the interviewer's questions, we perhaps went too far in establishing a contrast with the beauty queen who served as our first accomplice. Certainly the subjects in the second experiment gave her mediocre attractiveness ratings. What might the effects have been of our overshooting the mark? One effect that we failed to take sufficiently into account in planning Experiment II, stems from the reasonable assumption that as the physical attractiveness of the accomplice decreased in the eyes of the subjects, the importance attached to her liking for the subjects also declined. One can imagine a level of unattractiveness that would produce great indifference from a coed subject population exposed to indications of liking or disliking. We obviously did not produce this kind of indifference by our shift in accomplice, but what might the effects of a more modest difference in attractiveness be?

Let us start the discussion by making the assumption that it is more gratifying to be liked by a very attractive than by a moderately attractive person and also more devastating to be disliked by her. In short, information about the more attractive accomplice's feelings has considerably more impact. Sigall and Aronson (1969) have argued that pleasing an attractive evaluator should be most satisfying, while failure to please that person should be more disturbing. They present evidence to show that male subjects like an attractive girl who gives them a positive evaluation better than an unattractive positive evaluator. However, there is a reversal when the evaluation received is a negative one; under these circumstances the unattractive evaluator is liked slightly more than the attractive evaluator.

Table 6.9

Evaluation of the SP by Conditions and by Experiments (Meter Estimation, Social Attraction, and Competence)

		METER ESTIMATION		SOCIAL ATTRACTION		COMPETENCE	
		I	II	I	II	I	II
Similar Attitudes							
	Liked	+1396	+821	58.4	51.50	60.1	51.00
	Disliked	−642	+383	32.5	39.83	42.6	48.3
	Diff.	2038	1204	25.9	11.67	17.5	2.7
	$P_{diff.}$	n.s.		<.05		<.01	
Dissimilar Attitudes							
	Liked	+1852	+810	52.4	45.00	54.8	47.8
	Disliked	−38	−625	32.9	30.92	49.7	40.9
	Diff.	1890	1435	19.5	14.08	5.1	6.9
	$P_{diff.}$	n.s.		n.s.		n.s.	

These results support the assumption that attractive females carry greater impact in a mixed sex situation. Is there any evidence for the same kind of effect in the present experiments where the sex of the subject and the evaluator is the same? Table 6.9 presents attraction data for each measure selected from the liked and disliked conditions of both experiments. The values of interest are the difference scores between the degree of attraction for the liking accomplice and the degree of distaste for the disliking accomplice. If we compare these differences in Experiments I and II, we find that in five out of six comparisons there was a greater difference score in the first experiment than in the second experiment. Two of these difference-between-differences comparisons were significant. Both of these were in conditions where the accomplice and the subject had similar attitudes. In addition, in the similar attitudes conditions, the attractive person was always liked or respected *less* than the less attractive person when she disliked the subject. This is the intriguing, less obvious part of the Sigall and Aronson hypothesis, but the tendency only shows itself when the accomplice's attitudes are similar. In the dissimilar conditions the attractive accomplice is always appreciated *more* than the less attractive one. Thus we may say that there is good evidence for the greater impact of evaluation by an attractive person, and the evidence is especially strong when the person has similar attitudes.

And how might this greater impact in the experiment with the more attractive accomplice account for the major differences in the results of the two experiments? Let us make one more reasonable assumption: The more attractive an evaluator is, the more the subject will attempt to reduce the sting of a negative evaluation by seizing upon some feature of the situation that might justify such an evaluation. The subject in Experiment I who finds that a dissimilar other dislikes her, may comfort herself with the explanation that "it is not surprising when people with such different opinions do not like each other." In the condition in which the subject is disliked by a similar other, we would expect more signs of stress and discomfort. The results in this condition are unique in a number of respects. First, we have noted (Tables 6.2, 6.3, and 6.4) that subjects in this condition are most negative toward the accomplice regardless of the measure of evaluation. Second, we have also noted that subjects in this condition are particularly skeptical about the validity of the meter. This is exactly what we would expect if they were searching around for some way to discount the implications of being unexpectedly disliked. Finally, on an index of self-evaluation derived from summing the subjects' self-ratings on 12 personal characteristics, subjects in the similar-disliked condition tend to rate themselves more harshly than subjects in any other condition. It would appear that the subject is particularly devastated by the information that she is disliked not for her disagreeable attitudes, but for some inner quality that shines through her performance. She responds to this devastation either by doubting the validity of the information, by expressing reciprocated hostility, or some combination of both.

In Experiment II, our last assumption carries the further implication that there should have been less pressure on the subjects to wiggle away from the implications of being disliked. This may help us to understand why the results in the second experiment fall into an "additive" pattern. If the subjects in Experiment II did not care terribly much whether they were liked or disliked by the accomplice, we would expect them to be less emotionally involved and therefore more rational and objective in processing information about her and her reactions. The final step in the argument is to suggest that these detached subjects were less concerned with protecting their own self-esteem than with drawing a *reasonable* conclusion from the social information at hand. Whereas the first experiment involved the subject in attempts to protect her self-esteem, which affected her perceptions and evaluations, the second experiment put the subject more into an orientation of wondering how she should rate the other person to arrive at the most sensible response. What is more seemingly reasonable than to make a kind of algebraic summation of similarity and liking information? However much weight is differentially assigned to the two (within broad limits), a dissimilar disliking person would be liked least and a similar liking person would be liked most. This is precisely the pattern of observed results.

We should like to advance the proposition, then, that the perceptual-evaluative reaction to variations in accomplice similarity and liking depends on the importance for self-esteem of being liked. To be liked or disliked by a rather bland and unattractive person is not a matter of great moment. Under such circumstances our responses tend to reflect a rational weighing of the information given. To be liked or disliked by a very attractive person, on the other hand, involves and has consequences for the self. Here we tend to shape our responses in line with certain self-protective strategies. Especially included is a tendency to dislike and to attribute incompetence to a physically attractive accomplice who shares our attitudes and yet dislikes us. In order to maintain our self-esteem, we have to believe that such a person is something of an insensitive fool.

SUMMARY AND CONCLUSIONS: A POST MORTEM

The preceding two experiments hardly conform to the neat examples of laboratory experimentation offered in traditional psychology textbooks. The passage from hypothesis to procedure to results to interpretation has been tortuous and further complicated by the fact that our second experiment failed to replicate the first. We developed a hypothesis that seemed to point to a phenomenon that others have overlooked in predicting the effects of similarity on attraction. Whereas a number of psychologists have assumed, and demonstrated, that attitude similarity elicits attraction, it occurred to us that similarity could in some circumstances establish expectations that would lead to *less* attraction than dissimilarity. Specifically, the average subject should expect to be liked by a similar other and disliked by a dissimilar other. If these expectations were confirmed, we would not expect the subject to be particularly elated or distressed. To be liked or disliked when you do not expect it, however, should arouse stronger positive and negative feelings. This, essentially, was our (preferred) hypothesis of violated expectations.

We chose to support this hypothesis over two competing ones. The first of these we called the balance hypothesis. From the basic assumption that consistency or the fulfillment of expectation is itself rewarding, we might have predicted that the similar liking and the dissimilar disliking accomplices would have been liked more than accomplices in the remaining conditions. This prediction coincides with ours for the dissimilar case but is the reverse of our own prediction for the similar case. As a second alternative, we might have expected attitude similarity and liking to summate algebraically: to be liked by a similar person is the most gratifying, but to be disliked by a dissimilar person should incur the greatest reciprocal dislike. The former prediction coincides with the balance hypothesis but not our own; the latter prediction is the converse of both the balance hypothesis and our own.

It is generally considered an advantage when investigators can design an experiment in such a way that competing theoretical positions would make clearly different predictions. Even when one is successful in developing such a design, however, there is always the possibility that two or more relevant hypotheses are partially valid or that different theoretical processes underlie the responses of different subjects. Negative or nonsignificant results can thus reflect conflicting psychological pressures fighting each other to a standstill so that the condition means do not differ greatly from each other and there is extreme variability within conditions. Unfortunately, when negative or inconclusive results are obtained it is never easy to tell whether nothing is going on or whether too many things are going on at once.

In these experiments there was some support for each of the alternative hypotheses, depending on the measure of evaluation being attended to and the physical characteristics of the accomplice. The critical results are summarized in Figure 6.1 where the average scores for the being liked conditions are graphed for the most emotionally colored and the most rationally colored measure of attraction. This is merely a different way of presenting some of the data already presented in the tables, so that the two experiments and the different measures can be more readily compared. The expectancy violation hypothesis, predicting a preference for the dissimilar accomplice, was supported in Experiment I with the meter estimation measure. The balance hypothesis, predicting a preference for accomplices whose liking was consistent with their attitudinal similarity, was supported in Experiment I on the competence ratings. The additive hypothesis, predicting relative preference for the similar accomplice, was generally supported in the rating data for Experiment II.

Naturally, we did not wish or expect to obtain such complicated results. It is always easier to deal with data that either clearly confirm or clearly refute a theoretically derived hypothesis. We have tried to understand these complicated findings by making two basic assumptions: (a) ratings of competence are more colored by objective, rational considerations, than are estimates of one's true emotional reaction; and (b) one is likely to give more rational, objectively justifiable responses to evaluations from a moderately attractive person than to evaluations from an extremely attractive person. Armed with these assumptions,

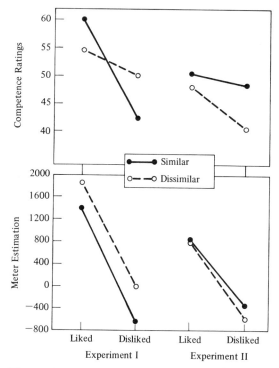

Figure 6.1
Effects of similarity and being liked on estimation of GSR meter readings and on competence ratings (uncertain conditions omitted).

we have tried to show that the additive hypothesis applies when there is minimal involvement, that the balance hypothesis applies when involvement is high but the measure refers to verifiable attributes in the person, and that the expectancy violation hypothesis holds under high involvement with a measure that is highly sensitive to the subject's emotional reactions.

We have been able to assemble some circumstantial evidence that is consistent with these speculations, but our explanation in terms of differential involvement and measurement sensitivity is obviously after the fact. However, there is no reason why the experimental design we have described could not be used to test the new and more complicated formulation in a precise way. To do so would require more careful manipulation of the involvement variable. This could be achieved by using the same accomplice in both versions of the experiment but varying her attractiveness by changes in her grooming (Sigall & Aronson, 1969) or perhaps her status and popularity on campus. It would also be interesting to find some other way of increasing and reducing the importance of being liked and to see whether the present patterns of results could be reproduced with this different way of manipulating involvement.

While the present results are complex and inconclusive, they suggest some important qualifications in appraising Byrne's position. First of all, we were unable to obtain a straight similarity-leads-to-attraction effect in either experiment in the absence of determinate information about being liked. On all three measures in each experiment the similar other was evaluated more positively than the dissimilar other in the uncertain conditions, where the subject did not know how one other "subject" evaluated her, but none of these differences ever came very close to statistical significance. This was a surprise to us because Byrne and his colleagues have shown again and again that even small variations in attitude similarity—much smaller than those introduced in the present experiment—are related to return ratings of attraction.

Byrne's position does receive support when all the similar and dissimilar conditions in Experiment II are compared. The additive model is obviously applicable under some conditions and with certain measures of attraction. However, our results do not confirm Byrne's proposition that liking is just another, if more powerful, attitude. The results of our first experiment show that attitude similarity and liking information can combine in rather paradoxical ways when the subject is highly involved and concerned with protecting his self-esteem.

At this point in the accumulation of research findings on the determinants of interpersonal attraction, it would seem premature to conclude that paper and pencil responses to paper and pencil similarities necessarily say something clearly and precisely about the role of similarity in everyday impression formation. The preceding experiments seem to indicate that, in a situation where information about liking is reliably conveyed, attitude similarity leads to attraction to the extent that the subject is uninvolved in the evaluation he receives and to the extent that the attraction measure is sensitive to rational rather than emotional considerations. People may feel that they *should* like others who share their attitudes, but the present experiments suggest that when the going gets rough and implications for self-esteem are heightened, it is easier to like the dissimilar person who dislikes us than the similar person. It remains to be seen whether other and better investigations along these lines bear this out.

REFERENCES

ARONSON, E., & LINDER, D. E. Gain and loss of esteem as determinants of interpersonal attractiveness. *Journal of Experimental Social Psychology,* 1965, **1,** 156–172.

ARONSON, E., & WORCHEL, P. Similarity versus liking as determinants of interpersonal attractiveness. *Psychonomic Science,* 1966, **5,** 157–158.

BERSCHEID, E., & WALSTER, E. *Interpersonal attraction.* Reading, Mass.: Addison-Wesley, 1969.

BRAMEL, D. Interpersonal attraction, hostility, and perception. In J. Mills (Ed.), *Experimental social psychology*. Toronto: Macmillan, 1969. Pp. 1–120.

BYRNE, D. Attitudes and attraction. In L. Berkowitz (Ed.), *Advances in experimental social psychology*. Vol. IV. New York: Academic Press, 1969. Pp. 35–89.

BYRNE, D., & CLORE, G. L., JR. Predicting interpersonal attraction toward strangers presented in three different stimulus modes. *Psychonomic Science*, 1966, **4**, 239–240.

BYRNE, D., & GRIFFITT, W. Similarity versus liking: A clarification. *Psychonomic Science*, 1966, **6**, 295–296.

BYRNE, D., GRIFFITT, W., & GOLIGHTLY, C. Prestige as a factor in determining the effect of attitude similarity-dissimilarity on attraction. *Journal of Personality*, 1966, **34**, 434–444.

BYRNE, D., LONDON, O., & REEVES, K. The effects of physical attractiveness, sex, and attitude similarity on interpersonal attraction. *Journal of Personality*, 1968, **36**, 259–271.

BYRNE, D., & RHAMEY, R. Magnitude of positive and negative reinforcements as a determinant of attraction. *Journal of Personality and Social Psychology*, 1965, **2**, 884–889.

DEUTSCH, M., & SOLOMON, L. Reactions to evaluations by others as influenced by self evaluations. *Sociometry*, 1959, **22**, 93–112.

GORDON, B. F. Influence and social comparison as motives for affiliation. *Journal of Experimental Social Psychology*, 1966, Supplement 1, 55–65.

HEIDER, F. *The psychology of interpersonal relations*. New York: Wiley, 1958.

JONES, E. E. *Ingratiation*. New York: Appleton, 1964.

JONES, E. E., & GERARD, H. B. *Foundations of social psychology*. New York: Wiley, 1967.

KERCKHOFF, A., & DAVIS, K. E. Value consensus and need complementarity in mate selection. *American Sociological Review*, 1962, **27**, 295–303.

LANDY, D., & ARONSON, E. Liking for an evaluator as a function of his discernment. *Journal of Personality and Social Psychology*, 1968, **9**, 133–142.

McWHIRTER, R. M., & JECKER, J. D. Attitude similarity and inferred attraction. *Psychonomic Science*, 1967, **7**, 225–226.

NEWCOMB, T. M. Autistic hostility and social reality. *Human Relations*, 1947, **1**, 69–86.

OSGOOD, C. E., SUCI, G. J., & TANNENBAUM, P. H. *The measurement of meaning*. Urbana, Ill.: University of Illinois Press, 1957.

SCHWARTZ, M. S. Effectance motivation and interpersonal attraction: Individual differences and personality correlates. Unpublished doctoral dissertation, University of Texas, 1966.

SIGALL, H., & ARONSON, E. Liking for an evaluator as a function of her physical attractiveness and nature of the evaluations. *Journal of Experimental Social Psychology*, 1969, **5**, 93–100.

WALSTER, E. The effect of self-esteem on romantic liking. *Journal of Experimental Social Psychology*, 1965, **1**, 184–197.

WALSTER, E., & WALSTER, B. Effect of expecting to be liked on choice of associates. *Journal of Abnormal and Social Psychology*, 1963, **67**, 402–404.

WINCH, R. F. *Mate selection: A study of complementary needs*. New York: Harper & Row, 1958.

STATISTICAL APPENDIX

The following statistical tables are included as an appendix for readers who wish a more detailed quantitative analysis of the data presented in Tables 6.1 through 6.8. Table A statistically summarizes data presented in Tables 6.1 and 6.5 of the text; Table B summarizes data in Tables 6.2, 6.3 and 6.4; and Table C summarizes data in Tables 6.5, 6.7, and 6.8.

Table A

Analysis of Variance Summary in Experiments I and II: Predicted Attitude Discrepancy Scores

Source	d.f.	Experiment I		Experiment II	
		MS	F	MS^a	F
Being Liked (A)	2	7.00	1.12	.32	.35
Similarity (B)	1	648.00	104.01*	46.93	52.09*
A $\times$ B	2	8.50	1.36	1.66	1.84
Error	$\begin{cases} 66(I) \\ 62(II) \end{cases}$	6.23		.90	

^{a} Because of unequal cell frequencies, comparisons were based on means rather than totals, with appropriate adjustments of the error term. Therefore, the mean square values are not comparable with those listed under Experiment I but the F-ratios should be.

* P < .001

Table B

Analysis of Variance Summaries in Experiment I: Meter Estimates, Social Attraction, Competence

Source	d.f.	Meter Estimate		Social Attraction		Competence	
		MS	F	MS	F	MS	F
Being Liked (A)	2	2547.0	19.98***	3095.0	19.39***	824.5	7.69**
Similarity (B)	1	84.0	.66	308.0	1.93	58.0	.54
A $\times$ B	2	180.0	1.42	89.5	.56	356.0	3.32*
Error	66	127.05		159.65		107.21	
$A^a \times$ B	2	351.56	2.77				
$A^b \times$ B	1					526.69	4.91*

* p < .05
** p < .01
*** p < .001

^{a} This orthogonal comparison tests the hypothesis that the preference for a dissimilar person under "liked" and "disliked" conditions shifts to a preference for a similar person under the "uncertain" condition.

^{b} This comparison ignores the "uncertain" condition.

Table C

**Analysis of Variance Summaries in Experiment II:
Meter Estimates, Social Attraction, Competence**

Source	d.f.	*Meter Estimate* MS	F	*Social Attraction* MS	F	*Competence* MS	F
Being Liked (A)	2	97.0	7.01**	87.5	8.88***	13.0	1.60
Similarity (B)	1	9.0	.65	69.0	7.01**	48.0	5.91*
A × B	2	4.0	.29	4.0	.41	3.0	.37
Error	62	13.83		9.85		8.12	

 * p < .05
 ** p < .01
 *** p < .001

section three

GROUP INFLUENCE UPON INDIVIDUAL BEHAVIOR

In this section, Cottrell examines the effects that the mere presence of others can have upon an individual's behavior and Gerard and Conolley consider the impact of others' responses in producing conformity behavior, which they assert represents one example of a general process whereby variations in information concerning others' behaviors produce systematic effects upon one's own behavior. Thus, the present section is principally concerned with the effects upon a subject's behavior of the presence of others and of variations in other's behaviors. It does not consider behavioral reciprocity, exchange, or interaction between two or more actors, which is the focus of Section IV. Both theory and research in this section follow the standard S-R or S-O-R paradigm found so frequently in psychology. Namely, one varies some stimulus and observes resultant variations in response (S-R), or one varies some stimulus, classifies respondents in terms of some characteristic or predisposition, and observes behavior as a function of both stimulus and organismic variables (S-O-R).

Cottrell begins his chapter on social facilitation with a question: "What is the effect of the mere presence of other individuals upon the performance of the single individual?" He goes on to rationalize the importance of the question by observing that: "Understanding the effects of the mere presence of others upon individual behavior is of fundamental importance to social psychology because this rudimentary social arrangement is included in almost all social relationships." One might add that this is also the potentially simplest social relationship to deal with conceptually and methodologically, and hence a rather natural beginning point for those interested in studying social influence and social interaction.

Cottrell, in his very intensive analysis, reviews a number of the principal studies in the area of social facilitation, and carefully outlines Zajonc's conceptual attempt to integrate a variety of findings wherein the latter utilizes some of the theoretical notions outlined in Hull-Spence learning theory. Cottrell then suggests some revisions of this conceptual system that make it more consistent with a number of more recent observations. Chapter 7 provides the reader with an excellent opportunity to follow the interaction between theory and data. The author permits the reader to witness the ongoing process whereby a given conceptual system leads to observations, some of which are inconsistent with the model's predictions, and then the model is revised for reasons of consistency and parsimony. And then the conceptual revision is again subjected to empirical test, and the process reiterates itself.

Cottrell's chapter is also instructive in a second important way. In considering the process of social facilitation, he provides an extensive review of empirical studies that have employed subject populations ranging from cockroaches to chickens to university sophomores. And in doing so, he clearly demonstrates the relevance of using various animal species for investigating theoretical statements concerning basic forms of social behavior and organization. The reader who is interested in a more extensive introduction to experimental studies of animal social behavior may want to consult books edited by Etkin (1964) or Zajonc (1969).

Chapter 8 by Gerard and Conolley also contains a message that has validity beyond a mere consideration of the topic of conformity. Namely, they observe that many areas in social psychology have been defined in terms of particular forms of social responding when a more fruitful approach, both conceptually and methodologically, would be to examine the common processes that underlie a variety of forms of behavior. Thus, they assert that conformity should be viewed as only one response classification of a more general theory concerning the effects of human information seeking in situations where the subject references and evaluates his own behavior against the behavior of others. McGuire in an earlier chapter in this book makes a somewhat similar observation when he characterizes early research on attitudes as an attempt to catalogue and find correlates of various beliefs, rather than to define and observe the general processes that underlie the development and change of attitudes.

Given this process orientation, Gerard and Conolley go on to report a series of carefully controlled investigations of conformity behavior. The latter are concerned with the effects that varying the number of persons who provide consistently discrepant information about a stimulus have upon a subject's own view of and behavior towards that particular event. The findings are inconsistent with prior major studies in this area, but we will not reveal the plot here.

Again the reader should remember that the two chapters in this section are only examples of conceptual and experimental paradigms that have been employed to investigate the effects that others, serving as social stimuli, have upon an individual's behavior. One could, for instance, also include here examples from the various paradigms that have been employed to investigate social imitation wherein the behavior of one or more persons serves as a model for another. The early work by Miller and Dollard (1941) on social learning and imitation, the studies by Bandura and others (1961, 1963a, 1963b) on the imitation of aggressive behavior, and the research by Baer and others (1964, 1967) on the use of operant conditioning methods for producing modeling behavior could all serve to represent other aspects of this important problem area.

REFERENCES

BAER, D., PETERSON, R., & SHERMAN, J. The development of imitation by reinforcing behavioral similarity to a model. *Journal of Experimental Analysis of Behavior,* 1961, **10,** 405–416.

BAER, D., & SHERMAN, J. Reinforcement control of generalized imitation in young children. *Journal of Experimental Child Psychology,* 1964, **1,** 37–49.

BANDURA, A., ROSS, D., & ROSS, S. Transmission of aggression through imitation of aggressive models. *Journal of Abnormal and Social Psychology,* 1961, **63,** 515–582.

BANDURA, A., ROSS, D., & ROSS, S. Imitation of film-mediated aggressive models. *Journal of Abnormal and Social Psychology,* 1963, **66,** 3–11. (a)

BANDURA, A., ROSS, D., & ROSS, S. Vicarious reinforcement and imitative learning. *Journal of Abnormal and Social Psychology,* 1963, **67,** 601–607. (b)

ETKIN, W. (Ed.) *Social behavior and organization among vertebrates.* Chicago: University of Chicago Press, 1964.

MILLER, N., & DOLLARD, J. *Social learning and imitation.* New Haven, Conn.: Yale University Press, 1941.

ZAJONC, R. (Ed.) *Animal social psychology: A reader of experimental studies.* New York: Wiley, 1969.

7

SOCIAL FACILITATION[1]

Nickolas B. Cottrell[2]

This chapter seeks to answer the question: "What is the effect of the mere presence of other individuals upon the *performance* of the single individual?" Understanding the effects of the mere presence of others upon individual behavior is of fundamental importance to social psychology because this rudimentary social arrangement is included in almost all social relationships. If we can specify the effects produced by the mere presence of others, then we have taken one step fundamental to understanding the multitude of variables that determine the performance of both human and infrahuman individuals in a variety of social settings.

Psychologists confronted the question of the effects of the mere presence of others quite early (e.g., Triplett, 1897). Educators who were concerned with comparing the efficiency of work done in class with homework also showed an early interest in this question (e.g., Burnham, 1905, 1910). Thus, there is a large literature of experimental research on the effects of the presence of others upon individual performance. This research was carried out in two experimental paradigms: the audience paradigm and the coaction paradigm. In the *audience paradigm* the investigator manipulates the presence of passive spectators as an independent variable. In the *coaction paradigm* the independent variable is the presence of others who work simultaneously and independently on the same task on which the subject is working. In both paradigms the dependent variable is the task performance of individuals.

The audience and coaction experiments used a wide variety of tasks and were conducted with subjects of several different species. Interestingly, the results of these studies point to two quite different conclusions. Some studies showed the *social facilitation of individual performance*—individuals with others present performed better than individuals working alone. Other studies, however, showed *performance decrements from audience and coaction*—

[1] Preparation of this chapter was supported in part by National Science Foundation Grant GS-1956.

[2] A number of individuals made extensive comments on drafts of this chapter, and, although they cannot be held accountable for the final product, I am especially grateful for the help of Robert Zajonc and my wife, Elinore Cottrell.

individuals performed better alone than when others were present. Until quite recently psychologists could add nothing to the tentative conclusions offered by the educational psychologist Burnham 60 years ago. In reviewing the results of contemporary research on the effects of audience and coaction he concluded: ". . . The question is relative to the kind of work done. . . . For some kinds of work the stimulus of the social group is needed. For some kinds of work . . . the environment of solitude is better [Burnham, 1910, p. 765]."

Recently Zajonc (1965, 1966) has offered a hypothesis that integrates these divergent results. Much of this chapter is concerned with presenting Zajonc's hypothesis and discussing the subsequent experiments that have tested this hypothesis. We shall begin by examining some studies that showed the social facilitation of individual performance. Then we shall turn to some studies in which audience or coaction produced a decrement in individual performance.

SOCIAL FACILITATION OF INDIVIDUAL PERFORMANCE

Meumann (1904) made one of the earliest reports of audience effects upon individual performance. He conducted extensive studies of muscular effort and fatigue using a finger ergograph. In this apparatus the subject's arm is strapped to the table and a weight is suspended from his finger. Upon signal, the subject must pull the weight as far and as rapidly as he can. A record is kept of the distance the weight travels each trial. On this simple task subjects very quickly reach a stable asymptotic performance level. Meumann found that when he entered the laboratory unexpectedly while a subject was working, performance shot far above asymptotic level. In later experiments he confirmed what was at first an accidental observation: The simple presence of a passive spectator boosts ergographic work beyond asymptotic level.

Travis (1925) studied the effect of an audience upon the performance of college students on the pursuit rotor. In this task the subject had to keep a flexible pointer on a circular target located on a disc which revolved at 60 revolutions per minute (rpm). The target was electrically wired so that if the pointer was held on target for one complete revolution, a counter registered a score of 10. Each subject practiced this task alone for 20 trials a day for several days. The average score per trial (20 revolutions) described the usual negatively accelerated learning curve. Improvement was rapid at first, but on later days the scores leveled out. When the subject showed no additional improvement for two consecutive days, he was considered to have mastered the task. The following day he found an audience of from four to eight upperclassmen waiting in the laboratory. The subject completed 10 trials under the quiet but attentive scrutiny of the audience.

Travis compared the average score made on the ten trials with an audience with the average of the highest ten consecutive scores made while working alone. It should be noted that using the highest ten alone scores, without regard to whether the individual could maintain that level consistently, probably over-

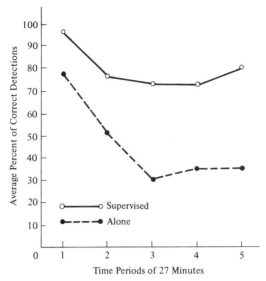

Figure 7.1
*Accuracy on a vigilance task performed alone
and under supervision (from data by Bergum
& Lehr, 1963).*

estimated performance while working alone. Nevertheless, 18 of the 22 subjects made better scores before an audience than when working alone. Under the assumption that it was just as likely for a subject to do better before an audience as alone, the likelihood that this result could have occurred by chance is less than two in a thousand ($p < .002$).[3] The difference between the means was not great (audience $\overline{X} = 177.42$, alone $\overline{X} = 172.76$), but it was statistically reliable, ($t = 2.818, p < .02$).

Bergum and Lehr (1963) studied the effect of an audience upon performance on a vigilance task. National Guard trainees were isolated in booths that contained a panel with 20 red lamps arranged in a circle. These lamps lit in a clockwise sequence at a rate of 12 rpm. At random intervals one or another of the lights failed to go on in its proper turn. The subject kept watch and was to press a button whenever a light failed to go on normally. Twenty subjects performed the task alone and the remaining 20 subjects were told that "from time to time a lieutenant colonel or a master sergeant would visit them in their booths to observe their performance." These supervised subjects were visited four times during testing. Figure 7.1 shows that the visits produced superior accuracy. The performance of both groups declined over time, due to fatigue, but the detection accuracy of the supervised subjects remained on the average 34 percent higher than the accuracy of the subjects working alone.

[3] Travis did not analyze his data with modern techniques for testing statistical hypotheses. Therefore, we have computed a binomial test (Siegel, 1956) and a t test for paired observations (Edwards, 1969) from his data.

Studies of coaction have also found social facilitation effects. The investigation of coaction began with Triplett's (1898) experiment, which, incidentally, was the first experiment of any sort in social psychology. It seems that Triplett became interested in coaction because of a recurrent pattern that he found in the records of contemporary bicycle races. The times for simultaneous competition were always the best. Next best were the times for paced races in which the cyclist is preceded by a tandem bicycle that sets the pace for him. Distinctly inferior performances were always made by cyclists racing alone against the clock.

Triplett proposed that the bodily presence of another rider was responsible for the dramatic differences between performance alone and in coaction. He tested this notion in a context far removed from professional bicycle racing. In his experiment Triplett instructed children to turn a fishing reel as rapidly as possible for a set time period. Sometimes they worked alone. At other times two children worked at the same time in the same room, each with their own reel. The results showed that the children worked faster in coaction than when alone.

Although studies of audience effects have usually used human subjects, studies of coaction have been performed with several other species. Some very pronounced social facilitation effects were reported by Chen (1937) from a study of ants. He observed 36 ants excavating nests alone, in groups of 2 and in groups of 3. On four successive days ants were placed in a milk bottle half filled with dry, sandy soil. The dependent variables were the time at which they began to build a nest and the weight of the earth they excavated during a six-hour test period. On the first and fourth days the ants were tested alone. On the second day ants were tested in pairs and on the third day in groups of three.

Table 7.1 shows that the performance of ants improved tremendously in coaction. Coaction reduced latency of digging to nearly one-sixth of that observed alone and more than tripled the amount of earth dug. On Day 4 the ants were tested alone again, and their performance subsided to the initial level.

Some powerful social facilitation effects have been observed in studies of behaviors such as eating and drinking. The work of Bayer (1929) and the more recent studies of Tolman (Tolman, 1964, 1965, 1968, 1969; Tolman &

Table 7.1

Nest Building by Isolated and Coacting Ants

	Successive Days			
	1	*2*	*3*	*4*
		GROUPS	GROUPS	
Treatment	ALONE	OF TWO	OF THREE	ALONE
Mean latency (per ant) of nest building in minutes	192	28	33	160
Mean weight (per ant) in milligrams of earth excavated during a 6-hour period	232	765	728	182

SOURCE. From data in Chen, 1937, pp. 424–427.

Wilson, 1965) have produced fairly consistent results: Substantial increments in eating are found when chickens are given food in the presence of others. Similar effects were found with puppies (James, 1953), rats (Harlow, 1932), rhesus monkeys (Stamm, 1961), armadillos (Platt, Yaksh, & Darby, 1967), and opossums (Platt & James, 1966). Figure 7.2 shows Harlow's data. In his experiment rats were fed alone or in pairs on successive days. The presence of others also enhances drinking in rats (Bruce, 1941).

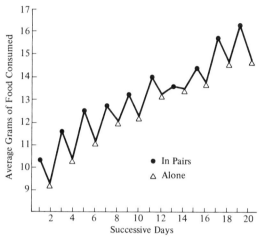

Figure 7.2
Feeding of isolated and paired rats (drawn from data reported by Harlow, 1932, Experiment 7).

Larsson (1956) has studied sexual behavior in male rats and found strong social facilitation effects. Larsson found that when three pairs of animals were placed in the same cage and allowed to copulate, the males reached a higher number of ejaculations per hour and achieved ejaculation more rapidly than did the males of solitary pairs of animals. The presence of other pairs of copulating animals in the same room, but each pair in a separate cage, had a similar but less pronounced effect.

In a series of studies on the effects of coaction, Allport (1920, 1924) administered several types of tests to students at Harvard College. The students were tested several times. On half of these occasions they worked alone in separate rooms, and the other half of the time they worked while seated in groups of four or five at a table so that each person worked independently on the same task (coaction).

Allport used five timed tasks: (a) In the *vowel-cancellation task* the subject was given columns of newspaper material and instructed to cross out all the vowels. (b) In the *reversible-perspective task* the subject viewed a drawing of a cube as shown in Figure 7.3. The cube can be perceived in two different orientations, either with corner B in front of corner A or with corner A in front of corner B. The subject was to rapidly alternate his perception of the orientation of the cube. (c) In the *multiplication task* the subject obtained the products of pairs of two-digit numbers. (d) In the *chain-association task* the subject was given a sheet of paper with a word written at the top. Upon signal he was to write beneath it the first word that came to his mind. This first response then served as the next stimulus word, to which another free association had to be made, and so forth, for a three-minute time period. (e) In the *problem-solving task* the subject read epigrams by Marcus Aurelius and Epictetus. After each passage the subject was given five minutes to write as many arguments *refuting* the passage as possible.

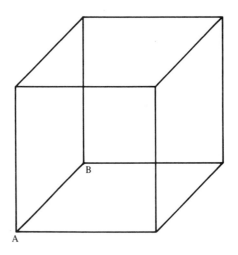

Figure 7.3

Most of Allport's results showed social facilitation. In the chain-association task, individuals wrote more associations in coaction than when alone. Co-action also produced more vowel cancellations and more reversals of perspective than did the alone condition. The subjects completed more multiplication problems in coaction than when alone. Also, they seemed to be equally accurate in both conditions. On the problem-solving task subjects wrote more refutations in coaction than when alone.

Allport suggested that the activity of individuals in coaction is enhanced by two factors:

The first of these is social facilitation. The movements made by others performing the same task as ourselves serve as contributory stimuli, and increase or hasten our own responses. This process is accompanied by a consciousness of impulsion. The second process is rivalry. Its occurrence is in direct proportion to the competitive setting of the group occupation, though a certain degree of rivalry seems natural to all coactivity [pp. 284–285].

Using some of the same tasks and procedures used by Allport, Dashiell (1930) conducted a series of experiments on the effects of audience and coaction. Dashiell found, as did Allport, that individuals made more chain associations and completed more multiplication problems in coaction than when alone. Dashiell also found that the presence of an audience had the same effect as coaction on these measures of performance.

The results reviewed above show an enhancement of the performance of individuals when working under observation or coacting with others. The results show social facilitation among several species and for many different behaviors. Moreover, the behaviors seem to be of the same general sort; they are all behaviors that are either instinctive or already well learned. This evidence suggests that the mere presence of others has a facilitative effect upon individual performance. However, there is also a large research literature that shows that audience and coaction *impair* individual performance.

PERFORMANCE DECREMENTS FROM AUDIENCE AND COACTION

Although subjects wrote more refutations in coaction during Allport's problem-solving task described above, the results of this task show a decrement in the quality of performance in coaction. For each subject Allport determined the proportions of the refutations written alone which fell into each of three quality classes: superior, intermediate, and poor reasoning. The same determination was made for the arguments each individual wrote in coaction. For six of the nine subjects, the proportion of "superior" refutations written alone was greater than the proportion of "superior" arguments written in coaction. Also, for six of the nine subjects, the proportion of "poor" refutations written in coaction was greater than the proportion of "poor" refutations written alone. These findings led Allport (1924) to modify his conclusions concerning coaction that were quoted above. ". . . It is the *overt* responses, such as writing, which receive facilitation through the stimulus of coworkers. The intellectual or implicit responses of thought are hampered rather than facilitated [p. 274]."

Studies of infrahuman organisms have also found performance decrements from coaction. Light is an aversive stimulus for cockroaches. Gates and Allee (1933) trained cockroaches to run a maze to escape from light into a dark bottle. The maze consisted of four runways which were constructed to form the letter E. The entire maze was suspended over a pan of water. A dark bottle at the end of the middle bar of the E afforded escape from light. Some roaches were tested alone, some in pairs, and some in groups of three.

Figure 7.4 shows the results plotted in terms of average minutes for a successful run averaged over blocks of five trials. Coaction clearly impaired performance in the maze. Coacting cockroaches almost always took more than twice as much time to reach the goal as did solitary cockroaches.

Coaction has also been found to impair learning by birds. Allee and Masure (1936) found that Australian parakeets trained alone learned a maze more rapidly and with fewer errors than birds trained in pairs. Klopfer (1958) found similar results for greenfinches learning to discriminate between two types of food.

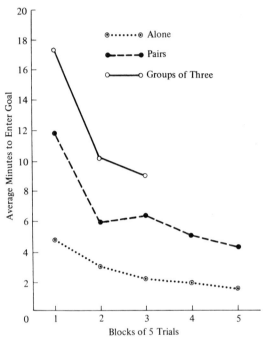

Figure 7.4
Maze learning in isolated and coacting cock-roaches: Average time per block of five successive trials (from Gates & Allee, 1933).

Some studies have also shown that the presence of an audience impairs individual performance. Pessin (1933) had individuals learn two lists of seven nonsense syllables by the serial anticipation method. The criterion of mastery was one perfect recitation of the list. Each subject learned one list alone in an isolated cubicle. While learning the other list, an interested spectator (who was Pessin himself) watched him through a window in the cubicle. Individuals learned most efficiently alone, mastering that list in an average of 9.8 repetitions. With an audience they required an average of 11.3 repetitions to reach mastery. The average number of errors made while learning alone was 36.6 and when under observation 41.1. Dashiell's (1930) studies of audience and coaction effects, described above, found that both audience and coaction increased the number of errors made in the multiplication of pairs of two-digit numbers.

We have just reviewed evidence that audience and coaction impair individual performance. These results are in opposition to those discussed earlier. However, there is also ample evidence that audience and coaction improve individual performance.[4] These divergent results do not seem to have been produced by significant differences in the procedures used in the various laboratories, since in two instances divergent results were obtained in both the laboratories of Allport and Dashiell.

INTEGRATING THE DIVERGENT RESULTS

Recently Zajonc (1965, 1966) pointed out a rather subtle consistency in these conflicting results and suggested how to bring them into harmony. He suggested that audience and coaction impair the acquisition of new responses and facilitate the emission of responses that are well learned or instinctive. We noted earlier that a common characteristic of the studies that showed social facilitation was that the behavior involved was well learned or instinctive. The studies that showed performance decrements from audience or coaction also seemed to share a common feature. The behaviors studied involved the learning of new responses. This generalization can be reformulated to suggest a way in which the facilitation and decrement findings are manifestations of the same psychological process.

First let us examine some new terms, *competitional situations, hierarchy of competing responses*, and *dominant response*. Most of the stimuli to which organisms respond elicit several different response tendencies at the same time. Some of these responses can be performed simultaneously. For instance, a motorist whose car begins to skid on an icy road may yell, turn his head, and depress the brake pedal all at the same time. However, some of the elicited responses cannot be performed simultaneously; they are incompatible and therefore in competition with each other. Thus the skidding motorist cannot simultaneously hold the steering wheel steady, turn it to the left, and turn it to the right. Performing one of these responses precludes performing either of the others at that particular moment in time. Spence (1956) has labeled such situations competitional.

The many competing responses elicited by the stimuli of a competitional situation can be ordered in a hierarchy on the basis of their probability of emission as overt behavior and the speed and vigor with which they are performed. Figure 7.5 depicts a hierarchy of competing responses. The most probable response is R^1 and it is called the dominant response. The other responses, R^2, R^3, and R^4, are called the subordinate responses.

Before returning to the audience and coaction results, let us examine the role of hierarchies of competing responses in the learning process. The learning process can be viewed as the modification of the hierarchy of competing responses elicited by the task stimuli. At the beginning of learning, the correct response has a low probability of emission. Some other response is dominant and so the subject's overt responses are mostly the wrong ones. As learning

[4] Dashiell's (1935) comprehensive survey of the findings of audience and coaction research shows the same pattern of conflicting findings.

progresses, the response to be learned is strengthened[5] and moves to the dominant position in the hierarchy, and the subject emits the correct response more and more frequently. The vicissitudes of students of foreign languages learning to cope with false cognates illustrate this process quite clearly. The beginning student of French is likely to say "crayon" when asked to give the English equivalent of the French "crayon." As he practices his vocabulary drills, the incorrect response grows weaker and the correct response grows stronger, and finally he says "pencil" every time he is asked to translate.

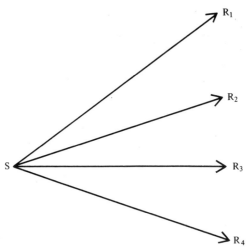

Figure 7.5
A hierarchy of competing responses. The responses are ordered vertically in order of their probability of emission as overt behavior.

Zajonc has proposed that audience and coaction have a single effect upon behavior. They increase the probability of emission of the dominant response. If the dominant response is the correct response, as is the case in well-learned or instinctual activities, then performance is improved, as in the studies which found social facilitation. If, on the other hand, the dominant response is an incorrect response, then it too will be facilitated and performance will suffer because the emission of the correct response will be postponed or prevented, as in the studies which found performance decrements in audience and coaction.

Zajonc took one further step in the integration of the audience and coaction findings. He attempted to specify the psychological process responsible for these findings. Zajonc (1965, 1966) drew on Hull-Spence theory (Spence, 1956) and proposed that the mere presence of others enhances the emission of dominant responses by increasing the individual's general drive (D) level.

---

[5] The various theories of learning (for surveys, see Deese & Hulse, 1967; Hilgard & Bower, 1966; Kimble, 1961) present different views of the conditions necessary for reinforcement.

HULL-SPENCE THEORY AND GENERAL DRIVE

To explicate this aspect of the hypothesis, we shall examine some material from contemporary research and theory on learning and motivation. Many psychologists distinguish between those variables that direct behavior and those variables that energize behavior. Hebb (1955), for instance, has used the analogy of the difference in function of the steering gear and the engine of an automobile. Some variables alter the direction behavior takes, but not the energy with which it is performed. Other variables alter the vigor and intensity of behavior, but do not determine the particular behavior performed. Many of the directing influences on behavior have been integrated under the term *habit* (recognizing, of course, that unlearned or instinctual response tendencies can also provide direction to behavior). What the organism will do when confronted with a particular stimulus depends on what activities have been learned and what activities have been extinguished. The term *motivation* integrates those variables that influence how frequently and vigorously the organism does what it has been trained to do.

The following are some examples of the effect of motivational variables upon the performance of learned responses. Horenstein (1951) trained hungry rats to press a panel to secure food. When this response was firmly established, she extinguished the animals under one of four different levels of motivation, either 0, 2, 12, or 23.5 hours of food deprivation, and observed the number of times each animal pressed the panel. Figure 7.6 shows the results in terms of the median number of responses for each group during the 15-minute extinction period. The greater the level of motivation during extinction, the more frequently the animals emitted the learned response. It is important to remember that the four groups shown in Figure 7.6 had previously received equal training during the learning stage and so it is reasonable to assume that they had learned the panel press response equally well.

In Horenstein's experiment the type of motivation varied during testing was the same (hunger) as that used to establish the instrumental response during training. There exists then the possibility that increases in motivation will increase the emission of learned responses only when the motivation is relevant to the conditions of learning the response. However, other experiments have shown that increases in motivation (or drive) which are irrelevant to the conditions of learning also increase the probability that a learned response is performed. For example, Webb and Goodman (1958) trained hungry rats to press a lever to secure food. After 60 trials of such training they were satiated for food and returned to the test box for two successive five-minute extinction test sessions. During the first session the animals pressed the bar an average of 1.8 times. In the second test period motivation was increased by flooding the box with water. This produced a dramatic increase in the incidence of bar pressing. The still satiated animals made more than four times as many presses (the mean was 8.4) as they had during the preceding five minutes.

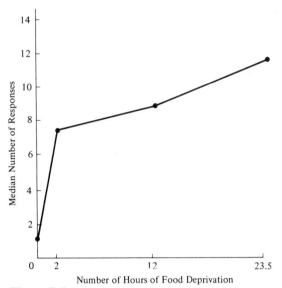

Figure 7.6
Effect of food deprivation upon panel pressing during extinction (from Horenstein, 1951).

Similarly, Miller (1948) showed that the irrelevant drive of shock can increase the occurrence of a response learned originally to secure food. He trained hungry rats to find food in a T maze. He then satiated them for food and tested them in extinction. During extinction half the animals were given a strong electric shock at the beginning of each trial. The shocked animals ran faster and made fewer errors in extinction than did the nonshocked animals. Thus increases in motivation (or drive) serve to energize learned responses regardless of whether the drive is the same as that which prevailed during original learning.[6]

Evidence like that reported above led Hull (1943) and Spence (1956) to propose the formal theory of learning and performance summarized in Equation 7.1:

$$S \qquad \rightarrow \quad \boxed{H_1 \times D = E_1} \qquad \rightarrow R_1 \qquad [7.1]$$

In the equation the symbols outside the box are observable events and those inside are unobservable theoretical constructs. The symbols denote the following:

(a)   S is a particular stimulus or set of stimuli.
(b) R_1 is a particular overt response.

---

[6] It is inappropriate to summarize all of the relevant evidence here. Detailed treatments of these topics may be found in texts on learning (Deese & Hulse, 1967; Kimble, 1961) and motivation (Bolles, 1967; Brown, 1961; Cofer & Appley, 1964).

(c) H_1 symbolizes the strength of the habit governing response R_1. The theory assumes that habit strength is an increasing function of the number of training trials on which S and R_1 have been paired.

(d)   D symbolizes general drive level. A wide variety of antecedent conditions, including appetitional needs such as hunger and thirst, and noxious stimuli such as electric shock, cold temperatures, intense light, or loud noises, are assumed to contribute to the organism's general drive level. Also, some individuals are more emotionally responsive than others and therefore are capable of higher levels of general drive.

(e) E_1 symbolizes excitatory potential. Equation 7.1 states that the capacity for a particular stimulus (S) to elicit a particular response (R_1) depends upon the excitatory potential (E_1) for that response. Excitatory potential is a multiplicative function of the strength of the habit governing the response (H_1) and general drive level (D).

Brown (1961, pp. 99–100) pointed out several implications of this theory which we have summarized below with special emphasis upon the role of general drive.

1.   Drive is conceived of as only a numerical multiplier and therefore cannot determine the direction behavior will take, that is, which response will occur. The direction of behavior depends upon which H has been established by training (innate or instinctive reactions to S can influence direction as well).

2.   The theory maintains the distinction made by learning theorists between *learning* and *performance*. Learning refers to unseen hypothetical changes (H) produced by training. Performance refers to overt behavior, for example, the frequency of occurrence of R_1, along with its amplitude and latency. The distinction is based on the observation that sometimes organisms do not perform well when there is no reason to believe that they have forgotten their habits, for example, the animals in Horenstein's (1951) experiment that were tested under zero hours of food deprivation.

3.   One cannot by merely observing overt behavior under a single set of conditions accurately estimate the respective contributions of D and H. A particular response may occur because of a high drive level and a weak H, or the reverse.

4.   Any operation that increases motivation can (within as yet unspecified limits) be substituted for another, since the D produced by each is identical. Thus, if a response has a high probability of being elicited by a stimulus when a subject is hungry, it should also be elicited (assuming that S, the stimulus, stays nearly the same) when the subject is thirsty or in pain. The results of Webb and Goodman (1958) and Miller (1948) summarized above provide some confirmation for this aspect of the theory.

To extend the theory to competitional situations, we need to take into account that S often elicits other incompatible habits at the same time that it elicits H_1. Equation 7.2 states that S also elicits another habit (H_2) and that the excita-

$$S \qquad \to \qquad \boxed{H_2 \times D = E_2} \qquad \to R_2 \qquad [7.2]$$

tory potential (E_2) for R_2 is a multiplicative function of the strength of the habit governing R_2 and general drive level. In a competitional situation, R_1 and R_2 are incompatible—both cannot occur at the same time.

Which response will occur in a competitional situation and how quickly and vigorously will it be performed? The theory assumes that these events depend upon the relative strengths of the excitatory potentials for the competing responses. The greater the difference between the excitatory potential for the dominant response (the one with the greater E value) and the excitatory potential for the subordinate response, the more likely is the dominant response to occur and the more quickly and vigorously it will be performed.

Performance in a competitional situation could be predicted by simple subtraction of the E values except for the often observed fact that hierarchies of competing responses are not completely stable over time. From time to time they undergo momentary fluctuations so that upon occasion the dominant response is displaced momentarily by one of the subordinate responses. A commonplace example of such a displacement may be found in the case of a shower bather who attempts to adjust the water temperature and finds to his chagrin that he has turned the faucet the wrong way. Hull-Spence theory conceptualizes these fluctuations in terms of oscillatory inhibition. The excitatory potential for each response is from moment to moment, reduced by a continually varying amount of oscillatory inhibition.[7] Moreover, the oscillatory inhibition for each response varies independently of that for other responses. Thus the value of E, which might be computed by quantifying D and H, is not a constant, but is instead conceived of as the central tendency of a whole range of E values, any one of which might be effective at a given moment. Figure 7.7A depicts the hypothetical distribution of E for two competing responses R_1 and R_2. The respective habit strengths are $H_1 = 3$ and $H_2 = 2$. D is assumed equal to 1. Since E_1 is usually greater than E_2, R_1 will usually occur. However, the two distributions are overlapped to indicate that upon occasion E_2 could be momentarily greater than E_1 so that R_2 could sometimes displace R_1.

What is the effect of increasing drive level upon performance in a competitional situation? Since D is assumed to multiply all habits equally, increasing D from 1 to 2 in our example would elevate the locations of the hypothetical E distributions as shown in Figure 7.7B. The figure shows that the distribution for E_1 is now centered at $E = 6$, and the E_2 distribution is now centered at

---

[7] The sources of oscillatory inhibition are numerous and all of them have not yet been identified. The observed variability in behavior from trial to trial, even when D and H have been kept constant, urge positing such a process (see Spence, 1956, p. 96 ff).

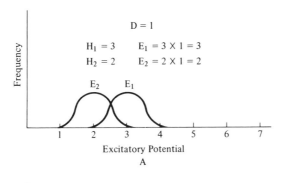

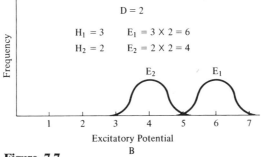

Figure 7.7

Relative frequency distributions of momentary excitatory potential (E) for two competing responses as a function of general drive level (D).

E = 4. However, the most important result is that increasing D also increases the difference between the two distributions. Figure 7.7B shows that the difference between E_1 and E_2 is twice as great as that shown in Figure 7.7A. As a result, the two E distributions now overlap very little, which means that there are fewer occasions when R_1 would be momentarily displaced by R_2, and also that R_1 will occur more quickly and vigorously than when D was equal to 1. Thus, increasing general drive level (D) in a competitional situation is assumed to increase the probability that the dominant response will be performed and also the speed and vigor with which it is performed. The concept of oscillatory inhibition deals with the fact that under apparently constant values of D and H, there is some variability in the speed and vigor with which the dominant response is performed, and also upon occasion it is displaced by one of the subordinate responses.

Thus the Zajonc hypothesis states that the mere presence of others enhances the emission of dominant responses by increasing the individual's level of general drive. If the appropriate responses are dominant, then the presence of others will improve performance by increasing the probability of correct responses. If, on the other hand, the appropriate responses are subordinate to stronger incorrect responses, then the presence of others will impair performance by increasing the probability of incorrect responses.

The summary of Hull-Spence theory presented above has, for the sake of brevity, omitted some details (e.g., see Spence, 1956, 1958; Spence & Spence, 1966) and also special cases and recent revisions (e.g., Broen & Storms, 1961). The validity of the hypothesis that the mere presence of others enhances the emission of dominant responses is not tied to the validity of Hull-Spence theory. The general drive concept seems useful because it integrates the evidence rather well and it also seems to be the best available conceptual tool to account for changes in performance that are not due to learning. If future experimental tests should invalidate this aspect of Hull-Spence theory, then we would need to seek other conceptual tools to link the variable of the presence of others to psychological processes. At present, however, the results of a number of experiments have shown the scientific utility of the general drive construct. An experiment by Lee (1961) is a good example of those studies.

Lee studied the effect of general drive level (D) upon the performance of three tasks which represented differing degrees of dominance of the correct response. The subjects first spent four trials practicing a 15-item paired-associates list by the anticipation method. Each pair consisted of two adjectives which previous work had indicated were highly associated with each other, for instance, absurd-stupid, brutal-unkind. Next the subjects worked for six trials on a transfer task of 15 paired-associate items. In this list five of the word pairs were retained from the training list (Unchanged Pairs). These pairs were assumed to represent a task in which the correct response was in a clear position of dominance, since there was both a strong preexperimental association within each pair, and also the subjects had just spent four trials practicing them. Five other pairs of the transfer list (New Pairs) were also assumed to represent a task in which the correct response was dominant. These were five adjective pairs with a strong preexperimental association within each pair, for instance, polite-gracious. Since the subjects had not practiced these pairs in the first stage, it was assumed that the correct responses for the New Pairs were not as dominant as were the correct responses for the Unchanged Pairs. Finally five pairs (Changed Pairs) were assumed to represent a task in which the correct response was not dominant. These were five pairs used in the first stage, but rearranged, for example, brutal-obscure, unclear-rustic, speedy-unkind, so that the required pairings were in opposition to both the preexperimental associations and also to the pairings during initial practice.

The high drive group consisted of individuals who achieved high scores on the Manifest Anxiety Scale (abbreviated MAS, Taylor, 1953). This is a self-report inventory which distinguishes individuals who have a high or low drive level in learning situations. The subjects in the high drive group also received painful electric shocks during the intervals between trials on the transfer list. The low drive group consisted of individuals who achieved low scores on the MAS and did not receive shocks.

The results shown in Figure 7.8 clearly confirm Hull-Spence theory predictions concerning the effects varying D. On those transfer pairs in which the correct response was not dominant (Changed Pairs), the high drive group made

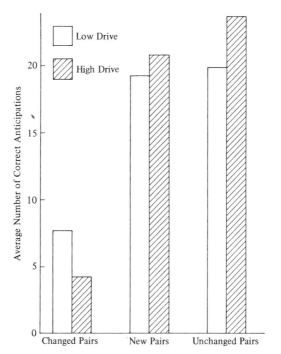

Figure 7.8
Mean number of correct anticipations on three types of paired-associates items as a function of general drive level (D) (drawn from data reported by Lee, 1961).

fewer correct responses than did the low drive group. When the correct response was dominant (New and Unchanged Pairs), the high drive group made more correct responses than the low drive group. Furthermore, the superiority of high drive to low drive was greatest on those pairs for which the correct response was most dominant (Unchanged Pairs).

STRATEGIES FOR TESTING THE ZAJONC HYPOTHESIS

The Zajonc hypothesis states that the mere presence of other organisms of the same species is a source of general drive, and therefore performance will be improved if the correct response is dominant and impaired if the correct response is not dominant. This hypothesis provides a plausible integration of the conflicting findings from studies of audience and coaction reviewed above. However, in the science of psychology, propositions are not validated by plausibility. They must be subjected to experimental test. A number of tests have already been made of Zajonc's hypothesis. Before presenting the results of these experiments, we will first consider some strategies to be followed in testing the hypothesis.

Competing Responses in Experimental Tasks

In formulating the hypothesis, Zajonc was required to make a number of assumptions about the competing responses elicited by the task stimuli in the various experiments he reviewed. In some instances these assumptions would probably be accepted without dispute. For instance, it is difficult to quarrel with the assumption that in the Travis study the correct responses for the pursuit rotor task were dominant at the time the audience was introduced; Travis had given his subjects nearly 100 trials of practice and these had yielded an asymptotic learning curve. In other studies, however, these assumptions are problematic. For instance, to interpret the results of Allport's studies of coaction in terms of Zajonc's hypothesis, one must assume that the responses involved in canceling vowels were dominant, and also that the responses necessary to refute arguments from Epictetus were not dominant. One could, however, take just the opposite position and argue that since Allport's college student subjects probably had more practice in writing essays in philosophy than in canceling vowels, the responses necessary for problem solving were dominant and the responses necessary for vowel cancellation were not dominant. If this interpretation is correct, then Allport's findings mean that the presence of coactors enhanced the emission of subordinate responses over dominant responses. The results of Allport's experiments and the others as well will remain ambiguous as long as there is dispute concerning which task responses are dominant and which ones are not.

To avoid ambiguous results, experiments to test Zajonc's hypothesis should use tasks in which response competition is fairly well understood. There should be independent evidence that the task stimuli elicit hierarchies of competing responses. In order to predict which response will be enhanced by the presence of others, there should also be independent evidence to indicate the dominant and subordinate responses. Furthermore, since the hypothesis implicates general drive as the psychological process responsible for enhancing the emission of dominant responses, tasks used in prior studies of the effect of general drive upon performance would be especially useful. In this way one could compare the effect of the presence of others with the effects produced by variables that are already acknowledged to be sources of general drive.

What Is Meant by "Mere Presence"?

Let us consider the manipulations that should serve as the independent variable in experiments to test the hypothesis. What is meant by "the mere presence of others"? Would any situation in which two or more organisms are present be an appropriate experimental treatment in an experiment to determine the effects of the mere presence of others? Definitely not, because in many of those situations the particular actions of the other present organism can also influence the subject's behavior. Zajonc (1966) has classified many of these influences under the rubrics of *cue effects* and *social reinforcement effects*.

Cue Effects. The responses of one organism can change the behavior of a second by providing cues for particular responses. This process seems to be responsible for Gurnee's (1939) finding that subjects working in groups learned a maze with 20 choice points faster than subjects working alone. The subjects working in groups had additional cues to direct their behavior which were not available to the subjects working alone. Unlike the subjects in most of the coaction experiments described above,[8] the grouped subjects in Gurnee's experiment heard the choices made by the other subjects and could then adjust their own responses accordingly. The finding that individuals make their perceptual judgments conform to the majority opinion (Asch, 1952) has instigated a vast research literature on the topic of conformity (See Chapter 8). Most of these demonstrations of conformity can be understood in terms of the publicly expressed judgments of others serving as cues which guide the individual's subsequent judgmental responses. Research on the topics of imitation and vicarious learning (e.g., Bandura, 1965; Miller & Dollard, 1941) provides additional evidence that in many settings the cues provided by the actions of others can guide the individual's responses.

Social Reinforcement Effects. A second way in which the particular responses of one individual can modify the behavior of another is by providing reinforcement. A *reinforcer* is any event occurring after a response which serves to increase the probability that the response will occurr subsequently. Greenspoon (1955) was one of the first to demonstrate that the responses of one organism can provide reinforcement for the responses of a second organism. He asked his subjects to say words at random for 50 minutes. Each time the subject emitted a plural word, the experimenter responded with verbal assent—"mmhm." The rate at which the subjects said plural words increased dramatically. Subsequent studies have shown that the application of head nods, smiles, and verbalizations such as "yes" and "I see" as reinforcers can produce profound effects upon the direction and rate of the individual's verbal behavior. As a matter of fact, a recent series of studies (Koenig, 1966; Sarason & Ganzer, 1962, 1963) found that social reinforcement can increase the rate at which individuals say negative and self-depreciating things about themselves. Social reinforcement can modify the probability of motor responses as well. Stevenson (1965) summarized the results of a number of experiments in which children play a game that involves dropping marbles into holes. The rate at which children perform this response can be increased dramatically if the experimenter (E) says "good" whenever the child drops a marble. There is no doubt that many responses can serve as social reinforcers for a wide variety of individual behavior.

Many different social situations include the mere presence of others and that is why Zajonc's hypothesis has great potential importance for social psychology.

---

[8] The results of some of the studies of coaction summarized above may be interpreted as instances of cue effects, rather than due to differences in D, since the overt response of the coactor were available to the subject as cues to guide his responses. This question of interpretation is examined later in the chapter.

If experimental tests support the hypothesis, then we have identified one of the many psychological processes that determine individual behavior in many social situations. However, experiments to test the hypothesis should use experimental manipulations in which the others are simply present and not doing anything else, such as providing cues or reinforcement for the subject's responses. Otherwise, the effects produced by the mere presence of others will be entangled with the effects produced by other variables.

EXPERIMENTAL TESTS OF THE ZAJONC HYPOTHESIS

The Zajonc hypothesis states that the mere presence of others is a source of general drive (D) for the individual and therefore enhances the emission of dominant responses. As mentioned above, in order to test this hypothesis, the investigator must use an objective method to identify the dominant response. This section of the chapter is organized in terms of the methods used to identify the dominant response. It begins with some studies in which the investigator established habits of different strengths during an initial period of training in the experiment itself. Next there are some studies in which the investigator mapped the dominant response by observing the subject's preferences for different response alternatives before manipulating the independent variable. Finally there are some studies which have used population norms to identify the dominant responses to the task stimuli.

Prior Training of the Dominant Response

Several years ago, Zajonc and Nieuwenhuyse (1964) developed a very sensitive technique for detecting the effect of general drive upon individual performance. Their procedure involved first establishing habits of different strengths by differential training of responses, and then placing these responses in competition with each other. In their experiment, drive was manipulated by means of motivating instructions, which in the high drive group promised the subjects a monetary reward for superior performance. Figure 7.9 shows for the two groups the frequency of emission of the various competing responses as a function of their habit strength (i.e., training frequency). In accordance with Hull-Spence theory, the figure shows that high drive enhanced the emission of dominant responses—responses governed by strong habits—at the expense of subordinate responses.

Two recent studies (Cottrell, Wack, Sekerak, & Rittle, 1968; Zajonc & Sales, 1966) used this procedure to determine whether the presence of an audience is a source of drive and therefore enhances the emission of dominant responses. In both experiments the first phase of the task established a set of verbal habits of different strengths. This was done by manipulating the frequency with which the subject pronounced each of ten nonsense words (e.g., *Afworbu, Zabulon*). The instructions described the task as learning to pronounce some

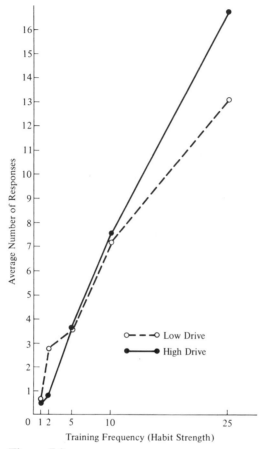

Figure 7.9

Frequency of response emission on pseudorecognition trials as a function of training frequency and drive level. Response frequencies averaged over subjects and trial blocks (redrawn from data reported by Zajonc & Nieuwenhuyse, 1964).

foreign words. Each subject pronounced two different words at each of five training frequencies (e.g., in the Cottrell et al., 1968, study the frequencies were 1, 2, 5, 10, and 25).

The test phase of the task placed the verbal habits in competition with each other. The instructions described this stage as a recognition task. The subject was told that the words he had been pronouncing would be flashed, one at a time, on a screen, and that sometimes the word would appear for only a very brief interval. He was to call out the word exposed and to make a guess when he was unsure. Each subject was tested for 160 trials, of which 120 were actually *pseudorecognition* trials. The stimulus on these trials was insufficient for recognition; it was a very brief (.01 sec.) flash of a stimulus which subjects in pretests had reported to be wordlike, but otherwise unrecognizable. Since the subject was instructed to call out one of the ten words on each trial, and since recognition was impossible on the pseudorecognition trials, the pseudorecognition trials placed the ten verbal responses in competition with one another.

Half of the subjects were alone during testing, and half of the subjects had an audience of two spectators. At the beginning of testing in the audience condition the experimenter brought in two students who, he said, were interested in watching the subject work on the task. Then the experimenter retired to the control room.

Figure 7.10 shows the results obtained by Cottrell et al. (1968).[9] The figure depicts the average frequency of emission of the competing verbal responses as a function of their habit strength—the frequency with which each word was pronounced during the first, training, phase of the task. The figure shows that relative to the alone condition, the presence of an audience enhanced the emission of the dominant responses (the two words pronounced 25 times each during training) at the expense of the subordinate responses. Zajonc and Sales (1966) obtained very similar results. These results parallel exactly those obtained by Zajonc and Nieuwenhuyse (1964) (See Figure 7.9) in which a known source of drive enhanced the emission of dominant responses. Thus the results of two studies (Cottrell et al., 1968; Zajonc & Sales, 1966) give strong support to the Zajonc hypothesis that the presence of an audience enhances the emission of dominant responses by increasing the individual's general drive level.

The increment in general drive produced by the presence of an audience can be examined more closely by using some of the detailed predictions from Hull-Spence theory. The theory states that E (excitatory potential) is a linear function of D (drive) and H (habit). Equation 7.3 gives the normal form of a linear equation.

$$Y = A + BX \qquad [7.3]$$

Equation 7.4 presents the equation for E as a function of D and H.

$$E = D \times H \qquad [7.4]$$

Equation 7.4 states that E is a linear function of H where D is the multiplier and plays the same role as B in Equation 7.3. In terms of the theory, then, the quantitative effect of increasing D while holding H constant is to increase the slope of the function relating observed response frequency to habit strength. In the three experiments discussed above the H factors were constant across treatments, training was identical in all treatments, and the stimulus series during testing was also identical in all treatments. The slope of the response emission function produced by the different treatments in the three experiments is shown

---

[9] Figure 7.10 also includes results from a third condition—mere presence—and these results are discussed in a later section.

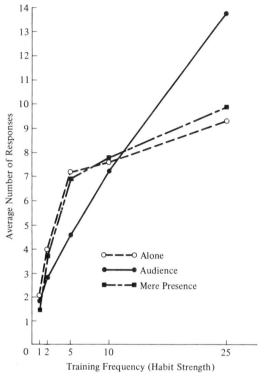

Figure 7.10
*Frequency of response emission on pseudorecog-
nition trials as a function of training frequency
and condition of testing. Response frequencies
averaged over subjects and trial blocks (from
Cottrell, Wack, Sekerak, & Rittle, 1968).*

in Table 7.2. This statistic is simply the slope of the line of regression of Y
(frequency of response emission) on X (training frequency).

The table shows that the results of the two audience studies are very similar.
In both studies the presence of an audience increased the slope by a factor of
approximately 2 above the slope of the alone condition. The slopes obtained by
Zajonc and Nieuwenhuyse (1964) are also of interest. They are, in general,
larger than those obtained in the audience studies. However, there is a remarkable similarity between the slope for the low drive condition and the slope
obtained in the two audience conditions. Perhaps this is not surprising in light of
the fact that in the low drive condition the experimenter remained in the same
room as the subject during testing and thereby constituted an audience.

Martens (1969) investigated the effect of an audience upon the learning and
performance of a complex motor skill. Since skilled performance involves a
sequence of organized responses (Fitts & Posner, 1967), it is not always possible to identify the relevant stimuli and responses as precisely as in the studies

reported above. Nevertheless, if the task is novel to the subject, it is reasonable to assume that the appropriate sequence of responses is relatively weak and subordinate to stronger, incorrect responses. Continued practice on the task should strengthen the correct responses and eventually bring them to dominance.

In Martens' study the subject was to intercept a moving target just as it reached a particular point in its course. He had to launch a rolling pointer which was mounted in a track with just the right amount of force so that the pointer reached the interception point at the same instant the target did. Error scores were computed by comparing the arrival times of the target and the pointer. The greater the difference in arrival times, the larger the error score. Half of the subjects were alone during their initial training trials and the other half had an audience of ten passive spectators. The learning phase was terminated when the subject reduced his error below a preset criterion of mastery. The two groups were then subdivided and half of each group was tested with an audience and the other half was tested alone.

The results give strong support to the Zajonc hypothesis. During initial learning, when presumably incorrect task responses were dominant, the presence of an audience produced inferior performance. In the testing phase, when presumably the appropriate responses were in a position of dominance, the presence of an audience produced superior performance.

Table 7.2

Slope of Function Relating Frequency of Response Emission on Pseudorecognition Trials to Training Frequency

		Treatment		
Study	ALONE	AUDIENCE	LOW DRIVE	HIGH DRIVE
Zajonc & Nieuwenhuyse (1964)[a,b]	X	X	.484	.681
Zajonc & Sales (1966)[c,d]	.215	.464	X	X
Cottrell, Wack, Sekerak, & Rittle (1968)[c]	.257	.488	X	X

SOURCE. From data in Cottrell et al., 1968, and data in Zajonc & Nieuwenhuyse, 1964.

NOTE. Frequencies per trial block of 30 pseudorecognition trials, averaged over subjects, were used in computing slopes.

[a] N = 12 per treatment.

[b] Data originally reported in percentages; these converted to frequencies by multiplying each by 30.

[c] N = 15 per treatment.

[d] Slopes originally reported multiplied by factor 30/43 to institute same relationship between scale on X and scale on Y as in other studies.

Mapping the Dominant Response from Subject Preferences

Imagine that a subject is confronted with a set of response alternatives and is asked to choose one of them. If the subject is asked to make this choice a number of times, then one can readily determine the dominant—the most frequently chosen—response alternative. According to the Zajonc hypothesis, if we now introduce coactors into the situation, the frequency with which the subject emits his dominant response should increase.

Goldman (1967) tested this derivation from the hypothesis in a study of color preference. For 30 trials individual subjects were shown a set of five samples of colored paper. On each trial the subject was asked to "pick the color you like at the moment." The subject wrote her choices on a piece of paper. Then half the subjects had 30 more trials alone, while the other subjects had their second set of 30 trials with four coactors who were also choosing colors. Since the subjects did not announce their choices publicly, the choices made by the coactors did not provide cues to guide the individual's responses. The results showed that coaction enhanced the emission of the dominant response. Subjects in coaction chose their most preferred color (as determined by their choices during the first block of 30 trials) more frequently than subjects who made their choices alone.

Strain (1967) found a similar effect of coaction upon the choice of color-oddity. Children showed a preference for the odd-colored piece of candy when choosing one from a dish of *M & M*'s. Making candy choices in coaction increased this preference for oddity.

Zajonc, Wolosin, Wolosin, and Loh (1970) studied the effect of spectators and coaction upon choice in a two-alternative task. The apparatus consisted of two lights with a telegraph key under each light. The subject's task was to predict which of the lights would be lit on each trial by pressing the appropriate key. The two events were not equiprobable. For half the subjects the left light was lit on 80 percent of the trials and the right light on 20 percent of the trials. For the other half of the subjects the positions of the frequently and infrequently occurring lights were reversed. The subject received three cents each time he correctly predicted the occurrence of the 20 percent light and three-fourths of a cent each time he correctly predicted the occurrence of the 80 percent light. Thus the expected values of the winnings for the two choices were equal (expected value is defined as the product of the probability of occurrence and the payoff for predicting that light[10]).

In the first session all subjects had 180 trials alone. The dominant response on this task was to press the key which predicted the 80 percent light. On an average of 63.7 percent of the trials the subjects predicted that the 80 percent light would occur. During the second session of 180 trials, which followed immediately, there were three different conditions in the experiment. One-third of the subjects continued to respond alone. One-third of the subjects were joined by a single student spectator who watched the subject quietly and attentively. One-third of the subjects executed the second session in coacting groups of three. In the coaction condition each subject sat in a separate booth with his own set of lights and keys and could not see the choices made by the coactors.

Figure 7.11 shows that all conditions increased the frequency of emission of

---

[10] The concept of expected value is discussed in detail in Chapter 9.

the dominant response during the second session. However, only in the audience and coaction conditions was the increase statistically reliable. Confirming the Zajonc hypothesis, both audience and coaction enhanced the emission of the dominant response.

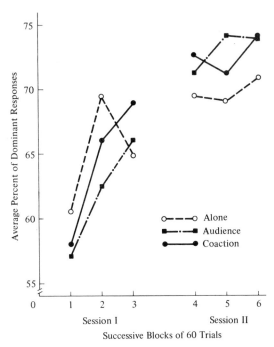

Figure 7.11
Average percent of dominant responses in a two-choice situation per block of 60 trials. The dominant response was pressing the key for the 80% light. During Session I all individuals worked alone (redrawn from data reported by Zajonc, Wolosin, Wolosin, & Loh, 1969).

Determining the Dominant Response from Population Norms

The studies summarized in this section used normative information (i.e., population norms) to identify the dominant response. This method of identifying the dominant response is similar to the method described above of mapping the dominant response from subject preferences. In those studies the same individuals who were subsequently tested in the experiment provided the response norms to the task stimuli. In the method of population norms, on the other hand, one set of individuals provides the response norms to the task stimuli, and another completely different set of individuals is tested in the subsequent experiment.

Spence, Farber, and McFann (1956) used normative information about the associative connections between words to construct a noncompetitional list and a competitional paired-associates list. The *noncompetitional list* consisted of 15 synonym pairs (e.g., adept-skillful, barren-fruitless), constructed to maximize the strength of the correct response tendencies—the association within each pair—and to minimize the strength of incorrect response tendencies—associations between members of different pairs. The *competitional list* of 12 pairs (e.g., barren-fruitless, arid-grouchy, desert-leading), was constructed to maximize incorrect response tendencies and to minimize the strength of the correct response tendencies. Spence et al. (1956) predicted and found that high drive tended to improve performance on the noncompetitional list (the correct responses were relatively strong on this list), and that high drive tended to impair performance on the competitional list (on this list the correct responses were superseded by many strong, competing, incorrect response tendencies).

Since the effect of drive upon the learning of competitional and noncompetitional lists is well established, a clearcut empirical implication of the Zajonc hypothesis is that the presence of an audience should also tend to improve performance on the noncompetitional list and to impair performance on the competitional list. Cottrell, Rittle, and Wack (1967) tested this derivation. There were four combinations of experimental treatments. Each subject learned either the competitional list or the noncompetitional list used by Spence et al. (1956). For half of each of these two groups of subjects learning was done alone, and for the other half there was an audience of two passive spectators. Figure 7.12 shows the results in terms of the mean number of errors made on 30 anticipation trials. The presence of an audience tended to decrease the number of errors made on the noncompetitional list, but tended to increase the number of errors made on the competitional list. The results of this study support Zajonc's hypothesis that the presence of an audience is a source of general drive. An audience had the same effect upon the learning of different types of paired-associates lists that had been produced by known sources of drive in previous studies.

Matlin and Zajonc (1968) studied the effect of an audience upon the latency of free association responses to verbal stimuli. The subjects were instructed that whenever they heard a verbal stimulus they were to say aloud the first word that came to mind. Half the subjects were alone while tested, and the other half had an audience of one passive spectator. Figure 7.13 presents the results and shows the mean latency of response averaged over subjects and stimuli for successive blocks of verbal stimuli. The presence of an audience descreased the latency of free association responses.

In order to support the Zajonc hypothesis, there must also be evidence that the responses accelerated by the presence of an audience were indeed the dominant responses to the verbal stimuli. A commonality score was computed which indicated whether the subject's responses were those frequently given by other individuals to the verbal stimuli; the more common the response, the more dominant it was assumed to be. The analysis indicated that the responses made

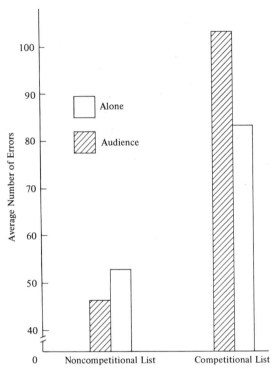

Figure 7.12
Mean number of correct anticipations on two types of paired-associates items as a function of the presence of spectators (redrawn from data reported by Cottrell, Rittle, & Wack, 1967).

by individuals in the audience condition had greater commonality than those made by individuals in the alone condition. Thus, the results of this study support Zajonc's hypothesis by showing that the presence of an audience decreased the latency of dominant free association responses.

Certain population norms can also be found in the behavior of cockroaches. As noted above, Gates and Allee (1933) found that the typical response of cockroaches confronted by a bright light is to run away from it. Zajonc, Heingartner, and Herman (1969) designed a maze and a runway for cockroaches that differ in the degree to which this dominant response to run away from light is the appropriate response. When placed in the apparatus a cockroach was exposed to a bright floodlight. He could escape from the light by entering a darkened chamber which served as a goal. Figure 7.14 shows the maze and runway and the placement of the floodlight for each. The maze and the runway were each housed in a 20-inch cube of transparent plexiglass. The walls of the alleys and the startbox were also constructed of transparent plexiglas.

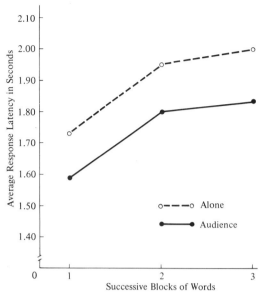

Figure 7.13

Average latency of free association responses to successive blocks of verbal stimuli by individuals tested alone and with a spectator. Latencies averaged over subjects and stimuli within each block. There were 30 verbal stimuli in blocks 1 and 3 and 32 in block 2 (redrawn from data reported by Matlin & Zajonc, 1968).

The runway, which is shown in the left side of Figure 7.14, was designed so that the cockroach's dominant tendency to run away from light coincided exactly with the responses required to reach the goal box; movement away from the floodlight would serve to bring a cockroach closer to the goal. On the other hand, a cockroach placed in the maze shown in the right side of Figure 7.14 was not so fortunate. Simple movement away from the floodlight would ultimately take a cockroach away from the goal of the maze and into a lighted cul-de-sac. In order to reach the goal of the maze a cockroach must overcome the dominant tendency to move as far away from the light source as possible.

According to the Zajonc hypothesis, the presence of other cockroaches would increase the dominant tendency to run away from the floodlight. Such an enhancement would lead to improved performance in the runway by decreasing the time spent reaching the goal. On the other hand, enhanced running away from the floodlight would prolong the time spent reaching the goal of the maze. Zajonc et al. (1969)[11] conducted two experiments to test these predictions.

---

[11] Zajonc (1968) reported a similar experiment.

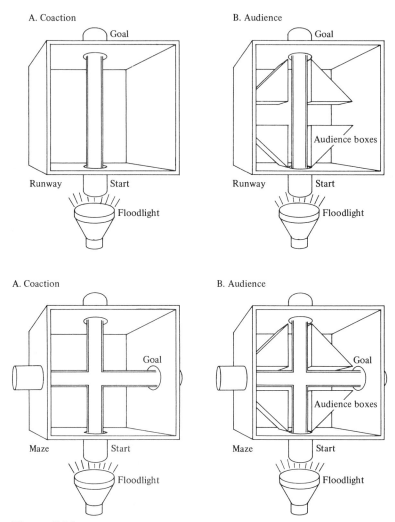

Figure 7.14
Diagrams of the runways and mazes used in experiments with cock-
roaches (from Zajonc, Heingartner, & Herman, 1969).

In the first experiment the escape behavior of cockroaches running alone was
compared to the escape behavior of roaches running in coacting pairs. Each
animal received ten trials and, for purposes of analysis, its score was the median
of its ten escape times. The subjects were 32 female cockroaches (*Blatta
orientalis*). Sixteen animals were tested alone—8 in the runway and 8 in the
maze. The remaining 16 animals were tested in coacting pairs—8 were tested
in the runway and 8 were tested in the maze. Table 7.3 shows the results. Confirming the hypothesis, the presence of coactors reduced time to escape in the
runway, but the presence of coactors increased time to escape in the maze.

Table 7.3

**Mean Time in Seconds to Escape from Light by
Paired and Solitary Cockroaches**

	Treatment	
Task	ALONE	COACTION
Runway	40.6	33.0
Maze	110.4	130.0

SOURCE. Zajonc, Heingartner, & Herman, 1969, p. 86.
NOTE. N = 8 in each condition; mean is average of individual medians of 10 escape trials.

The second experiment studied the effects of an audience. In order to confront the subject roach with an audience, a grandstand for cockroaches was constructed. It consisted of four boxes with clear plexiglass sides. When these boxes were in position, as shown in the lower portion of Figure 7.14, almost the entire extent of the walls of the runway or maze were in direct contact with the sides of the audience boxes. Thus, no matter where the subject roach might run, spectator roaches were always close by.

Forty female *Blatta orientalis* cockroaches were run for 10 trials. Half of the animals were tested in the runway and half were tested in the maze. Within each of these groups half of the animals were run with an audience of 40 cockroaches (10 in each audience box) and half with no audience present but with empty clean audience boxes in place. Table 7.4 presents the results. Confirming the Zajonc hypothesis, the presence of an audience decreased the time to escape in the runway, but increased the time to escape in the maze. Thus the results of these two experiments on cockroaches show that both the presence of coactors and the presence of an audience improve individual performance when the dominant response is correct, but impair individual performance when the dominant response is incorrect.

Table 7.4

**Mean Time in Seconds to Escape from Light by Cockroaches
with an Audience and Solitary Cockroaches**

	Treatment	
Task	ALONE	AUDIENCE
Runway	62.6	39.3
Maze	221.4	296.6

SOURCE. Zajonc, Heingartner, & Herman, 1969, p. 86.
NOTE. N = 10 in each condition; mean is average of individual medians of 10 escape trials.

While it may not be immediately obvious, studies of the social facilitation of eating have also used the method of population norms to identify the dominant response. One can readily observe that eating is the response that occurs most frequently when a hungry animal is confronted with the stimulus of food. Studies summarized in an earlier section showed that the presence of coactors enhances the emission of the dominant eating response—thus supporting the Zajonc hypothesis. There is, however, much evidence in this literature to indicate that the social facilitation of eating is also greatly influenced by the particular cues provided by the behavior of the coactor. For instance, in one of the earliest studies (Bayer, 1929) the introduction of a hungry coactor reinstated eating in a chicken which had just eaten to satiation (and for whom eating was presumably no longer the dominant response to the stimulus of food). Thus, the recent studies of the social facilitation of eating that have tested the Zajonc hypothesis have also been concerned with a comparative evaluation of mere presence and cue explanations of social facilitation findings. Therefore, examination of these studies will be postponed until a later section in which alternatives to the Zajonc hypothesis are considered.

OTHER INTERPRETATIONS OF AUDIENCE AND COACTION EFFECTS

This section evaluates two families of interpretations that have been proposed as alternatives to Zajonc's hypothesis. One family asserts that audience and coaction effects occur because the particular cues provided by the presence of others have directive effects upon individual behavior. Another set of interpretations questions Zajonc's proposal that the mere presence of others is a sufficient condition for increasing the individual's drive level, asserting that the presence of others must elicit anticipations of reward or punishment in order to increase drive level.

Audiences Are Distracting

Echoing a suggestion made originally by Meumann (1904),[12] Jones and Gerard (1967) have proposed that, ". . . the presence of others is distracting as well as motivating, and that the impairment of learning and complex problem-solving may be as much a direct effect of distraction as the increased prominence attached to nondominant solutions [p. 604]." They support their proposal by citing some of the results of two studies of audience effects, including Pessin's (1933) study of serial learning. There was a third condition in this study not mentioned in the earlier discussion of Pessin's results. In addition to learning one serial list alone and one list with a spectator, Pessin's subjects also learned a third list while subjected to mechanical distractors. These were a flashing light and a buzzer sounded at regular intervals. Like the audience con-

[12] Burnham (1905) and Allport (1924) have presented short summaries in English of Meumann's work.

dition, the mechanical distraction condition impaired the acquisition of a serial list. Subjects took more trials to achieve mastery in these two conditions than they did in the alone condition. Since an audience and mechanical distraction had the same effect of impairing learning, Jones and Gerard concluded that audiences influence performance by distracting the individual from his task. Their proposal suggests three somewhat different research hypotheses.

One hypothesis is that audiences are distracting and therefore the *audience effect* is to impair individual performance. The experimental evidence does not support this hypothesis. Some further results from Pessin's study call it into question. After mastering their lists, the subjects returned for a second day of testing on which they relearned the lists. On the second day performance was *better* in the audience and mechanical distraction conditions than in the alone condition. In these two conditions the subjects took fewer trials and made fewer errors to relearn the lists than in the alone condition. In terms of Zajonc's hypothesis, these results occurred because the presence of an audience improved performance when, as a result of mastering the lists on Day 1, the correct responses were dominant.[13] Although the results from Day 2 are not congenial to the Jones and Gerard position, they are not a clear confirmation of Zajonc's hypothesis either. One can argue that on Day 2 the habits governing the correct responses for the lists learned in the audience and mechanical distraction conditions were stronger than those for the list learned in the alone condition, since in these conditions subjects had more practice trials on Day 1 than did subjects in the alone condition. Thus the differences among conditions on Day 2 may be due to differences in habit strength, rather than to differences in drive. However, the results of other studies reviewed above do not suffer from this ambiguity of interpretation. These studies support the Zajonc hypothesis by showing that when the dominant response is correct, the presence of an audience improves performancy by increasing the frequency and speed of emission of the correct response (Bergum & Lehr, 1963; Martens, 1969; Matlin & Zajonc, 1968; Travis, 1925; Zajonc et al., 1969). Thus the experimental evidence refutes the hypothesis that an audience always impairs performance.

Another hypothesis that can be drawn from the Jones and Gerard position is that there are some kinds of audiences that can impair the individual's performance by distracting him. Studies of the effects of razzing and heckling support this hypothesis. For instance, Laird (1923) studied the effect of razzing upon performance on three tests of simple motor coordination, including a steadiness test. In this test the subject holds a thin metal stylus in a small hole in a metal panel. His task is to hold the stylus steady and to avoid contact with the panel. The stylus and panel are wired so that a buzzer sounds whenever the stylus makes contact. In Laird's experiment the dependent variable was the number of times the stylus made contact with the panel during the test period.

---

[13] This interpretation of Pessin's Day 2 results implies that the mechanical distractors were also a source of drive, since they also impaired learning and facilitated relearning. There is some evidence (Berlyne, 1967) that intermittent noise is a source of drive.

The subjects were fraternity pledges who worked individually for two sessions before an audience of the active members of the fraternity. During the first session the spectators were a passive audience; they watched quietly and attentively. During the second session the spectators tried to distract the subject by razzing and heckling him. They made discouraging and personally disparaging remarks about the subject and his performance. This razzing was quite distracting. In fact, Laird reported that he himself was so distracted that the records of two subjects had to be discarded because he "became unduly engrossed in the patter" and forgot to time the test periods. The results showed that the razzing impaired the subjects' performance as well. On the steadiness test all eight subjects made more errors (stylus contacts with the panel) when working before a razzing audience than when working before a passive audience. Under the assumption that it was just as likely for an individual to do better under razzing as before a passive audience, a sign-test was made which showed that the probability that this result occurred by chance was only eight in a thousand ($p = .008$). Razzing had a similar effect upon the other tests.

What bearing do these findings have on Zajonc's hypothesis? The answer is very little. This hypothesis concerns the effect of a passive audience upon individual performance, since its aim is to specify the effects of the mere presence of others. Evidence that razzing impairs performance tells us something about the effect of different kinds of audiences, but it does not add to our understanding of the effects of the *mere presence* of others.

A final hypothesis is that the presence of a passive audience always motivates the individual, thus tending to improve performance, but sometimes also distracts him from his task, thus producing inferior performance at times. Although this hypothesis is compatible with the pattern of findings reported above, it may be merely a description of past findings and add little to our understanding of them. In order to test the Jones and Gerard hypothesis experimentally, one must specify in advance the conditions under which a passive audience has the additional effect of distracting the individual and thus impairing his performance. At present Jones and Gerard have not made such a specification, and so their hypothesis is not testable in its present form. The Zajonc hypothesis provides a sharp contrast, for it specifies the conditions under which the presence of an audience should improve performance and the conditions under which an audience should impair performance. The hypotheses generated by Jones and Gerard are either not supported by evidence, irrelevant to the effects of the mere presence of others, or not testable in their present form. Jones and Gerard have not provided a viable alternative to the Zajonc hypothesis.

Coaction Effects Are Directive Effects

A much more plausible argument can be made that coaction effects are directive effects. Rather than, as proposed by Zajonc, the presence of coactors serving to energize the dominant responses elicited by the nonsocial, "task" stimuli, this interpretation proposes that cues provided by coactors have a *directive* effect upon the subject's performance. This position holds that the facilitation of dominant responses shown in studies of coaction occurs because stimuli produced by the responses of the coactor serve as *cues* to elicit the facilitated responses from the subject.

The social facilitation of eating in domestic chicks provides typical examples of the various types of directive effects that are possible in coaction. In this paradigm chickens are confronted with a pile of their customary food and the amount of eating and/or pecking done by each bird is observed. The results of such experiments are quite consistent—birds eat and/or peck much more in coaction than when alone. The responses of a coactor provide a wide variety of stimuli that are not available to a bird eating alone. There are at least three ways in which these stimuli might serve as cues to elicit eating responses from the subject.[14]

Imitation.   The goal response (in this case pecking) of the coactor might be a sufficient stimulus to elicit pecking from the subject. This interpretation assumes that more eating occurs in coaction because the subject chick has either learned in the past to peck when other chicks are pecking or that pecking in others instinctually elicits pecking. Both the sight of food and the sights and sounds of pecking coactors serve as cues to elicit the pecking response of the subject in coaction, whereas the sight of food is the only stimulus available to a subject eating alone.

Changing Nonsocial Stimuli.   The coactor's eating behavior may alter the nature of the nonsocial stimuli by, for instance, diminishing the size and altering the shape of the food supply. Enhanced pecking in coaction may occur because the sight of a rapidly diminishing food supply is a more effective stimulus for the elicitation of eating, than is the sight of food, which is the only stimulus available to the solitary chick.

Response-Produced Cues in Behavior Chains.   Eating behavior consists of a chained sequence of discrete pecking and consummatory responses. For a hungry chick, the sight of food is sufficient to elicit the first peck, but after that, other stimuli play important roles in maintaining and accelerating the chain of responses. Some of the cues that play such roles are those produced by the subject's own immediately prior eating behavior. Of these new cues produced by eating behavior, some are available only to the bird that is feeding (e.g., tactual and gustatory responses to bits of food in the beak and craw). However, some of these response-produced cues are identical to those that are produced by the eating behavior of a coacting bird (e.g., the sound of pecking). Therefore, the reason birds in coaction eat more than birds alone may be that in coaction the coactor's eating provides cues that maintain and accelerate the emission by the subject of the sequence of eating responses. Birds eating alone do not have this additional source of cues.

There is evidence that all of these processes contribute to social facilitation of

[14] See Tolman (1968a) for a more complete discussion of the role of the companion in the social facilitation of eating.

eating in chickens. Bayer's (1929) findings seem best explained by the imitation process described above. He found that the presence of a hungry (and pecking) coactor bird reinstated eating in a chicken which had just fed to satiation (and for whom eating was presumably no longer the dominant response to the stimulus of food). Tolman (1967, 1968a) found that with hungry birds, the rate of the coactor's pecking has a dramatic effect upon the amount of socially facilitated eating—the more the coactor pecks, the more the subject pecks. Tolman's findings seem to involve the second and third directive processes described above.

The findings of many of the coaction studies summarized earlier can be reinterpreted in terms of the directive processes described above. The results of Allport (1924), Chen (1937), and Dashiell (1930) may have occurred because the subjects imitated the goal responses of the coactors. (A close reading of Allport's and Dashiell's reports does not completely assure the reader that their procedures eliminated the possibility that a subject could observe the answers, words, etc. written by the coactors.) Chen's study also permits the interpretation that coaction affects individual performance because the behavior of the coactor alters the nonsocial stimuli. His findings may simply mean that wheras the average latency to initiate nest building in response to the stimuli provided by a bottle of soil is 192 minutes (See Table 7.1), the latency of nest building is much less when the sight of a partially dug nest (dug by the coactor) is also available as a stimulus. Larsson's findings (1956) may be due to the availability to subjects in coaction of additional response-produced stimuli that maintain and accelerate the emission of the chains of responses which comprise copulating behavior.

It seems quite certain that the cues provided by the coactor play a very important role in producing coaction effects upon individual performance. Perhaps in some instances these directive cues are entirely responsible for the findings obtained. But is this true in every case?

The answer appears to be no. First let us consider a recent study of the social facilitation of eating (Tolman, 1968). This experiment shows that the social facilitation of eating occurs even when the coactor is prevented from providing cues to direct the subject's behavior. In this study Tolman changed the coaction situation into an audience situation. The pecking of hungry (five hours food-deprived) isolated birds in the presence of food was compared with the pecking of hungry birds in the presence of food and a coactor that was separated from the subject by a barrier of clear plexiglass. This coactor was actually a spectator, since food was available to the subject only. Even with the feeding behavior of the stimulus bird eliminated in this way, the experiment showed that subjects pecked more in coaction than in isolation. Figure 7.15 shows the results of this experiment in terms of the average number of food pecks made by subjects during a seven-minute test period. The figure shows that subjects with a live coactor (which was actually a spectator) made 84 percent more food pecks than did subjects tested alone. These results indicate that the cues produced by a feeding coactor are not necessary conditions for the

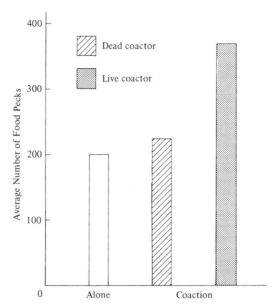

Figure 7.15
Average number of food pecks by solitary and coacting domestic chicks (from Tolman, 1968b, Experiment 3).

social facilitation of eating in chickens and therefore give support to the motivational process proposed by Zajonc.[15]

The results of two of the coaction experiments summarized earlier do not seem to be interpretable solely in terms of the directive processes described at the beginning of this section. In the studies of Goldman (1967) and Zajonc et al. (1970) we can be quite certain that the goal responses of the coactors were not available as cues to guide the subject's responses, because in these studies individuals in coaction made their task responses in private. Nevertheless, the presence of coactors enhanced the emission of the dominant response.

That some studies have shown that both audience and coaction produce similar effects upon individual performance also points to the conclusion that directive processes are not sufficient to account for *all* coaction results. Zajonc et al. (1969) found that both the presence of spectators and the presence of

[15] Tolman (1968b) has drawn a different conclusion from the results of these experiments: "It must be concluded that an organism's mere presence is not a sufficient condition for social facilitation of feeding in chicks [p. 282]." He based this conclusion on the failure of a mere presence condition to increase feeding. In this condition not only was the coactor's feeding behavior eliminated, but *all* of its behavior was eliminated by the expedient of killing it shortly before the feeding test. During the test the corpse of the stimulus bird was propped against the outside of the transparent barrier that separated the stimulus bird from the subject. As shown in Figure 7.15, the dead coactor condition did not increase feeding. Perhaps in completely eliminating the behavior of the stimulus bird in this way, Tolman eliminated its effective presence as well.

coactors increased the time for cockroaches to reach the goal in a maze and also decreased the time to reach the goal in a runway. In a study of human performance, Zajonc et al. (1970) found that both audience and coaction enhance the emission of the dominant response. Directive interpretations of audience effects are no doubt possible, but must be rather contrived, since a passive audience, by definition, maintains a "steady state," and does not signal to the subject which responses are correct and which are not.

Thus, particular instances of coaction effects may be entirely due to directive cues produced by the responses of the coactor. However, it is frequently possible to conceal from the subject those cues that might be provided by the coactor's responses, and thereby completely forestall the effects of directive processes in coaction. When there is doubt, perhaps parallel experiments on coaction and audience might be run and carefully compared. Obviously, if a coaction experiment is to provide evidence on the validity and limitations of the Zajonc hypothesis, one must carefully study the particular experimental arrangement to determine whether it provides potentially directive cues that are not available to a subject working alone.

Presence of Others: A Learned or Innate Source of Drive

Finally we shall examine a revision of the Zajonc hypothesis. Cottrell (1968) has recently proposed that the presence of others is a learned source of drive, rather than a source of drive which is innate or "wired-into" the organism, as is tacitly assumed in the Zajonc hypothesis. It is quite clear that the Zajonc hypothesis must be modified in some way because there is experimental evidence that shows that under certain circumstances the mere presence of others is not a sufficient condition for enhancing the emission of dominant responses. We shall first examine this evidence and then consider the rationale and details of the learned drive revision of the Zajonc hypothesis.

The Zajonc hypothesis assumes that the audience and coaction paradigms are representative of all situations in which species mates are merely present and neither providing cues nor reinforcements to direct the subject's behavior. As the evidence continues to accumulate, it seems more and more certain that the presence of spectators or coactors enhances the emission of dominant responses by increasing the individual's general drive level. However, is it the *mere presence* of others that is responsible for these effects? If so, then the presence of persons who are neither spectators nor coactors should also, according to the Zajonc hypothesis, enhance the emission of dominant responses.

The Sufficiency of Mere Presence of an Audience.   Cottrell et al. (1968) tested the *mere presence* derivation from the Zajonc hypothesis in the audience paradigm and used the pseudorecognition procedure described earlier. In an initial training stage, a set of verbal habits of different strengths was established for each subject. After that, the experimental treatments were administered. Finally, the testing stage placed the verbal habits in competition with one another. For each subject, one of three experimental treatments prevailed during testing. In the alone condition, the subject was alone during pseudorecognition testing. In the audience condition, two spectators sat six feet from the subject and watched him quietly and attentively. The spectators were actually confederates of the experimenter posing as subjects reporting to serve in an experiment on color perception. When they "learned" that their experiment would not begin until the experimenter had finished with the real subject, the confederates obtained the experimenter's permission to remain and watch the subject while they waited. The mere presence condition was very similar to the audience condition; two confederates posing as subjects sat six feet from the subject and remained silent throughout the test phase. However, the confederates in this condition wore blindfolds, purportedly to dark adapt them in preparation for their later experiment on color perception. Thus the stimulus persons in the mere presence condition were not really spectators, for although they could hear the subject's verbal responses, they could not see the task stimuli that prompted them.

Figure 7.10 shows that relative to the alone condition, the audience condition enhanced the emission of dominant responses at the expense of subordinate responses. The figure also shows that the mere presence condition was almost identical to the alone condition; it did not enhance the emission of dominant responses at the expense of subordinate responses.[16]

Clearly, the mere presence of others is not a sufficient condition to enhance the emission of dominant responses. In interpreting the results of the experiment described above, Cottrell (1968) has suggested that the presence of others in the audience paradigm will enhance the emission of dominant responses only when the spectators can evaluate the individual's performance. The blindfolds precluded the possibility that the "spectators" in the mere presence condition could evaluate the correspondence between the task stimuli and the subject's attempts to name these stimuli as they were flashed on the screen.

The results of two subsequent studies (Henchy & Glass, 1968; Paulus & Murdoch, 1971) that also used the pseudorecognition task point to a similar conclusion. Henchy and Glass used instructions to vary the extent to which the subject perceived that his performance during the test phase was being evaluated. In the alone condition the subject was given no special instructions concerning the evaluation of his performance. In the alone recorded condition the subject was instructed that specialists in human learning and perception would evaluate films and tape recordings of his performance. In the other two conditions two individuals sat quietly and watched the subject perform: In the expert condition the subject was told that these individuals were experts in human learning and perception and were interested in evaluating his performance, and in the nonexpert condition they were told that the observers were undergraduate students who wanted to watch a psychological experiment.

The results showed that the greatest enhancement of dominant responses was

---

[16] The slopes of the response emission functions show a similar result. The slope in the mere presence condition was .292, much less than the slope for the audience condition, .488, and very similar to the slope for the alone condition, .257.

produced by the conditions that emphasized the evaluation of the subject's performance—the expert and alone recorded conditions. In partial support of Zajonc's contention that the mere presence of others is sufficient to increase dominant responding, there was a difference of borderline statistical significance between the nonexpert and alone conditions.

The experiment by Paulus and Murdoch gives somewhat stronger support to the contention that evaluative factors and not the presence of others is responsible for enhancing the emission of dominant responses in the audience paradigm. Half of the subjects were given their pseudorecognition task alone, and the other half had two other persons present during testing. Within both of these groups half of the subjects were instructed that *after* the pseudorecognition task two undergraduate students would evaluate their performance on the task, and the other half of the subjects were not given these instructions. In the others present-evaluation condition the experimenter described the stimulus persons as individuals who were going to evaluate the subject's performance at the end of the session. The instructions in the others present-no evaluation condition described the stimulus persons as subjects who were adapting to the level of illumination in the experimental room in preparation for a later experiment.

There was one major change in the procedure of administering the pseudorecognition task. Whereas in previous studies (Cottrell et al., 1968; Henchy & Glass, 1968; Zajonc & Nieuwenhuyse, 1964; Zajonc & Sales, 1965) the subject *spoke* his verbal responses aloud during training and the subsequent testing, in the Paulus study subjects *wrote* their verbal responses privately both during training and testing. This procedure allowed Paulus and Murdoch to manipulate the physical presence of others orthogonally to the likelihood of a later evaluation of performance. The stimulus persons in the others present conditions were able to observe the task stimuli as they were presented to the subject, but they could not at that moment evaluate the appropriateness of the subject's responses to these stimuli, since on each trial the subject wrote his response in private.

Table 7.5

Slope of Function Relating Frequency of Response Emission On Pseudorecognition Trials to Training Frequency

| | *Later Evaluation Expected* | | |
	YES	NO	AVERAGE
Others Present	.643	.437	.540
Alone	.695	.492	.594
Average	.669	.464	

SOURCE. Paulus & Murdoch, 1971, p. 287.
NOTE. Frequencies per trial block of 30 pseudorecognition trials, averaged over subjects, were used in computing slopes.

Table 7.5 shows the slope for each condition of the function relating frequency of response emission on the pseudorecognition trials to habit strength (training frequency). The table shows that the greater the probability of evaluation, the greater the slope of the response emission function, thus indicating that the anticipation of an impending performance evaluation enhances the emission of dominant responses at the expense of subordinate responses. The table also shows that the presence of others did not enhance the emission of dominant responses; the slopes for the others present conditions are nearly identical to the corresponding alone conditions. The results show that the mere presence of others is not a sufficient condition to enhance the emission of dominant responses, but that these effects do occur when there is the anticipation of later praise or criticism.

The Sufficiency of Mere Presence of Coactors. There is also evidence to suggest that the mere presence of coactors is not sufficient to enhance the emission of dominant responses. Dashiell (1930) found that there are certain circumstances under which the presence of coactors does not produce the typical coaction effects upon individual performance. His studies implicated competition and rivalrous comparisons of performance, rather than the mere presence of coacting others, as the determinant of coaction effects. Dashiell separated rivalry and competition from the mere presence of coactors. The coaction effects found earlier by Allport (1920) did not obtain in the mere coaction condition of Dashiell's experiment, but in the competitive coaction condition the results were very similar.

Dashiell (1930) manipulated rivalry by means of explicit instructions to compete or not to compete. Klinger (1969) separated coaction and rivalry by manipulating the situational cues available to subjects. Klinger (1969) compared work done in two different coaction arrangements with work done alone. In the mere coaction condition two individuals worked simultaneously and independently on the same kind of vigilance task; they kept watch for irregularities in a repeated visual signal. There was no opportunity for the paired individuals to compare their detection accuracy with each other. The coaction-errors public condition was identical with the addition of two distinctive error signals that made public to both participants that a particular individual had made an error of detection. There were two alone control conditions, one with an error signal for the individual and one with no error signal. The results showed that mere coaction had little effect upon individual performance. The detection accuracy of individuals working in coaction was almost identical to that achieved by individuals working alone. In contrast, in the conditions in which errors were made public, coaction had a dramatic effect upon individual performance; individuals in coaction were 1.4 times as accurate as individuals working alone. When the error signal made possible rivalrous comparisons of performance, coaction had dramatic effects upon individual performance. In opposition to the Zajonc hypothesis, the mere presence of coactors had no effect upon individual performance.

THE MODIFICATION OF A HYPOTHESIS

How can the Zajonc hypothesis be modified to accommodate these inconsistent results? Henchy and Glass (1968) have suggested that apprehension about evaluations of performance may be a necessary condition for the occurrence of social facilitation effects. In a similar vein Jones and Gerard (1967) have suggested that social facilitation effects ". . . are mediated primarily through self-consciousness on the part of the subject, a concern with how he appears in the eyes of others [p. 607]." While these suggestions may account for the exceptions to the Zajonc hypothesis, how well do they account for the evidence that supports it? It is plausible to assert that among human beings the presence of others is drive-increasing only when it produces evaluation apprehension, self-consciousness about performance, etc. But what of the animal evidence? The explanatory terms of "evaluation," "self-consciousness," etc. are ill-suited for the analysis of the behavior of cockroaches, chickens, and rats.

The value of parsimony in explanation prompts us to attempt to account for the human and animal evidence with the same explanatory scheme. There is also empirical justification for seeking a unified explanation of the human and animal findings. Some studies of animals have also shown that the presence of species mates is not sufficient to increase the emission of dominant responses.

In a series of experiments on the social facilitation of eating in rats, Harlow (1932) examined the role of competition in producing coaction effects. He concluded, "The essential condition for the occurrence of social facilitation is the presence of rats unrestrained and actively competing with each other for food [p. 220]." The results of Harlow and Yudin (1933) point to a similar conclusion. In their studies monkeys were allowed to eat under three experimental conditions: alone; a competitive coaction condition in which the paired animals could, if they chose to, steal food from each other; and a coaction arrangement in which competition was not possible. Both versions of coaction produced increments in eating, but the increment in the noncompetitive coaction condition was rather small (23 percent) and possibly unreliable, whereas competitive coaction produced a very large (53 percent) increment that was also stable over all animals. Vogel, Scott, and Marston (1950) eliminated competition from their coaction condition in a study of dogs and found that dogs ran a 170-foot long alley to obtain food at the same speed in noncompetitive coaction as they did when tested alone.

There is also evidence from studies of animals that indicates that whether or not the presence of others will enhance the emission of dominant responses depends upon the individual's prior social experience. Harlow (1932, Experiments 3 & 4) tested two groups of rats for the social facilitation of eating. One group had been reared in isolation since weaning, and the other group had been housed in groups of four or five since weaning. The socially experienced group showed a strong social facilitation of eating effect. The isolation-reared group, however, did not; during testing the animals in this group ate the same amount when tested alone as they did when tested in a coacting group.

Other investigators have repeated Harlow's results using chicks (Tolman, 1964; Wilson, 1968) and dogs (James, 1960; James & Gilbert, 1955). Some of these investigators also found that when testing was continued over an extended period of time, the isolation-reared group eventually showed the social facilitation of eating. Thus these studies show that prior social experience is necessary for producing the social facilitation of eating. Animals reared in isolation eat the same amount when tested alone as when tested in a coacting group. Continued testing for the social facilitation of eating provides the necessary social experience and eventually isolation-reared animals come to eat more when fed in a group than when fed alone.

Presence as a Learned Source of Drive

Cottrell (1968) has attempted to integrate the findings that contradict and those that support the Zajonc hypothesis in a framework that is appropriate for the analysis of both human and animal behavior. He has suggested that the drive-increasing property of the presence of others is created through social experience and is not, as is implied by the Zajonc hypothesis, a biological given. This formulation states that the presence of others is a *learned source of drive* (Brown, 1961; Brown & Farber, 1968). It is assumed that at birth the stimuli produced by the mere presence of another organism are motivationally neutral; they neither increase nor decrease the individual's general drive level. Various aversive and gratifying events that serve to increase the individual's general drive level occur throughout the individual's life. Many of these events are spatially and temporally contiguous with the presence of others. For example, frequently others are present when an individual is praised or rewarded for his performance, and also when he is criticized or punished. Others are often the agents of frustration. Upon occasion other organisms will physically attack and harm the individual. There are also occasions when other organisms are a source of physical gratification to the individual, for instance, sexual gratification, contact comfort. With an increasing number of such encounters, the stimuli from the mere presence of others gradually lose their neutral quality and become, through classical conditioning, sufficient to increase the individual's drive level. Through experience the individual learns to anticipate subsequent positive or negative outcomes whenever others are merely present and not overtly doing anything that has motivational significance for him. It is these anticipations, elicited by the presence of others, that increase the individual's drive level. The mere presence of others is not a sufficient condition to increase drive; this presence must also elicit anticipations of positive or negative outcomes.

The precise processes by which these anticipations function to increase drive will not be discussed in detail here. The processes of incentive motivation, conditioned fear, and anticipatory frustration responses[17] may govern the functioning of these anticipations as a source of drive. However, future research may implicate other processes in addition to, or instead of, these.

The nature of the anticipations produced by the presence of others and the process that creates them are probably somewhat different for human and infrahuman species. In the case of audience effects upon human performance, individuals have presumably been "trained" by their past experience in that other persons who watch them as spectators often praise or criticize them. After such training similar social situations, such as the classical audience paradigm in which spectators can compare the individual's performance with an evaluative standard, will elicit anticipations of praise or criticism and thereby increase the individual's drive level. This analysis further assumes that in the individual's experience there have been some situations in which others were present but that typically did not result in praise or criticism. Such situations and others like them would not elicit anticipations of praise or criticism and would therefore remain motivationally neutral for the individual. Experiments described above (Cottrell et al., 1968; Henchy & Glass, 1968; Paulus & Murdoch, 1971) have shown that when anticipations of praise or criticism are eliminated the presence of others does not increase the individual's drive level.

Some evidence (Dashiell, 1930; Klinger, 1969) indicates that coaction effects upon human performance are mediated by rivalrous comparisons of performance. In terms of the learned drive interpretation, such comparisons themselves might constitute positive or negative outcomes for the coacting individuals, or these performance comparisons might serve as the basis for the subsequent dispensing of an external reward or punishment. Presumably, individuals are trained by their past experience so that when others are working on the same task at the same time, positive or negative outcomes are often the result. After such training, a new instance of coaction that produces rivalrous comparisons of performance serves to increase the individual's drive level. It is further assumed that in the individual's experience not every situation in which coactors were physically present typically produced rivalrous comparisons of performance. Presumably individuals come to discriminate such nonrivalrous coaction arrangements and these situations remain motivationally neutral for the individual. When a nonrivalrous coaction arrangement is encountered (as in the experiments of Dashiell, 1930; Klinger, 1969), the presence of coactors does not serve to increase the individual's drive level.

For animals the events that serve as either positive or negative outcomes differ from those of humans (it is difficult to conceive of, for instance, one cockroach praising another cockroach for his task performance). Nevertheless, the analysis of animal behavior is formally similar to that used above in analyzing human behavior. For newborn infrahuman organisms the presence of species mates is motivationally neutral. Through social experience, the presence

---

[17] These processes are part of the Hull-Spence theory and are discussed in detail by Brown, 1961; Brown and Farber, 1968; Cofer and Appley, 1964; Spence, 1956, 1958.

of species mates elicits anticipations of positive or negative outcomes. These anticipations serve to increase the individual's general drive level. When these anticipations are elicited by the presence of others in a new situation, then the individual's drive level is increased. As with human beings the training that establishes positive and negative anticipations also serves to establish discriminations as well. As a result of this training the individual comes to discriminate between those social situations that are a sign for impending reward or punishment, and those that are not. Thus the socially experienced animal will have its drive level increased by some situations in which species mates are present, but not in others.

Most of the research on animals has been on the social facilitation of feeding in coaction. The learned drive interpretation of those findings is as follows: When animals feed together in groups, they frequently steal food from each other and interrupt and frustrate each other's sequence of consummatory responses in other ways as well. Initially the stimuli from the presence of other animals are motivationally neutral. With continued instances of frustration, animals are "trained" to anticipate the frustration of their eating activities whenever other animals are nearby. These anticipations, rather than the mere presence of others, increase the animal's drive level and thus enhance the emission of the dominant eating responses elicited by the stimuli from food. This interpretation can account for all the evidence that the Zajonc hypothesis can, and also the evidence that is inconsistent with the Zajonc hypothesis—the evidence which suggests that competition for food is a necessary condition for the social facilitation of feeding (Harlow, 1932; Harlow & Yudin, 1933; Vogel, Scott, & Marston, 1950), and also the studies showing the crucial role of prior social experience in social feeding effects (Harlow, 1932; James, 1960; James & Gilbert, 1955; Tolman, 1964; Wilson, 1968).

The learned drive interpretation of audience and coaction effects has several advantages that encourage its further development. It retains the motivational process proposed by Zajonc that organizes a large body of evidence, and it can accommodate the evidence that is contrary to the Zajonc hypothesis. The learned drive formulation is parsimonious in that it uses the same broad outline in the analysis of both human and animal behavior. However, the scientific viability of this interpretation will only be established by empirical verification of its testable implications.

Future Evaluation of the Learned Drive Interpretation

Future research must further test the assertion that evaluative processes mediate audience and coaction effects upon human performance. If the learned drive interpretation is correct, then any particular demonstration of audience or coaction effects should contain cues for rivalry or evaluation that, if removed, should eliminate the effects produced by the presence of others. Hopefully, work of this kind will produce a general and systematic description of social arrangements in which the presence of others reliably elicits anticipations of evaluation and rivalry, and thereby increases the individual's drive level.

A major implication of the learned drive interpretation is that particular kinds of social experience are required to confer a drive-increasing function upon stimuli stemming from the presence of others. At birth these stimuli are assumed to be motivationally neutral. It is assumed that the presence of others becomes a source of drive as a result of consistent association with events that themselves are drive-producing. In studies with animals this assumption can be examined very directly. There is some evidence that withholding social experience of any kind by rearing animals in isolation eliminates the social facilitation of eating in coaction (Harlow, 1932; James, 1960; James & Gilbert, 1955; Tolman, 1964). However, previous research has shown that coaction can also facilitate behaviors other than eating (Chen, 1937; Larsson, 1956; Zajonc et al., 1969). Also audience conditions can produce social facilitation in animals (Tolman, 1968b; Zajonc et al., 1969). If the learned drive interpretation is correct, then rearing in isolation should eliminate the social facilitation effects found in these experiments. If the results of experiments of this kind indicate that prior social experience is necessary to produce social facilitation, then further studies with animals could determine the particular sorts of social encounters that are required.

Obvious ethical considerations forestall such drastic interventions into the lives of human neonates and infants. However, measures of individual differences in personality can be used to gain some understanding of the role prior social experience plays in audience or coaction effects upon human performance. Two recent studies of audience effects (Ganzer, 1968; Quarter & Marcus, 1971) also included individual difference measures that seem especially indicative of differences in prior social experience.

Ganzer studied the effect of an audience on the serial learning performance of individuals at three different levels of test anxiety. "Test anxiety" was measured by the test anxiety scale (Sarason, 1960), which is presumed to detect differences among individuals in their concern and anxiety about taking tests and having their performance evaluated. Presumably such differences among individuals are created in their past social experience—individuals score as highly test anxious because frequently in the past other persons have been highly critical of their performance, moderately test anxious individuals have had fewer of these harsh evaluations, etc. The subjects learned a serial list of nonsense syllables either alone or with a spectator watching them. The results showed that the presence of an audience impaired the learning of new material. The results for the first block of five trials were of especial relevance to the learned drive view. These results showed that the greater the individual's test anxiety, the greater was the impairing effect of the audience on learning new material. The difference between audience and alone treatments was greatest for highly test anxious individuals, the conditions did not differ among individuals of low test anxiety, and moderately test anxious individuals were in between. The results suggest that prior experience with harshly evaluative audiences make individuals more responsive to contemporary presence of a passive spectator, and thus provide some indirect support for the learned drive interpretation of audience effects upon human performance.

The findings of Quarter and Marcus also strongly suggest that presumed individual differences in prior social experience affect the magnitude of the audience effect upon human performance. Subjects performed a set of digit span tasks either alone or with two spectators sitting six feet away. Digit span tasks require subjects to listen to a spoken series of digits and then reproduce the series perfectly. Previous research has shown that increases in drive from nonsocial sources impair the performance of individuals on digit span tasks. Quarter and Marcus found that the presence of an audience also impairs individual performance on the digit span tasks. Of most relevance to the learned drive interpretation of audience effects was their finding that this audience effect was confined to individuals who were first born or only children. Later born children were equally proficient at digit span tasks when working alone as when working with spectators. Schachter (1959) has suggested that first born and only children are more responsive to socially induced stress and to evaluations made by other persons than are later born individuals.[18] It is plausible to assume that first born and only children have in their past histories, especially during the first years of life, more frequently had their performance monitored by their parents and been praised or criticized more often than later born individuals. If this line of reasoning is correct, then the findings of Quarter and Marcus lend some support to the learned drive interpretation of audience effects by showing that the audience effect is contingent upon the individual's prior social experience.[19]

REFERENCES

ALLEE, W. C., & MASURE, R. H. A comparison of maze behavior in paired and isolated shell-parakeets (*Melopsittacus undulatus Shaw*) in a two-alley problem box. *Journal of Comparative Psychology*, 1936, **22,** 131–155.

ALLPORT, F. H. The influence of the group upon association and thought. *Journal of Experimental Psychology*, 1920, **3,** 159–182.

ALLPORT, F. H. *Social psychology*. Boston: Houghton Mifflin, 1924.

ASCH, S. E. *Social psychology*. Englewood Cliffs, N.J.: Prentice-Hall, 1952.

BANDURA, A. Vicarious processes: A case of no-trial learning. In L. Berkowitz (Ed.),

---

[18] Recent research (see Sampson, 1965, and Warren, 1966, for reviews) has given some support to this formulation.

[19] Paivio (1965) has conducted an extensive program of research on individual differences in reactions to audiences. However, the associative characteristics of the performance tasks used are not well understood, and thus the relevance of the results to the Zajonc hypothesis is not clear.

Advances in experimental social psychology. Vol. 2. New York: Academic Press, 1965. Pp. 1–55.

BAYER, E. Beiträge zur Zweikomponententheorie des Hungers. *Zeitschrift für Psychologie*, 1929, **112**, 1–54.

BERGUM, B. O., & LEHR, D. J. Effects of authoritarianism on vigilance performance. *Journal of Applied Psychology*, 1963, **47**, 75–77.

BERLYNE, D. E. Arousal and reinforcement. In D. Levine (Ed.), *Nebraska symposium on motivation, 1967*. Lincoln, Neb.: University of Nebraska Press, 1967.

BOLLES, R. C. *Theory of motivation*. New York: Harper & Row, 1967.

BROEN, W. E., JR., & STORMS, L. H. A reaction potential ceiling and response decrements in complex situations. *Psychological Review*, 1961, **68**, 405–415.

BROWN, J. S. *The motivation of behavior*. New York: McGraw-Hill, 1961.

BROWN, J. S., & FARBER, I. E. Secondary motivational systems. *Annual Review of Psychology*, 1968, **19**, 99–134.

BRUCE, R. H. An experimental analysis of social factors affecting the performance of white rats. I. Performance in learning a simple field situation. *Journal of Comparative Psychology*, 1941, **31**, 363–377.

BURNHAM, W. H. The hygiene of home study. *Pedagogical Seminary and Journal of Genetic Psychology*, 1905, **12**, 213–230.

BURNHAM, W. H. The group as a stimulus to mental activity. *Science*, 1910, **31**, 761–767.

CHEN, S. C. Social modification of the activity of ants in nest-building. *Physiological Zoology*, 1937, **10**, 420–436.

COFER, C. N., & APPLEY, M. H. *Motivation: Theory and research*. New York: Wiley, 1964.

COTTRELL, N. B. Performance in the presence of other human beings: Mere presence, audience, and affiliation effects. In E. C. Simmel, R. A. Hoppe, & G. A. Milton (Eds.), *Social facilitation and imitative behavior*. Boston: Allyn & Bacon, 1968. Pp. 91–110.

COTTRELL, N. B., RITTLE, R. H., & WACK, D. L. The presence of an audience and list type (competitional or noncompetitional) as joint determinants of performance in paired-associates learning. *Journal of Personality*, 1967, **35**, 425–434.

COTTRELL, N. B., WACK, D. L., SEKERAK, G. J., & RITTLE, R. H. Social facilitation of dominant responses by the presence of an audience and the mere presence of others. *Journal of Personality and Social Psychology*, 1968, **9**, 245–250.

DASHIELL, J. F. An experimental analysis of some group effects. *Journal of Abnormal and Social Psychology*, 1930, **25**, 190–199.

DASHIELL, J. F. Experimental studies of the influence of social situations on the behavior of individual human adults. In C. Murchison (Ed.), *Handbook of social psychology*. Worcester, Mass.: Clark University, 1935. Pp. 1097–1158.

DEESE, J., & HULSE, S. H. *The psychology of learning*. (3rd ed.) New York: McGraw-Hill, 1967.

EDWARDS, A. L. *Statistical analysis*. (3rd ed.) New York: Holt, 1969.

FITTS, P. M., & POSNER, M. I. *Human performance*. Belmont, Calif.: Wadsworth, 1967.

GANZER, V. J. Effects of audience presence and test anxiety on learning and retention in a serial learning situation. *Journal of Personality and Social Psychology*, 1968, **8**, 194–199.

GATES, M. F., & ALLEE, W. C. Conditioned behavior of isolated and grouped cockroaches on a simple maze. *Journal of Comparative Psychology,* 1933, **15,** 331–358.

GOLDMAN, C. An examination of social facilitation. Unpublished manuscript. University of Michigan, 1967.

GREENSPOON, J. The reinforcing effect of two spoken sounds on the frequency of two responses. *American Journal of Psychology,* 1955, **68,** 409–416.

GURNEE, H. Effect of collective learning upon the individual participants. *Journal of Abnormal and Social Psychology,* 1939, **34,** 529–532.

HARLOW, H. F. Social facilitation of feeding in the albino rat. *Journal of Genetic Psychology,* 1932, **41,** 211–221.

HARLOW, H. F., & YUDIN, H. C. Social behavior of primates, I. Social facilitation of feeding in the monkey and its relation to attitudes of ascendance and submission. *Journal of Comparative Psychology,* 1933, **16,** 171–185.

HENCHY, T., & GLASS, D. C. Evaluation apprehension and the social facilitation of dominant and subordinate responses. *Journal of Personality and Social Psychology,* 1968, **10,** 446–454.

HILGARD, E. R., & BOWER, G. H. *Theories of learning.* (3rd ed.) New York: Appleton, 1966.

HORENSTEIN, B. Performance of conditioned responses as a function of strength of hunger drive. *Journal of Comparative and Physiological Psychology,* 1951, **41,** 210–224.

HULL, C. L. *Principles of behavior.* New York: Appleton, 1943.

HUSBAND, R. W. Analysis of methods in human maze learning. *Journal of Genetic Psychology,* 1931, **39,** 258–277.

JAMES, W. T. Social facilitation of eating behavior in puppies after satiation. *Journal of Comparative and Physiological Psychology,* 1953, **46,** 427–428.

JAMES, W. T. The development of social facilitation of eating in puppies. *Journal of Genetic Psychology,* 1960, **96,** 123–127.

JAMES, W. T., & GILBERT, T. F. The effect of social facilitation on food intake of puppies fed separately and together for the first 90 days of life. *British Journal of Animal Behavior,* 1955, **3,** 131–133.

JONES, E. E., & GERARD, H. B. *Foundations of social psychology.* New York: Wiley, 1967.

KIMBLE, G. A. *Hilgard and Marquis' conditioning and learning.* (2nd ed.) New York: Appleton, 1961.

KLINGER, E. Feedback effects and social facilitation of vigilance performance: Mere coaction versus potential evaluation. *Psychonomic Science,* 1969, **14,** 161–162.

KLOPFER, P. H. Influence of social interaction on learning rates in birds. *Science,* 1958, **128,** 903–904.

KOENIG, K. P. Verbal behavior and personality change. *Journal of Personality and Social Psychology,* 1966, **3,** 223–227.

LAIRD, D. A. Changes in motor control and individual variations under the influence of "razzing." *Journal of Experimental Psychology,* 1923, **6,** 236–246.

LARSSON, K. *Conditioning and sexual behavior in the male albino rat.* Stockholm: Almqvist & Wiksell, 1956.

LEE, L. C. The effects of anxiety level and shock on a paired-associate verbal task. *Journal of Experimental Psychology,* 1961, **61,** 213–217.

MARTENS, R. Effect of an audience on learning and performance of a complex motor skill. *Journal of Personality and Social Psychology*, 1969, **12,** 252–260.

MATLIN, M. W., & ZAJONC, R. B. Social facilitation of word associations. *Journal of Personality and Social Psychology*, 1968, **10,** 455–460.

MEUMANN, E. Haus- und Schularbeit: Experimente an Kindern der Volkschule. *Die Deutsche Schule*, 1904, **8,** 278–303, 337–359, 416–431.

MILLER, N. E. Theory and experiment relating psychoanalytic displacement to stimulus-response generalization. *Journal of Abnormal and Social Psychology*, 1948, **43,** 155–178.

MILLER, N. E., & DOLLARD, J. *Social learning and imitation.* New Haven, Conn.: Yale University Press, 1941.

PAIVIO, A. Personality and audience influence. In B. Maher (Ed.), *Progress in experimental personality research.* Vol. 2. New York: Academic Press, 1965. Pp. 127–173.

PAULUS, P. B., & MURDOCH, P. Anticipated evaluation and audience presence in the enhancement of dominant responses. *Journal of Experimental Social Psychology*, 1971, **7,** 280–291.

PESSIN, J. The comparative effects of social and mechanical stimulation on memorizing. *American Journal of Psychology*, 1933, **45,** 263–270.

PLATT, J. J., & JAMES, W. T. Social facilitation of eating behavior in young opossums. I. Group vs. solitary feeding. *Psychonomic Science*, 1966, **6,** 421–422.

PLATT, J. J., YAKSH, T., & DARBY, C. L. Social facilitation of eating behavior in armadillos. *Psychological Reports*, 1967, **20,** 1136.

QUARTER, J., & MARCUS, A. Drive level and the audience effect: A test of Zajonc's theory. *Journal of Social Psychology*, 1971, **83,** 99–105.

SAMPSON, E. E. The study of ordinal position: Antecedents and outcomes. In B. A. Maher (Ed.), *Progress in experimental personality research.* Vol. 2. New York: Academic Press, 1965. Pp. 175–228.

SARASON, I. G. Empirical findings and theoretical problems in the use of anxiety scales. *Psychological Bulletin*, 1960, **57,** 403–415.

SARASON, I. G., & GANZER, V. J. Anxiety, reinforcement, and experimental instructions in a free verbalization situation. *Journal of Abnormal and Social Psychology*, 1962, **65,** 300–307.

SARASON, I. G., & GANZER, V. J. Effects of test anxiety and reinforcement history on verbal behavior. *Journal of Abnormal and Social Psychology*, 1963, **67,** 513–519.

SCHACHTER, S. *The psychology of affiliation.* Stanford, Calif.: Stanford University Press, 1959.

SCOTT, J. P. Social facilitation and alleomimetic behavior. In E. C. Simmel, R. A. Hoppe, & G. A. Milton (Eds.), *Social facilitation and imitative behavior.* Boston: Allyn & Bacon, 1968. Pp. 55–72.

SIEGEL, S. *Nonparametric statistics for the behavioral sciences.* New York: McGraw-Hill, 1956.

SPENCE, J. T., & SPENCE, K. W. The motivational components of manifest anxiety: Drive and drive stimuli. In C. D. Spielberger (Ed.), *Anxiety and behavior.* New York: Academic Press, 1966. Pp. 291–326.

SPENCE, K. W. *Behavior theory and conditioning.* New Haven, Conn.: Yale University Press, 1956.

SPENCE, K. W. Behavior theory and selective learning. In M. R. Jones (Ed.), *Ne-*

braska symposium on motivation, 1958. Lincoln, Nebr.: University of Nebraska Press, 1958. Pp. 73–107.

SPENCE, K. W., FARBER, I. E., & McFANN, H. H. The relation of anxiety (drive) level to performance in competitional and noncompetitional paired-associates learning. *Journal of Experimental Psychology,* 1956, **52,** 296–305.

STAMM, J. S. Social facilitation in monkeys. *Psychological Reports,* 1961, **8,** 479–484.

STEVENSON, H. W. Social reinforcement of children's behavior. In L. P. Lipsitt & C. C. Spiker (Eds.), *Advances in child development and behavior.* Vol. 2. New York: Academic Press, 1965. Pp. 97–126.

STRAIN, G. S. Social facilitation of oddity preference by children. Paper presented at the meeting of the Midwestern Psychological Association, Chicago, May 1967.

TAYLOR, J. A. A personality scale of manifest anxiety. *Journal of Abnormal and Social Psychology,* 1953, **48,** 285–290.

TOLMAN, C. W. Social facilitation of feeding behavior in the domestic chick. *Animal Behavior,* 1964, **12,** 245–251.

TOLMAN, C. W. Emotional behavior and social facilitation of feeding in domestic chicks. *Animal Behavior,* 1965, **13,** 493–496.

TOLMAN, C. W. The feeding behaviour of domestic chicks as a function of pecking by a surrogate companion. *Behaviour,* 1967, **29,** 57–62.

TOLMAN, C. W. The role of the companion in social facilitation of animal behavior. In E. C. Simmel, R. A. Hoppe, & G. A. Milton (Eds.), *Social facilitation and imitative behavior.* Boston: Allyn & Bacon, 1968. Pp. 33–54. (a)

TOLMAN, C. W. The varieties of social stimulation in the feeding behaviour of domestic chicks. *Behaviour,* 1968, **30,** 275–286. (b)

TOLMAN, C. W. Social feeding in domestic chicks: Effects of food deprivation of nonfeeding companions. *Psychonomic Science,* 1969, **15,** 234.

TOLMAN, C. W., & WILSON, G. F. Social feeding in domestic chicks. *Animal Behavior,* 1965, **13,** 134–142.

TRAVIS, L. E. The effect of a small audience upon eye-hand coordination. *Journal of Abnormal and Social Psychology,* 1925, **20,** 142–146.

TRIPLETT, N. The dynamogenic factors in pacemaking and competition. *American Journal of Psychology,* 1898, **9,** 507–533.

VOGEL, H. H., JR., SCOTT, J. P., & MARSTON, M. V. Social facilitation and alleomimetic behaviour in dogs. 1. Social facilitation in a noncompetitive situation. *Behaviour,* 1950, **2,** 121–133.

WARREN, J. R. Birth order and social behavior. *Psychological Bulletin,* 1966, **65,** 38–49.

WEBB, W. B., & GOODMAN, I. J. Activating role of an irrelevant drive in absence of the relevant drive. *Psychological Reports,* 1958, **4,** 235–238.

WILSON, G. F. Early experience and facilitation of feeding in domestic chicks. *Journal of Comparative and Physiological Psychology,* 1968, **66,** 800–802.

ZAJONC, R. B. Social facilitation. *Science,* 1965, **149,** 269–274.

ZAJONC, R. B. *Social psychology: An experimental approach.* Belmont, Calif.: Wadsworth, 1966.

ZAJONC, R. B. Social facilitation in cockroaches. In E. C. Simmel, R. A. Hoppe, & G. A. Milton (Eds.), *Social facilitation and imitative behavior.* Boston: Allyn & Bacon, 1968. Pp. 73–88.

ZAJONC, R. B., HEINGARTNER, A., & HERMAN, E. M. Social enhancement and impairment of performance in the cockroach. *Journal of Personality and Social Psychology,* 1969, **13,** 83–92.

ZAJONC, R. B., & NIEUWENHUYSE, B. Relationship between word frequency and recognition: Perceptual process or response bias? *Journal of Experimental Psychology,* 1964, **67,** 276–285.

ZAJONC, R. B., & SALES, S. M. Social facilitation of dominant and subordinate responses. *Journal of Experimental and Social Psychology,* 1966, **2,** 160–168.

ZAJONC, R. B., WOLOSIN, R. J., WOLOSIN, M. A., & LOH, W. D. Social facilitation and imitation in group risk-taking. *Journal of Experimental Social Psychology,* 1970, **6,** 26–46.

8

CONFORMITY[1]

Harold B. Gerard
Edward S. Conolley

In any social group norms of opinion and conduct exist. These observed regularities have been commented upon since ancient times, but their empirical study began only in the recent past. Social influence is the medium through which society is held together and sustained. This appears to us to be an obvious truism, but it was no mean feat of insight for the ancient philosophers who reported on it. We must realize that beliefs about the origins of social man and society were steeped in myth, magic, and mystery.

The earliest experimental studies on record date back a mere 70 years to the turn of the century. It was at that time that psychologists began to study what was later to be referred to as "group effects." Also, at about that time, the French, mainly through the work of Emile Durkheim, established a sociological tradition which had as its focus the study of group effects in the larger societal frame. As the new disciplines of sociology and social psychology developed, the study of conformity and social influence processes continued to remain a center of attention. The scope and amount of empirical work carried out by scientists in both disciplines has increased at an ever-accelerating rate since those early years. In social psychology most of the work has been done in laboratory settings, and in recent years sociologists as well have found it advantageous to use the laboratory to isolate aspects of social life.

The study of conformity behavior has provided a bridge between the study of basic psychological processes and concern with social behavior in the everyday world. Contemporary American society has been characterized as conformist, and commentators on the current scene often invoke conformity as an explanation for many social ills and excesses. The concerns expressed by politicians and editorial writers are often reflected in the problems social scientists choose to work on. The major complaint we hear these days is that society's concerns are not sufficiently reflected in the problems academics choose to study. This kind of pressure from practitioners and commentators has led to a somewhat unfortunate state of affairs in a number of problem areas.

[1] The writing of this paper was in part supported by National Science Foundation Grant No. GS-392.

PROLEGOMENON

In the study of conformity, the social psychologist has, to some extent, lost sight of his problem. Rather than having psychological processes as his focal concern, he has often simply cataloged conditions that do or do not lead to conformity. We, as social psychologists, are concerned with the structure and dynamics of the person. We presumably study the conditions that do or do not lead to conformity not because we are interested in conformity per se, but because comparing conditions under which a subject tends to conform or not conform might provide the basis for making inferences about the workings of the inner person. At least, this is how the present authors view the study of conformity behavior. A vast number of experiments have been run where there is only a very dim recognition, if any, as to the task of the basic scientist. Much of the research deals with what Jones and Gerard (1967) refer to as empirical generalizations. In psychology such generalizations merely relate responses to stimulus conditions without considering the intervening organismic process that might mediate the stimulus-response relationship. To know that a subject conforms more to the political opinions of someone who is reputed to be an expert on politics than to the opinions of an ordinary citizen is not very interesting unless we ask questions as to what hypothetical states and processes inside the person's head might predict such a relationship. The social psychological "person" we are talking about is an idealized entity constructed by the social psychologist that consists of a hypothetical set of parts and internal processes which, because they are hypothetical, cannot be observed directly. The specifications of this person are designed to explain observed relationships we already know, like the example we just gave, and can also predict relationships we do not as yet know. We speak about the person we actually run in the experiment as the *subject*, and we reserve the term *person*, for the idealized construction we make inferences about from the behavior of subjects exposed to different experimental treatments.

The physicist studying spin resonance in the idealized atomic nucleus makes adjustments in the magnetic field surrounding a particular crystal specimen (his subject) and in the current applied to a coil surrounding the specimen and observes the minute changes induced in the crystal (the power absorbed by it) on a meter that measures the magnetic effects on the surrounding coil. His interest is not simply in watching the meter needle wiggle as he changes the magnetic flux, amplitude, or frequency of the current applied to the coil. Rather he systematically varies experimental parameters (such as flux and frequency) in an attempt to study the nuclear resonance process and the nuclear interaction that take place within the crystal lattice that are consistent with the induced changes, as measured by the meter, that are caused by the parametric variations.

The social psychologist inquiring into basic inner-personal processes takes the same scientific approach. He observes the effects upon some response or set of responses of systematic variation of stimulus conditions. What distinguishes the social psychologist from other kinds of psychologists has to do with the kind of processes, that is, theories he constructs (and not with the stimuli he presents or the responses he measures). This and the other chapters in the volume provide the readers with a range of theoretical positions.

The psychologist designs his experiments in such a way that they capture the conditions necessary for making inferences about processes that are assumed to occur within the organism. Thus, if we propose that uncertainty about an opinion will lead the person (the idealized social-psychological one) to seek information that will reduce that uncertainty (thus making him vulnerable to social influence), we have to create the conditions necessary for examining the tenability of this assertion. We require at least two stimulus situations that differ in the amount of uncertainty they will induce in an experimental subject, and we must also make available at least two response alternatives from which we may infer the strength of the subject's tendency to seek information (conformity might be one indicator of such a tendency) in order to reduce the uncertainty he is assumed to be (or not to be) experiencing. Many studies of social influence are based either explicitly or implicitly on some variant of this basic hypothesis, that uncertainty will lead the person to seek information.

Some of the work has been concerned with conditions that do or do not lead to uncertainty. Other studies have been concerned with the kind of information the person seeks in order to reduce his uncertainty. Still other studies have examined the types of psychological states about which the person does experience uncertainty. Because other people are a potential source of information, the person tends to rely on them. They augment the information he himself possesses. When he is uncertain of some belief or opinion he will, therefore, often seek out other people who might provide him with necessary information. If he finds that his opinion differs from that of others, one possible response the person may make is to change his opinion so that it agrees with the others. A major reason why conformity has been so popular as a response is that it is easy to record and measure. When the psychologist decides to use a particular response measure, he arranges the experimental situation in such a way that the subject can respond in that way or not with greater or lesser strength or frequency. As we shall see later in the paper, whether or not he conforms to the others, or selects alternative responses will depend upon a number of factors in the situation. By relating conformity (or other responses) to the systematic variation of these situational factors, inferences are possible as to the inner-personal processes under investigation.

Some Theoretical Considerations

Conformity has been used as a measure not only for studying the vicissitudes of opinion uncertainty but also as a measure of what Jones and Gerard (1967) have referred to as *reflected appraisal*. In these studies the subject's conforming response is conceived of as an attempt to enhance or maintain his status in the eyes of someone else. That is, under certain circumstances, the person will tend to curry favor or avoid some punishment by expressing agreement with someone else.

In their treatment of social influence processes, Jones and Gerard distinguish two generic kinds of dependence upon others, *information* and *effect dependence*, both of which make the person vulnerable to social influence. They see the socialization process as resting on both types of dependence. Beyond childhood, information and effect dependence continue to embed the person in his social world. The human infant is helpless at birth and is completely dependent on others for survival. Although the nature of this dependence changes as the person matures, he nevertheless remains dependent throughout his life. The ascetic, who chooses a life of isolation, is a very rare exception. The child's basic needs for food, comfort, and affection place him at the mercy of significant others in his immediate environment. Their ministrations provide the "effects" that serve to satisfy his needs. As the child's needs get shaped by his social milieu, they become more subtle and differentiated. With this increasing complexity of both his need repertoire and the variety of effects that might satisfy those needs, the person develops a second order need, a need for information relating his strivings and fears to features of his environment that might be relevant to those fears and strivings. Thus, basic biological needs are the foundation for effect dependence which, in turn, leads to subsequent information dependence. In the early years, the child's parents are the source of both effects and information, but as he matures his world becomes populated by larger and larger numbers of mediators and potential mediators of effects and information.

The person's complex set of needs combined with the often very complex set of skills and actions necessary to satisfy those needs places a very high premium on information about various aspects of what Jones and Gerard refer to as the *action sequence*. Let us consider the nature of that sequence. In deciding whether or not to take a particular course of action, the person is confronted with the necessity of evaluating and comparing his current state of affairs with the state of affairs that might result from his taking the contemplated course of action. He will compare his present outcome level with the possible outcome level associated with the contemplated course of action. He also requires information as to the actions required to get from where he is to where he might be and concerning the skills required to perform these actions. For much of this evaluation, he may refer to other people. Most social referencing behavior occurs rapidly and at an implicit level. A quick glance at someone else or some momentary reflection about what someone told him on a previous occasion may provide the person with a basis for evaluating some aspect of the action sequence. Jones and Gerard distinguish several types of information acquisition processes: instruction, advice, observational learning, empathic cognizance, and social comparison (1967, pp. 128–131). The last mentioned of these, social comparison, has, for a variety of reasons, been the focus of attention of a large number of research workers over the past twenty odd years, and the work we will describe grows out of that tradition.

Information acquisition appears to occur through two distinct types of social comparison, *comparative appraisal* and *reflected appraisal*. In comparative appraisal the person uses the behavior of others as bench marks, so to speak, to evaluate himself. In reflected appraisal he forms an impression of some aspect of himself from the behavior of others that is directed toward him. Thus, one obvious distinction between the two types of appraisal is that reflected appraisal is mediated by face-to-face confrontation, whereas comparative appraisal need not be. Charles Horton Cooley (1902) used the term *looking-glass self* to refer to this process of reflected appraisal. In both his concept and ours, there is the basic idea that the person can see an image of a part of himself reflected in the behavior of others toward him. Reflected appraisal is based on both information and effect dependence. The person will tend to place considerable weight on information about himself proffered by or solicited from someone who is in a position to provide "effects" for the person. That is, by someone who has power over him. Thus a child is more likely to be influenced by his own teacher's impression of him than by the teacher of some other class. Comparative appraisal is based strictly on information dependence. Whether the person can or cannot be rewarded or punished by the other person will tend to have no bearing on whether or not he will conform to the other's opinions.

In self-evaluation by comparative appraisal, the person is attempting to estimate where he stands relative to some person or persons. Comparative appraisal requires that the attribute in question be elicitable as an overt performance or behavior of some sort. Psychologists have studied comparative appraisal of beliefs, opinions, attitudes, abilities, and emotions.

There has been relatively little work by experimental social psychologists on reflected appraisal. Work by Jones (1964) is an exception. Research instead has been more concerned with the process of comparative appraisal. The reason for this may be that comparative appraisal appears, at least at first glance, to be somewhat less intuitive and less obvious, and, given a choice, psychologists prefer to study the nonobvious. To many psychologists it seems trivial to note that a person will be influenced more by someone who has power over him than by someone who does not. Less obvious is the assertion that the subjective validity of our opinions is often anchored in our group memberships. The southern segregationist does not consider that he is prejudiced because his opinion of Negroes is popular in the south. It is difficult for an egalitarian-minded northerner to understand this fundamental fact in the segregationist's psychology. He cannot understand why the segregationist should hold what seems to him to be such antidemocratic views.

This is not to say that reflected appraisal is simpler as a process than comparative appraisal; there is the added complexity of the face-to-face encounter in the former process. Comparative appraisal, on the other hand, is much more pervasive than would appear at first glance. It is as pervasive as the air we breathe. That we require air for survival was, however, a poorly understood fact until recent times. As we shall see, our knowledge of the comparative appraisal process is still rather primitive.

Research Strategy

Much research has attempted to establish empirical generalizations that should be as true of real life as they are of the laboratory. This reflects a misunderstanding of the would-be purpose of the typical laboratory experiment on social influence processes. As we shall see, laboratory situations are most often sufficiently dissimilar to real-world social influence situations so that it would be very unlikely that a particular finding relating some set of stimulus conditions to a tendency to conform or not to conform would be applicable to real life. The typical laboratory experiment in social psychology is run in a university setting using a ready source of subjects—college students. So we have the peculiar situation of a rather exotic stimulus situation being responded to by a rather atypical human subject population. How then are we able to draw meaningful inferences from data thus collected? A question that is often asked of the experimental social psychologist is, "How can you generalize from the behavior of college sophomores?" "How do you know if a factory worker or a business executive would respond like college sophomores?" Unfortunately, we are subjected to the same sort of critical attack from misguided individuals within our own discipline. They ask that experiments be replicated with different subject populations, not only within our own culture but cross-culturally as well. We are not about to devote our valuable time to trying to create experimental situations that would be responded to in the same way by people everywhere. In social psychology that task is virtually impossible. If we want to study social influence processes among young children, we have to devise experimental situations that will appeal to them. If we were studying social influence processes among the Iatmul of central New Guinea, we would have to create conditions that would be appropriate for the world of the Iatmul.

We have the basic faith that human beings are human beings and that social influence phenomena occurring anywhere and at any time can be interpreted within the same basic conceptual framework. The human species has developed such rich and varied ways of satisfying biological and social needs that the student of social psychology must first know a great deal about the particular world of a prospective subject population before he can design a laboratory experiment that will engage someone from that cultural milieu in the manner required to test the specific hypothesis under investigation. He must first, as it were, crack the code of meanings attached to very complex events within that milieu. The experimental social psychologist would have to become an anthropologist in order to do the preliminary work of mapping out the life space of a would-be subject population.

Fortunately, there is a nice shortcut to all of this. Given the abiding faith in basic universals of humankind, the social psychologist might just as well work with a subject population he knows something about and that is close at hand—the students in his classes. A major virtue of using college sophomores as subjects is that the psychologist himself was once a college sophomore. In spite of the generation gap, he pretty much knows what the world of the contemporary sophomore is like and can therefore create experimental conditions that will "hook" a student in ways that are appropriate for studying what it is he wants to study. By careful preliminary pilot work with a number of subjects drawn from the student population at hand, he will usually be able to make the adjustments in procedure necessary to approximate the stimulus conditions that will induce the perceptions he wants to relate to certain response tendencies. In his preliminary work he will also attempt to provide the subject with response alternatives that will meaningfully reflect the hypothetical end state of the psychological process under investigation. The strategy of using college students as subjects also has the additional virtue that the same subject population is also available to his social psychological colleagues at other universities who make up most of the audience to whom he reports his findings. They, therefore, can check his results or run related experiments using much the same procedures. This helps to standardize techniques.

For example, one method the psychologist might use to vary uncertainty is to attempt to create stimulus conditions that differ in degree of novelty. In order to know what is novel or familiar to the subject, the experimenter must perforce know something about the subject's past experience. This is where familiarity with the subject's culture enters the picture. If he wanted to induce degrees of novelty in an Iatmul subject population, he would undoubtedly use different procedures than he would with UCLA sophomores. The psychologist refers to these procedures as *operations*. If he were using different subject populations, he would probably use different operations to induce the same hypothetical state.

Once the particular operations for inducing novelty in a specific sample of subjects have been established, he must also provide the subjects with response alternative operations that will reflect different levels of information seeking. Just as in the case of inducing different uncertainty levels, there are many possibilities for "measuring" the strength of the subject's desire for information. One technique used by Schachter (1959) was to give the subject a choice of being with other people or being alone. Schachter inferred that the extent to which a subject chose to be with other prople reflects the strength of his desire for information. A person might want to be with others for a variety of reasons, but one of these reasons could certainly be a desire for information. Testing what reason or reasons might underlie a subject's desire to be with others provided the basis for Schachter's original work and the work of a number of psychologists who were stimulated by Schachter's studies. There are many intriguing questions surrounding this work that have to do with the legitimacy of inferring a subject's desire for information from his desire to affiliate with others. It is unfortunate that here, too, some workers in the field have lost sight of the original purpose of the work, which was to elucidate comparative appraisal by assessing the strength of the subject's affiliation desire as it is affected by variations in stimulus conditions.

In the conformity literature, the subject's vulnerability to social influence is also viewed, in part, as reflecting a desire for information. As in the case of an affiliative response, there may be a number of determinants of a person's vulnerability to social influence other than the uncertainty underlying his desire for information. For example, a subject may yield to the opinion of another person in order to curry favor with that other person (this would invoke reflected appraisal). He may be absolutely certain that his opinion is correct but may dissemble in the face of disagreement and behave as though he agrees with the other person. Here we enter a very rich domain of questions that concern the relationship between overt compliance to the opinions of others and covert acceptance of those opinions. The development of dissonance theory and the research that has grown out of the dissonance tradition was, in part, stimulated by considerations of the relationship between overt compliance and covert acceptance.

From the foregoing we can see that the same basic process may be studied using a wide variety of experimental operations. The required psychological conditions may be induced by using various techniques. For example, uncertainty may be induced by differences in novelty, by perceived disagreement with others, by procedures that might induce lowered self-ability estimates, etc. The kinds of response alternatives that might be offered to the subject might also be selected from a wide variety of possibilities. The same basic underlying state might be reflected in an affiliative response, a conforming response, an influence attempt, misperceptions of various kinds, a rejection response, etc. Any particular stimulus operation we choose may inadvertently induce unwanted perceptions in all or some subjects that may interfere with or obscure the process we wish to study.

In examining a particular experiment, there are three basic things to consider: (a) the particular stimulus conditions confronting subjects in the different experimental treatment combinations, (b) their responses to those stimulus conditions, and (c) the experimenter's interpretation of the process mediating stimulus and response. We must remember that the stimulus conditions themselves as well as the responses are mute as to mediating mechanisms. It is the psychologist who makes the data talk. It is he who assumes that the stimulus conditions produced certain psychological states which set some assumed process in motion which eventuates in the observed response. Whether or not the process actually occurred is a meaningless question. The question at hand is rather, "Can we make sense out of the relationship between stimulus conditions and responses by assuming that such and such a process mediated the relationship?"

Given the raw stimulus conditions and the raw responses, it is usually possible to concoct a number of different mediating mechanisms. The number of such interpretations is limited only by the scientist's ingenuity in concocting them. Some interpretations may seem more plausible than others in view of other relevant data that may exist. Some interpretations may be more parsimonious than others.

Part of the art in psychological experimentation involves the ability to create specific, uncontaminated perceptions. Alternative interpretations of experimental results are based upon considerations of the sorts of percepts experimental treatments may have induced other than those percepts the experimenter assumed were induced. Alternative interpretations may also be based on alternative meanings attributed to the subject's particular response. In designing an experiment, it is important to eliminate, by careful manipulation and measurement, as many alternative interpretations as possible. A deep consideration of the various techniques we might use to test alternative interpretations require much more space than we have allotted to us for this paper.

This chapter, like some others in this volume, is organized around a particular response measure. In terms of the foregoing discussion, this seems like an arbitrary focus. We are interested in social comparison processes, and conformity is only one of a number of possible manifestations of comparison tendencies. The only justification we can give for agreeing to write such a chapter is that a large amount of research has been conducted using conformity as the dependent measure. Furthermore, most of these studies use a similar methodology. We shall now examine the specific methodology used in studies of conformity.

METHODOLOGY

Following the early attempts by the French sociologists, LeBon, Tarde, and Durkheim, to understand the influences of social pressure, several investigators in the United States attempted to bring the study of social influence into the experimental laboratory. Allport (1920) compared a person's evaluation of the pleasantness of odors and the magnitude of weights when the person was alone to those evaluations when he was in the presence of others. Allport found that the person was more conservative and made less extreme judgments when in the presence of others than when he was making judgments alone. Moore (1921) went a step further and exposed subjects to both a majority opinion and an expert opinion on ethical judgments, language usages, and musical preferences. He found that both sources of influence had a marked effect on individual judgments.

Since these early investigations of social influence, three different types of experimental situations have been employed in much of the research. Consider first the procedure introduced by Sherif (1935) in which the subject makes judgments of the extent of perceived movement of a pinpoint of light in a completely darkened room. In actuality, the light is stable and only appears to move (the autokinetic illusion). The judgmental task confronting the subject is extremely ambiguous since objectively correct answers do not exist. The subject hears the judgments of other group members who actually give predetermined judgments set up by the experimenter. The subject then makes an estimate himself, and the experimenter records the extent to which the subject's judgments were affected by the group judgments. Sherif found that not only is the subject influenced by the other people's judgments but that this "group effect" tends to persist in the absence of those who were originally responsible for it. Others have used variants of this technique.

A second type of experimental procedure was used by Festinger and his associates (Back, 1951; Festinger & Thibaut, 1951; Schachter, 1951; and Gerard, 1954). In this research the task confronting the subject is somewhat less ambiguous, but there still is no objectively correct answer since the judgments are individual opinion statements. In this research subjects typically state their opinion about some issue. One issue used in some of the studies involved a fictitious case history of a juvenile delinquent named "Johnny Rocco." Subjects were asked to judge whether Johnny's plight was his own fault or whether he was a victim of circumstances beyond his control. The experimenter recorded the amount and patterning of influence attempts among group members. It was found that group members do attempt to influence each other's opinions and further that if these attempts are unsuccessful the person often changes his own opinion or attempts to reject the uninfluenceable person from the group.

A third procedure, similar to that of Sherif, was invented by Asch (1951, 1952, 1956). The method is simple and utilizes judgmental stimuli that are very unambiguous. The virtue of using an issue about which there is a clearly correct judgment is that the situation creates a clear and present conflict between the subject's tendency to make the correct judgment and his tendency to yield to an incorrect judgment endorsed by a group of peers who in actuality are confederates of the experimenter.

Festinger's group discussion procedure that utilizes an issue on which a range of opinion is likely to exist within any given group, permits one to study the relative acceptance or rejection of those holding extreme opinions as well as other related phenomena. With Sherif's procedure it is possible to drastically change the subject's initial estimate of how far the point of light appeared to move, thus providing a rather sensitive indicator of the magnitude of the group effect. But the Asch procedure is the only one that induces a sharp conflict between the two competing tendencies of giving the correct response or the group's response. While in the two other procedures there is considerable individual variability in reaction to them, in the Asch situation nearly every subject, at least initially, experiences the same conflict. The subject's reaction to this conflict is thus brought under a fair degree of control. By appropriate manipulation of aspects of the situation that can be superimposed or varied within the same basic setting, and by observing the subject's responses to these variations, it is possible to draw inferences about the nature and dimensions of the conflict and its resolution. We believe that one of the main tasks of social psychology is the thorough study of the informational inputs that produce conflict, the course of the conflict itself, and the state of the person following resolution of the conflict. The Asch paradigm, and variants thereof, provide excellent mediums for studying conflict in which one of the inputs is information from other persons.

In order that the reader might more fully understand the Asch situation, we now paraphrase a description of it by Jones and Gerard (1967, pp. 387–389). The basic setting is as follows. Eight undergraduate male students sit facing a blackboard, and the experimenter informs them that they are participating in an experiment concerned with the accuracy of visual perception. He then places two white cards about three feet apart on the blackboard sill. The left card has a single vertical line on it; the card on the right has three vertical lines, each of a different length, one of which is equal in length to the single line on the left-hand card.

The experimenter then asks each subject to decide which of the three comparison lines on the right is equal in length to the single standard line on the left. He then asks them to announce their judgments, one after the other, beginning with the leftmost person in the row. On this first trial, each subject announces his judgment in turn. The comparison lines are clearly different in length, and no one has any apparent difficulty in judging since it is quite obvious which one is equal to the standard. The second trial, with a different set of lines, also runs off with no apparent difficulty. On the third trial, however, something strange happens. As the first few subjects announce their judgments, all concurring with the first subject, the next to last subject appears to be quite upset. He has been squinting, tilting his head, leaning forward; he is obviously distressed. When it is his turn, he hesitates for a long time but finally announces his judgment with much less conviction and confidence than he did on the first two trials. The final subject, with no apparent distress, then announces his judgment which concurs with the first few subjects. Before the next set of cards are put up, the next to last subject asks the experimenter to explain the task again. The experimenter answers that the task consists merely of stating which of the three comparison lines is equal in length to the standard. On the fourth trial, the next to last subject again appears to experience the same difficulty and distress as he did on the previous trial. During the remaining fourteen trials, he, and only he, continues to exhibit periodic marked disturbance.

To get a more complete understanding of what is happening here, let us look at the situation from this particular subject's point of view by reconstructing his thoughts during the sequence of judgment trials. This reconstruction, paraphrased from Jones and Gerard, is based upon material from interview protocols reported by Asch (1956). A paraphrasing of the subject's thoughts after the experimenter had given the instructions might be as follows.

This task should be quite easy since I know my eyes are quite good. Wonder what he's trying to find out. Let's see, there's the first pair of cards. That's easy, line 2 is the correct one. Let's see what the first guy says. Yep, line 2 it is. Yes, the others agree, and now it's my turn. "Line 2." Naturally the last guy agrees too. That makes it unanimous. O.K., there's the second pair of cards. That's easy too; it's line 1. That's right, we all agree. Here comes the third pair. That's line 3. This sure seems easy. Wait a minute, what did the first guy say. Line 2. What's going on here? Am I seeing things or hearing things? The third guy just said line 2. Maybe my head is tilted or I'm positioned incorrectly. No, whichever way I look at it, it still looks like line 3. The fourth guy just said "2." Hmm, there must be some explanation for this. Wow, the fifth and then the sixth guys both said line 2. Is this some kind of optical illusion? What am I going to say, it's my turn? I know I'm right, but they might think I'm some kind of a nut if I disagree with them.

They all can't be wrong—or can they? Maybe they're just playing Follow-the-Leader. Yeah, that must be it, the first guy made a mistake and they're all just following along like sheep. But why should they? What do I do? Well, it's my turn so I'd better tell him what it looks like to me. "Line 3." Wow, what a pall just came over the room! They must think I'm some kind of a jerk. But what else could I do, I was asked to call them as I see them. Maybe this isn't going to be so easy after all. The last guy just went with the others. I sure would have felt better if he'd agreed with me! I'd better ask the experimenter what it's all about; maybe I'm doing something wrong . . . No, he says I'm doing what I'm supposed to. Let's see what happens with the next set of cards. That seems quite clear, it's line 1, see what the first guy says. He just said line 2! But that's clearly too short! One of us is nuts! The second guy just said 2. Well, here we go again. Sure is getting hot in here. I wish I could have a drink of water. How could they see it so differently from me? It either is or isn't right. There are no two ways about it! The third guy just said 2! Well, I guess I'm going to stand out like a sore thumb again! Maybe I ought to go along with the crowd. What's the difference anyway—it's only an experiment. But then I'm supposed to tell him which one *I* think is correct. I wish I had more time to think this over. I really feel uncomfortable. I've always assumed people see things the way I do. Maybe I just don't see things clearly, and they are actually right. If I say line 1, I may be wrong, and then I'll really be conspicuous. At least if I agree with them, we'll all either be right or wrong together, and maybe that's the best thing. It's my turn. What should I do? "Line 2." There, I said it. He seemed pleased now and I feel a little better about it. But why did I do it; it still looks like line 1 to me [pp. 388–389].

We see that the situation was quite hard to explain from this particular subject's point of view. There is, however, a perfectly reasonable explanation for what he was experiencing. In actuality, he was the only real subject, and the others were accomplices of the experimenter. On twelve of the eighteen trials, the others announced prearranged false judgments and were completely unanimous in their choice of comparison line.

The above idealized account of the thoughts of our hypothetical subject gives some indication of the conflict involved and the psychological forces that contribute to the conflict. At first glance, the line judgments may seem too inconsequential to be used in the study of important psychological processes. In actuality, however, a very important skill is involved. Throughout his life, the subject has learned to put a great deal of trust in his ability to make estimates of the kind required in the experimental setting. On the other hand, he has also learned to rely on other people as important sources of such information. The subject believes that the others possess essentially the same perceptual capacities as he does and are reporting what they actually see. How then can there be the observed discrepancy between these two sources of information? These considerations make up the informational side of the conflict.

There is also the problem of "standing out like a sore thumb," as our hypothetical subject stated. In addition to being concerned about being correct, the subject is also concerned about the kind of impression he is making on the others. He assumes that the others expect him to agree with them. By reporting what he sees, he will frequently disagree with the others, which he assumes will displease them and thus will be likely to lead to his losing status in their eyes. This, he assumes, will lower the degree to which he can rely on them for outcome mediation in the future. These considerations make up the normative side of the conflict. Thus, we see both information and effect dependence are implicated in the conflict experienced by the subject.

The subject has only two courses of action open to him. He can announce the line he believes is correct or he can voice the group choice. Each alternative has both positive and negative implications for him. If he states the choice he believes is correct, he is being true to himself and is doing what the experimenter asked him to do. On the negative side, he risks possibly being incorrect and also incurring the disfavor of the others. If he yields to the group choice, the situation is reversed; he is false to himself and the experimenter, but he does not run the risk of displeasing the group. Furthermore, if he is wrong, at least he is not alone. The subject's resolution of this conflict depends upon such things as the importance he attaches to being true to himself versus the importance of avoiding potential ridicule and loss of status. The relative weights of these two prospects depend upon many social and nonsocial aspects of the situation and upon certain of his own idiosyncrasies. Here we would expect to see the simultaneous operation of both underlying personality dispositions as well as momentary fleeting social influences.

Some highlights of Asch's first experiments should be mentioned at this point. His main concern was to examine the effects of the situation just described on the subject's frequency of "yielding." Data were gathered from 123 college student subjects with an additional 37 subjects in a control group where they simply ran through the series of visual judgments. With only one or two exceptions, every control subject made the judgments without any errors, suggesting that the task itself was quite unambiguous. However, when confronted with the incorrect group consensus, only about one-fourth of the subjects were completely correct on all trials. Experimental subjects on the average made between four and five errors out of a possible twelve. Even though the average subject made four or five errors, there were wide individual differences among subjects. Some did not yield on a single trial, whereas others yielded on all twelve trials.

Asch did not observe an increase in the yielding effect over time. Instead he found that if a subject yielded at all he tended to do so quite early in the series of judgments. Likewise, those subjects who started out being independent tended to remain so throughout the series of judgments. This may seem somewhat paradoxical since with successive disagreements we might expect the subject's confidence to decrease to the point where he might yield to the group's judgment later in the series. This point will be discussed more fully in a later section.

In examining the hypothetical subject's running commentary, it is clear that he has two very important concerns. He is concerned with being correct and also with what the others will think of him. This is clear from the extensive postexperimental protocols reported by Asch, from which our commentary was constructed. This anecdotal data suggest that both comparative appraisal and reflected appraisal are engaged by this type of situation.

We pointed out earlier that the person's uncertainty about some aspect of the action sequence arouses comparative appraisal. Outcome dependence on other persons, which is affected by what others think of him, arouses reflected appraisal. To understand these two processes better, let us examine the details of the situation confronting the subject in the Asch situation to see which variables tend to elicit one or the other process.

A detailed consideration of the forces at work in the Asch situation led Gerard (Deutsch & Gerard, 1955) to devise a refinement of the technique in which data from several subjects may be gathered simultaneously. The subjects are seated side by side and separated visually from one another by partitions. In his cubicle, each subject has a panel of lights on which the choices of the other subjects are displayed. There are also buttons on the panel that he can press to indicate his choice to the others. The stimuli to be judged are projected on a screen in front of the subjects. The critical feature of this technique is that the choices of the "others" are predetermined and controlled by the experimenter. All of the subjects are led to believe that the "others" are making the responses they see on their panel of lights. In actuality all subjects are in the same parallel situation and all respond simultaneously when their turn comes up. Since the stimuli are quite unambiguous, the experimenter can arrange the situation so that the subjects are led to believe that the "others" have made a judgment different from their own. A further refinement of this technique is that all of the experimental instructions are tape-recorded and presented to the subjects through earphones. This contributes greatly to the control and uniformity of the experimental situation from group to group. Through further equipment elaboration, it is possible for the experimenter to gather data on several variables in addition to the subjects' choice of comparison line. For example, the response latency or time it takes the subject to make his choice, his confidence in the correctness of the choice, and physiological measures of the stress induced by the conflict have been recorded in various studies.

A BRIEF REVIEW OF THE RESEARCH

Our review will cover only the research using the technique developed by Asch and further refined by Gerard. Asch's results led Deutsch and Gerard to consider the relative contributions of the two self-appraisal processes to the yielding behavior of the subjects. They felt that if the subject could state his judgments in private where he could not be held publicly responsible for them, reflected appraisal effects should be minimal. They, therefore, compared a situation in which the subjects were physically isolated from each other with Asch's face-to-face situation. Both comparative and reflected appraisal should occur in the face-to-face situation, whereas in the cubicle situation comparative appraisal should predominate. Comparing the amount of conformity in both situations would provide the basis for estimating the relative contribution of each process. The results showed that there was more yielding in the face-to-face than in the anonymous treatment. When confronting the others in a face-to-face situation, subjects yielded on an average of 7.08 out of a possible 24 critical trials. However, when they were visually isolated, and therefore presumably not identifiable to the others, they made an average of 5.92 yielding responses. This difference presumably reflects the operation of both processes in one situation and predominantly comparative appraisal in the other.

Research by Mouton, Blake, and Olmstead (1956), also manipulated the subjects' anonymity by using a similar bogus consensus procedure. Four subjects, seated in separate rooms, were each asked to estimate the number of metronome clicks they heard on each of a series of nine trials. Prerecorded voices of the "others" gave incorrect estimates on six of the nine trials. In the public nonanonymous treatment each subject (including, of course, the members of the fictitious majority) announced his name before giving his judgment, whereas in the anonymous private treatment no names were announced. Considerably more yielding occurred in the public treatment. Furthermore, this difference was due primarily to subjects who had scored high in "submissiveness" on a previously administered personality test. This combined effect of the manipulated experimental treatment of anonymity and a highly relevant personality trait lends additional support to the assumption that a face-to-face setting engages reflected appraisal. The results of these experiments clearly show that conformity pressure tends to be greater when the subject can be publicly identified with his judgment, and support the notion that this heightened pressure is due to the effect of adding reflected appraisal to the ever-present effect of comparative appraisal.

Informational Features of the Situation and Comparative Appraisal

When a person has to choose between alternatives, his task becomes more difficult the more similar the alternatives are. The terms *ambiguous* or *equivocal* are used to characterize stimulus situations that confront the person with this type of difficulty. The greater the ambiguity, the more uncertain the person will be and therefore the greater will be his need for information that will help him make his choice. One important source of such information is other people. We would expect, therefore, that the more ambiguous the stimulus material to be judged, the more likely will the subject depend on the judgments of others and hence the greater will he tend to yield to the others. Several investigators have reported data supporting this expectation.

Asch (1952) reported several experiments, one of which was designed to explore the role of stimulus ambiguity. In this experiment, the standard line was presented with only one comparison line, and the subject was to judge whether the comparison was shorter, longer, or equal in length to the standard. On the critical trials the size of the discrepancy between the two lines was varied systematically, whereas on the neutral trials both lines were of equal length and the accomplices reported the two as equal. As was predicted, the amount of yielding was greater the smaller the discrepancy between the two lines. In other words, the more ambiguous the judgment the greater was the influence of the group. These results were also confirmed by Conolley (1964) using a non-face-to-face "simulated group" procedure similar to Deutsch and Gerard. It was found in that study that even when the absolute level of ambiguity was quite high, increasing it even further resulted in even greater yielding.

Deutsch and Gerard varied another type of ambiguity. The subject responded twice to the same series of 18 visual judgments as in Asch's original experiment. During one series the cards were exposed on each trial while all of the subjects made their judgments. During the other series, the cards were exposed for only a few seconds and then removed before the first subject announced his judgment. This "memory series" produced much more yielding than the series in which the judgmental stimuli remained in view. Apparently the subject was more vulnerable to the social information when the physical information was absent.

When judgmental stimuli are ambiguous, the subject may assume that "several heads (or pairs of eyes) are better than one." Under normal circumstances, the subject has no reason to believe that the others are any more likely to be correct than he is. Therefore, it would seem reasonable that the larger the group of others making the visual judgments the greater would be the impact on the subject and the greater should be the observed yielding. Asch (1951) varied the number of accomplices with whom the subject found himself in disagreement from only one other subject to majorities as large as 16. His results showed that opposition from one other person had only a minimal effect, this increased sharply when the subject was opposed by two people, and still further when a third person was added to the majority. Beyond 3, however, there appeared to be no further increases in conformity. We shall return to a fuller discussion of this effect in the last section of this chapter.

Asch (1951) conducted several variations of his experiment in which the subject found a "partner" among the others. In one case, a member of the pre-instructed majority chose the physically correct line on every trial. This procedure drastically reduced the yielding of the naive subject. Apparently having one other person in agreement with him insulated the subject against the effects of disagreement with seven or eight other people.

Gerard and Greenbaum (1962) created a situation in which a member of the majority joins the subject at some point in the judgment series. Data from earlier studies indicated that when the subject is next to the last to respond, the last person is seen as a good-for-nothing culprit since he had a clear choice of going along with the others (which he did) or agreeing with the subject. Assuming that a subject tends to become more uncertain with each successive disagreement, Gerard and Greenbaum predicted that if the last subject in a group of four (the subject himself was the third person to respond) switched to agreement with the subject late in the series, there would be a dramatic increase in his attractiveness. The reasoning here is that the later the subject is joined by a partner, the more uncertainty will be reduced and therefore the more attractive will the partner subsequently become. We can thus make derivations about comparative appraisal that concern the subsequent attitudes the person will have toward an information source. The general procedure was very similar to the one used by Deutsch and Gerard, but at some point in the series of trials, Subject 4 (the last subject) switched to agree with the subject, who was Subject 3, by choosing the correct comparison line. Deutsch and Gerard found that when the subject wrote his judgments down, his yielding to the bogus consensus was virtually eliminated. Since it was important that the subject not yield to Subjects 1 and 2, Gerard and Greenbaum incorporated this procedure. The experiment varied the trial on which Subject 4, after initally disagreeing with the subject, switched over to him and made the same line choice (the correct one) as the subject made for the remaining trials. The data tended to support the prediction that when preswitch uncertainty was high, the attractiveness of Subject 4 increased greatly when he switched to agree with the subject. That is, the later the switch the more attractive was Subject 4 to the subject.

The Effect of Ability Estimates on Conformity

When discussing stimulus ambiguity and its effects on yielding, we mentioned that the subject's estimate of his own ability was a determinant of his decision to yield or remain independent. That is, a person's information dependence on others is determined in part by the degree of expertise he attributes to himself relative to the others. Several experiments have studied the effects of differential self-ability attribution on the person's tendency to yield to group pressure. The general procedure for these studies involves a two-stage experiment. In the first stage, the subject is either given bogus feedback in a judgment task about his performance (Goldberg & Lubin, 1958; Mausner, 1954a; Gerard, 1961) or about the performance of the others (Mausner, 1954b), or he is given some special information that will make him an expert (Snyder, Mischel, & Lott, 1960). In the second stage, he is exposed to discrepant judgments from the others in the usual manner. The general finding is the same in all of these studies and confirms the prediction that the greater the subject's assumed ability relative to the others, the greater his independence in the face of the discrepancy.

It might be assumed from the uniform results of this type of experiment, that the high-ability person experiences little difficulty in remaining independent and that it is only the low-ability person who is influenced by majority judgment. Consideration of this question led to two studies which examined the psychological impact of self-other disagreement on individuals of different ability (Smith, 1936; Gerard, 1961). The Gerard experiment used the line judgment task and subject cubicles used by Deutsch and Gerard. Ability was varied by giving the subject false information about his performance on a prior task. He was told that he was either better than the others, approximately equal to the others, or poorer than the others in the required ability—regardless of his actual ability level. Since the purpose of the experiment was to study the psychological impact on the subject of discovering that his judgments deviated from the group consensus, the situation had to be arranged to prevent the subject from yielding. This was accomplished by having everyone's judgments on a given trial displayed simultaneously. In this way, the subject did not know about the consensus until he had responded. As in previous experiments, the subject was exposed to a false but unanimous consensus on his display panel so that he found himself a deviate on twelve of the eighteen trials; the false consensus was correct on the remaining six trials.

The results showed that the greater the subject's ability relative to the others, the greater was the stress he experienced as measured by the change in his skin resistance. In other words, the psychological impact of the self-other disagreement was greatest on those subjects who had been led to believe they were high in ability. How might we interpret this puzzling finding? It should be remembered that the majority had presumably made their judgments independently, and it was therefore not simply a situation in which the group followed the leader. Therefore, the dilemma facing the high-ability subject could not be resolved in this way. The group consensus very likely appeared to be highly credible, and therefore when the subject's own ability was high, he was confronted with two highly credible sources of information that were discrepant with each other. This presumably created a conflict that was difficult to resolve, and was reflected in the high-ability subject's greater emotional reactivity. Smith (1936) found similar results in an experiment that was not as carefully controlled.

The experiments discussed earlier found an inverse relationship between the subject's ability and his conformity to the others. This particular laboratory situation presumably engenders informational dependence in which the subject has ability data that dictate the relative reliance he should place on himself and the others; the greater his ability relative to others, the less does he, therefore, yield. When, however, the situation is arranged so that the subject cannot yield, as in the Gerard experiment, and a high degree of credibility is attached to the majority judgment, the nature of the basic conflict is revealed. When the credibility of the information supplied by the group is high (in the above experiment each of the others presumably arrived at the same judgment independently), increasing conflict is generated by increasing self-credibility. The conflict thus revealed appears to be between response tendencies based upon the two sources of information, each with a particular credibility attributed to it.

Acceptance by the Group and Reflected Appraisal

In the experiments described earlier in which the person was publicly identified with his decision to conform or deviate, we found evidence that reflected appraisal occurs, that is, conformity was greater when he was publicly identified with his judgments than when he was not (Deutsch & Gerard, 1955; Mouton, Blake, & Olmstead, 1956). Further, this ought to be more pronounced the greater the person's effect dependence on the other group members. When A is effect dependent on B, B's appraisal of A has consequences for A's future out-comes. A therefore tends to behave so as to elicit a positive evaluation from B. A at least attempts to avoid displeasing B, for if he does he may place his prospective outcomes in jeopardy.

Presumably a certain amount of effect dependence exists in a public situa-tion. The others, by virtue of their status as peers, can offer subtle rewards or impose punishments. Just what these rewards and punishments are is not clear. There have been several attempts to study reflected appraisal systematically by adding explicit effect dependence over and above that which normally exists in this kind of an experimental situation. We would expect that an increase in effect dependence would lead to an increase in conformity.

In one of the experimental conditions of the Deutsch and Gerard study, sub-jects were told that groups making the fewest errors would receive tickets to a play. These instructions thus introduced a group goal, the desire for which presumably induced mutual effect dependence. The results of this treatment showed a striking increase in the number of group-influenced errors, with many subjects yielding on nearly all of the critical trials.

Thibaut and Strickland (1956) varied effect dependence in their *group set* condition by informing the subjects that the experimental task was a test of cooperative ability and also stressed that each group was competing on this dimension with other groups. The subjects in this condition also evaluated each other before the task, thus making reflected appraisal a very salient feature of the situation. In the *task set* condition, the experimenter stated that he was primarily interested in the accuracy of individual judgments, thus under-emphasizing effect dependence. The subjects, seated in separate cubicles, were given an unfamiliar task of judging the "friendliness" of four separate arrangements of 24 thumbtacks that were to be regarded as representing per-sons in a group. The apparent friendliness of the tack arrangements was sug-gested by variations in the homogeneity of the color and shape of the tacks and by differences in the density of their dispersion. The experimenters had arranged the tack displays so that a particular ordering of the four arrangements would naturally be favored by the subjects.

The procedure called for the subjects to rank order the arrangements and communicate their choice to each of the other five subjects by a written ballot. These ballots were intercepted and replaced by substitutes that indicated a consensus of the group opposed to the subject's initial ordering. The results showed that in the group set treatment, approximately 60% of the subjects changed in the direction of the fictitious majority, whereas in the task set treat-ment, only 30% changed. The difference between these two conditions offers strong evidence for the effectiveness of reflected appraisal in inducing con-formity.

Half of the groups in this experiment were composed of freshman pledges recruited from a campus fraternity, and the other groups were composed of complete strangers. There was significantly more conformity within the pledge groups than within the groups of strangers, which offers still further evidence of the operation of reflected appraisal if we assume that persons who know each other will be more concerned than strangers about the impression they are making on each other.

Commitment and Conformity

Earlier we referred to Asch's finding that when a subject starts out by conforming he tends to continue to conform, whereas if he starts out by being independent he continues to be independent. It appears as though the subject continues to do what he initially committed himself to doing. Gerard (1963), in reanalyzing data from the Deutsch and Gerard experiment, found that the tendency for the initially independent subject to remain independent occurred only in the face-to-face situation. In the anonymous cubicle situation subjects who started out being independent were just as likely to yield later on as remain independent. It therefore looks as though in Asch's experiment public commitment operated to sustain independence.

In their experiment Deutsch and Gerard manipulated commitment by having the subject in one condition write his choice down before the judgments were announced. This self-commitment treatment reduced yielding to a minimum which suggests that a commitment can be induced either by having the subject's behavior acknowledged publicly or by contriving to force him to acknowledge an initial private decision.

Gerard and Rotter (1961) and Gerard (1965) found that the person accommodates his attitudes to his commitment to yield or to remain independent. The discrepancy confrontation with the others brings into question the credibility the subject should attribute to his own and the others' judgments. A judgment is a performance based upon a person's ability. We find that there is a marked tendency for the subject to make ability attributions that are commensurate with his decision to either deviate from or conform to the others. These attributions serve to justify the behavior and make easier similar behavior in the future. The person's gradual accommodation to a sequence of similar acts illustrates what has been referred to in the real world as brainwashing. Each successive discrepant act makes subsequent acts easier. A slight, relatively innocuous discrepant act makes possible future acts that are more discrepant with the person's original inclination.

A Detailed Look at an Experiment

An experiment conducted by Gerard, Wilhelmy, and Conolley (1968) investigated the effects of the size of a unanimous discrepant majority on the vulnerability of a deviate. The focus here was thus on an aspect of comparative appraisal. On the face of it, one would guess that the greater the number of people who disagree with the person, the more uncertain would he feel about his opinion. Thus, we would predict that with increasing majority size, the subject would be more likely to yield to the majority opinion. This apparently reasonable prediction does not fit the facts of several earlier experiments. The earliest work on the effects of group size was reported by Asch (1951) in which a lone subject confronted a disagreeing unanimous majority. The subject did tend to yield more the greater the size of the disagreeing majority, but "the effect appeared in full force with a majority of three [p. 188]." Asch ran groups with majorities as large as sixteen and found no appreciable increase in the tendency for the subject to conform beyond that displayed with a majority of three. An explanation for this finding that comes to mind immediately is that when confronting a disagreeing majority of three the subject gives in completely and therefore yields on practically all of the critical trials. This, however, cannot possibly be the explanation, since the subjects in that treatment yielded on an average of about one-third of the critical trials. In all of the reported research using Asch's stimulus material, subjects tend, on the average, to give a greater number of independent judgments than conforming ones.

Rosenberg (1961), using stimuli similar to those used by Asch, observed much the same group size effect. It has been nearly 20 years since Asch reported his original finding which is one of the most oft-quoted findings in social influence literature. The fact that it does appear to violate common sense expectations probably accounts for the wide attention the finding has received.

What does the "majority size three effect" imply? The finding is usually quoted as illustrating an empirical generalization purportedly discovered in Asch's laboratory. The generalization would have it that a typical person (whatever that concept means) will react with maximum uncertainty when finding himself in disagreement with three other people. The empirical generalization believers argue that the effect would hold for most or nearly all issues. There is, however, evidence to the contrary. Goldberg (1954), Kidd (1958), and Conolley (1964) report different results in experiments utilizing ambiguous stimulus material. When the issue about which the subject finds himself at variance with the group is ambiguous, there doesn't seem to be any consistent group size effect. Ambiguous stimuli provide a great latitude for disagreement. This being the case, the subject may conclude that his guess is as good as anybody else's regardless of how many other subjects disagree with him. This would be more likely to happen to the extent that the subject was, for some reason, strongly committed to his opinion. Ambiguous issues also make it easier for the subject to relinquish his own opinion without violating self-imposed strictures about "sticking to his guns." These two assumed tendencies act in opposite directions. The first would serve to make the subject more steadfast, whereas the second would make him more vulnerable. Which tendency would win in any given situation depends on a number of other moderating factors. We might expect much greater intersubject variability with ambiguous as compared with unambiguous judgmental issues.

Where does all this leave us? We certainly cannot draw any empirical generalizations about the effects of group size. The typical real world situations we might want to generalize about are much too complex to have some silly "group majority size three effect" applied to them. We would venture to guess that some of our colleagues actually believe that the effect is a reliable one irrespective of the issue context. Rather than take the effect as gospel, which it apparently is not, we should puzzle over the basis for it within the specific laboratory situation Asch used.

Asch, in a later publication (1956), provided us with a possible clue to the perceptions of the subject that might account for the plateau. Asch conducted extensive postexperimental interviews with his subjects. Statements such as, "A lot of them just copied what the other one said," and "I felt they weren't sure of themselves and were just copying" suggest that the subjects perceived that the others were being influenced by the first subject's judgment; that in so doing they were not thinking for themselves. In an attempt to explain what was happening, the subject assumed that the group was following the first person, who, for some strange reason, was making incorrect judgments. He believed that the judgments of the rest of the majority were dependent on the first person's response. If a subject believed this, the impact of the majority judgment would be blunted. He could maintain that his disagreement about the correct stimulus line was only with the first person who was leading the others astray.

In Asch's experimental context, it may be that beyond some majority size, seemingly three, adding additional "sheep" would add no increment to the group effect. What would happen if the subject were unable to entertain this "sheep hypothesis"? Majority sizes larger than three might then have an additional impact if each person in the majority was perceived by the subject as responding independently.

Gerard, Wilhelmy, and Conolley (1968) devised an experimental situation in which the subject, in one condition, perceived the majority as all making their judgments independently. In a second condition it was possible for the subject to perceive that the others were following the first respondent. Within each of these basic conditions, group size was varied from two through eight. In the group size two condition, the subject found himself in disagreement with one other person, whereas in the group size eight condition he was disagreeing with seven others.

The procedure, which we now quote from the original publication, was as follows:

> The subjects, who were seated in adjacent cubicles, received their instructions over headphones. Although they were not visible to each other, each viewed the same series of 12 stimuli projected twice on a screen 20 feet away. The subjects' task on each trial was to choose one of three comparison lines that matched a standard.
>
> At the outset the group was told that each person had been assigned a number at random except the "observer-recorder" who would keep a record, on the answer sheet provided, of the choices made by each person, including himself. They were further told that each person was to respond in turn according to his subject number by depressing one of the buttons on his response panel corresponding to the comparison line which he chose as correct. The observer-recorder, who

did not depress a choice button, was to record his judgment after all of the others had indicated theirs.

In the "contingent" condition, the subjects were further instructed that when a person depressed his response button it would light the appropriate light on the subject display panels in all the other booths. They were also told that this arrangement would allow the observer-recorder to see the choices of the others on his display panel so that he could record them and that *it also allowed each person to see how all the others were answering.* In the "independent" condition, the subjects were instructed that when a person depressed his response button it would light the appropriate light on the display panel of the observer-recorder *only.*

Each subject was privately informed at the beginning that he was the observer-recorder, and he assumed that the others had been assigned Subject Nos. 1, 2, etc. The choices of the others were pre-programmed to be unanimous and in disagreement with reality on 14 of the 24 trials so as to duplicate Asch (1952).

The sequence of events was as follows: A stimulus was projected on a screen in front of the subjects, each of whom could see the stimulus and his display panel. The experimenter then asked "Subject 1" to push his choice button, followed by "Subject 2," etc., and finally he asked the observer-recorder to indicate his own choice on the prepared answer sheet.

The overall design was a 2 × 7 factorial, with two levels of perceived contingency and seven levels of group size. Due to the limitations of subject availability, boys only were used for Group Sizes 2, 4, 6, and 8, with girls only at Sizes 3, 5, and 7. Half of the subjects at each group-size level were exposed to the contingent and the other half to the independent condition. Due to the constraints imposed by group size, the number of subjects were somewhat unequal across the group-size treatments [p. 80]. . . .[2]

In any experiment it is important to determine whether or not the intended perceptions of the subject were in fact induced by the various treatments. In this particular experiment, it was critical that subjects in the contingent condition perceive that the others might possibly be following the leader and that they perceive that no such following was possible in the independent condition. On a postexperimental questionnaire, the subject was asked who he thought could see the judgments as they were made. Out of 77 subjects in the independent condition, 65 stated that only the observer-recorder could see the others' judgments. In the contingent condition, 51 out of 77 subjects believed that each person in the group could see the others' judgments. This suggests that we did set up the conditions necessary for the subject to entertain the "sheep hypothesis" in the contingent condition, and also that it was not possible for him to do so in the independent condition. We, of course, do not know for sure whether the subject in the contingent condition did in fact believe that the others were following the leader.

The conformity data are presented in Table 8.1. An analysis of variance indicates no effect of perceived contingency nor of an interaction between perceived contingency and group size. There is, however, a substantial effect of group size. The principal component of this effect is the linear one. That

---

[2] The *n*'s are given in Table 8.1.

is, yielding appears to increase steadily with increasing group size. The data do indicate considerable up-and-down variation as well, which appears to be accounted for by a sex effect. Boys were run in the even-numbered group sizes, and girls in the odd-numbered group sizes. There is an overall sex effect in our data in that males yielded on an average of 3.25 trials and females yielded on an average of 4.16 trials. Correcting for this effect by multiplying the means for the odd-numbered groups by .781 (3.25/4.16, the ratio of boy to girl yielding) washes out the up-and-down effect. The only remaining effect is the strong linear one.

Table 8.1

Mean Number of Group-Influenced Errors for Each Treatment Combination of Perceived Contingency and Group Size

| | *Group size* | | | | | | | OVERALL EFFECT OF CONTINGENCY |
	2	3	4	5	6	7	8	
Perception of contingency								
No	1.63	2.44	4.12	4.00	3.25	5.30	4.19	3.56
Yes	1.88	3.44	3.13	5.40	3.50	4.37	4.24	3.71
Average for both treatments	1.76	2.94	3.64	4.70	3.38	4.84	4.22	
	(16)[a]	(18)	(16)	(20)	(24)	(28)	(32)	

SOURCE. Gerard, Wilhelmy, & Conolley, 1968, p. 86.
[a] The figures in parentheses indicate the *n*'s in each group-size treatment, with boys at even-numbered and girls at odd-numbered group sizes.

Clearly, we did not replicate the leveling off at majority size three (this would have been the group size "four" treatment in our experiment). What we expected to find, of course, was a leveling off in the contingency condition and a linear increase in the independent condition, that is, an interaction between perceived contingency and group size. What we found was a linear increase under both treatments. Looking across the table, and remembering that there is a sex effect, we see a very steady increase that suggests that if we had run groups larger than eight we would have had a larger effect. The reason we limited group size to eight was that if we got the leveling off for group size "four" under the contingent condition we would have been able, with the group size treatments we did run, to demonstrate the predicted interaction between perceived contingency and group size.

How can we account for our not having replicated Asch's effect in the contingent condition? There was a major difference between our procedure and the one used by Asch that might give us a clue. He ran his subjects in a face-to-face situation, whereas we ran our subjects in booths where they could not see each other. Asch used actual accomplices, whereas we used "electrical stooges."

It might be that when subjects are run in booths it is more likely that they will attribute independence to the others even when they are given explicit instructions to the contrary. Rosenberg (1961), however, found leveling off at majority size three, and he ran his subjects in booths. His data, thus, rule out the booth versus face-to-face factor as the basis for the difference between our results and those of Asch.

It is possible that, questionnaire data not withstanding, the manipulation of contingency was not really convincing and that the subjects in the contingent condition responded as though there were no contingency. When they were asked after the experiment if the subjects could see each other's judgments, they recalled the earlier instructions to that effect and answered the question accordingly. What we are saying is that in spite of the fact that most subjects in the contingent condition indicated on the questionnaire that everyone could see everyone else's judgments, during the experiment they may have acted as though this were not true.

The discrepancy between our results and those of Asch and Rosenberg is thus still unexplained. It may be that some unknown factor other than perceived contingency may have been operating in their studies that produced the leveling off. As in much of the social psychological literature, we find a loose end which certainly deserves further exploration.

We started out to account for Asch's leveling off phenomenon which appears to violate common sense, and instead we found that common sense holds up very well; the greater the number of people with whom the subject finds himself in disagreement, the more he tends to yield his opinion. We found that this was unabated up through a majority of seven regardless of whether or not there was the possibility for perceived contingency. These data are consistent with the idea that the greater the number of people in the majority the greater will be the uncertainty induced in the subject. Further research is needed to determine the conditions under which this finding holds and those under which it does not.

REFERENCES

Allport, F. H. The influence of the group upon association and thought. *Journal of Experimental Psychology,* 1920, **3,** 159–182.

Asch, S. E. Effects of group pressure on the modification and distortion of judgments. In H. Guetzkow (Ed.), *Groups, leadership, and men.* Pittsburgh, Pa.: Carnegie Press, 1951. Pp. 177–190.

Asch, S. E. *Social Psychology.* Englewood Cliffs, N.J.: Prentice-Hall, 1952.

Asch, S. E. Studies of independence and conformity: A minority of one against a unanimous majority. *Psychological Monographs,* 1956, **70**(9, Whole No. 416).

Back, K. W. Influence through social communication. *Journal of Abnormal and Social Psychology,* 1951, **46,** 9–23.

CONOLLEY, E. S. Social influence on visual discrimination judgments. Unpublished master's thesis, San Diego State College, 1964.

COOLEY, C. H. *Human nature and the social order.* New York: Scribner, 1902.

DEUTSCH, M., & GERARD, H. B. A study of normative and informational social influence upon individual judgment. *Journal of Abnormal and Social Psychology,* 1955, **51,** 629–636.

FESTINGER, L., & THIBAUT, J. Interpersonal communication in small groups. *Journal of Abnormal and Social Psychology,* 1951, **46,** 92–99.

GERARD, H. B. The anchorage of opinions in face-to-face groups. *Human Relations,* 1954, **7,** 313–326.

GERARD, H. B. Some determinants of self-evaluation. *Journal of Abnormal and Social Psychology,* 1961, **62,** 288–293.

GERARD, H. B. Emotional uncertainty and social comparison. *Journal of Abnormal and Social Psychology,* 1963, **66,** 568–573.

GERARD, H. B. Deviation, conformity, and commitment. In I. D. Steiner & M. Fishbein (Eds.), *Current studies in social psychology.* New York: Holt, 1965. Pp. 263–277.

GERARD, H. B., & GREENBAUM, C. W. Attitudes toward an agent of uncertainty reduction. *Journal of Personality,* 1962, **30,** 485–495.

GERARD, H. B., & ROTTER, G. S. Time perspective, consistency of attitude, and social influence. *Journal of Abnormal and Social Psychology,* 1961, **62,** 565–572.

GERARD, H. B., WILHELMY, R. A., & CONOLLEY, E. S. Conformity and group size. *Journal of Personality and Social Psychology,* 1968, **8,** 79–82.

GOLDBERG, S. C. Three situational determinants of conformity to social norms. *Journal of Abnormal and Social Psychology,* 1954, **49,** 325–329.

GOLDBERG, S. C., & LUBIN, A. Influence as a function of perceived judgment error. *Human Relations,* 1958, **2,** 275–280.

JONES, E. E. *Ingratiation: A social psychological analysis.* New York: Appleton, 1964.

JONES, E .E., & GERARD, H. B. *Foundations of Social Psychology.* New York: Wiley, 1967.

KIDD, J. S. Social influence phenomena in a task-oriented group situation. *Journal of Abnormal and Social Psychology,* 1958, **56,** 13–17.

MAUSNER, B. The effect of prior reinforcement on the interaction of observer pairs. *Journal of Abnormal and Social Psychology,* 1954, **49,** 65–68. (a)

MAUSNER, B. Prestige and social interaction. The effect of one partner's success in a relevant task on the interaction of observer pairs. *Journal of Abnormal and Social Psychology,* 1954, **49,** 557–560. (b)

MOORE, H. T. The comparative influence of majority and expert opinion. *American Journal of Psychology,* 1921, **32,** 16–20.

MOUTON, J. S., BLAKE, R. R., & OLMSTEAD, J. A. The relationship between frequency of yielding and the disclosure of personal identity. *Journal of Personality,* 1956, **24,** 339–347.

ROSENBERG, L. A. Group size, prior experience, and conformity. *Journal of Abnormal and Social Psychology,* 1961, **63,** 436–437.

SCHACHTER, S. Deviation, rejection, and communication. *Journal of Abnormal and Social Psychology,* 1951, **46,** 190–207.

SCHACHTER, S. *The psychology of affiliation.* Stanford, Calif.: Stanford University Press, 1959.

SHERIF, M. A study of some social factors in perception. *Archives of Psychology,* 1935, No. 187.

SMITH, C. E. A study of the autonomic excitation resulting from the interaction of individual opinions and group opinion. *Journal of Abnormal and Social Psychology,* 1936, **30,** 138–164.

SNYDER, A., MISCHEL, W., & LOTT, B. E. Value, information, and conformity behavior. *Journal of Personality,* 1960, **28,** 333–341.

THIBAUT, J. W., & STRICKLAND, L. H. Psychological set and social conformity. *Journal of Personality,* 1956, **25,** 115–129.

section four
SOCIAL INTERACTION

The reader is warned that the transition from the conceptual systems required in Sections II and III to those of Section IV is a major one, insofar as there is a major shift in the complexity of the phenomena investigated. In effect, we step from the relatively well-charted domain of classical social psychology to the more recent and relatively unexplored areas of social interaction and interdependence. We leave behind for the most part the S-R and S-O-R models upon which most of the previously reported research is based, and arrive in a problem domain in which the task of conceptualization is more difficult, where the number of experimental paradigms are more limited, and for which appropriately powerful analytic techniques, including statistics, are yet to be developed.

The complexity of this problem area can be partially represented by citing several examples from Zajonc's (1966) excellent book on experimental social psychology. He observes that in order to characterize social interaction one must add dimensions of complexity to the S-R model. He first characterizes a social reinforcement paradigm for the individual actor in the following terms:

$$R_j \rightarrow K_i \rightarrow R_i \qquad \text{[IV.1]}$$

R_i denotes the behavior of the subject being observed and K_i are the rewarding and punishing behaviors for R_i, produced by another person R_j.

By extending this S-R model for one actor to encompass situations of social interaction where the behaviors of both individuals afford rewards and punishments to the other, namely to situations of social interdependence, the patterning of relationships between the individuals and their behaviors becomes markedly more complex. For example, following Zajonc's exposition, in order to characterize an instance where two persons are mediating rewards for one another (cooperation as defined by Zajonc), one would need a representation of the following sort:

$$R_i - + \rightarrow K_i - + \rightarrow R_i - + \rightarrow K_i - + \rightarrow R_i$$
$$\mid \qquad \uparrow \qquad \mid \qquad \uparrow$$
$$+ \qquad + \qquad + \qquad + \qquad\qquad [\text{IV.2}]$$
$$\downarrow \qquad \mid \qquad \downarrow \qquad \mid$$
$$R_j - + \rightarrow K_j - + \rightarrow R_j - + \rightarrow K_j - + \rightarrow R_j \quad \text{etc.}$$

where plus ($+$) means reinforces or mediates positive rewards.

Similarly, negative mutual reinforcement or the blocking of positive reinforcement (competition as defined by Zajonc) would require the following representation:

$$R_i - + \rightarrow K_i - + \rightarrow R_i - + \rightarrow K_i - + \rightarrow R_i$$
$$\mid \qquad \uparrow \qquad \mid \qquad \uparrow$$
$$- \qquad - \qquad - \qquad - \qquad\qquad [\text{IV.3}]$$
$$\downarrow \qquad \mid \qquad \downarrow \qquad \mid$$
$$R_j - + \rightarrow K_j - + \rightarrow R_j - + \rightarrow K_j - + \rightarrow R_j$$

where minus ($-$) refers to the mediation of negative reinforcement or the blocking of positive reinforcement.

These representations are in themselves simplifications. The reader can imagine, for example, situations in which one person mediates positive rewards for the other who in turn mediates negative rewards, or where an individual's prior response, for example, R_i, mediates negative reinforcement for his own subsequent response, for example, $R_i - - \rightarrow K_i - - \rightarrow R_i$. In addition, one can imagine the increases in complexity that would occur if a third person were added to the interaction. Returning to IV.2 and IV.3, it is also apparent that the traditional procedure of treating the S as an independent variable (R_j in the $R_j \rightarrow K_i$ sequence in IV.3), and measuring its impact upon some dependent variable (R_i in IV.1) is not feasible. For in IV.2 and IV.3, there is no easy separation between independent and dependent variables. Each person's behavior (R_i and R_j) serves both as a response to a prior own and other's behavior, as well as part of the stimulus to own and other's subsequent behaviors. (For a further discussion of this problem, the reader may want to review Chapter I of Thibaut and Kelley's (1959) now classic book, *The Social Psychology of Groups*.)

The study of social interaction thus involves an order of complexity beyond individual social psychology, and for this reason its emergence as an experimental area of inquiry is relatively recent. Its advent was hastened by the early work of Bales (1950) in developing a methodology for classifying and measuring verbal interaction sequences (Chapter 15 of the present volume reviews Bales' work in some detail). Its progress has been markedly affected by three concurrent and related theoretical and empirical developments: (a) the social exchange paradigms introduced by the sociologists Homans (1961) and Blau (1964) and by the social psychologists Thibaut and Kelley (1959); (b) the development of game theory as a mathematical, economical, and psychological theory of choice in situations of social interdependence which emerged from the initial work of the mathematician Von Neumann and the economist Morgenstern (1944); and (c) the collaborative efforts by Fouraker, an economist, and Siegel, a psychologist (1963), in studying the social psychological bases of interpersonal bargaining.

In the first chapter of this section, Chapter 9, the present author briefly reviews the development of game theory as an experimental social psychological paradigm, and the utilization of the Prisoners' Dilemma Game as a technique for investigating cooperation and competition. He then goes on to examine the goals of players in this interpersonal setting, and to stress the importance of distinguishing goals (one's long-term objectives) from strategies (the instrumental acts one initiates to achieve one's objectives). The final sections of the chapter are devoted to the problem of achieving methods for assessing social goals relatively independently of strategy. Eventually, to understand the behaviors of participants in a situation of social interdependence, it will be, of course, necessary to assess the utilities persons assign particular outcomes (goals), and the strategies that they utilize to affect both their own and the other person's behavior in an attempt to achieve their more valued (higher utility) outcomes.

In the subsequent chapter, Kelley and Schenitzki describe the conceptual and experimental paradigm developed by Fouraker and Siegel for studying conflict and bargaining behavior in the economic situation of bilateral monopoly. They then review the findings that Fouraker and Siegel obtained in experiments designed (a) to test alternative formal economic models of bargaining, and (b) to evaluate the effects of the presence or absence of information concerning other's potential profits as well as variations in maximum potential joint profit upon the bargainers' behavior. The reader may wish to note that the preceding affords a comparison between two important types of conceptual and research strategies in social psychology. The first involves testing very precise quantitative predictions which follow from formal quantitative models, an approach used by social psychologists working principally with mathematical models of learning or decision making; the second is comparable to the majority of current research conducted by social psychologists, where predictions derive from less precise verbal theories, and are made in terms of simple orderings between variables, such as "more than" and "less than."

Kelley and Schenitzki then discuss further uses and various adaptations that the Fouraker-Siegel paradigm can serve in investigating social interaction in a setting of interpersonal bargaining. They report a series of studies which were designed to examine the social psychological processes that might be associated with players' success or failure in obtaining solutions which would maximize joint profit. They conclude by discussing the utility of the paradigm for social psychological research, and by raising an issue which confronts most social psychologists: "Posed here is one of the central, day-to-day conflicts for the social psychologist—whether to drift toward the level of greater complexity and realism (toward social science problems), or toward the level of greater simplicity and analysis (toward psychological or even biological science problems), or to maintain an intermediate and perhaps unique position between his social science and psychological science colleagues."

The final chapter in this section, Chapter 11 by Stryker, considers the phenomena of coalition formation. In a fundamental sense the study of coalitions is conceptually even more complex than the research reported on games and bargaining. The reader will recall that the unit of observation for the research reported by this writer and Kelley and Schenitzki was the dyad, the two-person group. Coalitions, by definition, imply at least three-person groups. And, as the sociologist Simmel observed at the turn of this century, there is a marked difference in the complexity of relationships when a group of two is augmented by one additional member. In effect, one increases the potential interdependencies from one ($A \rightleftharpoons B$) to six ($A \rightleftharpoons B$, $A \rightleftharpoons C$, $B \rightleftharpoons C$, $AB \rightleftharpoons C$, $AC \rightleftharpoons B$, and $BC \rightleftharpoons A$).

Stryker, following the earlier work of Gamson (1964), first defines coalition formation as a process that involves the joint use of member resources to determine the distribution of rewards and punishments in a situation where the maximization of rewards requires coordination between some participants and conflict with others. Given this definition, he considers the various conceptual and experimental paradigms that have been employed in an attempt to understand coalition behavior. The influence of social exchange, bargaining, and game theory as conceptual frameworks for investigating social interaction are again apparent in this discussion. The author concludes this incisive review with a series of questions which must be confronted by future investigators of coalition behavior if, indeed, major theoretical and experimental advances are to be made.

In concluding this section introduction, we would again note that these chapters are representative of theoretical and empirical research on social interaction. The reader desiring a more complete review of this area will want to familiarize himself with one or more of the social exchange theories referenced previously. In addition, the work of Schelling (1960) provides a fundamental appreciation of the role and range of possible strategic behaviors in conflict situations involving individuals and nation-states.

REFERENCES

BALES, R. *Interaction process analysis.* Cambridge, Mass.: Addison-Wesley, 1950.
BLAU, P. *Exchange and power in social life.* New York: Wiley, 1964.
FOURAKER, L., & SIEGEL, S. *Bargaining behavior.* New York: McGraw-Hill, 1963.

HOMANS, G. *Social behavior: Its elementary forms*. New York: Harcourt, 1961.

SCHELLING, T. *The strategy of conflict*. Cambridge, Mass.: Harvard University Press, 1961.

THIBAUT, J., & KELLEY, H. *The social psychology of groups*. New York: Wiley, 1959.

VON NEUMANN, J., & MORGENSTERN, O. *Theory of games and economic behavior*. Princeton, N.J.: Princeton University Press, 1944.

ZAJONC, R. *Social psychology: An experimental approach*. Belmont, Calif.: Brooks-Cole, 1966.

9

GAME BEHAVIOR AND SOCIAL MOTIVATION IN INTERPERSONAL SETTINGS[1]

Charles G. McClintock

The investigation of choice behavior through the use of simplified games is a relatively recent area of theoretical and empirical concern within experimental social psychology. It considers both why and how individuals make decisions in situations where one person's welfare is determined not only by his own actions, but also by those of other participants. In effect, game behavior occurs in a social setting where there is interdependence between players insofar as each can affect, but in most instances not completely determine, their own and the others' outcomes. For this reason, games provide a convenient paradigm for investigating the motives that underlie and the strategies that evolve in situations of social interaction.

Consider, for example, the game of poker. Any player's outcomes are not only dependent upon his own plays, but also upon those of the other players. Formally, the game of poker may be described as involving considerations of *utility* and *strategy*. We can assume that each player is motivated to maximize the *utility* of some outcome—points, money, prestige, or retention of his garments—by adopting some set of *strategies* or choice rules. To be successful, to maximize some desired outcome, the player's strategy must take into account the motives and strategies of the other players since no individual player can completely determine the outcome of the game. By investigating behavior in such games, we hope to begin to understand the motives and strategies that characterize man's relationships to others in similar situations of social interdependence.

[1] The author wishes to acknowledge support on this chapter from Grant No. R01, HD03258, National Institute of Child Health and Human Development, and National Science Foundation Grant No. GS-3061.

DEVELOPMENT OF AN AREA

Historically, the area of game theory and research evolved from attempts within the field of economics to develop formal mathematical models to prescribe appropriate rules for decision making in situations where there were two or more decision makers in competition for limited economic resources. The earliest decision theory models of human behavior described how a single individual should make rational decisions so as to maximize the *expected value* of his outcomes. To do so, the models asserted that an individual should consider the *utility* (amount of dollars, the degree of prestige, the number of bushels of some valued commodity) attached to a given decision alternative, and the *probability* that the alternative would occur. Faced with various choices or alternatives, the models held that a rational decision maker should select that decision rule which would yield the highest product of these two variables, utility and probability, and thus provide the maximum expected value. For example, faced with a maximum problem such as choosing between a bet where you have a 50-50 chance of winning $1.00 versus one where you have a 1 in 10 chance of winning $6.00, you "should" choose the latter because it would maximize your expected payoff: ($6.00 $\times$ .10 = $.60) is greater than ($1.00 $\times$ .50 = $.50).

The problems in utilizing the preceding individualistic decision model for prescribing rational decision making in many economic situations was initially described by Von Neumann and Morgenstern (1944) in their classic book *Theory of Games and Economic Behavior*. First, they observed that an economic environment involving a single decision maker is a rarity—comparable to the situation faced by Robinson Crusoe. Crusoe, they assert, given estimates of his own wants, the resources available to him, and the probabilistic nature of the environment, could indeed select alternative actions to maximize his resulting satisfactions in terms of food, shelter, defense, being rescued, and so on. However, in contrast to Robinson Crusoe, the authors in a compelling argument set forth the reasons why the more usual multi-person economy, a social exchange economy, necessarily represents a radically different decision environment than that of an individual isolated on an island:

> Consider now a participant in a social exchange economy. His problem, has, of course, many elements in common with a (individual) maximum problem. But it also contains some very essential elements of an entirely different nature. He too tries to obtain an optimum result. But in order to achieve this, he must enter into relations of exchange with others. If two or more persons exchange goods with each other, then the result for each one will depend in general not merely upon his own actions but on those of the others as well. Thus, each participant attempts to maximize a function (his above-mentioned "result") of which he does not control all variables. This is certainly no maximum problem, but a peculiar and disconcerting mixture of several conflicting maximum problems. Every participant is guided by another principle and neither determines all variables which affect his interest [pp. 10–11].

In effect, Von Neumann and Morgenstern set forth some of the reasons why formal decision models which prescribe rational decisions for individuals in relation to the physical environment are inadequate for prescribing rational behavior for individuals whose own outcomes are dependent not only upon their own behavior but also upon that of other persons. In their book, they go on to develop a formal theory of games which prescribes rational behavior for decision makers who know what they want and who are socially and economically interdependent. Their theoretical models take into consideration several social contexts: (a) two-person, strictly competitive, *zero-sum* games, in which the joint outcomes of players sum to zero ("my wins are your losses and vice versa"), and in which communication between participants may or may not occur; (b) multiple-person games of the same zero-sum or competitive order in which coalitions between participants may or may not be formed; and (c) *non-zero-sum* games which are not strictly competitive since players' outcomes do not necessarily sum to zero, and in which various types of cooperation or collusion become possible. The latter instance includes games in which certain choices may simultaneously yield to both players positive or negative outcomes.

Von Neumann and Morgenstern and others interested in formal game theory have constructed a number of more or less rigorous mathematical models that can be used to help designate what are "rational" rules for economic and social decision making. These models make a number of assumptions concerning the social nature of man, and the type of environment in which he functions. Most generally, they deal with situations in which individuals are competing for scarce resources. They assume that all the participating individuals are motivated to maximize their own supply from some limited set of mutually valued commodities. In this setting, one fundamental rule advises all players of a competitive game, who are assumed to be motivated to win as much of a commodity as possible, to recognize like predispositions in the other participants, and to make decisions so as to minimize their own maximum possible loss.

Consider, for example, an administration faced with a decision to call or not call the police to campus in the midst of a student strike, and student strikers faced with a decision of whether or not to forcefully occupy the administration building. Furthermore, assume that this is a zero-sum situation, an instance of pure conflict, insofar as the students' gains are the administrations' losses, and vice versa. Finally, let us postulate that the payoffs or values for each of the four possible outcomes have the characteristics indicated in Figure 9.1, where the number to the left in each mutual payoff cell represents the value of that joint choice for the students, and the value to the right the value for the administration.

Given this situation, there is, according to game theory, an optimal strategy for both players given the above values of the various outcomes. The administration observe that if they call the police, the worst that could occur is that the students would occupy the administration building and they evaluate this occurrence as -8. If they do not call the police, the worst that could happen is that the students would occupy without police presence and they evaluate this outcome as —4. The students can also calculate that given either administration action, a strategy of occupying has a higher payoff than not occupying. Given a minimax strategy on the part of both contestants, the rational way to play is for each player to make a choice that minimizes the losses the other can inflict. For the administration, the minimax choice is not to call the police; for the student strikers, the choice is to occupy the administration building. This analysis obtains only when one assumes that adversaries are motivated to do as much harm to each other as possible, and that each knows that the other has this orientation and has the intelligence and information to take advantage of this knowledge. Needless to say, these are very restrictive assumptions in viewing the behavior of men in most situations of social interdependence.

		ADMINISTRATIONS' CHOICES	
		Call Police	*Not Call Police*
STUDENTS' CHOICES	*Occupy*	+8, —8	+4, —4
	Not Occupy	—1, +1	—9, +9

Figure 9.1
Zero-sum, competitive game between students and administration.

Some of the early empirical investigations of game behavior in social psychology were directed towards evaluating such mathematical models and the rules they prescribed for rational human behavior (Rapoport & Orwant, 1962). For instance, studies were conducted to ascertain whether players in competition actually made choices so as to minimize their maximum losses. However, more recent research in social psychology departs from earlier work based on the economic theory of games in two major respects: (a) it has emphasized the operation of various social motives underlying a variety of forms of behavior in situations of social interdependence rather than the single motive to maximize own gain or minimize loss in situations of strict competition; and (b) its principal theoretical orientation has been redirected toward describing behavior in situations of social exchange rather than constructing formal rules for rational choice behavior; that is, it focuses upon the description of factors that affect interpersonal decision making and exchange rather than upon the construction and testing of formal mathematical models based upon assumed human motivational predispositions. These differences are, of course, matters of degree. Many experimental social psychologists remain not only cognizant of the formal mathematical models developed by the economists and the decision theorists, but also rely heavily upon certain assumptions, mathematical structures, and methodologies that were employed in these original areas of theoretical and empirical concern.

THE TWO-PERSON NON-ZERO-SUM GAME:
THE PRISONER'S DILEMMA GAME

Most recent social psychological research in game behavior has employed two-person non-zero-sum games in which communication between the two participants is restricted. As noted earlier, non-zero-sum refers to those games which are not strictly competitive, and hence the outcomes afforded players do not necessarily sum to zero. The game paradigm most frequently employed in this research and displayed in Figure 9.2 is the Prisoner's Dilemma Game (PDG).

The paradigm, which is attributed to A. W. Tucker, considers the dilemma of two suspects who are arrested by the police. Both have been involved in a crime, although there is insufficient evidence to prosecute them. The district attorney talks to each one alone. Each is aware that if neither provides State's evidence, both will receive at most minor sentences for vagrancy. Each is informed that if he confesses for both, he will be freed in order to obtain sufficient evidence to imprison the other. Finally, each knows that if both confess, each will receive the relatively heavy sentence appropriate to the crime. Numbers representing the number of years of imprisonment can be attached to these various outcomes and the choice situation then characterized in a game or payoff matrix as follows:

		PRISONER 2	
		Confess	*Not Confess*
PRISONER 1	*Confess*	$-7, -7$	$0, -10$
	Not Confess	$-10, 0$	$-1, -1$

Figure 9.2
Classic Prisoner's Dilemma situation.

By convention the outcomes to Player (Prisoner) 1 are represented by the numbers on the left-hand side in each matrix cell, those for Player (Prisoner) 2 on the right.

Let us review the decision situation or game from Prisoner 1's standpoint. He observes that if he does *not confess*, he will spend either ten years or one year in prison depending upon whether Prisoner 2 confesses or not. If, on the other hand, he *confesses*, he will spend either seven years or zero years in prison, depending again on the other's choice. If Prisoner 1 is motivated to minimize his possible stay in jail, he should obviously prefer the confession alternative for he is better off regardless of what Prisoner 2 chooses. But, the same arguments hold for Prisoner 2, and if he confesses as well, they both spend seven years in prison. Hence, both are far worse off by confessing than if they both had not. What is the most rational choice? Should Prisoner 1 decide not to confess? If he doesn't confess, and Prisoner 2 does, then he receives a ten-year sentence, and his colleague goes scot-free. Hence the dilemma. This is certainly no simple maximum problem, but "a peculiar and disconcerting mixture of several conflicting maximum problems," as Von Neumann and Morgenstern have observed, and no simple prescriptive rule provides an answer as to what is "rational" behavior.

There exists another way of conceptualizing the structure of a PDG situation. If one defines cooperative behavior as behavior in which "promotively interdependent goals" are dominant (Deutsch, 1949), or as behavior that constitutes or leads to mutual reinforcement (Zajonc, 1965), then a "not confess" choice may be viewed as a form of cooperation—it maximizes the other prisoner's likelihood of minimizing his jail sentence (zero or one year) and permits the most favorable joint outcome, namely, a one-year sentence for both prisoners. And if one views competitive behavior as behavior in which "contriently interdependent goals" are dominant, or alternatively as behavior that leads to negative reinforcement (or the prevention of mutual positive reinforcement), then a "confess" choice may be viewed as a form of competition—it maximizes the other prisoner's jail sentence (seven or ten years) and permits one to exploit the other's cooperation (zero years for self, ten for other). Viewed in this manner, the PDG becomes one of selecting cooperative or competitive forms of behavior.

Rather than attempt to determine what is or should be rational behavior for the players of PDG, most social psychological research today utilizes the game as a paradigm for investigating behavior in situations of social interdependence in which players have the option of cooperating or competing, and asks what types of variables influence the level of cooperative and competitive behavior of individuals in such situations.

A more typical form of a PDG employed by experimental social psychologists concerned with cooperative and competitive game behavior is found in Figure 9.3 in which Player 1 chooses the rows, and Player 2 the columns. The payoff on the left in any given cell is again that afforded Player 1; that to the right that afforded Player 2. Hence, an AX choice provides both players with 5 points; an AY choice results in −4 for Player 1 and 6 for Player 2; a BX choice gives 6 points to Player 1 and −4 to Player 2; and a BY choice affords both −3 points. The reader can define cooperation and competition in the present instance.

PLAYER 2

		X	Y
	A	5, 5	−4, 6
PLAYER 1			
	B	6, −4	−3, −3

Figure 9.3
Typical Prisoner's Dilemma matrix.

Research studies employing the PDG paradigms have produced a number of findings relative to factors influencing cooperative and competitive behavior (See Gallo & McClintock, 1965; Becker & McClintock, 1967; Vinacke, 1969). It has been observed, for example, that: (a) the level of cooperative and competitive behavior in an interpersonal setting is affected by the changes in the numerical values of payoffs in a game matrix such as increasing the points lost for competing (Rapoport & Orwant, 1962), but not by differences across a wide range of monetary rewards associated with a given set of numerical values in a payoff matrix (Deutsch, et al., 1967); (b) ideological considerations such as the player's predisposition toward internationalism (Lutzker, 1960) or his level of authoritarianism (Deutsch, 1960) can affect his predisposition towards cooperative behavior; (c) fixed strategies on the part of the other player (a certain proportion of cooperative or competitive choices) do not affect the level of competitive play (McClintock, et al., 1963), but a varied strategy, which in effect rewards the other player for cooperative choices and punishes him for competitive ones, produces more cooperation than fixed cooperative or competitive strategies (Bixenstine & Wilson, 1963; Deutsch et al., 1967); (d) prior mutually rewarding experiences produce more cooperative behavior among subjects than nonrewarding or punishing experiences (Harrison & McClintock, 1965); (e) permitting communication between players increases the level of cooperative behavior (Loomis, 1959; Deutsch, 1958); and (f) paranoid schizophrenics, as contrasted with nonparanoid and normal samples, are more likely to be cooperative when dealing with a simulated "tough" other player, and to be more competitive when confronted with a "tender" player who always selects a cooperative choice (Harford & Solomon, 1965).

PROBLEMS WITH THE PDG

Two major problems can be identified in studies employing the PDG. The first relates to the assumption that players' choices are motivated by the numerical payoffs represented in the various cells which are assumed to be isomorphic with the players own values; a second problem has to do with a confusion between motivation and strategy. Let us examine the first problem in some detail, and then review sources of confusion regarding the second. In doing so, we will introduce a new game paradigm, the Maximizing Difference Game (MDG), which we hope to demonstrate avoids some but not all of the problems of the PDG.

Motivation and Utility: A Structural Analysis

As long as one accepts the previously given definitions of cooperation and competition, there does not seem to be any major conceptual difficulties in employing the Prisoner's Dilemma Game to study such forms of social behavior. However, when one proceeds one step further, and asks the questions, "What are the players attempting to do in the game?" "What utility functions or goals might they be attempting to optimize or satisfy?" one is forced to investigate in detail the motivational structure of the Prisoner's Dilemma and other games. In doing so it becomes apparent that more than one motive may underlie a response that has cooperative or competitive implications for the other player, and in some instances the same motive may lead to cooperation or competition depending upon the manner in which the player analyzes the game.

In reviewing the structural properties of the payoffs in a PDG, it is apparent that if we postulate that players can have various social motives or goals, then the numerical values in the cells can take on radically different meanings depending upon which motive dominates. On the basis of both phenomenological and logical analysis, four outcome goals suggest themselves as possible orientations that a given player might assume: (a) maximization of joint gain (cooperation); (b) maximization of own gain (individualism); (c) maximization of relative gain (competition); and (d) maximization of other's gain (altruism). One can ask what are the choice implications, given the dominance of one of these motivational states, for a player confronted with the classic PDG.

Since an altruistic response, permitting the other player to get more points than oneself, is a relatively infrequently observed choice within the context of the PDG paradigm, the present structural analysis will be restricted to the other three predispositions: maximizing own gain, maximizing relative gain, and maximizing joint gain. If we assume that a player may on any given trial of a game attempt to maximize his outcomes in terms of one of these three predispositions, we can look at the structure of the game, and ask what would be appropriate choice or decision rules.

Evaluating the PDG game (See Figure 9.3) in terms of Player 1, we note that an attempt to *maximize joint gain* leads to an A choice insofar as the highest joint outcome, 10, is obtained if Player 1 chooses A, and Player 2 chooses X. Had Player 1 selected B, then the joint outcomes would have been 2 if the other had selected X, and —6 if he selected Y. Obviously, to maximize joint gain, 10 is preferable to 2, and 2 is preferable to —6. So the rational strategy for maximizing joint gain for Player 1 is an A choice.

If, on the other hand, Player 1 is concerned with *maximizing own gain*, he might prefer B to A, since an X response by Player 2 yields him 6 and a Y, —3, which are preferable to the 5 and —4 he would potentially obtain if he had selected A and the other had selected X or Y. In other words, a B choice minimizes his maximum possible loss. The rationality of this choice must come into question, however, as noted earlier, when one considers the interdependence structure of the game. Since Player 2 is faced with the same options, should he make the same analysis of the dominance structure of the game, he should prefer Y, and hence a joint BY choice obtains, and both receive —3. For reasons of efficiency, as noted in our earlier discussion of the PDG, the joint AX choice is certainly to be preferred to the joint BY choice since it affords both players positive outcomes. But to obtain an AX choice, both players have to resist the temptation to take advantage of the other player's A or X choice since an AY choice leads to the highest own and relative payoff to Player 2, and a BX choice leads to a similar payoff for Player 1. What choice should rationally dominate in this instance in terms of own gain motivation becomes problematic—with trust, an A or X; without it, a B or Y.

Finally, if Player 1 is concerned with *maximizing relative gain*, then a B choice dominates. In so choosing, he receives 10 points more than Player 2 if Player 2 selects X, versus 0 advantage if the other selects Y; had he selected B, then there is no relative advantage or disadvantage if the other chooses Y, whereas he would receive 10 points less than the other if the other selects X.

Summarizing what we have observed about the PDG in terms of its motivational structure, we can note: (a) an A choice for Player 1 and an X choice for Player 2 maximizes joint gain; (b) there is no clear strategy for maximizing own gain; and (c) a B choice for Player 1, and a Y choice for Player 2 dominate in terms of each player maximizing his relative gain.

Because of the motivational ambiguity as to the appropriate choices for own gain maximization, it is difficult to employ the PDG for purposes of motivational analysis for determining why a player chose a response which may be defined as cooperative or competitive in terms of the outcomes it affords the other. Namely, each choice option may reflect one of two motives. A cooperative choice (A or X) may be made to maximize joint or own gain with trust; a competitive choice (B or Y) may be made to maximize own or relative gain.

The Maximizing Difference Game (MDG)

In an attempt to overcome some of the ambiguity discussed above, the present author devised the Maximizing Difference Game (MDG). As indicated in Figure 9.4, the motivational structure of this game is somewhat different from that of the PDG. There are still clear cooperative and competitive choices insofar as an A or X response permits the other positive reinforcement, and a B or Y choice blocks the other from being positively reinforced. But more importantly, in this game, there is no confusion about the dominant choice for own gain maximization. If, indeed, Player 1 wants to maximize joint gain, he should prefer an A response; if he desires to maximize own gain, then considerations of minimizing own loss and efficiency should dictate an A response since a payoff of 6 is better than 5 if Player 2 chooses X, and he should be indifferent between outcomes of 0 and 0 if Player 2 chooses Y; and finally, if he wants to maximize relative gain, then a B choice should dominate since only in the BX cell does he have an opportunity for achieving more points than the other player.

One cannot differentiate own gain from joint gain motivation in the MDG as it is by definition impossible to differentiate three separate motives in a two-choice situation. But, unlike the PDG, in the MDG we do know that a B or Y choice should be made for one motivational reason, namely, the player is attempting to maximize relative gain. Thus, one has at least a relatively unfounded measure of the motive to maximize relative gain.

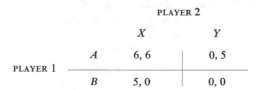

Figure 9.4
A maximizing difference game matrix.

In effect, what we have asserted is that the utility structure of a non-zero-sum game is not reflected directly in the numerical payoff structure of that game, and that we cannot know what the numbers in the matrix mean to the player until we know his goals. If the payoffs in the cells were utilities (they represent the value of a choice taking into consideration the subject's motives), then it is obvious that a player in a MDG would make an A or X choice if he is a rational being. But the numbers may not be utilities; they may be only points to be given to himself and the other. And the value of these points is a function of the player's orientation towards himself and the other player.

MOTIVATION: PHENOMENOLOGICAL DATA

In order to determine whether the utility of points might vary as a function of the motivational predispositions of players in a MDG, the author asked players to verbally report their reasons for making particular choices during the course of a MDG game. The principal reasons given for choices fell within the following categories:

1. To try to get as many points as possible for myself.
2. To keep the lead.
3. To catch up with the other player.
4. To help the other player get more points.
5. To get as many points as possible for both of us.
6. To get the other player to play differently.
7. To try something new.
8. To learn something about the game or the other player.
9. For no precise reason.
10. For another reason (explanation given).

In a subsequent study using the preceding list, 30 male undergraduates in Belgium and in the United States were requested on each of 100 trials to indicate which cell in the matrix they preferred, and for which of the 10 reasons. Table 9.1 presents the results of the study in terms of reasons given for preferences for the four possible joint outcomes. Although we will not comment in detail upon these results, several findings are relevant here. First, across both the Belgian and American samples, 85 percent of the reasons given for cell preferences fell in categories reflecting one of four motivational goals; maximizing own gain (Reason 1), maximizing joint gain (Reason 5), maximizing relative gain for self (Reasons 2 and 3), and permitting other to maximize relative gain (Reason 4). The remaining 15 percent of the reasons fell into categories which were more strategic or information seeking in nature such as to get the other to change his strategy, to learn something about the game, or to try something new. It should be noted that the strong preference shown for the mutually cooperative AX cell is not characteristic of subjects' choice behavior in situations where phenomenological data are not collected. The very act of jointly asking subjects what outcomes they prefer and why seems, not surprisingly, to generate a more cooperative orientation.

We observe further that although the proportions of individual cell preferences for the two cultures are quite similar (See column on the far right of Table 9.1), Americans were more likely to give the reason, "trying to get as many points as possible for myself" for both mutually cooperative (AX) and competitive advantage choices (AY and BX) than Belgians (See final row in Table 9.1). Such findings indeed illuminate one of the values of phenomenological data. Namely, they may reveal instances where the same response may have different meanings for the respondents. In this case, these differences seem systematically linked to cultural factors.

Strategic Analysis

We have thus far considered choice behavior as a function of the goals or motives of the players. This represents, of course, an oversimplification of the decision process insofar as choice behavior must take into consideration at least two variables: motives (goals) and strategy (instrumental acts). A choice in a game may represent a simple and direct expression of a goal. However, the relationship between goal and choice may be more indirect. Consider the following example. Suppose that in the MDG, you are motivated to maximize your own gain. To do so, you make an A choice. However, the other player is motivated to maximize his relative gain and continues to make Y choices. As a result, you end up in the AY cell which affords you 0 points and the other player 5. In an attempt to change the other's goals, you begin to make B responses which lead to the joint choice of BY and afford both you and the other player 0 points. In effect, you may be attempting to convince the other player that he is losing possible points by not changing his motivational state. In this instance, then, a B choice on your part does not reflect the *goal* of competing and attempting to maximize relative gain, but a *strategy* devised to convince the other player to make choices which will permit you to realize your goal of maximizing own gain.

How an investigator views the question of goals versus strategy has a major impact upon the theory he emphasizes, and the type of investigations he pursues. In general, there have been four approaches taken:

1.   To not distinguish between strategies and goals, and to treat choices as a measure of cooperation and competition given the outcome definitions

Table 9.1

Percent of Time Particular Reason Given for Cell Choices in The MDG for U.S. and Belgian Samples across 100 Trials
(If reason given less than 3 percent of time, it is recorded as — in the table.)

Cell Choices	Sample	Goal Choices					Strategic Choices				Total Choice of Cell
		1	2	3	4	5	6	7	8	9–10	
Mutually cooperative (AX)	U.S.	25.1	—a	—	—	67.5	—	—	—	—	64.6
	Belgian	5.0	—	—	—	81.1	—	—	—	—	59.1
Competitive advantage (AY, BX)	U.S.	30.8	8.7	23.2	—	—	5.9	—	3.5	3.6	22.8
	Belgian	13.5	21.2	43.2	—	—	3.9	7.4	5.3	—	23.8
Altruistic (AY, BX)	U.S.	6.0	—	—	57.3	—	—	—	15.8	10.3	6.1
	Belgian	—	—	—	79.9	—	—	3.9	8.2	3.2	9.3
Mutually competitive (BY)	U.S.	26.8	—	—	—	—	19.5	14.9	15.4	17.0	6.4
	Belgian	8.5	15.2	—	—	—	21.8	20.1	17.1	11.9	7.7
Total reason given	U.S.	29.9	2.3	5.8	4.6	43.9	3.6	2.0	3.6	4.0	
	Belgian	7.4	7.4	10.9	8.9	48.7	3.2	5.0	4.3	3.9	

Cell Choices Defined

AX   Mutual cooperation choices and motives permits own and joint gain maximization.

AY, BX   Competitive advantage permits maximization of relative gain. AY for Player 1; BX for Player 2.

AY, BX   Altruism permits other to maximize relative gain at player's expense. AY for Player 2; BX for Player 1.

BY   Mutual competition blocks other from maximizing joint, relative, or own gain (also prohibits player from doing the same).

Goal Choices (1–5) and Strategic Choices (6–10) Defined

Number	Reason
1	To try to get as many points for myself as possible.
2	To keep the lead.
3	To catch up.
4	To help the other get more points.
5	To get as many points as possible for both of us.
6	To get the other to play differently.
7	To try something new.
8	To learn something about the game of the other player.
9	For no precise reason.
10	Other.

[a] If reason given less than 3 percent of the time, it is recorded as —.

discussed previously. The great majority of studies in game behavior fall into this category.

2. To treat strategy as an independent variable and to measure the effects of variation in the other player's strategy upon cooperative and competitive game choices. This approach is the same as 1 except in the employment of other's strategy as an independent manipulation.

3. To assume that the numbers in the game matrix represent utilities, the goals of the players, and given this assumption to ask what strategies persons use to accommodate to one another in situations of social interdependence. This approach is taken by H. Kelley (1968):

> It should be emphasized that interdependence is the central concept in this approach, not rewards and costs. Rewards and costs, or some similar concepts of outcomes, payoff, or reinforcement, are necessary for the analysis of interdependence, but I do not regard it as the task of the social psychologist to solve the conceptual and measurement problems associated with this component of the analysis. If he does so concern himself, the social psychologist will not be likely to be able, in the foreseeable future, to get on with the analysis of the intrinsically social psychological aspects of the problem [p. 408]. . . .

4. To assume, contrary to 3, that the problems of defining and measuring social goals (rewards and costs) does indeed lie within the province of social psychology particularly when these emerge from soical situations. In doing so, one cannot help but recognize the difficulties of this endeavor. Yet one can indeed question whether one can understand decision making in situations of social interdependence without measuring rather than assuming the goals of participants. In effect what one is asserting is that an understanding of goals is an essential prerequisite to understanding the meaning of strategy. It is for this reason that the present author has focused primarily on measuring social motivation. The remainder of this chapter will examine the development of a research strategy directed towards determining such goals.

SOCIAL MOTIVES AND CHOICE BEHAVIOR: THE MDG

We have already discussed the structural properties of a MDG in terms of its utility for distinguishing the goal of maximizing relative gain from those of maximizing joint and own gain. We have further cited evidence that subjects report that most of their outcome preferences are for reasons of attaining a particular goal, and that their actual choices represent a direct means of achieving these goals. In order to explain further how the game paradigm can be used to investigate social motives, we will first review some of the methodological problems associated with its use. Next we will review some of the dependent measures which have been used to characterize players' choice behavior. Finally, in this section we will review some of the variables which have been hypothesized to affect the relative dominance of the various social motives that may operate in situations of social interdependence such as the MDG. And in doing so, we will consider some of the principal findings which have been obtained using the MDG paradigm.

Methodology

Task. The task in game situations generally involves two players who are visually isolated from one another and who make a series of repeated choices between two alternative responses. The nature of the interdependence structure between players is displayed in a matrix of joint outcomes before each subject. The joint choice outcomes are not displayed on a given trial until both players have completed their respective choices. Communication between players is not permitted. Whether cumulative scores across trials are displayed and in what format depends upon the theoretical orientation of the study.

Subject Selection. An obvious first step in any empirical investigation is the selection of subjects. In game research, as in most other areas of social psychological investigation, the primary group employed as subjects is college students. One generally assumes that the basic laws of social behavior observed in a non-random sample of students drawn from a particular campus will be the same as the total population of students for that campus, for students in general, and for the population of "normals" in a given culture. This assumption is tenuous, and at some point in the research process it must be stated as an hypothesis and subjected to empirical test. However, this requirement is generally deferred until regularities in the behavior of experimental groups of college students are observed. And since, unfortunately, relatively few regularities or basic laws of social behavior have been found across the college samples investigated, the necessity of broadening one's universe of subjects has not yet been very compelling.

The selection of subjects for particular experimental conditions within a given investigation involves another set of sampling decisions which are in some ways more important than that of limiting one's universe to college students. In psychological research, one generally differentially manipulates an independent variable or selects subjects on the basis that they differ in terms of some variable, for example, male versus female or freshmen versus seniors. Then one observes how these systematic variations affect the behavior of subjects in some experimental situation.

For example, in one of a series of studies on the effect of prior experience upon behavior in the MDG, McClintock and McNeel (1967) manipulated the degree of positive reward members of a dyad afforded each other. They then observed the effects of these manipulated differences in prior experience upon cooperative and competitive behavior of dyad members in a MDG. In a subsequent study in this series (McClintock, Nuttin, & McNeel, 1970), subjects were selected in terms of prior patterns of friendship and non-friendship, and then their cooperative and competitive behaviors were observed in the same game situation.

In both instances, the subjects were drawn nonrandomly from univeristy classes. However, in the first study, subjects were randomly assigned to the prior experience conditions to ensure that the only variable that might produce systematic differences in the subjects' behavior in the MDG was the experimentally manipulated difference in prior experience. In the second instance, subjects were selected on the basis of a set of already existing attitudes (friendly versus nonfriendly).

The importance, within a given study, of randomly assigning subjects to experimental conditions, or systematically assigning them to conditions on the basis of measured attributes cannot be overstressed. The most fundamental premise of scientific research is that one *controls* all "relevant" variables except those one *manipulates* (prior experience provided subjects) or those one *measures* (actual prior patterns of friendship). Random or systematic selection and assignment of subjects to conditions are essential procedures in meeting this premise.

Subject Instructions.   Instructions in game research must be considered a potential manipulation since they affect the set or orientation with which the players approach the game. In general, if one is *not* concerned with manipulating and measuring the effects of instructional set upon game behavior, one provides the same instructions to all subjects. In such instances, one is still confronted with the problem of what type of common orientation one wants to provide. In game research, this is an important and somewhat difficult problem. If one is interested in cooperative and competitive behavior, or in the motivational or strategic bases of such behavior, one may obviously affect the subjects' behavior by the manner in which one defines the nature of the game task. There is no such thing as neutral instructions, although there are probably varying degrees to which a given set of instructions may produce more or less cooperative or competitive choice behavior, or various strategic or motivational orientations.

For instance, the very use of the term *game* may produce a more competitive set, or relative gain orientation, on the part of the subjects than the term *task*. Or instructing players to obtain as many points for themselves as possible may yield a different task expectation than providing no instructions regarding the accumulation of points. A safe assumption is that instructions will have some systematic effect upon subjects. Given this assumption, one does not ask how to eliminate the effects of instructions, but what effects one would like to produce. One obvious goal is to ensure that the instructions themselves do not produce one predominate motivational set on the part of subjects since this reduces the likelihood that one's manipulations will produce expected differences in subjects' behavior. To accomplish this end, most studies in game behavior have attempted to utilize instructions that emphasize neither cooperation nor competition as appropriate behavior.

A problem closely associated with that of attempting to avoid giving subjects a particular motivational set in game research is that of ambiguity. In order not to invoke a particular predisposition towards the task, there has been a tendency to make the instructions ambiguous in the same manner as one uses ambiguous pictures in various standardized projective personality tests, such as, the TAT, the Rorschach, or measures of achievement and affiliation. Such ambiguity, while being less likely to produce a particular motivational set, may lead to a misunderstanding of the basic social interdependence structure of the task. Thus, one is confronted with a potential trade-off between predisposing the subjects motivationally, and confusing them in terms of the structural properties of the game.

In most studies utilizing the MDG, the present author has used instructions that are relatively neutral in suggesting cooperative or competitive behavior. The term *game* is used. The nature of the interdependence in outcome structure is illustrated in several demonstration trials. Subjects are provided with detailed information concerning: (a) the signaling of when a trial is to begin; (b) the choice options they have and how to express them; (c) the meaning of display panels which provide simultaneous information on own and the other player's choices after both have completed their choice; (d) the manner in which own and/or other's cumulative points are displayed; (e) the fact that they are not to communicate verbally with one another, and will make choices across a number of trials; and (f) the desirability that they should not discuss the study with other students until some specified date in the future.

In summary, the instructions serve to acquaint the players with the nature of the game and their behavioral alternatives. In most studies, except those in which the instructions serve as a manipulation (e.g., describing the other player as a "friend" or an "opponent"), an attempt is made not to predispose the subject through instruction strongly in favor of one of the two available choice alternatives.

Experimenter Effects. One major methodological problem, whose importance has been dramatically demonstrated in a number of recent experimental studies, is the effect, often unintentional and unrecorded, that an experimenter has upon a subject's behavior. This effect derives mainly from two sources, namely, the experimenter's communicating different expectations to subjects than he intended, and the experimenter's expectations affecting his own judgmental responses in the role of an observer of the subject's behavior.

Let us consider several instances or examples where in game research such effects may produce biased findings, that is, lead one to make false assertions concerning one's findings. Consider, for example, a game study that employs both male and female experimenters in a game situation involving only male players. Let us assume that because of scheduling difficulties the female experimenter is responsible for running most subjects in one experimental condition, and the male experimenter in a second. Furthermore, we will assume that significant differences in the players' behavior are observed as a function of the experimental condition to which they were assigned. Now we are indeed faced with an immediate and insoluble dilemma. Are the observed differences a function of the experimental manipulation, or of systematic differences in subjects' expectations towards experimenters of different sexes? Obviously, to answer this question, the effects of the sex of the experimenter upon subjects' expectations must either be controlled in some manner or measured.

The preceding example presents a very obvious source of experimenter effect which is generally recognized in game research literature. For example, in studies conducted with the MDG, experimenters are generally given a minimal role by utilizing tape-recorded instructions which are the same for all players, and the sex of the experimenter is controlled across experimental conditions. In effect, an attempt is made to minimize experimenter-subject interaction to preclude unforeseen sources of experimenter influence, and to ensure that when such interaction does occur, the experimenter is a relatively standard or controlled stimulus object for all participants.

Minimizing subject-experimenter interaction also reduces the likelihood of systematic error or bias entering into a study due to the experimenter's own expectations concerning how certain subjects should behave given particular experimental manipulations. Such expectations may operate at an unconscious level to influence an experimenter to behave differentially toward subjects, and hence produce systematic differences between experimental groups. Consider a study utilizing different sexed dyads and a male experimenter. The experimenter may, in effect, change the nature of his instructions by intonation, gesture, or other modes of communication when he is interacting with female subjects as contrasted to male subjects. Or the hypothesis he is testing may selectively distort his observations and data recording in a manner consistent with his expectations.

Robert Rosenthal, in his book *Experimental Effects in Behavioral Research* (1966), provides examples of such perceptual distortions in the physical and biological as well as the social sciences. Reductions in the latter forms of systematic error can be achieved by utilizing persons to interact with the subjects who do not know the hypotheses of the study, by employing precise procedures for human observation and recording, and by substituting electrical-mechanical or electronic devices for human observation in actually recording and analysing data.

Measures of the Dependent Variable

Proportion of Competitive Choices. The most frequently employed measure in research on non-zero-sum games, including the MDG, is the overall proportion of cooperative and/or competitive responses over a series of trials where cooperation and competition are defined in terms of the outcome possibilities which one player's choice affords the other player. Because there are only two choices possible in the MDG, one need only to report the proportion of one of the types of responses, for example, competitive. And since one is dealing with a repeated measure (the game remains the same and is repeated across trials), one generally describes the time course of choices for a given player by dividing his total sequence into trial blocks, for example, ten-trial blocks.

Given the proportion of competitive choices by a player within ten-trial blocks, it is then possible to utilize a standard analysis of variance design in which one's experimental manipulations define the major between treatment effects and the ten-trial blocks are assessed as within treatment effects. Simply stated, one can ascertain whether one's manipulations produced a difference in players' overall level of competitive choices and/or differential changes in the manner in which players made choices through time. In terms of the motivational assumptions in the MDG, one attempts to ascertain the effects of various manipulations upon the predisposition to maximize own and joint or relative gain.

In employing an analysis of variance or any other statistical design, it is important to note that in a "fair" game, where players' outcomes are actually dependent upon their own and the other player's choices, one is dealing with correlated measures, that is, the behavior of the subject has an influence on the other. Hence, one's statistical unit of analysis is the mean proportion of competitive responses for a two-person group (dyad). This has the practical implication that one must double the number of subjects to obtain some prespecified sample size of subjects.

Proportion of Matched Choice. A second simple type of analysis which provides descriptive data at the dyadic level is to determine the proportion of joint choices occurring over trials. It will be remembered that in a 2×2 game there exist four possible outcomes: mutual cooperation, mutual competition, and two states of unilateral competition-cooperation. Again one can assess changes in properties of dyadic choice states through time. For example, it has been generally observed that through the course of play the proportions of mutual cooperative or competitive states increase relative to the unilateral states. Psychologically, this suggests that the members of a dyad tend towards some stable choice state.

Variance Analyses. Two types of questions can be addressed by a variance form of analysis of choice behavior developed by Messick and McClintock (1967): (a) to what extent do members of a given dyad develop similar choices through time, and (b) to what extent do dyads within a given experimental condition develop similar patterns of responding through time? To obtain estimates of within and between dyad homogeneity one can expand some of the standard methods of analysis of variance. Such measures indicate what is going on within a given dyad through time in terms of the variability of individual choices, and to what degree there is increasing or decreasing similarity of choices between dyads subjected to the same experimental manipulations. In studies conducted to date, it has generally been observed that the behavior of individual dyad members becomes increasingly similar to one another through time, but that the variability between dyads within a condition is subject to a variety of patterns of change depending upon the particular experimental manipulation.

State-Conditioned Propensities. Measures of conditioned propensities have been developed by Rapoport and Chammah (1965), and provide another means of describing the relationship between dyadic states and individual propensities. In effect, these descriptive measures are simply the computed conditional probabilities of an individual's making a cooperative choice after each of the four possible prior dyadic states: X being the proportion of individual cooperative choices following a mutually cooperative choice, Y being the proportion of individual cooperative choices following a state in which the other competed unilaterally, Z being the proportion of cooperative choices following a state in which self competed unilaterally, and W being the proportion of cooperative choices following a mutually competitive state. Psychologically, Rapoport and Chammah suggest that the X propensity is related to "trustworthiness," Y to "forgiveness," Z to "repentance," and W to "trust." Whether this is indeed the case remains an empirical question.

Transition Probabilities. Another measure which provides information about the dynamics of decision making in a two-person game situation is the probability of a given dyad going from one joint state on a given trial (T) to the same or another state on the subsequent trial (T + 1). Thus, if a given dyad moves from a mutually cooperative state to a mutually competitive state 10 times over a series of 100 trials, we can describe the transition probability of this event as .10. In terms of an actual experimental example, data from a study reported by McClintock and McNeel (1967) indicated that the probability of remaining in a mutually cooperative state for subjects in a condition with a high monetary reward for cooperation was .738 whereas the probability for a similar transition for subjects in a low reward condition was .463.

The preceding represent various ways in which choice behavior has been described in game research. It should be observed that the field of social psychology is just beginning to confront some of the measurement problems that derive from considerations of people in interaction. To date, most of the measurement and statistical techniques developed reflect an individualistic approach to an understanding of social phenomena where some stimulus is manipulated and the responses of the individual measured. It is undoubtedly the case that, as has occurred in the physical sciences, social psychology will increasingly be confronted with constructing more dynamic and probabilitistic models and measures of human interaction processes. Such problems are obviously even more important for those investigating stategy and interpersonal accommodation than for those who utilize games as a method of assessing individual social goals or motives.

Empirical Studies and the MDG

Given the preceding methodological orientation, a number of studies have been conducted employing the MDG to ascertain the effects of various factors upon the motivational orientation of players. In this brief review we will focus on studies that have investigated the motivational effects of variations in four categories of independent variables: (a) characteristics of the player, (b) task characteristics, (c) characteristics of the other, and (d) the nature of the social relationship.

Two subject characteristics that have been investigated in relationship to the goals underlying subjects' choice behavior are those of age and culture. McClintock and Nuttin (1969) conducted identical studies in the United States and Belgium to assess changes in the dominance of the motive to maximize relative gain in second, fourth, and sixth grade boys. They observed that in both cultures the frequency of relative gain choices (competitive) increased significantly from the second to the fourth to the sixth grades, and that the American children sampled were more competitive in the second and fourth grades than those in Belgium. Subsequently, the author and Masanoa Toda conducted similar studies in Greece and Japan. The results for all four cultures across grade level and trials is presented in Figure 9.5. It can be seen that the proportion of relative gain choices increases with age and with trials in all cultures, and that there are also systematic differences in choices between the various cultural groupings.

Kubička (1968), in a study utilizing Czechoslovakians who were fourteen years old, found an interaction between two other individual characteristics, sex and intelligence, and competitive behavior. He observed that more maximizing relative gain choices (competition) were made by the less than the more intelligent boys, and by the more than the less intelligent girls when the strategy of the other was preprogrammed to be cooperative. The less intelligent boys and girls were found to be more relative gain oriented than their brighter counterparts when the strategy of the other was a simulated "tit-for-tat," namely, the subject received as the other's choice his own choice on the prior trial. He observed that the less intelligent boys and the more intelligent girls tend to exploit another's cooperative play to improve their relative position, whereas it is the bright students of both sexes who respond to the notion that in a tit-for-tat situation only cooperative behavior can provide substantial positive own reward.

The major task manipulation that has been utilized in the MDG involves changing the monetary payoffs associated with the numerical entries, thereby increasing the positive payoffs for joint gain play in relationship to the payoffs for relative advantage play. If, indeed, the goals of the subjects are affected by the monetary utility of the payoffs, one might anticipate the costs of mutual competition would increase as the value of mutual cooperation increased. McClintock and McNeel (1967) report in a study employing Belgian college students that dyads who had an opportunity to win $13.20 over a series of 100 trials made significantly more choices reflecting own and joint gain maximization than relative gain maximization than those who could win $1.32 over the same number of trials. However, even given a significant statistical difference, high reward dyads still made noncompetitive responses only about 50% of the time. In effect, the high reward subjects were still willing to forego considerable material gain which would have obtained if they had maximized joint gains to ensure that they would have more points than the other, or at least, not fall appreciably behind the other in score.

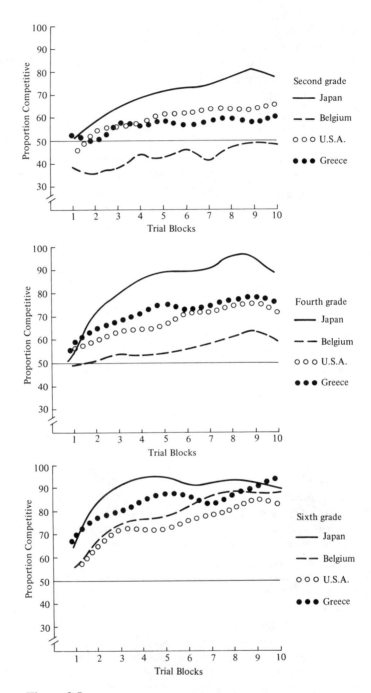

Figure 9.5
Proportion of competitive choices (maximizing relative gain) by grade level and culture across ten ten-trial blocks.

Studies also have been conducted in which the perceived characteristics of the other player are manipulated. McClintock and McNeel (1967) observed three groups of players: one where players had not interacted previously, one where players participated in a prior task which evoked the perception of the other as being friendly, and one which evoked the image of the other as hostile. Afforded an opportunity to play the MDG, these groups differed in their choice behavior. Competition or relative gain behavior was observed most frequently between "strangers" and least frequently between "friends." In a second study in this series McClintock, Nuttin, & McNeel (1970), it was observed that in comparing strangers and sociometrically chosen friends and non-friends, the strangers again made the most relative gain choices and the friends the fewest. Varying another perceived characteristic, namely the sex of dyad partner, it was found that the proportion of relative gain choices was similar among like sexed partners, but decreased significantly for both players in mixed sex dyads (McNeel & McClintock, 1970). This latter finding would tend to indicate that differences in sexual role expectations affect the likelihood of relative gain maximization or competition. In another investigation, Gallo[2] conducted a study in Hawaii employing the MDG in which he paired Caucasians, Japanese-Americans, and Caucasians and Japanese-Americans. He observed that differences in the nationality of partner did not affect choice behavior.

Finally, several studies utilizing the MDG have been undertaken which have some implications for the interaction process, or the outcomes of the interaction process itself. McClintock and McNeel (1966) report that players who are permitted to view both their own and the other players' cumulative scores through the course of the game make more relative gain choices than those who have access only to their own cumulative scores. This would suggest that the opportunity to compare own and other's outcomes facilitates relative gain motivation. Marwell, Radcliff, and Schmitt (1969) report that players who are behind compete more than those who are ahead. In terms of the other's strategy, both Gallo, Irwin, and Avery (1966) and Kubička (1968) report that simulated "tit-for-tat" strategies produce more cooperative behavior (maximizing own or joint gain choices) than a cooperative other strategy or a fair game in which the experimenter does not control the strategy of the "other." Gallo (1969) also observed that subjects confronted with a "tit-for-tat" strategy not only cooperate more, but also form a more favorable impression of the other player.

We have briefly outlined some of the theoretical and empirical relationships that have been investigated using the MDG paradigm. These studies seem to clearly indicate that a number of parameters associated with the individual, the task, or the other person in the situation can affect the relative dominance of those social motives postulated to underlie cooperative and competitive behavior in situations of social interdependence.

---

[2] Personal communication from investigator.

FUTURE RESEARCH ON MOTIVATION AND GAME BEHAVIOR

As is often the case in describing research paradigms in social psychology, the particular approach one describes is in a state of continuous modification and change. We have noted previously that there are fundamental problems in using a 2×2 game matrix such as the PDG or the MDG to assess social motives.

First, if there are more than two motives operating, one cannot measure them in any simple and direct way when players have only two choices. Nevertheless, such measurement is necessary for any detailed determination of Ss goals. Second, the reiteration of the same game lacks flexibility as a technique for assessing the relative strength of particular motives. Specifically, utilizing the same game with the same payoff structure for many trials provides little information as to what would happen if players were provided more or less points for choices that serve a given motivational disposition as related to other motivational dispositions, nor does it allow one to ascertain how the operation of several goals may be combined in a situation to affect the player's choice behavior.

A third difficulty arises with the 2×2 game paradigm given that one is always confronted with the problem of whether one can differentiate motives (goals) from strategy (instrumental acts) and, if so, how? The clearest separation of goals from strategy occurs in games characterized by a clear motivational dominance structure, that is, in games such as the MDG in which, given a particular goal (e.g., maximizing relative gain), a particular choice is dictated regardless of the choice of the other player. However, even here strategy considerations enter when multiple trials are presented to Ss, and when Ss can see clearly the total interdependence structure of the situation, as they can in a matrix presentation of games.

For these reasons, Messick and McClintock (1968) constructed a 2×2 decomposed game paradigm in which S's attention is focused on the outcomes which are a direct result of his own behavior, and considerations of interdependence are relegated to the background. An example of six possible classes of games given three motives and two choices is given in Table 9.2. It can be seen that in these decomposed games the subject has complete control over the payoffs that he and the other player will receive as a function of his own choice of A or B. Furthermore, one can observe the greater flexibility in varying the point values associated with given motives, and for pitting one motive against another. While the use of decomposed games seems a reasonable approach, the adequacy of the method as a measure of motivational disposition has yet to be completely tested. However, it does not seem possible to measure motivation and strategy simultaneously. The utilization of decomposed games approach seeks to minimize strategic considerations in order to obtain less confounded measures of motivational dispositions. Once such a method for assessing motivational dispositions is developed, one can return again to the question of the strategies players utilize in interpersonal settings to achieve their goals, and the various ways in which they accommodate one another.

Table 9.2

Six Classes of Two-Choice Decomposed Games with Examples

		Choice	
		A	B
1. Own, joint, relative gain lead to same choice (A)	Own	8	6
	Other	2	3
2. Own, relative gain lead to same choice (A), joint controlled (A, B)	Own	8	6
	Other	2	4
3. Own, joint gain lead to same choice (A), relative controlled (A, B)	Own	8	7
	Other	2	1
4. Own and relative lead to same choice (A), joint controlled (A, B)	Own	8	7
	Other	2	3
5. Own and joint lead to same choice (A), relative to other choice (B)	Own	8	7
	Other	2	0
6. Relative leads to one choice (A), joint to other (B), own controlled (A, B)	Own	8	8
	Other	2	5

CONCLUSION

In this chapter, we have briefly reviewed the use of the game paradigm for assessing social motivation in a social setting where some degree of interdependence exists between two persons. We have further presented a conceptual orientation which asserts that three major motives operate in two-person non-zero-sum game situations: own gain (individualism), relative gain (competition), and joint gain (cooperation). We next considered several types of experimental game paradigms which can be used to assess these motives: the PDG, the MDG, and Decomposed Games, noting advantages and problems inherent in each paradigm. In addition, some major methodological issues in game research were discussed, as well as some of the principal findings to date.

It should be noted that the present state of conceptual and empirical work in the area of game behavior is in rapid transition. The predominantly descriptive, atheoretical effort to relate various factors to cooperative and competitive behavior is coming to a close. Emphasis is increasingly being placed upon the development of theoretical models to account for those individual and interpersonal processes which underlie cooperative, competitive, and related forms of social behavior. In this redirected effort, attempts are increasingly being made to utilize theoretical developments in related areas (as is illustrated by Kelley and Schenitski's work on bargaining, outlined in the next chapter), to find methods which will permit a more precise identification and scaling of motives and strategies, and to construct more valid conceptual models, whether descriptive or prescriptive, of decision making in situations of social interdependence. We close with the observation that, although investigating the dynamics of interpersonal behavior is a relatively new area of experimental inquiry in social psychology, its importance is indeed obvious when one considers the significant quantity of time human beings spend in interaction with other human beings in situations where their outcomes are mutually determined.

REFERENCES

BECKER, G. M., & McCLINTOCK, C. G. Value: Behavioral decision theory. In P. R. Farnsworth (Ed.), *Annual Review of Psychology,* Vol. 18. Palo Alto, Calif.: Annual Reviews, Inc., 1967. Pp. 239–264.

BIXENSTINE, V. E., & WILSON, K. V. Effects of level of cooperative choice by the other players in a prisoner's dilemma game. Part II. *Journal of Abnormal and Social Psychology,* 1963, **67,** 139–147.

DEUTSCH, M. An experimental study of the effects of cooperation and competition upon group process. *Human Relations,* 1949, **2,** 199–231.

DEUTSCH, M. Trust and suspicion. *Journal of Conflict Resolution,* 1958, **2,** 265–279.

DEUTSCH, M. Trust, trustworthiness, and the F scale. *Journal of Abnormal and Social Psychology,* 1960, **61,** 138–140.

DEUTSCH, M., EPSTEIN, Y., CANAVAN, D., & GUMPERT, P. Strategies of inducing cooperation: An experimental study. *Journal of Conflict Resolution,* 1967, **11,** 345–360.

GALLO, P. S. Personality impression formation in a maximizing difference game. *Journal of Conflict Resolution,* 1969, **13,** 118–122.

GALLO, P. S., IRWIN, R., & AVERY, G. The effects of score feedback and strategy of the other on cooperative behavior in a maximizing difference game. *Psychonomic Science,* 1966, **5,** 401–402.

GALLO, P. S., & McCLINTOCK, C. G. Cooperative and competitive behavior in mixed-motive games. *Journal of Conflict Resolution,* 1965, **9,** 68–78.

HARFORD, T. C., & SOLOMON, L. The effects of game strategies upon interpersonal trust in paranoid schizophrenic samples. Paper presented at the Eastern Psychological Association Convention, 1965.

HARRISON, A., & McCLINTOCK, C. G. Previous experience within the dyad and co-operative game behavior. *Journal of Personality and Social Psychology,* 1965, **1,** 671–675.

KELLEY, H. H. Interpersonal accommodation. *American Psychologist,* 1968, **23,** 399–410.

KUBICKA, L. The psychological background of adolescent's behavior in a two-person non-zero-sum game. *Behavioral Science,* 1968, **13,** 455–466.

LOOMIS, J. L. Communication, the development of trust, and cooperative behavior. *Human Relations,* 1959, **12,** 305–315.

LUTZKER, D. R. Internationalism as a predictor of cooperative game behavior. *Journal of Conflict Resolution,* 1960, **4,** 426–435.

MARWELL, G., RADCLIFF, K., & SCHMITT, D. Minimizing differences in a maximizing difference game. *Journal of Personality and Social Psychology,* 1969, **12,** 158–163.

McCLINTOCK, C. G., HARRISON, A., STRAND, S., & GALLO, P. S. Internationalism, isolationism, strategy of the other player and two-person game behavior. *Journal of Abnormal and Social Psychology,* 1963, **67,** 631–636.

McClintock, C. G., & McNeel, S. P. Reward and score feedback as determinants of cooperative and competitive game behavior. *Journal of Personality and Social Psychology,* 1966, **4,** 606–613.

McClintock, C. G., & McNeel, S. P. Prior dyadic experience and monetary reward as determinants of cooperative behavior. *Journal of Personality and Social Psychology,* 1967, **5,** 282–294.

McClintock, C. G., & Nuttin, J. M. Development of competitive game behavior in children across two cultures. *Journal of Experimental Social Psychology,* 1969, **5,** 203–218.

McClintock, C. G., Nuttin, J., & McNeel, S. Sociometric choice, visual presence, and game-playing behavior. *Behavioral Science,* 1970, **15,** 124–131.

McNeel, S., & McClintock, C. G. Sex of partner and game behavior. Unpublished manuscript, University of California, Santa Barbara, 1970.

Messick, D. M., & McClintock, C. G. Motivational bases of choice in experimental games. *Journal of Experimental Social Psychology,* 1968, **4,** 1–25.

Rapoport, A., & Chammah, A. *Prisoner's dilemma.* Ann Arbor, Mich.: University of Michigan Press, 1965.

Rapoport, A., & Orwant, C. Experimental games: A review. *Behavioral Science,* 1962, **7,** 1–37.

Rosenthal, R. *Experimenter effects in behavioral research.* New York: Appleton, 1966.

Vinacke, W. E. Variables in experimental games: Toward a field theory. *Psychological Bulletin,* 1969, **71,** 293–317.

Von Neumann, J., & Morgenstern, O. *The theory of games and economic behavior.* (2nd ed.) Princeton, N.J.: Princeton University Press, 1947.

Zajonc, R. B. *Social psychology: An experimental approach.* Belmont, Calif.: Wadsworth, 1966.

10

BARGAINING[1]

Harold H. Kelley
Dietmar P. Schenitzki

INTRODUCTION

It is common for the seller of a product to have considerable leeway in the price he can charge, and for a prospective buyer, knowing this, to bargain with him in order to purchase the product at a favorable price. The process of bargaining occurs at all levels of economic life, in retail buying as well as in wholesale transactions and in the purchase of raw materials. It also has its parallels in realms where the transaction is not a matter of money versus goods, but involves, for example, the exchange of services (roommates deciding who will do what cleaning job), trading favors (political "log-rolling," with an agreement to support one another's programs), allocating territory (settlement of boundary disputes between nations), or using limited resources (teenage sisters trading off the use of their clothes or deciding which program the TV set will be tuned to). Inasmuch as they involve processes of social perception, communication, and persuasion, the strictly "economic" bargaining transactions are of much interest to the social psychologist. And insofar as he sees the possibility that investigation of such transactions will also yield information about a broad class of apparently analogous noneconomic social transactions, the social psychologist concerned about conflict processes finds bargaining to be a major focus of his research.

The present chapter begins with the research on economic bargaining conducted at Pennsylvania State University in 1958–1959 by the late Sidney Siegel and Lawrence E. Fouraker (Siegel & Fouraker, 1960). We will consider their experimental paradigm and major results, and then, some of the subsequent work by other investigators who have pursued questions raised by Siegel and Fouraker's research or have employed their procedure to investigate other problems.

The research by Siegel and Fouraker represents an impressive and rather

[1] Preparation of this chapter was facilitated by National Science Foundation Grant GS-1121X.

unusual instance of interdisciplinary collaboration, that between an experimental social psychologist (Siegel) and a theoretical economist (Fouraker). Principles and theories from economics provided the specifications for the bargaining task as well as contrasting predictions about the results the negotiations would yield. The setting and methods of the social psychological laboratory were employed to test these predictions and social psychological concepts (e.g., level of aspiration, rivalry, cooperativeness, communication) were introduced to account for departures from the predicted results. From the point of view of economics, Siegel and Fouraker's procedures provided an opportunity to empirically test classical theories which previously had only been evaluated intuitively against complex and imperfect naturalistic data. Within social psychology, this research can be considered one of the pioneering experimental forays into the thickets of "economic" conflict and its resolution.

Social psychologists, of course, have investigated various other types of conflict for many years and in many separate studies. In other chapters of this book, the reader will find experimental paradigms involving interpersonal conflict of opinions and attitudes or conflict of beliefs about correct solutions to problems. These are all instances in which the consequences for the individual of holding one opinion or another or of expressing one belief or another, are rather ambiguously defined. In contrast, the research inspired by economic conflict (of which the chapters on coalition formation, Chapter 11, and game behavior, Chapter 9, afford other examples) involves as its central feature the effort to specify in terms of some concrete and scaleable units the consequences of various events (individual action, joint decisions) for the several persons. Thus, the common aspect of these economic procedures is the set of payoffs or scores described in numerical terms. It is these numbers by means of which the investigator makes his analysis of the situation for the purpose of formulating hypotheses about its probable consequences, and in terms of which he performs his analysis of the results of his investigation. The strengths and weaknesses of this procedure will become clear to the reader as he learns about the Siegel and Fouraker paradigm and its uses.

THE EXPERIMENTAL PARADIGM: BARGAINING IN BILATERAL MONOPOLY

The Bargaining Situation

The basic situation is one in which a single buyer of a specific commodity interacts with a single seller of that commodity. Economists refer to this situation as *bilateral monopoly*. The buyer and seller each has available a profit table which specifies the amount of profit he will make for each possible transaction between them. They bargain over how many units of the commodity the buyer will purchase (quantity) and the price he will pay for each unit. The profit tables, examples of which are given in Table 10.1, show for each possible combination of price and quantity the profit each party will receive if their final agreement or "contract" is as specified. Blanks in the table indicate that losses would be involved in the indicated transactions (profits would be negative).

Table 10.1

Profit Tables Used in Bargaining

| | Seller's Profit Table | | | | | Buyer's Profit Table | | | |
| | QUANTITY | | | | | QUANTITY | | | |
PRICE	8	9	10	11	PRICE	8	9	10	11
240	1190	1350	1430	1430	240				
230	1120	1260	1320	1300	230				
220	1050	1170	1210	1170	220				
210	980	1080	1100	1040	210	50	0		
200	910	990	990	910	200	120	90	33	
190	840	900	880	780	190	190	180	143	91
180	770	810	770	650	180	260	270	253	221
170	700	720	660	520	170	330	360	363	351
160	630	630	550	390	160	400	450	473	481
150	560	540	440	260	150	470	540	583	611
140	490	450	330	130	140	540	630	693	741
130	420	360	220	0	130	610	720	803	871
120	350	270	110		120	680	810	913	1001
110	280	180	0		110	750	900	1023	1131
100	210	90			100	820	990	1133	1261

SOURCE. Adapted from Siegel and Fouraker, 1960, Appendix B, pp. 113–115.

Let us pause for a moment to inquire about the origin of the two profit tables. A point to be emphasized is that the research begins with or assumes these tables. It does not "test" them or prove in any sense that they are more plausible or typical than any other set of tables might be. The investigation concerns only what will happen *given these tables*. The particular tables exemplified in Table 10.1 are, however, not entirely arbitrary. They are derived from certain plausible economic assumptions about the relation between price and quantity for the producer or initial acquirer of goods (the seller in the paradigm) and for the person who then resells or passes the goods along to customers in a market (the buyer).

The reason for the variations in profits as we scan up and down the table (e.g., along a given quantity or Q column) is obvious: the higher the price, the more the seller makes and the lower the price, the more the buyer makes. At a given Q, the joint profit (i.e., the total to be made by both bargainers) is the difference between the seller's cost of procuring the items and what the buyer can manage to resell them for, depending upon the demand for them. Thus, for a given Q there is a constant amount of joint profit to be divided between the buyer and seller, and the only question is how much of this amount each will receive.[2]

The variations between the columns of the tables reflect the different ways in which the seller's cost and the buyer's income are assumed to vary with quantity. The unit cost of supplying the commodity is assumed to *increase* as the seller has to provide a larger quantity. As his zero profit entries in Table 10.1 show, if he must provide 10 units his costs are 110 each but if he must provide 11 units his costs are 130 each. On the other hand, the average price at which the buyer can resell the commodity is assumed to *decrease* as he has more units to sell. As the zero profit levels in the buyer's table show, if he has 9 units to sell, he will be able to get 210 per unit for them but if he has 11 units to sell, he will find it necessary to sell them at somewhat less than 200. By virtue of these constraints, the profit to be made *per item* declines as quantity increases. For the circumstances summarized in Table 10.1, the profit per item declines with increasing quantity as follows: 128.75 for $Q = 8$, 120.00 for $Q = 9$, 102.30 for $Q = 10$, and 79.18 for $Q = 11$. Given this decrease in profit per item with increasing Q, the *total* profit to be made by the pair (Q $\times$ profit per item) bears a nonmonotonic relationship to Q, first increasing and then decreasing as Q increases. (The reader can easily understand this point by obtaining the products of successive pairs of numbers, the first member of each pair being taken from an ascending series and the second member, from the corresponding position in a descending series. For example, $1 \times 10 = 10$, $2 \times 8 = 16$, $3 \times 6 = 18$, $4 \times 4 = 16$, and $5 \times 2 = 10$.) In short, there is an optimum intermediate quantity that yields the greatest joint profit. In Table 10.1, this is $Q = 9$ which yields a total profit to the pair of 1080. Larger and smaller quantities yield less, 1030 for $Q = 8$, 1023 for $Q = 10$, and 871 for $Q = 11$.

Given profit tables for the seller and buyer, the problem is to predict the outcome of their bargaining, that is, what price and quantity they will agree upon. These predictions are made by taking into account the *form of negotiation* and the *amount of information* possessed by each party. With regard to the first, there are various procedures the two might follow to arrive at a contract. One common practice is that one party (e.g., the seller) sets a price for his commodity and then the other party (the buyer) decides how many units he wishes to purchase. This does not constitute bargaining in the usual sense, but it is one form of procedure by which agreement can be reached. This form of negotiation, termed *price leadership*, has been investigated by Fouraker and Siegel (1963) but will not concern us here. Another procedure and the one of present interest is that of full-fledged bargaining. The parties make successive offers and counter-offers of price and quantity until they can mutually agree on a contract specifying how much of the commodity will be exchanged at what price.

[2] Bargaining along one of these quantity columns, in what is referred to as a *constant-sum game*, is exemplified in studies by Chertkoff and Conley (1967) and Komorita and Brenner (1968).

The second important condition affecting the outcome is the amount of information each party possesses. In the condition we will refer to as *complete information*, each one knows both his own and the other's profit table. In *incomplete information*, each one knows only his own profit table. The first case might prevail in a business in which the production and market conditions are so well known and thoroughly analyzed that either the buyer or seller can sit down and calculate not only his own but the other's profits for various contracts. The second case would apply to instances in which each party has full information pertaining to his particular phase of the business but is totally ignorant as to those aspects which affect the other party's costs and revenue. Of course there is also the mixed case, investigated by Siegel and Fouraker as well, in which one party has complete information and the other, incomplete. As to whether any or all of these are realistic in the sense of being characteristic of certain real business settings, the research is silent. It reveals only what are the consequences of the bargaining process given one or another of these information conditions.

The reader may wonder whether a businessman ever knows even his own profits with the precision implied by these profit tables. The answer to this must be given from two perspectives: (a) We are considering cases in which the person has gathered the information and made the calculations necessary to at least convince himself that he knows or can anticipate the consequences of his various decisions. The profits indicated in the table may be only those anticipated by the bargainer and not what he will actually realize. This, at least, is the psychologist's view of the matter, although not necessarily the economist's. (b) Unless we assume the bargainers possess this knowledge of their profits, the analysis of the problem cannot even begin. Without the assumption, we can make neither plausible predictions as to what persons will do nor reasonable interpretations of what we observe them to do. This inability derives from our intuitive understanding that without knowledge of their profit implications, each party will be bewildered as to what contracts to accept or reject. The functions and necessity of the assumptions regarding knowledge by each party of his own profits will become clearer as we proceed with the problem.

The Experimental Procedure

Before proceeding to a consideration of the predictions made regarding what contracts will be agreed upon under the various conditions of information, it is necessary to describe Siegel and Fouraker's experimental procedure in some detail.

The subjects used in the research to be considered here were undergraduate college students, all males except one, enrolled in an elementary economics course and recruited to take part in a research project in which they could earn some money. A large number were scheduled for each session (those present at the various sessions ranged from 16 to 30), and when each subject arrived at the assigned room he was given a number. After all had arrived, these numbers were exchanged for a second number randomly drawn. The second numbers had previously been paired on a random basis and one number of each pair had been designated, again on a random basis, as the buyer (the other being the seller). Independently, one number of each pair had been randomly designated as the person to initiate the bargaining with his partner. In this manner, it was insured that each subject's role and partner were determined by chance and independently of any of his many possible relevant properties and predispositions (preferences as to role or partner, time of arrival for the experiment, social class, knowledge of business activities, etc.).

Once the role assignments and pairings had been made, the sellers were sent to one room and the buyers to another, where they were given further instructions. The subjects in each room were told whether they were buyers or sellers and each person was given a profit table and a printed set of instructions. The instructions were read aloud to them and each one kept his own copy for possible reference throughout the experimental session. The instructions were as follows:

This is a research project supported by the Social Science Research Center, which has made funds available for conducting these experiments. If you follow instructions carefully, you will be able to gain a considerable amount of money which you may keep. If you are not careful you may go home with nothing.

Each of you will be randomly paired with another student. One of you will be selected to act as the seller of X, the other will act as the buyer of X. The significant factor in your relationship is that each of you is unique. That is, if you are named as the seller of X, you are the sole seller—the other person can buy from only one source. If you are the buyer of X, you are the only buyer—you, in turn, will distribute the product. The seller can sell to no one else, and the buyer can buy from no one else. Because of this situation, in order for either of you to make a profit, you must reach an agreement.

You will be supplied with a table showing various profit levels you can attain, and the prices and quantities to be exchanged in order to reach certain levels of profit. The seller's table is derived from his costs and reflects the condition that his profits vary directly with price. The buyer's table is derived from what he can distribute profitably, and therefore varies inversely with price. To this extent your interests are opposed; that is, the seller wants to sell at high prices, and the buyer wants to buy at low prices. However, an agreement as to price and quantity must be reached if you are to realize any profit. *It is in your interest to get the largest possible profit, since that is the amount that you will take home.*

Across the top of the table are various quantities of X; along the left-hand side of the table are listed various prices of X. The numbers in the body of the table represent the profits associated with the various combinations of price and quantity.

The profits that you will earn will be based on the actual position of price and quantity you agree on as a result of your bargaining.

The following steps outline the procedure to be followed:
1. One of you will be selected to start the bargaining.
2. Your respective bids will be in terms of both price and quantity.

3. You should start bargaining from a position which is quite favorable to you, since you will probably have to make concessions to reach an agreement.

4. You must either accept the offer of the other party, or make a counter-offer until an agreement is reached.

5. Bargaining is done in good faith (i.e., any bid offered by you at any time and turned down by your rival may be subsequently accepted by him).

6. No final agreements which involve losses for either party will be acceptable.

7. You should reach an agreement within an hour; however, additional time will be allowed, if needed. In no case will more than two hours be allowed.

8. Your offer is made by writing a price and quantity bid *only* on available slips of paper.

9. The profit table shows some possible prices and quantities; however, you are permitted to use values not given in the table. If you choose a price and/or quantity in between two values shown on the table, then the profit you will take home will be in between those shown on the table.

10. Have you any questions [Siegel & Fouraker, 1960, pp. 19–21]?

The questions asked had to do with interpreting the profit tables and were answered by means of specific examples. It was emphasized that the profit each subject achieved by virtue of the contract would become his personal property. (The amounts in Table 10.1 represent the number of cents each person could receive.) The time limit on the bargaining and the "good faith" rule were also stressed at this point.

After the instructions were completed, the subjects were taken individually into a large room containing 30 separate cubicles, each with a desk and chair. These cubicles were formed by partitions which prevented the seated subjects from seeing each other. Each one was then told whether he was to begin the bargaining or to wait for the other's first offer. After all were seated, a general signal was given for the bargaining to begin.

A subject recorded his bid or offer on a sheet of paper provided for this purpose and then held it up over his head. A research assistant then took it to his opponent whose identity was completely unknown to him. When a subject received the sheet, he could either accept the offer or write a counter-offer on a different sheet that had been provided for his offers. When he held this over his head, the assistant picked up both sheets and took them to the other player who was then permitted either to accept the counter-offer or to make a new one of his own on his sheet. Then, again, both sheets were returned to the opponent. This procedure of offers and counter-offers was continued until one person finally accepted an offer the other had made. At that time, each person was given a slip of paper showing the agreed-upon price and quantity and his own profit. The bargainers were then sent, one at a time, to separate rooms, one for buyers and another for sellers. Here they signed their slips and exchanged them for the cash payoffs. As each person appeared, one at a time, for his money, he was asked not to discuss the experiment with anyone in order not to bias subsequent research.

It is convenient here to consider some of the controls and constraints that were introduced by the above procedures. A first type can be regarded as experimental controls serving to reduce or eliminate the effect of variables regarded as irrelevant to the problem under investigation. We have already noted an example of this, namely, the procedure for random assignment of subjects to partners and roles which prevents irrelevant personal factors from having systematic biasing effects. Other procedures can be regarded as constraints necessary to place the experiment in the particular domain of interpersonal relationships the investigators intend to study. The profit tables and certain of the rules for the interaction were designed to create a bargaining situation which corresponds to a specific model from the economic marketplace. For example, according to the rules and particularly Rule 4 in the procedure, the outcome of the process is determined bilaterally and by mutual agreement. This is in contrast to the procedure more typical in research with simple experimental games (as with the Prisoner's Dilemma Game) in which each party independently and unilaterally decides upon his action and then the joint consequences of the two unilateral decisions are made known. The purpose of the bilateral control rule and associated rules is, of course, to create a situation of bargaining rather than one resembling, say, a battle or an economic contest. That is to say, Siegel and Fouraker's rules were designed to enable an interchange between the interdependent parties which has no effect upon their outcomes but which permits exchange of information. The essense of bargaining is that it permits the parties to *talk* about their relationship before *doing* anything about it. This is different from the usual "game" procedure in which every action has an effect on the other party with the consequence that the communication between the parties is inextricably entangled with actions which affect (help or hurt) each other.

The rules that essentially instruct the subject in how to bargain (3, to start high; 6, not to accept a loss; and 5, the good faith rule) also fit this second category inasmuch as they constrain him to play a role that is presumably realistic for the economic marketplace. Experienced bargainers probably start with high bids and plan to make concessions, and within the strictly economic context, they would not be expected to accept an agreement yielding them a loss. In the latter connection, experimental subjects might in fact accept losses, but then we would be concerned about the completeness of our analysis of the incentive structure of the situation for them. If they are acting with regard to, say, affiliation motivation or a desire to escape from the bargaining situation itself, and therefore accept contracts which are not in their interests as specified by the bargaining tables, then our theoretical analysis based upon those tables is incomplete and our subjects' behavior does not afford appropriate tests of the theories derived from the tables. Siegel and Fouraker's sixth rule is an attempt, more or less by fiat, to avoid this situation. Of course, it may simply operate to produce an apparent rather than a real conformity of the subjects' behavior to the basic economic assumptions (profit maximization) and serve to screen the investigator from evidence that this assumption is sometimes violated. Siegel and Fouraker's principal means of insuring that subjects have a strong motivation to maximize their profits was the use of monetary incentives. These were set at a high enough level that they were probably of meaningful value to the subjects. (The two subjects were able to share a joint payoff of around ten dollars.)

The good faith rule, which prohibits haggling or reneging on prior offers, probably affords an appropriate simulation of the case of recurring relationships among businessmen. When my opponent is a person with whom I will have to do business on repeated occasions, it is in my long-term interest to maintain a reputation of integrity with him by making good my offers to him. The good faith rule constrains the experimental subjects to act in this manner even though their interactions are on a one-time only basis with anonymous opponents.

A third class of procedures falls between the first two in terms of the functions it serves. These procedures provide controls by delimiting the region of the bargaining domain under study, but the nature of the excluded factors is not such that all or even most investigators of bargaining would regard them as irrelevant. Of course, what is irrelevant and what is relevant depends largely upon the investigator's purposes, so this category is not a clear one. Nevertheless, it is rather easily exemplified by reference to the present study. We refer to the procedures used, as Siegel and Fouraker put it, to "minimize interpersonal reactions between subjects [p. 22]": the use of separate rooms, cubicles, anonymity of opponents, interaction by way of intermediaries, payoff one at a time, etc. As Siegel and Fouraker observe, "This procedure eliminates certain variables which may well be important in bargaining—variables connected with interpersonal perceptions, prejudices, incompatibilities, etc. [pp. 22–23]." Their reason for minimizing these factors which other investigators might regard as highly relevant is that of *control*—to reduce the "irrelevant" variability among pairs that would have resulted from the subjects' diverse reactions to one another's personal appearance and manner.[3]

This third class of procedures is further illustrated by the limitations placed upon the subject by Rules 1, 2, and 7. These rules were undoubtedly introduced by Siegel and Fouraker in order to narrow the range of events that could occur in the course of their sample of bargaining sessions, and in that sense the rules constitute experimental controls. However, they jointly define a very special type of bargaining situation, one in which there is (a) no communication except of quantity and price bids, (b) no opportunity to refuse to make any offer or to be silent and not reply to the opponent's offer, and (c) no meaningful alternative to reaching agreement.[4] It is probably most common in bargaining situations, including the strictly economic ones, that each party has one or more alternative sources with which to deal, should he be unable to

---

[3] It must be noted that controls of this sort often entail subtle dangers. It is possible that subjects treated in this highly individual and isolated manner may wonder whether they are bargaining against another real person as alleged, or are in fact being given a fixed schedule of offers and counter-offers. The latter procedure is a common tool for gaining further control over the interaction. Subjects may be aware of such procedures and suspect their use even when in interaction with real persons.

[4] Only one of their 57 pairs failed to come to agreement within the two-hour period.

reach agreement with the party at hand. As a consequence, the threat of going to the alternative parties is a prominent aspect of the bargaining process and it is often invoked, either implicitly or explicitly, through elaborations of the communication content beyond information about preferred contracts. This aspect of bargaining is minimized in the Siegel and Fouraker procedure. (And, of course, this limitation is suggested by their describing their procedure as an instance of bilateral monopoly, that is, a situation where there is only one seller and one buyer.) This is not to say that threats are entirely eliminated. Each party has available the threat of extending the required negotiation time and even of refusing ever to agree. In other investigations (e.g., Fischer, 1969; Kelley, 1966; Kelley, Beckman, & Fischer, 1967; Hornstein, 1965), the conditions pertaining to communication and alternatives to agreement have been relaxed so that investigation can be made, for example, of the conditions under which threats are made and of reactions to threats.

Theory and Hypotheses

Siegel and Fouraker review the various theories in economics which yield predictions as to what agreements (in terms of quantity and price) bargainers in the bilateral monopoly situation will reach. These predictions can be summarized by reference to Figure 10.1, which is simply a scatterplot showing the relation between the buyer's and seller's profits for each of the contracts in Table 10.1 that yield both parties zero or greater profits.

In the literature of theoretical economics, ranging from the classics of Marshall (1890), Edgeworth (1881), and Pareto (1909) to the recent works of Von Neumann and Morgenstern (1947), Boulding (1950), and Schelling (1960), Siegel and Fouraker find varying treatments of the bilateral monopoly situation. As a consequence, they have at hand an hypothesis to cover almost every possible outcome of their experiments. This is not a criticism of Siegel and Fouraker but simply a description of the state of the relevant theory as they find it. In many ways, this circumstance heightens the potential significance of their work insofar as it may serve to indicate some of the conditions determining when one theory or another will be correct.

On the question of the quantity at which the bargainers will settle, while some economists have regarded this as unpredictable, a larger number have found reasons to expect the settlement to be at the value yielding maximum joint profit or MJP ($Q = 9$ in Table 10.1). It is assumed that each of the participants will act so as to maximize his own total profits. Under circumstances such as those summarized in Table 10.1 and Figure 10.1, an agreement on any contract other than one with $Q = 9$ results unnecessarily in one or both bargainers getting less profit than he might if a contract with $Q = 9$ were specified. For example, if the bargainers are about to agree on the contract $Q = 11$ and $P = 170$, it will be in their mutual interest (i.e., promotive of their respective interests in profit maximization) to shift to the contract $Q = 9$ and $P = 160$. (This shift is shown by the solid arrow in Figure 10.1.) In the same vein, at many points one bargainer can, at little cost to himself, greatly increase the other's profits—as he may have to in order to get the other to agree. (An instance of this sort is illustrated by the dotted line in Figure 10.1.) Thus, Siegel and Fouraker generally adopt the view that ". . . the two parties, if they behave rationally and in their respective self-interests, will be forced inexorably to a contract at the quantity which maximizes their joint benefit [p. 9]."

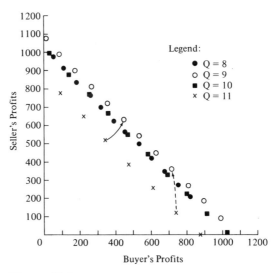

Figure 10.1
The relation between buyer's and seller's profits.

As to the information necessary for bargainers to achieve agreement on one of the contracts yielding MJP, Siegel and Fouraker note that most of the theories imply complete information in the sense that each party knows both the supply and the demand factors which provide the framework for the negotiation. Presumably, this would mean that at the point of tentative agreement on a non-MJP contract, one or both of the bargainers would be able to calculate or determine a different contract, one with MJP, which would be better for both of them.

Considering the "possibly more realistic case of bargainers who know only the circumstances pertinent to their own functions [p. 14]," Fouraker had earlier proposed that the negotiators would converge on one particular contract among those yielding MJP. His argument was that in the absence of information about the other party's profits, the seller would start at high prices and make concessions by decreasing his offered price. At each price level he would designate a quantity that would yield himself maximal profits. The set of bids this would yield is shown in the left portion of Table 10.2, designated by the circled contracts, and the progression of offers is indicated by the arrow. Similarly, the buyer would start with low prices and make upward concessions in price, offering at each price level the quantity yielding maximum profits for himself.

His general movement is indicated by the arrow in the right half of Table 10.2. The reader will note that the joint consequence of the two sequences would be an agreement at Q = 9 in the neighborhood of P = 180, with the seller making more profit than the buyer.

Table 10.2

Bargaining Movement Hypothesized by Fouraker

	Seller's Profit Table					Buyer's Profit Table			
	QUANTITY					QUANTITY			
PRICE	8	9	10	11	PRICE	8	9	10	11
240	1190	1350	1430	1430	240				
230	1120	1260	1320	1300	230				
220	1050	1170	1210	1170	220				
210	980	1080	1100	1040	210	50	0		
200	910	990	990	910	200	120	90	33	
190	840	900	880	780	190	190	180	143	91
180	770	810	770	650	180	260	270	253	221
170	700	720	660	520	170	330	360	363	351
160	630	630	550	390	160	400	450	473	481
150	560	540	440	260	150	470	540	583	611
140	490	450	330	130	140	540	630	693	741
130	420	360	220	0	130	610	720	803	871
120	350	270	110		120	680	810	913	1001
110	280	180	0		110	750	900	1023	1131
100	210	90			100	820	990	1133	1261

SOURCE. Adapted from Siegel and Fouraker, 1960, Appendix B, pp. 113–115.

Fouraker's analysis affords a prediction that Q = MJP even under incomplete information (and also that the final price will be a particular one). This analysis notwithstanding, Siegel and Fouraker expected that there would be greatest attainment of MJP when both bargainers have complete information, and less frequent attainment when one or both has incomplete information.

With regard to price, Siegel and Fouraker found three different predictions in the economic literature: (I) The specific price determined by the process described by Fouraker's analysis, outlined above. (This is referred to as the *marginal intersection hypothesis*, inasmuch as the price is located at the intersection of the marginal cost function and the marginal revenue function.) Depending on the particular economic parameters of the situation (i.e., the facts concerning supply and demand), this price may yield one or the other bargainer a lion's share of the possible profit. (II) The specific price determining an equal division of the total profit between the buyer and seller. (III) A random symmetric distribution of prices reflecting differences between the various buyers and sellers in their toughness in bargaining. This would yield an average value equal to that specified by II but would involve a distribution of prices around this average.

Hypothesis II seemed most plausible under conditions of complete information and the hypothesis was so stated. This is based on the simple assumption that when they know what profits each other obtains for various contracts, each bargainer will insist that he obtain as much as the other. Their mutual insistence on this condition can only be resolved by a 50–50 split of the profit. The question remaining, then, was whether Hypothesis I or III would give the better description of the results obtained under incomplete information.

The reader may wish to consider what assumptions are involved in the preceding hypotheses regarding the psychological scale properties of the numbers in the bargainers' profit tables. At first glance, it seems that equal numerical distances are assumed to represent equal psychological units, for example, that the psychological distance between the profit values of 120 and 140 is the same as that between 700 and 720. This seems implied in the assumption of profit maximization, that the person is as concerned about each unit in the upper region of the profit scale as he is about each unit in the lower region. Yet, strictly speaking, all that is assumed is that he is concerned *to some degree* about each unit of profit regardless of how many units he is already assured. In other words, the only assumption is that he exerts effort to gain every possible unit of profit. Whether he places equal value on each additional increment of profit is irrelevant as long as he places some value on it.

Similarly, the evaluation of the bargaining outcome in terms of joint profit seems to entail an assumption of interpersonal comparability of the psychological units of value. Thus, a profit division of 900 and 180 will be treated as equivalent to one of 450 and 630. Yet, this involves merely a decision by the investigator as to what equivalence categories he will establish for the analysis of his data. No assumption is involved here as to the equivalence *for the subjects* of equal increments in their respective profits and there is certainly no implication that they regard, say, the various MJP contracts as of equivalent satisfactoriness. The evaluation of outcomes in terms of joint profit involves adopting an extraindividual perspective—the perspective of the pair or a "social welfare" perspective—and requires no assumption whatever about the individual evaluations. At certain points in the analysis, there *is* an assumption that individuals do make interpersonal comparisons and act on the basis of the resulting evaluations. For example, such assumptions are involved in the expectation that contracts yielding equal profits will prevail under conditions of complete information.

Design and Results

The reader will note that Siegel and Fouraker's hypotheses are of two types: (a) predictions as to specific values to be obtained in certain conditions, and (b) predictions as to differences to be obtained between different conditions. The first are the predictions of Q and P values that the bargaining will yield, and the second have to do with differential outcomes under different information conditions. Predictions of the first type are characteristic of work with explicit quantitative theoretical models (e.g., mathematical models of learning). Those of the second type, more typical in experimental social psychology, reflect the use of more ambiguous theories that only yield predictions of a gross quantitative sort such as "X will be greater than Y." When the investigator has a theory of the first type, he can simply create the specified experimental condition and take measurements to determine whether the resulting values correspond adequately to those predicted by his theory. In the second case, he must run several different conditions and compare them. He can draw no conclusions from the results of any one condition alone.

Having predictions of both types, Siegel and Fouraker followed a procedure that is a blend of the two just described: they ran one condition at a time and (apparently) checked its results against their models before running the next one. Over five successive experimental sessions, they varied conditions and, at the end, compared the results from successive runs much as the usual experimentalist would compare the various simultaneously conducted conditions in his experimental design. However, no experimental design in the usual sense was used.

The stepwise procedure followed by Siegel and Fouraker has obvious advantages for exploratory work in a new area. It enables the experimenter to adjust his procedures from one session to the next and, thereby, to evolve a highly effective representation of the conditions he wishes to investigate. On the other hand, the dangers and limitation are equally obvious. As we shall see, some of the adjustments made from one occasion to the next may render the conditions questionable as to their comparability. And even if the experimenter maintains a procedure that is standard in all respects except those he wishes to investigate, he runs the risk that successive samples of subjects will not be comparable, due to changes in who is present in the settings from which subjects are selected, who volunteers or is otherwise selected for the experiments, and information available to potential subjects via "leakage" about details of the experiment.

The conditions for four of the experimental sessions are summarized in Table 10.3. (A fifth session, concerned with "levels of aspiration" assigned to the subjects, will be disregarded here.) The first three sessions provided comparison of three degrees of information. In Session 1 both bargainers' information was incomplete, that is, each knew only his own profits. In Session 2, one bargainer's information was incomplete but the other bargainer knew both sets of profits. (In this case, the person with incomplete information was also unaware of the informational difference whereas the one with complete information knew of this difference.) And in Session 3, both bargainers had complete information. The various tables for these three sessions were derived from a given set of economic parameters, as indicated by the fact that the maximum joint profit, hypothesized prices, and related values were identical for the three sessions. However, they were presented in different formats. In the tables used in Session 1, the subject read price entries for various combinations of quantity and profit values. This format was not feasible for a table providing complete information, so the tables in Sessions 2 and 3 presented profit entries for various combinations of price and quantity. Also, apparently because of the greater space required to present both sets of profits in the complete information table, the tables used in Sessions 2 and 3 were smaller with fewer rows and columns than the tables in Session 1.

Table 10.3

Summary of Conditions in the Four Experimental Sessions

		Table Format			Table Values				
Ses- sion	Information Condition	ROWS	COL- UMNS	EN- TRIES	MJP	SECOND LARG- EST JP	Q AT MJP	PRICE PER HY- POTH- ESIS I	PRICE PER HY- POTH- ESES II & III
1	Incomplete- Incomplete	Quantity	Profits	Price	1080	1070	9	180	150
2	Complete- Incomplete	Price	Quantity	Profits	1080	1070	9	180	150
3	Complete- Complete	Price	Quantity	Profits	1080	1070	9	180	150
4	Incomplete- Incomplete	Quantity	Profits	Price	1000	940	4	150	225

Siegel and Fouraker did not discuss the matter but they apparently assumed that these variations in table size and format did not matter when the first three sessions were compared for evidence as to the effects of various information conditions. It is difficult to estimate how much difference such variations in format might make. Minimally, it appears that the tables were not equally easy to read and, because of different requirements for calculating interpolated values, may have placed different obstacles in the path of agreement. In any case, the comparison of the first session with the later two for the purpose of making inferences as to the effects of information is far from ideal, inasmuch as the three sessions differ in other respects (date of session, size of table, table format) as well.

Session 4 was conducted under the same incomplete-incomplete information condition and with the same table format as Session 1. It differed from 1 only in that the table values were derived from different parameters. These were selected so as to create a larger gap between the values of the MJP and the next largest joint profit. These parameters also yielded different price predictions for the several hypotheses. Except for its later position in the sequence of sessions, with all the possible consequences for subject differences and subtle procedural differences that position entails, Session 4 is to be compared with 1 in order to determine how attainment of MJP under incomplete information is affected by how different MJP is from other joint profit values. This difference is shown in Figure 10.1 as the distance between the "frontier" set of values (the circles) and the next ones. Siegel and Fouraker speculate that if this difference is small, subjects may not attain MJP because the advantage it affords over adjacent values is not "sufficiently large to justify their continued bargaining [p. 34]." "It was predicted that the use of tables which in this way increased the cost of deviating from the optima would reduce the acceptability of contracts adjacent to the optima and thus would increase the uniformity with which contracts at the optimal quantity were reached [p. 35]."

The major results from the four experimental sessions are summarized in Table 10.4. Considering first whether dyads tend to reach agreements yielding MJP, it can be seen that in the first three sessions 6 out of 8 dyads do so in the complete-complete condition, 7 out of 15 in the complete-incomplete condition, and only 4 out of 11 in the incomplete-incomplete condition. These results confirm Siegel and Fouraker's hypothesis that joint profit would be more dependably maximized the greater the amount of information. They applied a simple test of the likelihood of obtaining the predicted order by chance in order to demonstrate the statistical significance of this result.

A comparison of Sessions 1 and 4 suggests the validity of their hypothesis that the greater the mutual advantage of the MJP in relation to the next largest amount of joint profit, the more dependably it would be achieved. It should be noted that most of the pairs not reaching MJP did agree on one of the adjacent quantity values (i.e., one yielding near MJP). In fact, only three pairs failed to come within one unit of the optimal quantity (two in Session 1 and one in Session 4).

One may ask whether the frequency of achieving MJP is greater than chance in each of the four sessions? For example, even the four cases of MJP in Session 1 may reflect a significant tendency to arrive at MJP. This question is difficult to answer without having a model of what "chance" behavior in the situation would be. Inasmuch as there were 17 quantities in Session 1 on which the bargainers might agree with mutual profit, the 4 agreements on $Q = 9$ (and the 9 agreements on $Q = 8$, 9, or 10) are obviously more frequent than would be expected if the bargainers selected mutually profitable contracts by chance. However, this criterion seems to be rather weak in the sense that to reject this hypothesis still leaves us in the dark as to how they do reach MJP. We would never seriously have entertained the hypothesis that bargainers, even the inexperienced experimental subjects, would settle the problem by selecting randomly among all possible mutually profitable contracts.

With regard to the prices agreed upon by the bargainers, a comparison of the average values in Table 10.4 with those listed in Table 10.3 for Hypothesis I versus Hypotheses II or III reveal that the latter hypotheses are generally supported. Siegel and Fouraker's statistical demonstration of this point consists of t tests used to show that the obtained averages differ significantly from those predicted by Hypothesis I but not from those predicted by Hypotheses II and III These results tend to disconfirm Fouraker's view of the process which formed the basis for Hypothesis I. Bargainers do not follow the procedure he specified, of starting at a favorable price and making concessions in terms of price and, at each price level, specifying a quantity that yields oneself maximum profit. At least, they do not do this consistently enough that it has the expected consequence for the price level at which the bargainers converge. No data are presented as to the nature of the bargainers' successive offers or the degree to which they correspond to Fouraker's expectations.

Table 10.4

Results for the Four Experimental Sessions

Session	Number of Pairs	Number on MJP	Average Price	Average Difference in Profits
1	11	4	141	580
2	15	7	148	152
3	8	6	150	12
4	11	10	228	295

Hypotheses II and III predicted the same average price but II predicted relatively small variance around this price (the one yielding a 50-50 split). Siegel and Fouraker test this difference in variance indirectly. If all bargainers come close to the price yielding a 50-50 split (as indicated by Hypothesis II), the members of each dyad will tend to gain the same profits and the differences between buyer's and seller's profits in each dyad will be small. If, on the other hand, bargainers agree on a wide range of prices, and only *on the average* yield the midrange, equal-split price (per Hypothesis III), the average differences between buyer's and seller's profits will be large. The last column in Table 10.4 suggests that Hypothesis II is supported for the more complete information conditions (Sessions 2 and, particularly, Session 3) and Hypothesis III for the incomplete information conditions. In the former cases, in which one or both bargainers have full information, it appears that such information is used not only to insure maximizing the joint profits but also to insure relatively equal profits for the two parties. This, of course, is particularly true when both parties have full information. In contrast, in the absence of information, not being able to compare their outcomes, the bargainers settle on a variety of prices with the result that one's profits are often larger than the other's.

Table 10.4 summarizes virtually all the results from the four experimental sessions. Although the data were available from the bid sheets the subjects had passed back and forth, Siegel and Fouraker did not systematically analyze the process of bargaining. They report their informal observations about various aspects of the process (e.g., that subjects in the complete-complete condition of Session 3 start with more modest initial profit requests) and present concession curves from sample pairs. However, they made no systematic use of the available data on these points. As we shall consider in detail in the next section, this lack of process analysis leaves considerable ambiguity as to how to account for one of their central findings, that pairs settle on MJP contracts even under the condition of incomplete-incomplete information. To anticipate a bit, we may note that the single detailed hypothesis the authors present as to how bargainers might obtain the MJP, that proposed earlier by Fouraker, is not confirmed, at least in terms of the average prices at which agreements were made (the Hypothesis I values). Yet bargainers did tend to reach the MJP quantity or come close to it. If this is not by way of the process envisioned by Fouraker, how did it occur? A close analysis of their data might have suggested the answer to this question.

It should be emphasized that this criticism of the failure to analyze process data can be leveled at a large majority of investigations on such topics as group decision making (Kelley & Thibaut, 1969), conflict resolution (Shure, et al., 1966), persuasion, etc. The most common procedure is to measure the end products of the process (e.g., quality of group decision, payoff to the conflict-ing parties) but merely to speculate about the nature of the intervening or mediating process. This reflects clear difficulties and complexities involved in obtaining and analyzing process data, but also a considerable conceptual vague-ness about the process (well illustrated by Siegel and Fouraker's comments on the subject) and a certain laziness in approaching the matter.

In their data analysis, Siegel and Fouraker also illustrate another practice in psychological research the merits of which are often debated. They examined their evidence as it pertained to their *a priori* hypotheses but did not pay any attention to trends in the data they did not happen to predict. There are sharp differences of opinion on this point and Siegel took a strong position on the matter, being understandably doubtful about the degree of confidence that can be placed in *post hoc* findings extracted by searching through the data (Siegel, 1964). The opposing viewpoint emphasizes the inadequacies of present theories in social psychology. These inadequacies make it desirable not to limit oneself to testing for regularities that are anticipated in advance, but also to keep one's eyes open for regularities to which his present theories may not sensitize him. For an example of the latter approach to the investigation of bargaining, the reader is referred to Kelley (1966) and Kelley, Beckman, and Fischer (1967). There is a continuing tension between these emphases on testing versus discovery in research—between the deductive and the inductive method. The present authors believe that the two approaches are not incompatible but represent differ-ent stages in the research. The adroit investigator can switch back and forth between the necessary roles, with emphasis on hypothesis testing in early stages of the research (though not totally so since he should consider what measures not suggested by his theory might later prove to be of interest) and with a shift of emphasis, after the hypothesis-related data are in, to the inductive role.

One strong merit of Siegel and Fouraker's work is that they present their data in greater detail than that required merely to show its relevance to their hypotheses. Thus, the interested reader has an opportunity to discover over-looked regularities himself and to use these as a basis for developing leads for further theoretical analysis and research. To the degree investigators "over-report" their results in this manner, it is often fruitful for the newcomer to a given field, as a means of gaining new theoretical insights, to examine closely the data presented in the research reports rather than to accept as complete and precise the authors' verbal summaries of their research.

FURTHER USES AND ADAPTATIONS OF THE PARADIGM

The Process of Attaining Maximum Joint Profit

On reading Siegel and Fouraker's monograph, the present authors were struck by the theoretical importance of their central finding, that bargainers were able to agree on contracts yielding maximum joint profit. Little explanation seems required for the achievement of MJP under conditions of complete-complete information: both parties could see what were the mutually advantageous contracts and could propose agreement on one of them. But the bargainers tended also to attain MJP *even under conditions where both information and communication were quite limited*, that is, in the incomplete-incomplete information condition and with communication limited only to bids and counterbids. This result was especially provocative because not only were the bargainers operating under the handicap of restricted information and communication, but they were also oriented primarily toward maximizing their respective individual outcomes, and little concerned about the total profit. Thus, it appeared that two self-interested parties, interdependent in a mixed motive relationship, were able to work together to "solve," so to speak, their "cooperative" problem which was to gain jointly as much from the situation as possible. Apparently by some sort of implicit process, they were led to a joint result toward which neither had been directing his efforts. This made it seem doubly important to understand the nature of the process of attaining MJP. Conditions of poor information and communication, along with emphasis on self-interest, are common enough features of interpersonal and intergroup relationships that any understanding we can gain of the processes by which any form of cooperation can evolve despite these limitations is potentially of great significance. To put the point more specifically, virtually all relationships are of the mixed motive type represented in the Siegel and Fouraker paradigm. That is, they involve both competitive and cooperative components. To the degree the cooperative aspects are fulfilled and the total input of resources to the members is thereby maximized, the competitive aspects of the relationship will tend to be less disruptive. The larger the total gains for the pair, the greater the likelihood that each party will be able to gain a share which meets his needs and expectations. Thus, processes that promote the attainment of MJP are likely to reduce competitive conflict.

Our question, then, was how the subjects had managed to attain MJP. We were particularly concerned about discovering whether this outcome reflected some unique *property* of the Siegel and Fouraker situation, and hence, might not be relevant to a broader class of situations, or whether it derived from a process common to a wide range of interpersonal conflicts. With the hope that the latter would prove to be true, we embarked on a series of analyses and experiments to attempt to identify the pertinent process. The results of this venture are presented in detail in Schenitzki (1962) and are summarized in Kelley (1964).

Theory and Hypotheses.   As noted earlier, Siegel and Fouraker's monograph provided little information about process and no answer to the question of how bargainers attain MJP. In their summary of the typical pattern of bargaining, they stated, "The search for efficient means of making concessions tended to lead the bargainers to solutions on the Paretian optima [MJP]" and that the ". . . succession of bids served to . . . enable the subject to find means by which concessions could be made to the opponent without making offers below the aspiration level [p. 90]." But as to what these "means" were and how the bargainer discovered them, no more specific answer was given.

Their one detailed hypothesis which had process implications, the marginal intersection hypothesis proposed by Fouraker, specified that each bargainer would start at a favorable price and make his concessions in terms of price, the buyer starting low and increasing his offered price and the seller starting high and reducing his. It was further assumed that at each price level, the bargainer would specify a quantity yielding himself maximum profit. These tendencies would produce a series of bids such as indicated by the arrows in Table 10.2 which would converge at a given price on the quantity yielding MJP. As we thought about the situation, it seemed more plausible that each bargainer would define his starting point and successive concessions in terms of his own profit (rather than price). At each profit level, he might give some consideration to the concerns of the other party. Thus, the seller would offer the contract with the lowest price at each of his profit levels and the buyer would offer the contract with the highest price. On close inspection, it is apparent that this process would yield sequences of moves identical with those predicted by Fouraker's hypothesis. Thus, Siegel and Fouraker's results based on the Fouraker hypothesis are relevant to ours. And their results *disconfirm* this type of hypothesis: the agreements reached were distributed widely over the possible MJP contracts. They were not concentrated on the particular subset of contracts at or near the intersection of the two specified lines of concessions.

Process data demonstrate the inappropriateness of these two hypotheses with even greater precision. An analysis of the pattern of bidding in our data (to be described below) showed no tendency for bargainers selectively to propose, at a given profit level, contracts with prices favorable to the other person. At a given profit level, a bargainer offered contracts with prices favorable for the other party no more often than would be expected by chance. In their succession of offers, rather than following a line of contracts such as shown in Table 10.2, bargainers were found more characteristically to explore successive levels of profit. This is illustrated in Table 10.5, which is excerpted from the tables Schenitzki used (Siegel & Fouraker, Appendix E). Here the seller first offers four contracts in the profit range 720–750, then offers four more contracts in the range 585–630, and then four in the range 525–540. In retrospect, this pattern of concession making is also suggested by the concession curves Siegel and Fouraker present for a dozen of their pairs. Many of these graphs show a stepwise pattern of concessions, that is, a series of steps or plateaus, rather than a steady decline in the subject's own profits. Both patterns of results are consistent with what is a reasonable procedure for the subject to follow with incomplete information—to explore several different contracts at or near a given profit level before lowering his goals and trying for agreement at a new lower level.

Table 10.5

Illustration of Exploration of Successive Profit Levels by Seller

	Seller's Profit Table					Buyer's Profit Table			
	QUANTITY					QUANTITY			
PRICE	3	4	5	6	PRICE	3	4	5	6
375	765	900	975	990	375	135	60		
360	720	840	900	900	360	180	120	0	
345	675	780	825	810	345	225	180	75	
330	630	720	750	720	330	270	240	150	0
315	585	660	675	630	315	315	300	225	90
300	540	600	600	540	300	360	360	300	180
285	495	540	525	450	285	405	420	375	270
270	450	480	450	360	270	450	480	450	360
255	405	420	375	270	255	495	540	525	450
240	360	360	300	180	240	540	600	600	540
225	315	300	225	90	225	585	660	675	630
210	270	240	150	0	210	630	720	750	720
195	225	180	75		195	675	780	825	810
180	180	120	0		180	720	840	900	900
165	135	60			165	765	900	975	990

SOURCE. Adapted from Kelley, 1964, p. 244.

This pattern of concession making suggested to us that a concept-formation process might form the basis of MJP attainment under incomplete-incomplete information. In the tables of possible contracts used by Siegel and Fouraker, the MJP is always associated with contracts having a certain attribute, namely, a certain quantity. Thus, in Table 10.5, if the bargainers agree on any contract involving the quantity 4, they attain MJP. This fact is a consequence of the economic model from which Siegel and Fouraker derived their profit tables. However, it constitutes a rather special condition if one considers a broad range of negotiation situations. In many of these, the several agreements yielding MJP may have no attribute in common. Given this special condition, one may ask the question: is it possible for bargainers to learn the concept that bids incorporating a certain quantity are better than others? If so, they might then focus their bargaining on that particular quantity with the result that their final agreements would very likely yield MJP.

The answer is that it is possible, at least in principle, for the (incomplete information) bargainers to learn that bids with certain quantities are better than others. This assumes that they follow the procedure just described in making their successive bids. For example, consider the effect from the buyer's point of view of the seller's tendency to suggest several contracts at a given profit level before dropping down and proposing contracts at a lower level. Referring again to Table 10.5, it can be seen that as the seller tries out various contracts yielding a profit of 720–750, the buyer might observe that his own profit is highest for those contracts with Q = 4. The same is true when the seller explores various contracts in any other fairly narrow range (e.g., 585–630 or 525–540). Thus, as long as the seller explores successive "isoprofit" regions, the buyer's profits will tend to be higher for bids involving 4 than for neighboring bids with other quantity values. Of course, the same will be true from the seller's point of view if the buyer explores successive profit regions in his table. The consequence is that both bargainers will have an opportunity to form the concept "contracts with Q = 4 are best." If either one learns this concept and limits his subsequent proposals to contracts with this attribute, its presence in the final agreement and the attainment of MJP is assured.

Once specified with this degree of clarity, the way to test this concept-formation idea was quite apparent. The basic condition underlying the explanation is that all the MJP contracts are characterized by some particular attribute identifiable by the bargainers (in the present case, by a particular quantity). If the concept-formation explanation is correct and if this condition is violated (if the MJP contracts are made indistinguishable as far as the bargainers are concerned), then their ability to attain MJP should be sharply reduced. To test this, we modified the Siegel and Fouraker tables, rearranging the location of profits within them so that MJP was no longer associated with Q. This rearrangement, of course, makes no sense in terms of the economic theory that generated the original work, but it provided a simple and obvious way to test our ideas about the social-psychological processes involved in MJP attainment. Our first hypothesis was that the attainment of MJP would be disrupted to the degree the association between it and Q was attenuated. Table 10.6 shows rearranged versions of the bargaining tables in Table 10.5. In this case, the association between MJP and Q has been almost entirely eliminated. Inasmuch as MJP equals 960 for these tables, the circled values (not specially designated in this manner in the tables used by the bargainers) show that MJP occurred about equally often for each value of Q. We expected MJP to be attained less frequently by bargainers who used this type of table then by those who used the type shown in Table 10.5.

A second and less obvious way to test the concept-formation hypothesis is found within a special analysis of the bargaining process obtained with the original tables. Inasmuch as the argument assumes that one or both parties explore their "isoprofit" zones in making successive bids, it follows that pairs in which the bidding actually fits this pattern should more frequently attain MJP than pairs in which bidding is unsystematic or follows some other pattern. An index of how well the bidding fits the assumed pattern is provided by a count for each person of how many of the bids he receives with the critical Q value also yield him higher profits than neighboring bids with other Q values. This index can be high only if the initiator of the bids is being systematic in the manner described. And only if this index is high does the bargainer have a basis for forming the appropriate concept. Our second hypothesis then was that this index, the number of "locally optimal" offers with Q = 4, would distinguish pairs that attain MJP from those that do not, this being true for the original tables but not for the rearranged ones.

Table 10.6

Jumbled Version of Table 10.5

	Seller's Profit Table					Buyer's Profit Table			
	QUANTITY					QUANTITY			
PRICE	3	4	5	6	PRICE	3	4	5	6
375	975	990	765	(900)	375			135	(60)
360	900	720	(840)	900	360		180	(120)	0
340	(780)	675	810	825	345	(180)	225		75
330	720	630	750	(720)	330	0	270	150	(240)
315	585	675	630	(660)	315	315	225	90	(300)
300	540	540	(600)	600	300	360	180	(360)	300
285	450	(540)	525	495	285	270	(420)	375	405
270	(480)	360	450	450	270	(480)	360	450	450
255	375	(420)	270	405	255	525	(540)	450	495
240	300	180	(360)	360	240	600	540	(600)	540
225	315	(300)	90	225	225	585	(660)	630	675
210	150	270	0	(240)	210	750	630	720	(720)
195		75	(180)	225	195	810	825	(780)	675
180	(120)	0	180		180	(840)	900	720	900
165		(60)	135		165	990	(900)	765	975

SOURCE. Adapted from Kelley, 1964, p. 247.

Procedure and Results. A comparison was made of bargaining outcomes for three types of tables, varying in the degree of association between MJP and Q. The *strong association* tables, similar to those presented in Table 10.5, were the ones used by Siegel and Fouraker. The *weak association* tables were constructed by randomly rearranging the entries within each row of the original table just as the tables in Table 10.6 were constructed by rearranging the entries in each row of Table 10.5. This rearrangement completely eliminated the association between MJP and Q. The *moderate association* tables were constructed by shifting enough of the entries within each row so as to reduce but not entirely eliminate the association between MJP and Q.

The bargainers were students in educational psychology courses. When they arrived at their usual classroom, they found the chairs had been placed in pairs, back-to-back. Each was randomly given a seat number and package of instructions and materials. This seat assignment and the materials determined the pairs of bargainers, which one was buyer and seller, which one made the first offer, and which set of tables (strong, moderate, or weak) they bargained from. Sex was disregarded in forming the pairs and the evidence provides no indication of any difference between male, female, or mixed-sex pairs.

When all the subjects were assembled, the experimenter read the instructions aloud with them, and illustrated the procedure of exchanging bids on the blackboard in front of the room. The instructions were similar to those used by Siegel and Fouraker with several exceptions: (a) they did not bargain for real money, but were merely told to treat the situation as if real money were involved; (b) they were warned that no conversation was permitted; (c) the subjects were in close proximity to each other and directly passed back and forth the sheet on which they listed their successive offers and counter-offers; and (d) the several experimental conditions represented by the different versions of the tables were run simultaneously.

In the main experiment, 19 pairs bargained with the strong, 19 with the moderate, and 21 with the weak association tables. It was necessary to eliminate 3 pairs from the moderate condition because of misunderstanding or because one member had to leave before reaching agreement. In a second experiment, only the strong and weak tables were used, 24 pairs with the former and 25 pairs with the latter. One strong pair and 2 weak pairs were eliminated because of failure to understand or follow instructions.[5]

The results from the two experiments were quite consistent. They disconfirmed our first hypothesis but were largely consistent with the second. With regard to the first, the rate of attaining MJP was approximately the same for the three sets of tables representing the three degrees of association between MJP and Q. In Experiment I, the numbers of pairs attaining MJP for the strong, intermediate, and weak tables were, respectively, 9 of 19, 11 of 16, and 13 of 21. In Experiment II, the numbers for the strong and weak tables respectively were 18 of 23 and 15 of 23. It is clear that MJP was attained with considerable frequency in all these incomplete-incomplete information conditions, but it was attained no less often with the modified tables than with the original ones. Thus, the process of MJP attainment does not depend on the special pattern of information generated by the specific economic assumptions underlying Siegel and Fouraker's tables. It might be noted that only 2 of the 102 pairs missed MJP by more than one degree in our results.

To test the second hypothesis, we first counted for each person how many of the offers he received with $Q = 4$ yielded him higher profits than adjacent offers

---

[5] This experiment also involved an unsuccessful attempt to vary the subjects' orientations to the bargaining, whether a "group goal" or an "individual goal" orientation. This experimental variation made little difference and can be disregarded here.

with other values. We then examined the relation between this index and whether or not the pair attained MJP. Consistent with our hypothesis, a relation was found between frequency of "locally optimal offers with $Q = 4$" for bargainers using the original (strong association) tables, but not for bargainers using the modified tables. However, the relationship for the strong association tables was present to a significant degree only for the person who had finally concluded the bargaining by accepting the other person's bid. In other words, if in the strong association condition, we examined the pattern of bids offered the person who finally accepted the terminating bid, in those cases where this bid yielded MJP, he was especially likely to have been presented with a sequence of offers that would have enabled him to form the concept "$Q = 4$ is best." This is a pattern which is generated by a succession of offers such as shown in Table 10.5.

The Systematic Concessions Model.   The lack of difference between the three experimental conditions in rate of attaining MJP definitely ruled out concept-formation as a necessary mechanism in the process. Attaining the concept that a certain Q was best was not possible with the weak association tables and yet bargainers using these tables reached MJP contracts as often as did those using the original tables. This result was also completely incompatible with Fouraker's marginal intersection hypothesis and our earlier hypothesis which also were based on the particular pattern of profits presented in the Siegel and Fouraker tables.

On the other hand, the process analysis indicated that attainment of MJP depends on a pattern of systematic exploration of isoprofit regions. Given these results, we were forced to seek a new conception of the process. The one we now believe to be correct is simple, fits the various findings, and has implications for a broad class of negotiation situations. It might be referred to as a *systematic concessions* model and is illustrated in Figure 10.2. While each of the time frames in this figure shows both bargainers' profits for the various contracts, we will assume that each one knows only his own profits. That is all the information they are given and the present model makes no assumptions they ever learn more than that. Knowing only the profit each contract yields himself, the bargainer has no choice but to begin by proposing contracts for which his profits are high. As he finds these to be unacceptable to the other party, he then proposes contracts yielding somewhat lower profits, and so on. As he makes successive concessions, each time dropping his level of aspiration, he enlarges the set of contracts he himself considers acceptable. Thus in Figure 10.2, as time progresses, the set of contracts the buyer considers acceptable becomes larger, and the same occurs for the seller. The prediction of their final agreement is simply a matter, then, of predicting where these two sets of acceptable contracts will *first* overlap. As shown in Figure 10.2, the two sets are likely to intersect first on the contracts located along the outer edge of the total set. Located there, of course, are the MJP contracts. In other words, by virtue of their successive concessions, their sets of acceptable contracts are most likely to have in common first those contracts yielding MJP.

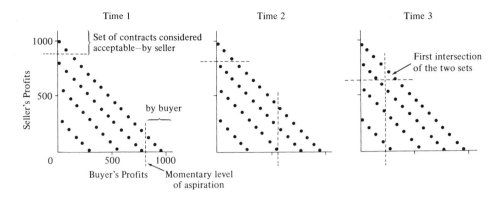

Figure 10.2
The systematic concessions model of bargaining (from Kelley, 1964, p. 248).

It should be emphasized that the process we conceive is cue-independent. That is, it assumes nothing about the bargainers' ability to identify or distinguish among the various contracts. Each one need know only the profit each contract provides him, nothing more. In that important respect, the model is consistent with the results from our experiment where we destroyed the relation between MJP and the quantity attribute without producing any reduction in MJP attainment. Thus, the process as we now view it is independent of the special configuration of profits present in Siegel and Fouraker's tables. Consequently, it is more likely than we had thought at the outset that their results on MJP attainment have general applicability to interpersonal negotiations.

This view of the process makes no assumptions about the bargainers' relative rates of concession making. If these are different, the agreement may be toward one or the other extreme of the MJP set (as in Figure 10.2 where the seller's profit exceeds the buyer's) rather than near the middle. This is consistent with Siegel and Fouraker's conclusion and our own findings that there is wide variation among the dyads that obtain MJP in the profit differential between the two bargainers.

The model *does* assume that concessions are made systematically, with fairly good exploration of the various possible contracts at a given profit level before moving on to less profitable ones. Where successive bids are selected in an unsystematic manner, MJP should be obtained less often. However, the attainment of MJP on the basis of systematic concessions requires only that one individual behaves systematically and that the other one terminates the process by accepting the highest offer available to him. Inasmuch as the one person's systematic pattern is likely to generate as the highest offer one that involves MJP, the pattern of offers made by the person who terminates the bargaining (the acceptor) is irrelevant. Only the pattern of offers made by the other person should affect MJP achievement. This inference is supported by the process data described above. The more systematic the bids offered the person whose acceptance terminates the bidding, the more likely it is that the contract will be in the MJP set.

The model is also consistent with the results from Siegel and Fouraker, comparing Sessions 1 and 4, that MJP is attained more often the more it is separated from the next largest joint profit. As can be seen in Figure 10.2, the more the outer line of values is separated from the next line, the greater the likelihood that the first overlap of the two sets of acceptable contracts will consist exclusively of values on that outer line.

Implications of the Model. The main impetus for the development of the systematic concessions model was provided by a finding of *no difference* between the various conditions in Schenitzki's experiment. A result of no difference is usually not a very secure basis for interpretations because a poorly conducted investigation, with inadequate subjects, poorly defined independent variables, and unreliably measured dependent variables, tends to be biased toward this result. However, the systematic concessions model was credible to us because of its consistency also with several sets of positive results, as described in the preceding section. Since then, the model has gained credibility as its implications for other situations have been investigated and confirmed. The general point is that a model of a phenomenon becomes acceptable as an accurate account of that phenomenon to the degree (a) it accounts for existing facts, and (b) yields testable and valid predictions about as yet unexamined aspects of the phenomenon.

In the present case, one implication of the model is that if bargainers do not make their concessions in a systematic manner, they will not attain MJP. On the hypothesis that one source of nonsystematic concessions might be over-concern for one another's profits (as in a highly cooperative relationship), Schenitzki (1962) designed a procedure in which the bargainers were explicitly instructed to try to maximize their joint profits. It was emphasized that each one would gain half of the total profit they both made, and it was suggested that the total might be maximum even though the profits shown for one bargainer or the other were low. The instructions concluded with the summary statement, "So it is in your interest to cooperate with your partner so that you both make the largest profit possible." This "group goal" condition was compared with the usual "individual goal" condition in which each bargainer was told to get the largest possible profit for himself and not to pay any attention to how much profit he thought the other player might be getting. All bargaining was conducted under incomplete-incomplete information conditions and with communication restricted to the exchange of offers.

A comparison of the two conditions showed that MJP was attained by 10 of the 12 individual goal subjects (consistent with the earlier results) but by only 4 of 12 group goal pairs ($p < .05$ by Fisher exact test). The reasons for this are made fairly clear by the accompanying process and questionnaire data. (a) In the group goal condition, the bargainers made fewer offers and counter-offers and the acceptor more often terminated the bargaining by accepting a contract yielding him less profit than another contract already offered. (b) In their reasons for accepting the offer, given in a post-session questionnaire, the acceptors more often referred to the other person's (inferred) outcomes. The implication, of course, is that in their pursuit of MJP, the group goal oriented bargainers tried to take account of one another's profits as well as their own, but made errors in doing so. In the absence of a sound basis for inferring the other party's profits, these inferences were often based on erroneous cues. For example, the other party's repetition of a given offer was taken to indicate that his profits were very high and, thus, that the contract was a good one for the pair.

These results show a paradoxical situation, in which even though *explicitly* trying to obtain MJP, the cooperative bargainers did so less often than the individualistically oriented ones who, as we have shown, attain it *implicitly*. Further conditions in Schenitzki's experiment showed that this deficiency in the group goal pairs' performance is eliminated when they are permitted to communicate more freely. (In the free communication condition, they were not allowed to reveal their profits but could communicate their evaluative reactions to one another's offers.) However, their poor performance with limited communication makes one wonder how often it happens in real interpersonal negotiations that the implicitly generated consequences of selfishly oriented parties are superior to the more socially conscious actions of cooperatively oriented persons. One also wonders how often it is true that well-intentioned but uninformed persons make unnecessary concessions and unwise decisions on the basis of erroneous inferences about one another's preferences, with the results that one or both enjoy less good outcomes than they might otherwise.[6]

The systematic concessions model also seems to be applicable to more complex bargaining situations than that of Siegel and Fouraker. Thus, whereas all the research reported above employs the particular bargaining format developed by Siegel and Fouraker, there is some evidence that the model derived from that research is not limited in its applicability to that particular format. We refer

---

[6] Morgan and Sawyer (1967) provided similar evidence of a tendency for cooperatively oriented subjects (in their case, friends) to attempt to give the other person what they erroneously think he wants. They also found this tendency to be reduced by exchange of information between the two as to what they expect and desire. However, because of the different reward structure of their bargaining situation, the well-intentioned but erroneous inferences led to higher total payoff than did the informed ones. Pairs of boys were given the task of agreeing on one of the following seven packages in which the two numbers refer, respectively, to the number of cents each boy will receive: (0, 30), (25, 25), (50, 20), (75, 15), (100, 10), (125, 5) and (150, 0). Before the bargaining, each boy was asked privately to tell the experimenter the most he thought he could win and the least he thought he might win. When these expectations were not made public, the friends tended to agree on the 75–15 package but when the experimenter announced the expectations, the boys tended to agree on the 25–25 package. The authors observed that these results "suggest that in the absence of information, friends develop and act upon false expectations about the other's preferences." The favored person typically started with a request for the 150–0 package or a similar high one, and this is taken by his partner to mean that he wanted a lot. ". . . The less favored person is inclined to let the other *have* a lot if he really seems to want it. Thus they are likely to reach an outcome that neither really prefers, in the kind of well-intentioned misunderstanding that friends are frequently prone to [p. 147]." The important difference from Schenitzki's experiment was that misunderstanding yielded the cooperating subjects a higher total outcome than did accurate understanding.

here to the more complex and realistic bargaining procedure used by Kelley (1966) in a study of bargaining between pairs of students in a classroom. Examples of what the bargaining tables for the two players might be like are shown in Table 10.7. The situation is similar to that of collective bargaining negotiations in which the two parties usually have a list of issues raised by one or both of them. In Table 10.7, the bargainers confront three issues. The letters down the side represent the eight possible ways they might resolve each issue and the values in the table are the payoffs to each player of each particular settlement. The bargaining is concluded when they have agreed on a settlement point for each issue. Thus, a possible final contract might be G on Issue 1, E on Issue 2, and B on Issue 3. As can be seen, the issues are not of equal importance to each party and an issue of high importance to one may be less important to the other. Their interests are in conflict on each issue but, because of varying importance, this is not a case of pure conflict. That is, on some issues one party can greatly increase the other's payoff at relatively little sacrifice to his own. The total set of possible contracts the pair might specify provide a plot of values rather similar to that shown in Figure 10.1. That is, the relationship is a mixed motive one: each party desires an overall settlement pattern favorable to himself but the two parties have a common interest in achieving patterns of settlement that yield good outcomes to both rather than less good ones. For example, the settlement pattern of GEF is better for both parties than a settlement pattern of CDH.

This bargaining task was used in a class on group processes, the members of the class being paired off on repeated occasions (never in the same pairings) in order to bargain for point scores that counted as an important portion of their course grades. The two bargainers sat back to back and were required to communicate by written messages. They were allowed to communicate anything they wished including information about their profits, but they were not allowed to show one another their profit tables. Analysis was made of procedures commonly used by the bargainers, procedures they learned over the series of successive bargaining sessions, and procedures that enabled them to attain the greatest total profit from the interaction.

The analysis pertinent to the systematic concessions model involved the tendency of a bargainer to propose various contracts (patterns of settlement points such as BEF) at a given level of total profit before moving to less profitable proposals. Each person's successive contracts were examined to determine the frequency of variations around a given profit level. A contract was considered to be a "variation" of an earlier one if it yielded the negotiator within five points of what the earlier one yielded and if it yielded him more points on at least one issue and fewer points on at least one other issue. (They were dealing with five issues rather than three as shown in Table 10.7.) The latter condition was applied to eliminate contracts that represented simple concessions from earlier proposals. About half of the "complete package" proposals (that is proposals encompassing all five issues) met these criteria. This type of variation was found to be somewhat more common during the later bargaining sessions, after the students had gained familiarity with the task, than during the earlier ones. This suggests the students learned that the exploration of such variations (i.e., systematic concessions) was a valuable bargaining procedure. At the end of the series of sessions, 21 of the 22 students endorsed the idea of trying out different combinations of items at a given level. More directly to the point, there was evidence that such exploration promoted the joint profit. Dyads in which both persons frequently (i.e., on more than half of their five-item offers) proposed variations of earlier contracts more often came close to the maximum joint profit than did dyads in which only one or neither did so (77 percent vs. 39 percent).

Table 10.7

Bargaining Tables Used in the Classroom Study

	Payoff Table for Player I				Payoff Table for Player II		
	ISSUE				ISSUE		
	1	2	3		1	2	3
A	1	21	11	A	20	11	100
B	11	21	21	B	19	18	94
C	19	21	29	C	18	23	87
D	24	21	34	D	16	27	77
E	28	20	38	E	13	29	61
F	34	20	44	F	9	34	38
G	44	20	54	G	8	40	32
H	51	19	61	H	7	45	24

In a situation of this type in which several different issues are being settled at once, the systematic concessions model has another implication. Exploration of a given profit level becomes limited or even impossible if settlement is reached on some issues before others. Only if all issues are dealt with at the same time can the best patterns of settlement be attained. Thus, achievement of MJP would be promoted by negotiating the entire contract at once rather than one issue at a time. The evidence from the classroom study is consistent with this point. As they learned how to bargain, the students increasingly started out by proposing complete packages in their first offers. And over successive sessions, they sharply decreased in their tendency to reach definite agreement on one issue before the others were settled. Finally, it was found that if they reached firm agreement on some items before others, their total profits tended to fall farther short of the maximum joint profit than otherwise. Thus, it was in their mutual interest to juggle all five issues at once rather than to settle them one at a time.

We must be careful in generalizing from this result, however. Under certain conditions, there may be marked advantages to approaching a negotiation problem by piecemeal settlement. Thus, Fisher (1964) describes the benefits of "fractionating" the conflict into smaller issues that can then be settled one at a time. The fractionation principle seems to apply to conflicts of a more political nature which involve questions of principle, power, prestige, and ideology. There may be little basis for agreement in such instances but often concrete matters may be split away from the principles and settled on more pragmatic terms. The present suggestion, that all issues should be considered and settled at once, probably applies more to strict economic bargaining.

Variations in Strategy of Bargaining

It is possible to investigate the consequences for the *pair members* of different bargaining procedures, as in the research described above, but it is also possible to study the consequences for the *individual bargainer* of following one or another strategy in his bargaining. And this is readily subjected to experimental control by simulating one of the bargainers, presenting a standardized pattern of offers and messages to the other party (the experimental subject), and analyzing the effects of the particular strategy.

An example of this experimental procedure, employing the Siegel and Fouraker situation, is provided by Hatton (1967). His subjects were all assigned the role of buyer and initiator of the bargaining. They bargained against confederates who followed one of two programmed schedules in presenting counter-offers. The two parties sat face-to-face but were not permitted to talk. They exchanged offers by means of cards provided for the purpose. They were acting under conditions of incomplete-incomplete information, each knowing only his own profits for various contracts. The bargaining context was provided by profit tables adapted from one of those used by Siegel and Fouraker (Appendix E). The confederate followed either a yielding or a demanding schedule of offers. In the first case, he made large and rapid concessions from an extreme opening bid and then made smaller but consistent concessions as the bargaining proceeded. With the demanding schedule, the confederate began with the same extreme opening bid and made concessions slowly, presenting many offers that yielded the subject no profit, and occasionally repeating offers. Both schedules were designed to make no concessions beyond a specified point. The yielding schedule was programmed to reach this point on its twenty-eighth offer and the demanding schedule on its fifty-ninth offer. In both cases, the pattern of offers made by the confederate tended to follow the systematic concessions pattern portrayed in Table 10.5. Apparently as a consequence of this, all agreements were on the same quantity value, the one yielding MJP in the original tables (Hatton, Personal communication). This made it possible to disregard quantity and to use as the major dependent variable the price the subject, as buyer, finally agreed to pay for the commodity.

The subjects were Negro high school girls who had been selected from a larger sample as perceiving whites to be highly prejudiced against Negroes. In some cases, the confederate against whom they bargained was a Negro girl and in other cases, a white girl.

Hatton's results show that the relative effects of the yielding versus demanding schedules depend upon whether the confederate is Negro or white. The subjects persisted longer (and hence, gained more favorable prices) when bargaining against the yielding white opponent and the demanding Negro opponent. (Statistically, in the two-way analysis of variance design, neither race nor schedule had an effect but there was a significant interaction between them.) In other words, there was no overall difference between the yielding and demanding schedules in their effectiveness—in how much they induced the buyer to increase his offered price. One schedule was more effective in the hands of one type of confederate and the other schedule in the hands of the other type.

The incomplete nature of Hatton's study severely limits making interpretations as to the nature of interaction between Negroes and whites. We refer here, of course, to the absence of data from white subjects or from the other Negroes in his original sample (those attributing less prejudice to whites). However, Hatton's results do illustrate in a vivid way the dilemma a bargainer faces in deciding whether to adopt a hard, unyielding line or a conciliatory, agreeable one. The dilemma stems from the fact that in some relationships it is desirable (or at least profitable) to be tough but in others, it is better to be agreeable. The problem, of course, is to "read" the particular relationship correctly and to know in advance which approach will be the more effective one.

The bargaining situation lends itself readily to the experimental manipulation of behavioral patterns on one side of the social interaction. Investigation of different strategies has typically involved simpler bargaining problems than that developed by Siegel and Fouraker. More commonly the problem involves the simple purchase of one item so the question is simply the price at which the purchase will be made. The relationship is then one of pure conflict of interest since the buyer and seller are dividing up a fixed amount of profit between themselves. (This is often referred to as a *constant-sum game*.) Typically, however, they do not know each other's break-even (zero profit) points so they don't know the total amount they are dividing (incomplete-incomplete information). In this setting, studies have been made of extremity of initial offer (Chertkoff & Conley, 1967; Liebert, Smith, Keiffer, & Hill, 1968) and rate of concessions (Chertkoff & Conley, 1967; Pruitt & Drews, 1969). The reader will also note the possibility of having a prearranged fixed schedule as opposed to one which is made contingent upon the subject's offers. The latter is illustrated by Komorita and Brenner's (1968) schedule which made concessions proportional to those made by the subject, either 1/10 as large, 1/2 as large, or equal to them.

Effects of Levels of Aspiration

Hatton's research highlights the importance of the prior attitudes and expectations which subjects bring to the bargaining situation. Other studies bear on the same general fact, that the course and outcome of bargaining are affected in major ways by what might be called noneconomic factors, that is, factors not reflected in the profit tables. The interested reader is referred to Kelley, et al. (1969), Krauss (1966), and Shure, et al. (1966).

The approach of the experimental social psychologist to factors of this type is to attempt to manipulate them in a controlled manner. This is in contrast to the procedure more typical of personality research where existing attitudes and orientation differences are first measured and then incorporated into the experimental design. A simple but powerful example of the manipulation of personal variables is provided by Siegel and Fouraker's variation of level of aspiration. The level of aspiration is one important way in which bargainers may differ as they enter a negotiation situation. That is, they may have quite varied ideas of how much they can expect to get out of the exchange and of how much they will be satisfied with.

In a bargaining task with MJP equal $9.60, conducted under conditions of incomplete-incomplete information, Siegel and Fouraker induced a low level of aspiration in a randomly designated member of each pair and a high level for the other member. This was done by reference to a second part of the study in which the subject would have an opportunity to double his profits. He could participate in the second part only if he made a profit of at least $2.10 (or $6.10 in the high condition) in the bargaining. Thus, it was very important for the subject to achieve the designated level. We might assume that given these rules, a person's satisfaction with his profit in the bargaining would increase sharply as the profit increased from $2.09 to $2.10 (or from $6.09 to $6.10, as the case may be). This is the conceptual definition of level of aspiration that Siegel had proposed earlier (1957), that is, as a point on the scale of objective values at which there is the largest increase in psychological utility (increase in feelings of satisfaction or change from dissatisfaction to satisfaction).

The results from 11 pairs showed clearly (and not surprisingly) that the levels of aspiration affected the profits each one made. The average player with a low level of aspiration gained $3.35 while the average player with a high level gained $6.25. In all but 1 of the 11 pairs, the low man settled for a smaller profit than did the high man. Siegel and Fouraker note that the bargaining tended to take a longer time in this experiment than in their other sessions, but all pairs reached agreement when told they would be given no extension of time.

It should be noted that the magnitude of MJP was such that both players could achieve their assigned levels of aspiration, though we may infer from the long bargaining times that they often experienced serious difficulty in reaching mutually satisfactory agreements. In a recent experiment, Kahan (1968) varied the magnitude of the levels of aspiration in relation to the total possible outcome. His investigation yielded the highly plausible generalization that as the pair of levels of aspiration become too high to be satisfied within the limit set by the MJP, the bargainers have a great deal of conflict and a low rate of agreement.

We can think of a person's level of aspiration, essentially as Siegel proposes, as a psychological transformation of the objective (or tabled) profit values—a transformation which increases the value of some profits and decreases, at least relatively speaking, the value of others. Siegel and Fouraker promoted this transformation by adding an extra rule or contingency to the bargaining relationship. However, persons also spontaneously transform the objective values in various systematic ways without the intervention of the experimenter. Thus, Thibaut and Kelley (1959) assume that a person's level of aspiration for his outcomes in a relationship (referred to as his *comparison level*) depends upon what values are made salient to him and are seen as possible of attainment. From this general formulation, we would expect a person's level of aspiration in a bargaining experiment to depend on such things as the profits he sees the other party obtaining (if these are made known) and the profits suggested by the table as being attainable.

The primary evidence as to the effects of the other party's outcomes comes from the strong tendency for subjects to insist on equal profits in situations where they know what each other is getting. If each one will only be satisfied with what the other one gets, the only resolution permitting mutual satisfaction is for both to receive the same profit. As noted earlier, Siegel and Fouraker found evidence of this in their Session 3 with *complete-complete* information. Six of eight pairs achieved an equal division of the MJP and the profit differences in the other two cases were very small. Morgan and Sawyer's (1967) finding of the high attractiveness of an equality solution among boys, both friends and nonfriends, has the same implication.

The effect on level of aspiration of the profits presented in the bargaining tables is suggested by the results mentioned above from Siegel and Fouraker's study of levels of aspiration. The reader will note that the low man typically surpassed his assigned level more than did the high man, the relative advantage being $1.25 versus $.15. (Siegel and Fouraker did not remark upon this difference, but it is significant, with a two-tailed t test, at $p < .10$.) The implication is that the high profit values the low man sees in his table, over three-fourths of which are above $2.10, cause him to set his sights above the assigned level and not to be entirely satisfied with achieving merely that level. Some such interpretation also seems necessary to account for the long bargaining times in these interactions. Otherwise, why should the set of assigned levels, both easily satisfied in view of the size of the MJP, present such barriers to agreement?

Kelley (1966) found that satisfaction with outcomes was affected by the level of profits attainable in prior bargaining sessions. This effect seems to require an interpretation in terms of level of aspiration. From one session to the next (separated in time by several weeks) the entire level of scores available, as in the tables in Table 10.7, was raised or lowered. Then, at the end of each session, subjects were asked whether they prefered to bargain from the tables they had used that day or from the ones used on the preceding session. A sizeable majority of those who expressed a preference did so for the tables yielding higher scores. Consistent with the Thibaut and Kelley formulation, this result suggests that what the bargainer regards as satisfactory, his level of aspiration, is affected by his experienced outcomes from previous similar encounters.

EVALUATION OF THE EXPERIMENTAL PARADIGM

The investigation and results we have summarized above give some idea of the fruitfulness of the Siegel and Fouraker paradigm as a means of investigating bargaining processes. It seems fairly clear that the procedure yields stable results and provides sensitive discriminations between different experimental conditions. With fairly small numbers of cases in each treatment, Siegel and Fouraker were able to distinguish the effects of different information conditions, different configurations of profits, and different levels of aspiration. (The reader will recognize that the number of cases for statistical purposes is the number of dyads. The individuals in each dyad are so highly interdependent in their behavior that they may not be treated separately in the analyses.) And Schenitzki's and Hatton's experiences with the procedure seem to have the same implication that the procedure provides a useful site for comparing different conditions and samples.

An outstanding feature of the paradigm is its high degree of adaptability to diverse problems. Already noted has been its use to compare different information conditions, different payoff structures (e.g., different degrees of gap between MJP and next largest joint profit), different pre-game orientations or sets, and different types of interpersonal relationships. In work subsequent to that reported here, Fouraker and Siegel (1963) varied the procedure in order to investigate other types of economic transactions. For example, they investigated the case of *price leadership* in which the seller specifies a price and the buyer then decides how much to buy. (The reader might find it interesting to predict what the outcome of this process would be if, for example, the decisions were made on the basis of the profit tables in Table 10.1 with complete-complete information. Hint: the agreements do not yield MJP.) With this procedure, they also varied whether the pair made only one transaction or made successive ones. The latter procedure provides a more realistic approximation to the usual real-life situation in which seller and buyer have a continuing, relatively stable relationship and repeatedly carry out business transactions.

We have also noted the ease with which the paradigm is modified to permit investigation of different basic questions. The work on bargaining between two subjects tends to focus on the consequences for the pair (e.g., success in attaining MJP, time to reach agreement, post-game attitudes) of different conditions. However, the procedure is easily modified to provide evidence on the type of questions likely to be raised by each bargainer as he pursues his own interest; namely, what are the consequences for him of following one strategy rather than another. The indicated modification, of course, is to control or program the behavior of one bargainer and study his effect upon his partner, the experimental subject. The reader will note that this modification returns to the more classical social psychological experimental paradigm, similar to that found in general experimental psychology, in which the subject responds to a controlled social stimulus. This is in sharp contrast to the original Siegel and Fouraker procedure in which the ambient conditions are controlled but the interaction is free and spontaneous. The latter then requires an analysis and interpretation of the interaction process if one is to understand the observed relation between various conditions on the one hand and various outcomes on the other.

Other possible modifications of the paradigm might be in the direction of making more salient other aspects of the bargaining process. This would include more complete communication and a more plausible possibility of nonagreement with specified consequences. Drawing their inspiration from other examples of bargaining (e.g., collective bargaining negotiations between labor and management representatives), other experimentalists have designed bargaining paradigms that emphasize these other features. These are also mixed motive, incomplete information models but they emphasize more explicitly (a) threat, for example, threat of withdrawal from the negotiation, and (b) misrepresentation of the information each person controls in order to gain advantage. The interested reader is referred to Fischer (1970), Kelley (1966), and Kelley, Beckman, and Fischer (1967). An excellent behavioral analysis of collective bargaining negotiations is provided by Walton and McKersie (1965).

The issue is too complex to discuss fully here but we must mention the problems of incentives and motivation which run through all this type of bargaining and gaming research. The central problem is that of knowing the psychological value of the various outcomes and possible changes in these values during the course of the interaction. The values of the profits specified by the experimenter's tables depend upon the individual bargainer's goal—whether it is to maximize his own profits (as the economic analysis assumes), merely to reach some minimum amount of profit, to maximize both persons' profits, to maximize the other person's profits, to beat the other person (maximize the difference), or to hurt the other person. If the experimenter does not know which of these goals (or which combination) his subjects are pursuing, he will have a difficult time interpreting their behavior.

We may note that there are several rather different approaches to this problem: (a) Exhortation of the subjects to adopt one or another orientation, for example, to maximize only their own scores. This relies on the willingness of subjects to cooperate with the experimenter and upon their ability to suspend for the duration of the experiment whatever other tendencies they may feel. Little is known about either their willingness or ability in these respects. (b) Use of high monetary incentives to attempt to insure that subjects are primarily and mainly motivated to maximize their own profits. (c) Induction of specific goals, as by setting specific levels of aspiration or group goals. These are usually induced by specific payoff rules such as Siegel and Fouraker's rule that attaining a specified level is necessary to have an opportunity to double one's profits, or Schenitzki's rule that total profit will be divided equally between the two bargainers. (d) Assessment of individual differences in goals before the interaction, with subsequent analysis of bargaining outcomes for pairs of individuals having different goal patterns. An example is provided by Kelley, et al. (1970). (e) Assessment of shifts in individual goals during the course of the interaction, as the bargainers experience threats, difficulty, boredom, time pressure, salience of their next appointments, etc. This requires using some sort of questionnaire probes introduced during the interaction and entails problems of how the measurement procedure itself may influence the interaction process. For an example of this approach, the reader is referred to Shure, et al. (1966). (f) Development of evidence and theories about how the individual's goals are affected by information and events in the bargaining process. Examples have been indicated above in the discussion of how information about the other party's outcomes and the range of tabled profit values affect the profit levels that bargainers regard as minimally acceptable.

These comments will perhaps convince the reader that the analysis of motivation is of central importance to the understanding and prediction of the bargaining process. These comments also illustrate what must surely be clear to the reader by now, that the bargaining process is exceedingly complex in terms of the psychological processes involved. Interacting in a tangled interplay are a number of different processes—learning, perception, communication, concept formation, attribution, motivation—each of which is complicated and incompletely understood in its own terms. The question of strategy of research inevitably arises: What are the relative gains to be derived from studying these processes as they interact in the bargaining situation as compared with the gains to be derived from simpler studies in which one specific psychological process is isolated for special investigation. The latter might be illustrated by studies of impression formation (Anderson, 1965) or intention inference (Jones & Davis, 1965), both of which are certainly component processes of bargaining. In the opinion of the present authors, decisions about the level of complexity of social phenomena at which to direct one's research efforts are made almost entirely on the basis of intuition and personal interest.

Undoubtedly, psychological processes, such as social perception, must eventually be understood as they operate within complex social contexts. However, it is not clear whether: (a) this understanding can be accomplished only after they are thoroughly understood in simpler contexts, (b) the problems for analysis in simplified circumstances should be specified only on the basis of understanding of the complex settings, or (c) there should be a continuous interplay between investigations of complex phenomena and more analytic studies. We leave these questions unanswered because we are not sure of the answers. This is one of the central day-to-day conflicts for the social psychologist —whether to drift toward the level of greater complexity and realism (toward social science problems), or toward the level of greater simplicity and analysis (toward psychological or even biological science problems), or to maintain an intermediate and perhaps unique position between his social science and psychological science colleagues.

Siegel and Fouraker's motivation in their research was clearly that of solving a social science problem, one posed by economic theories. The basic question was, given certain *initial* assumptions about the reward or payoff structure of their relationship, what agreements will bargainers reach? We have already noted that the Siegel and Fouraker experiments constituted only a limited test of the economic theory. Their work did not bear on the question of whether or not the assumed cost and revenue functions are appropriate for any given class of situations. Nor did they bear on the question of the "ecological representativeness" of any particular set of experimental conditions they investigated (for example, various conditions of information, communication, etc.). Their experiments provided merely a test of what the bargaining process would yield, *given* certain profit tables and certain procedural and informational constraints.

Their work does illustrate very clearly the role of experimental social psychology in relation to economic thought. The relations they observed between payoff structure and initial conditions on the one hand and bargaining outcomes on the other hand could be interpreted only in the light of mediating individual and social interaction processes. Thus, the experimental studies provided tests of certain *added* assumptions which explicitly or implicitly form the basis for the economists' predictions. For example, economists *explicitly* assume that persons act to maximize their profits. All of Siegel and Fouraker's results are consistent with that assumption although with some qualifying ideas, for example, that bargainers especially act to increase their profits up to the level they find others to be achieving, or up to levels they find it necessary to reach for other purposes. Schenitzki's analysis of the process necessary for MJP attainment suggests something about what economists *implicitly* assume, namely that in his pursuit of maximum profits, economic man acts systematically, persistently, and thoughtfully. The economists' predictions may be incorrect, even for the assumed structure of payoffs and procedural rules, if these further added assumptions are unwarranted. It is the role of the experimental social psychologist to test these aspects of the phenomenon. He does not, of course, test the validity of the initial assumptions about the structure of payoff tables.

From the point of view of psychological science, there is little of interest to be found either in the original Siegel and Fouraker work or in Schenitzki's analysis of the process. No new psychological phenomena are revealed nor are new insights gained regarding familiar phenomena (e.g., level of aspiration, motivation, social comparison processes). It is, rather, at the level of *interpersonal processes* that the work has its primary significance. The research reveals with greater clarity than existed before, the processes that mediate between individual behavior tendencies on the one hand and collective consequences on the other.

Several other lines of investigation have been conducted on the same general point, as summarized in Kelley and Thibaut's (1969) discussion of simple behavioral tendencies which mediate solutions to common interest problems. The same general conclusion is indicated by these diverse lines of work: As individuals pursue their own individual interests and do so within the confines of limited understanding and information, under certain conditions the joint consequences of their actions will be to their mutual benefit. The problem is that the necessary conditions, constituted by factors external to the individual such as variations in reward structure or process constraints, are not always present. (An example of the effects of process constraints is the bargaining procedure which permits MJP attainment vs. the price leadership procedure which mitigates against it.) As a consequence, for reasons quite external to themselves—quite aside from their propensities and their intentions, one set of interdependent persons may be able to achieve good collective outcomes but another similar set may not. There exists a gap, then, between individuals and their properties on the one hand and the social welfare on the other. This gap is bridged by social process and it is for the analysis of this process that research on bargaining is relevant and important.

REFERENCES

ANDERSON, N. H. Primacy effects in personality impression formation using a generalized order effect paradigm. *Journal of Personality and Social Psychology,* 1965, **2**, 1–9.

BOULDING, K. E. *A reconstruction of economics.* New York: Wiley, 1950.

CHERTKOFF, J. M., & CONLEY, M. Opening offer and frequency of concession as bargaining strategies. *Journal of Personality and Social Psychology,* 1967, **7**, 181–185.

EDGEWORTH, F. Y. *Mathematical psychics.* London: Paul, 1881.

FISCHER, C. S. The effect of threats in an incomplete information game. *Sociometry,* 1969, **32**, 301–314.

FISHER, R. Fractionating conflict. In R. Fisher (Ed.), *International conflict and behavioral science.* New York: Basic Books, 1964. Pp. 91–109.

FOURAKER, L. E., & SIEGEL, S. *Bargaining behavior.* New York: McGraw-Hill, 1963.

HATTON, J. M. Reactions of Negroes in a biracial bargaining situation. *Journal of Personality and Social Psychology,* 1967, **7**, 301–306.

HORNSTEIN, H. A. The effects of different magnitudes of threat upon interpersonal bargaining. *Journal of Experimental Social Psychology,* 1965, **1**, 282–293.

JONES, E. E. & DAVIS, K. E. From acts to dispositions: The attribution process in person perception. In L. Berkowitz (Ed.), *Advances in experimental social psychology.* Vol. 2. New York: Academic Press, 1965. Pp. 219–266.

KAHAN, J. P. Effects of level of aspiration in an experimental bargaining situation. *Journal of Personality and Social Psychology,* 1968, **8**, 154–159.

KELLEY, H. H. Interaction process and the attainment of maximum joint profit. In S. Messick & A. H. Brayfield (Eds.), *Decision and choice.* New York: McGraw-Hill, 1964. Pp. 240–250.

KELLEY, H. H. A classroom study of the dilemmas in interpersonal negotiations. In K. Archibald (Ed.), *Strategic interaction and conflict.* Berkeley, Calif.: Institute of International Studies, University of California, 1966. Pp. 49–73.

KELLEY, H. H., BECKMAN, L. L., & FISCHER, C. S. Negotiating the division of a reward under incomplete information. *Journal of Experimental Social Psychology,* 1967, **3**, 361–398.

KELLEY, H. H., SHURE, G. H., DEUTSCH, M., FAUCHEUX, C., LANZETTA, J. T., MOS-

COVICI, S., NUTTIN, J. M., JR., RABBIE, J. M., & THIBAUT, J. W. A comparative experimental study of negotiation behavior. *Journal of Personality and Social Psychology,* 1970, **16,** 411–438.

KELLEY, H. H., & THIBAUT, J. W. Group problem solving. In G. Lindzey & E. Aronson (Eds.), *Handbook of social psychology.* (2nd ed.) Vol. IV. Reading, Mass.: Addison-Wesley, 1969. Pp. 1–101.

KOMORITA, S. S., & BRENNER, A. R. Bargaining and concession making under bilateral monopoly. *Journal of Personality and Social Psychology,* 1968, **9,** 15–20.

KRAUSS, R. M. Structural and attitudinal factors in interpersonal bargaining. *Journal of Experimental Social Psychology,* 1966, **2,** 42–55.

LIEBERT, R. M., SMITH, W. P., KEIFFER, M., & HILL, J. H. The effects of information and magnitude of initial offer on interpersonal negotiation. *Journal of Experimental Social Psychology,* 1968, **4,** 431–441.

MARSHALL, A. *Principles of economics.* London: Macmillan, 1890.

MORGAN, W. R., & SAWYER, J. Bargaining, expectations, and the preference for equality over equity. *Journal of Personality and Social Psychology,* 1967, **6,** 139–149.

PARETO, V. *Manuel d'économique politique.* Paris: M. Giard, 1909.

PRUITT, D. G., & DREWS, J. L. The effect of time pressure, time elapsed, and the opponent's concession rate on behavior in negotiation. *Journal of Experimental Social Psychology,* 1969, **5,** 43–60.

SCHELLING, T. C. *The strategy of conflict.* Cambridge, Mass.: Harvard University Press, 1960.

SCHENITZKI, D. P. Bargaining, group decision making, and the attainment of maximum joint outcome. Doctoral dissertation, University of Minnesota, 1962.

SHURE, G. H., MEEKER, R. J., MOORE, W. H., JR., & KELLEY, H. H. *Computer studies of bargaining behavior: The role of threat in bargaining.* Santa Monica, Calif.: System Development Corporation, Document SP-2196, 1966.

SIEGEL, A. E. Sidney Siegel: A memoir. In S. Messick & A. H. Brayfield (Eds.), *Decision and choice.* New York: McGraw-Hill, 1964. Pp. 1–23.

SIEGEL, S. Level of aspiration and decision making. *Psychological Review,* 1957, **64,** 253–262.

SIEGEL, S., & FOURAKER, L. E. *Bargaining and group decision making.* New York: McGraw-Hill, 1960.

THIBAUT, J. W., & KELLEY, H. H. *The social psychology of groups.* New York: Wiley, 1959.

VON NEUMANN, J., & MORGENSTERN, O. *Theory of games and economic behavior.* (2nd ed.) Princeton, N.J.: Princeton University Press, 1947.

WALTON, R. D., & MCKERSIE, R. B. *A behavioral theory of labor negotiations.* New York: McGraw-Hill, 1965.

11

COALITION BEHAVIOR

Sheldon Stryker[1]

INTRODUCTION

Inherent in any social relationship of more than two persons, groups, organizations, or societies is the possibility—some would say the strong probability—of coalition behaviors. Given three persons, two can gang up on the third; given three nations, two can join together to combat the one remaining. It is the ubiquity of the possibilities for and the fact of coalitions in social life that make systematic inquiry into such behaviors worth pursuing.

The Coalition Situation Defined

"A coalition is the joint use of resources to determine the outcome of a decision in a mixed-motive situation involving more than two units [Gamson, 1964, p. 85]." This chapter is concerned with the experimental study of coalitions defined in this way.

A close look at the definition will clarify that concern. The key notion is that of a *mixed-motive situation*, best understood in contrast to two others: *pure coordination* and *pure conflict*. The terminology comes from an analysis of games of strategy (Schelling, 1958). In a pure coordination game, the participants share interests which can be maximally achieved by all at the same time; the "problem" of interaction reduces to the purely technical one of rationally organizing joint resources to maximize returns. In a pure conflict game, two persons are involved in a zero-sum situation: Any gain obtained by one of the participants means an equivalent loss for the other. Extended to more than two persons, pure conflict implies a situation in which no person can gain through coordinating his actions with another, either because there are constraints prohibiting such coordination or because he can achieve as much or more of some scarce value by acting on his own (Gamson, 1964, pp. 84–86). When two persons are involved, a mixed-motive game exists if a player must choose be-

[1] I am grateful to William A. Gamson for a critical reading of this chapter in an early stage of preparation. I am especially grateful to Charles McClintock for a detailed and perceptive editorial review of the chapter.

tween competing motivations to coordinate his actions with those of the second player or alternatively to act in opposition to that other player. The Prisoner's Dilemma Game, discussed in Chapter 9, is a much-studied variant. With more than two persons, a mixed-motive situation is one in which maximization of rewards dictates coordination with some and conflict with other participants in a system of interaction.

Behaviors which simultaneously involve coordination with some and conflict with others obviously imply a setting in which more than two social units (people, groups, organizations, societies) are interacting. The most frequently studied case is that of the triad, the three-member situation. The reason is clear: The triad is the simplest (by virtue of being the smallest) case in which coalitions as here defined become possible.[2] But there is no limit, apart from the lower limit of three, on the number of units in interaction consistent with the possibility of a coalition; indeed, we shall pay some attention to research involving more than three units.

The remaining elements in the definition of a coalition are *resources, joint use,* and *decision.* "A resource is some weight controlled by the participants such that some critical quantity of these weights is necessary and sufficient to determine the decision. Two or more participants will be said to be using their resources jointly if they coordinate their deployment of resources with respect to some decision [Gamson, 1964, pp. 82–83]." Potential resources are almost infinitely variable; any quality or object that can be brought decisively to bear on a decision qualifies as a resource. Money would qualify as such a weight in many social interactions; votes are another common resource. Finally, the term decision implies a conscious, deliberate act of terminating some problematic question or issue.

Many interaction patterns to which the language of coalitions has been applied—some of which have been studied experimentally—do not fit the definition provided above. Two nations reach a nuclear nonproliferation pact. A group of students collectively construct a story about a TAT picture on which all agree, with pairs of them being more mutually reinforcing or supportive of one another's contributions than they are of anyone else's. The members of a family argue about where to go on vacation, eventually going where the mother and children, rather than the father, prefer. The members of a club pool their money to buy a boat that none alone can afford. Fifty-one senators vote the same way on a bill, passing it, without benefit of caucus or strategy meeting. Sizable majorities of the poor and of elderly property owners vote against a school bond referendum, whereas young middle-class voters vote for it. None of these examples accords with our definition (although each is prototypical of behaviors which have been discussed using the word "coalition"), either because maximization of reward for a given social unit called for "pure coordination," or because joint utilization of resources did not occur, or because no deliberate, conscious act of deciding took place.

---

[2] There is another, more substantive, reason for focusing on the triad. If Caplow (1968) is correct, the triad is the building block from which all social organization is constructed.

Consider, on the other hand, the following illustrative instances. In a race for a political nomination the second and third men (in terms of the number of delegates' votes controlled) join forces in order to prevent the leading candidate from winning the nomination, agreeing that one of them will be the nominee for the position at issue and the other will receive a high appointive position if the candidate wins the general election. Three brothers wish to go out on a sailboat that can carry only two; two mutually choose one another and leave the third behind. Political parties of the left in France agree to support one another's candidates in parliamentary elections, rather than run opposing candidates, so that they can concentrate the opposition to candidates representing a right-wing party. Two airlines merge to enable them to compete more effectively with a third.

In all of the foregoing examples, some goal or gain is available the maximization of which requires the cooperation of some and the exclusion of other of the units participating in an interactive situation. And there are resources which may be utilized in effecting a decision with respect to that goal or gain. These, then, are coalition situations.

The Nature of Coalition Questions

What is it we wish to know about such situations? Put another way: What classes of behaviors are to be conceptualized as variables of the theories about coalitions we wish to develop and test? First, we wish to know which, if any, of the potential coalitions in a given situation is most likely to be formed. In the convention illustration previously used, are the two candidates with fewer committed delegates going into the convention the most likely to join together? Is there, then, general validity to the "strength is weakness" paradox, in the sense that to control the most resources, when one's resources are insufficient in themselves to determine an outcome, is to assure that one will be left out of a winning coalition? Will, as is implicit in our example, power be a crucial determinant of coalition formations? Are similarities of social characteristics or of interests other than those directly involved in the coalition situation also important determinants? Where power and similarity conflict, which will predominate? Assuming that there are tangible rewards associated with a coalition victory, other than the rewards issuing from domination itself, how will these be distributed? According to the resource contributions of the participants in the coalition? Or according to some other principle?

If other things are equal and it is true that two weak units are more likely to coalesce in opposition to one initially stronger, is there any strategy the stronger can adopt to prevent this from happening? Given three or more units involved in lengthy interaction over a series of issues, will the coalitions that form evidence a high degree of stability? Or will there be shifting liaisons? Finally, assuming—as we have every right to do—that the answers to such questions will not be simple, but rather will vary with types of social units, types of interactive settings, and so on, our last major question is: Can we specify the conditions—the *units, determinants, payoffs, strategies, stability*—under which general answers to coalition behavior questions will be more or less true?

These, clearly, are not trivial questions. If the experimental study of coalitions sheds light on such questions, we will have gained considerably in our attempt to build a social science that is "relevant," that is germane to much that is of importance in social life.

Early Theoretical Interest in Coalition Questions

Although the experimental study of coalition questions is relatively new, attention to such questions is not. The most proximate sources of interest include sociology, political science, and the variety of disciplines that have looked at the structure and processes of decision making.

The formal sociological concern with the relevance of number of social units to social structure in the writings of Georg Simmel (1950) called attention to the coalition potentialities of the triad. An insightful example is his account of the means by which the ancient Incas implemented necessary decentralization of political rule, while minimizing potential threat to the central rulers. They divided a newly conquered tribe into two approximately equal parts, placing over these parts supervisors with just noticeably different rank. This arrangement met the ends of the central rulers, suggests Simmel, for if the supervisors had been of greatly different ranks they would have recognized the right of one of them to lead in a coalition against the central rulers; and if they had been of precisely equal rank, they could have come to an easy agreement concerning leadership on the grounds of purely technical efficiency. Given a slight difference in rank, however, one supervisor would stake claims to leadership to which the second would not accede (1950, pp. 165–166).

Political scientists interested in the relationships among nation-states have investigated coalitions in terms of the concept of *balance of power*.[3] Beyond this, political scientists have explored coalition behavior in the context of national (Luce & Rogow, 1956) and state (Francis, 1962) legislative systems, and in the context of judiciaries (Schubert, 1964).

Still another area with a theoretical interest in coalition behavior is the multidisciplinary investigation of decision making. This work has been strongly influenced—directly or indirectly, in "ideology" if not in more technical fashion—by mathematical game theory. Game theory is preeminently a theory of decision making in situations where not all of the relevant variables are controlled by any one participant in the game.[4] Introduced by Von Neumann and

---

[3] As Zinnes (1970) notes in her exploration of the relevance of the experimental literature on coalitions to the central issue of balance of power theories—namely, the problem of stability of international systems premised on such balance—by and large, the coalition formation and the balance of power literatures sidestep one another. The major exception is Riker (1962), to which reference will be made at another point in this chapter.

[4] Many have bemoaned the fact that the essentially frivolous connotation of the word *game* belies the import of the work done under the rubric of game theory. It appears we are stuck with the language, and, that being the case, we must remind ourselves that the theory purports to have something to say about even such serious topics as warfare.

Morgenstern (1944) and developed from earlier work by Von Neumann, the theory is normative rather than descriptive (i.e., it seeks to say what *should* be done if one has certain goals rather than what *will* be done), although it may be interpreted as having certain descriptive implications.[5] The mathematics of the theory have been well developed for the two-person, zero-sum case, in that rules for arriving at unique solutions exist. Such solutions do not, in general, exist for the N-person, non-zero-sum case. Since coalition situations, by definition, have these characteristics, unique solutions are not generally available for coalition situations. Thus, what goes under the label of a game theory of coalition behavior is "in the spirit of," but is not technically derivable from, game theory. At any rate, game theory speaks, in interesting albeit incomplete ways, to questions of coalition formations and payoffs.

Contemporary Theories of Coalition Behaviors

The theoretical work from which most contemporary analyses of coalitions by social psychologists derives was initiated in response to purported limitations, for sociological purposes, of the game theory treatment of coalitions (Caplow, 1956). Arguing that the Von Neumann-Morgenstern discussion "concealed . . . the assumption of equality of power among the three players, even when they have different possibilities of gain or loss," Caplow further argued that this assumption did not "fit many triads of sociological interest in which the typical gain consists of domination over other triad members, and not in an external reward to be obtained by a given coalition [1956, p. 489]."

Distribution of Power Theory. As an alternative, Caplow proposed a theory developed from four assumptions:

> *Assumption 1.* Members of a triad may differ in strength. A stronger member can control a weaker member, and will seek to do so.
> *Assumption 2.* Each member of the triad seeks control over the others. Control over two others is preferred to control over one other. Control over one other is preferred to control over none.
> *Assumption 3.* Strength is additive. The strength of a coalition is equal to the sum of the strengths of its two members.
> *Assumption 4.* The formation of coalitions takes place in an existing triadic situation, so that there is a precoalition condition in every triad. Any attempt by a stronger member to coerce a weaker member into joining a nonadvantageous coalition will provoke the formation of an advantageous coalition to oppose the coercion [1956, pp. 489–490].

Applying these assumptions to six triad types differing in the way in which "strength" is distributed among members of the triad, Caplow predicted the typical coalition(s) that will form. The triad types and the predictions made for each are presented in Table 11.1. To illustrate how Caplow arrives at his predictions, consider Type 2, the one-strong/two-equally-weak case.

---

[5] There are a number of useful introductions to game theory, varying in the sophistication demanded of the reader. Two good introductions are to be found in Hurwicz (1945) and Shubik (1954).

Table 11.1

Triad Types and Predicted Coalitions in the Triad

Triad Type	Weights Assigned by Vinacke-Arkoff	Coalitions Predicted by Caplow	Coalitions Predicted by Game Theory
1. $A = B = C$	1-1-1	any	any
2. $A > B, B = C, A < (B + C)$	3-2-2	BC	any
3. $A < B, B = C$	1-2-2	AB or AC	any
4. $A > (B + C), B = C$	3-1-1	none	none
5. $A > B > C, A < (B + C)$	4-3-2	BC or AC	any
6. $A > B > C, A > (B + C)$	4-2-1	none	none

SOURCE. Stryker & Psathas, 1960, p. 218.

One member is stronger than the other two, but not much stronger. Again, all three members seek a coalition since to be isolated is unequivocally disadvantageous. However, the three possible coalitions are no longer of equal advantage.[6] Consider the position of B. If he forms a coalition with A, he will (by virtue of the coalition) be stronger than C, but within the coalition he will be weaker than A. If, on the other hand, he forms a coalition with C, he will be equal to C within the coalition and stronger than A by virtue of the coalition. The position of C is identical with that of B, so that other things being equal, the coalition BC will be formed and the individually strongest member of the triad will ordinarily turn out to be the weakest after the formation of the coalition [1956, p. 490].

Game Theory. The game theoretic alternative[7] asks which coalitions will form, on the assumptions that players in a game will act to maximize their returns from the game, and that the players understand the consequences of a given "move" for ultimately winning or losing. The predictions made for a game in which players relate in triads modeled after the Caplow types are also given in Table 11.1; for three of the six triad types, the predictions made by Caplow and from game theory differ. One arrives at the prediction that any coalition is equally likely to form in the one-strong/two-weak triad runs since any player must observe that only in a coalition can he be guaranteed of winning, and that any of the three possible coalitions can win if it is formed. Further, he must note that no one can demand more than half of what there is to win through coalition, for such a demand can only result in the remaining two players forming a coalition. If the logic of this argument is followed, no coalition is more likely than any other, and only equal divisions of the spoils are likely.

The differences in the predictions of game theory, which stresses winning regardless of one's relative power, and Caplow's theory, which emphasizes forming coalitions so as to maximize the amount of control one has over others, provide the basis for the first experimental study of coalition formation. Before

[6] Caplow is contrasting the Type 2 triad with the Type 1.

[7] As developed by Vinacke and Arkoff (1957).

reviewing it, we will briefly note a variety of theoretical perspectives that developed subsequent to this study. Stating them now may enable the reader to better visualize the context out of which each arises.

A Specification of Distribution of Power Theory. Vinacke and Arkoff (1957) interpreted Caplow's original theory as referring to perceptions of power structure. If coalition behavior based on game theoretic reasoning is taken to be rational, then, by implication, behavior developing from perceptions of power structure is irrational. Caplow (1959) found this paradoxical, since he viewed his theory as imputing rationality to participants in triadic relationships. He resolved the apparent paradox by modifying the original theory to specify one of three situations in which coalitions could occur—*continuous, episodic,* or *terminal*—and by suggesting that his original theory fit the first of these situations by virtue of the way in which his Assumption 2 was stated: "Each member of the triad seeks control over the others. Control over two others is preferred to control over one. Control over one is preferred to control over none." This assumption implies that the object of coalition is to control the joint activity of the triad and to secure rewards inherent in the situation itself.

In contrast, the episodic situation is one in which the object of coalition is to secure advantage in each of a series of distributions of rewards occurring periodically and under predetermined conditions. It assumes that "each member of the triad seeks a position of advantage with respect to each distribution of reward. A larger share of reward is preferred to a smaller share; any share is preferred to no share [Caplow, 1959, p. 489]." In such situations, the need to enter coalitions in all but Type 4 and Type 6 triads will be clear to each member, equal distributions of rewards will be suggested, and coalitions will tend to be limited to particular episodes. Consequently, Caplow argues, in the episodic case the predictions flowing from his power distribution theory and those from game theory are precisely alike.[8]

Minimum Resource Theory. Formulated by Gamson, this theory takes as its most general hypothesis that "any participant will expect others to demand from a coalition a share of the payoff proportional to the amount of resources which they contribute to a coalition [1961b, p. 376]." Thus, every participant brings to coalition situations a "parity norm" which specifies what all participants "deserve" to receive of the rewards available.[9] Participants can be expected to seek to maximize their rewards; this, together with the parity norm, leads to the hypothesis that the "cheapest winning coalition" will form, that is, that a coalition will form in which the total resources of coalition members are as small as possible and still sufficient to win. This is so because, given that a participant will expect his parity price and will get it, he will maximize returns

---

[8] The terminal situation, less important for present purposes, is one in which the coalition is directed toward a single, final redistribution of power. It, too, requires a modification of Assumption 2: "Each member of the triad seeks to destroy the others and to add their strength to his own [Caplow, 1959, pp. 490–491]." Under this assumption, Caplow predicts that any coalition will form in Type 1 triads, BC coalitions will form in Types 2 and 3, and no coalitions will form in Types 4, 5, and 6.

[9] At this point, there is contact between coalition theory and such theoretical ideas as are summarized in the phrase *distributive justice* (Homans, 1961).

when he maximizes his resources in relation to the total resources of the coalition. Referring back to the triad types given in Table 11.1, minimum resource theory predicts for the Type 5 triad that BC coalitions will form; it permits differentiating between AC and BC coalitions in a way not permitted by the original Caplow theory. For all other triad types, the Gamson and the Caplow predictions are the same.

A closely parallel statement, leading to identical predictions, is developed by Riker (1962). Riker asserts the *size principle*: Coalitions will be created just large enough to assure winning, and no larger. The size principle takes two somewhat different forms. The first form is that already given. The second amends the first to say that coalitions will be created just as large as participants *believe* will insure winning, and no larger. The second leaves room for participants to "play safe" by forming coalitions somewhat larger than would actually be necessary to win.

Probability of Reciprocated Choice Theory. It is the Type 5 triad for which Caplow and Gamson make different predictions. Caplow, it will be recalled, predicts either the AC or BC coalition for this case; Gamson predicts the BC coalition. Chertkoff (1967) suggests that a modification of Caplow leads to predictions for this triad type more consonant with experimental evidence than are either the Caplow or the Gamson predictions. Instead of assuming that coalitions are equally likely when choices are reciprocated, says Chertkoff, suppose we examine the proportion of times given coalition choices are made by each member of the Type 5 triad. By Caplow's earlier reasoning, A is indifferent as between B and C; half of his choices will be B, half will be C. B will always choose C. C will prefer A and B equally; his choice will be A half the time, C half the time. Multiplying the proportions of individual choices gives the probability of reciprocal choices between pairs. Thus, BC coalitions should occur 50 percent (1.00 × .50) of the time; AC coalitions should occur 25 percent (.50 × .50) of the time; AB coalitions should not occur (.50 × .00); and no coalitions should occur the remaining 25 percent of the time. If the no-coalition cases are allowed to choose anew, the proportion of reciprocated choices should be repeated, and eventually the ratio of BC to AC coalitions should go to 2:1.

Expected Reward Theory. While explicitly not a finished product, another theory has been developed by Chertkoff (1970) to account for available evidence. This theory assumes that people subscribe both to the parity norm and to the logic of game theory. Thus they believe that division of rewards should in part reflect contributed resources. Since all potential coalition partners are to some extent equal in that one cannot win without the other, expected rewards should be modified toward equality from the levels called for by strict application of the parity norm. Chertkoff proposes that available data are best described by a formula in which expected rewards are midway between those given by the parity norm and those given by equal divisions.[10]

He also proposes that the extent to which the parity norm division will be

---

[10] The coefficient of ½ is simply regarded as a reasonable first approximation.

modified toward equality will vary for individuals as a function of individual differences and situational variables, and is to be established by research. Chertkoff would predict coalition preferences[11] from differences in expected rewards, although he argues that such preferences will not vary in direct proportion to the ratio of expected rewards, but rather will reflect much more complicated determinants.

Competing Definitions of the Situation Theory.   Psathas and Stryker (1965) contend that coalition theories in general have dealt only perfunctorily with the processes by which coalitions are formed, and that there is reason to believe that detailed attention to such processes is necessary for an adequate theory of coalition outcomes. They suggest that the process of coalition formation be conceptualized in terms of rival definitions vying for dominance. In the typical triadic situation, forming a coalition involves a series of choices (to approach or to wait to be approached by another, what other to approach, what offer to make to another, how to respond to offers made by another). Each choice, they argue, will be premised on some definition of the situation in which interaction occurs, and each choice will contribute to some redefinition of the situation. Initial definitions will be structured by the conditions of interaction, including such matters as differences in power (both real and perceived) among triad members. Redefinitions will reflect inferences drawn from the bargaining process—who offers what to whom. Coalitions take shape when definitions match, in particular when a given participant in interaction can bring at least one other participant to share his definition of the situation. We will look more closely at this theoretical approach to coalition behavior at a later point in the chapter.

THE EXPERIMENTAL STUDY OF COALITION BEHAVIOR

The Vinacke Paradigm

If we exclude from consideration studies of triads which use the language of coalitions but which do not meet the definitional criteria explicated above (Mills, 1954; Strodtbeck, 1954; Borgatta & Borgatta, 1963), the first experimental study of coalitions is that reported by Vinacke and Arkoff (1957). It is appropriate for many reasons to focus on the experimental paradigm used in this work. The study explicitly contrasted Caplow's distribution of power theory with a game theoretic account of coalition formation, and in so doing set the tone for subsequent theoretical developments. Vinacke and his students have been the most consistent contributors to the experimental literature on coalitions, and, as we shall see, numerous other investigators have taken their leads from Vinacke's work.

The Phenomenology of the Paradigm.   Assume that you are a male member of an introductory psychology course and that you have volunteered to partici-

---

[11] As opposed to actual coalition outcomes.

pate in an experiment to be conducted by a member of the faculty of the department of psychology. Appearing at an assigned hour, you are ushered into a room[12] along with two others who share your characteristics. Along with your fellow subjects, you take a seat at a table with nothing out of the ordinary about it (i.e., no partitions erected to prevent face-to-face contact, no microphones on the table, etc.). On the table is a parcheesi board, with the spaces around the edge of it numbered from 1 to 67 from a point which is labeled START. On the table as well is a hopper, which contains green, blue, and red buttons with numbers from 1 to 4 printed on them.

You are given a sheet of paper with the following instructions on it, and are requested to read these and to keep them available for reference:

> This game is a contest between three players. Before each game each player will draw a counter out of a hopper. The number on this counter will determine the player's strength for that game. You will move by multiplying your weight times the value of a die, thrown by the experimenter. For example, if you draw a weight of "2" and the die comes up "3," you will move six spaces. A prize of 100 points will be given to the winner or winners, except that it will be divided in the case of ties. At any time during the game any player may form an alliance with any other player. In this event, players entering into an alliance must decide upon how they will divide the prize if they win. After forming an alliance, players join forces and proceed to the position represented by their combined acquired spaces; thereafter, they use their combined weights in moving. Any player may concede defeat if he or she considers his or her position to be hopeless.[13]

You then watch a demonstration of how to play the game, accompanied by an explanation which is an iteration of the instructions you have read. Three counters are placed into the hopper. You and your fellow subjects each draw one counter; yours has the number "2" on it, one of your fellow subject's has the number "2" on his as well, and the other's has the number "3." You place your counters on the board at the point marked START. The experimenter then throws a single die; it comes up "5." Your counter is then moved to the space numbered "10," so is the counter of your fellow subject who also drew a counter marked "2," and the counter of the third subject is moved to space "15."

The experimenter notes that one of you may wish to form an alliance with another, and that you should indicate that desire by offering one of the others some proportion of the 100-point prize. The other can accept or reject the offer, counter your offer with another directed at you, or make an offer to the third subject. You are told that anyone can make a coalition offer to anyone, but that once a player says (in effect) "I accept that offer," an alliance is formed for that game.

---

[12] The physical features of this room need not be specified. Some studies using the paradigm have recorded interaction or have used observers to keep track of bargaining proposals, and for these the facilities of the typical small groups laboratory are useful. But, fundamentally, a study using the paradigm can proceed in virtually any room without impairment.

[13] I am grateful to W. E. Vinacke for supplying these instructions.

Suppose, notes the experimenter, you reach an agreement after the first throw of the die with the subject who has drawn the "3." A counter representing the coalition is placed on space "25." The die is thrown again, coming up "2." Your coalition counter is moved ten spaces to space "35." The counter of the player left out of the coalition is moved from space "10" to space "14."

You are asked if you have any questions. If you ask a question about the rules of the game, you are answered by a reference back to the instructions. If you ask if you are supposed to make alliances, the experimenter answers, "That's up to you."[14]

When questions have been dealt with, the experiment proper begins. Counters are placed in the hopper, are drawn, and so on. You play 18 games. Most of the time, coalitions are formed before the die is actually thrown and the omitted player concedes victory to the coalition.[15] In a few instances, the game is played all the way to conclusion. Sometimes no coalitions are formed before the game is won. As play goes on, the experimenter keeps records, but you keep no records of coalitions joined or points won, nor do your coplayers. In all probability, they, like you, find it impossible to keep track of how anyone stands in relation to the others over the games played.

The Variables and Their Operationalization.   Vinacke and Arkoff structured their study as a test of the comparative accuracy of the predictions about coalition formations given in Table 11.1. The Caplow predictions, it will be recalled, flow from a consideration of the distribution of power among members of a triad; the game theory predictions follow from a consideration of what a "rational" man would do if he understood completely the consequences of his actions and if he sought to maximize gains available through interaction.

Obviously, the comparative test of these theories requires a situation in which the independent variable of power or strength can be manipulated to form triads with the six precoalition structures specified in the Caplow hypotheses. Vinacke and Arkoff, as noted, developed a simple game modeled after parcheesi. To win, it is necessary to move a counter over a series of spaces from START to HOME, either alone or in coalition, before other players in the game do so.

To give operational meaning to the power variable, they assigned to triads numbers which conformed to the power structures required by the triad types. These assigned numbers are shown in Table 11.1. (It should be clear that an infinite set of numbers would meet the ordered relationships.) For example, Caplow's Type 2 triad, the one-strong/two-equally-weak case, was assigned the numbers 3-2-2; the Type 5 triad was assigned the numbers 4-3-2. The rules of the game provide that each player move his counter at a rate equal to the product of the number he drew prior to each game and the number appearing on a die cast by the experimenter. All players move their counters at each throw of the die. Thus, the outcome of any given game, if no coalition forms, is completely

---

[14] From personal correspondence with W. E. Vinacke.

[15] This was true in 70 percent of the games (Vinacke & Arkoff, 1957, p. 409). Players did not have to reveal the number drawn; most do so voluntarily (Vinacke, 1959). Of course, once the die is thrown, weights are revealed.

determinate: That person, or those persons, drawing the highest weight in a given game win. Strength or power, then, is represented by these weights, which translate to advantage in the game prior to coalition formations.

It is the fact that individual weights can be added together and coordinated to the spaces on the game board that makes the experimental game fit the assumptions underlying Caplow's predictions. And it is the fact that in three of the triad types—2, 3, and 5—any coalition can win the game, irrespective of the preplay weights that are drawn, that permits the comparative test of game theory and Caplow's theory.

Coalition outcome is the variable predicted by Caplow's theory, and it is the major dependent variable in the Vinacke and Arkoff study. The opportunity to form coalitions is, of course, the prime requisite of the experimental paradigm, and it is clear that the game rules provide this opportunity. A count of the frequency with which coalitions are formed and of the frequency with which players with given weights form coalitions can easily be made. Such counting is facilitated by the rule that makes a coalition, once agreed upon, binding for the duration of a game.

The paradigm makes possible the systematic collection of other types of data. Game theory permitted the hypothesis of equal division between coalition partners of the spoils available in a situation in which any coalition could win. However, it seemed to Vinacke and Arkoff a reasonable inference from power structure theorizing that payoffs would reflect differences in strength. As has been noted, the rules of the experimental game require that a division of the 100-point prize available in the game be agreed upon before a coalition is considered formed. Such agreements on prize division, then, constitute a second dependent variable. In this initial work, no formal or public cumulative score was kept (this becomes a variable in later research). And, as noted previously, the conditions of play probably made it impossible for any player to accurately assess his cumulative winnings, particularly in relation to other players.

Also potentially available for analysis are data on the initiation of coalitions. Vinacke and Arkoff are ambiguous about just what behavior is being reported as "initiation." While it is conceivably possible, using this paradigm, to record the entire bargaining pattern, to establish frequencies of who offers to ally with whom and what splits of the prize are suggested, it is practically impossible to do so accurately given the rush of face-to-face conversations, interruptions, and so on during the game. Thus, Vinacke and Arkoff simply report data on the member of the triad initiating the offer to form a coalition. This seems to refer to the first offer eventually culminating in a coalition, but it may refer to the first offer to ally made in the game,[16] whether or not a coalition between the player who offers and his target actually forms.[17] Vinacke and Arkoff also counted the number of offers to coalesce made in each game. Although no use

[16] This appears to be the data provided in a report (Vinacke, 1959) which incorporates the data of the first study. Yet the two sets of data do not coordinate precisely in any obvious way.

[17] See the note to Table 11.3.

is made of these data in their initial report, in a later one that incorporates findings from the first research (Vinacke, 1959), this count is used as an index of competitiveness.

Finally, given the design used in this study, informal data reflecting such variables as motives and motivation, reasoning and rationalizations, appeals and "gut" reactions to the experimental experience can be gathered from the uncontrolled conversation that accompanies experimental play. Systematic use of such data, however, is for all practical purposes precluded by the impediments noted above in connection with recording the bargaining process.

Methodology. Much of the foregoing discussion of the Vinacke and Arkoff experimental paradigm has been methodological, in one broad sense of that term. Here we will concern ourselves with those features of their design not yet reviewed.

Subjects were 90 male students from an introductory course in psychology who volunteered to participate in the experiment. Each student was assigned to a triad; thus 30 groups of 3 were constituted. Each triad played 18 games, divided into 3 series of games; each series included 1 game representing each of the 6 forms of power distribution specified by Caplow in his initial theoretical paper. Thus each triad played 3 games under each of the types of triads given in Table 11.1. Since, again, there were 30 triads, there were 90 instances of games played under each power structure condition.

To control for the potential effect of the sequential position of the triad types within the series of games, the order of the games was systematically arranged according to a Latin square design[18] which varied the sequence of the types in the three series.

Although the games played under each power structure condition were replicated in each series, it was not necessarily the case that a player was assigned the same initial strength in each replicated game. The attachment of a weight to a player in a given game was left to chance: Each player drew his weight for a particular game from a hopper in which had been placed three counters marked with appropriate weights. The order of draw was controlled by rotation, with each player drawing first, second, and last the same number of times. Players were given letter positional designations, A, B, or C, depending on the weight drawn in a given game. By chance, then, players might (or might not) play each position once in the three games under each power structure condition. In those instances where a triad type called for more than one player with the same weight, the counters placed in the hopper were of different colors and attached to letter designations. For example, when the condition called for three players with the weight "1," a green counter was A, blue was B, and red was C.

Other than the controls achieved by rotating the order of the games and the order of drawing for weights, there were apparently no systematically instituted controls utilized in the study. To some degree, the randomization achieved

[18] A Latin square is an arrangement such that each treatment, in this case experimental condition and sequence of games, appears once and only once in each column and each row of a square matrix. Such a design facilitates certain kinds of analyses of resulting data.

through chance selection of weights controls for individual differences among players, although it is entirely conceivable that the same player in a triad might select the same weight in each of the three plays of the games of a particular type. To some degree, as well, the restriction of the subject population to males in an introductory psychology course in a single university controls variation in a number of potentially relevant social structural and personality variables (e.g., it can be expected that such a population is relatively homogeneous by social class).

What about the motivation of the participating subjects? There is, of course, the prize of 100 points available in the game; but it cannot be expected that this in itself would strongly motivate participants. It seems clear that Vinacke and Arkoff rely on the familiarity of their subjects with games in general, and on the assumptions that their subjects understand that in such games one is "supposed" to play to win and that they are willing to treat the experiment as falling into the class of such games. In the report itself, we are told that "there was every indication that the game succeeded in arousing keen interest and strong competition [1957, p. 408]." Other than this assertion, no support for the motivational assumptions is provided. There are, however, two external supports for the general adequacy of these assumptions. On the premise that the male role in our society calls for more competitiveness than does the female role, the apparent fact that males play this game more competitively than do females (See, e.g., Vinacke, 1959; Vinacke el al., 1967) suggests that there is some basis for the motivational assumptions made. Beyond this, we might be permitted by the literature on the subject role—by the evidence that students do adopt the definitions of the situation explicitly or implicitly held by the experimenters—to draw the inference that the subjects in this study were adequately motivated.

Findings. The Vinacke and Arkoff research developed as a comparative test of implications drawn from Caplow's theory and from game theory, and the major predictions derived from these theories concerned the coalitions that would form given particular distributions of precoalition power. Both theories predict that any coalition is equally likely in triad Type 1; both predict that no coalitions will form in triad Types 4 and 6. Game theory predicts that any coalition is equally likely in the remaining triad Types 2, 3, and 5; whereas Caplow predicts the BC coalition in Type 2, either AB or AC in Type 3, and either AC or BC in Type 5.

Table 11.2 makes it apparent that where one player can win outside of any coalition, in Types 4 and 6, coalitions are formed comparatively rarely,[19] although they do in fact occur. Vinacke and Arkoff (pp. 411–412) read this evidence as being more consistent with Caplow than with game theory, suggesting that the former ". . . allows for some coalitions in these types." This imputed allowance is premised on Caplow's (1956, p. 490) remark to the effect

---

[19] The difference in proportions of noncoalitions in Type 4 as compared with Types 1, 2, 3, and 5 is significant at the .01 level. This is also true of Type 6 (Vinacke & Arkoff, 1957, p. 409).

that in these triad types "extraneous" means of inducing coalitions might operate.

In Type 1, all coalitions occur with considerable frequency, a fact consistent with both theories. The distribution of coalitions, however, very nearly departs from the chance model as a consequence of an underrepresentation of AC coalitions. No reason for this seems to exist, and the authors conclude that it may well be due to chance.

Table 11.2

Coalitions Formed in the Six Types of Power Patterns in Triads

Allies	Type 1 (1-1-1)[a]	Type 2 (3-2-2)	Type 3 (1-2-2)	Type 4 (3-1-1)	Type 5 (4-3-2)	Type 6 (4-2-1)
AB	33	13	24	11	9	9
AC	17	12	40	10	20	13
BC	30	64	15	7	59	8
Total	80	89	79	28	88	30
(No Coalition)	10[b]	1	11	62	2	60
χ^2	5.43	59.61	12.19	.93	47.07	1.40
d.f.	2	2	2	2	2	2
p	>.05	<.01	<.01	<.70	<.01	<.50

SOURCE. Vinacke & Arkoff, 1957, p. 409.

NOTE. N = 90 games for each type.

[a] The figures in parentheses show the power of the three members, e.g., in Type 1, A = 1, B = 1, and C = 1. In computing χ^2, it was assumed that each pair would occur an equal number of times by chance.

[b] There were two three-way coalitions in this type; in a sense these might be considered to be mutual nonaggression pacts.

In each of the remaining three triad types, the distributions are significantly different from the chance distribution of equal proportions of all coalitions. In Type 2, the coalition of the two weaker players is by far the most frequent, as Caplow predicts. In Type 3, both AB and AC occur much more frequently than does BC, again as Caplow predicts; the rather large difference in frequency of the two predicted coalitions is, however, unexplained. And in Type 5, where Caplow predicts either the AC or BC coalition, it is true that these predominate. Again, however, there is a large difference in the number of AC and BC coalitions; the latter appear roughly three times as often as the former. This result is inexplicable in terms of the initial formulation of Caplow's theory—indeed, he explicitly states that, "whether the differential strength of A and B will make them more attractive to C lies outside the scope of our present assumptions [p. 490]."

Vinacke and Arkoff conclude that the results of their work support Caplow and therefore require the rejection of an interpretation in terms of game theory (p. 410). Bolstering this conclusion are the data in Tables 11.3 and 11.4 reporting initiation of offers to form coalitions and divisions of the prize. In Types 1 and 3, positions initiate relatively equally. In the remaining types, the distributions depart substantially from equality by position, with the weaker positions in each case most likely to initiate offers.

The divisions of the prize appear to reflect the influence of power structure. Vinacke and Arkoff (p. 410) read these data to say that where differences in strength are perceptually pronounced, extreme divisions of the prize occur (Types 4 and 6); where the players are equal or relatively equal in strength, equal divisions of the prize predominate (Types 1 and 2); and where one participant is weaker than the other two, moderately unequal splits are characteristic (Types 3, 5, and 6). Although the data are not presented in detail, Vinacke and Arkoff indicate that, when unequal divisions occur, the stronger player reaps the major share. They also note that it is players equal in strength who are most likely to arrive at 50-50 divisions and to do so without bargaining.

Finally, in data not given here, Vinacke and Arkoff analyze the coalitions

Table 11.3

Member of the Triad Initiating the Offer to Form a Coalition

Initiator	Type 1 (1-1-1)	Type 2 (3-2-2)	Type 3 (1-2-2)	Type 4 (3-1-1)	Type 5 (4-3-2)	Type 6 (4-2-1)
A	21	17	28	2	18	4
B	26	40	18	32	26	19
C	26	31	27	20	43	26
Total[a]	73	88	73	54	87	49
x^2	.69	9.17	2.49	25.33	11.24	15.50
d.f.	2	2	2	2	2	2
p	>.70	<.01	<.30	<.01	<.01	<.01

SOURCE. Vinacke & Arkoff, 1957, p. 410.
NOTE. N = 90 games for each type.
[a] In certain instances it was impossible to decide who initiated the offer, hence Ns differ slightly from those in Table 11.1. There are also offers made when no coalition was formed, especially in Types 4 and 6.

Table 11.4

Kinds of Agreement Reached in Six Types of Power Patterns in Triads

Division of Prize	Type 1 (1-1-1) N	%	Type 2 (3-2-2) N	%	Type 3 (1-2-2) N	%	Type 4 (3-1-1) N	%	Type 5 (4-3-2) N	%	Type 6 (4-2-1) N	%
50-50	48	60	62	70	31	39	11	39	41	47	7	23
30-70 to 49-51	25	31	21	24	30	38	3	11	39	44	9	30
1-99 to 29-71	7	9	6	7	18	23	14	50	8	9	14	47
Total	80[a]	100	89	101	79	100	28	100	88	100	30	100
x^2	31.64		56.59		3.98		6.96		23.36		2.60	
d.f.	2		2		2		2		2		2	
p	<.01		<.01		<.20		<.05		<.01		<.30	

SOURCE. Vinacke & Arkoff, 1957, p. 411.
NOTE. N = 90 games for each type.
[a] Two triple coalitions omitted.

formed in the six triad types for each series of games taken separately. They suggest that the third series might be a better test of the game theory predictions because some learning will have taken place by virtue of playing the first two series; the players will have come to a better understanding of the game and will therefore be able to play more rationally. Their data indicate that, while players do apparently learn that coalitions are unnecessary in triad Types 4 and 6 and necessary in the remaining types, no great differences in the proportions of various coalitions exist among the three series.

Critique. Many of the critical remarks that might be directed at the experimental paradigm just reviewed are equally pertinent to a variety of greater or lesser modifications of it which we shall look at in the next section of this chapter. In order to minimize redundancy, these will be reserved for that next section. One point ought be stated, however, before any critical remarks are made: To have made this paradigm the focus of this chapter implies a belief in its fundamental worth. Still, the paradigm is open to a number of criticisms on various levels. We will start with the more detailed and concrete and proceed to the more general and abstract.

Consider, first of all, the cases of no coalition shown in Table 11.2 for the Type 3 triad. For this triad, Caplow predicts that the weak man, A, will form a coalition with either of the two strong men. Vinacke and Arkoff see the data as supporting this prediction and conclude that it is indeed true that the initially weakest player will be strongest in the sense of being most assured of being part of a winning coalition. Now, recall the rules of the game. Games are permitted to end without coalitions being formed. When they do, the winner will be that player who drew the highest weight. In Type 3, there are two equally strong men, B and C. Thus, without a coalition B and C will both be winners in these games. In point of fact, the outcome will be precisely the same as if a BC coalition had formed. If, then, the 11 games shown in Table 11.2 as ending with no coalitions formed are treated as implicit BC coalitions, these can be added to the 15 explicit BC coalitions. The distribution of coalitions would then be 24 AB coalitions, 40 AC coalitions, and 26 BC coalitions for Type 3 triads. Since now the data would show that the weak man was included in 64 coalitions, when by chance he is expected to appear in 60 of the 90 coalitions, we would not be likely to conclude that in this situation the weak man was strong by virtue of being assured a place in a winning coalition.

One must also question the propriety of the statistical treatment of the data. The only statistical tool used is chi-square. Chi-square assumes the independence of the events represented by the frequencies whose distribution is compared with some chance model. Only when this assumption is met is the application of this statistical test legitimate. Given that each triad played three games of each type, that is, that 30 triads each contribute roughly three times[20] to the instances of coalitions, initiations, or prize divisions recorded under each type, it

---

[20] Roughly, in that not all games eventuate in coalitions, so that there are not precisely 90 coalitions, initiations, or prize divisions.

is clear that the assumption of independence is violated when the data from the three series of games are lumped together. Analysis of the data from the first series of games alone would not be subject to this criticism.

Another specific statistical criticism seems warranted. There are, of course, a variety of chance models against which a particular observed distribution can be evaluated. The analyst must select that model making most sense given the problem and the data at hand. Vinacke and Arkoff choose the same chance model for each of their major analyses, as shown in Tables 11.2, 11.3 and 11.4, that being the "chi-square" model of equal frequencies. This seems to make eminently good sense in the case of coalitions and initiators, given both the nature of the categories of coalitions and initiators used and the question asked of the data. But does it make equally good sense for prize divisions? Note the categories of divisions. The first is a single point (50-50) on the range from 100-0 to 0-100. Does it make sense to assert that chance—random splits of the prize— would produce fully one-third of the prize divisions at this single point, with another one-third falling between splits of 30-70 and 49-51, and the final one-third in the 1-99 to 29-71 segment of the total range? Might it not make better sense to visualize the chance' distribution of prize divisions as a normal curve with a mean at the 50-50 point? One could then compute the number of cases to be expected at the point 50-50 ± one, two, or three standard deviations and compare the observed distribution of prize divisions against the expected.

A large share of the costs of running experimental groups is in bringing subjects together at the same time in the same place. Once such groups are available, it seems wasteful to use them for an experiment which, apart from instructions, consumes only a few minutes; indeed, the temptation is to gather as much information from them as possible. There are analytic techniques available to deal with correlated or repeated measurements. However, usually one must plan in advance his data-gathering procedures so that the requirements of these techniques are met. In general, procedures must not be "mixed"; and, unfortuantely, the Vinacke and Arkoff procedures are mixed. Given the way in which weights were attached to players, any subject might or might not draw the same position in two or even all of the games played in a particular triad type. Thus, the data are neither completely independent observations nor repeated measurements, and the application of efficient analytic techniques becomes impossible.

Furthermore, while it is sometimes inconvenient and difficult to do so, subjects can be recruited in blocks and assigned randomly to triads. This should be done for two reasons: Strictly speaking, many of the tests of statistical significance require it; without random assignment, an undiscoverable systematic bias may characterize the resultant data.

It is necessary to ask whether the motivational assumptions made by the investigators are warranted. As stated earlier, it seems rather clear that the award of points would not suffice to motivate players strongly to win, and the theories being examined assume such competitive motivation. Is it reasonable, then, to rely on subjects' experience with the norm of competitiveness in games in general and on their propensity to adopt the role of subject? To some degree, as we have suggested, it probably is. But in sufficient degree to be worrisome, it probably is not. In the first place, the absence of any real indeterminacy—except at the point of drawing weights—is likely to decrease competitiveness; here the analogy to the normal games people play breaks down. But, much more importantly, many investigators who have used the Vinacke paradigm or a modification of it (See, e.g., Stryker & Psathas, 1960; Trost, 1965; Vinacke, 1959) report behaviors which deny the existence of fully competitive orientations: A player in an unassailably strong position will nevertheless offer to form a coalition with a weak player; a player who understands the game will instruct others, even advising coalitions against himself; players will toss a die to determine who will coalesce with whom. These behaviors are comparatively infrequent, but they occur with enough regularity to cast a shadow over easy acceptance of the motivational assumptions built into the paradigm as initially developed.

Players in the experimental game deal with one another on a face-to-face basis. Given the considerable confusion of continuous conversation and the added confusion from playing a series of games in which the weights in the game change, one's own weight and one's weight relative to other players, and it becomes difficult to believe that players "know the score." It is the literal rather than the figurative sense of this phrase with which we are concerned here.[21] Recall that no public record of wins and prize shares is kept. Undoubtedly, subjects make some attempt to keep score, but also undoubtedly, cannot do so with any accuracy. The relevance of these observations is indicated by the finding (Bond & Vinacke, 1961; Hoffman, Festinger, & Lawrence, 1954; Emerson, 1964) that when cumulative scores are publicly kept, those who trail in the scores tend to coalesce regardless of the form of the power structure. Thus, data that are read as evidence of the influence of power structures on coalition behavior may be in part a function of varying degrees of confusion among players.

The most general criticism that can be leveled at the Vinacke paradigm is that it is not appropriate as a means of dealing with the major question posed by Vinacke and Arkoff, namely, the comparative validity of the game theory versus the Caplow theory of coalition formation. Caplow's theory developed out of a consideration of ". . . many triads of sociological interest in which the typical gain consists of domination over other triad members, *and not in an external reward to be obtained by a given coalition* [1956, p. 489, italics added]." It is moot that the experimental paradigm represents this case.

Beyond this cavil—a response might well be that whatever Caplow's intention, his reasoning fits the category of coalition situations which the paradigm does adequately represent—it may have occurred to the reader that the predictions about coalition outcomes stemming from game theory and those deriving

---

[21] We will concern ourselves in the next section with an implication of the complexity of the experimental design and consequent failure to "know the score" in its figurative sense.

from a model predicated on random behavior are precisely the same. In triad Types 1, 2, 3, and 5, game theory predicts that all coalitions are equally likely; a random model generates these predictions as well. Now, whatever "rationality" may mean in the context of game theory, it does not mean "chance." And it is impossible to decide on the basis of coalition outcome data alone which of these may have operated, since the data are consistent with either. Focus on the bargaining process might provide differentiating data, but, as has been suggested above, the paradigm is not well suited to systematic observation of that process. Implied in this criticism is a more general point concerning problems of interpreting the relationship between process theories and outcome data, to which we will pay more attention in the next section of the chapter.

The Introduction of Control Variables. Our concern now is with representative examples of research making use of the Vinacke paradigm, but modifying it by introducing control variables. (We will reserve for later treatment work which introduces more substantial changes in procedure.) We will ask what modifications are made, what their methodological or theoretical purposes may be, and what findings they have produced. There are certain characteristic problems of these designs, whether in original or modified form, and we will take note of these. What follows is not, it should be stressed, a complete review of the literature, but rather of studies that have been selected to make useful points.

The first studies, those involving the introduction of control variables, are largely the work of Vinacke and his students. Vinacke (1964) introduced *cumulative score, delayed payoff,* and *immediate payoff* along with the *game-by-game* condition earlier used by himself and Arkoff. Except for these new elements, the design was identical to that used by Vinacke and Arkoff in 1957. Cumulative score was intended to increase competitiveness and interest in the game (Vinacke, 1959). It arose in part out of statements by subjects in the game-by-game situation, where each game is intended as an isolated event, that knowing where they stood in the sequence of games would have affected their bargaining. This condition was introduced by providing a cumulative record of points won by each subject after each of 18 games played. The delayed payoff variation also sought to motivate subjects and arose from observing that the behavior of players in earlier work would differ were the prize more substantial. In this condition, a cumulative score was kept, players were told that 1 cent per point one would be paid after the experimental session, and a special prize of $10.00 was offered the player of each sex with the highest total score. Because some groups apparently did not believe that payments would in fact be made and because some groups in the delayed payment condition evolved a strategy of "permanent triple alliance" thus awarding all the points available to a particular player,[22] a condition of immediate payoff was contrived: 1 cent per point was paid at the end of each game, and a prize of 50 cents was promised a winner in each triad (pp. 122–123).

[22] They did so in order to guarantee that a triad would produce the "grand" winner, agreeing to an equal split of the $10.00.

This study used both males and females triads. An earlier report (Vinacke, 1959) had shown that the sexes played the experimental game differently. In language adopted later, males were more likely to use an *exploitative* strategy, females an *accommodative* one. In the female triads, more games were played without coalitions, more triple coalitions were formed, more coalitions occurred when one player could win without coalition, less bargaining tended to occur, and less disporportionate prize distributions were the rule. Males, in short, tended to take competition and winning seriously; females tended to be more concerned with reaching mutually acceptable solutions.[23]

While cumulative scores and payments of money reduced the differences between male and female coalition outcomes, Vinacke argued that the underlying difference in strategy remains. For males, cumulative scores resulted in coalitions of those who were behind in the series of games, regardless of the triad power structure. For females, cumulative scores produced increased bargaining, but seemed not to alter outcomes. Monetary awards increased triple alliances and equal prize divisions in male triads. Interestingly, Vinacke interprets this as reflecting increased competitiveness (pp. 141–142), while at the same time interpreting the generally higher frequency of such behaviors among females as evidence of an accommodative strategy.

Kelley and Arrowood (1960) proposed that a simplified version of the Vinacke-Arkoff game would produce results more in conformity with game theoretic predictions, arguing that the complexity of the initial experimental procedure precluded the understanding that game theory assumes. Using only the Type 5 game with weights 4-3-2, they further simplified the task by having each player retain the same weight throughout the games. Twenty triads played from 10 to 70 games (26 on the average), while another 10 triads played 20 games each. Kelley and Arrowood found that the distribution of coalitions in first play of the game conformed reasonably well to the Vinacke-Arkoff conclusion that 3-2 coalitions were most frequent, 4-2 coalitions less frequent, and 4-3 coalitions least frequent; that the frequencies of coalitions in the initial three plays of the game were in the same order, but departed less from chance expectations than in the first play; and that the frequencies of the various coalitions in the last set of three games failed to depart from a chance model. Further, while the strong man got a higher proportion of the prize in early games, he did less well in later games. They interpreted these findings to say that subjects in the Vinacke and Arkoff situation initially misperceive the strong weight as implying power but that they achieve a more correct understanding of the irrelevance of weight after a very few trials, and thenceforth behave in accordance with this correct understanding,[24] and the game theoretic predictions.

[23] Vinacke (1964) prefers not to identify these strategies with sex per se: Some males play the game with an accommodative strategy and some females with an exploitative strategy. Chaney and Vinacke (1960) show that men of higher educational levels tend to be accommodative.

[24] Kelley and Arrowood also argue that the Caplow predictions will hold when power is "real" rather than "illusory." This segment of their study will be dealt with later.

Vinacke, Crowell, Dien, and Young (1966) introduced the variable of information in an attempt to deal with this issue. They noted that complexity was intended to enhance interest, that eliminating complexity makes probable the development of fixed routines and so loss of interest, and that one possible consequence is that players will mix alliances simply to relieve boredom. They also suggested that under conditions of simplified play, members of the triad can keep a reasonably accurate cumulative score, and that the Kelley and Arrowood findings might reflect the tendency under this condition for losers to coalesce. In brief, they argued, Kelley and Arrowood had not established that players will behave rationally in the game theory sense (p. 182).

The above investigators designed a study that reproduced the Vinacke and Arkoff procedure, except that triads played six successive games in each of four triad types, 1, 2, 4, and 5, ordered randomly, and except for the information conditions. The latter involved providing randomly designated subjects with information about alternative strategies, the first strategy following Caplow's reasoning and the second strategy following game theory. Information about both strategies was provided, without suggesting that one was preferable, to one, two, or all members of a triad. Triads first played two games under the original instructions and then the information condition was introduced. Sixty-nine triads, 35 male and 34 female, recruited from introductory psychology classes and rewarded with laboratory credit, took part in the experiment.

Findings for Type 2 and 5 triads[25] were that the incidence of coalitions of weaker players is consistently high under all conditions; that, except for male triads in which all players are informed, the frequency of coalitions of weak players does not decrease in later as compared with earlier games played; and that information did not affect entry into coalitions. Postgame questionnaire responses indicated that these results were not attributable to the failure of the information conditions to "take," but also indicated that, particularly for females, triads evidencing greatest understanding of the objective irrelevance of weights formed fewer weak coalitions. Evidence further indicated that the more members of a triad who were characterized by a desire to win, the lower the incidence of coalitions of weak players. The authors conclude that the chief effect of understanding is to increase the motivation to win, and not to increase rational play in the style of game theory.

Vinacke, Lichtman, and Cherulnik (1967) introduced a chance, or *stochastic*, condition as opposed to a *deterministic* condition. In the latter condition, as in the original Vinacke-Arkoff study, all players moved their counters on the roll of a die (in this case a pair of dice were used to speed up play). In the stochastic condition, each player cast the dice and moved independently. Thus, "gambling" was possible: Players could choose to risk winning without coalition with some probability of success. In order to vary the inclination to gamble, *short board* and *long board* conditions were introduced by using game boards with 49 and 89 spaces, respectively. (The assumption was that if the

---

[25] The data for the other triad types are not reported.

distance to be covered was short, a player might feel that he could rely on a few lucky roles of the dice, whereas over a longer haul he could not.) Other than the specified changes, the design reproduced Vinacke and Arkoff's. Ten male and ten female triads, again students, were assigned to each of the experimental conditions, and triad Types 1, 5, and 6 were used. Three games of each type were played, with the order of types counterbalanced.

In brief, the findings were that, as expected, fewer coalitions occurred under stochastic and short board conditions in Type 1 and Type 5 games; that more weak coalitions were formed in the Type 6 game under the stochastic condition; and, that, whereas sex differences of the previously observed sort continued to exist, they were sharply attenuated where gambling was encouraged.

The Vinacke Paradigm Modified. Stryker and Psathas (1960) focused on the Type 3 triad, the two-equally-strong/one-weak case, in an attempt to check the Vinacke and Arkoff finding that to be weak is to be strong, that is, to be included frequently in the coalitions formed. Beyond that, however, they were interested in examing the consequences of *relative* weakness. Simmel (1950) contended that the advantage the weak man[26] has in a triad with two strong others is independent of his own intrinsic strength and ". . . is determined exclusively by the strength which each of (the other members) has relative to the other. . . . The only important thing is that his superadded power gives one of them superiority [p. 157]." An extension of the perception of strength interpretation of Caplow implies that variations in the relative strength of the weak man would make a difference. Simmel further suggested that the weak man draws maximal advantage where there is contention between the two more powerful members of the triad and where he is free to choose which way he will throw his strength.

Thirty-six male undergraduates were randomly assigned to 12 triads. The triads were assigned randomly, within the requirements of a Latin square,[27] to play 12 games, each game characterized by one of three weight conditions, one of two contention conditions (present or absent) between strong players, and one of two contention conditions (present or absent) between the weak and one strong player (one way of varying the weak man's freedom of choice). The weight conditions varied the weak player's weight in the games among 1, 3, and 5, with the two strong players' weights always being 6. Contention was created by instructing appropriate players that they "have been enemies of long standing and cannot form a coalition." In all other respects but one, the procedure was the same as that of Vinacke and Arkoff: Stryker and Psathas forced coalitions by requiring the replay of games ending in a tie.

The results indicated that the weak man enters coalitions at precisely the rate anticipated by chance and that when he does enter a coalition he receives

---

[26] Simmel (1950) discusses the "to be weak is to be strong" thesis using the phrase *tertius gaudens,* which translates to "the third who enjoys."

[27] It was initially planned to run three Latin squares in order to examine possible trial effects. This was not accomplished. Thus the study confounds possible order of games and trial effects and there is no way of examining these clearly.

less than half of the prize. The data also showed that the relative weight of the weak man does not affect his chances of being included in the winning coalition, but that when he is included, in general, his share of the prize rises with his weight. Simmel's conjectures about the optimal circumstances for the weak man were supported by the evidence of this study.

Reflecting on their data and the procedures used to produce them, Stryker and Psathas argued that no reliable conclusions could be reached through these procedures concerning the comparative validity of the Caplow and game theories of coalition behavior. Both theories develop from assumptions about the *process* by which coalition decisions are made. To use a coalition *outcome* as evidence that a given *process* has operated is extremely risky, unless that process can only lead to one outcome and that outcome can only result from one process. They suggested that this ideal circumstance was not present in their work or in previous work using the Vinacke paradigm, that Caplow outcomes can arise from game theoretic bargaining and vice versa. They also noted the difficulty in drawing inferences about the validity of game theory predictions when outcomes corresponding to game theory predictions are precisely those that random behaviors could produce. Asserting that only greater attention to the bargaining process itself can provide answers to the original Vinacke and Arkoff question, they also contended that the original Vinacke and Arkoff paradigm fails to produce the necessary data: Competitive bargaining was comparatively absent, keeping accurate track of such bargaining as did occur was extremely difficult, and the face-to-face situation introduced extraneous and uncontrolled variance into the data.

To obtain more adequate data to test the Caplow versus game theory predictions, Psathas and Stryker (1965) screened triad members from one another and permitted only written messages routed through the experimenter. They hoped to eliminate the reticence of subjects to compete vigorously and to facilitate the recording of offers. Except for eliminating a condition that forced a single coalition, the design followed that of the Stryker and Psathas (1960) study. The experimental design was a 9 × 9 Latin square with three replications. Each of 27 triads composed of subjects recruited in blocks of 27 were assigned randomly to triads and to cells in a Latin square design. They played nine games, each game characterized by one of three weight conditions (weak man's weight 1, 3, or 5 and the two strong men's weight 6) and one of three contention conditions (no contention, weak/strong contention, and strong/strong contention).

Outcome data closely reproduced the findings of Stryker and Psathas (1960): The weak man entered coalitions no more frequently than one would expect by chance, his likelihood of entering a coalition was not consistently related to relative weakness, and prize divisions reflected contention conditions and the weight of the weak man. Data on prize divisions are given in Table 11.5 for the first study and the replication; the greater competitiveness in the replication— evidenced by more prolonged bargaining sequences—is indicated in these data, but the results of the two studies are essentially alike.

Table 11.5

Frequency of Various Proportions of Prize Obtained by Weak Man in Coalitions, by Contention Conditions and Weight of Weak Man: Original Study and Replication

		Proportion of Prize to Weak Man					
		ORIGINAL STUDY			REPLICATION		
Contention Condition	*Weight of Weak Man*	50%– OVER	1–49%	p[a]	50%– OVER	1–49%	p[a]
No contention	1	2	7	.09	3	11	.03
	3	2	5	.23	6	15	.04
	5	3	5	.36	5	10	.16
W-S contention	1	1	7	.04	1	14	.001
	3	1	8	.02	2	8	.06
	5	2	5	.23	3	11	.03
S-S contention	1	4	7	.27	23	4	.001
	3	8	4	.19	24	3	.001
	5	10	2	.02	25	2	.001

SOURCE. Psathas & Stryker, 1965, p. 129.

[a] Probability of obtaining a split this or more imbalanced if true probability is .5 (binomial test).

It proved abortive in the study described above to relate bargaining behavior to coalition outcomes given the large number of combinations of behaviors possible—who initiates what level of offer to which target? Insufficient games were run to generate clear patterns of such behavior between various weight and contention conditions. Convinced that the source, the object, and the level of offers, as well as the state of contention between, and weights assigned to, participants, interact to structure later bargaining choices, Psathas and Stryker turned to a simulated triadic situation. Simulation was used to avoid having to recruit and to run the large number of triads required to examine the effects of each of the above variables in a free bargaining setting. That is, it would have required observing an enormous number of triads to obtain sufficient data for analyzing each of the types of situations to be simulated.

Subjects recruited from sociology classes were assigned randomly in sets of 20 to the nine situations in which players might find themselves playing the previous games. These nine situations are indicated by the rows of Tables 11.6 and 11.7. Each is distinguished by a contention condition, a source of offer, and a target of offer. Three of the situations represented in Table 11.6 involve the weak man as the target of an offer. The weak man can receive an offer from either of the two strong men under the no contention condition (Situation 1) and under the strong/strong contention condition (Situation 3); which of the two he receives an offer from makes no logical difference in the context of the game. Under the weak/strong contention condition, the weak man can receive an offer only from the strong man with whom he is not in contention (Situation 2).

Table 11.6

Means and Frequencies of Weak Man's Reciprocal and Nonreciprocal Counteroffers, by Contention Condition, Source, Target, and Level of Offer, and Weight of Weak Man: Simulation Study

Offer — Counteroffers Made When Level of Offer Is: / WEIGHT OF WEAK MAN IS:

SITUATION	CONTENTION CONDITION	SOURCE	TARGET	TARGET OF COUNTEROFFER	60 1 $\bar{X}$	60 1 N	60 3 $\bar{X}$	60 3 N	60 5 $\bar{X}$	60 5 N	50 1 $\bar{X}$	50 1 N	50 3 $\bar{X}$	50 3 N	50 5 $\bar{X}$	50 5 N	40 1 $\bar{X}$	40 1 N	40 3 $\bar{X}$	40 3 N	40 5 $\bar{X}$	40 5 N
1.	No	S_1	W	S_1	44.7	15	45.0	14	41.5	13	50.0	13	50.9	11	50.8	13	51.0	5	55.0	4	56.0	5
				S_2	36.0	5	42.5	6	40.7	7	45.0	7	41.0	9	43.5	7	49.4	15	48.2	16	46.3	15
2.	W-S_2	S_1	W	S_1	44.8	20	49.7	20	43.5	20	52.3	20	50.3	20	49.8	20	56.3	20	51.0	20	48.5	20
3.	S-S	S_1	W	S_1	46.5	16	45.3	15	40.9	16	50.4	11	50.8	12	48.0	10	49.1	7	49.0	8	37.5	4
				S_2	31.5	4	32.2	5	30.2	4	41.8	9	34.5	8	36.6	10	43.2	13	43.8	12	41.9	16

SOURCE. Psathas & Stryker, 1965, p. 131.

Table 11.7

Means and Frequencies of Strong Man's Reciprocal and Nonreciprocal Counteroffers, by Contention Condition, Source, Target, and Level of Offer, and Weight of Weak Man: Simulation Study

Counteroffers Made When Level of Offer Is:

SITUATION	CONTENTION CONDITION	SOURCE	TARGET	TARGET OF COUNTEROFFER	60 WEIGHT 1 $\overline{X}$	N	60 WEIGHT 3 $\overline{X}$	N	60 WEIGHT 5 $\overline{X}$	N	50 WEIGHT 1 $\overline{X}$	N	50 WEIGHT 3 $\overline{X}$	N	50 WEIGHT 5 $\overline{X}$	N	40 WEIGHT 1 $\overline{X}$	N	40 WEIGHT 3 $\overline{X}$	N	40 WEIGHT 5 $\overline{X}$	N
4.	No	W	S_1	W	31.5	10	38.4	16	38.0	15	38.5	10	42.3	11	40.5	10	30.0	4	33.3	3	33.3	3
				S_2	48.5	10	60.0	4	58.0	5	50.0	10	51.1	9	51.1	10	47.8	16	45.4	17	46.8	17
5.	No	S_2	S_1	S_2	42.1	12	41.2	12	41.4	11	44.0	10	43.3	9	46.4	7	40.9	9	43.0	6	41.0	5
				W	24.8	8	37.5	8	38.9	9	29.0	10	35.9	11	40.4	13	35.9	11	39.3	14	42.0	15
6.	W-S_2	W	S_1	W	36.2	8	37.1	14	37.9	14	37.8	9	39.5	10	41.0	10	30.0	4	37.5	4	43.5	10
				S_2	35.5	12	31.0	6	29.3	6	39.6	11	41.0	10	44.1	10	41.2	16	41.9	16	43.2	10
7.	W-S_2	S_2	S_1	S_2	46.0	16	45.6	14	46.2	16	48.4	11	48.7	10	46.6	11	41.7	7	42.0	6	45.0	7
				W	21.2	4	32.5	6	35.0	4	26.1	9	37.0	10	39.2	9	30.7	13	35.7	14	39.8	13
8.	W-S_2	S_1	S_2	S_1	44.2	20	46.2	20	48.6	20	47.1	20	50.0	20	50.0	20	44.2	20	43.6	20	43.9	20
9.	S-S	W	S	W	32.6	20	40.0	20	45.6	20	32.4	20	37.0	20	46.4	20	29.4	20	41.8	20	46.9	20

SOURCE. Psathas & Stryker, 1965, p. 132.

The six remaining situations involve a strong man as the recipient or target of an offer, and these are represented in Table 11.7. Two are under the no contention condition; a strong man can receive an offer either from the weak man (Situation 4) or from the second strong man (Situation 5). In the weak/strong contention condition, it is necessary to distinguish the situations of the strong man who is not in contention with the weak man from the situation of the strong man who is: the former may receive an offer from either the weak man (Situation 6) or the other strong man (Situation 7); the latter may receive an offer only from the second strong man (Situation 8). Finally, under the strong/strong contention condition, a strong man (which is a matter of indifference in the logic of the game) can receive an offer only from the weak man (Situation 9).

Subjects were fed offers of 60 (more than half the prize available), 50 (half), and 40 (less than half) points, and were asked to make the one best counteroffer that would maximize their eventual rewards in the game. Each subject "played" nine games, three under each level of offer, with the weak man's weight varying among 1, 3, and 5. The questions investigated were: When players have a choice, to which of the potential coalition partners do subjects turn in response to an offer from a given source at a given level? And what are the levels of counteroffers made?

Highlighting the results are the following: (a) The higher an offer made to a player, the more likely is that player to reciprocate (direct his counteroffer to the source of the initial offer). (b) In general, when a player makes a reciprocating counteroffer, he offers more to his potential coalition partner than he does when he makes a nonreciprocating counteroffer (the exception: when the strong man is responding to offers from another strong man). (c) The counteroffers of the strong man are affected by the weight of the weak man more consistently than are the counteroffers of the weak man himself. (d) The weak man tends to offer more to potential partners in response to lower offers from them, while the characteristic strong man response is to make higher counteroffers to offers of 50 points than to offers of either 60 or 40 points.

While this work was in progress, Kelley and Arrowood (1960) published their study questioning the basis of the Vinacke and Arkoff findings. To check their conclusions and to probe further possible determinants of coalition behavior, Psathas and Stryker had 20 triads play six games of the Type 3 form, with one player being consistently assigned weight 1, two assigned weight 6, and no barriers to coalitions interposed. All subjects responded to postgame questions about their perceptions of the relevance of weights as bases for bargaining decisions. Ten of the 20 triads also responded to brief questionnaires before the first, second, and fifth games. No differences in coalition behavior were discerned between triads responding to questions in the course of play and those who did not. Once again, the weak man entered coalitions no more frequently than expected by chance, and once again the weak man's share of the prize reflected his weight. There were no differences between early and late games in the frequency with which the weak man entered coalitions. Nor was there any progression toward a greater incidence of 50-50 splits of the prize, as might be expected from Kelley and Arrowood's work.[28]

Questionnaire responses were classified into two categories, *weight relevant* and *weight irrelevant*, the former reflecting answers implying that one or another weight carried more power in the game *and* that one or another weight deserved more of the prize by virtue of its greater power. All but one subject gave weight-relevant responses before the first game, most specifying that players with weight 6 were most powerful. By the end of the play, weak men moved considerably toward weight-irrelevant responses; strong men continued to provide weight-relevant responses, although now many of them saw weight 1 as most powerful. In short, there is indeed learning in the game, but that learning is differentiated by power position held.

Table 11.8

Frequencies of Various Proportions of Prize Obtained by Weak Man in Coalitions by Views of Power Relevance of Initial Weight: Learning Study

	Weak Man's Prize	
Viewpoint	OVER 50%	UNDER 50%
Weak man's views:		
W-man equal to or stronger than S-man	11	7
W-man weaker than S-man	4	17
Strong man's views:		
At least one S-man sees W-man as equal to or stronger than S-man	13	13
Neither S-man sees W-man as equal to or stronger than S-man	2	11
Both:		
W-man and at least one S-man see W-man as equal to or stronger than S-man	10	3
Other combinations	5	21

SOURCE. Psathas & Stryker, 1965, p. 141.

Further analysis of the data indicates that views of the relevance of weight strongly affect game outcomes. Table 11.8 presents the evidence for the weak man's share of the prize when he enters the coalition. When the two strong men form coalitions, in 15 of 21 instances they split the prize 50-50. In five of the six exceptions, at least one of them sees the weak man as having greatest power.

Willis (1962) extended Caplow's coalition theory to the tetrad (the four-person group) and used a modification of the Vinacke paradigm to test the extension. Selecting from 17 tetradic power structures, he predicted that for the type with a 4-4-3-2 initial distribution, the two-way coalitions of 4-3 and the

[28] It must be remembered that Kelley and Arrowood used the 4-3-2 triad.

three-way coalitions of 4-3-2 would be most likely; for a 5-3-3-2 initial distribution, he predicted the two-way coalitions of 5-3 and 5-2 and the three-way coalition of 3-3-2. Willis introduced monetary rewards and an element of chance into the game in order to increase participant interest. From 88 male and 56 female students of the University of Helsinki, 36 same-sex tetrads were formed. Each tetrad played 20 games of one of the two power distributions, with randomly assigned weights being held throughout the series of games. Players moved individually on a 100-space game board on the toss of a die. If the die came up even, the player or coalition moved the number of spaces equal to his (or its) weight; if the die came up odd, the player or coalition did not move. Thus, while probability of winning related closely to weight, the winner was not completely predetermined. A cumulative score was kept by each player, and the player in each tetrad winning the most points was given a 1-in-36 chance of winning 3000 Finnmarks (about $9.30). Before each game, a two-minute negotiation period was set aside for coalition formation.

Data indicated that predicted two-way coalitions occurred more often than nonpredicted coalitions,[29] but not significantly so. The predictions for three-way coalitions, on the other hand, were strongly supported. Some tendency for the weak players to be excluded from two-way coalitions and for strong players to play alone existed. In two-way coalitions it was typically the stronger of the pair who initiated the coalition and he typically received the greater share of the prize, but not in a degree proportional to the power differential. With power relations constant, higher shares of the prize went to players who made offers than those who waited for offers.

Willis believes the greater complexity of the tetrad (there are 13 two- and three-way coalitions possible) and the introduction of chance into the game accounted for the relative failure of the two-way coalition predictions. He offers as an alternative to Caplow's theory an "exclusion of the most powerful member" principle to account for the three-way coalition findings. He notes that, while for the particular tetrads he studied, no distinction between these alternatives is possible, for certain tetradic structures the two approaches provide varying predictions. In general, Willis stresses the qualitative difference between the triad and the tetrad, observing that the latter provides the first possibility of countercoalitions (coalitions formed in response to initial coalitions) and also that coalition size becomes a consideration.

Critique. Many comments appraising the Vinacke paradigm have already been made. Perhaps the most significant of these concerns the difficulty in interpreting data in terms directly relevant to the process theories of coalition behavior. The point merits emphasis: Given that the same outcomes can be produced by a variety of processes, to use outcomes as the measure of the degree to which a specified process is operative is unwarranted. This dictum applies with most force to Vinacke and Arkoff's attempt to test the Caplow and game theory predictions. It is further illustrated by the fact that Vinacke argues that males

---

[29] The prediction is for *initial* coalitions formed within the tetrad.

use an exploitative strategy and females an accommodative strategy, and yet both obtain very similar (under certain conditions) coalition outcomes.

Closer attention to the processes through which coalitions are reached is obviously necessary. The Vinacke paradigm in its original form does not seem conducive to generating requisite data of requisite quality. Given the complexities of a multistage bargaining process, screening subjects and requiring written messages by themselves do not solve the problem, although they may be a first step.[30] Chertkoff (1970) has suggested one way of dealing with the gap between bargaining and coalition outcomes: Make the bargaining offers themselves the major dependent variable of coalition studies. This, however, seems rather like throwing out the baby with the bath, if one is indeed interested in coalition formation rather than bargaining per se.

We must treat at least briefly a critical issue thus far raised only by implication—the "meaning" of conceptual variables in relation to the adequacy of one's operational procedures. The problem is posed most clearly by the concept of power. There is a vast literature on the concept, and little agreement on its meaning. But, within the context of coalition research, power is supposed to mean advantage in gaining access to some goal. The particular question relevant here is whether Vinacke's operational procedures are coordinated to the concept so defined. Thibaut and Kelley (1959) and Kelley and Arrowood (1960) argue that they are not, in that—as a game theoretic analysis shows—in most of the triadic structures studied none of the assigned weights give any advantage to a player if he does not enter a coalition, since he cannot attain the goal outside of a coalition. Kelley and Arrowood (1960), in the second half of the research reported earlier, developed a game in which assigned weights do carry advantage in or out of coalitions. The weights represent the number of points a player earns on each trial if he plays the game independently. Further, they required bargaining for shares of the prize only after a coalition is agreed to, rather than as a precondition for a coalition. Thus a given player was less dependent on entering a coalition and had less to lose if agreement on a split of the prize was not reached within the coalition. He did not have to enter a coalition to win at least some points, and the weights represented "real" as opposed to "illusory" power. Using the weights 4-2-0, Kelley and Arrowood showed that the coalition distribution approximates the Vinacke and Arkoff results for the Type 5 triad and that this result becomes more firm as play goes on.

Some comment on the limitations of work done with the Vinacke paradigm or its derivatives is also necessary. First, such results as have been obtained are limited to the constant-sum case, where the prize remains fixed regardless of the power of the players in the game. In many situations with coalition potentials, rewards vary with the amount of power a coalition can muster. Whether the weak man would have in the variable-sum game the advantage he is claimed

---

[30] Insofar as it seeks to have applicability outside the experimental situation, coalition theory must at some point incorporate the complexities introduced by face-to-face communication.

to have in the constant-sum case is doubtful at best, if the reward available to a coalition of two strong men is appreciably higher than the reward available to a coalition including the weak man. Second, the work that has been done is largely limited to what Caplow called the continuous, rather than the episodic or terminal, situation. In part, this is an artifact of experimenters' desire to maximize information obtained from subjects. But, whatever its source, it is clear that the games played are not regarded as discrete units by players. This being the case, an important variable has been neglected in the research thus far —differential reinforcement (Chertkoff, 1970). Whether a player wins or loses a game, and the division of the prize he is able to claim in that game, can be expected to have an important impact on the play of the next game. Such a variable must either be examined or controlled; it cannot be neglected.

An Alternative to the Vinacke Paradigm. While there have been a number of situations devised for the experimental study of coalitions—for example, Kelley and Arrowood's (1960) approach or the completely different one taken by Weick (1966)—the major alternative to the Vinacke paradigm in the literature at present is Gamson's (1961a) convention design. The convention design was elaborated to test the minimum resource theory developed by Gamson (1961b). The paradigm developed purports to deal with "full-fledged coalition situations" in which:

1. There is a decision to be made and there are more than two social units attempting to maximize their share of the payoffs.
2. No single alternative will maximize the payoff to all participants.
3. No participant has dictatorial powers, i.e., no one has initial resources sufficient to control the decision by himself.
4. No participant has veto power, i.e., no member must be included in every winning coalition [p. 374].

The paradigm calls for information on the initial distribution of resources, the payoff for each coalition, nonutilitarian strategy preferences (player's inclination to join another player independent of that other's control of resources), and effective decision point (the amount of resources necessary to control the decision). It assumes that players have the same information about relevant variables, that they do not distinguish among payoffs in the same payoff class,[31] and that every player has a rank ordering of nonutilitarian preferences. The theory predicts that, where the total payoff to a winning coalition is constant, players will choose among alternative coalition strategies by maximizing the ratio of their resources to the total resources of a coalition and, to do this, players will favor the cheapest winning coalition. Finally, the theory posits that coalitions will actually form only given reciprocal strategy choices between two players. The predictions of coalitions are the same as Caplow in five of the six situations in Table 11.1. The exception is Triad Type 5; here Caplow predicts either AC or BC, Gamson predicts BC.

___

[31] Payoffs that may differ, but do not differ sufficiently to make a difference to players, belong to the same payoff class.

The initial test of the theory (Gamson, 1961a) involved 120 subjects recruited from social fraternities, organized into 24 groups of 5 consisting of 3 men from one fraternity and 2 from another. Subjects were told they were to participate in a study of political conventions and that each would play the role of delegation chairman at the beginning of a set of conventions. They were given sheets with the number of delegates each chairmen controlled. The convention "prize" consisted of political patronage "jobs" which chairmen could win by forming coalitions to control the majority of the votes. To form a coalition, an agreement of the division of patronage jobs was first necessary.

The variables of the theory were operationalized as follows: The number of votes controlled by each chairman of a total of 101 votes were the resources available, the payoff consisted of a given number of jobs attached to each winning coalition, subjects were assumed to have a nonutilitarian preference for members of their own fraternity, and a simple majority—51 of 101 votes—was designated as the effective decision point.

Table 11.9

Initial Distribution of Resources and Payoff for Three Experimental Situations

		Player				
Convention		RED	YELLOW	BLUE	GREEN	WHITE
1	Votes	20	20	20	20	20
	Jobs	100	100	100	100	100
2	Votes	17	25	17	25	17
	Jobs	100	100	100	100	100
3	Votes	15	35	35	6	10
	Jobs	90	100	0	90	0

SOURCE. Gamson, 1961a, p. 567.

Three conventions were structured in the manner indicated in Table 11.9. Subjects were screened from one another. At a signal, they raised a card with the color of the single chairman with whom they wished to bargain at that point; if they wished not to bargain, they raised their own card. If reciprocal choices occurred, the pairs entered a "smoke-filled room," where they could discuss for three minutes the division of jobs that would be theirs if they ended up in a winning coalition. If they agreed on a division and controlled the necessary majority of the votes the convention was concluded. If they agreed, but did not control the necessary majority, they returned to the convention to choose and to bargain as a unit until a coalition having a majority was formed. If they did not agree, they returned separately to the convention to choose anew and to bargain. Bargaining sessions between a coalition and another chairman or coalition of chairmen were organized to resemble delegations with single spokesmen for coalitions. To avoid listing payoffs associated with all possible coalitions, subjects were told that any winning coalition would receive the highest number of jobs associated with any member and that any losing coalition would receive no jobs. A cash prize was given to the person at each position who received the most jobs. Gamson sought to prevent interdependence between conventions by telling subjects that, given how prizes were awarded, nothing was to be gained by punishing someone in a given convention for having a high total from previous conventions, and by prohibiting any commitments beyond a single convention. Bargaining sessions were tape-recorded.

The theory predicts both individual choices of potential coalition partners and actual coalitions (the result of a combination of choices). In Convention 1, no individual choice is more likely than any other on the first round. When two coalitions have formed without a majority being reached, two "players" have 40 votes each and the third has 20 votes. The theory predicts that players with 40 votes will choose the one with 20. The predictions concerning both choices and coalitions were confirmed. In Convention 2, the theory predicts that the cheapest coalition of Red-Blue-White will form, therefore, that Red, Blue, and White will choose one another. These predictions were confirmed. However, the theory also predicts that Green and Yellow will prefer to choose among Red, Blue, and White (even though these choices will not be reciprocated). This prediction was not confirmed: Green and Yellow chose one another beyond chance expectancies. Convention 3 represents a situation we have not yet encountered: Different payoffs are attached to different winning coalitions. Here, too, in contrast to the first two conventions, a winning coalition can form in one rather than two steps. Convention 3 provided mixed results for the theory. The number of stages necessary to reach a majority strongly affected coalition strategies, with the fewest steps being preferred. The distribution of final coalitions did not support the theory. However, where the number of steps was held constant (i.e., with attention limited to three-man minimal winning coalitions), the theory was supported in that the predicted coalitions of Yellow-Green-White, Red-Yellow-Green, and Blue-Green-White were the first to meet in potentially winning bargaining sessions in 12 of 17 opportunities.

With respect to bargains reached concerning job divisions, in general, in all three conventions job shares reflected initial resources whether or not the coalition members were in fact the cheapest winning coalition; equals divided jobs equally when they bargained, and those with most resources received higher proportions of the jobs when unequals bargained.

Gamson concludes that the theory is generally supported, but that it needs to be modified to account for its failure to predict initial choices of players who do not become members of the predicted winning coalition and to account for the preference for a strategy that brings victory in one step rather than two. Since he interprets this preference as arising out of a quest for certainty of winning, he suggests that the probability of a prospective strategy being successful be introduced into a modified theory.

Burris and Frye (1966), in an experiment comparable to Gamson's, had subjects compete for grade points rather than jobs in two conventions. In one, the distribution of votes was 49-15-15-15-7; in the second, 25-25-17-17-17. In the first, 49 and 7 preferred one another and this coalition formed most frequently. The three 15s also preferred the 49. In the second, the predicted winning coalition of the three 17s occurred most often. The 25s preferred each other, contrary to the minimum resource theory.

Chertkoff (1966) used Gamson's convention design to study the probability of success as a variable in coalition formation, although Chertkoff's variable was the probability of success of the coalition in a later election, while Gamson's was the probability of effecting a winning nominating coalition. In a three-man nominating convention, with A controlling 40 votes, B 30 votes and C 20 votes, subjects were told that A had varying probabilities of .50, .70, and .90 of being elected, while B and C always had .50 probabilities. They were provided jobs to divide, but were told that the jobs would not be theirs unless their man won the election. In a control condition in which probability of succuss was not mentioned, the weakest available partner was preferred. When players had equal probabilities of success, no differential preferences existed. When A had the higher probability of success, he was preferred despite the fact that he bargained harder for a greater share of the jobs. On the other hand, Trost (1965) and Willis (1967) found that where probability of success was a variable, either no coalitions or coalitions between weak players were preferred. Chertkoff (1970) cites the possibility that these results reflect the difference between intragroup and intergroup conflict (See also Vinacke, 1964). He interprets the results of his research as supporting Riker's version of minimum resource theory, in that coalitions larger than the cheapest may form if players believe this necessary to win.

While we have been looking at laboratory research, it is worth noting that Gamson (1962) tested his theory with data on presidential nominating conventions from 1900 to 1952. Successful prediction occurred, but was modest. However, as Gamson noted, "In many ways, the modest success here in situations characterized by so many unique historical features is more satisfying than neater but more easily obtained experimental results [in a laboratory setting] [p. 171]."

TOWARD A MORE COMPREHENSIVE THEORY OF COALITION BEHAVIOR

A Summary of Findings

What are the facts to which an adequate theory of coalition behavior must be responsive? Certainly, the most impressive single fact is the variability of the behavior. The weak man does and does not get into coalitions beyond chance frequency. The strong man is and is not left out of coalitions. The cheapest winning coalition does and does not form most often. And so on. It is clear that, unless the findings of research thus far prove to be artifacts of methodology rather than reflections of the way it really is, no simplistic theory will do. This last assertion suggests the crucial gap in available evidence: We do not really know how well the current findings will stand up. Thus, the greatest need is for replication, for research that will provide some indication of the stability of the findings thus far produced.

1. However explained, bargains that are struck in the process of arriving at coalition agreements reflect real or imagined resources in the hands of bargainers. When resources are equal, prize divisions are equal. When resources are unequal, the lion's share goes to the bargainer with the most resources, although it appears that differential rewards are not strictly proportional to differences in resources, but are modified toward equality.

2. It appears that those who are behind as the result of previous coalition arrangements will, if the opportunity affords itself, coalesce in opposition to one who is ahead. While this may only be true in continuous interaction where rewards are constant and where status differentials are minimal or nonexistent, it is still a fact that a theory must recognize.

3. It also appears that the introduction of chance into coalition situations reduces the frequency of coalitions.

4. Coalitions will form even where there seems to be no objectively defined need for them.

5. That males and females tend to utilize different strategies when faced with coalition decisions seems to be reasonably descriptive of reality.

Apart from straightforward replication, it would be important for theoretical development to know the degree to which any findings of current coalition research can be generalized across coalition situations as Caplow (1959) defined them. Gamson's findings with the convention paradigm gives some confidence that certain findings will hold for the episodic as well as for the continous situation; it remains to be seen what may hold for terminal situations, clearly the most difficult to study experimentally. (Terminal situations are those in which a coalition is directed toward a single, final redistribution of power.) And it would be extremely useful to have findings for the case Caplow developed his original theory to explain—the case in which rewards are internal to the triadic relationship, rather than emanating from outside.

The Gaps in Extant Theories

No existing theory can account for the variety of facts that coalition research has produced. Perhaps there is no more convenient way of visualizing the problems existing theories have with the data than by summarizing Gamson's advice to partisans who wish to demonstrate experimentally their theories (1964, pp. 103–106). He suggests that the minimum resource theorist build a good deal of conflict into his situation, see that subjects are competing for something really valued, prohibit free communication while bargaining, keep the situation simple so that the coalition with smallest resources can be easily identified, and begin by enhancing the saliency of the parity norm. To the minimum power theorist[32] he suggests that conflict be maximized, that competition be for something so important that what one "ought" to get becomes secondary, that subjects be placed in a setting where an offer can be quickly met by a better offer, that the situation be kept simple so that subjects can readily see whose power can change a losing coalition into a winning one, that subjects be kept from developing trust in one another, that subjects have no established relationships and no prospects of developing them, and that subjects be indifferent or hostile toward one another so that they are not bothered by someone consistently losing. The anticompetitive theorist (one impressed by the accommodative strategy sometimes used in coalition games) should keep conflict to a minimum and the stakes only symbolic; he should make subjects feel they are in a polite game where sportsmanship and proper play are more important than winning. Gamson (1964) only half facetiously offers what he terms *utter confusion theory* as a way of "accounting" for the findings that do not fit other theories of coalition behaviors. He suggests that the confusionist demonstrate his theory by introducing complex variables to preoccupy subjects with rules and information to be assimilated that will allow little time to consider strategy, using very short time limits to increase pressure for quick coalitions, minimizing differences between alternative coalitions and maximizing differences between coalition and no coalition, using unsophisticated subjects who do not know one another and will not meet one another again, preventing stable relationships from developing in the course of the experiment, and making accurate communication extremely difficult.

Comparable advice could be given the theorist wishing to demonstrate other possible theories discussed early in this chapter. We shall not go through the exercise. Rather, we shall simply iterate that no existing theory accounts for the full range of facts produced by coalition research.

A Framework for the Development of Coalition Theory

In the Introduction, to this chapter a brief statement of a "competing definitions of the situation" orientation to the explanation of coalition behavior was presented. Although the word "theory" was used in that context, it must be admitted that it is unwarranted in any technical sense. Rather, what is stated constitutes a point of view, the rudiments of a framework within which a theory proper might be constructed. We seek now to extend that framework and to move toward a theory.

The point of view is a venerable one, fundamental to the more general theoretical framework called symbolic interaction.[33] Its basic dictum is attrib-

---

[32] This rubric is used by Gamson to refer essentially to game theorists.

[33] For a rather thorough exposition of this framework, see Stryker (1964).

utable to W. I. Thomas: "If men define situations as real, they are real in their consequences [Thomas & Thomas, 1928, p. 572]." It enters coalition research in the work of Psathas and Stryker (1965). As stated there:

> Coalition outcomes are the end-result of decisions with respect to bargaining behavior. In a triadic situation, a member of a triad must initially choose whether to initiate bargaining or not, what level of offer to make if he chooses to initiate bargaining, and to which of two others he will direct his offer. If a member of a triad receives an offer, he must choose to accept or reject, to reciprocate that offer or not, and what level of counteroffer to make. Every initial offer can be expected to be contingent on some definition of the situation. This definition can be expected to be a function of perceptions of the conditions under which the interaction takes place. Every offer can be expected to contribute to definitions structuring counteroffers. Similarly, every counteroffer made can be expected to affect definitions, and so on, to the termination of bargaining [p. 142].

Presumably, bargaining ends when members of a projected winning coalition come to share definitions; and, when they begin with conflicting definitions, a critical question is whose definitions are basic to the joint definition.

What will shape definitions with which the process of bargaining begins? First of all, persons enter any interaction with a history, and this history has provided them with labels whose meanings consist in their action implications. "This is a game" implies the appropriateness of a certain pattern of behavior. "This is a struggle for scarce goods" implies the appropriateness of another pattern. In the absence of cues in the immediate situation, or given ambiguity in those cues, this past history will be called upon to "make sense" of the immediate situation, to suggest how one is to behave until the situation becomes clarified. Often there are reasonably adequate cues in the immediate situation—in the experimental games we have been reviewing, in the instructions given, in the analogies suggested, and so on. A particularly important kind of cue exists in anything that serves to define the relative status of those in a system of interaction, for such definitions are central to conceptions of justice, equity, and parity.[34]

Whatever cues are utilized, persons will arrive at some definition that enables them to act. And their acts will serve to redefine the situation for everyone in it. Paying attention to one potential partner rather than another serves to define for both their rank order of attractiveness and so contributes to their sense of bargaining position. Offering little to another in effect tells him that he is not deserving for want of resources, power, or whatever. Rejection of such an offer is a denial of the attributed definition and the assertion of an alternative. If definitions meet, agreements will be reached.

The only direct evidence that definitions of the situation affect coalition behaviors is found in Psathas and Stryker (1965), who in one phase of their research attempt to discover the definitions held by players before the play of

---

[34] For a general statement of the relevance of status to coalition behavior, see Anderson (1967).

games. The evidence seems clear that the coincidence of given definitions under-lay the bargains struck. It is, as well, a reasonable inference from their data that in the Vinacke game those who hold the high weights make power differen-tials a central element in their definitions, while those assigned low weights are sensitive to cues suggesting alternative bases for projecting rival definitions.

But there is considerable indirect evidence from coalition studies to support the view being proposed, for in terms of it quite diverse findings take on some degree of order. Weights in the Vinacke game, analyzed logically, are meaning-less in many of the triad types. But subjects introduced to that game will try to make sense of it; to do so they will make use of whatever cues are available. Weights are in that game for some purpose, and experience is likely to suggest that they be considered as resources. The concept of resources in turn introduces definitions of equity and parity, that is, proper resolutions of the game—equal returns for equal contributions, unequal returns for unequal contributions. The evidence is that the parity norm operates, although not precisely—prize divi-sions for unequal weights tend to be modified toward equality. There are a number of possible explanations of this, stemming from a definition of the situation orientation; for example, the clash of parity definitions with defini-tions emerging from bargaining positions and threat potentials (Isard & Smith, 1968), or the definition of the situation as a game requiring justice and fairness since one is being handed an advantage rather than earning it.

Consider the finding that males and females play the game differently. The finding fits nicely into what is known about male and female roles in this society. A sex role, like any general role, serves as a definer of appropriate behaviors over a wide variety of situations. Particularly where cues are ambiguous, we can expect such sex role definitions to affect behavior. It is interesting from this point of view that introducing chance narrows the differ-ence between the way males and females behave in the Vinacke situation. Introducing chance makes the situation less ambiguously a game in the usual sense of that word, and so legitimates competition to a greater degree.

Consider, too, the finding that those who fall behind in total score in games where cumulative scores are kept tend to form coalitions regardless of their relative power position. Such behavior makes sense if, as Anderson (1967) sug-gests, participants define themselves as status equals and so equally deserving of the rewards available in the game. In terms of this view, we can also understand the finding (Willis, 1962, p. 371) that advantage lies with the person who initiates offers rather than with the person who waits to receive them. His offers, being first, have a stronger chance of shaping the definitions leading to decisions in the game.[35]

It is, however, insufficient to leave the statement in this general form. The ideas must be drawn together into a theory; they must be organized to specify

---

[35] While the assertion that initiating actions have stronger impact on definitions seems to have general validity, that advantages necessarily accrue to the initiator is dubious on the basis of data in Psathas and Stryker (1965) indicating the interaction of relative power position of offerer and target and level of the offer.

hypothesized relationships among variables. Unfortunately, we do not know enough to specify these relationships. Whereas the point of view we are considering leads us to be open about those variables that structure definitions of the situation, the theory must be developed from a relatively restricted set of variables if it is not to be utterly vapid. We seem to know some of the variables. Relative status and relative power serve as initial definers, as do analogies drawn to previous game (in the narrow, "play" sense) experience, and as do the general roles through which people are tied to social structure. In the bargaining process itself, the initiation of offers, their direction, and their level appear to be of consequence. But at least one crucial class of information is missing, without which a theory cannot really be stated. We must know more about the "staying power" of given kinds of definitions, their ability to withstand attack or denial, and the probability that definitions of a given kind will hold as against definitions of another kind. We need more information of the sort suggested by the finding (Psathas & Stryker, 1965) that those assigned strong weights in the Vinacke game "resist" learning the objective irrelevance of those weights.

Necessary Modifications of Experimental Paradigms

If the above assessment is accurate, it serves as a statement of the next stages in the experimental study of coalitions and suggests modifications of extant experimental paradigms. Required are techniques of ferreting out definitions brought to the experimental situation and developing within it. The intrusion of questionnaires at strategic points is one way of gathering such information, but has obvious shortcomings. Perhaps a technique, suggested by Scheff (1967), of supplying each participant with a partner to whom he must explain his proposed and actual actions could be used. Potential users of this technique, however, must be warned. Forcing participants to verbalize in this way may well organize and rationalize actions to an extent not generally characteristic of such actions. Further, it is probable that introducing a partner also introduces a new range of social expectations into the coalition situation.

Second, we need designs in which competing definitions are deliberately introduced and manipulated. Various procedures suggest themselves—providing rules or other cues with contradictory implications, or using stooges to carry out actions implying given definitions. Above all, we need designs that permit efficiently recording, in ways suitable for detailed analysis, the entire coalition bargaining process. Perhaps a stooge design that enables the investigator to conserve his subject resources for triad studies by not consuming three subjects at a time, would permit the controlled observation of the necessary very large number of bargaining sessions. Or perhaps, as suggested elsewhere (Psathas & Stryker, 1965), a reasonable alternative is the use of computer simulation. Whatever the research strategy chosen, and whatever the difficulties in implementing a research strategy, the ubiquity and importance of coalition phenomena justify the outlay of scientific resources.

REFERENCES

ANDERSON, R. E. Status structures in coalition bargaining games. *Sociometry*, 1967, **30**, 393–403.

BODIN, A. M. Family interaction, coalition, disagreement and compromise in problem, normal, and synthetic family triads. Technical Report No. 8, 1965, Office of Naval Research, Grant 4374(00).

BOND, J. R., & VINACKE, W. E. Coalitions in mixed-sex triads. *Sociometry*, 1961, **24**, 61–75.

BORGATTA, M. L., & BORGATTA, E. F. Coalitions in three-person groups. *Journal of Social Psychology*, 1963, **60**, 319–326.

BURRIS, J. C., & FRYE, R. L. The effects of initial resources of individuals upon their selection of a partner in the formation of coalitions. Paper presented at Southeastern Psychological Association meetings, 1966. Cited in Chertkoff (1970).

CAPLOW, T. A theory of coalitions in the triad. *American Sociological Review*, 1956, **21**, 489–493.

CAPLOW, T. Further development of a theory of coalitions in the triad. *American Journal of Sociology*, 1959, **64**, 488–493.

CAPLOW, T. *Two against one*. Englewood Cliffs, N.J.: Prentice-Hall, 1968.

CHANEY, M. V., & VINACKE, W. E. Achievement and nurturance in triads varying in power distribution. *Journal of Abnormal and Social Psychology*, 1960, **60**, 175–181.

CHERTKOFF, J. M. The effects of probability of success on coalition formation. *Journal of Experimental Social Psychology*, 1966, **2**, 265–277.

CHERTKOFF, J. M. A revision of Caplow's coalition theory. *Journal of Experimental Social Psychology*, 1967, **3**, 172–177.

CHERTKOFF, J. M. Social psychological theories and research in coalition formation. In S. Groennings, E. W. Kelley, & M. Leiserson (Eds.), *The study of coalition behaviors*. New York: Holt, 1970. Pp. 297–322.

EMERSON, R. M. Power dependence relations—Two experiments. *Sociometry*, 1964, **27**, 282–298.

FRANCIS, W. L. Influence and interaction in a state legislative body. *American Political Science Review*, 1962, **56**, 953–960.

GAMSON, W. A. An experimental test of a theory of coalition formation. *American Sociological Review*, 1961, **26**, 565–573. (a)

GAMSON, W. A. A theory of coalition formation. *American Sociological Review*, 1961, **26**, 373–382. (b)

GAMSON, W. A. Coalition formation at presidential nominating conventions. *American Journal of Sociology*, 1962, **68**, 157–171.

GAMSON, W. A. Experimental studies of coalition formation. In L. Berkowitz (Ed.), *Advances in experimental social psychology*. Vol. 1. New York: Academic Press, 1964. Pp. 82–110.

HOFFMAN, P. J., FESTINGER, L., & LAWRENCE, D. H. Tendencies toward group comparability in competitive bargaining. *Human Relations*, 1954, **7**, 141–159.

HOMANS, G. C. *Social behavior: Its elementary forms*. New York: Harcourt, 1961.

HURWICZ, L. The theory of economic behavior. *American Economic Review*, 1945, **35**, 908–925.

ISARD, W., & SMITH, T. E. On social decision procedures for conflict situations. In Peace Research Society (International), The Hague Conference, *Papers,* 1967, **8,** 1–29.

KELLEY, H. H., & ARROWOOD, A. J. Coalitions in the triad: Critique and experiment. *Sociometry,* 1960, **23,** 231–244.

LUCE, R. D., & ROGOW, A. A. A game theoretic analysis of congressional power distributions for a stable two-party system. *Behavioral Science,* 1956, **1,** 83–95.

MILLS, T. M. Coalition pattern in three person groups. *American Sociological Review,* 1954, **19,** 657–667.

PSATHAS, G., & STRYKER, S. Bargaining behavior and orientations in coalition formation. *Sociometry,* 1965, **28,** 124–144.

RIKER, W. *The theory of political coalitions.* New Haven, Conn.: Yale University Press, 1962.

SCHEFF, T. J. A theory of social coordination applicable to mixed-motive games. *Sociometry,* 1967, **30,** 215–234.

SCHELLING, T. C. The strategy of conflict: Prospects for a reorientation of game theory. *Journal of Conflict Resolution,* 1958, **2,** 203–264.

SCHUBERT, G. *Judicial behavior.* Chicago: Rand-McNally, 1964.

SHUBIK, M. *Readings in game theory of political behavior.* Garden City, N.Y.: Doubleday, 1954.

SIMMEL, G. *The sociology of Georg Simmel,* K. H. Wolff (Ed.). Glencoe, Ill.: The Free Press. 1950.

STRODTBECK, F. L. The family as a three person group. *American Sociological Review,* 1954, **19,** 23–29.

STRYKER, S. The interactional and situational approaches. In H. T. Christensen (Ed.), *Handbook of marriage and the family.* Chicago: Rand-McNally, 1964. Pp. 125–170.

STRYKER, S., & PSATHAS, G. Research on coalitions in the triad: Findings, problems and strategy. *Sociometry,* 1960, **23,** 217–230.

THIBAUT, J. W., & KELLEY, H. H. *The social psychology of groups.* New York: Wiley, 1959.

THOMAS, W. I., & THOMAS, D. S. *The child in America.* New York: Knopf, 1928.

TROST, J. Coalitions in triads. *Acta Sociologica,* 1965, **8,** 226–243.

VINACKE, W. E. Sex roles in three-person game. *Sociometry,* 1959, **22,** 343–360.

VINACKE, W. E. Puissance, strategie, et formation de coalitions dans les triades dans quatre conditions experimentales. *Bulletin du C.E.R.P.,* 1964, **13,** 119–144.

VINACKE, W. E., & ARKOFF, A. An experimental study of coalitions in the triad. *American Sociological Review,* 1957, **22,** 406–414.

VINACKE, W. E., CROWELL, D. C., DIEN, D., & YOUNG, V. The effect of information about strategy on a three-person game. *Behavioral Science,* 1966, **11,** 180–189.

VINACKE, W. E., LICHTMAN, C. M., & CHERULNICK, P. D. Coalition formation under different conditions of play in a three-person competitive game. *Journal of General Psychology,* 1967, **77,** 165–176.

VON NEUMANN, J., & MORGENSTERN, O. *Theory of games and economic behavior.* Princeton, N.J.: Princeton University Press, 1944.

WEICK, K. E., & PENNER, D. D. Triads: A laboratory analogue. *Organizational Behavior and Human Performance,* 1966, **1,** 191–211.

WILLIS, R. H. Coalitions in the tetrad. *Sociometry,* 1962, **25,** 358–376.

WILLIS, R. H. Coalitions in a three-person inessential game. Paper presented at Midwestern Psychological Association meetings, 1970. Cited in Chertkoff (1970).

ZINNES, D. A. Coalition theories and the balance of power. In S. Groennings, E. W. Kelley, & M. Leiserson (Eds.), *The study of coalition behaviors.* New York: Holt, 1970.

GROUP STRUCTURE AND MEMBERSHIP

By and large social psychologists have been predominantly concerned with the social psychology of the individual. As one considers the more complex social phenomena of the impact of the group upon individual behavior and of social interaction, current theories and methodologies reflect a greater variety of professional traditions including anthropology, economics, and sociology as well as psychology. When one examines the problem area of group structure and membership within units ranging from small groups to large organizations, the major conceptual and empirical contributors are found among social psychologists with a more sociological background. It is at this level of analysis that the familiar sociological constructs of role, position, norm, status, and power are introduced into the conceptual and experimental paradigms of social psychology. And the central focus of theoretical and empirical concern becomes understanding the development and change of more or less structured relationships between actors involved in some common task.

In the first chapter of this section, Ziller begins by considering what is meant by the constructs *group* and *group membership*. He then reviews a number of studies that have attempted theoretically and empirically to determine the effects of homogeneous and heterogeneous group composition upon one or more dimensions of individual and group performance. As an example, he describes a research paradigm employed by Hoffman and Meier (1961) to manipulate group composition and measure productivity. After critically reviewing this paradigm and the results it produced, the author turns to a more phenomenological approach developed by Levy (1964) in which perceived homogeneity and heterogeneity of others is related to attraction to the group. The major thrust of Levy's argument is that a first requisite to research in this area is to ascertain whether a participant perceives himself to be a member of the given group, and whether he views the group as being homogeneous or heterogeneous in its membership. This phenomenological point of view, which enjoyed relatively low status during the era of strict behaviorism, is beginning to reemerge in social psychological research. As a result, increasing stress is being placed upon assessing the subjects' perceptions and interpretations of a given stimulus, task, or manipulation.

Chapter 13 provides us with an example of a conceptual paradigm concerned with one type of heterogeneity within a group, namely that of status distribution. Burnstein and Katz consider the problem of a rational division of labor between group members asking principally how and under what conditions a group can achieve an equitable distribution of status consonant with the successful performance of some task. In two preliminary studies, the authors describe an experimental paradigm for investigating this problem area, and assess the effects of change in status upon members' performance, as well as conditions that induce a group to redistribute status.

After establishing that changes in status distribution do affect performance and that groups work towards optimal distribution of status, the authors report three additional studies which investigate the conditions under which it is more or less difficult to obtain such an optimal distribution, and how group members accommodate to changes in status. The present chapter, beyond its substantive contribution, provides yet another example of how research can be carried out in a cumulative stepwise fashion. Each study represents a logical and empirical derivative from previous studies.

Chapter 14 by Cohen, Berger, and Zelditch is concerned with the conceptual and empirical utility of the concept of status, and its role in determining the forms of social interaction that occur in groups. After reviewing prior studies of status, they set forth and illustrate the reasons why it has been impossible to develop a cumulative body of knowledge in the area. Their general argument is important in all areas of social psychology. In effect, they cite the need for research that makes explicit its conceptual and definitional framework and employs more or less standardized experimental paradigms: "More generally, we assert that the failure of these studies to be cumulative is due to the lack of a framework that guides the design and conduct of each individual piece of work. To us, such a framework consists of an abstract formulation of the problem containing one or more empirical generalizations about the phenomena, a theoretical explanation of generalization and a standardized empirical situation in which to evaluate and extend the theory." (The present writer might inject the observation that one principal purpose of this book is to provide the reader with examples of problem areas that have been more or less abstractly formulated, and for which standardized experimental paradigms have been developed.) The authors conclude by presenting one conceptual and empirical framework for investigating the distribution of status and its effects upon the behavior of group members.

In Chapter 15, one of the authors of the preceding chapter, Zelditch, outlines even more explicitly an example of a conceptual model for investigating the relationship between (a) the authority structure of organizations, (b) the performance expectations of its members, and (c) the possible forms of change deriving from inconsistencies between (a) and (b). In developing the model, the author defines a set of logical requirements for characterizing the authority structure of an organization, explicitly defines performance expectations in terms of an actor's evaluation of his capacity relative to other actors, and enumerates forms of authority rights which a superior may have relative to a subordinate.

Subsequent to his conceptual statement, the author goes on to describe in detail a research paradigm in which certain aspects of an organization are simulated. He notes that simulation is used rather than more highly controlled laboratory experiments because "organizational theory is in a very primitive state of development and guarantees the irrelevance of very few properties of naturally occurring organizations." In effect, the author is arguing that there currently exists insufficient information concerning the functioning of organizations to know, in investigating any given hypothesized relationship, all the variables which can and should be controlled. On the other hand, since one can make some judgments about the relevance of certain variables, only part of a real organization need be generated or simulated. Describing this as a *heuristic* simulation, he then identifies the relevant organizational features to simulate given his conceptual model.

After defining the characteristics of the organizational simulation, Zelditch describes in detail the types of measurement and analytic techniques which can be employed for assessing the resultant behavior. As noted in the first chapter of this book, measurement and analysis are integral components of a theory. Chapter 15, more than any other in this volume, illustrates the utility of developing these as an intrinsic part of one's conceptual model. The chapter concludes with the enumeration of some limited findings which derive from the conceptual and experimental paradigm, and a discussion of possible future developments.

The final chapter is also fundamentally concerned with the variable of status, namely, with understanding the "origins and development of task and social-emotional leadership role differentiation in groups." Utilizing the prior work of Bales and Slater (1955) as his principal theoretical and methodological orientation, Burke goes on to revise some of their assumptions and to develop more refined methods for measuring the behavior of group members. In particular, the author is methodologically concerned with obtaining a more valid assessment procedure for determining the relative and absolute amount of social-emotional and task performance behavior by various group members.

After discussing the above revisions, the author presents two studies. The first examines the relationship between the perceived legitimacy of a task by group members, measured ex post facto, the degree of differentiation between task and social-emotional leadership roles, and member inequality in task participation. In the second study the variables are the same, but in this instance the perceived legitimacy of the task is manipulated. The results are consistent across the two studies. It might be noted that the juxtaposition of studies provides an example of an excellent research strategy. One first makes an analysis utilizing an ex post facto "manipulation" of one's independent variable. In the present instance this involves classifying subjects after the first study in terms of their perception of the legitimacy of the task, and determining whether differences on this variable are related to role differentiation and task participation. Then, and most importantly, one replicates the study utilizing an actual manipulation of the same independent variable, task legitimacy, and measures its impact upon the same dependent variables. The latter, of course, represents a more powerful test of one's theory. Burke concludes his chapter with a discussion of possible strategies of future research for investigating task and socioemotional role differentiation in groups.

REFERENCES

BALES, R., & SLATER, P. Role differentiation in small decision-making groups. In T. Parsons, R. Bales, et al. (Eds.), *Family, socialization, and interaction process.* New York: Free Press, 1955. Pp. 259–306.

HOFFMAN, L. & MEIER, N. Quality and acceptance of problem solutions by members of homogenous and heterogenous groups. *Journal of Abnormal and Social Psychology,* 1961, **62,** 401–407.

LEVY, L. Group variance and group attractiveness. *Journal of Abnormal and Social Psychology,* 1964, **68,** 661–664.

12

HOMOGENEITY
AND HETEROGENEITY
OF GROUP
MEMBERSHIP[1]

Robert C. Ziller[2]

The relation between characteristics of a group's members, such as similarity or dissimilarity of race, age, ability, or personality, and the manner in which the group functions is a significant theoretical problem, as well as an applied one. For example, in assembling a group of men to guide a deep probe into space, the composition of the team is crucial. Not only must the team be efficient, but the members must also be compatible over long time periods and under conditions of confinement with no opportunity to change personnel. A hostess faces a similar problem in arranging a dinner party.

Group composition is also the junction of individual and social psychology. When individuals are assembled into a group, their perception of themselves and of the persons within and outside the group tends to change, as does the perception of the individual by the others. An understanding of the confluence of individuals and groups is one of the crucial concerns of social psychology.

This analysis begins with a brief description of some of the earliest investigations of homogeneous and heterogeneous groups in the areas of genetics, education, and political science. Four approaches to the study of the homogeneity and heterogeneity of groups are then described. Finally, two models for the study of group composition are presented, which derive from one of the four previously described approaches. The first model varies the homogeneity or heterogeneity of groups with regard to one or more member characteristic and

[1] This chapter is Report One under contract between the University of Oregon and the U. S. Navy, Office of Naval Research.

[2] I must underscore the contribution of Harold M. Proshansky, the editor of this section. He has been a partner in structuring this paper, and any of its merits derive in part from his acute scholarship and editorship.

assesses the differences in group performance that follow. The second model considers how variations in a group member's perception of the spread of differences among other group members affects his behavior.

Genetics

In a review of literature concerning the incest taboo, Lindsey (1967) outlines several genetic explanations of the phenomenon. The most relevant concepts for our purposes are *heterosis* or hybrid vigor, which refers to the relatively greater rate of growth, size, fertility, and comparable characteristics in hybrids when compared to their parents; and *inbreeding depression*, which refers to the tendency of closely inbred animals to show a reduction in fertility and resistance to disease.

The most general theoretical observation is that genetic diversity is associated with the organism's increased biological adaptability to the environment, thereby maximizing the survival potential of the species. An inbred animal is more rigidly specified biologically and is relatively incapable of varied biological responses to environmental demands leading to reduced survival potential.

At the very least, genetic theories suggest through analogy that heterogeneous groups are more consistent than homogeneous groups in their performance across situations, that is, under varied conditions of task demands. Indeed, there is some support for this hypothesis. In a study of group size (Ziller, 1957), a tendency was observed for six-man groups to perform at a more consistent qualitative level across problem solving tasks than were individuals or groups of smaller size. Of course, it could be argued that the size variable alone might explain the differences and that heterogeneity is a superfluous explanation. This indeed would tend to be the case if all persons were alike. However, it seems more reasonable to assume that each individual brings different experiences and talents into the group, leading to a wider variety of resources within a group. Thus, there is a higher probability that a larger group will be in a position to match the task demands with personnel resources. As the tasks change, new resources may be selected from a larger pool. The result is greater consistency of group performance across situations, or, in a sense, increased survival potential in a problem-solving situation.

Education

Educators have often proposed that classroom groups composed homogeneously according to some measure of academic ability are more likely to benefit from instructional processes than are randomly composed groups. It is usually assumed that homogeneous groups provide a more even distribution of potential for understanding among classroom members, that this permits more efficiency in communication and learning, and that instruction is thereby more comparable to that at the individual level. In other words, it seems to be assumed that in the classroom learning proceeds from the teacher to a student and from this student to the next in some chainlike manner. On this basis, the efficiency of learning is a direct function of the slowest person in the series.

Conversely, if a parallel rather than a serial interpretation of the classroom setting is proposed (using an electrical analogy, see Voiers, 1955), and if each pupil is looked upon as a single learning unit, the least efficient student need not retard the class's progress. Moreover, the superior members of the class may increase class efficiency by offering models of superior individual learning which might be effectively imitated by the less effective class members.

Homogeneous ability grouping has been tried in the public schools for 70 or 80 years (Goldberg, Passow, & Justman, 1966) and has been studied systematically for at least 40 years, but the homogeneity versus heterogeneity problem remains unresolved and the practice little enlightened. The failure of these studies is usually attributed to the limitations of I.Q. as a single selection criterion for homogeneity, to poor experimental designs, to difficulty of evaluating achievement in education, and to the failure to assess the effects of grouping on teachers and administrators.

Political Science

A third area of research involving heterogeneity and homogeneity of group membership concerns the organization of a state into a monolithic structure, as opposed to a collection of competing subgroups or pluralistic societies (Kariel, 1961). Generally, it is assumed that if the membership is similar in its beliefs, the organization tends to become controlled by the persons who represent the central membership. Moreover, in time, social pressures are applied to make the group increasingly homogeneous. On the other hand, if the group is pluralistic (composed of a variety of subgroups or individuals), the probability of participation, challenge, and competition across subgroups is maximized, power is shared, and the identity of the subgroups is preserved. The power of the subgroups and individuals that make up the membership is preserved through the complexity of the structure, which precludes control by a few. Since the organizational structure is constantly in a state of flux, new coalitions are constantly in the making. Control of the organization is thus shared, because there is no simpler alternative.

THEORETICAL APPROACHES TO THE STUDY OF HOMOGENEOUS AND HETEROGENEOUS GROUPS

Initially the studies of group homogeneity and heterogeneity were atheoretical. The investigator was often content to show that superiority of group performance was associated with either homogeneous or heterogeneous groups. One of the earliest studies (Gurnee, 1937) found that human groups of homogeneous sex learned a maze in less time than did heterogeneous groups. More recently, more theoretical approaches have been in evidence. Three examples of these approaches are described here, including studies of status congruence, reinforcement, and social comparison.

Status Congruence and Incongruence

If a set of individuals is to be ordered in terms of status on each of two variables, such as age and power, a condition of status congruency obtains if the positions of each individual in the set is equivalent for both dimensions. For example, if the oldest person in the group is also the most powerful and the youngest is the least powerful, a condition of status congruence exists. Status incongruence would obtain under conditions where the youngest member was the most powerful (Ziller & Exline, 1958; Exline & Ziller, 1959). In a sense, congruity of status with regard to a single individual may be viewed as intrapersonal homogeneity.

In the studies cited above, heterogeneity of age was found to be positively related to group problem-solving effectiveness when the subjects were male. When the subjects were female, however, groups composed homogeneously according to age were superior to heterogeneous groups. The results were explained in terms of status congruence. Age and power are congruent for men, but incongruent for women. Older women may be perceived by younger women, and indeed by themselves, as possessing less power in some very broad sense associated with reproduction, sexual attractiveness, and mobility. Thus, in female groups heterogeneous with regard to age, a condition of status incongruence was created. Moreover, status incongruence interfered with problem-solving effectiveness because the efforts of the group members were diverted from the task demands to conflicts arising from attempts by the members to establish conditions of status congruence.

A number of other behavioral consequences for group members may be seen to derive from conditions of status incongruence. The ability of the members of groups under conditions of status incongruence to predict their behavior in relation to that of other members is less reliable, their self-esteem is perceived as threatened, and the members' behavior will be more self-centered, thus leading to increased group conflict. All of these factors contribute to losses in effectiveness of group performance.

Member Similarity and Reinforcement

A second attempt to examine homogeneity and heterogeneity at a more fundamental level grows out of the work by Byrne and Nelson (1965). They propose that persons are attracted to persons who support and generally reinforce their life style. Moreover, those who are most likely to support the life style of another tend to have a similar life style. A higher rate of reinforcement is associated with higher attraction, and higher attraction is associated with higher similarity. This "law of attraction" has been found to hold for similar and dissimilar attitude statements and economic similarity and dissimilarity (Bryne, Clore, & Norchel, 1966). Persons similar in attitudes and socioeconomic status tend to be more attracted to each other. Similarly, one can propose that members of homogeneously composed groups will tend to emit a greater number of positive reinforcements to the members because of greater similarity in values and attitudes, leading to a higher probability of reinforcement.

Social Comparison

A third fundamental approach to the phenomenon of homogeneity and heterogeneity of group membership involves Festinger's theory of social comparison (1954). Festinger proposed that in the absence of direct physical standards (physical reality), people will seek to satisfy their need for self-evaluation through social standards—by comparing themselves with other people (social reality). These social comparisons can yield stable self-evaluations only when a person compares himself with someone similar to himself on the characteristic in question. If the other is too different, the subject will simply categorize him as different (contrast) rather than search further for similarities. Therefore, persons will seek out others who are similar to themselves or try to make those persons near to them more similar in order to facilitate self-evaluation and social comparison.

In terms of our present problem, this suggests that groups that are initially heterogeneous move in the direction of homogeneity. This trend may be especially strong under conditions of unchanging group membership (closed groups). Under some circumstances, however, homogeneity may be detrimental to group performance. For example, it has been proposed that in groups in which the membership is in a constant state of flux (open groups), the members are less interpersonally oriented, less status striving, less inclined toward captious criticism, and therefore more creative (Ziller, 1965). Here, then, by creating open-group conditions, the heterogeneity of the group may be maintained against the press for similarity posited above. Thus, the concept of group homogeneity and heterogeneity may be useful in developing a theory of open and closed groups (Ziller, 1965).

Group Training as Opposed to Selection of Members

In addition to the previous three theoretical orientations that are relevant for understanding the role of homogeneity and heterogeneity in group functioning, there remains the theoretical and pragmatic issue of how to obtain either homogeneous or heterogeneous groups. Two methods have been proposed: training and selection. Selection, although more economic, has a number of problems associated with it. The first and perhaps most difficult one is measurement. In most experiments and in studies of grouping in the classroom, group members are selected on the basis of a single variable, such as intelligence. Other variables that may be involved are assumed to be randomized. Nevertheless, the effects of group homogeneity according to a single variable may be attenuated by a variety of effects from other salient member characteristics, particularly as the group's tasks change. One may attempt to increase group homogeneity by matching on several variables, but it is pragmatically difficult to compose groups that are homogeneous on more than a few variables. In response to this difficulty, some investigators favor using more global measures of similarity, such as sociometric choices or self-selection to group membership (Roby & Rosenberg, 1954). The selection problem is compounded, of course, by the unavoidable problem of changing group membership.

Perhaps a more workable and flexible approach is training for homogeneity or heterogeneity. Here the powerful tool of behavior modification may be employed in groups (Bavelas, Hastorf, Gross, & Kite, 1965). First, task demands similar to the desired behavior must be incorporated in the group situation. Then behavior consistent with the demands of the situation is reinforced by a trainer or other group members, leading to increased frequency of the desired behavior. Reinforcements may, of course, be given for either homogeneous or heterogenous behaviors.

Another training technique that may generate heterogeneity was employed by Maier and Solem (1952), who taught groups to consider the minority opinion by simply informing the leader that this was behavior expected of the leader. Indeed, here the trainer may be seen as reinforcing the leader's behavior.

TWO EXPERIMENTAL PARADIGMS

Two paradigms of research concerning group homogeneity and heterogeneity will be presented. Both may be said to emanate from the "similarity of membership and reinforcement" approach to the problem area. The major difference between the two paradigms concerns the number of conceptual links between group composition and group productivity (See Figure 12.1).

In the first paradigm group composition involves homogeneity and heterogeneity of the personality characteristics of the members. Group productivity concerns the group's problem-solving effectiveness. The model largely ignores the members' perceptions of the group (did the members perceive the members of the group as being similar or dissimilar?), the affective structure of the group (was the group cohesive?), and group processes (how much conflict was observed?).

In the second model it is recognized not only that composing groups in a given manner may be associated with an increase or decrease in group productivity (quality of decisions, creativity, or units of production, for example), but also that the associative link between composition and productivity is mediated by affective group structure and group processes. The problem of mediating constructs is inherent in small group research. Having composed a group in a certain way (See Figure 12.1) does not insure a certain hedonic tone, satisfaction, or lack of conflict in the group (affective group structure). Furthermore, groups composed similarly may use different group processes. Decisions may be submitted by one or all group members. Ideas may be submitted by a few or many members. And evaluations and positive reinforcements may be many or few, quite apart from or only partially related to how the group is composed. Indeed, the member's perception of group composition could be a more significant variable than the composition itself (See Figure 12.1). The second paradigm considers that studies that examine both group composition and the members' perceptions of group composition are necessary.

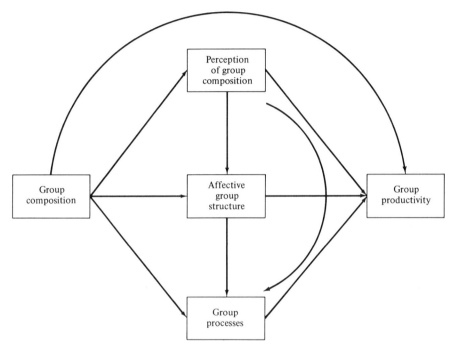

Figure 12.1
Conceptual links between group composition and group productivity.

It is apparent from the order of presentation of the components in Figure 12.1 that the emphasis in the second paradigm is on the extended linkage between group composition (or perceived group composition) and group productivity. This emphasis may be misplaced, however. At this stage in the conceptual and empirical development of the framework, it may be more feasible to study more proximal links, such as between-group processes and group products or group composition and the perception of the group by the members.

EXPERIMENTAL PARADIGM I

A series of three studies by Hoffman (1959; Hoffman & Maier, 1961; Hoffman & Maier, 1966) are representative of research using the first paradigm. They associate group composition (similarity and dissimilarity of personality profiles) with group performance and group satisfaction over time. This design derives from studies of individual personality and problem-solving performance where groups are formed of individuals selected on the basis of a given personality measure and productivity in a problem solving situation is assessed. The underlying conceptual framework for this research derives from the work of Maier (1930) and Duncker (1945) in the area of individual problem solving. Maier and Duncker proposed that persons with many "directions" available, that is, those capable of many restructurings of their perceptual field, are more likely to be successful problem solvers than persons who are inflexible and adhere to a single direction.

Hoffman and Maier assumed that "direction" operates in the same way in groups as in individuals. Heterogeneous groups have a variety of possible directions available that derive from the varied perceptual and cognitive structures of their members. Hence, heterogeneous groups should arrive at higher-quality group solutions.

In the three studies discussed here, the main thrust concerns the link between group composition and group productivity, with a secondary interest in the link between group composition and affective group structure. Ignored, however, is the link between group composition and group processes. In addition, the paradigm ignores the subject's perception of the group. Thus, if the subjects were homogeneous or heterogeneous with regard to race and the study was conducted in an American university, the members' perceptions of the group would not be taken into account. And if one does not know what the members' perceptions might be under conditions of race heterogeneity, or for that matter under conditions of heterogeneity of various personality characteristics, then one is forced to make a number of tenuous assumptions that variations in perception of group composition or in group process do not affect the extreme linkages between group composition and productivity.

Perhaps the most limiting assumption of Paradigm 1 is that homogeneity or heterogeneity is nonspecific; that is, the generalizations are not contingent upon the variable used to select the subjects. The model also assumes, implicitly, that homogeneity or heterogeneity has wide implications and that one may expect to find a variety of correlates and consequences. It would seem that a contingency model would be more appropriate where the association between homogeneity and heterogeneity of group membership and group productivity is dependent upon the specific variable upon which the members are homogeneous and upon the specific task demands. For example, heterogeneity of intelligence in terms of Guilford's facets of intelligence (1967) may be associated with creativity, but homogeneity of personality may be associated with satisfaction with problem solution.

The independent variable in all three studies by Hoffman and Maier was homogeneity or heterogeneity of group membership. The dependent variables included quality and inventiveness of group problem-solving solutions on two or more tasks, acceptance of problem solutions, and the members' attraction to the group.

Study I

In the first study in the series (Hoffman, 1959), it was hypothesized that nonhomogeneous groups produce higher-quality solutions than do homogenous groups. As stated earlier, this hypothesis derived from an extrapolation of findings from individual problem-solving behavior associating flexibility of personality and individual problem-solving effectiveness. Thus, it was proposed that nonhomogeneous groups with the inherent varied perceptual and cognitive structures of their members would yield higher quality-solutions than would homogeneous groups.

The second hypothesis proposed that, when compelled to provide an answer to a problem where there is no objectively correct solution, nonhomogeneous groups either fail to agree on a solution and resist change or produce inventive solutions. Homogeneous groups, on the other hand, produce few inventive solutions, but either fail to agree or to accept an alternative solution offered to them. Here, problems having no objectively good solution are referred to as *acceptance* problems. The quality of the solution to acceptance problems can be judged only in terms of the members' personal values and standards. Since there is no correct answer that can be demonstrated by some principle of science or logic, the "correct" answer is determined by "social reality" or group agreement on the solution. Given these task demands, it was proposed that differences in affective structures (e.g., satisfaction with the group) in nonhomogeneous groups should produce conflict. The result of such conflict is difficult to predict, but if the values involved are not central to the members of the group, there is a high probability of easy resolution of the conflict. Indeed, the group is likely to generate a unique and interesting solution under these conditions. Presumably, moderate conflict is associated with creativity. On the other hand, if the issues are central, conflict is less likely to be resolved and nonhomogeneous groups in particular are more likely to fail to agree on a solution.

The third hypothesis proposed that, "for homogeneous groups there is no relationship between the degree of satisfaction with the solutions and their quality. . . . For nonhomogeneous groups, there is a positive relation between the degree of satisfaction with and the quality of the solutions [p. 28]." The hypothesis derives from the assumption that only a limited number of "directions" will evolve from members of homogeneous groups and that these will tend to be incorporated into the solution and approved unanimously. In nonhomogeneous groups, conflict is more probable, since a greater number and variety of proposals must be incorporated into the group solution. Thus, in nonhomogeneous groups unanimous satisfaction may be expected only in those groups with high-quality solutions, where a breadth of ideas have been used in the solution. Heterogeneity, then, is associated with more directions, and if more directions are accepted, a higher-quality solution evolves.

Method. Unlike many small-group studies, the subjects were members of meaningful, long-term groups, which insured some commitment by the members to the groups. The subjects were sophomore, junior, and senior students in an undergraduate course in human relations. Nevertheless, the life space of the subjects also included membership in other groups with other norms, frames of references, and personal orientations that could operate against the presence of the independent variable—heterogeneity or homogeneity of group membership.

The Guilford-Zimmerman Temperament Survey (1949) was used as the basic device for creating homogeneous or heterogeneous group compositions. "It was assumed that the ten trait measures provide a sample of the personality characteristics such that subjects with similar profiles are likely to be more similar than those with dissimilar profiles [p. 28]." This approach has the advantage of including a wide sample of personality characteristics in formulating the groups rather than attempting to isolate a single personality characteristic, which too often is tenuous at best, and has the disadvantage of being nonspecific. Kendall's tau was used to determine the correlation between the ten-score profiles of every pair of students in the laboratory section of the class.

Three types of four-person groups were assembled in the first study. Type 1 groups (homogeneous) were composed of persons with high correlations between their ten-score personality profiles. Type 2 groups were composed of persons with both high negative and high positive profile correlations. In these groups, some members were assumed to be the same in personality profiles, whereas others were opposite in personality profiles. Type 2 may be said to be mixed or somewhat heterogeneous. Type 3 groups consisted of persons whose profiles were neither positively nor negatively correlated. The members of these groups were assumed to possess unrelated personality profiles.

However, when it was subsequently found that only 4 of the original 15 Type 2 groups continued to assemble, these 4 groups were combined with Type 3 groups to comprise the nonhomogeneous groups. The number of groups of each type initially established were, respectively, 20, 15, and 22, for a total of 57 groups. A comparison of the algebraic and absolute sums of correlations between profile scores for the three types of groups provided statistical evidence that there were distinct qualitative differences in the personality mixtures of each group type. Although students were assigned to these different types of groups purely on the basis of their personality characteristics, comparisons of the various types of groups also indicated no differences in sex composition.

Comments on Method.   It is noteworthy that the subjects completed all facets of the experiment in the laboratory phase of their class. In this way, the students perceived the series of events as a learning exercise rather than an experiment in which the experimenter might have a personal stake.

Several methodological problems emerged in the procedures for forming groups. The method of determining high and low homogeneity of personality profiles (Kendall's tau) did not differentiate among homogeneous groups, which derived largely from mutually high scores on one of the ten scales or from mutually high scores on one of the other ten scales. Homogeneity with regard to specific personality patterns could not be determined because there were too few cases in each cell. Thus, we are compelled to accept homogeneity as a transcending characteristic: that high correlations between profiles that derive largely from one heavily weighted scale out of ten has a similar meaning to high correlations between profiles that derive from another heavily weighted scale out of ten. The use of a personality profile with fewer components may prove more amenable to further analyses and obviate the necessity of assuming that homogeneity is nonspecific with regard to traits or measures.

The experimental groups were composed of four persons. No attempt was made to control for sex, intelligence, or sociometric attractiveness of the groups. Fortunately, upon analysis no significant differences were found on these variables between groups. Nevertheless, it is important that the effects of these and similar variables be considered in initially forming groups. It may be hypothesized, for example, that minority group members (females, American Negroes, physically disabled, or older persons) tend to scan the environment and are more aware of the ratios involving their own category of persons in relation to the total population. It should be noted that an evaluation of sex composition was made in the second study in the series.

Selecting the group size for small-group research is a problem that can be too easily overlooked. There always exists, of course, the pragmatic question of one's ability to recruit enough subjects for study. Aside from this constraint, there are few theoretical guidelines for defining what group size is appropriate. There is some evidence, for instances (Ziller & Behringer, 1965), that heterogeneity of group membership may have a more significant impact in two-man groups as opposed to three- and four-man groups. Moreover, higher-order interactions among uncontrolled variables are more probable and more difficult to trace in larger groups. This would suggest that the dyad be used unless there are some cogent theoretical reasons to use groups of a larger size.

On the positive side, it should be pointed out that the groups in the present study met over a relatively long period of time. This contrasts with the usual laboratory group that often meets for an hour or less. The longer-term meetings may help to intensify the experimental conditions. Other approaches that may intensify the potential effects of variations in group composition include isolation of the group for days or weeks in duration or creating an expectation on the part of members that they will be involved in extended interaction with a particular group (Altman & Haythorn, 1967). Experimental approaches for increasing the significance of the group for the individual member will do much to increase the validity and generality of results from laboratory experiments.

Group Tasks.   The first of the problems presented to the group in the present study was the Mined Road problem (Lorge, Tuckman, Aikman, Spiegel, & Moss, 1955). It was administered in the next to the last meeting of the semester. In this problem the group was asked to identify with a five-man guerrilla team that is attempting to return to its own lines. In order to do so, the men must cross a road that is known to be heavily mined. The problem is to determine the best method for crossing the road safely, quickly, and without evidence to the enemy of crossing. Various scrap materials, such as ropes and lumber, are scattered around the area.

A score was derived from a content analysis of the proposed solution in terms of the feasibility of the method used to cross the road, safety, concealment of clues, and time taken to solve the problem. The reliability of initial and repeated scoring by the same judges two weeks later of 19 solutions was .84.

The second problem was the Change of Work Procedure problem developed by Maier (1952). There is no objectively "best" solution; the best solution is that which is most acceptable to the group, the one they are willing to carry out. Some solutions can be considered more or less inventive, however.

The problem involves a role-playing situation. Three workers perform three different jobs in hourly rotation. In order to achieve greater efficiency, their supervisor asks the group to work at fixed instead of rotating positions. The problem is essentially the resolution of the conflict between capitalizing on individual ability for higher production or freedom from monotony through rotation. Three types of solutions are usually found: refusal to change (old solution), acceptance of the supervisor's suggestion for the most part (new solution), and compromise or inventive solutions. Reclassification of the types of solutions after a two-week interval by the same judges showed almost perfect agreement with the initial classification.

Measures of member satisfaction with the solution were also obtained. For the Mined Road problem the measure of satisfaction took the form of the question, "Were you satisfied with: (a) the entire solution, . . . (e) practically none of the solution?" For the second problem the students were asked, "How satisfied are you with the solution reached by the group?" Again, a five-point scale was used.

It is not at all clear that the tasks provided valid and reliable measures of productivity. One way to increase validity and reliability is to use a number of problems in deriving the dependent measures of problem-solving productivity. In this way, similar results across problems serve to support the reliability and validity of the measure of the dependent variable. Indeed, if several widely disparate types of problem-solving tasks are used, the generality of the results are more assured. Hoffman and Maier were apparently aware of this, because in the second study in the series (1961), two additional problems were used.

Results.   The first hypothesis proposed a relationship between heterogeneity of group composition and group productivity. A simple t test was used to examine the reliability of the difference between homogeneous and heterogeneous groups' performances on the Mined Road problem (See Table 12.1). As predicted, homogeneous groups obtained a significantly lower quality of solution ratings than did heterogeneous groups. The effect was not very strong, as a one-tailed test of significance was required to obtain significance. Given the controversy of the theory of homogeneity or heterogeneity of group membership, the use of a one-tailed test rather than a mere conservative test seems somewhat cavalier. In fact, in the second study in the series, the more conservative two-tailed test was used.

Hoffman also proposed that heterogeneous groups, because they are more flexible and capable of more "directions," develop more inventive solutions to problems. In order to test this proposition, solutions to the second problem were classified as "old," "new," or "inventive." Differences between groups are presented in Table 12.2. The chi-square value for the contingency table composing the homogeneous and nonhomogeneous groups is 2.88, which is not significant at the .05 level of confidence.

Table 12.1

Comparison of Scores on Mined Road Problem

	Tau	Mean*	SD	Number of Groups
Homogeneous	+	44.5	28.63	13
Nonhomogeneous	0, —	63.1	28.53	17

SOURCE. Hoffman (1959), p. 30.
* One-tailed t test that the mean of nonhomogeneous groups is greater than the mean of the homogeneous groups is significant at the .05 level.

In considering inventive solutions alone, however, only 2 (16 percent) of the 12 homogeneous groups, as against 7 (41 percent) of the 17 nonhomogeneous groups, produced such solutions. Although the results were not statistically significant, the author suggested that the resolution of conflict generated in certain nonhomogeneous groups resulted in ideation creativity. The results of the second study confirmed this result and they were statistically significant.

Table 12.2

Number of Groups Producing Each Type of Solution

Group Type	Tau	N	Type of Solution		
			OLD	NEW	INVENTIVE
Homogeneous	+	12	4	6	2
Nonhomogeneous	0, —	17	2	8	7

SOURCE. Hoffman (1959), p. 30.

An analysis of the results pertaining to the third hypothesis revealed no significant differences between the satisfaction of homogeneous as opposed to heterogeneous group members. A significant association was found between the members' satisfaction with the solution to the problem and the quality of the solution in both types of groups. And for both homogeneous and heterogeneous groups, where the group generated the inventive solution, the members of the group were almost unanimously satisfied with the solution (Table 12.3).

In summary, the first study in the series indicated that there was no significant difference between homogeneous and heterogeneous groups regarding satisfaction with the solution to the problem. It was found, however, that heterogeneous groups were superior in their solutions to the first problem and tended to submit more inventive solutions in the second problem.

Table 12.3

Relation between Type of Solution and Satisfaction with the Solution (Change of Work Procedure)

	Type of Solution	
Group Type	OLD OR NEW	INVENTIVE
Homogeneous Number satisfied		
Four	3	2
Less than four	7	0
		p = .15
Nonhomogeneous Number satisfied		
Four	6	6
Less than four	4	1
		p = .24
Total Number satisfied		
Four	9	8
Less than four	11	1
		p = .03

SOURCE. Hoffman (1959), p. 30.

Study II

As has already been indicated, a second study was conducted which employed a similar classroom setting and used the same independent and dependent variables. In addition, three more problem-solving tasks were introduced. These tasks involved conflicts in values, personal conflicts, and the distribution of a bonus.

The Mined Road problem, used in the first study, was administered in the first meeting of each group. The Student Assistance Fund problem, a role-playing case developed for the second study, was administered in the fourth meeting. In this problem each member of a group was assigned the role of a different student who was deemed qualified for financial assistance from a university fund. Each "student" was told that he qualified on one or more attributes. Each was also told that he needed $1500 for the next academic year, but the total available funds were only to be $3000 for the year. The group had to decide on how to allocate the money in the future. Conflict was induced by the provision that the total amount of money was less than that needed by all group members combined and not enough for any one member if they divided the money equally. The chance of reaching agreement was reduced further by giving the subjects opposing standards for allocating money among themselves. The method developed for allocating funds among students in the future was scored for quality.

The Painter-Inspector Argument problem (adapted from Maier, Solem, & Maier, 1957), another role-playing case in which a leader was assigned randomly within each group, was administered in the sixth laboratory session. A painter, an inspector and rough primer, a shop steward, and a foreman meet to settle an argument between the painter and the inspector. The argument reflects a basic conflict in the entire shop and requires an analysis of the shop as a system rather than as a collection of persons, but few groups were able to get beyond the initial argument and identify the total shop problem.

The Change of Work Procedure problem (Maier, 1952) described previously was administered in the eighth session. The Point Distribution problem was administered in the tenth session. Each group was given 19 points to distribute among its members as a bonus for participating in the experiment. The points were to be used to raise the final grade of the student. Each subject knew his own position in the class relative to the tentative cutting points for grades indicated by the instructor. The groups were given 40 minutes to arrive at a decision and were told that no fractional or negative points were to be given and that failure to agree would give each subject four points—a total of 16 for the group. Since no objective standard of quality could be applied to the solutions, this problem was used to evaluate fairness or acceptance of solutions.

Whenever possible, Hoffman and Maier combined the data collected in the first and second studies. In the present study heterogeneous groups produced a higher proportion of high-quality solutions than did homogeneous groups in three of the four problems with quality components (See Table 12.4).

By combining the results of both studies, it was also possible to analyze the groups according to homogeneity according to sex (see Table 12.5). There was a tendency for mixed-sex groups to produce higher quality solutions than all-male groups. It seems likely that sex homogeneity and sex heterogeneity, being more apparent than personality homogeneity or heterogeneity, served to heighten the subjects' awareness of the heterogeneity-homogeneity variable and thereby intensified its effect. It was also found that satisfaction with the problem solutions was about the same in the homogeneous and heterogeneous groups.

Hoffman and Maier, in reviewing their findings, suggested that solutions with high quality and high acceptance can be obtained from groups in which the members have substantially different perspectives on the problem (heterogeneous groups), and in which these differences are expressed and used by the group in arriving at the final decision. However, if heterogenous groups are simply more attractive or interesting for the group's members (affective group structure in the paradigm of Figure 12.1), conclusions by Hoffman and Maier might be more simply explained in terms of motivation or curiosity among heterogeneous group members. If members of heterogeneous groups are more mutually stimulating, they may attend to each other to a higher degree, leading to superior and more inventive solutions. The results of the third experiment, reported below, tend to militate against this latter explanation, however.

Table 12.4

Quality of Solutions by Homogeneous and Heterogeneous Groups

	Present Study		Combined Studies	
	HOMO-GENEOUS	HETERO-GENEOUS	HOMO-GENEOUS	HETERO-GENEOUS
Mined Road Problem				
Percentage above median[a]	30%	57%	21.7%*	52.6%*
M	55.9	65.3	45.9*	64.3*
SD	34.6	29.9	32.1	29.3
Number of groups	10	21	23	38
Student Assistance Fund				
Percentage above median[a]	36%*	80%*		
M	44.2	50.9		
SD	17.5	12.8		
Number of groups	14	20		
Painters and Inspectors				
Percentage above median[a]	54%	56%		
M	16.5	15.1		
SD	10.5	13.9		
Number of groups	13	16		

SOURCE. Hoffman and Maier (1961), p. 402.

[a] The median score was determined from the results of the four-person groups, including residual groups not assigned to either the homogeneous or heterogeneous types.

* Percentage or mean difference significant at the .05 level.

Study III

The third study in the series compared homogeneous and heterogeneous groups formed in the same way as those in the two previous studies and under the same class-laboratory conditions. Homogeneous and heterogeneous groups were compared with regard to their members' attraction to the group. The four measures of this attraction were based on liking, problem-solving ability, choice of ingroup versus outgroup members as companions, and choice of ingroup versus outgroup members regarding problem-solving ability.

At the end of the two-hour laboratory periods in the fifth, eighth, and eleventh weeks after the group had been established, subjects completed sociometric questionnaires. Each subject rated every other member of his own group on a nine-point scale according to how much he liked him and again according to his problem-solving and role-playing ability. Each subject also chose three people from the entire laboratory section whom he would most like to have in his group, once because he liked them and a second time on the basis of their problem-solving ability.

The mean of the three ratings through which each subject reported how much he liked the other members of his group was used as an index of his attraction to the group on the basis of liking. The mean of his three ratings of problem-solving ability represented his attraction to the group, on the basis of this variable.

Two indices of attraction were derived from each subject's choices as a function of how often he chose his own group members from all the people in his laboratory section. Since the sections varied in size from 11 to 21, an index was developed which reflected the greater mathematical probability of making an ingroup choice in the smaller section. Indices based on the liking choices and on the problem-solving choices were computed to measure each subject's attraction to his group.

Table 12.5

Homogeneous-Heterogeneous Differences in Solution Quality to the Mined Road Problem in Groups of Different Sex Composition (Combined data: 1959 and present studies)

	All Male		*One Female*		*Two or Three*[a] *Females*		*Total*	
	HOMO-GENE-OUS	HET-ERO-GENE-OUS	HOMO-GENE-OUS	HET-ERO-GENE-OUS	HOMO-GENE-OUS	HET-ERO-GENE-OUS	HOMO-GENE-OUS	HET-ERO-GENE-OUS
Percentage above median[b]	12.5*	66.7*	0.0	33.3	50.0	72.7	21.7*	52.6*
M	34.8*	75.1*	37.7	54.1	64.1	72.2	45.9*	64.3*
SD	35.8	31.3	11.3	24.4	35.3	31.9	32.1	29.3
Number of groups	8	9	7	18	8	11	23	38

SOURCE. Hoffman and Maier (1961), p. 404.

[a] Data from one homogeneous group in the 1959 study that consisted of four women are included in the two or three females category.

[b] The median score was determined from the results of all four-person groups, including residual groups not assigned to either homogeneous or heterogeneous types.

* Mean or percentage difference between homogeneous and heterogeneous groups is significant at the .05 level by t test or chi-square test, respectively.

The results confirmed Hoffman's earlier findings. On none of the four measures were the homogeneous groups significantly more attractive to their members than the heterogeneous groups, nor was there any indication of a trend in this direction on successive measurements. It was concluded that, in this setting, there is no evidence that group members with similar personalities become more attracted to each other than do those with dissimilar personalities.

DISCUSSION

This series of studies is seen to be less than optimally systematic in terms of Figure 12.1, which outlines various hypothetical associations between group perception and problem-solving processes and products. Only in the third study is a systematic attack made upon the question of group composition and group acceptance. Overall, then, there is a tendency in these studies to hasten toward the more distal association between variables in the nexus before examining or even exploring more proximal relationships, such as those between group composition and group perception.

This suggests that future research be directed toward the analysis of other associations in the structure of crucial relationships. With the accumulation of findings, the models of these relationships may be expected to become more integrated.

For example, if a positive association is established between group membership heterogeneity and group productivity and between group membership heterogeneity and ease of assimilation of new members (Ziller, 1965), it may be anticipated that over time, when membership changes are inevitable, the differences between homogeneous and heterogeneous groups would be magnified. The series of studies presented here seem to have passed over consideration of the meaning of the concept of homogeneity or heterogeneity of group composition toward the discovery of distal productivity correlates, seeking safety in empiricism rather than first building upon a thorough analysis of the independent variable and possible mediating processes. Indeed, the Paradigm 1 approach may reflect a distrust of theory or at least a preference for empiricism, and the hope that through empiricism more fundamental processes may somehow be deduced.

In terms of these three studies, we now know that heterogeneity of group composition (as created by the testing technique described here) is associated with group productivity in a wide variety of problem-solving tasks. But homogeneity or heterogeneity is not related to group attraction. Since the intervening associations remain unknown, it is still something of a tour de force rather than a scientific explanation. A phenomemon has been described, but not explained.

The Hoffman-Maier paradigm for the study of homogeneity or heterogeneity of group membership is somewhat similar to that used by students of group size. The initial studies were concerned with the association between group size and group productivity, but later studies were more concerned with group processes and group products under various task demands (Thomas & Fink, 1963). A satisfactory theoretical approach to group size has yet to emerge.

At the outset of this chapter, a number of theoretical approaches to the problem of homogeneity or heterogeneity of group composition were proposed. These included status incongruence, similarity and positive reinforcement, and social comparison. It would be relatively simple to study rate of reinforcement and parity of reinforcement among members of homogeneous and heterogeneous groups as they were composed by Hoffman and Maier. This alone would bring us closer to understanding group processes associated with productivity and offer the possibility of using a well-developed theoretical framework.

Perhaps, however, one of the more basic descriptive experiments in the study of homogeneity or heterogeneity of group membership has yet to be attempted. This basic experiment concerns the perception of homogeneous or heterogeneous groups by the group members themselves (See Figure 12.1). The members' perception of the group is a fundamental property of the group. The first step in a research program concerning group composition should, therefore, be concerned with the members' perception of the group and the concomitants of these perceptions. One can assume that even under the complex group composition conditions created by Hoffman and Maier, members of a group develop hypotheses about the nature of the group. These hypotheses, whatever they may be, are also presumed to influence the behavior of the group members. For example, if the members in some way view the group as simplex rather than complex (capable of being described here with a few concepts rather than with many concepts), various behavioral correlates of these perceptions are anticipated. Members who perceive the group as complex may be less concerned about acceptance by the majority of the group members and, thus, may submit more extreme problem-solving solutions. Experimental Paradigm II involves a direct analysis of the members' perception of group properties.

EXPERIMENTAL PARADIGM II

In a series of studies by Levy (Levy, 1964; Levy & Richter, 1963; Levy & Steinmeyer, 1967) groups are treated as perceptual objects. Thus, if each member of a collection of individuals is given some value on a particular dimension, such as dangerous-safe, groups can be composed which will differ from each other in their means and variances for that dimension. Treating such groups as stimuli permits study of the effects of variations in these properties on the perception and behavior of the observer. This approach seeks to establish the meaning of homogeneity or heterogeneity of a set of social stimuli through the individual perceiver's evaluation rather than on the *a priori* basis of the experimenter's judgment (See Krech, Crutchfield, & Ballachey, 1962, p. 19).

In the cognitive approach underlying Levy's paradigm, the stimulus and the response are mediated by the individual's perceptions (Stimulus → Individual Perception → Response). Essentially, the approach is phenomenological. In this regard, Asch (1952) notes that "the paramount fact about human interactions is that they are happenings that are *psychologically represented* in *each* of the participants." Psychological interaction between persons occurs: "between entities both of which are systems which perceive, feel, and understand [p. 142]."

As Scheerer has observed (1954, p. 107), the individual's perception of the stimulus is a cognitive representation, and this representation can be conceived of as causing behavior. The phenomenal field, such as the perception of the group by the individual member, is considered a cause, an intervening variable or an explanatory construct of the individual's behavior under certain conditions.

This paradigm is in the direction of a minimal social approach. The problem is stripped of its extraneous variables and assumptions. Instead of making tenuous assumptions about the perceptions of the group members, here we examine how the individual gains information and understanding of the group and how he acts in and upon his environment on the basis of these perceptions (Scheerer, 1954).

The usual criticism of this paradigm (Spence, 1950, 1951) is that the intervening representation is difficult to observe and unnecessary and that a cognitive representation tends to complicate the investigation prematurely and unnecessarily. To this must be added the shortcoming that the phenomenological approach may simplify the investigation by shortening the chain of associations and omitting certain assumptions, but not without some concurrent costs. One critical cost is associated with the ability to measure and interpret the subject's reports. The meaning of self-reports are illusive at best. The opposing arguments are that it would be premature to base exploratory concepts on molecular connections of S-R because they have been isolated from the total complex organization. An analysis of the perceptual aspects of the stimulus and of the response in their total settings should precede a more narrow analysis (Sheerer, 1954, p. 93).

A major limiting assumption of this paradigm is that the perception of a field of objects in which the self is not included is similar to the perception of a field of persons in which the perceiver is included with the group. Again, of course, this is subject to empirical test. When the subject is somewhat detached from the perceptual field, greater objectivity may be assumed. Moreover, when included within the perceptual field rather than being outside it, different problems of information search obtain. For example, when the observer is a member of a minority group (e.g., a Black American) and is included in a group heterogeneous with regard to race it is probable that the self is less likely to be weighted properly in the perceptual field. The minority member may even fail to add himself to the number of the minority. At other times membership may act to increase the salience of the minority and add to the perceived number of the minority. For example, the minority candidate for political office may overestimate the minority-majority ratio.

The studies by Levy investigated the relationships between groups shown pictorially and determined independently to be homogeneous or heterogeneous and the degree to which individuals found these groups attractive. Also studied was the relationship between the personality needs of the subjects and their attraction to homogeneous or heterogeneous groups. The independent variable was always the variability of the portrayed group members, as determined by an independent group of raters.

Method

Stimulus Material.   In a first study (1961), Levy scaled facial photographs of males on four dimensions: good-bad, reliable-unreliable, dangerous-safe, and tense-relaxed. On the basis of these data, 24 sets of five photographs each were formed. The sets of five were made up so that for each of the four dimensions there were two sets having the same mean value on a particular dimension, but widely differing variances. In addition, for each dimension three different mean values of attractiveness (high, medium, and low) were represented with no picture being included in more than one set. Thus, as indicated in Table 12.6, six different sets of pictures were presented for each dimension.

Subjects.   Seventy subjects, 31 men and 39 women, participated in this experiment in partial fulfillment of a requirement in a college introductory psychology course.

Procedure.   The experiment was conducted in two parts. Each subject took part individually. In the first part the subject was required to make 12 choices from 12 pairs of picture sets. One pair was presented at a time. Each pair consisted of two sets of pictures with the same mean value on a particular dimension (good-bad, etc.) but differing in variance (high or low). The pairs were presented in randomized order over subjects, first with respect to dimension and then with respect to mean value within dimensions.

The two sets of pictures were presented simultaneously, side by side on a rack in front of a subject. The left-hand location of the high- and low-variance sets were varied according to the prescribed random order. The subjects were told that this was one of a series of studies concerning the question of what makes some people "interesting or attractive to others." They were then asked

Table 12.6

Means and Variances for Picture Sets

Attractiveness values and variance levels	Dimension							
	GOOD–BAD		RELIABLE– UNRELIABLE		SAFE– DANGEROUS		RELAXED– TENSE	
	M	S^2	M	S^2	M	S^2	M	S^2
High								
High	85.8	79.8	77.6	109.6	75.0	185.6	76.6	106.4
Low	85.1	5.0	77.4	2.8	74.8	8.6	76.4	4.0
Medium								
High	51.6	39.2	51.8	39.8	52.4	50.4	51.2	55.4
Low	50.0	2.8	50.6	2.0	52.6	.4	51.4	2.8
Low								
High	24.2	82.2	25.6	115.2	27.0	100.4	24.6	102.0
Low	25.4	10.8	22.2	6.2	29.0	4.8	25.0	1.4

SOURCE. Levy (1964), p. 662.

to choose from a pair of picture sets which group, as a group, they would "prefer meeting and getting to know." The instructions indicated that each set was to be considered as a whole and that there were no right or wrong answers.

Two or three days following the picture judgments, the subjects completed the Edwards Personal Preference Schedule (EPPS) by appointment with the departmental clinic secretary. Three men and three women either failed to keep their appointments or did not complete the test, thereby reducing the number of subjects in this part to 64.

Results. In analyzing the data with regard to choice of variance, the 17 subjects who chose the high variance set 50 percent of the time were eliminated because this response was interpreted as indicating no preference. Of the remaining 53 subjects, 38 chose the high variance set 7 or more times out of 12, and 15 chose the high variance set 5 or less times. This difference in preference is significant beyond the .001 level by a two-tailed criterion for the binomial test. Levy concluded that higher-variance groups were more likely to be chosen as the more attractive. Since the 17 subjects who chose the high-variance set only 50 percent of the time were not included in the final analysis, the data indicate a more cautious interpretation.

The preference for high-variance groups may not apply to high, medium, and low mean values of the faces on the various dimensions to the same degree. In order to determine whether or not the preference for high-variance groups was generalizable across the three value levels (high, medium, and low mean values), three binomial tests were performed. In each case, the comparison was made between the number of subjects who made three or four choices (out of four) in favor of the high-variance set against the number making one or no choices (out of four) in this direction. For the high mean value the numbers were 42:6, for the medium mean value 22:27, and for the low mean value 24:22. A statistical analysis indicated that for pictures with high mean values, heterogeneous groups (high variance) were preferred to homogeneous ones.

Obviously there is no statistical significant difference between the medium and low value levels. Thus, the preference for high variance in groups of faces is only significant in the case of groups with highly valued facial features.

Finally, a score was ascribed to each subject consisting of the number of times, overall, that he chose the high-variance set. These scores for the subjects were then correlated with each of the 15 Edward's Personal Preference Schedule need scores, a broad spectrum personality inventory. Only one of the correlations reached significance at the .05 level of confidence, n Autonomy $(-.27)$. Since ten tests of significance were calculated, the one significant result may well be attributed to chance.

DISCUSSION

In contrast to the first paradigm, the present perceptual paradigm represents a more highly controlled approach. The stimulus materials are, to a large extent, under the control of the experimenter. The experimenter presents the faces to be viewed and the dimension (group variance) that differentiates the two sets. This is in great contrast to the first paradigm, where selective attention by subjects to various differences among group members is probably a significant source of error variance.

The visual displays in Levy's studies should be extended to include different races and stimulus materials other than faces or faces only, thereby extending the generality of the results. Similarly, the subjects might be extended to include persons of other ages and races. For example, the present results may simply indicate that subjects of college age and background prefer higher-variance groups. Older subjects from different backgrounds may prefer lower-variance groups.

The task is also one in which the subjects may lack personal involvement. The task is academic, distant, and aseptic, suggesting a cognitive rather than a conative set to the stimulus materials. The subjects are reminded that they are in a study, which may suggest that they are to communicate with the investigator according to the norms of behavior associated with such interactions. The subjects may be expected to present themselves according to their perceived expectations of the investigator.

The results of this study demonstrate that variance is a discriminable attribute of social groups and that on the whole it is a favorably regarded attribute. When given a choice, subjects report groups having the greater amount of variance as more attractive. This obtains, however, only when the two groups between which the individual must express a preference are both favorably regarded. Heterogeneity is valued in a group when all the elements in the group are regarded favorably.

Possibly the most significant contribution of Levy's perceptual paradigm is that the individual's perception of the groups has become a subject of psychological inquiry. While person perception has enjoyed a long and productive history of research in social psychology, group perception has been largely ignored. Levy has posed the question of the preference for homogeneous as opposed to heterogeneous sets of persons. Preference for group homogeneity or heterogeneity is but one of the many propositions that evolves from the general area of inquiry concerning group perception. Similar inquiries are suggested concerning group size, group structure in terms of communication networks (Shaw, 1964), and various facets of group heterogeneity. For example, it may be proposed that minority as opposed to majority group members (i.e., Negroes and whites in the United States) report different preferences for various ratios of Negro and white members in a group.

Ziller and Behringer (1967), for example, proposed that visually distinguishable minority group members in contrast to majority members (Negro vs. white) tend to report different perceptions of the percentage of a specific variety of objects in a tachistoscopically presented heterogeneous field of elements (10 percent, 20 percent, 30 percent, 40 percent, 50 percent, 60 percent, 70 percent, 80 percent, and 90 percent black elements). The associations between various characteristics of the elements (objects vs. faces) in the perceptual field and the percentage of these elements in the field were also explored in relation to the subject's estimates of the percentage. The results of the two experiments suggest that both functional factors (race and community of the perceiver—3 percent of one community and 30 percent of another were Negro) and structural factors (number of different elements in the field, proportion of elements in the field, and brightness of the focused elements) are associated with percentage perception and the meaning of the percentage of elements. The meaning of the ratio of elements in the field was examined by presenting a field of 60 objects varying with regard to the percent of objects of a particular variety and asking the subjects to respond to the display in terms of Osgood's semantic differential (1957). The study of homogeneity or heterogeneity of group composition is fundamental to the study of prejudice.

OVERVIEW

Two paradigms for the study of homogeneity and heterogeneity of group membership have been outlined here. They are distinguished largely by the number of potential intervening variables that are bypassed in the analysis of the relationship between the independent and dependent variables. In the model used by Hoffman and Maier, the major thrust of the inquiry concerned the relationship between group composition (homogeneity or heterogeneity) and group productivity. Largely ignored were the intervening variables of group perception, affective group structure, and group processes.

The second model was simply concerned with the individual's perception of two sets of persons varying in heterogeneity. Other relationships in the sequence of variables presented in Figure 12.1 must be explored before we can hope to understand experiments that attempt to examine group composition and group productivity. Finally, future research should attempt to combine the first and second models, so that group characteristics and the member's perceptions of these characteristics can be examined concomitantly.

It is probably evident by now that the writer is convinced by the evidence and personal bias that the optimum general strategy for the composition of long-term groups is heterogeneity of selection according to a wide variety of variables followed by group training in accordance with the task demands, followed in turn by constant changes in group membership in order to preserve the heterogeneous base. For short-term groups with a well-demarcated task, selection may be preferred to produce groups homogeneous according to a crucial characteristic or array of characteristics.

The assumption underlying the heterogeneous composition of long-term groups (e.g., a college faculty or student body) is that the alternative of homogeneous composition is inherently narrowing. Homogeneous as opposed to heterogeneous groups, almost by definition, may be expected to hold a more narrow range of concepts and more rigid limitations on the kinds of behavior deemed acceptable. Thus, for example, it is now proposed that the initial reasons for homogeneous composition also implant a set toward preservation of homogeneity. Moreover, this assumed set toward homogeneity tends to be associated with a sharpening of the basis for homogeneity, increased narrowing of the width of the working categories, and increased exclusiveness or nonresponsiveness. Groups that attempt to preserve heterogeneity, on the other hand, may be expected to strive for increased heterogeneity, leading to increased category widths and increased inclusiveness and responsiveness to external influences. Using an approach paralleling Paradigm II as described here, the aforementioned propositions are subject to empirical test.

Earlier it was proposed that homogeneity and heterogeneity of group composition must be considered in terms of the planned group tenure. Short-term and long-term groups were assumed to present different situational demands. More generally, it is proposed that group composition must respond to the situational demands. It is now proposed that since the situation is usually in a constant state of flux and since stability of group composition is most difficult to achieve (except, perhaps, in the case of the family), group training may be a more realistic alternative for matching group characteristics and situational demands.

When the tenuous nature of groups is considered along with the varied task demands, the investment required for composing groups homogeneously for a given task demand seems highly uneconomical. The task requirements may be expected to change and change in group membership is inevitable. In each case the effort spent on selection is nontransferable and must be counted as a loss.

On the other hand, training of members and groups under conditions of changing membership is more transferable. The departing member carries the newly learned skills to a new group, and members who remain in the group should be capable of redeveloping the group and assimilating new group members. Unfortunately systematic approaches to group training have not flourished in social psychology. It is hoped that this deficiency may be remedied.

If I can be permitted one more backward look, it is astonishing that the problems outlined here have been ignored by social psychologists for so long. The transformations that follow the introduction of the individual into a group are not only intriguing, but also raise crucial theoretical issues concerning the bridge between individual and social psychology. Heterogeneous versus homogeneous group members' perceptions of other individuals and other groups is but one case in point.

REFERENCES

ALTMAN, I., & HAYTHORN, W. The ecology of isolated groups. *Behavioral Science,* 1967, **12,** 169–182.
ASCH, S. E. *Social psychology*. Englewood Cliffs, N.J.: Prentice-Hall, 1952.

BAVELAS, A., HASTORF, A. H., GROSS, A. E., & KITE, W. R. Experiments on the alteration of group structure. *Journal of Experimental Social Psychology*, 1965, **1**, 55–71.

BYRNE, D., CLORE, G. L., & NORCHEL, P. Effect of economic similarity-dissimilarity
on interpersonal attraction. *Journal of Personality and Social Psychology*, 1966,
4, 220–224.

BYRNE, D., & NELSON, D. Attraction as a linear function of proportion of reinforcements. *Journal of Personality and Social Psychology*, 1965, **2**, 884–889.

DUNCKER, K. On problem solving. *Psychological Monographs*, 1945, **58**(5, Whole
No. 270).

EXLINE, R. V., & ZILLER, R. C. Status congruency and interpersonal conflict in
decision-making groups. *Human Relations*, 1959, **12**, 147–162.

FESTINGER, L. A theory of social comparison processes. *Human Relations*, 1954, **7**,
117–140.

GOLDBERG, M. L., PASSOW, A. H., & JUSTMAN, J. *The effects of ability grouping.*
New York: Teachers College Press, 1966.

GUILFORD, J. P. *The nature of human intelligence.* New York: McGraw-Hill, 1967.

GUILFORD, J. P., & ZIMMERMAN, W. S. *The Guilford-Zimmerman temperament survey.* Beverly Hills, Calif.: Sheridan Supply, 1949.

GURNEE, H. Maze learning in the collective situation. *Journal of Psychology*, 1937,
3, 437–443.

HOFFMAN, L. R. Homogeneity of member personality and its effect on group problem-solving. *Journal of Abnormal and Social Psychology*, 1959, **58**, 27–32.

HOFFMAN, L. R., & MAIER, N. R. F. Quality and acceptance of problem solutions by
members of homogeneous and heterogeneous groups. *Journal of Abnormal and
Social Psychology*, 1961, **62**, 401–407.

HOFFMAN, L. R., & MAIER, N. R. F. An experimental re-examination of the similarity-attraction hypothesis. *Journal of Personal and Social Psychology*, 1966, **3**,
145–152.

KARIEL, H. *The decline of American pluralism.* Stanford, Calif.: Stanford University Press, 1961.

KRECH, D., CRUTCHFIELD, R. S., & BALLACHEY, E. L. *Individual in society.* New
York: McGraw-Hill, 1962.

LEVY, L. H. Group variance and group attractiveness. *Journal of Abnormal and
Social Psychology*, 1964, **68**, 661–664.

LEVY, L. H., & RICHTER, M. L. Impressions of groups as a function of the stimulus
values of their individual members. *Journal of Abnormal and Social Psychology*,
1963, **67**, 349–354.

LEVY, L. H., & STEINMEYER, C. H. Variance matching in information-source preference and judgment in social perception. *Journal of Personality and Social Psychology*, 1967, **7**, 265–270.

LINDSEY, G. Some remarks concerning incest, the incest taboo, and psychoanalytic
theory. *American Psychologist*, 1967, **22**, 1051–1065.

LORGE, I., TUCKMAN, J., AIKMAN, L., SPIEGEL, J., & MOSS, G. Solutions by teams
and by individuals to a field problem at different levels of reality. *Journal of Educational Psychology*, 1955, **46**, 17–24.

MAIER, N. R. F. Reasoning in humans. I. On direction. *Journal of Comparative Psychology*, 1930, **10**, 115–144.

MAIER, N. R. F. *Principles of human relations.* New York: Wiley, 1952.

MAIER, N. R. F., & SOLEM, E. R. The contribution of a discussion leader to the quality of group thinking: The effective use of minority opinions. *Human Relations,* 1952, **5,** 277–288.

MAIER, N. R. F., SOLEM, E. R., & MAIER, A. A. *Supervisory and executive development.* New York: Wiley, 1957.

OSGOOD, C. E., SUCI, G. J., & TANNENBAUM, P. H. *The measurement of meaning.* Urbana, Ill.: University of Illinois Press, 1957.

RAY, W. S. Complex tasks for use in human problems. *Psychological Bulletin,* 1955, **52,** 134–149.

SCHEERER, M. Cognitive theory. In G. Lindsey (Ed.), *Handbook of Social Psychology.* Cambridge, Mass.: Addison-Wesley, 1954. Pp. 91–137.

SPENCE, K. W. Cognitive versus stimulus-response theories of learning. *Psychological Review,* 1950, **57,** 159–172.

SPENCE, K. W. Theoretical interpretations of learning. In S. S. Stevens (Ed.), *Handbook of Experimental Psychology.* New York: Wiley, 1951. Pp. 690–729.

THOMAS, E. J., & FINK, C. F. Effects of group size. *Psychological Bulletin,* 1963, **60,** 371–384.

VOIERS, W. D. Bombing accuracy as a function of the ground school proficiency structure of the B-29 bomb team. *Research Report,* Air Force Personnel & Training Research Center, Lackland Air Force Base, San Antonio, Texas, 1955.

ZILLER, R. C. Group size: A determinant of the quality and stability of group decisions. *Sociometry,* 1957, **22,** 165–173.

ZILLER, R. C. Toward a theory of open and closed groups. *Psychological Bulletin,* 1965, **64,** 164–182.

ZILLER, R. C., & BEHRINGER, R. D. Motivational and perceptual effects in orientation toward a newcomer. *Journal of Social Psychology,* 1965, **66,** 79–90.

ZILLER, R. C., & BEHRINGER, R. D. Race and ratio perception: A perceptual model of a social phenomenon. Unpublished manuscript, University of Oregon, 1967.

ZILLER, R. C., & EXLINE, R. V. Some consequences of age heterogeneity in decision-making groups. *Sociometry,* 1958, **47,** 57–66.

GROUP DECISIONS
INVOLVING EQUITABLE
AND OPTIMAL DISTRIBUTION
OF STATUS[1]

Eugene Burnstein
Stuart Katz

Efficient group performance usually requires a rational division of labor. Among other things this means that certain persons are expected to contribute a great deal to the group product and to strongly determine its value; others are expected to contribute little and to have slight influence on its value. Usually a member's power to determine group performance depends on his competence. If people want the best possible joint outcome, such an arrangement must appear eminently logical. Moreover, because individuals in everyday life usually differ in ability, it should be commonplace for members to award control to the more able. Thus a person will know from logical analysis as well as from experience that joint outcomes suffer when the skillful and unskillful determine group performance in equal measure. The obvious implication is that when individuals vary in competence and care about their joint outcome, they readily agree to have the contribution of the skillful performer count for more than that of the unskillful.

Despite the flawless logic, the reader is probably suspicious of this argument. Ordinary experience tells us that invidious distinctions are not accepted gladly; and even in *ad hoc* laboratory groups, differences between members along a value-laden dimension such as responsibility or power are not likely to be achieved without difficulty. The term *status* is used here to refer to such differences. Specifically, we are concerned with the extent to which an individual's performance is permitted to influence, contribute to, or determine the outcome for the group. As will be shown, sometimes one can specify exactly how much difference in status should exist among members in order to produce the maxi-

[1] This research was supported by National Science Foundation Grant 570.

mum benefit for the group. Let us call such a distribution of status *optimal*. The studies that follow are concerned with the problems encountered by groups in deciding to distribute status optimally. The difficulties to be examined arise when status distinctions that are optimal for the group as a whole are unjust to individual members.

Often the degree to which people differ in status is not commensurate with the extent to which they differ in competence. For instance, consider two high school students, P and O, neither of whom can afford college tuition and thus cannot continue their education unless they receive scholarships. They take an exam which will be used by a committee in allocating the limited number of scholarships available. P does slightly better than O. As a result the former is awarded a scholarship whereas the latter is not. Intuitively this is neither just, fair, nor equitable, because the slight superiority of P over O on the exam is hardly commensurate with the gross differences in their life chances produced by the committee's decision which in effect permits P a college education but denies it to O. Furthermore, the members of the scholarship committee as well as P and O probably recognize this and are upset and embarrassed, albeit to different degrees. Even if they believe that selection according to ability bene-fits society as a whole, the immediate inequities to individuals are difficult to ignore. An analogous but less poignant dilemma is created in the present study: sometimes optimal status distinctions, which in the long run are most beneficial for the group as a whole, violate common standards of equity, in that they are disproportionately large compared to the differences in ability among members.

The social psychological conception of equity (Adams, 1965; Blau, 1964; Homans, 1961; Leventhal & Bergman, 1969) generally has been formulated in terms of the relationship between two ratios: (a) the profit a person receives for his performance relative to the investment he makes by virtue of this per-formance; and (b) the profit comparable others receive, relative to the invest-ment they make. Investments may be reflected simply by the time, energy, or skill the person devotes to the activity. Profits depend on the rewards received minus the costs incurred. Note that rewards refer not only to material benefits but also to the prestige, respect, and affection given by others for engaging in the activity. Similarly, costs refer not only to material losses, due either directly to the present activity or to foregoing attractive alternative activities, but also to the disrespect or disaffection shown by others. Inequity, by definition, increases as the ratios depart from equality, and this will occur if there is a change in the individual's invesment or profit relative to that of others. Thus if P worked extremely hard to prepare for the exam while O did nothing but convince a brilliant friend to stand in and both P and O were awarded scholarships, an inequity would still exist. While they profited equally, P's investment was con-siderably greater, making their respective ratios of profit to investment unequal.

Inequities are assumed to have noxious effects. Those who benefit (their pro-fits increase or their investments decrease relative to others) as well as those who are injured (their profits decrease or their investments increase relative to others) are said to experience embarrassment and perhaps guilt or anger if the injustice is especially strong. Such emotional consequences would in all likelihood be enhanced when, as in the present studies, the gains or losses are public. Therefore, the individual desires to maintain or restore equity and will act to satisfy this desire. For example, in work by Adams (1965), individuals who were over-rewarded in terms of their qualifications for a job tended to increase their output if they were paid by the hour (an increase in their investment) and to decrease their output by lavishing extra care on their work if they were paid by the piece (a decrease in their profits as well as an increase in their investment).

While there is reasonably good evidence that the person will attempt to restore equity when the decision is his alone to make, it is not at all clear that restoration will be undertaken when it requires collective action, or, if undertaken, that it reflects a collective desire for equity. One should not infer that members are striving for justice merely because their decision happens to be just. Most group decisions, including those which correct an injustice, depend on the coordination of individual preferences. For instance, if some members of our scholarship committee want to weigh a student's need more heavily than his ability, while others wish to give ability greater weight, no awards at all could be made until they first decided how to coordinate or combine these different preferences. Now, suppose the opportunities for these committee members to communicate are very limited and/or they must commit themselves to a position ahead of time, before discussion. Further suppose they would like to agree as quickly as possible and with as little bickering as possible. That is to say, the efficient coordination of individual choices is important but problematic. Under these conditions, which to some extent obtain in many experiments on group decisions, each member will want to take a position that will be acceptable to his partner. If standards of equity (or any other decision rule for that matter) are perceived as shared and salient, the person may well use them as a guide in selecting such a position to espouse. Hence, equitable behavior can occur because members wish to facilitate agreement and not because they are concerned that justice be done.

A similar point has been made by Schelling (1960): Among a range of possible decisions (in our case, various distributions of status) there may be some which for several reasons (e.g., precedent or mathematical simplicity) are compelling foci for agreement, independent of their equity; thus, the agreement ". . . may not be so much conspicuously fair or conspicuously in balance with estimated bargaining powers as just plain 'conspicuous' [p. 69]." One classic illustration is a tacit bargaining situation (no explicit communication between participants is permitted) in which two individuals must coordinate their decisions to apportion $100 between them so that the sum of the amounts each requests for himself does not exceed the amount to be divided. A 50-50 split is almost inevitable. This would be equitable if $50 had approximately the same value to both individuals. How about if one individual happens to be a pauper and the other a millionaire?

In addition, there is the obvious consideration that selfishness may dominate.

If some members benefit from an inequity and will be deprived of this benefit when equity is restored, the problem of coordinating individual decisions to achieve agreement could be tricky. Vested interest can weaken inclinations to fairness, particularly when the inequity is perceived as desirable for the membership on other grounds. Thus, because an inequitable distribution of status is recognized as necessary in order that the group as a whole benefit from their performance (e.g., it makes for a more rational division of responsibility), certain members may be provided with sufficient justification for enjoying their unexpected eminence. At least they may not rush to redress matters. Whereas in other circumstances, say, when the members cannot argue that the group as a whole will benefit from a more rational distribution, the embarrassment over their unfair advantage might readily induce them to redistribute status more equitably. The issue then is whether an inequity which benefits some and harms others will be sufficiently distressing to *both* sets of individuals to induce them to agree on collective action to restore equity, independent of the desire to agree for reasons unrelated to equity (say, in order to minimize bickering).

PRELIMINARY STUDIES

The first two experiments were mainly designed to explore a method we hoped to use throughout our research. It had two important advantages. The variables could be manipulated with reasonable precision and a detailed sample of behavior could be obtained continuously over time. However, the procedure was highly artificial. Thus we were uncertain that subjects would become engaged or that considerations of equity would affect the simple responses involved. These preliminary studies were conducted to learn if more or less standard equity effects, some of which have been found in realistic settings (e.g., Adams, 1965), could be observed under our rather antiseptic conditions.

One effect of inequity observed by Adams has already been mentioned. This involved changes in individual performances which reduced an inequity based on over- or underpayment. In the present experimental situation the comparable result would be indicated by appropriate changes in the effort a member devotes to the group task. We are interpreting status as a reward which the group confers on a member, and his effort as a member's investment in group activity. Thus, when abruptly stripped of responsibility, a member's effort should decrease. When he is suddenly awarded additional responsibility, his effort should increase.

The second equity phenomenon we hoped to observe has to do with the circumstances which induce groups to redistribute status. Our procedure permits changes in status to occur only when the group explicitly decides to institute them. Equity theory implies that after a long interval of stable performance abrupt changes in status should be avoided if possible. Decisions of this kind will be resisted until there is appreciable evidence that the promotion or demotion is warranted and, thus, equitable.

Consider the member who performed extremely well for a period of time and had been awarded high status by his co-workers. He has accumulated much profit (respect, prestige) and has made a sizable investment (effort, skill). If at a later point he begins to perform poorly, his investment will appear to decline relative to his profit. As a result, in time his ratio of profit to investment will become uncomfortably large compared with that of other members, and according to the theory an inequity will exist. The group then will be induced to restore equity. One way is to reduce the status (the profit) of this member. (Theoretically, there are other possibilities, but they are precluded by our experimental procedure. For example, the others could attempt to goad this member into improving his performance. Aside from being unreliable, goading would be extremely difficult because discussion is ruled out during performance.) A similar analysis can be made when a low status member who performed incompetently for a long period begins to improve. In either case the strength of the inequity will depend on an accumulation of instances that are discrepant with past experience. Given a long past history of stable differences in status and performance, the profit to investment ratios would not be much affected by a few discrepant events. Therefore, sudden changes in status, those made at the first sign of changing performance, are unlikely. In fact, if status and performance have been stable, an abrupt promotion or demotion can itself be inequitable.

Resistance to an abrupt change may be weakened, however, if members believe their joint profits will be enhanced as a result; that is, they might expect the cost incurred by quickly raising or lowering the status of a few members of legendary skill or incompetence will be compensated by an overall increase in value of the group outcome which they foresee will result from these changes. Thus, additional justification, for example, a clear awareness that a member's performance has reliably fallen or improved, may not be needed and the decision can be made rapidly. This would not be the case if a group believes its chances of achieving an attractive outcome are nil, regardless of how status is allocated. In the latter circumstance there is unlikely to be much compensation for an embarrassingly abrupt redistribution of status. As a result, such decisions will be avoided until there is reliable evidence of a change in performance which justifies the decision. In brief, the likelihood of a group decision to upgrade or to downgrade members or the speed with which it is made should depend directly on the extent to which the decision will improve the group's chances of success.

Experiment I

In our first experiment performers are made to differ in apparent ability on a group task. Initially a member's status, how much his performance counts in determining the group outcome, is perfectly correlated with his apparent ability—the more successful the performer, the more his performance counts. Thus, initially the distribution of status is completely equitable as well as optimal, and remains so for a large number of trials. Then, in one condition the competence of the most responsible member, the individual who had been most successful, suddenly decreases; in a second condition, the competence of the least responsible member, the individual who had been least successful, suddenly increases. A group has the option to redistribute responsibility following each and every trial block. As will be seen, up to the point at which the dramatic change in performance is introduced, this option is almost always ignored by the members. At that point, however, it is quickly seized. In short order a decision is made to redistribute status more rationally, by downgrading the high status member whose performance is faltering or upgrading the low status member who is rallying. When this is done at the first sign of a change in performance, the group appears to give little consideration to the members' past efforts. Hence, their decision is rational (given the shift in relative competence it will maximize the value of the group outcome), but according to equity theory it is unfair.

Our main interest' centers on the consequences of such decisions for the effort a member expends on the group task. Equity theory suggests that the effects of downgrading are likely to be quite different from those of upgrading. Specifically, a member will decrease his effort if he has displayed great competence for an extended period of time and is abruptly downgraded following a decline in his performance; conversely, a member will increase his effort if he has displayed little competence in the past but is suddenly upgraded following an improvement in his performance.

Procedure. We will describe the general features of our procedure here in detail and only give brief consideration to them in the later experiments. The Group Reaction Time Apparatus that was used in all of our studies consists of individual panels and a control console operated by the experimenter. Each panel contains stimulus lights, failure signals, and reaction keys. In the present experiment, simple reaction times were observed for four-man groups. In all conditions the onset of a white light on the subjects' panels constituted the critical stimulus. Subjects were required to press their reaction keys as quickly as they could after its onset. They were informed that a reaction will be considered "successful" if, and only if, it occurs within a certain specified time interval following stimulus onset. Reactions that had longer latencies were defined for the subjects as "failures," and they were signaled by red "failure" lights on the subjects' panels. Actually, the appearance of the failure light was controlled by the experimenter independently of the person's reactions and according to a fixed schedule described below. The subjects sat within two to three feet of each other and could easily observe each other's panels and the appearance of failure lights (for additional information about the apparatus, see Zajonc, 1965).

Immediately after coming to the laboratory, the four subjects were seated in front of their individual panels and the operation of the stimulus lights and reaction keys was explained. Baseline reaction time data were obtained first in a series of 20 trials. Subjects were instructed to press their reaction keys as quickly as they could upon the onset of the stimulus lights on their panels. After a "ready" signal, the stimulus light was turned on by the experimenter. In all cases the subject's reaction turned off his stimulus light, and his reaction time was recorded by the experimenter. The subjects were told that their tasks would be to work as a group in playing a simple game. The game was described as follows:

> Fifty similar groups will be run in this study of team performance. Each group will have the same opportunity to earn a number of points. At the end of the study, the four members of the group with the most points will each receive $10.00. In order to receive points at least two or more members must press quickly enough to beat the red "failure" light. The latter will appear on a member's panel when he does not press within a fixed interval of time after the signal. [The failure signal remained on for 12 seconds.] On each trial, if two or more members beat the failure light, the group is eligible to receive points. However, since each member will be assigned a different number of points to contribute to the group total, the amount of points the group receives will depend on which members beat the failure light. If a member does not beat the failure light, he can contribute nothing. If only one member is successful, the group receives no points regardless of the number of points he is assigned.

One block of five trials was given so that subjects might become accustomed to working against the failure signal. After this practice block, the experimenter distributed counters which indicated the number of points each member could contribute to the group's total if his reaction was ostensibly "successful," and if there was at least one other member with a "successful" reaction. The group member whose baseline reaction time was shortest appeared to have made only one failure out of the five practice trials. For his "good" performance he was given a counter labeled "100." The member with the second shortest baseline reaction time was made to appear to have made two failures, and received a counter labeled "80." The member with the third fastest baseline reaction time evidenced three failures and was awarded a "40" counter, while the member with the slowest baseline reaction time was made to fail four times on the practice trial block, and was awarded the "20" counter. We shall refer to these subjects of different ranks as R-1, R-2, R-3, and R-4, respectively.

On the practice block, and for three successive blocks, the appearance of the failure signal was controlled in the following manner: R-1 was made to appear successful on 90 percent of the trials over these four trial blocks, R-2 on 70 percent, R-3 on 50 percent, and R-4 on 30 percent. Following the practice block, at least two members were regularly made to succeed. This, of course, enabled the subjects to contribute points to the group's total on all trials.

Immediately after the fifth trial block, it was explained that henceforth after every block of five trials, the members would be asked to vote on whether they wanted to change the rank assignments. Each subject was given a ballot on which he was privately to record his vote. After the first vote, which took place immediately after the sixth trial block, and after all subsequent votes, the experimenter would examine the ballots in front of the members and indicate whether or not there was a unanimous vote favoring change. When such unanimity occurred, the group members were given a few minutes to discuss and to agree on what changes to make in the assignment of ranks. The experimenter always reallocated the points according to the decisions reached by the groups.

The pattern of success remained constant for two more trial blocks. On the ninth block changes in apparent success were instituted according to the requirements of two experimental conditions. In Condition I, R-1 subjects were reduced from 90 percent to 40 percent of apparent success, while all the remaining ranks were brought to 60 percent. On the tenth trial block R-1 subjects were further reduced to 20 percent success and remained at this level thereafter. All other ranks in this condition remained at 60 percent success level from the ninth trial block on. Twenty groups were run in the above manner.

In the 20 groups of Condition II, R-4 subjects were made to appear successful on 60 percent rather than 30 percent of the trials, while the remaining three group members were successful only 40 percent of the time. On the tenth trial block R-4 subjects were moved up to 80 percent of apparent success and continued at this level until the conclusion of the experimental session. The remaining three group members in Condition II continued at 40 percent of success from the ninth trial block on. The experimental session was terminated when (a) no unanimous "yes" vote occurred across 15 blocks of five trials each; (b) no second unanimous "yes" vote occurred within three blocks after the first reallocation of ranks; or (c) no unanimous "yes" vote occurred within one block after the second reallocation of points.

Results.   Figure 13.1 shows the average reaction times in milliseconds for R-1 subjects in Condition I and for R-4 subjects in Condition II. The data are presented in three segments. The first shows performance on the last baseline trial block (fourth trial block) and on the first trial block when the failure signals were first introduced. There is a clear effect evident in figure 13.1, with R-4 subjects in Condition II showing a greater improvement in performance than R-1 subjects in Condition I.[2] Of course, these former subjects saw themselves succeeding on only one out of five trials, whereas the latter saw themselves succeeding on four out of five. However, this effect cannot be unequivocally attributed to the introduction of failure signals alone because these two categories of subjects also differed in their baseline reaction times. The data for the initial segment of Figure 13.1 were therefore treated by analysis of covariance, which showed these changes in R-4 versus R-1 subjects' performances to be significant even when corrected for the initial baseline differences.

The second segment of the results shown in Figure 13.1 deals with the effects of the further success manipulation, which was designed to lead ultimately to a change in rank assignments. The curves in the second segment of Figure 13.1 begin immediately after the experimenter assigned points differentiating the members' contributions to the group total, trial block 6. They end prior to any changes in rank assignments which were instituted by the groups themselves, that is, on trial block 10. Both R-1 and R-4 subjects show a slight improvement in performance up to trial block 8. But as soon as the percent of apparent

---

[2] Unless otherwise specified, all the findings discussed in this paper are significant at the alpha level of .05 or better.

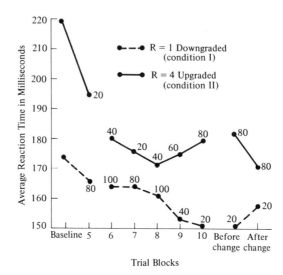

Figure 13.1

Average reaction time for R-1 subjects in Condition I and R-4 subjects in Condition II over various segments of the experimental session. Figures at the points of the graph indicate percent of apparent success for the given trial block (from Burnstein & Zajonc, 1965b, p. 22).

success begins to change (on the ninth trial block), there are clear changes in performance. For members whose apparent success begins to decline (R-1 in Condition I), performance shows a definite improvement from that trial block on. On the other hand, subjects who become more successful on trial block nine (R-4 in Condition II) show a decided drop in performance. These results are entirely consistent with previous studies (Zajonc, 1962; Zajonc & Taylor, 1963) in which a similar negative correlation between the probability of success and performance was found. In these previous studies, however, performance feedback was accurate.

In all groups a reallocation of status took place as a consequence of changes in the apparent success of the group members. On the twelfth trial block, 19 of the 40 groups agreed to make a change in rank assignments, and by the fourteenth, all groups made appropriate changes. (By *appropriate* is meant that, in Condition I, R-1 subjects were downgraded, and, in Condition II, R-4 subjects were upgraded in rank. If a status reallocation did not involve R-1 in Condition I or R-4 in Condition II, it was considered "inappropriate.") When the 20 R-1 subjects of Condition I were reduced in status in this four-man hierarchy, 7 of them were downgraded to the lowest rank, 6 to the third rank, and 7 to the second. Of the 20 R-4 subjects in Condition II, 8 were upgraded to the highest rank, 5 to the second highest, and 7 to the third.

The third segment of Figure 13.1 shows the average reaction time for R-1 subjects in Condition I and for R-4 subjects in Condition II on the blocks immediately following their respective demotions and promotions. It is evident that upgrading affected performance favorably, while downgrading affected it adversely. Again, however, the groups differed in reaction time on the block preceding change, and a covariance technique was therefore applied to these data. The F ratio for the adjusted effects of shifts in rank was significant. Answers to a postexperimental questionnaire indicated that subjects in each condition were sensitive to individual differences in apparent performance. For example, the mean number of failures attributed to members of different ranks during the first 10 trials was as follows (the actual number of failures induced by the experimenter is given in parenthesis): R-1, 1.0 (1); R-2, 3.6 (3); R-3, 5.2 (5); R-4, 6.8 (7).

Experiment II

The second experiment was similar to the first in most respects except that in one condition there were higher expectations of achieving a valuable outcome than in another. When these expectations had been created, the group found it could improve its chances still further by redistributing status. As before, this involved downgrading R-1 or upgrading R-4, both of whose performances suddenly changed. Clearly, if the group waited a decent period in order to be certain of R-1's decline and R-4's improvement, it would render the decision more equitable. But to do so would endanger the group's chances of winning. This justification for not waiting long before redistributing status, however, exists only to the extent that the group believes its opportunities to win are already fairly good. Thus, it was expected that "unsuccessful" groups, who should feel their chances are poor, regardless of *who* has *how much* responsibility, if they made such a decision at all, would require more trials before redistributing, than "successful" groups, who believe they have a good opportunity to win.

Procedure. Aside from the manipulation of group success, the procedure was identical to that of the preceding study. Recall that in describing the task to the participants, the following was given as the criterion for group success: "At the end of the study, the four members of the group with most points will each receive $10.00. *In order to receive points at least two or more members must press quickly enough to beat the red failure light. . . .* If only one member is successful, the group receives no points regardless of the number of points he is assigned."

The pattern of success was identical to that in Experiment I for the first eight trial blocks. On the ninth block, group and individual success were manipulated by the experimenter according to the requirements of four experimental conditions. In *Condition I*, R-1 subjects were reduced to 40 percent of apparent success, while all the remaining ranks were brought to 60 percent. On the tenth trial block R-1 subjects were further reduced to 20 percent success and remained at that level throughout. The minimal criterion of group success (i.e., at least two members succeeding) was met on every trial. In *Condition II*, the changes in individual performance were identical to that in Condition I. However, individual successes were so spaced within a block that the criterion of group success was met only on two of the five trials. Thus, the groups in this condition failed to meet the minimal performance criterion of two or more members beating the red "failure" light on 60 percent of the trials, chosen at random.

In *Condition III*, R-4 subjects were made to appear successful on 60 percent of the trials, while the remaining three members were successful only 40 percent of the time. On the tenth trial block, R-4 subjects were moved up to 80 percent of apparent success and continued at this level until the conclusion of the experimental session. The remaining three members continued at 40 percent of success from the ninth trial block on. Group success was continuous. In *Condition IV*, changes in individual performance were identical to those in Condition III. However, as in Condition II, successful individual performances were spaced so that the group met the success criterion on only 40 percent of the trials. Hence, in Conditions I and II the marked incongruence between performance and status was achieved by reducing the apparent success of R-1 subjects, and in Conditions III and IV, by increasing the apparent performance of R-4 subjects. At the same time, groups in Conditions I and III met the minimal performance criterion and received points 100 percent of the time, whereas those in Conditions II and IV met it only 40 percent of the time. Thus groups in the former conditions would be more likely to win the prize for most points than groups in the latter. Ten groups were observed in each condition.

Results.   Subjects' ratings of how likely their group was to win the prize for the most points and how well it performed during the first and second half of the session give some indication of our effectiveness in manipulating group success. The mean ratings of the likelihood of winning the prize are presented in Table 13.1. There is a significant difference between continuous versus intermittent success. The evaluation of group performance during each half of the experiment is presented in Table 13.2. Again, group success accounts for an appreciable amount of the variance. The difference between the halves was also significant.

Table 13.1

Mean Estimates of the Likelihood of Winning the Prize

	Group Success	
Direction of Change	CONTINUOUS	INTERMITTENT
R-1 reduced to R-4	7.2[a]	8.5
R-4 increased to R-1	6.7	8.7

SOURCE. Burnstein and Zajonc (1965a), p. 354.
[a] 1 = Certain of winning; 13 = Certain of not winning.

Table 13.2

Mean Evaluation of Group Performance during the First and Second Halves of the Trials

| | *Group Success* | | | |
| | CONTINUOUS | | INTERMITTENT | |
Direction of Change	FIRST HALF	SECOND HALF	FIRST HALF	SECOND HALF
R-1 reduced to R-4	4.8[a]	5.3	4.5	6.9
R-4 increased to R-1	4.7	5.1	4.8	7.4

SOURCE. Burnstein and Zajonc (1965a), p. 354.

[a] 1 = Performed extremely well; 13 = Performed extremely poorly.

The first time each group had an opportunity to discuss how to reallocate points, the experimenter observed and ranked each member in terms of the amount to which he participated. On 5 occasions, however, these rankings could not be made; therefore, participation data are available for only 35 groups. The number of members falling into each participation rank as a function of the status (points) assigned them is presented in Table 13.3. Although we have no data on the reliability of these rankings and have therefore not analyzed these results further, there seems to be a strong positive relationship between the amount of participation and status, especially when the highest status member (R-1) is to be reduced to the lowest status, which is somewhat curious. We will return to this finding in the next study. Let us now consider the shifts in status. In Conditions I and II, an *appropriate* change is one that demotes the R-1 subject to *any* lower rank; in Conditions II and IV it is a change that raises the R-4 subject to *any* higher status. The *optimal* change in the former two conditions is that which displaces R-1 to R-4; in the latter conditions it is that which displaces R-4 to R-1. The number of groups making appropriate or optimal changes at various points in the experimental session is shown in Table 13.4. One group in Condition IV did not reallocate status at all over 15 blocks. The effects of group success are significant for both appropriate and optimal changes. It is clear that groups working with continuous success redistribute status in a rational manner sooner than groups working under intermittent success.

Results of the two preliminary experiments seemed quite satisfactory. Sooner or later almost all groups decided to distribute status in an appropriate or optimal fashion. As expected, groups that already had a good chance of achieving a valuable outcome made this decision more rapidly than those who had only a poor chance. We assumed that equity would constrain groups from making such a decision until they were certain of the apparent increment or decrement in a member's performance. However, these constraints would be less effective under continuous success conditions, where the group's chances were good, and there was considerable justification in trying to improve them further, than under intermittent success, where they were already poor and there was little justification in trying for improvement. Thus, groups in the former condition would be less likely to hold off on their decision for a decent interval (when upgrading or downgrading would be more equitable). Moreover, it seems that effort, in terms of reaction time, changes when status is redistributed. As equity theory would predict, if a member is abruptly demoted, his effort decreases, and if he is suddenly promoted, his effort increases.

Table 13.3

Number of Members Falling into Each Participation Rank as a Function of the Status (Responsibility) Initially Assigned Them

	R-1 changed to R-4 (Conditions I and II)			
	PARTICIPATION RANK			
Initial Status	1	2	3	4
R-1	11	3	2	0
R-2	3	5	6	2
R-3	1	3	8	4
R-4	2	4	6	4

	R-4 changed to R-1 (Conditions III and IV)			
	PARTICIPATION RANK			
Initial Status	1	2	3	4
R-1	7	9	2	1
R-2	6	4	7	2
R-3	3	4	8	4
R-4	2	3	6	8

Table 13.4

Number of Groups Making Appropriate and Optimal Changes as a Function of Group Success

	Trial Block on Which Change Was Made			
Condition	9–10	11–12	13–14	15 OR NO CHANGE
Appropriate Changes				
(I, III) Continuous Success	12	5	3	0
(II, IV) Intermittent Success	5	10	3	2
Optimal Change				
(I, III) Continuous Success	8	5	7	0
(II, IV) Intermittent Success	1	8	6	5

SOURCE. Burnstein and Zajonc (1965a), p. 356.

STATUS AS A REWARD

Experiment III

The findings from our preliminary research are consistent with equity theory, but at the same time they are open to other interpretations (e.g., see Burnstein & Zajonc, 1965a, 1965b) because of certain weakness in the experimental design. For example, there is no direct evidence that a member's position in the group was important to him. It merely seemed plausible that status would be rewarding and that abrupt changes in status without regard to past performance would be perceived as unfair. If status was not rewarding, then no inequity was produced by the abrupt promotions and demotions, and the observed effects must be due to some process other than restoring equity. Note also that the members had little choice *how* to redistribute status. The extent to which a member's performance determined the group outcome was indicated by the value on his counter, and these values were fixed. The counters could be shifted about among members but the values themselves could not be altered. Someone had to have "100," "80," "40," and "20," and it was clear who ought to have "100," or "20," even if the group would have preferred another set of values which imposed smaller (or greater) distinctions. The members, therefore, had no opportunity to decide between an *equitable* and an *optimal distribution of status*. The choice was mainly one of timing, between imposing an optimal distribution right now or waiting awhile. Perhaps, by fixing the precise amounts a performance must count and thereby eliminating alternative distributions, the experimenter removed an important source of conflict.

How then can we be more certain that a particular group decision violated equity? There is no lack of means. For example, in the context of the preceding experiments there might have been other conditions in which groups had much less past experience which justified a member's initial status before being faced with the necessity of promoting or demoting him. If only a very limited sample of performance by high or low status members is available before a shift in performance occurs, then the ratio of profit to investment will be based on a small number of cases and can be readily affected by the shift. In this case, when there is little justification for tenure in R-1 or R-4, sudden changes in the distribution of status should seem less inequitable and occur more rapidly, with minimal effect on effort. This is one of several possibilities. The following study (Burnstein & Wolosin, 1968) takes advantage of some others. It creates conditions in which a large number of alternative distributions of status are available, some being more equitable than optimal (and vice versa). In addition, for certain conditions status is made a highly significant reward for the person; in others it is insignificant. Optimal distributions of status involving the former should produce strong inequities while those involving the latter should not.

Our general proposition is that an optimal distribution of status which creates an inequity will be more difficult to achieve than one that does not. To clarify these circumstances, that is, the conditions under which equity is violated, let us consider the following example. Two individuals are engaged in a group task that extends over a long series of trials. After each trial the group receives a payoff in which each member shares equally. The value of the joint outcome depends on which performer succeeds and how much his performance counts. Say the maximum value of the joint outcome for any trial is 20 cents and the two individuals can decide the extent to which each of their performances determines the outcome. Thus, they may share responsibility for the outcome equally so that each performer adds 10 cents to the outcome if he succeeds and nothing if he fails; in this case, when *both* succeed they win the maximum, 20 cents, and when *either* one fails and the other one succeeds they obtain one-half of the maximum, 10 cents. Of course, if both fail, they receive nothing for that trial. Suppose, however, they decide that one of them should have higher status, say, that his performance should count for three-quarters of the joint outcome, 15 cents, and that the other's performance should count for one-quarter, 5 cents. Now when both succeed, they still obtain the maximum of 20 cents. But, if only one succeeds, the joint outcome is either 15 cents or 5 cents, depending on which member is successful.

If each member is equally likely to succeed it makes no difference, in terms of the expected value of their joint outcome, how status is allocated. On the other hand, when one member is more likely to succeed than the other, it makes a considerable difference. In the latter case, the value of their joint outcome can be maximized if and only if the more successful performer is given greater weight. It is important to observe that in this hypothetical situation the weights given to performers are combined additively, when they succeed, to determine the value of the group outcome. Given this rule for combining individual performances, it is clear that when individual differences in the likelihood of success exist, regardless of the size of the difference, the rational solution is to assign total responsibility to the more successful performer. Only then will the group be able to achieve an outcome of maximal value. Table 13.5 demonstrates that having each performance count equally or having one count more than the other has no effect on the outcome if members are equally successful. But when one member is more successful than the other, they will obtain their most profitable joint outcome only if the former is given complete responsibility—regardless of whether he is a great deal or just slightly better.

We make the same two assumptions as before (but this time it is possible to show what happens when they do not hold). First, a group decision to assign one member higher status than the other is, among other things, public recognition of the respect in which he is held as a performer. It legitimizes his superiority. When this cannot be assumed, the consequences for optimizing status are quite different, as will soon be clear. Second, the effort and skill a member commits to the task denote his investment. This is demonstrated to others by the frequency with which one performs successfully. It is well known, however, that success does not always reflect effort. What happens in this case is also demonstrated.

Table 13.5

The Relationship between the Expected Value of a Joint Outcome and the Probability of Success (Ps) of Two Performers (A and B) When They Are Assigned Equal or Different Weights

	$Ps(A)$		$Weight(A)$		$Ps(B)$		$Weight(B)$	Expected Value
No difference in Ps	.7	×	10	+	.7	×	10	14
	.7	×	15	+	.7	×	5	14
	.7	×	20	+	.7	×	0	14
Small difference in Ps	.8	×	10	+	.6	×	10	14
	.8	×	15	+	.6	×	5	15
	.8	×	20	+	.6	×	0	16
Large difference in Ps	.9	×	10	+	.5	×	10	14
	.9	×	15	+	.5	×	5	16
	.9	×	20	+	.5	×	0	18

SOURCE. Burnstein and Wolosin (1968), p. 418.

In the present experimental setup, the optimal or rational distribution of responsibility is one in which the more successful member's performance is permitted to completely determine the joint outcome. Since status is ordinarily a reward, it follows that such a distribution will be more inequitable, and therefore more difficult to achieve, when individual differences in performance are small than when they are large. When differences are large the more successful performer, by virtue of his extraordinary effort and skill, has made a much larger investment in the activity than has his co-worker; thus, large differences in reward are justified and there is no appreciable violation of equity in the former's receiving the overwhelming share of responsibility for the group outcome. When, however, differences in performance are small, the superior performer has made an only slightly greater investment than his partner; under these conditions very large differences in reward are unjustified, and the assignment of complete responsibility to the superior performer would create an appreciable inequity even though it would produce the best joint outcome.

As before status is defined in terms of the responsibility associated with a position. If a person's position is to be a source of the embarrassment which is assumed to accompany an injustice, it is critical that status be interpreted as the group's evaluation of the individual performer, that it be seen in large part as reflecting the esteem in which his performance is held. Were it not possible to interpret status as an evaluation of the individual performer, or were such evaluations inconsequential to the performer, gains or losses in status would have no significance as rewards or costs. This implies that when distinctions in terms of status are instituted but do not reflect an evaluation of consequence to the group or the performer, equity is not likely to be violated, even if the difference in status is grossly disproportional to the difference in individual performance.

In the following experiment, in addition to the case in which assigned status reflects an important evaluation, we will examine two conditions in which decisions to increase the status of the more successful performer and to decrease that of the less successful performer should have little significance as rewards or costs: (a) where individual success or failure is not determined by effort or skill but by some external agent such as the experimenter or chance; and (b) where task performance is perceived to reflect a totally unimportant proficiency.

Procedure. The apparatus and general procedure were similar to that of the preliminary experiments except that (a) group size was reduced to two, (b) chips instead of counters indicated responsibility, and (c) additional instructions were used to vary the significance of status. As soon as possible after coming into the laboratory the two subjects were introduced to one another and told that they would be working as a group after they mastered their individual tasks. After the practice trials, the subjects were told:

> A group will receive points when at least one member, either of you, presses fast enough to prevent the failure light from coming on. If either member beats the failure light, he contributes his points to the group total. If both members beat the failure light, the sum of both members' points is added to the group total. If neither member beats the failure light, the group gets nothing for that trial. The number of points a member can contribute is indicated by the number of poker chips he has—here are 10 chips for each of you [p. 420].

Examples were then given of how the group's total would depend on whether each member had the same or a different number of chips, and, whether one or both players succeeded or failed. For instance,

> . . . if one member has 15 chips, and the other member has five chips, then if only the first member beats the failure light, the group gets 15 points; if only the second member beats the failure light, the group gets five points; and if both members beat the failure light, the group gets 20 points. If neither member beats the failure light, the group gets nothing. Is this clear? All groups participating in the study have the same point system and thus the same chance to earn points [p. 420].

At this point, the task-importance induction was given to the subjects. Groups were assigned randomly to one of three importance conditions:

Important Performance (IP)
Let me now briefly give you some background on what you will be doing. Each of you will perform a reaction-time task.[3] This is one of the oldest and still one of the most widely used tasks in studying individual differences in sensory-motor capacity. Originally, in the 1870's, psychologists were interested in the efficiency with which a person responded to various classes of stimuli. For example, would visual signals produce a more rapid reaction than auditory signals? From such work much was learned of how the central nervous system processes information

[3] The reader who is unfamiliar with the reaction time literature should be warned that the statements made to the subjects are completely contrived, for example, the relationship between reaction time and intelligence or personality, and have no factual basis.

transmitted by the different senses. Early research established that individual differences in reaction time reflected differences in sensory-motor functioning in the central nervous system. As a result researchers began to wonder whether people with slow reaction times were different in other respects from those with quick reaction times.

During and since the second World War, using much the same task that you will perform here, these experimenters found that, indeed, intellectual functioning and personality adjustments were significantly related to reaction-time performance. For example, individuals with fast reactions tended to be more flexible and adaptive in adjusting to environmental changes, more creative in solving problems, generally more intelligent, better able to endure strong stresses, and psychologically better adjusted. Those with slow reaction time tend to be more rigid and maladaptive in dealing with a changing environment, relatively uncreative in problem-solving, less intelligent, unable to endure strong stresses, and rather maladjusted. Moreover, reaction-time differences are quite consistent. If one person is faster than another initially, he remains faster.

The task you will be engaged in, thus, has played a long and productive part in research on the individual personality and its capacities. We are using it here in a slightly different way, as a measure of your performance in a simple game when you are operating as a team playing against others [pp. 420–421].

Unimportant Performance (UP)
Let me orient you to what you will be doing. Each of you will perform a simple reaction-time task. This is a common kind of response in psychological experiments because it is very convenient to work with. It is a very simple thing to do, merely pressing a button or closing a switch. Anyone can do it without training and it is easy to observe and measure. Also, reaction time is influenced mainly by the situation. It is unrelated to intellectual or personality traits. Although individuals differ in reaction time, this difference does not seem to have any significance in terms of the person's creativity, intelligence, or psychological adjustment. There are just as many intelligent, creative, well-adjusted people who have long reaction times as have short reaction times. Moreover, although one person in a given situation will respond somewhat more quickly or somewhat more slowly than another person, and this difference is consistent within the situation, that is, if he is initially slower, he remains slower and if he is faster, he remains faster in that situation, this difference in response speed very often is reversed in another, different situation. Reaction time is merely an uncomplicated, convenient, and easily measured response which reflects the situation. We are using it here as a performance device in a simple game to observe how you as a team play against others [p. 421].

Chance (C)
You may be interested to know that each member of the group has a different time to beat. That is, the failure interval will be different for each member of the group. The times have already been assigned at random before the experiment began. One of you will have a relatively long or "easy" time to beat, and the other will have a somewhat shorter, "hard" time to beat. Therefore, whether you succeed or fail has little to do with your own ability, and depends on which interval you happened to be assigned to. Is this clear? [p. 421].

One trial block of five trials was given so that the subjects might become accustomed to working against the failure signal. On the first two blocks of five trials, the fixed schedule of failures for each subject was initiated. For one member (chosen at random) the schedule allowed him ostensible success 50% of the time—that is, out of 10 trials (two blocks) he succeeded half the time and failed half the time. The other member had one of three failure schedules: also 50% success, 70% success, or 90% success. The schedules were drawn from a random number table so that in every two trial blocks, the proportion of failures was constant. There were, thus, three levels of performance difference: a relatively large difference of 40% (50-90), a relatively small difference of 20% (50-70), and no difference (50-50). The subjects were then reminded that they had 10 poker chips. These poker chips represented the number of points that each could contribute to the group total if he were successful on a particular trial. They could redistribute these chips in any way they wished after each trial block.

Results.   When the superior performer (R-1) gains all 20 points and the inferior performer (R-2) possesses none, the group has distributed responsibility so as to maximize the value of its outcome. The ease with which this is achieved may be seen in the rate with which the inferior member loses points over trial blocks. This is shown in Figures 13.2, 13.3, and 13.4 for the 50-90, 50-70, and 50-50 conditions, respectively. It is apparent that when members are equally likely to succeed (50-50), there is no systematic change in the distribution of points over blocks. Hence, in the following analyses the 50-50 condition is omitted unless otherwise stated. In both the 50-70 and 50-90 Chance conditions, groups rapidly achieve an optimal distribution of points, and by the fourth block nearly all of them have completely divested the inferior performer of control over the outcome. This process is somewhat slower when performance reflects an important skill and when the difference between R-1 and R-2 is relatively small. Thus, the inferior performer loses points most slowly over trial blocks in the IP/50-70 condition and, excluding the Chance groups, most rapidly in the UP/50-90 condition.

As before, after every block of five trials each member indicated whether and how he wished to change the distribution of points. The ballots were shown to the experimenter, and if both expressed a preference for change, they engaged in a brief discussion to decide on a specific redistribution. In each group R-1's and R-2's own preferences were compared to the obtained distribution of points, that is, the distribution agreed to in the group decision. These are presented in terms of difference scores over six blocks in Table 13.6. They denote the number of points the inferior member feels he himself should have, and the number of points the superior member judges his partner should have, each of these values being subtracted from the actual number of points that they jointly decide to give to the latter for the next block of trials. A positive value indicates that the superior member preferred fewer points for the inferior performer than the latter actually received as a result of the decision; a negative value indicates that the superior member preferred more points for the inferior performer. The

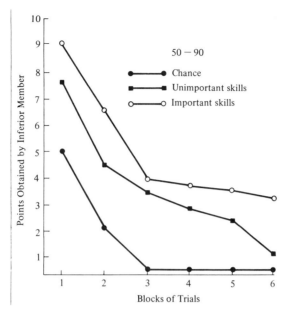

Figure 13.2
*Mean number of points given to the inferior per-
former on the basis of a group decision when
difference in performance between members is
large (from Burnstein & Wolosin, 1968, p. 422).*

algebraic sums of the differences over the five trial blocks were subject to analysis
of variance. A reliable main effect for performance importance was obtained. As
status becomes increasingly significant, R-1 prefers to assign more points to or
confer higher status on his inferior partner than the latter feels he should
receive.

Discussion.   If a rational assignment requires marked discrepancies in status,
inequities occur (a) as the individual differences in task proficiency decrease,
and (b) as status becomes an increasingly significant reward or cost. Inequities
are said to have foreseeable interpersonal consequences, such as embarrassment,
guilt, or anger, which individuals prefer to avoid. Hence, if other means of
maintaining equity are precluded, there should be great difficulty in achieving an
optimal distribution of status when individual differences are small and the
status conferred on the person is public recognition that he possesses or lacks
a valuable trait. It is in these circumstances that the conflict between achieving
an optimal distribution of status and avoiding inequity is most intense.

Findings on the speed with which groups achieve such a distribution of
status support this analysis. Small differences in proficiency in an area of performance that had great importance to the person occasioned the greatest resistance to redistributing status, whereas large performance differences that had

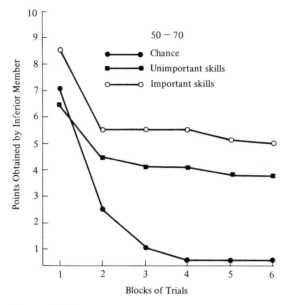

Figure 13.3

Mean number of points given to the inferior per-
former on the basis of a group decision when
difference in performance between members is
small (from Burnstein & Wolosin, 1968, p. 423).

little significance to the individual occasioned the least. Since the subjects kept a running record of their own and their partner's successes and failures, it cannot be argued that the results reflected increased difficulty in discriminating relative superiority as the difference between members decreased. Such an argument is also inconsistent with the abrupt demotion of the inferior performer in the Chance condition even when individual differences were relatively small. More-over, the rapid achievement of a rational redistribution in both Chance condi-tions precludes another rather powerful alternative interpretation, which is that the difficulty is due merely to the subjects' lack of understanding of what assign-ment is necessary to maximize the expected value of their outcome.

Data on group decision time give further support to this argument. A tape recording was to be made of each discussion on the allocation of points. Due to experimenter and equipment malfunctioning, this was only obtained in about half of the groups in the IP and UP conditions. From these tapes it was deter-mined which member initiated the discussion, whether his act was relevant to bargaining over points, and, if so, whether it took the form of an offer ("Why don't I give you five of my chips?") or a demand ("You ought to give five of your chips to me.") The length of time required to reach agreement about reallocating status was also obtained. These partial data are presented in Table 13.7 for the first group discussion. Note that in the condition thought to pose little difficulty (UP/50-90), the least time was required.

Table 13.6

The Mean Number of Points Obtained Minus the Mean Number Preferred by the Inferior and Superior Member for the Inferior Member over Trial Blocks in the 50-90 and 50-70 Conditions, in which Performance Reflects Chance (C), Unimportant (UP), or Important (IP) Factors

		Trial blocks							
		1	2	3	4	5	6	Σ	$|\Sigma|$
C/50-90	Obtained-inferior's pref.	1.8	1.0	-0.2	0.0	0.0	0.0	2.6	3.0
	Obtained-superior's pref.	0.3	0.6	0.2	0.0	0.0	0.0	1.1	1.1
UP/50-90	Obtained-inferior's pref.	0.0	-1.0	-1.0	-0.3	0.7	0.5	-1.1	3.5
	Obtained-superior's pref.	-1.0	-0.6	-0.8	-0.6	0.7	-0.2	-2.5	3.9
IP/50-90	Obtained-inferior's pref.	0.0	-1.0	0.0	-0.2	0.0	0.0	-1.2	1.2
	Obtained-superior's pref.	-2.6	-3.0	-1.4	-1.0	-1.7	-1.0	-10.7	10.7
C/50-70	Obtained-inferior's pref.	1.0	-1.6	0.0	0.0	-0.2	0.0	-0.8	2.8
	Obtained-superior's pref.	-1.0	-0.3	-0.5	-0.2	0.8	0.2	-1.0	3.0
UP/50-70	Obtained-inferior's pref.	1.3	0.3	1.1	1.5	-0.2	0.3	4.3	4.7
	Obtained-superior's pref.	0.3	-0.2	0.5	0.1	-0.2	-1.0	-1.5	2.3
IP/50-70	Obtained-inferior's pref.	0.8	0.8	0.7	0.9	0.1	0.1	3.4	3.4
	Obtained-superior's pref.	1.4	-1.7	-1.9	-1.2	-1.2	-1.5	-6.1	8.9

SOURCE. Burnstein and Wolosin (1968), p. 425.

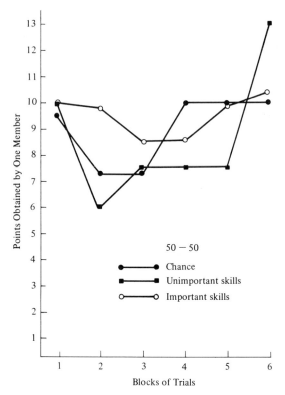

Figure 13.4
Mean number of points given to a performer on the basis of a group decision when there is no difference in performance between members (from Burnstein & Wolosin, 1968, p. 423).

Table 13.7

Initiator, Type of Act Initiated, and Decision Time during the First Discussion

Condition	Groups	Initiating Performer	Act	Group Decision Time (secs.)
50-90	1	Inferior	Offer	29
IP	2	Inferior	Offer	23
50-90	1	Inferior	Offer	8
UP	2	Inferior	Offer	8
	3	Inferior	Offer	10
50-70	1	Inferior	Offer	41
IP	2	Inferior	Offer	34
50-70	1	Superior	Demand	12
UP	2	Inferior	Offer	19
	3	Inferior	Offer	20

SOURCE. Burnstein and Wolosin (1968), p. 427.

The present experimental setup attempted to preclude alternative means of maintaining equity other than by avoiding an optimal distribution of status. Whereas the results suggest that we were at least in part successful, it would be unrealistic to assume complete success. It therefore might be worthwhile to consider what other means of maintaining equity existed that might not have been ruled out by our procedure. There are few sources of evidence to guide our conjectures. In Table 13.7, for all but one of the taped groups, discussions are *always* initiated by the inferior performer (the one about to be demoted) who makes an offer to his partner. A similar trend appeared in our preliminary research where R-1 participated more than other members in group decisions, especially when he would suffer most as a result, that is, when he would be demoted to R-4. This curious finding can now be given some interpretation: participation and influence in decision making provided an unforeseen avenue for restoring equity. But first let us consider the additional evidence for such an interpretation. Recall from Table 13.6 that in those conditions where an optimal distribution of status would produce the strongest inequity, the inferior performer is more likely to prefer such a distribution than the superior performer. That is to say, the unsuccessful individual is more severe with himself than is his successful co-worker. Moreover, if we take as a measure of relative influence in decision making the absolute difference between a member's own preference and the distribution agreed upon by the group, it appears that in these very same conditions the inferior performer also exerts greater influence (See Table 13.6).

Given these data, what conjectures can be made about interpersonal tactics to maintain face and minimize embarrassment? Keep in mind that individual differences in performance were quite clear. Not only was each member's success or failure observed by his partner, but each kept a continuous record of these events. Everyone involved, including the experimenter (to the extent that his opinion was relevant to the subjects), possessed perfect information on the performance of the two members. Hence, we can assume that R-2 recognized his own inferiority and with some justice felt that this inferiority was apparent to the others. Although he would like to change this evaluation, it is soon obvious to him that his performance cannot be improved. There is, however, another area of activity—the decision to distribute status—which is equally important in determining the value of the group outcome. If the inferior performer understands what is required before his more successful partner does, he may be able to recoup respect and compensate for the humiliation of being divested of responsibility. Were this stratagem used in the present situation, we would expect (and did observe) the inferior performer to initiate the decision-making discussion and to advocate an optimal distribution of status more frequently than the superior performer, especially when the difference in performance is relatively small or when the responsibility assigned to on individual is of particular significance to him.

Admittedly, in advocating such a distribution, the inferior performer may seal his fate, since his partner is likely to accede to his request and from that point his performance will count for little. At the same time, martyrdom has its rewards. First, while the superior performer may agree that a significant redistribution of status is called for, he might counter with something less severe. The inferior performer would certainly expect this if he had any inkling of his partner's preferences. Second, a rational distribution of responsibility could be foreseen as inevitable; by initiating a policy that can belittle him, the inferior performer not only exhibits the admirable trait of altruism but at the same time displays an acute understanding of organizational problems. In short, through such face-saving tactics an inferior performer may gain compensatory benefits, for example, being recognized as the "causal locus" for selfless and intelligent social planning (See Bem, 1967; Jones & Davis, 1965; or Kelley, 1967 for a general analysis of such processes).

The attempts to maintain or restore equity on the part of the less successful performer can complement rather nicely the tactics of his partner who has a similar end in mind. Again, since the performance situation is quite unambiguous, R-1 not only recognizes his partner's inferiority but, equally important, he may be rather certain that R-2 is aware that this recognition exists. If the superior member further assumes that his partner wishes to obtain the most valuable outcome possible under the circumstances and that he understands how status must be redistributed to achieve this result (these are not dangerous assumptions for they are readily tested during the discussion), he can relax and allow his partner to take the lead in arranging matters. Hence, he in part reduces the embarrassment of benefiting from an inequity by having the victim initiate the process. Furthermore, research on post-decision behavior (Brehm & Cohen, 1962) suggests that by not compelling compliance and by giving his partner the opportunity to initiate and control the decision to redistribute status, the more successful member may increase the other's commitment to a hierarchy that under other conditions would be considered unfair.

It would probably be wise, as well as interesting, not to attempt to preclude such tactics aimed at maintaining equity but to build them into the design as a variable. For instance, it follows from the above considerations that when compensatory actions that do not endanger the value of the group outcome are possible (e.g., the inferior member may be given a larger share of the joint payoff, more affection, or greater "idiosyncrasy credit" than ordinarily would be the case), a rational division of responsibility involving differences in status that are not commensurate with the differences in performance may be achieved with less difficulty. This then is the next issue we investigated.

COMPENSATING FOR AN INEQUITABLE DECISION

Experiment IV

In the preceding study it was conjectured that members benefiting from an inequity attempted to reduce its sting via rather subtle and indirect compensations (e.g., allowing their partner the major role in deciding how to redistribute status). If this is correct then we should be able to facilitate optimal but inequitable decisions by making such tactics legitimate and easy to employ. Presumably when a specific compensation procedure is immediately available, it should not be difficult for the donor and the recipient to coordinate their actions. Indeed, the fact that compensation is legitimate and expected may minimize whatever loss of pride or embarrassment a person experiences when he depends on the largesse of the other. Equity is restored with poise, and face is preserved.

In the present experiment members make two decisions: (a) how to distribute responsibility for the next block, a decision identical to that observed in the last study, and (b) how to divide the profit from the preceding block. The second decision makes salient for the group a legitimate avenue of compensation. By allowing the inferior performer a larger share of the outcome than he ordinarily might receive, any inequity produced by optimizing responsibility is to some extent mitigated. As a result, there should be less hesitancy in having some performers count for more than others.

This line of reasoning assumes that the two decisions are independent of each other. Suppose they are not. Indeed, as is often the case in everyday affairs, suppose they are positively correlated, with increased responsibility going hand in hand with an increased share of the joint outcome. Now the second decision—how to divide the outcome—could in no way compensate for the first, but, in fact, would be an additional source of inequity. In other words, if the interdependence between these two decisions was such that as a member is upgraded, his share of the profit increases, and as he is downgraded, it decreases, then the inequity is exaggerated. If it is unfair when status differences are incommensurate with differences in performance, then it is even more unfair under such conditions when a member's status determines his portion of the joint outcome.

Procedure. In general the experimental situation was similar to that of the last study, with a few important changes. Again each member began with 10 chips denoting his status or the points his successful performance added to the group total. Each point won was said to be worth 2 cents to the group. Thus if both members beat the failure light on any trial the group would win 20 points or 40 cents and if this happened over 5 consecutive trials the group would have earned 2 dollars for the trial block. A second set of 20 so-called outcome chips was also given to each member at the same time as he received the 10 status chips. The outcome chips were said to represent the proportion of the group's winnings that would be credited to a particular member. A single outcome chip was worth 2.5 percent of what was earned by the group on the immediately preceding block of trials. Thus at the end of the initial set of 5 trials each performer was credited with 50% of their joint outcome, since both had received 20 outcome chips. Each member's capacity to determine this outcome, their status, was also equal since both could contribute 10 points. At the end of the first block of trials, however, the group could decide to change the distributions, that is, to distribute status and winnings unequally.

Correlated and *uncorrelated* decision procedures were used to govern changes in status and outcome. Subjects in the *uncorrelated* decisions situation were told that after every block, if both desired, they would have an opportunity to redistribute status for the following block, as well as the outcome obtained on the preceding block, the former decision always being made before the latter. At the same time certain restrictions were placed on the second decision. It could only be made if the members also agreed to redistribute status. Moreover, when there was a shift in status, regardless of how big or small, *at least one* outcome chip had to change hands. Either member, however, could receive the latter. It was up to the group to decide. In brief when a decision was reached, say, to increase the status of the superior performer by giving him more responsibility, the group must also reapportion their joint profits from the last block at least one chip worth. This could just as well mean an increase in profit for the superior performer and a decrease for his partner or vice versa.

The purpose of introducing these rather cumbersome restrictions was to minimize resistance to an unequal sharing of the outcome. There is some evidence for normative pressures toward equal sharing which might be particularly strong when apportioning the outcome had no instrumental connection with achieving that outcome (Morgan & Sawyer, 1967).

In the *correlated* decisions condition, if the superior performer was given *n* additional status chips (and the inferior performer was deprived of this number), then he must also be given *n* additional outcome chips (and his partner must be deprived of this number). Hence, the two decisions are perfectly correlated. However, since there are 20 outcome chips and only 10 chips denoting status, the inferior performer could not be completely deprived of a share of the outcome. Even if status was distributed optimally, that is, if the inferior performer was totally stripped of responsibility, he would still receive 25 percent (10 chips worth) of the joint outcome obtained on the preceding block of trials. Of course, his partner would receive 75 percent (30 chips worth).

A final modification in procedure involved individual performance. We have implied that it is not the absolute level of performance that determines whether an optimal distribution of status is inequitable but the amount by which the individuals differ in performance. Thus, when individual differences are small an optimal distribution should be more unfair than when such differences are large. To check this assumption, two equally small individual differences were produced, but each was based on different absolute levels of performance. In one condition (70-90) an individual succeeded on 70 percent and his partner on 90 percent of the trials; in another (50-70) the comparable values were 50 percent and 70 percent. These two relatively small differences were contrasted with a third in which individual differences were larger, with one individual succeeding 50 percent of the time and the other 90 percent. Here an optimal distribution of status should have been more equitable. Performance was made highly significant for the individual by the use of the Important Performance instructions described in the preceding experiment. When performance was terminated each member filled out a questionnaire in which they rated their relative influence on decisions and the fairness of the decisions.

Results.   Similar to the findings in the preceding study, large differences in performance (50-90) encourage a more optimal distribution of status than small differences (50-70 and 70-90). The latter two conditions do not reliably differ in their decisions regarding status, nor as we shall see, do they differ in apportioning outcomes. The curves in Figures 13.5 and 13.6 demonstrate this, with the inferior performer losing more responsibility over blocks in the 50-90 than in the 50-70 or 70-90 conditions. The effect, however, is dampened considerably when the two decisions, status and outcome, are correlated. At each level of performance, status tends to be distributed in a more optimal (and thus more inequitable) fashion under uncorrelated conditions than under conditions in which status and outcome are correlated.

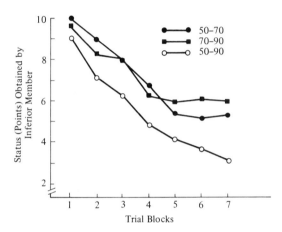

Figure 13.5
Mean number of points given to inferior performer under three conditions of performance differences when an uncorrelated decision procedure is used by the group.

For correlated groups profit sharing is tied to status. Thus to learn how the outcome is apportioned between members, the reader should merely substitute in Figure 13.6 "outcome chips" for status on the ordinate, with a maximum value of 20 and a minimum of 10. For uncorrelated groups, decisions as to how the outcome will be shared are not necessarily determined by the distribution of responsibility. Yet they are related to the latter in an interesting, if not paradoxical, fashion. This is shown in Figure 13.7. Notice that when performance differences are large and, as was shown, the inferior member is eventually deprived of nearly all responsibility for the outcome, he receives a significantly larger share of this outcome than when performance differences are small. Hence, the performer who is only slightly inferior to his partner is not so severely downgraded as one who is greatly inferior, but at the same time he is not treated to as generous a portion of the joint outcome.

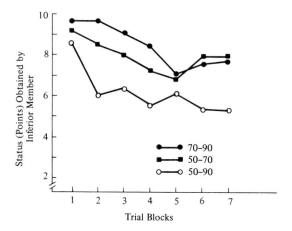

Figure 13.6

Mean number of points given to inferior per-former under three conditions of performance differences when a correlated decision procedure is used by the group.

Similar to the preceding study, inferior performers seem to exert more influence than their partners in decision making. Following each trial block the subjects indicated to the experimenter their individual preferences regarding the distribution of responsibility and outcome. Over the seven blocks under correlated conditions the group decisions regarding status more often approximated the inferior performer's preference within 66 percent of the groups, more often the superior performer's within 20 percent, and within the remaining groups the decision approximated each performer's preference with equal frequency. Under uncorrelated conditions the comparable values were 60 percent, 20 percent, and 20 percent, respectively. An identical trend appeared in apportioning the outcome. Under correlated conditions, the inferior performer's preference approximated the group decision more frequently in 53 percent of the groups; the superior performer's preference approximated the group decision more frequently in 13 percent of the groups; and each approximated the decision with equal frequency in the remaining groups. Comparable frequencies for the uncorrelated conditions were 47 percent, 20 percent, and 33 percent, respectively.

Parallel differences appeared on the postexperimental questionnaire when members rated themselves and their partners for relative influence in decision making (unspecified as to responsibility or outcome). Under correlated conditions the inferior performer perceived himself to be more influential in 40 percent of the groups, in 25 percent he perceived his partner to be more influential, and in 33 percent he perceived equal influence; the superior performer perceived himself as more influential in only 13 percent of the groups, in 73 percent of the groups he saw his partner as more influential, and in 13 percent of

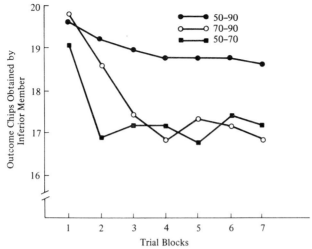

Figure 13.7

Mean number of outcome chips given to inferior per-former under three conditions of performance differences when an uncorrelated decision procedure is used by the group.

the groups he perceived equal influence. The pattern was quite similar under uncorrelated conditions.

Ratings of fairness are shown in Table 13.8. In general, the distribution of status is thought to be more fair by dyads with an uncorrelated decision procedure than by those with a correlated procedure. Moreover, there is a general marginally significant tendency for inferior performers to view the decision as more fair than their partners. This tendency is marked for inferior performers when decisions regarding status and profits are uncorrelated, *despite the fact that they are by far the most severely downgraded.* In respect to dividing the outcome, there is an indication, again marginally significant, for members burdened by a correlated procedure to consider the apportionment less fair than those with an uncorrelated procedure.

Discussion. Our main findings suggest that if equity can be restored without difficulty, inequitable but rational group decisions are facilitated. When earn-ings are tied to status (the correlated condition), equity is unattainable; indeed, if status is optimally distributed, the rule for parceling out profit forces the group to aggravate an already unjust arrangement. Publicly labeling a member's per-formance as worthless to the group is no doubt embarrassing to all concerned, but how much worse if at the same time they must halve this performer's earn-ings. Thus, the correlated decision procedure can be foreseen to create an intolerable interpersonal situation were status to be optimally distributed, and it is not surprising that the latter is avoided. However, when members are free to divide the joint outcome as they see fit (the uncorrelated condition), it becomes

Table 13.8

Mean Ratings of Fairness for the Distribution of Status and of Outcome

	Fairness of Status					
	Correlated Decision Procedure			*Uncorrelated Decision Procedure*		
	RATERS			RATERS		
Performance Difference	INFERIOR s	SUPERIOR s	$\overline{X}$	INFERIOR s	SUPERIOR s	$\overline{X}$
50-70	3.3[a]	7.3	5.3	1.3	5.0	3.2
70-90	5.8	4.1	5.0	1.5	4.2	2.8
50-90	3.9	4.7	4.3	1.8	3.4	2.6
	$\overline{X}$ 4.3	5.4		1.5	4.2	
	Fairness of Outcome					
50-70	3.0	5.1	4.0	3.2	5.9	4.5
70-90	5.4	4.3	4.8	5.8	3.7	4.6
50-90	7.5	8.6	8.1	4.7	5.2	4.9
	$\overline{X}$ 5.3	6.0		4.6	4.9	

[a] 1 = extremely fair; 13 = extremely unfair.

possible to compensate for and thus to reduce the injustice of a demotion which is incommensurate with performance. An optimal group decision, which entails such changes, becomes less burdensome and more readily achieved. Indeed in the condition where the inferior performer was most deprived of status, a high level of compensation seemed to legitimize the deprivation; that is, the near optimal distribution of status was perceived as completely fair.

SOME LIMITS ON EQUITABLE BEHAVIOR

Experiment V

In our earlier discussion we observed that compensatory activity could have other functions beside that of restoring equity. Thus, group members may not behave equitably merely to avoid the unpleasantness of doing or being subject to an injustice. For instance, the superior performer might think that being relatively lenient and permitting his partner to dominate the group decision would be good tactics for insuring the inferior performer's acceptance of a decision which will not at all be to his benefit. In addition, it was suggested that the concept of equity provides a common standard for the selection of mutually acceptable decisions. As a result, bargaining may be facilitated, individual choices are more readily coordinated, and the maximal joint outcome is achieved more rapidly. Again this is a function which in and of itself has little to do with reducing the embarrassment and antagonism associated with an injustice. The question then is whether and to what extent will equitable interpersonal behavior occur when ends irrelevant to equity are unlikely to be served. More specifically, suppose a member did not have to worry about the acceptance of the group decision or about coordinating his choice with that of the partner. Would he still behave equitably?

Procedure.   Two levels of performance differences were used, 50-70 and 50-90. As usual dyads were able to redistribute responsibility following each trial block, but not the joint outcome, which was to be shared equally. Instructions were of the Important Performance type. The major experimental manipulation had to do with the locus of decision making. In one condition, the distribution of status was decided by the superior performer alone; in another, the decision was made by the inferior performer. A control condition involved the distribution of status by group decision, as in the previous experiments. Discussion was always permitted before the decision, but in the two experimental conditions a single member determined whether a change in status was warranted and what that change should be. It was assumed that if one person decides how status will be distributed, there is no need for him (or his partner) to be concerned with problems of coordination and mutual acceptance. Thus by completely centralizing decision making, equitable behavior is deprived of at least some important "latent functions."

Results.   As in the earlier experiments, inferior performers consistently lose more points over trials when the difference in performance is large (in the 50-90 condition) than when the difference is small (in the 50-70 condition). However, in the present study we are mostly concerned with the distribution of status when standards of equity are irrelevant to coordinating individual choices. If under these conditions self-interest dominates, we should find that the inferior performer is downgraded less when he alone decides how status is to be redistributed and is downgraded more when this decision is made by his partner, than when the decision is made jointly, that is, when the issue of coordination is important. Note that this is quite different than what might be expected on the basis of their private preferences; in our past studies the inferior performer consistently advocated a *larger* reduction in status for himself than did the partner.

The predicted effects are obtained only in the 50-70 conditions. In the 50-90 situation the distribution of responsibility does not differ reliably over blocks as a function of who makes the decision. This is shown in Figure 13.8. Preferences for a particular distribution of status demonstrate a similar effect. An examination of Table 13.9 indicates that when the performance difference is small and the distribution of status is made by group decision, the inferior performer tends to be relatively severe with himself. He is more lenient, however, when he alone chooses the distribution. On the other hand, the superior performer is relatively lenient under group decision conditions but becomes more severe when he is solely responsible for the decision. Thus, individuals behave in terms of their vested interests when given the opportunity (if the

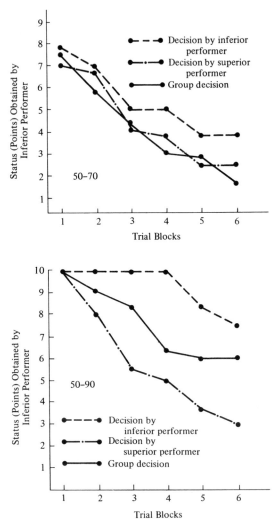

Figure 13.8

Mean number of points (responsibility) given to inferior performer as a function of the locus of decision making and the difference in performance.

individual alone decides), and they compromise their interests when forced to (if the decision must be a joint one). In brief, we have demonstrated what, perhaps, should have been obvious to begin with, that standards of equity will be bent in a self-serving manner when they are not instrumental for coordinating individual choices and insuring their mutual acceptance.

Table 13.9

Status (Points) Preferred for the Inferior Performer

Performance Difference	Trial Block	Decided by Group		Decided by Superior Performer		Decided by Inferior Performer	
		INFERIOR PERFORMER'S PREFERENCE	SUPERIOR PERFORMER'S PREFERENCE	INFERIOR PERFORMER'S PREFERENCE	SUPERIOR PERFORMER'S PREFERENCE	INFERIOR PERFORMER'S PREFERENCE	SUPERIOR PERFORMER'S PREFERENCE
50-70	1	8.75[a]	10.00	7.75	8.50	9.50	10.00
	2	8.00	9.00	7.50	7.00	9.50	9.50
	3	8.25	8.75	6.25	5.50	9.00	9.00
	4	5.50	6.50	4.50	5.25	9.50	9.00
	5	6.00	8.75	4.50	3.75	7.75	9.00
	6	5.50	8.50	3.75	3.50	7.75	7.00
50-90	1	6.25	7.00	7.50	6.50	7.50	9.00
	2	5.00	5.75	6.75	6.25	6.00	7.75
	3	4.25	4.50	5.50	5.50	5.25	6.00
	4	3.00	3.50	5.00	4.00	5.00	4.00
	5	2.75	2.50	4.50	3.00	3.75	4.25
	6	1.00	2.25	3.00	2.50	3.50	2.50

[a] This value denotes the mean number of points preferred for the inferior performer. Both members initially have ten points each.

Discussion. Aside from facilitating or inhibiting the expression of self-interest, the locus of decision making can also affect the face-work that occurs when there is mutual embarrassment. Maintaining face is an intricate process that as Goffman (1959) points out requires collusion between partners. The opportunity for such collusion is likely to vary depending upon whether the potentially embarrassing decision is to be made jointly or by a single individual. Earlier we suggested that the expression of preferences to the experimenter afforded members a tactical opening in what was otherwise a rather constrained situation for face-work. It gave them a way of presenting themselves so as to counter the impression of being unfairly advantaged or disadvantaged. This conjecture can now be detailed by contrasting the tactical possibilities of group decision and individual decision situations.

A member no doubt is aware that his intention to behave in a self-interested fashion is incompatible with his intention to behave equitably. When he is solely responsible for the decision, his choice will clearly reflect one or the other motive. However, if the decision is to be made jointly, his intentions can be disguised and need not be reflected in his choice. Our previous studies found that inferior performers were relatively severe and superior performers relatively lenient in the preferences they express about particular distributions of status. Relative leniency or severity was considered an attempt to mitigate the inequity that follows from an optimal distribution of status. However, we did not assume that given the opportunity the preferred distributions of status would actually be implemented. To the contrary, since if nothing else mattered both performers would like to achieve high status. Yet to act completely in terms of one's own vested interests is awkward especially when they conflict with the interests of the partner.

The statement of preference may provide a way of resolving this dilemma. The inferior performer, by preferring a drastic redistribution of responsibility, can appear to himself and others in the situation as intelligent ("I bet I know more than my partner about what has to be done for our group to win"). And the superior performer, by preferring a mild redistribution, can appear considerate ("I'm asking for less than my partner is probably willing to give"). While presenting themselves in a favorable light, each at the same time may believe that their particular interests, for which they are loath to plead, will be recognized by the partner when the decision is made. But in any case, if worse came to worse, both know that they will have considerable control over the actual distribution of status. Although the inferior performer may hope his partner will recommend a less drastic distribution ("He must understand my embarrassment") and the superior performer may hope his partner will advocate a more rational one ("He surely knows there's a winning arrangement"), neither is bound to his preferences; and if the group decision happens to move in an undesirable direction, the members can warn that it is unacceptable.

Thus, by engaging in face-work a person does not really endanger his vested interests and if all goes well, he and his partner could maintain a good opinion of themselves. This would not be the case, however, unless the decision to distribute status is made jointly. When the decision is in the hands of a single member, it is clear that the latter cannot depend on his partner taking a more severe or more generous line than his own. In other words, a group decision enables the nimble individual to display a desire for equity or at least to disguise a more selfish desire, and at the same time doesn't really jeopardize his vested interests. Such tactics are precluded if it is clear to all that he alone determines the distribution of status.

To summarize, if standards of equity are unimportant for coordinating choices or for insuring their acceptance by others, they tend to be violated or at least they seem less effective. This appears especially likely if decision making is centralized. More specifically, our findings suggest the actual distribution of status which is determined by a single member may be less fair and more self-serving than one which is jointly determined, because under the former but not under the latter conditions the "latent functions" of interpersonal equity are irrelevant. This state of affairs is also reflected in the statements of preference. Since they have little tactical value—neither performer can give the appearance of being selfless or considerate without actually distributing status in a selfless or considerate fashion—the preferred distributions of status become more self-serving, with the inferior performer being less severe and the superior performer less lenient than they are under group decision conditions.

It is noteworthy, however, that the violations of equity are not gross. In fact, if we review the several studies presented in this paper, it appears rare for the inferior performer to be completely deprived of status. When this does occur status has no real personal significance. Nor is the inferior performer deprived of much of his share of the group outcome. Doubtless in a face-to-face situation such as ours the individual inhibits self-serving behavior, especially since it demeans the other. Nevertheless, when a joint decision must be made regarding the distribution of status, there is fairly good evidence that group members try to behave equitably and to compensate another for his losses, even if the inequity is justifiable on rational grounds. It is not difficult to conjecture why this is so. Invidious distinctions, even when they benefit the group as a whole, create antagonisms. Members are unlikely to work together effectively unless they are convinced that the distinctions are justified. Under these conditions, group activities that demand coordination among members cannot easily be sustained. Equitable behavior, in and of itself, thus becomes functional, to the extent that it induces individuals of low as well as high status to accept their lot. In fact, such an integrative function is nicely suggested by one of our "paradoxical" findings: when a decision is made to severely reduce the status of the inferior performer, he perceives this decision as completely fair (much more so than those less severely downgraded) if at the same time he is well compensated. Thus, rational group decisions and fair group decisions often may conflict, but, in viable groups, mechanisms are created to reconcile rationality and fairness.

REFERENCES

ADAMS, J. S. Inequity in social exchange. In L. Berkowitz (Ed.), *Advances in experimental social psychology.* Vol. 2. New York: Academic Press, 1965. Pp. 267–299.

BEM, D. J. Self-perception: An alternative interpretation of cognitive dissonance phenomena. *Psychological Review,* 1967, **74,** 183–200.

BLAU, P. M. *Exchange and power in social life.* New York: Wiley, 1964.

BREHM, J. W., & COHEN, A. R. *Explorations in cognitive dissonance.* New York: Wiley, 1962.

BURNSTEIN, E., & WOLOSIN, R. J. The development of status distinctions under conditions of inequity. *Journal of Experimental Social Psychology,* 1968, **4,** 415–430.

BURNSTEIN, E., & ZAJONC, R. B. The effect of group success on the reduction of status incongruence in task-oriented groups. *Sociometry,* 1965, **28,** 349–362. (a)

BURNSTEIN, E., & ZAJONC, R. B. Individual task performance in a changing social structure. *Sociometry,* 1965, **28,** 16–29. (b)

GOFFMAN, E. On face-work: An analysis of ritual elements in social interaction. *Psychiatry,* 1955, **18,** 213–231.

HOMANS, G. C. *Social behavior: Its elementary forms.* New York: Harcourt, 1961.

JONES, E. E., & DAVIS, K. E. From acts to dispositions: The attribution process in person perception. In L. Berkowitz (Ed.), *Advances in experimental social psychology.* Vol. 2. New York: Academic Press, 1965. Pp. 220–226.

KELLEY, H. H. Attribution theory in social psychology. In D. Levine (Ed.), *Nebraska symposium on motivation.* Lincoln, Nebr.: University of Nebraska Press, 1967. Pp. 192–238.

LEVENTHAL, G. S., & BERGMAN, J. T. Self-depriving behavior as a response to unprofitable inequity. *Journal of Experimental Social Psychology,* 1970, **5,** 153–171.

MORGAN, W. R., & SAWYER, J. Bargaining, expectations, and the preference for equality over equity. *Journal of Personality and Social Psychology,* 1967, **6,** 139–149.

SCHELLING, T. C. *The strategy of conflict.* Cambridge, Mass.: Harvard University Press, 1960.

ZAJONC, R. B. The effects of feedback and group task difficulty on individual and group performance. *Human Relations,* 1962, **15,** 149–161.

ZAJONC, R. B. The requirements and design of a standard group task. *Journal of Experimental Social Psychology,* 1965, **1,** 71–88.

ZAJONC, R. B., & TAYLOR, J. J. The effects of two methods of varying group task difficulty on individual and group performance. *Human Relations,* 1963, **16,** 359–368.

14

STATUS CONCEPTIONS AND INTERACTION: A CASE STUDY OF THE PROBLEM OF DEVELOPING CUMULATIVE KNOWLEDGE[1]

Bernard P. Cohen
Joseph Berger
Morris Zelditch, Jr.[2]

INTRODUCTION

The study of small face-to-face groups has been a central area of sociological and social psychological research for more than two decades. Although a large literature has accumulated in this area, it is hard to conclude that we have a definitive body of cumulative knowledge. The discipline of small groups is extremely heterogeneous—many diverse problems studied by investigators from quite different traditions fit under this rubric; hence, it is probably too much to expect that a cumulative body of knowledge would emerge from the whole of the diverse field of small groups. Even when we look at a particular problem or tradition within the small groups literature, we do not find the cumulative growth of knowledge one expects in a scientific discipline. We reviewed the problem of the relationship between status conceptions and social interaction and found the major result to be that status conceptions affect the way people interact with one another. This idea began the research tradition, and it appears that the research has illustrated and exemplified this idea rather than extended it and made it more precise.

[1] Work on this chapter was partially supported by National Science Foundation Grant GS-1170.

[2] This paper is based on material from a forthcoming monograph, *Status Conceptions and Power and Prestige*. The authors gratefully acknowledge the assistance of Barry Askinas and H. Lee Freese.

Our research concern was to extend this idea; but as a byproduct we were led to examine the question of why previous work had not progressed further in building a body of cumulative knowledge. We were led to consider the conditions necessary to promote the development of a cumulative body of knowledge and to examine whether these conditions have been present or absent in previous research on status conceptions and social interaction. This chapter then is a case study of the problems that inhibit the growth of cumulative understanding of a phenomenon and a presentation of what we regard as essential elements in promoting this development.

The research tradition that concerns us deals with the effect on social interaction of the way in which actors define social situations. The conceptions which actors form of themselves and other actors have profound effects on the way they interact with one another. Here we owe to Robert Ezra Park (1928) an important insight: that status conceptions organize the behavior of individuals in social situations. Most of us still use Park's formulation: individuals classify themselves and others in terms of already established status categories. Such categories function both cognitively and normatively and provide individuals with information about how they should behave. In the absence of such categories, social situations are ambiguous, behavior is unpredictable, and individuals in such situations are anxious and tense.

The significance of Park's formulation cannot be overestimated. Imagine what it would be like to visit a close friend in the hospital, but not to be able to distinguish doctors from other visitors? A strange man walks into the room and orders you to leave, or he asks you to step outside and informs you that your friend has some dread disease, or he walks in and orders your friend to take off his clothes. Of course, the truth is that social arrangements hardly ever permit such situations to arise, or if they arise, to persist for long. Most of the time, the required definitions occur almost instantaneously, and even largely without conscious thought, so that most people are unaware that they are obeying a rather profound sociological law.

Not only can we all think of examples that fit Park's formulation, but 40 years of research has been guided, explicitly or implicitly, by Park's thesis. Reports ranging from casual observation to highly controlled experimentation document the phenomenon that Park isolated in contexts ranging from race relations to professional organizations, from permanent rigidly organized and hierarchized groups to temporary, informal unorganized groups.

Yet after 40 years and numerous field and experimental studies, it is difficult to point to a body of cumulative knowledge that represents our understanding of the relation between status conceptions and interaction. Can we, for example, say when status conceptions organize interaction and when they fail to organize interaction? Certainly one needs at least a partial answer to this question if one wants to apply Park's insight to new situations. Unfortunately, the body of literature in this tradition does not provide clear guidelines for approaching our question or for answering other similarly fundamental questions: What is it about status conceptions that organizes interaction? What features of interaction are organized by status conceptions? And, how do status conceptions organize interaction? Indeed, as one examines the literature on status conceptions and interaction, one cannot find a set of general questions that are consistently asked. In the absence of such a set of general questions, how can we say what the efforts of this tradition "add up to"?

We would like to review the literature and spell out the theoretical and empirical advances that have been made in studying the phenomenon and in extending and refining our conception of it. The end product of a cumulative research tradition is a body of scientifically (and, hopefully, practically) useful general knowledge soundly buttressed with empirical support. But we cannot present such a review; we cannot with confidence collect assertions that meet our standards of generality and evidential basis. We are reluctantly forced to conclude that in the sense of an identifiable end product, the research tradition begun by Park has not been cumulative. Why is this so?

It is our contention that this research tradition has not been cumulative because the studies have not addressed themselves consistently to a set of general and fundamental questions, questions such as those we raised above. The failure to ask these questions does not reflect on the merit of the studies taken individually, but results from implicit assumptions about the strategy of research. Rather than be critical of individual investigators, we question some of these implicit strategies. For example, there are many who believe that we can ask about the conditions under which status conceptions organize interaction only *after* we have a large body of studies to examine. We take a diametrically opposite position. We argue that such a body of studies will not provide an answer to the question unless the studies are conducted with the question in mind and are designed to provide an answer.

More generally, we assert that the failure of these studies to be cumulative is due to the lack of a framework that guides the design and conduct of each individual piece of research. To us, such a framework consists of an abstract formulation of the problem containing one or more empirical generalizations about the phenomenon, a theoretical explanation of the generalization, and a standardized empirical situation in which to evaluate and extend the theory. Without such a framework, it is impossible to develop a cumulative body of knowledge since it is inconceivable that a large number of separate studies would independently ask and answer the same set of fundamental questions. Furthermore, when one examines a study in concrete details, every study is unique; it was done in a particular place, at a particular time, with a particular set of subjects measured by a particular set of operations. Only by abstracting from these particulars and fitting studies into an abstract structure can we begin to compare and combine studies to see what they add up to.

Granted that such a framework is necessary, why can't we impose a new theoretical structure upon an already existing body of literature? Roughly speaking, we can. But in so doing we encounter serious problems of interpretation (does a given study meet or fail to meet the conditions of our abstract formulation?) and of comparability across studies. Hence, we regard imposing a structure on an existent body of results as a highly inefficient means of developing cumulative knowledge.

The purpose of this chapter then is to demonstrate first of all the need for an *a priori* framework around which to build a cumulative program. That is, to show that the questions we desire to answer not only will not be answered but won't even be asked in the absence of such a framework. Second, we intend to present part of the framework we have developed for the problem of the relationship of status conceptions to interaction and to show that it indeed does guide research both in terms of the questions that are asked and the methods by which answers are sought. To accomplish our purposes we must show why a collection of studies in the absence of such a framework is not cumulative; in addition, we must illustrate the problems that arise in attempting to impose a framework on an existent literature, and finally we must present an abstract framework and demonstrate that it provides clear directions for future research and the cumulation of knowledge.

To show that our understanding of the relation between status conceptions and interaction has not advanced beyond Park, we propose to make an intensive and detailed examination of three studies rather than do an extensive review of the literature in this area. We will put these three studies under a microscope, so to speak, because they represent many of the problems we confront when we attempt to "add up" knowledge from different investigations. A comment is necessary on the sense in which these studies are representative. They are not typical of the quality of research relating status to interaction, rather they are among the best studies that have been done. Neither are they typical in any quantitative sense, that is, they are not the types of studies that are most frequently done. The three studies we have chosen do, however, represent a broad range of analytic problems and generate the kinds of questions one would ask of the whole of the literature.

THREE STUDIES OF STATUS AND INTERACTION

The studies we have chosen are: *Social Status in Jury Deliberations* by Fred L. Strodtbeck, Rita M. James, and Charles Hawkins (1957); *Some Effects of Power on the Relations Among Group Members* by Jacob I. Hurwitz, Alvin F. Zander, and Bernard Hymovitch (1953); and *Some Consequences of Power Differences on Decision Making in Permanent and Temporary Three-Man Groups* by E. Paul Torrance (1955). As we examine these three studies, the reader should keep in mind the questions we raised earlier:

1. Under what conditions do status conceptions organize interaction?
2. What is it about status conceptions that organizes interaction?
3. What features of interaction are organized by status conceptions?
4. How do status conceptions organize interaction?

Our plan is first to describe the studies in detail and then to analyze the problem of assessing such studies in the absence of an abstract framework. Only when we have indicated the problems of assessment will we turn to our own formulation of the phenomenon. We will not present all the elements of our theoretical framework but will concentrate on two of its core elements. These are (a) an abstract empirical generalization which we believe captures the central phenomenon of this research tradition and (b) a standardized experimental situation that enables us to test a wide range of propositions. Hopefully, this will be sufficient to show how the framework solves many of the problems we point to and to document our assertion that research guided by such a framework will be cumulative. At the very least, we can show that the generalization itself adds something to previous knowledge because it provides one answer to the question of conditions under which status conceptions organize interaction. Let us now consider each of the studies.

Social Status in Jury Deliberations

Strodtbeck, James, and Hawkins (1957) considered the question of whether or not status differences of the larger community manifested themselves in jury deliberations. They argue, "if there is evidence that the status differences of the larger community become manifest in the deliberation, then it may be expected that a similar generalization of status will be found in other interactional contexts. . . [p. 713]." In other words, they treated their study as an instance of the phenomenon of status generalization. To represent status differences in the larger community they chose as independent variables, occupation of juror and sex of juror. They were concerned with how these variables operate to determine interaction roles in mock juries. Their dependent variables, measuring interaction roles, included: (a) who was chosen as foreman; (b) relative participation in jury deliberations; (c) votes received in answer to the question, "who do you believe contributed most to help your group reach its decision?" and (d) a measure of perceived fitness as jurors.

Their study was based upon 49 deliberations of 12-member juries, where the jurors were selected at random from regular jury pools. The jury deliberations were recorded, transcribed, and scored in terms of Bales' Interaction Process Analysis (Bales, 1950). The jurors listened to a recorded trial, deliberated, and returned the verdict, all under the customary discipline of the bailiffs and the court. Two civil trials were used as the basis for the deliberations. In the first (29 deliberations), the plaintiff sought compensation for injuries incurred in a two-car collision. In the second (20 deliberations), a young child sought compensation for facial disfigurement incurred in a fire alleged to have been caused by a defective vaporizer. A total of 588 different jurors were involved (49 $\times$ 12).

The authors found that both sex and occupational status were associated with being chosen as jury foreman and with relative rates of participation in the deliberations. Men were more frequently chosen as foremen than women, and males participated more in the jury deliberations than females. Furthermore, men received more choices as "helpful juror" than women. In examining occupational status, the authors found that proprietors were most frequently chosen as jury foremen, followed by clerks, skilled workers, and unskilled laborers, in that order. The same ordering held for percentage rates of participation in the jury deliberations. When the choice of "helpful juror" was correlated with occupation, proprietors were most chosen, and unskilled laborers least chosen, and the clerical and skilled categories fell in between with virtually the same number of choices.

Twenty-eight of the juries were asked the question: "The jury pool is made up of people from all walks of life. However, if a member of your family were on trial and you had your choice, which of the following kinds of people would you prefer to make up the majority of the jurors who would hear your case: business and professional people, clerical and white-collar workers, skilled workers, or unskilled workers?" For respondents who were proprietors or in clerical occupations, the preferred occupation of a juror followed the order proprietor, clerical, skilled, laborer. Among skilled workers, a choice of other skilled workers as jurors displaced the choice of clerical workers in the ordering. The choices of laborers were ordered quite differently: skilled, proprietor, laborer, and clerical.

Finally, other jurors were asked to choose "four of your fellow jurors whom you would best like to have serve on a jury if you were on trial." Here the authors were concerned not with generalized conceptions of other occupational groups, but with evaluations of particular persons. They wanted to know "if the selections made on the basis of face-to-face contact were similar or different from stereotyped choices." They found that for all respondents, other jurors with proprietors' occupations were most chosen and other jurors with laboring occupations were least chosen. By comparing the responses to the two types of questions where the respondents were from different but comparable samples, the authors noted that the differences between occupations, when the question was based on face-to-face experience, were less sharp than when the question was based on occupational categories in general.

Some Effects of Power on the Relations among Group Members

Hurwitz, Zander, and Hymovitch (1953) investigated the relationship between perceived power of any individual to influence other members of his group and egodefensive behavior. These authors based their study on previous work, particularly that of Lippitt, Polansky, and Rosen (1952) who found that "those high in attributed power make more frequent attempts to influence the behavior of others than do *lows* . . . whereas lows engage in approval seeking behavior more than do *highs* [in Hurwitz, Zander, & Hymovitch, 1953, p. 483]." The study was designed to test this conception using members of discussion groups in a controlled situation.

Perceived power of any individual to influence other members of his group was defined as the extent to which his opinions on a given topic would, in their judgment, carry weight. Participants in a mental hygiene conference were selected so that discussion groups in this conference would contain participants high in perceived power and participants low in perceived power. Since it was impractical to obtain a measure of perceived power of each individual in advance of the conference, the authors assumed that perceived power to influence would be highly correlated with prestige in the mental hygiene field; hence, the participants were selected by two knowledgable judges who were "qualified to judge the prestige of these persons in the eyes of fellow professionals." They chose half of their sample to be high in prestige and half to be low, in order to maximize the likelihood of "getting a reasonably good spread in the independent measure of perceived power to influence." The sample for this study consisted of 42 persons working in the general field of mental hygiene. The participants were mainly social workers, teachers, counselors and guidance workers, psychiatrists, psychologists, and nurses.

The 42 individuals attended a one-day laboratory conference which discussed mental hygiene problems. Each individual participated in four wholly different groups, discussing four separate topics, each for 30 minutes. The groups were arranged so that no two individuals met more than once in any group, and each group contained both high and low prestige members. The process of reshuffling the participants generated 32 different discussion groups.

The discussion topics were selected on the basis of the following criteria: sufficient generality in content to avoid favoring any professional groups by virtue of their particular training or experience; sufficient breadth of scope to minimize the likelihood of definite previous opinions; sufficient controversialness to insure differences in opinion; and unidimensionality in content to permit ratings along one continuum. The problems for discussion were: (a) To recommend a type of agency or institution in the field of mental hygiene to which the subjects would prefer to make a sizeable contribution—one emphasizing environmental change wholly, one emphasizing therapy wholly, or one emphasizing both of these; (b) the extent to which recent changes in the role of women generate helpful or harmful consequences to our society from the point of view of mental hygiene; (c) the possible effect (ranging from extremely negative to extremely positive) of greater federal participation in local preventive mental health efforts; and (d) the effect on the mental health of the American people of an effective worldwide scrapping of atomic bombs in the coming year.

The dependent measures were obtained after each of the 30-minute sessions. The authors measured each subject's liking for each of the individuals with whom he had just met, his perception of how much each member liked him, and his perception of the extent of verbal participation of each member. In addition, during each discussion an observer recorded the length and frequency of remarks made by each group member, thus obtaining an "objective" measure of participation.

For our purposes, the principal finding of this study was a relationship between prestige and frequency of communication as noted by the group observers: highs consistently communicated more frequently than did lows; lows tended to communicate more frequently to highs than highs did to other lows; and since highs also communicated more frequently to other highs, "it is of course not surprising to find highs receive more communications than do lows." (Although the authors analyzed their data in terms of perceived power to influence, it is reasonable for us to consider the relationship as one of prestige to communication, since the authors originally selected their participants on the basis of prestige and also reported that only three of the participants were differentially classified on the measure of prestige and the measure of perceived power to influence.)

In terms of their interest in egodefensive behavior, the authors found that individuals perceived high in power to influence were liked somewhat more than individuals perceived low in power to influence. More importantly, the lows liked highs considerably more than highs liked lows. The authors interpreted this liking as a way to reduce feelings of uneasiness that lows experience in their relation with highs. Furthermore, there was also a marked tendency for highs to like lows less than other highs and also less than lows liked other lows. Finally, individuals tended to underestimate the ratings they received on being liked and to overestimate the amount of participation of others. This underestimation of being liked was interpreted as defensive in the sense that if one does not get one's hopes too high, one cannot be disappointed, whereas the authors interpreted the overestimation of the amount of participation of others as due to the lower expectations of the amount lows should participate in discussions.

Some Consequences of Power Differences on Decision Making in Permanent and Temporary Three-Man Groups

Torrance (1955) conducted a study of Air Force crews central to our interests. He was particularly concerned with the effects of power differences on decision making in permanent groups with uniform, well-established, and clearcut hierarchial structures. He was interested in separating the consequences of power from the consequences of patterns of behavior developed as a result of enduring interaction. For that reason Torrance was particularly interested in comparing the decision-making behavior of permanent groups with that of similarly constituted temporary groups. The argument here seems to be that permanent groups may have allocated power to make decisions in ways that differ from the formal hierarchy of the group. If that is the case, one should see differences between permanent and temporary groups that cannot be attributed to the formal hierarchy, since both types of groups have the same hierarchy.

Torrance studied three-man B-26 bomber crews in an experimental situation where each crew was confronted with four different experimental tasks. Each crew was composed of a pilot, a navigator, and a gunner. The pilot as the aircraft commander has the final authority to make crew decisions regardless of differences in rank. The navigator is a commissioned officer and may even outrank the pilot; he makes many decisions, and as a commissioned officer may exercise certain power over the commander, an enlisted man. The gunner, in Torrance's words, "is definitely the low man on the totem pole."

Torrance studied 62 permanent and 32 temporary crews. The permanent crews had been together for several months and had reached the final stage of their crew training. The temporary groups were drawn from the same type of personnel; each had a pilot, a navigator, and a gunner, but they were arranged so that no man was with a member of his regular (permanent) crew.

Each group had to solve four decision-making problems, varying in nature and difficulty. The problems were:

1. The Maier Horse-Trading Problem: "A man bought a horse for $60 and sold it for $70. Then, he bought it back for $80 and sold it for $90. How much money does he make in the horse-trading business?" Each individual was first asked to write on a slip of paper his solution, without conferring with anyone. The group was then asked to confer and reach a group decision.

2. The Dot Estimation Problem: The task was to estimate the number of dots on a 16-by-21 inch card that had 3155 black dots scattered evenly but not geometrically over a white background. Here again, each subject was asked to write his individual estimate on a slip of paper and then the group was asked to confer to decide on the best estimate. For this problem, each individual was asked to write on a slip of paper the number of dots he really thought there were after the group had reached a collective decision.

3. The Projective Story Problem: This task involved an ambiguous picture about which subjects could construct a story by "projecting" their own feelings into the picture. In this task Torrance used a sketch of a conference group. The subjects were instructed to write within a five-minute limit a story about the picture. After each individual had written his own story, the crew was asked to agree upon and to write within a ten-minute limit a crew story about the same sketch.

4. The Group Survival Problem: For this problem the crew was told that they had been downed in enemy territory and they were to arrive at a solution to the problem of surviving in this situation.

In addition to the data on individual and group decisions, the group discussions were observed using the Bales categories of Interaction Process Analysis[3] and a very brief questionnaire was administered to all participants.

---

[3] Bales' Interaction Process Analysis is a technique for observing and categorizing behavior in discussion groups. Each simple sentence is scored according to who says it, to whom it is said, and which one of 12 types of behavior it represents. The 12 mutually exclusive categories according to which each sentence is classified are: (1) shows solidarity, (2) shows tension release, (3) shows agreement, (4) gives suggestion, (5) gives opinion, (6) gives orientation, (7) asks for orientation, (8) asks for opinion, (9) asks for suggestion, (10) shows disagreement, (11) shows tension, (12) shows antagonism. For a fuller description of his technique, see Chapter 16.

In general, Torrance's results showed that influence corresponded with command position on the B-26 crew. In the horse trading problem, for example, the pilots were most successful and the gunners least successful in influencing the crew to accept their correct solutions. In the group projective story, 58 percent of the pilots had strong influence whereas only 37 percent of the navigators and none of the gunners exerted strong influence in the group story. For the survival problem, on the basis of self-ratings, 41 percent of the pilots said they had the most influence on a decision; 8.8 percent of the navigators and none of the gunners felt that they had the most influence on the group decision.

On the group survival problem, Torrance reported interaction data on the crew members. Here he noted that navigators contributed 40.7 percent to the total participation in contrast to 34.1 percent and 25.2 percent for pilots and gunners respectively. He also pointed out that pilots, navigators, and gunners differed somewhat in the categories of their interaction. In sum, he noted that certain types of interaction tended to characterize the occupants of each position.

While influence tended to correspond to command position, there were some interesting anomalies in the results which Torrance reported. Consider, for example, the dot problem. If one looks at one measure, influence corresponds to the command structure; on the other hand, if one looks at an alternative measure, there are discrepancies in the influence-command relationship. Thus, if we examine Torrance's results, reproduced here in Table 14.1, we see that the pilot influenced the group most when he had a poor answer, the navigator was less influential when he had a poor answer, and the gunner was least influential when he had a poor answer. On the other hand, the failure to influence when they had the best answer shows an interesting result; that is, the navigators failed to influence the group when they had the best answer the fewest number of times. Here we see that using "successful influence with a poor decision" as our measure, influence corresponds to the command structure, but using "failure to influence when they had the best answer" as our measure, the influence pattern does not coincide with the command structure—the navigator having the fewest failures.

Table 14.1

Consequences of Power Differences on Influence of Crew Decision on Dot Test

| | *Percentages* | |
Position	TIMES HAD BEST ANSWER BUT FAILED TO INFLUENCE	TIMES INFLUENCED DECISION WITH POOR ANSWER
Pilots	50.0	21.0
Navigators	46.1	14.5
Gunners	64.0	11.3

SOURCE. Torrance (1955), p. 603.

As we noted earlier, Torrance was concerned with the difference between temporary and permanent groups. He summarized his results as follows: "On all four problems, influence was directly and clearly in accord with the power structure of the group. In general, the effects were somewhat lessened in the temporary crews [p. 491]." Close examination of his tables, however, indicates that the effects are somewhat more complicated. In the horse-trading problem he noted that temporary crews achieved more correct solutions than permanent crews, and, on his measure of "failures to influence given the correct answer," the temporary crews had fewer failures at each position of the command structure than the permanent crews. Furthermore, the gunners had only slightly more failures to influence when they had the correct answer than did the navigators. These data suggest that having the right answer was more important than the command structure in the temporary groups. However, when one examines the dot problem and the conference group story, one sees a somewhat different picture. For both of these problems it appears that more influence was accomplished in the temporary than in the permanent crews, but what is more important is that there was as clearcut a correspondence between the command structure and the amount of influence in the temporary as in the permanent crews. Unfortunately, Torrance's measures were confounded somewhat by incorporating the effects of attempts to influence, successful influence, and self-change in response. Hence, we must be somewhat cautious in interpreting the data with respect to the difference between permanent and temporary crews.

ANALYSIS OF THE THREE STUDIES

In these studies we have three well-conducted investigations of somewhat different phenomena. Yet taken together they do not provide answers to the general questions we have posed. We could, for example, regard Torrance's interest in the difference between permanent and temporary crews as a concern for the conditions under which status conceptions affect interaction. But abstractly we have to ask what it is about permanent and temporary crews that we want to conceptualize. Surely it is not simply that permanent crews have a prior existence. Torrance himself speculates that stable patterns of interaction are the important feature of this prior existence. But there are some stable patterns of interaction which may be totally irrelevant to the problem at hand. Hence, the theoretical task is to formulate those elements of previous interaction patterns that are relevant.

When we consider the other questions we have raised, we either find little information to aid us in formulating abstract and general answers or we find concrete features of these studies that may lead to many alternative abstract formulations. Thus, for example, when we ask what is it about status that affects interaction, we find in these studies either different features of status or correlates of status as the foci of interest. What is it that sex, occupational status, perceived power to influence, prestige in the mental hygiene field, Air Force rank, and command position in a crew have in common? Do they have enough in common to treat them as instances of the same abstract idea? If one begins with an abstract formulation and looks for an empirical manifestation of the idea, there is an explicit rationale to guide the investigator's behavior. In the absence of such an explicit rationale, the particular interests of an individual investigator guide the direction of his own study, and this may make it more or less useful at some later point for a general formulation. Thus, whereas Hurwitz, Zander, and Hymovitch look at their study primarily in terms of egodefensiveness, the present authors examine it from an entirely different perspective; and precisely those features that are of most interest to the original authors detract from our efforts to use the study in our general formulation. Almost every effort to use this literature to formulate generalizations encounters the same problems of comparability. The studies employ (a) diverse independent variables, (b) diverse research settings, (c) diverse dependent variables, and (d) diverse interpretations of their results. Let us consider each of these issues in turn.

Diverse Independent Variables

The primary independent variables in these three studies are occupational status in the jury study, perceived power to influence in the mental hygiene conference study, and command position in the Air Force crew study. The first thing to note is that these primary independent variables are formulated at different levels of abstraction; the value of the occupational status variable for each individual participating in the jury study is given extrinsically by the society at large, whereas perceived power to influence is an aggregate of ratings made by the participants in the conference study. Apart from the issue of measuring these variables, there is the issue of the type of abstraction involved. To most sociologists, occupational status is an *instance* of a more general conception of a hierarchically ordered variable, whereas perceived power to influence would be regarded by many as a *correlate* of this more general notion of status. To so regard perceived power to influence immediately raises the question of the invariance of the correlation—under what conditions is perceived power to influence highly correlated with status?

Constrasting command position with occupational status and with perceived power to influence pinpoints additional issues. Command position involves formal allocation of authority and, with it, legitimate rights to exert influence. Does this make command position a different sort of beast from either occupational status or perceived power to influence? Depending upon how one formulates an abstract notion of status, one could answer yes or no to this question; and if one answers yes, he may not want to regard the three studies as comparable. In the absence of an abstract formulation of status, regarding the studies as comparable or not becomes largely a matter of individual taste, and if the comparison of studies is solely a matter of individual taste, we can hardly hope for an accumulation of knowledge across a series of studies.

Although the three variables we have discussed were the primary independent variables, there were other "independent" variables as well. In the jury study, for example, the jurors were both male and female. In the mental hygiene conference study, the participants not only varied by sex but also had different occupations—psychiatrist, psychologist, social worker, and so forth. In the B-26 crews, Air Force rank as well as command position varied. Sometimes these additional variables were highly correlated with the primary independent variable of the study, and sometimes they were not. Unfortunately, with the exception of sex in the jury study, these three studies do not provide us with information about the relationship of these other variables to the primary variable of the study. Do they introduce confounding effects? Do they strengthen the reported relationship, that is, the relationship of the primary variable to influence? Or are they without effect? Strodtbeck and Mann (1955), in another paper based on the same research, report on the independent effect of sex on jury participation, but that is the only additional information we have. In the absence of adequate controls on these other variables, one cannot answer the questions we have posed. This is not to criticize these authors for not instituting appropriate controls. In doing such a study there are an infinite number of controls one could introduce, and without appropriate guidelines it is impossible to say which control should or should not be used. Rather, we simply want to point out once again the need for an abstract formulation of the problem in order to provide guidelines for the introduction of controls in experimental research.

The use of concretely different independent variables, as well as the presence of additional independent variables in these studies, makes it difficult to use the results to answer the question: What is it about status that affects interaction? Similarly, the diversity of independent variables bears on the question: Under what conditions does status affect interaction? Let us consider the second question. Although the authors do not provide definite information, it is easy to infer the operation of more independent variables than those they report. In the jury study, for example, jury members differed with respect to variables like style of dress, manner of speaking, and poise. These variables could be regarded as cues to the occupational status of the participant. In the Hurwitz et al. study, these factors would not be cues to "perceived power to influence" although there might have been similar factors providing each individual with cues as to the prestige of the other members of the group, and, after all, prestige was nearly perfectly correlated with perceived power to influence. In the Torrance study, on the other hand, each member was aware of the command position of the other members of the crew and there were highly visible and unambiguous symbols of Air Force rank.

We can use these examples to illustrate how one formulates the conditions under which status affects interaction and the implications of alternative formulations. To state two extreme positions, we could either say that status operates only if each member is fully aware of the relative status of *every* member of the group, or we could assert that status operates even if *no* member of the group is aware of the relative status of *any* member of the group. In other words, we could assert that awareness is a necessary condition; the opposite extreme argues that awareness is not a necessary condition. Posing these bald extremes should give some hint as to the range of possible formulations. We could, for example, introduce the idea of *degree of awareness* and argue that each variable, such as style of dress, operates to increase degree of awareness. Or, to take another strategy, we could treat awareness as a sufficient condition for status to affect interaction. Our contention here is that having the studies available does not restrict our theoretical options. It is possible to make a case using these three studies for or against any of the alternative formulations we have illustrated.

If we consider the two extreme positions that awareness is or is not a necessary condition for status to affect interaction, we can point to further implications for the analysis of these studies. If we take the position that status does not affect interaction unless each member is aware of the relative status of every member, we would not regard our three studies as comparable. While it seems obvious that the crew members in the Torrance study all meet this necessary condition, it would be difficult to argue that every juror is aware of the occupational status of every other juror. Futhermore, to add an additional complication, the awareness position does not allow for inaccurate social perception. What do we do, for instance, with two individuals who have clearcut beliefs about the hierarchy of group members, but whose beliefs are perfectly inversely correlated?

The awareness position has one virtue in that for some studies it would allow us to forget about potentially confounding variables because these variables are too subtle for individuals to perceive. Furthermore, asserting this necessary condition allows us to institute appropriate controls for the cues arising in group interaction that are likely to be interpreted in status terms.

If we take the position that status affects interaction even if there is no awareness, we still must raise the question of whether or not it operates more strongly when the participants are aware of the hierarchy. Hence, by itself, taking this position does not resolve the question of whether the studies are comparable or not.

Although we are arguing for the necessity of an abstract formulation of the problem, it is clear that no abstract formulation will conclusively answer the question of comparability of these three particular studies. Such a formulation would provide guidelines for comparing the studies and for raising theoretical and empirical problems, but the comparison will always rest, in large measure, on interpretation. But we should emphasize that an abstract formulation is oriented to the future; its purpose is to inform the design and conduct of future studies, and the studies that are so informed will raise fewer questions of comparability. Studies conducted in terms of a formulation that posits awareness as a necessary condition will all be comparable to the extent that their designs provide for a realization of this necessary awareness.

Diverse Research Settings

The three studies we have presented represent a range of possible settings in which to study these kinds of phenomena. In the Hurwitz, Hymovitch, and Zander study, the experiment was conducted in a field setting in the context of a mental hygiene conference; in the jury studies the setting was an actual court situation modified only to the extent that the subjects heard tape recordings of the trial rather than the actual trial and the context was the entire system of the administration of justice. The Torrance study, although conducted in the field at an Air Force base, most closely approximated a laboratory experiment, but in the context of the Air Force as an organization.

Many of the issues we have already discussed in connection with the independent variables of these studies also apply to the discussion of the diversity of research settings. Here let us only consider two additional issues. On the one hand, we should examine the possibilities and limitations for experimental control in each of these settings. On the other hand, we should concern ourselves with the impact of the context in which the research took place upon the results of these studies.

Every piece of research takes place in a setting that is unique in time and space. There are features of the setting that are peculiar to that setting and not relevant to generalizations about the phenomena of central interest. Some of these unique features can be dealt with by experimental means or through measurement and therefore discounted, but it is never possible to remove all of the unique elements of the situation that affect the variables of concern. Hence, while it is possible to argue that the Torrance study provided many more opportunities for control of unique situational variables than the Hurwitz, Hymovitch, and Zander study, and to argue that greater control of these factors is desirable, simply moving to a more controlled situation does not solve the problems that concern us. For even in the purest of laboratory situations there are unique effects that cannot be eliminated.

Given the position we have just enunciated, must we conclude that any statements we make about any one of these studies must be conditionalized by statements about the unique features of the study? Clearly the answer to this question must be no, for to answer it positively denies the possibility of general statements. How then do we handle these unique situational factors? We distinguish two types of features idiosyncratic to the particular research setting.

The first type consists of those features that can be formulated as instances of abstractly stated conditions. For example, in each of these studies the groups were involved with tasks that required cooperative performance among group members. Ignoring the particular content of the task in each of these three studies, we can formulate them as instances of an abstract idea. The abstract property we choose here is what we call collective valued tasks. By this we mean that the task requires actors who work together, taking the behavior of the others into account, and that actors want to succeed at the task.

The second type of unique situational element is the type that either cannot be formulated as an instance of an abstract condition or for which there is no desire to so formulate it. For example, the fact that the juries listened to tape recordings of a trial may certainly have produced different deliberations from those that would have occurred had the juries witnessed actual trials. How one should formulate this as an instance of some abstract notion, or indeed whether one should bother, depends upon the theoretical orientation guiding one's approach to the research. From our point of view, although this factor may have had important effects, we choose to ignore it and to regard the effects as irrelevant. Of course, this increases the risk of error in interpreting the jury study. In order to compensate for possible erroneous interpretation that could result from ignoring these idiosyncratic factors, we are forced to test our ideas in many studies rather than rely on a single study. By definition, idiosyncratic factors will not repeat themselves in different studies; hence, if our relationship holds up across many different situations, we are safe in eliminating the idiosyncratic features of one situation as an explanation of the relationship between status and interaction.

The distinction we have made in our analysis leads to two conclusions. First, that one cannot regard the unique elements of a setting as instances of abstract conditions unless one has an abstract theoretical formulation to apply to the setting. Second, in the absence of a theoretical formulation, one is left with only the second type of unique element. Confronted with the unique features of a single study, an investigator has no basis for choosing those elements which conditionalize his findings and those elements which can be ignored. It is always possible, looking at the jury study alone, to say that the result occurred only under Condition X, where the investigator is free to choose his own X. Clearly that is an intolerable situation. Now, it may be that an empirical result is an artifact occurring only under some Condition X which is a unique feature of a study, but a decision concerning artifacts can never be made in interpreting a single study and indeed it is our view that the determination of what is an artifact can only be made from the perspective of the theory. In other words, we are once again arguing for the necessity for a theoretical formulation in order to determine what features of the research setting must be controlled and what features of the research setting can be ignored.

The remaining issue that we want to consider in this section is the problem of the context in which the research is done. Certainly one does not want to ignore these contexts or regard them as irrelevant. In the first place the context has an important impact on the subjects' definitions of the status variables. We have already illustrated this in our discussion of independent variables. Do we want to regard each of these contexts as an instance of some abstract condition which qualifies the interpretation of each of these studies? Do we want to treat the three contexts as instances of different abstract conditions? Do we want to postpone the issue, acknowledging that the context is important but regarding it as a problem for future formulation? Can we postpone the question? Certainly Air Force rank would have a different significance in any context outside of the Air Force. Here again in the absence of stated theoretical concerns it is difficult, if not impossible, to answer these questions. One can caution that it appears that too much attention to the context leads to regarding the studies as irrelevant to one another, whereas focusing on the phenomena and more or less suppressing contextual differences may enable one to think creatively about the processes involved.

To sum up, the differences in setting of these three studies involve many differences in situational elements and striking differences in the contexts of the research. To take all of these differences seriously rules out the possibility of general statements and general knowledge. To interpret these diversities in the absence of an explicit theoretical formulation leaves the interpretation totally a matter of individual taste. A theoretical formulation, on the other hand, provides guidelines for making decisions about appropriate conditions; and, perhaps most importantly, a theoretical formulation allows one to say when a given setting or a given context is totally inappropriate for the problem at hand.

Diverse Dependent Variables

When we raised the question, "What is it about interaction that is affected by status conceptions?" we implicitly recognized that interaction is complex, has many properties, and these properties can be measured in many different ways. Which of these properties are invariantly related to one another and which we want to select out and assert as being affected by status conceptions are questions that cannot be answered in general at present. However, these studies dramatically illustrate the necessity for asking these questions and for making choices. In the jury study, the principal dependent variables were the choice of jury foreman and the amount of participation in the deliberations. Participants were also asked questions concerning their satisfaction with the quality of the deliberations and their evaluation of other participants. For example, they were asked, "Who do you believe contributed most to help your group reach its decision?" Strodtbeck et al. attempted to ascertain influence by measuring the jurors' initial opinion, prior to the deliberation, concerning what to award the plaintiff. Finally, two quasi-sociometric questions were asked concerning the makeup of the jury if "a member of your own family were on trial." The first of these asked the jurors which of the four occupational classes they would prefer to make up a majority of the jury, while the second asked them to choose "four of your fellow jurors whom you would best like to have serve on the jury."

The dependent variables employed in the mental hygiene conference study were primarily measures of liking for other participants and of participation of each of the participants. In addition, each conferee reported his perception of how much each other member liked him and his perception of the extent of verbal participation of each. Whereas in the jury study the measure of participation employed Bales' Interaction Process Analysis, Hurwitz, Hymovitch, and Zander simply recorded the length and frequency of remarks made by each group member.

The Air Force crew study also measured influence and participation and the measure of participation involved Interaction Process Analysis. In the horse-trading task, the dot task, and the group story task, individual answers were compared with group answers to determine the amount of influence of the various group members. The technique in the group story task was to tag salient aspects of an individual's story and then to note the frequency of occurrence of these aspects in the group story. In the survival problem, the interaction of the group was analyzed according to Bales' twelve categories. In addition, a questionnaire measured the individual's perception of the amount of effort he put out to influence the crew's decision, his opinion about who had the most influence, his agreement with the decision, and his satisfaction with the decision.

These basic measures in the Torrance study were transformed in various ways to arrive at the dependent variables in his analysis. For example, sometimes he presented as his dependent variable "percentage of Failures to Influence"; other times he presented "Times Influenced with a Poor Decision." In the dot task, he employed a more direct measure, that is, the mean deviation score between crew estimates and individual estimates made after the crew decision.

In order to analyze the diversity of these dependent variables, we must move to a more abstract level. Ignoring the details, we can argue that these three studies are concerned with participation and influence as two principal features of interaction. These two dependent variables are somewhat traditional concerns among small group analysts and have been employed in a large number of studies, including those which focus on status factors. The additional variables of the Hurwitz, Hymovitch, and Zander investigation (those of liking and perception of liking) are also traditional. These liking variables are somewhat different in character from participation and influence as the patterns of interrelationships among these three kinds of variables reveal. Previous research has shown a consistent relationship between amount of participation and degree of influence, but how well a person is liked is not consistently related to either how much influence he has or how much he participates. Bales and Slater (1955) have distinguished between a task leader and a social-emotional leader. The task leader is highest on participation and on influence but usually not highest on being liked. The social-emotional leader is usually best liked but not usually high on participation or influence. Their analysis suggests that liking variables are somewhat distinct from participation and influence variables. It would thus seem that at present it is not appropriate to attempt to integrate these three kinds of abstract variables in one conceptualization. Intuitively it seems that any formulation of the effects of status factors on interaction should be able to handle both participation and influence. Whether or not such a formulation will also eventually handle the relation of status conceptions to liking is a question for the future.

Our listing of the various measures and transformations of these measures at the beginning of our discussion of dependent variables reveals a second problem. Although there is considerable overlap among the abstract variables of these three studies, there is much less overlap in the particular indicators of these abstract variables. Consider, for example, the use of Bales' Interaction Process Analysis versus simply noting the frequency and length of remarks as measures of participation. In the Bales system, a unit is a single complete thought, usually a single complete sentence, whereas the unit for measuring the amount of participation in the mental hygiene conference study is the time unit of a single speech of an individual. To date, there has been no research demonstrating invariant relationship between these two types of units. It is reasonable to question, on theoretical grounds, the equivalence of these measures. Hence, it would not be at all surprising if the two studies produced quite different results with respect to propositions concerning status and participation. Although we are willing to regard these two measures as equivalent, it should be clear that we are doing so by fiat. It is only our assumption of the equivalence of these two measures that allows us to compare the findings of the three studies on the relationship of status to participation.

Another example of what might be termed the indicator problem is the use of three quasi-sociometric indicators in the jury study. What, for example, is the relationship of choice of foreman to our guiding orientation, "Status conceptions organize interactions"? While certainly most sociologists would argue for a relation, such an argument involves a lengthy chain of reasoning. In the interests of theoretical progress, it is desirable to make that chain of reasoning explicit. It is not enough to simply assert that choice of foreman is an indicator of status. While we might grant that assertion, it is still debatable whether it is the most appropriate, or, indeed, at all appropriate, as an indicator of status in the jury studies. The issue of appropriateness becomes more clearcut when one compares the findings on the choice of foreman question with the findings on the other two sociometric questions. It is certainly as reasonable to argue that questions concerning the kinds of people you would prefer to make up the jury and which of your fellow jurors you would like to serve on a jury are indicators of status conceptions. Yet, the relation to occupation of the chosen person differs markedly for each of these three questions. The occupational ordering of the chosen on the foreman choice is much more clearcut than the ordering on the other two questions, and least clearcut when the criterion for choice was "four of your fellow members." Examining the manifest content of each of these questions does suggest that they are somewhat different, but only with an abstract formulation of status conceptions can we make explicit what the differences are and provide some basis for deciding which to use as our indicator, or some basis for understanding differential findings across indicators.

Strodtbeck et al. do provide a rationale for using the two questions concerning choice of fellow juror. They wanted to know if the selections made on the basis of face-to-face contacts were similar to stereotyped choices. Unfortunately, they do not provide similar rationale for the choice of foreman as an indicator. Second, the use of different indicators virtually guarantees variability of the findings, both from the point of view of measurement error and from the point of view that these indicators tap overlapping but not completely equivalent aspects of the abstract variables. Finally, our interpretation requires us to pay attention to some cases where there are diverse findings across indicators and to ignore other cases of such differences; the only justification for doing that is in the service of a theoretical conception of the phenomena involved. Here again we see the urgent need for an abstract formulation of the problem.

Diverse Interpretation of Results

Before concluding our analysis of these three studies, we must look at the explanations offered by the investigators for their findings. Strodtbeck, James, and Hawkins propose no thoroughgoing explanation. They note that the phenomena is yet to be explained. They regard their study as an indication of status continuity; that is, statuses in the large community are replicated and account for differentiation in the jury situation.

Hurwitz, Hymovitch, and Zander focus on the egodefensiveness among group members with low power to influence and the manifestations of this egodefensiveness in interaction. These authors are only concerned with prestige as a correlate of perceived power to influence and their main interest is in the relation between perception of power and egodefensive behavior. Indeed, although perceived power to influence coincides with judges' ratings of prestige in all but three cases, the ratings of prestige are only an expedient to assist in the composition of the groups. (One can also look at status in these groups as a device by which to produce differences in perceived power to influence rather than as a focus of concern.) They regard the interpretation of their results as consistent with the assumption about egodefensive behavior with which they began their study.

Torrance is more concerned with a structural conception of power than with individual conceptions of power. That is, he is concerned with the relationship of influence among individuals and the power structure of the group— a conception of power that ties it more closely to status than is the case in the Hurwitz, Hymovitch, and Zander study. In our view, status in the group is an essential ingredient in Torrance's interpretation, whereas it is only one of several possible ways to produce differences in perceived power in the mental hygiene conference study. Torrance interprets his results as clearly indicating a relationship between the power structure of the group and influence. Consistent with his concern for a structural view of power, he focuses on the differences between permanent and temporary groups, asserting that the effects of the power structure are somewhat lessened in the temporary groups.

The first thing that we note about these interpretations is that they are at somewhat different levels of abstraction. Strodtbeck et al. deal descriptively with the relation of occupational status to interaction in the jury deliberation, leaving the task of explaining *why* occupational status is related to participation, influence, and satisfaction for future analysis. It is interesting that although Strodtbeck et al.'s study was done in 1954, no subsequent efforts to embed their results in a theoretical explanation have appeared, despite their call for such explanations. Whereas the notion of status continuity from the larger society is an explanatory idea, it does not fulfill the requirements of a systematic explanation, as Strodtbeck well recognizes.

Hurwitz, Hymovitch, and Zander attempt to integrate their study into a traditional psychological orientation that has emphasized the manifestations of ego functions in group behavior. Although their assumptions are abstractly formulated and are certainly more general in scope than their particular study, they have not yet achieved a systematic explanation. In the first place, their argument essentially hinges on one assumption: "Individuals with relatively little power to influence others behave toward others with more power in an essentially egodefensive manner." While they proceed to discuss this assumption, it is not clear which of their additional assertions are keystones in the argument and which are merely illustrative. For example, they say, "This defensiveness probably results from the fact that individuals high in the power hierarchy are generally regarded by other group members as being able to help them achieve some of their goals. The power to influence possessed by the highs makes the other group members want to be favorably regarded by them, and since these highs can exercise their power so as to help or hurt others, they generate feelings of uneasiness in other group members. Consequently, group members perceive highs and behave toward them in ways calculated to reduce this uneasiness [1953, p. 800]." Certainly one would not want to hold these authors to this rather informal interpretation containing such unexplicated notions as "uneasiness," yet the authors state that their study was designed to check the accuracy of these conceptions among members of discussion groups.

The theoretical discussion in their study illustrates a subtle and difficult problem in the construction of explanatory theories. On the one hand, the authors appear to be asserting abstract general statements for the purpose of explanation; on the other hand, they seem to be attempting to capture the subjective, descriptive language of the "feeling states" of their subjects. As a description of feeling states, one need not question the transition back and forth between levels of abstraction and the loosely postulated relationship between properties of the group and individual perceptions of these properties. The language of feeling states is essentially metaphorical, and the difficulty with metaphors is that the audience is free to read many unintended connotations into them. Thus, for example, there are a variety of different interpretations of what the authors call "feelings of uneasiness." It is not clear which of these interpretations the authors intend. Are these feelings unobservable internal states of a subject? Are they features of the atmosphere of the group? Do they have behavioral manifestations? Are they intervening variables? This list of possible interpretations employs ideas that are different types of concepts having different functions in a theory. One treats a group level property differently from an individual level property. Similarly, one treats an observable entity differently from an inferential construct. If one is concerned with theoretical explanation, it is important to clarify the elements of a formulation. The usage of ideas that are different types of abstraction, without clearly explicating them and without specifying the relationships among them, is a serious drawback. While, for example, it may be appropriate to relate "feelings of uneasiness" to perceived low power to influence and to underestimation of choices received on a liking measure, one can do so only by recognizing that "feelings of uneasiness" are then treated as unobservable intervening variables. Such explicit recognition thereby constrains the reader from reading into "feelings of uneasiness" connotations incompatible with its usage in the explanatory system. What we are arguing for is explicit exposure of the chain of reasoning that allows one to connect properties of the group situation with perceptions of these properties with behavioral reactions observed in the group.

The difficulties brought about in the absence of explicit chains of reasoning are well illustrated by the fact that the authors report the relationship of the subjects' perceived power to influence and judges' ratings of prestige but nowhere report the relationships of both of these variables to the occupational status of the individuals. We can infer a chain of reasoning here: occupational status → prestige → perceived power to influence; this implies that one would find the same high degree of correspondence between occupational status and perceived power to influence that they report for the relation between judged prestige and perceived power to influence. But the fact that judged prestige is on a different level of analysis from both occupational status and perceived power to influence may alter the expected relationship. After all, the judges are "outside the system," and their evaluations of occupational status may represent different processes from those represented by the evaluations of the group members. While in considering only the Hurwitz, Hymovitch, and Zander study this criticism may not be serious, it does become important when one wants to compare their study with either the jury study or the Air Force crew experiment.

Although Torrance titles his study "Some Consequences of Power Differences," and interprets his results in terms of the power structure of the group, he implicitly assumes a one-to-one correspondence between the command position and the distribution of power. Indeed, he does not formulate his notion of power structure at all, except to say that his study deals with decision making in permanent groups with uniform, well established hierarchical structures. That this abstract notion of power structure contains problems is illustrated by his statement, "A number of studies suggested that the consequences may be due as much to patterns of behavior developed as a result of interaction as to power itself [p. 483]." This seems to suggest that patterns of behavior developed in interaction are independent of a power structure, a position that some sociologists would find quite debatable. Furthermore, the interchangeability of hierarchical structure and power structure is an assumption that requires analysis. On the one hand if there were one-to-one correspondence between position in the hierarchy and power, one would expect a high correlation of perceived power to influence and occupational position in the mental hygiene conference study, but Torrance's own results, which show that navigators are sometimes more influential than pilots, would lead to a different expectation for the Hurwitz, Hymovitch, and Zander study. Clearly formulating this assumption, which could take many different forms, would aid us both in examining Torance's results and in comparing the Air Force study with the mental hygiene conference study.

The major difficulty in comparing and integrating the interpretations of these three studies is that the concepts employed overlap, but one cannot say in any precise way how much they overlap. The use of different levels of abstraction in their concepts and different kinds of constructs for their most abstract notions, makes it extremely difficult to compare their explanations and interpretations.

Summary

It is clear that the three studies we have analyzed all demonstrate that status conceptions do affect interaction. In that sense, they represent demonstrations of Park's basic assumption in three rather diverse situations, but our analysis has shown that it is difficult to say that these studies advance our knowledge beyond Park's original statement.

In this section we demonstrated the need for an abstract theoretical formulation for our knowledge of the relationship of status conceptions to interaction to be cumulative. We illustrated that unequivocal answers to the general questions we posed are not possible if we merely use the three studies themselves. The studies did not consider the questions: Under what conditions do status conceptions affect interaction? What is it about status that affects interaction? What aspects of interaction are affected by status? How does status affect interaction? When we turned to particular studies with these questions, we either found no information bearing on them or material consistent with several possible alternative answers. We contended that the outcome of our analysis would have been the same for any set of similarly general questions, and, furthermore, we argued that in order to advance our knowledge beyond Park, we must begin to answer some of these general questions.

In the course of our analysis, we pointed to problems of comparing two or more studies. We emphasized that regarding two studies as comparable or incomparable itself rests on a set of assumptions. We indicated some of the points of comparison where these assumptions are required and argued that these requirements underscore the need for an abstract formulation.

Comparing and interpreting these three studies have also shown that details of the design, conduct, and analysis of a particular study can be extremely important. Since there are a multitude of such details in any given study, it is impossible for an investigator to treat every detail with equal concern. We argued that an abstract formulation provides guidelines whereby the investigator can treat some details as central and other details as irrelevant.

We should digress to note that it is always possible to interpret any study after the fact and also to make comparisons among studies, but those interpretations and comparisons often rest on *ad hoc* assumptions, rarely made explicit and, indeed, often changing from one study to the next. Insofar as we can make one *ad hoc* assumption to interpret the first study, and change it when approaching a second study, we have not constrained ourselves at all, and any interpretation is as good as any other. A consistent and explicit theoretical formulation, however, constrains the ways in which we can interpret these three studies. While it is always necessary to interpret, it is desirable and may even be necessary for our interpretations to be constrained for them to be cumulative.

An Abstract Formulation of Relationship of Status Conceptions to Interaction

We believe that the previous analysis has demonstrated the necessity for abstractly formulating our ideas about the relationship between status conceptions and interaction. It is also our position that there is no unique formulation of this problem. A theorist focuses on certain elements that he regards as central and attempts to formulate these elements and their relations. There is no *a priori* reason why another theorist could not select different elements as central to his formulation and arrive at a theory as good or better than the first theorist's. Therefore, we do not intend to argue that our formulation is unique or even the only reasonable one. We hope that other theorists will attempt alternative formulations or formulations that supercede our own. The position we are prepared to defend vigorously is that any explicit, abstract formulation is better than no formulation.

We believed that a fruitful way for us to begin was to attempt to formulate the phenomena from the point of view of a given actor whom we call P. The resulting theory is known as a P-centric theory, thereby emphasizing that certain conditions must be met before the theory can be applied to any given actor. In more familiar terms, by making our formulation P-centric, we take seriously the traditional sociological injunction that an actor's "definition of the situation" determines his response to the situation. It also captures the fact that when he is interacting with one actor, an Air Force captain may be a high status person, whereas with another actor, such as a five-star general, the captain may be low status. The P-centric nature of the formulation enables the same assertions to be applied to actors with quite different definitions of the situation, once their differences are "plugged into" the conceptualization. Lest some readers regard the P-centric nature of the formulation as excessively limited, we should make it clear that the limitations in our opinion are not at all severe. It is possible to apply P-centric formulations to large groups by successive applications to the individuals making up these large groups.[4] Furthermore, by treating the phenomena from the point of view of each actor, we are able in an explicit and reproducible fashion to exclude those individuals in a situation for whom the theory does not apply, that is, those individuals who are outside the scope of the theory. We will illustrate how our formulation allows this after we have developed our key ideas.

Our actor, P, is reacting to himself and to other actors in the situation. We treat these other actors as objects of P's orientation and use the letter O to keep from repeating the cumbersome phrase "objects of orientation." P himself may be an object of his own orientation, and we distinguish this special object by using the letter P'. Thus, our formulation deals with relations between P, the actor, and P' and O as the objects of his orientation. For the sake of simplicity, and without any loss of generality, we deal with systems involving only one other actor, O. Our formulation can deal with many actors as the objects of P's orientation, but that would not alter the nature of the conceptualization and would greatly complicate the exposition. So, while our discussion deals only with systems containing one P reacting to P' and one O, the reader should bear in mind that the formulation can be applied to many P's, each of which has many Os in his interaction situation.

The starting point for our formulation is an attempt to explicate the idea of a status conception. We do this by introducing the notion of a *diffuse status characteristic*, where the characteristic is an attribute of an actor that signifies to himself and to others that he holds a certain status. Most of the studies we have examined deal with interaction between actors who differ with respect to some status attributes. What are the significant aspects of these differences? First of all, the differences involve *differential evaluations* of actors. The notion here is that one actor is better or worse than another actor. These evaluations are not about specific performance of the actors but are very generalized and diffuse (e.g., it is better to be a professional than a laborer, rather than, it is better to be able to solve a mathematical problem than not). Second, associated with the perception of differences in a status attribute are beliefs about different abilities, capacities, or other attributes of actors at specific tasks or in specific situations. In other words, perception of a status attribute arouses *specific expectations* about performances on specific tasks, such as "Men are better at mechanical puzzles than women." One of our key ideas, then, is that the perception of a status attribute triggers belief systems that are attached to this status attribute. In addition to these beliefs about specific performance in specific situations, there are also generalized beliefs associated with status attributes. We call generalized beliefs such as "Whites are smarter than Negroes," or "Officers are gentlemen," *generalized expectations*. We use

[4] Successively applying a P-centric formulation to arrive at propositions about groups can be called "the composition problem." While we do not wish to minimize the technical issues in solving the composition problem, we do believe that the necessity for solving them does not in principle limit the usefulness of a P-centric formulation.

these three notions of differential evaluation, the presence of specific expectations, and the presence of generalized expectations to define in abstract terms
what we mean by a diffuse status characteristic. We formulate the notion of a
diffuse status characteristic from the point of view of a given actor, P. Formally
the definition is as follows: A characteristic, D, is a diffuse status characteristic
from the point of view of P if, and only if (a) it has two or more states that are
differentially evaluated; (b) to each state, X, of D there corresponds a distinct
set, δ, of specifically associated, evaluated states of performance characteristics; and (c) to each state, X, of D there corresponds a distinct general expectation state, GES_x, having the same evaluation as the state D_x.

Thus, for example, skin color for a given actor may or may not be a diffuse
status characteristic. If the actor differentially evaluates the states, white and
black, regards whites as better able to solve mathematical problems than blacks,
and generally regards whites as superior to blacks, then for that actor, skin
color is a diffuse status characteristic. Note that the way we formulate the notion
does not require that skin color be a diffuse status characteristic for every
actor. Furthermore, our formulation allows the possibility, perhaps realized in
the case of the black militant, for skin color to be a diffuse status characteristic
for an actor where black is the state more highly evaluated than white, where
specific abilities are associated with being black, and where there is the generalized expectation of superiority in being black.

Our interpretations of the studies we have considered suggest that occupational status, command position, Air Force rank, mental hygiene specialty, all
may represent diffuse status characteristics. Since we don't have the responses
of each individual P in these studies, in order to interpret them we must assume
that each of these variables represents a diffuse status characteristic for most of
the subjects involved in the studies. If we were to redo each of these studies
from the point of view of this formulation of a diffuse status characteristic, we
would, of course, attempt to check on the presence of each of these elements in
each participant's definition of the situation. We believe that our formulation
captures some of the central ingredients of the idea of a status conception
without too closely tying the formulation to concrete instances. The virtue of
not tying the formulation too closely to concrete instances is well illustrated
by the historical changes that are currently taking place in the area of race.
Whereas a few years ago it was clear that for the vast majority of the population, both white and Negro, race had the properties of the diffuse status characteristic; the states, Negro and white, were differentially evaluated and there
were clear expectations associated with these states. But recent events appear to
be altering the beliefs associated with race. Thus, those who do not generalize
about whites and Negroes are Ps for whom race no longer fits the properties of
diffuse status characteristics.

In our formulation we rely heavily on the notion of a self-other expectation,
that is, a belief about oneself, relative to the others with whom one is interacting. These expectations may be quite specific, such as, "Relative to O, I am
more likely to solve mathematical problems. Thus, I have a high-low self-other

expectation." The expectation may be quite generalized, in which case we speak of a generalized expectation state. Once again, the self-expectation is relative, but this time relative to an entire class of Os. For example, relative to women, P' (a male) is smarter. For simplicity of exposition, we will treat the self-other expectations as taking on only two values, + and —.

We believe that expectations can be generalized to continuous variables having many degrees of + and —, but that is a problem for future work. In speaking about expectations, we will use the following notation (+ —) where the first symbol in the parentheses refers to the state of *self* and the second to the state of *other*. Thus, if a person believes that he has high ability at the dot problem and his partner has low ability, with respect to that problem he is a (+ —).

In our discussion we deal with specific performance expectations as attached to specific abilities or specific characteristics, and we will use interchangeably the terms *state of specific characteristic* and *state of a performance expectation*.

The next task is to conceptualize interaction. Earlier we suggested a direction that an abstract formulation of interaction variables might take. We regarded our three studies as principally concerned with participation and influence as two central features of interaction. Basing our thinking on the work of Berger and Conner (1969), we conceptualized the important aspects of interaction in terms of four kinds of observable behavior:

1. The actors either give or do not give *action opportunities*. These action opportunities are socially distributed chances to perform, for example, when one person asks another for his opinion.
2. The actors either contribute a *performance output* or do not. Thus, when A tells B his opinion, he is contributing a performance output.
3. An evaluation is made of the performance output, that is, either positive or negative. We will call this evaluation a *unit evaluation* so that when A tells B that he has a good idea, or that he agrees with his opinion, he is giving B a positive unit evaluation.
4. One member influences another. B changes his mind as a result of a unit evaluation of his performance by A.

Typically members of a group who are high in participation receive many action opportunities, are high in performance outputs, receive positive unit evaluations, and influence other members. That is, we argue that these four elements are highly interrelated and also highly correlated with total participation. It is therefore, reasonable to treat these four elements, and indeed total participation as well, in terms of a more abstract idea. This we label the *observed power-prestige order of the group*. In this notion we attempt to capture the idea that the interaction behavior of group members is a manifestation of the power and prestige they have in the group. We believe that the concept of an observed power-prestige order captures much of the task-relevant aspects of interaction.

Having formulated the idea of a diffuse status characteristic and the idea of an observable power and prestige order, we now need to characterize the situations in which interaction takes place. The studies we have examined all involve a collective task in which the group members are cooperating and are interdependent. It is also reasonable to assume that on these tasks the group members want to be successful; hence, we posit the existence of a collective, valued task as a condition under which status conceptions are related to interaction. But the interaction situation must also have other properties. We assume that these tasks each involve an ability. Since we have already posited the interdependence of actors (the task is collective), it follows that a given actor, in order to maximize his own success and/or the success of the group, must be able to assess the abilities and contributions of the other group members relative to himself. Whether a juror votes for a high award or a low award depends upon his assessment of the merits of the arguments put forth by the other jurors. Whether the gunner changes his estimate of the number of dots depends upon his assessment of the relative abilities of the pilot, the navigator, and himself.

We label this requirement for assessing abilities as *the pressure to assign* condition. In other words, task performance requires the formation of self-other expectations with respect to the ability that is instrumental to successful task completion. The assignment of expectations is a trivial matter and one not likely to be affected by status conceptions where the actor knows how much of the specific ability he and the others possess. We therefore require that the task situation involve no basis for the assignment of expectations to self and other except the states of the diffuse status characteristic. Given a group situation where (a) there is a collective valued task, (b) there is pressure to assign, and (c) there is no basis other than a status characteristic that provides information about the abilities of the actors in the situation, we are ready to formulate a generalization about the phenomena.

> When members of a group are differentiated with respect to a diffuse status characteristic external to the task situation, this differentiation determines the observable power and prestige order within the group whether or not the diffuse status characteristic is related to the group task.

In formulating this generalization we have taken a stance with respect to the general questions we raised at the outset of this chapter. The generalization incorporates the conditions under which status conceptions affect interaction, it indicates those features of status that affect interaction, and it posits those elements of interaction that are affected by status. Furthermore, we believe that this generalization captures the principal findings of the studies we have examined.

Our abstract generalization does not deal with the question of how status conceptions affect interaction. The theory that we have formulated, which we call the Theory of Status Characteristics and Expectation States (Berger, Cohen, and Zelditch, 1966), deals explicitly with that question. That theory constitutes an explanation of the generalization we have presented here. It contains a set of propositions that relate the elements of a diffuse status characteristic to specific performance expectations and enables us to formally deduce our generalization. We do not present the theory here, since it would require a lengthy exposition and is not central to the main purposes of this chapter. It would also be interesting to take our generalization and the theory and reanalyze the three studies which began this chapter, as well as other studies of status reported in this book. But we leave this for the reader to do. It remains for us to show how our formulation, that is, the generalization and the conditions under which it holds, serves as a guide to research. In the next section we will describe our standardized experimental situation and indicate how its features are related to our formulation.

A Standardized Experimental Setting

The formulation of the problem we presented in the last section enables us to employ an experimental paradigm for studying the relationship between status conceptions and the observed power and prestige order in a group. In examining our three studies, we raised many issues of comparability from one study to another. But the features of these studies that raised issues of comparability were not central to our concerns; hence we sought an experimental situation that would rule out most of the extraneous variables in these prior studies. Our intention was to construct a standardized situation that could be used repeatedly to study different aspects of the phenomena of status conceptions and would insure comparability across a large number of studies. In contrast to many current experimental designs that contain experimental treatments and one or more "control groups," this strategy allows rigorous comparisons to be made across different experiments. In other words, a particular study can use all previous experiments employing the standardized situation as control groups without the problems of interpretation we described in our analysis of the three studies.

The standardized experimental situation we shall describe captures the properties that we used to characterize these situations in the previous section. In particular, the task and interaction conditions directly incorporate the elements we have described. We should point out, however, that we did not logically derive the properties of our standardized experimental situation from our formulation. Rather, central features of the standard experimental situation preceded our present formulation and indeed contributed to our theorizing. On the other hand, our theoretical work introduced modifications into our conception of the standardized experimental setting. The setting that we have used represents the outcome of a long developmental program in which both theory and experimentation mutually influence one another. As a result of this program, we now have a situation, calibrated and standardized, which we are using to test propositions concerning status conceptions and interaction. This is not to say that all technical problems in experimenting on status and interaction have been solved, nor that we have been able to achieve all of the features we desire in our standardized experimental situation. Our technology is not sufficiently advanced so that simply defining a desired feature of the situation guarantees that we can implement that desire. Nevertheless, both several years of previous experience with studies of power and prestige and our explicit theoretical account of the conditions which must be met in order to study these problems have provided us with guidelines for designing and conducting our experiments. We are convinced that these guidelines are much sounder than the usual *ad hoc* hunches. Furthermore, they have defined new problems for us, both technological and theoretical, in those areas where there is a discrepancy between a desired feature of the standardized setting and our ability to implement that desire.

The standardized experimental setting has three basic features: (a) it operationalizes our basic theoretical concepts, (b) it permits the kinds of variations in conditions that are important to our formulation, and (c) it provides the opportunity for a high degree of control over those features of the process that are, in the light of our formulation, crucial to what takes place. The principal feature of the standardized experimental situation is that subjects do not directly interact with one another and in fact do not see one another. Since subjects are not in face-to-face contact, any cues about status or task performance are completely under the control of the experimenter. For this degree of control, however, we pay a price: both the strength of experimental manipulations and the credibility of the situation are somewhat less than they would be in face-to-face interaction situations. We regard the price as modest, but even so we are currently exploring closed circuit television as a way of enhancing the credibility and the impact of our experimental manipulations. Packaging this situation for closed circuit television appears promising, but it is too early to report definitive results.

The standard experiment has a manipulation phase, an experimental phase, and a postexperimental interview and debriefing phase. In the manipulation phase, subjects can be told their states of the diffuse status characteristic, the experimenter can assign general expectation states to the subjects, or he can assign states of the specific performance characteristic and thus put subjects into one or another of the performance expectation states. These manipulations can take place either through verbal instructions or through the administration of preliminary "tests." For example, the experimenter can tell the subjects in the manipulation phase, "I see one of you is a junior college student and one of you is a university student," and thus discriminate the subjects on a diffuse status characteristic.[5] When we want to manipulate states of a specific performance characteristic, we typically "test" the subjects' individual abilities and report their scores prior to having them perform the group task.

In the experimental phase, two or more subjects participating at one time repeat n identical trials (where a trial is used in the same sense as in a learning experiment), in each of which there is a binary choice decision-making prob-

---

[5] This assumes that from the point of view of each subject, level of education *is* a diffuse status characteristic. The P-centric nature of the theory, of course, requires us to evaluate whether each subject associates the set of beliefs with states of the characteristic required by the theory.

lem. Each trial has three stages. The first stage requires each subject to make an initial choice between the two alternatives of the binary choice task. After each subject has made his initial choice, he is told how the other(s) made an initial choice. After this feedback of other(s) initial choice(s), the subject makes a final choice. After his final choice a new trial begins.

On each trial of the decision-making task, the subject is presented with an ambiguous stimulus which has been extensively pretested to insure its ambiguity. For example, one of our tasks uses as stimuli large rectangles made up of 100 smaller black and white rectangles. The subject is to decide whether the stimulus is more black than white or more white than black. The task is presented to the subjects as measuring an ability which we call *contrast sensitivity*. The experimental instructions emphasize the importance of this ability and the fact that it is not related to other abilities about which the subjects may know their relative standing.

Communication between subjects is completely manipulated by the experimenter. This is accomplished by an Interaction Control Machine (called ICOM). ICOM consists of three kinds of equipment: (a) subject consoles; (b) a host experimenter's panel; (c) a master control unit. Each subject sits in front of a subject console, partitioned off from other subjects so that he cannot see them, and makes his decisions by using buttons on his console. His decision appears to him as a light on the panel, and information about the choices made by others appears in the same way. The master control unit contains all circuits of the machine, and connects all subject consoles so that communication from subject to subject passes through, and can be manipulated by, the master unit, which is typically located in a separate room. The host experimenter's panel duplicates all indicator lights, and has a relay release button for clearing all lights on the subject consoles; it allows an experimenter in the room to monitor the entire process.

The basic dependent variable is the difference between the final and initial decisions of the subject. If the subject does not change his initial decision, he is said to make a *self-response*; if the subject does change, he is said to make an *other-response*. (We use S-response as an abbreviation for self-response and O-response for other-response.) The probability of a self-response measures the degree to which the subject is influenced by others.

We want the experiment to operationalize the components of the power-prestige order and the conditions regarded as important in the development of power-prestige orders. It will be recalled from the previous section that the components of the power-prestige order are: (a) *action opportunities*, or socially distributed chances to perform; (b) *performance outputs*, or problem-solving attempts; (c) *unit evaluations*, or evaluations of a particular performance output or person at the moment of a performance output—which may or may not show itself in an observable reward, such as praise or blame; and (d) *influence*, the change of a judgment or decision as a consequence of the unit evaluations or performance outputs of other members of a group.

In the Berger-Snell (1961) model of how differences in power-prestige come about, two important conditions are: (a) the *agreement or disagreement* of actors, and (b) the *commitment of actors to a final decision.* The first is important because it suggests to actors that they have different states of the specific ability characteristic. The second is important because they cannot simply ignore this fact; they must resolve their disagreements in favor of one or the other actor. These conditions of the expectation process must be kept in mind in devising experiments, because failure to control them means that much will take place that we do not understand. For example, if subjects differ in the rates of disagreement with others, and we have no control over this disagreement, we will have no control over the differences in power-prestige that come about.

How are these features of the formulation defined by operations in the experiment? Action opportunities are given to each subject by the experimenter who requires the subject to make an initial choice independent of the choice made by others in the situation. The choice itself is the performance output. Influence is measured by the probability of a self-response. Unit evaluations are not directly observable but we assume are in $1:1$ correspondence with the self- or other-response. For example, if Subject 1 and Subject 2 disagree and Subject 1 decides, "I am right and he is wrong," then we assume Subject 1 makes a self-response. If Subject 2, on the other hand, decides, "I am wrong, he is right," this unit evaluation produces an other-response. Disagreement is identified in the experiment with the difference between one subject's initial choice and other subject's initial choice. Commitment to a decision is identified with the final choice of each standard trial, the result of which is a score that counts toward success or failure. Performance-expectation states are, of course, unobservables, and are not directly identified with operations of the experiment.

We should point out that our operationalization enables us to control two important features of the process. The first is the distribution of action opportunities to subjects and the second is their rates of disagreement. Since these elements are usually correlated with one another and usually correlate with influence of one actor on another, it is desirable to look only at one property of the power and prestige order at a time, holding constant the other elements. In natural settings an actor at the bottom of the power and prestige order typically takes few action opportunities and typically also has low influence on other subjects. If we want to see how such an actor would react if he were given and took action opportunities, we would have to arrange this experimentally. This is controlled by the structure of the standard trial, where each subject is required to make an initial and a final choice—in other words, each subject has the same action opportunities.

As we mentioned earlier, the disagreement or agreement of subjects in their initial choices is a second crucial feature of the power-prestige process, although the part it has to play is different. Disagreement fundamentally determines the stability or instability of self-other expectations. If, for example, a subject believes that both he and his partner are good at the task, and then he finds that they disagree, what can he think? A sufficient number of such disagreements should lead to a differentiation of his beliefs. They can't both be right if they are constantly disagreeing. On the other hand, if a subject believes that he is good at the task, and his partner is poor and finds that in independently made choices they both agree, what can he think? A sufficient number of such agreements should lead to the belief that they are equals. It is therefore important in studying this situation to be able to control the amount of disagreement that takes place. This is accomplished by ICOM which gives the experimenter complete control over, and ability to manipulate, the communication that takes place between subjects.

In this standardized situation, then, the principal dependent variable is a measure of influence, whereas the independent variable is some manipulation designed to indicate to the subjects that they possess different states of some status characteristic. The conditions we formulate are realized either through explicit instructions from the experimenter or through the control of communications using ICOM. The description of contrast sensitivity is designed to create a valued task for the subjects. Defining it as a new ability, we attempt to realize the requirement that subjects have no basis for forming expectations. This condition also requires us to make use of only one status characteristic differentiating subjects. Since the subjects do not see one another, the experimenter can severely limit the status cues available to subjects and thus guarantee that only a single diffuse status characteristic differentiates them.

The efforts to meet the requirements of a collective task include the structure of the decision-making trial as well as the instructions from the experimenter. Since the other person's opinion lights up on a subject's panel, it is difficult for him to avoid "taking the other into account." By emphasizing that we are interested in group performance rather than individual decisions, we attempt to remove the constraints a subject may feel in using the other person's opinion and changing his own initial decision. (Some subjects, for example, feel that it is cheating to use the other person's opinion.) Although it may appear that creating a collective task is the easiest condition to realize, it turns out to be more difficult than anticipated.

The final phase of the experiment, the experimental interview, is designed to determine two things: whether the subject met the conditions of the formulation and whether the independent variable of the study was indeed a status characteristic from his point of view as required by the P-centric nature of the formulation. Intensive questioning attempts to determine whether each subject meets the requirements or should be excluded from the analysis. Thus, for example, a subject who reports that he was very concerned about his own level of contrast sensitivity and therefore did not use his partner's opinions as that would give him a false reading of his own ability is excluded from the data analysis as violating the collective task condition. While the data from the interview phase are not as reliable as the decision-making data, they do provide insights that affect both the theoretical formulation and the experimental procedures.

In this situation, the manipulation (what it is and how it is carried out), the decision-making phase (what the task is and what properties it must have), and the interview phase (what questions are asked and how the information is employed) are all explicitly guided by the theoretical formulation. A number of studies have been conducted that use this standardized experimental situation and are designed to extend our understanding of the relation of status conceptions to interaction. These include studies of educational level as a status characteristic (Moore, 1968), Air Force rank as a status characteristic (Cohen, Berger, & Zelditch, forthcoming), race as a status characteristic (Seashore, 1968; Cohen, Kiker, & Kruse, 1969).

CONCLUSION

The purpose of this chapter has been to examine why our knowledge of the relationship between status conceptions and interaction has not been cumulative and to present a strategy that will promote the development of cumulative knowledge. We have argued that an abstract theoretical framework is a necessary condition for cumulative research. The elements of this framework are: one or more abstract generalizations, a set of conditions under which these generalizations may be expected to hold, a theory that explains the generalizations, and a standardized experimental situation in which to test and extend the theory. The standardized experimental situation, in turn, is informed by the generalizations and attempts to realize the conditions under which the generalizations will hold.

The problems of comparison and interpretation of existing studies dramatically illustrate the need for an abstract theoretical framework. But such a framework does not spring full-blown into existence. Where does one begin? Here our analysis of the three prior studies is instructive. Not only does the state of existing literature on a particular phenomenon motivate the quest for an abstract formulation; it contributes to the content of that framework as well. When one approaches a body of previous research with a general question, the partial answers and even the *way* in which a particular study fails to answer the question may be productive of insight and direction. Our formulation of a diffuse status characteristic owes much to asking and attempting to answer explicitly the question of what command position, occupational status, and sex have in common.

From our presentation, it also should be clear that an analysis of the existing literature cannot of itself provide a theoretical framework. If we did not have some elements of our theory and experimental situation, we would not have analyzed the three studies in exactly the way we did. Nevertheless, even in the absence of these elements, we could have usefully analyzed existing studies as a starting point if we asked questions such as: What do these studies say about the conditions under which X and Y are related? The first step in developing a body of cumulative knowledge is to ask a general theoretical question.

REFERENCES

BALES, R. F. *Interaction process analysis.* Reading, Mass.: Addison-Wesley, 1950.

BALES, R. F., & SLATER, P. E. Role differentiation in small decision-making groups. In T. Parsons & R. F. Bales (Eds.), *Family, socialization and interaction process.* Glencoe, Ill.: Free Press, 1955. Pp. 259–306.

BERGER, J., COHEN, B. P., & ZELDITCH, M., JR. Status chararacteristics and expectation states. In J. Berger, M. Zelditch, Jr., & B. Anderson (Eds.), *Sociological theories in progress.* Boston: Houghton Mifflin, 1966. Pp. 29–46.

BERGER, J., & CONNER, T. L. Performance expectations and behavior in small groups. *Acta Sociologica,* 1969, **12,** 4, 186–198.

BERGER, J., & SNELL, J. L. A stochastic theory for self-other expectations. Technical Report No. 1, 1961, Stanford, Calif.: Laboratory for Social Research.

COHEN, B. P., BERGER, J., & ZELDITCH, M. *Status conceptions and power and prestige.* Manuscript in preparation.

COHEN, B. P., KIKER, J. E., & KRUSE, R. J. The formation of performance expectations based on race and education: A replication. Technical Report No. 30, 1969, Stanford, Calif.: Laboratory for Social Research.

HURWITZ, J. I., ZANDER, A. F., & HYMOVITCH, B. Some effects of power on the relations among group members. In D. Cartwright & A. F. Zander (Eds.), *Group dynamics.* New York: Harper & Row, 1960. Pp. 800–809.

LIPPITT, R., POLANSKY, N., & ROSEN, S. The dynamics of power. *Human relations,* 1950, **5,** 37–64.

MOORE, J. C., JR. Status and influence in small group interactions. *Sociometry,* 1968, **31,** 47–63.

PARK, R. E. The bases of race prejudice. *The Annals,* 1928, **140,** 11–20.

SEASHORE, M. J. The formation of performance expectations in an incongruent status situation. Unpublished doctoral dissertation. Stanford, Calif.: Stanford University, 1967.

STRODTBECK, F. L., JAMES, R. M., & HAWKINS, C. Social status in jury deliberations. *American Sociological Review,* 1957, **22,** 713–719.

STRODTBECK, F. L., & MANN, R. D. Sex role differentiation in jury deliberations. *Sociometry,* 1956, **19,** 3–11.

TORRANCE, E. P. Some consequences of power differences on decision making in permanent and temporary three-man groups. In A. P. Hare, E. F. Borgatta, & R. F. Bales (Eds.), *Small groups.* New York: Knopf, 1955. Pp. 482–491.

15

AUTHORITY
AND PERFORMANCE
EXPECTATIONS
IN BUREAUCRATIC
ORGANIZATIONS[1]

Morris Zelditch, Jr.[2]

INTRODUCTION

Monocratic authority was a fundamental principle of the classical theory of organizations. Authority in an organization is *monocratic* if it satisfies the rule that:

> All authority over a subordinate is exercised by one and
> only one superior. (1)

What is meant by (1) is, first, that immediate superiors have a right to expect compliance with any authentic command that does not violate a basic community norm; second, that no other official has the right to expect compliance with any command in conflict with that of a subordinate's immediate superior. The result is a typical treelike structure, of the kind shown in Figure 15.1, in which channels of communication are restricted and vertical.

A subordinate such as D can communicate with another such as G only by going through B, A, and C. C, although superior in authority to D, can communicate with D only by going through B and A. Even A can communicate directly with D only by assuming direct responsibility for the consequent behavior of D, that otherwise is the delegated responsibility of B. The purpose of all

[1] Work on authority and evaluation structures in organizations in this chapter was partly supported by National Science Foundation Grant G23990.

[2] I am particularly grateful to Joseph Berger and William Evan for their contributions to this chapter.

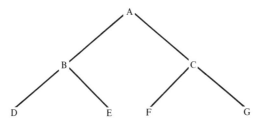

Figure 15.1
Classical organizational hierarchy.

this is to assure that superiors are accountable for the performance of their subordinates. For in classical organizational theories, A was responsible for the performance of B and held B responsible for the performance of D. D could not be blamed by A if D's performance was poor, because D was regarded only as complying with instructions from B. None of E, F, or G could be blamed, because they had no authority over D and lateral communication was not permitted. C could not be blamed, because he could have communicated with D only if B had permitted it. Only B could blame D directly for poor performance; by anyone else in the organization it was B, not D, who was given credit or blame for D's performance. The effect of all this is not only to securely fix credit and discredit, but to make the whole organization the efficient expression of a single will—that of A.

Rationality played an equally important role in the classical theory of organizations. An organization is rational if it satisfies the rule that:

All appointments and promotions are based solely on
possession of the necessary qualifications for office.   (2)

The point, of course, is to assure that appointment is not ascribed, does not depend on belonging to the right family, the right social class, or the right political party. Merit alone should determine appointment. Rationality as a principle is independent of monocratic authority (Udy, 1959), and it was rationality rather than monocratic authority that was for Weber the mark of the specifically *modern* bureaucratic organization, the aim of which was "the exercise of control on the basis of knowledge [Weber, 1947, 339]."

Principles (1) and (2) taken together seemed to classical theorists to imply a third, the identity of the authority and skill structures of an organization, or the superior knowledge of superiors.

Superior authorities possess superior knowledge.   (3)

For if (1) is true, a superior is called on to evaluate his subordinate's performance; and it is natural to suppose that he is competent to do so—in particular, that he is more competent to do so than the subordinate. Furthermore, if (2) is also true, the strictly graded levels of the organization guaranteed by (1) should correspond to similarly graded levels of merit; for it is natural to suppose from (2) that the higher the level achieved within the organization, the greater the official's merit.

We are concerned in this chapter with the fact that neither (1) nor (3) are true of all organizations. For example, in professional organizations (hospitals, universities, research organizations) the "professional," whether administratively in a subordinate position or not, is relatively autonomous in matters that require technical competence (diagnosis of patients, content of lectures, choice of research problem). He may be advised by superiors, but not directed. Where purely administrative decisions are involved (additions to plant, financing, maintenance) an administrative hierarchy exists in which the professional is directed, not advised. But even administrative decisions, if they require professional competence (appointments, promotions, dismissals), tend to be in the hands of collegial bodies representing the dominant professional group. Furthermore, where evaluations of skills and accomplishments are concerned, the organization may solicit and rely on outside opinions of members of the profession rather than rely solely on evaluations by administrative superiors.[3] Thus, authority in professional organizations is *collegial* rather than monocratic, that is, it is held by one's colleagues rather than one's superiors. And, although appointment and promotion do depend on technical qualifications, it is possible, and often happens, that administrative subordinates possess qualifications equal or superior to those of their superiors.[4]

Not only are (1) and (3) sometimes not true, there is evidence to suggest that when (1) is not true it is *because* (3) is not true. That is:

> Without the superior knowledge of superiors, organizations   (4)
> are not monocratic.

For example, there has been a marked change in the skill structure of the armed services. Middle-ranking officers and enlisted men have become technical

---

[3] See particularly Clark, 1961; Freidson, 1963; and Goss, 1961. On the professions in general, see Goode, 1957; and Hughes, 1951, 1958. For their effect on bureaucratic organization, see Hall, 1967, 1968. On various particular professional organizations, see Glaser, 1964; Coser, 1962; Kornhauser, 1960; Marcson, 1960, 1961; and Scott, 1965.

[4] The relative autonomy of technically proficient subordinates is noticed also in craft organizations. In such organizations, the subordinate plans his own work procedure, including the tools he will use, which he often provides himself; the materials he will need; and the work routines he will follow. He commands an empirical lore often greater than that of the foreman, respecting his own craft, and the authoritative acts of his superiors are confined to the coordination of different crafts, the identification and specification of goals, settling the terms of exchange, and similar decisions that do not interfere with craft institutions themselves (Stinchecombe, 1959).

specialists of one sort or another, and have come to possess skills not possessed by their commanders. The effect has been to weaken the military command structure, in the sense that such technicians favor bypassing the chain of command in between-echelon communications and increasing lateral communication and coordination at the expense of hierarchical communication and coordination (Janowitz, 1960).

Implied in (4) is an underlying process by which the authority structure of an organization is made to depend on the relative capacities of members of an organization to perform their organizational tasks. The main purpose of this chapter is (a) to investigate the nature and conditions of this underlying process, and (b) to construct an experimental setting in which such an investigation can be made.

We undertake the first of these two tasks in Part I, which analyzes the nature of beliefs people hold about performance capacities, the nature of authority structures, and especially the conditions under which the former bears causally on the latter—for it is clear from the present evidence that (4) is no more invariably true than (1) or (3). For example, in industrial organizations experts with specialized knowledge are often used to advise "line" officials, officials responsible for the operative decisions of the organization. All authority is concentrated in the hands of the line officials (who, indeed, are called "line" officials precisely because of their place in the chain of command) and the staff may advise them, but not direct them. In such organizations staff-line conflict is endemic (Dalton, 1950, 1959; Moore and Renck, 1955), but this may be because the experts are often inferior to line officials in resources and rewards, although superior in knowledge, education, and often social class. If beliefs about competence determine the sort of authority structure found in bureaucratic organizations, the process is more complicated than (4) implies, or depends on conditions not stated in (4). What these conditions are, how they are related to (4), and more precise definitions of the central concepts in (4), are given in Part I.

Part II of this chapter is concerned with a standardized experimental setting in which the nature and conditions of the process underlying (4) can be investigated. There has been some objection to studying anything so complex as an organization in a setting so simple as a laboratory. But it has not been possible in the natural setting of an organization to isolate the process underlying (4), because so many other organizational processes also bear on authority; nor has it been possible to find naturally occurring organizations in which theoretically important conditions of the process vary while other task and interaction conditions remain the same. Part II, therefore, describes a simulated organizational setting, in particular one with a complex division of labor and a hierarchy of status and authority, in which it is possible to isolate and control the process underlying (4).

A brief summary of findings and their implications for organizational theory is provided in part III.

I. THEORETICAL FORMULATION

Performance Expectations

A *performance expectation* is an inferred state of an actor's capacity, relative to another, to perform some given task.[5] Thus:

$$\text{Jones is a better volleyball player than Smith.} \qquad (5)$$

is a performance expectation. It should be noted that (5) is different from:

$$\text{Jones made a marvelous spike.} \qquad (6)$$

which is a *unit evaluation*, that is, an evaluation of one instance of Jones' actual behavior. Whereas (6) is an event that has actually occurred, (5) is an inference about what Jones is capable of; it is an expectation held by Jones that something like (6) is likely. It is because of such expectations, for example, that Jones probably allows Smith to use so little of the court space.

Performance expectations are subjective, relative, and specific. They have to do with what Jones thinks, not with his objectively verifiable capacities; with his performance compared to Smith, not with his absolute ability; with his ability to do something specific, not with his general ability. Thus, (5) should be prefixed: "Jones believes that . . ." and would be incomplete if either "Smith" or "volleyball" were omitted. Smith might hold a different performance expectation; Jones might believe that he is a better volleyball player than Smith, but a worse one than Doe; and Jones may be better than Smith at volleyball, but worse than Smith as a sociologist.

Example (5) is a *differentiated* performance expectation, that is, an expectation that one person is better than another; as opposed to an *undifferentiated* performance expectation, that is, an expectation that two people are equally good or equally bad. Differentiated performance expectations emerge in social interaction when there is disagreement among actors and they are committed to arriving at a final decision of some sort (Berger & Snell, 1961; Berger & Conner, 1969). Disagreement implies that either Jones knows better than Smith, or that Smith knows better than Jones; a decision-making task forces them to choose which of these two is correct, as opposed to just ignoring their differences. But not all performance expectations are formed in this manner, that is, from interaction itself. Often they already exist, prior to any specific instance of interaction, being attached to the *statuses* individuals occupy in a social group. For example, because Jones is a "coding supervisor" in a research organization, Smith may infer that Jones is more competent than he to direct coding activities,

[5] The formulation of expectation theory used here is based on Berger & Snell, 1961; Berger, Cohen, & Zelditch, 1966; Berger & Conner, 1969; and Berger, Conner, & McKeown, 1969.

even though he has no prior knowledge of Jones' actual ability. Characteristics from which people make such stereotyped inferences, such as education, race, sex, and occupation or organizational position, are called *status characteristics* (Berger, Cohen, & Zelditch, 1966).

For the sake of simplicity of formulation, the components of an expectation state may be thought of as dichotomous, as "high" or "low," "$+$" or "$-$." For the sake of greater precision, performance expectation states may in general be represented by expressions of the form:

$$\text{Subject [Self, Other]} \tag{7}$$

in which "subject" is filled in by some sign for the individual from whose point of view the expectation state is regarded, and "self" and "other" by that individual's expectations for himself and some specified other. The characteristic with respect to which the expectation is held is given by the context of the expression, because no two characteristics are ever represented in one such expression. Thus, if from S's point of view we regard S and O, and the context shows the characteristic in question to be knowledge of sociology, $S[-\ +]$ represents S's belief that O knows more sociology than S.

Given some external criterion, such as the respective positions of S and O in a formal status hierarchy, expectation states may be called *consistent* or *inconsistent* with the criterion. For example, $S[+\ -]$, $S[-\ -]$, and $S[+\ +]$, are all inconsistent with an authority structure in which S is the subordinate of O, whereas $S[-\ +]$ is consistent with such a structure. It is particularly the inconsistency, in this sense, of performance expectations and authority that concerns us in this chapter.

Authority

Using Barnard's definition, we will say that *authority* "is the character of a communication . . . in a formal organization by virtue of which it is accepted by a contributor . . . as governing the action he contributes . . . [1938, 163]." Barnard's view of authority placed rather equal stress on two somewhat different features of an authority relation: First, on the *acceptance* of commands by subordinates, and their reasons for doing so; but second, on the *authentication* of commands, on showing that they originated in an office that had a legitimate claim on the subordinate, and were within the legitimate sphere of competence of that office. A communication would unfailingly carry authority if identified as coming from the right source, meaning a source with a legitimate right to make it; and if it fell within the subordinate's *zone of indifference*, meaning the zone within which the subordinate would be willing to comply without regard to the content of the communication, that is, without himself deciding whether it was right or wrong.

Barnard made acceptance largely a matter of inducements: A subordinate complied for the same reason that he participated at all, to serve his own interests (e.g., to earn his salary). Most theories of authority have in this respect been more influenced by Weber who makes acceptance depend on legitimacy, and therefore on the existence within the organization of a normative order, an order in which authority holds a central place. *Legitimacy* is a matter of regarding it as right and proper that a particular official issue a particular sort of command. It was Weber's view that the exercise of pure power could not for long hold an organization together; its stability depended on acceptance by subordinates of the *right* of superiors to exercise authority (1947, part III). Authority could therefore be viewed as a system of rights more or less recognized in the organization, and, in particular, more or less recognized by subordinates.

Not *every* subordinate must accord legitimacy to *every* superior. A subordinate might not believe in the legitimacy of his superior; he might, instead, simply recognize that there exists in the organization some ultimate source of authority, and be aware that his own superior has been authorized to exercise authority by this ultimate source (Scott, Dornbusch, Busching, & Laing, 1967). The subordinate might even, as an individual, doubt the legitimacy of *any* source of authority whatever, so long as others in the organization believe in it. For in that case he would be aware of the existence of the rights of his superior even though he did not believe in them. He would be aware, that is, that others would support the exercise of these rights. Because of them, that is, because of the existence of such rights and of support for them, the superior would be able to control the distribution of inducements in the Barnardian sense. If the subordinate valued the inducements, he might accept the conditions on which they were offered, namely, compliance. While his compliance would depend purely on the fact of his superior's power, it is nevertheless the existence of a normative order governing authority, of a system of rights, that determines his action.

The purpose of all this, which has no immediate part to play in our analysis, is simply to justify looking at authority in terms of various sorts of rights. Although a finer and more exhaustive analysis is possible, we will here treat these rights as falling into three classes: *directive* rights, which are rights to instruct others in the performance of their assigned tasks; *evaluative* rights, which are rights to evaluate the consequent performance; and *allocative* rights, which are rights to give or withhold inducements for participation.

A holds *directive* rights over B if B must consult the opinion of A before taking any action not specifically authorized by A, and if B must comply with any instruction originating with A. If A does not hold such rights over B, B is *autonomous*, at least so far as A is concerned. For example, a doctor holds directive rights over drug therapies administered by nurses, but is himself comparatively autonomous. No nurse may give an injection not authorized by a doctor, and any injection that he authorizes must be given; on the other hand, the doctor need not ask permission of the chief of service to order such an injection, and if an injection is suggested by the chief the attending doctor may regard it as advice, not as a direction.

A more elaborate analysis than this is possible of *evaluative* rights, of their kinds, conditions, and sources; but what matters at the moment is only *who* is evaluated for performance of some task, T. Suppose A is the ultimate source of authority in an organization. Suppose further that he delegates directive rights to B, who in turn directs the performance of C, who actually performs T. Now A may either evaluate B for the performance of C, or evaluate C directly. In the first case, B is *accountable* for the performance of T, and hence of C; in the second case, it is C who is accountable. In a military command structure it has usually been the case that each officer is accountable for the performance of all his subordinates; whereas, in the typical university department the chairman is not held accountable for the research of his department members, who are themselves directly accountable for what they do. We shall find that this makes a great deal of difference to the authority-expectation process, for incompetent supervision of C by B may not have much effect on C if it is B, and not C, who is blamed for the consequences.

B holds *allocative* rights over C if B controls the distribution of inducements offered by the organization for C's participation. Furthermore, to the degree that C cares about these inducements, and to the degree that they are not readily available in some other way, control over their allocation gives B power over C. If B holds such power, B is capable of compelling compliance from C without regard to the legitimacy of his authority from any other point of view, and without regard to the legitimacy C grants to any of his other actions. The simplest of such allocative rights are of course the right to hire and fire, the right to determine wages or salaries, the right to recommend advancement, transfer to a better unit, or in some other way to sponsor better employment (e.g., recommending a graduate student for a job or an intern for a residency). Obviously, the true degree of autonomy of a subordinate depends not only on the organization of directive and evaluative rights, but also on the degree to which his immediate superior controls the allocation of inducements, sanctions, or rewards.

These rights may all be viewed as distributed over a *pair* of offices, that is a single authority relation, with respect to a single kind of activity or task. For this reason, authority structures, which are collections of such relations, are very much more complicated than would at first sight seem likely. For even the same two offices may be organized into more than one authority relation, and many different authority relations may exist in one authority structure. For example, to analyze a hospital ward one must keep in view the fact that the doctor-nurse relation, the chief-of-service–attending-doctor relation, and the chief-of-service–intern relation are all different and each is in itself different in technical as opposed to administrative situations. Any very summary description of authority on the ward as a whole is therefore to be viewed with some suspicion.

Conditions under Which Authority Depends on Performance Expectations

According to (4), monocratic authority relations are maintained only if they are consistent with performance expectations. For example, (4) makes the superior authority of B over C depend on the expectations $B[+ \ -]$ and $C[- \ +]$.

We know this formulation to be too simple, and must consider, therefore, the conditions under which (4) will be true. Here we consider three conditions that have so far appeared to be important: the degree to which tasks of the organization are routinized, the accountability of officials for their own performance, and the orientation of officials to their tasks.

A task is *routinized* if every step in its performance is determined by explicit rules written by the organization. Close-order drill is highly routinized; planning a psychological experiment is not. Note that the rules in question originate in the organization itself. Physicians, for example, learn many rules in medical school that serve to guide their conduct in hospitals, but they do not count as organizational rules. What matters from the hospital's point of view is that the physician uses his own judgment and knowledge of principles, not manuals provided by the organization (although there are such manuals, e.g., those governing the use of drugs, which make drug use among the more routinized of hospital procedures). The distinction is easily made because *routines* are altered at the will of the organization; professional training is not.

Routinizing organizational activities has two effects: (a) it makes the behavior of subordinates so bound by rules that little occasion arises for the exercise of judgment by their superiors; and (b) it makes the behavior of superiors so bound by rules that when they do exercise authority almost nothing is implied about their personal capacities. There is little to signify either competence or incompetence in a company commander's executing correctly a right turn in a parade. He does manage to coordinate the activities of his unit with that of others, but whether he has superior knowledge or not is not revealed by this fact. These two effects have a further effect: in routine tasks, performance expectations of particular individuals, independent of their office, neither emerge from the exercise of authority nor determine the activities of the organizational unit. If the subordinate *were* superior in knowledge to his superior, there would be no occasion to discover it nor any way in which the fact would determine their respective activities. A highly routinized organization, therefore, could tolerate a good deal in the way of incompetence in superiors without noticing the effect on its authority structure.

A member of an organization is *accountable* for performance of a task, T, if the blame for failure or the credit for success is his; in other words, if it is he who is evaluated for a successful or unsuccessful outcome. We may suppose members of an organization to be concerned about their performance evaluations; in fact, from one point of view we may regard an authority structure as an arrangement of the ways in which members of an organization are evaluated —for what and by whom (Scott, Dornbusch, Busching, & Laing, 1967). Incompetent management may from this point of view be regarded not only as a threat to efficient performance of organizational tasks, but also to fair and reasonable evaluations of officials. This threat is of two kinds: (a) If a subordinate, C, is held accountable for the outcome of T by some ultimate source of authority, A, but A has delegated directive rights over C to B, then incompetent direction by B threatens C with blame for errors that are not his own; and (b) If B

holds evaluative rights over *C*, but *B* is incompetent to evaluate, then incompetent evaluation by *B* threatens *C* with blame for creditable performance. In both cases, the authority relation of *B* to *C* is likely to be sensitive to performance expectations. But very often *C* is accountable in neither of these two senses for often *A* holds *B*, not *C*, accountable for the performance of *C*, giving to *B* full directive and evaluative rights over *C*; at the same time *B*, instead of holding *C* accountable for the outcome of *T*, holds *C* accountable only for compliance with his directives. Thus, *C* will expect to be told what to do and will do what he is told. Nor is *C* threatened by *B*'s incompetence, for if *B* fails at the task it is *B* who is blamed, and *B* himself evaluates *C* less for performance than compliance. And if *C* is not accountable for performance of *T*, the authority of *B* over *C* is very probably independent of performance expectations.

This presumes, of course, that the subordinate *C* does not care about the outcome of the task. If he cared about the outcome, even if he were not himself blamed for it, he would nevertheless care if *B* were performing the task poorly. His attitude in the latter case is *task-oriented*. Consider those tasks for which there are a correct and an incorrect decision, however difficult it may be to decide which decisions are correct and which incorrect. Diagnosis of an illness is such a task. It is sometimes difficult to say whether or not a diagnosis is correct, but doctors typically believe that there *is* some correct decision. An individual is *task-oriented* if making the correct decision is what matters to him. Not only does a doctor believe there is a correct diagnosis, he cares that he has made it. But some organizations, for example, those called by Clark and Wilson (1961) *utilitarian* organizations, do not require such an orientation of their members and their members typically do not have such an orientation. The goals of the organization are distinct from those of the members, and so long as the latter are served the former do not much matter; the effect being that, so long as the members are offered incentives for compliance it will not matter to them that they believe their superiors to be making *wrong* decisions, providing they are not accountable for them.

Task-orientation, routinization, and for that matter all other variables used in the present formulation are analytic in the sense that they characterize not whole organizations but specific authority-expectation situations. For example, a hospital attendant views a hospital as a utilitarian organization, a doctor does not; his tasks are routinized, a doctor's are not. Furthermore, administrative decisions made for a doctor have a different character than professional decisions, and he has a different attitude towards them. Therefore no organization as a whole is everywhere characterized by any of the variables of our theory, and its statements all make reference to specific relations and activities.

The Expectation Hypothesis

A more precise formulation can now be given to (4), precise in the sense that its conditions can be made more definite, precise also in the sense that its independent and dependent variables can be made more exact:

> Given task-oriented, accountable subordinates and un-
> routinized tasks, if performance expectations are incon-
> sistent with differential authority rights, subordinates
> of the organization are autonomous; otherwise they are
> not.   (8)

It is to (8) rather than (4), that we will be referring when in the future we refer to the *expectation hypothesis*. This hypothesis makes two sorts of predictions. First, assuming the conditions as given, it claims that the authority structures of an organization are determined by performance expectation states. Collegial authority structures should occur in the case of $S[+\ +]$, $S[+\ -]$, and $S[-\ -]$ expectation states (where S stands for a subordinate's point of view) and monocratic authority in the case of $S[-\ +]$. Second, it suggests, as (4) did not, alternative directions of change in organizational structure if no change is to take place in authority structures. These appear from (8) to be: (a) an increase in routinization, (b) a decrease in the commitment of participants to successful task outcomes, and (c) a displacement of accountability to higher levels of the organization. Among other things, all this implies that an organization that is highly routinized, utilitarian, and in which only superiors are accountable, need *not* rely on the superior knowledge of superiors to maintain a monocratic authority structure—an implication we would not have drawn from the formulation given in (4).

It will come as no surprise that (8) is consistent with the evidence so far obtained from professional organizations; it was largely by examining that evidence that (8) was formulated. Nevertheless, some important questions remain. Is it possible that instead of playing the role of conditions, task-orientation, accountability, and routinization are themselves the causal determinants of collegial authority, while the effect of performance expectations is wholly spurious? What we know about professional organizations does not seem to rule this out. On the other hand, is it possible that these conditions are too restrictive? Janowitz's studies of the Air Force, for example, may imply that performance expectations determine authority structures even where participants are not, in our specific sense, task-oriented and accountable; in which case (8) is true, but too narrow. The present state of our knowledge does not answer either question very definitely.

II. STANDARDIZED EXPERIMENTAL SETTING

Task, authority, and interaction conditions in part II follow the conceptualization of an experiment by Evan and Zelditch (1961) in which 45 college students believed they were employed by a national survey research organization to code the face sheet of a survey questionnaire. The codebook given was incomplete; if a subject, S, encountered difficulties he was to consult his supervisor, who was responsible for final decisions. After a brief period of experience in the organization, S was shifted to a supervisor (a confederate of the experimenter) who was even less competent than he, about as competent, or more competent (as the previous supervisor had been). The supervisor gave not only technical, but also administrative commands, because of the importance this distinction had assumed in the literature on professional organizations (See, for example, Goss, 1961). Relevant observables were performance, autonomy, compliance, and legitimacy of authority.

Here we confine our attention to just two observables, autonomy and compliance, and we omit purely administrative relations. In other respects, however, the organizational setting and methods of manipulating variables are identical with those in the Evan-Zelditch experiment. Basic features of the organizational setting are described in the first section. The four basic phases of the experiment, the structure of a decision-making trial during its task phases, methods of manipulating basic variables and conditions, and ways of analyzing and measuring results are described in subsequent sections.

Organizational Setting

Experiments simplify. They strip away those parts of the real world that are theoretically irrelevant to whatever processes they investigate. But organizational theory is in a very primitive state of development and guarantees the irrelevance of very few of the properties of naturally occurring organizations. Only a few, such as size, are quite obviously irrelevant. (For further discussion, see Zelditch & Hopkins, 1961; Zelditch & Evan, 1962; and Zelditch, 1969). The strategy adopted here, therefore, is *hueristic simulation*, that is, simulation that is relatively rich in realistic properties of naturally occurring organizations. Although clearly not the real thing, the simulation described here is nevertheless closer to it than would be desirable in an experiment based on a more secure body of knowledge.

The features our laboratory organization ought to have, because they may be relevant to the way in which its authority structure responds to inconsistent performance expectations are:

1. The laboratory organization should have a specific and explicit function and should exist in the minds of the members as an entity independent of their own participation in it.
2. It should perform, or appear to perform, some repeated activity directed at the attainment of its purpose.
3. Its offices should be distinct in their functions, with fixed spheres of competence, governed by explicitly formulated rules of conduct, and recognizable as entities apart from the individuals occupying them.
4. Activities of participants should be coordinated through a formal system of status and authority.
5. From the point of view of participants, inducements to participate should be given for performance and should represent wage or salaried employment.

Accordingly, the simulation of the organization we construct here will have as constant features the above five properties, as well as properties required by the expectation hypothesis itself.

To create these properties, the authority-expectation experiment recruits subjects through an employment office to work supposedly for a national research organization. The inducement to participate is the usual wage for the function S actually performs in the organization. S should understand that he is employed for part-time work on a project that is brief. In a university, it is of course easiest if the university employment service is used and if the organization is said to be a university affiliated research organization.

From S's perspective, the organization's division of labor is relatively simple (See Figure 15.2): *Coders* are trained to classify questionnaires according to given rules and to record their classification in a manner usable by IBM data-processing equipment (about which they are briefly instructed); *coding supervisors* have substantive knowledge of the material being coded, some training in the field of the research, some resources to deal with difficult questions (such as the *Dictionary of Occupational Titles* of the U.S. Census Bureau), are administratively responsible for supervising the coders (e.g., checking and keeping their records of employment), and make final decisions on questions about which they are consulted by the coder; a *project director* is responsible for the project as a whole, is the ultimate source of authority, is the source of rules, evaluations, and sanctions, and trains the coders. During their training period, while Ss are being instructed in the performance of their task, they may also be instructed in the authority structure of the organization (who is responsible to whom for what) and in some of its basic regulations (how to sign in and out, how to keep records of performance, and that code sheets must be initialed to be accepted by the supervisor). Other divisions of the organization, such as its IBM operation and its interviewing staff, are implied but never seen by S.

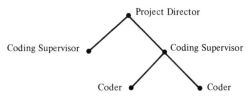

Figure 15.2
Formal organization of National Social Surveys, Inc., coding section.

The communication structure of the organization is the feature of it that looks least like a "real" organization. First, Ss are not permitted to communicate with each other after the training period (several may be trained at one time), ostensibly because independence of judgment, hence working in separate rooms, improves reliability; but, in fact, because the informal organization of work groups may obscure the effects of the experiment, and, even if not, the possibility of social influence would make it impossible to treat each S as a statistically independent observation. Furthermore, all Ss must be given identical questionnaires to code, a fact that would be immediately evident if they were in the same room. Second, Ss do not actually meet nor deal face-to-face with their supervisors. The only superior they meet is the project director who trains them. Ss are merely told that if they encounter difficulties they must call their supervisor on the phone and are given his extension, but no room number. The purpose of this is to help control the effect of status characteristics, and to reduce as far as possible the personal impressions of the supervisor. Some status characteristics are bound to operate, and must therefore be manipulated by E. For example, it supports the role of the project director if he is thought to be a professor, and the role of the coding supervisor if he is thought to be a graduate student. The lowest level of the organization is best occupied by undergraduates. In this manner the status structure is made to coincide with the authority structure. But confederates will sometimes have attributes that obscure this simple structure, such as black or yellow skin color, a beard, or a deceptively young face; facts that are not so apparent over the telephone.

With a little additional training, S could well play the supervisor's instead of the coder's role, offering an illuminating opportunity to study the exercise of authority by superiors who hold various expectation states. But wherever they are located in the organization, there can be only one subject role in any one authority-expectation experiment. All other roles must be played by confederates. The purpose is to eliminate the interactive character of authority. A subordinate who is in the state $S[+ \, -]$ interacts differently with a superior who himself is in the state $S'[- \, +]$ than he does with one who is in the state $S'[+ \, -]$ (where S' identifies a superior). If both are naive Ss at the same time, and are allowed free interaction, it becomes impossible to disentangle the effects of this interaction in the results of the experiment.

The great dependence on confederates, both to create complexity of organizational structure and to manipulate the experiment's independent variables, means that great care must be taken in their training, and a good deal of time budgeted for rehearsals. Of course, each confederate must have as complete a script as possible, as well as a thorough understanding of the role he is to perform.

A fair degree of realism can be created by using actual rooms of an actual research organization, or anything similar, with such props as scattered old boxes of IBM cards, boxes of old questionnaires, codebooks of other projects, and so on; although the price is high if an actual ongoing research organization is co-opted, because the telephones used by the Ss must not receive incoming calls during the experiment, and all activities not part of the experiment must be rigidly controlled by the experimenter. For this reason, it is best to run such experiments during short holidays or at night.

Structure of Paradigm Experiment

The paradigm authority-expectation experiment is made up of four phases: (a) an instruction phase, (b) a baseline phase, (c) an expectation phase, and (d) post-session interviewing and debriefing. In the instruction phase, the project director trains coders in their task. In the baseline and expectation phases, the coder works under the supervision of a coding supervisor for a series of n identical decision-making trials, the ith trial of which requires the coder to classify a response to one item of a standardized questionnaire into one of r classes, according to a set of rules provided by the project director. The interview phase validates manipulation of the independent variables and fixed initial conditions of the experiment and debriefs S. We will consider the nature and functions of the instruction phase first. We will then consider the structure of the basic decision-making trial of the experiment, which is common to both the baseline and expectation phases. A discussion of the use of this trial, first in the baseline and then in the expectation phases, follows. A discussion of the nature and functions of the interview phase concludes the section.

In the *instruction* phase the project director trains coders in their task. If there are k conditions of the experiment, coders are trained k at a time. The subject becomes familiar with the codebook and how to use it, with the purpose of coding, with the nature and requirements of the IBM punch card, and with such elementary rules as the importance of confining "don't know" responses to those instances in which the survey *respondent* does not know how to answer a question, *not* those in which the *coder* does not know how to code the respondent's answer. As much as possible the training should resemble the actual process of training a coder.

For any one experiment, coders who later receive different expectation treatments are nevertheless trained at the same time, and therefore are given identical treatment during the instruction phase. However, the instruction phase is an important manipulation phase from the point of view of differences in initial conditions between experiments. It is during the instruction phase that task-orientations, accountability, and authority structure are manipulated.

There are two important features of the coder's task-orientation: his identification with the goals of the organization, and his belief in the importance of a correct answer if these goals are to be achieved. During the instruction phase, when the purpose is to simulate the atmosphere of a professional research organization, great emphasis is given to the scientific importance of the research and the dependence of that research on the validity of the results, that is, on the accuracy of the coding. All this is omitted when instead it is the purpose of the experiment to simulate a more utilitarian organization.

The authority structure of the organization may be varied for two rather different reasons. First, changes in the authority structure of the organization are, after all, the dependent variable of the experiment, and it is possible to make the experiment more sensitive and more precise by restricting in various ways the parts of the structure that may change. Second, accountability is an important condition of the expectation hypothesis, for presumably S's responses are quite different if he knows that the project director is evaluating *him* for what is taking place compared to an authority structure in which someone else is responsible; it may therefore be manipulated as an independent variable in some experiments.

If it appears advisable to restrict the possible effects of the experiment, the choice, if S is a coder, is between emphasizing autonomy or compliance. To emphasize compliance but eliminate autonomy, more emphasis is given in the instruction period to consulting the superior if the coder is in any doubt; in fact, it is made clear that the coder *must* consult the superior, but less emphasis is given to complying with the decisions made by the superior. To emphasize autonomy but eliminate noncompliance, more emphasis is given in the instruction period to the fact that *if* S consults his superior he *must* comply with the superior's decision, but less emphasis is given to the obligation to consult the superior; instead, it can be said that the coder *may* call his superior if he requires advice. Four possible initial conditions result: consulting the superior and complying with his instructions both required; autonomy permitted, but compliance required; autonomy not permitted, but compliance an option; or autonomy and compliance both free to vary. Obviously the results of an experiment in one of these classes are not readily comparable with the results in another. (The Evan-Zelditch experiment allowed both autonomy and compliance to vary, within limits, at the same time.)

As for the distribution of evaluation rights in the organization, two things must be made clear to the S: First, it must be clear that it is the project director, not the coding supervisor, who evaluates performance and allocates rewards and sanctions. This is easily conveyed if the project director, while training the coders, mentions that *he* will check the results of their work after some trial period. Second, Ss must be told either that *they* have the final responsibility for the accuracy of their coding or that their *superior* does. Because all code sheets must be initialed, and S knows that there is a check procedure (recoding by another coder), he knows that who makes mistakes, and how many are made, are known quantities. The question in the coder's mind, of course, is who is blamed for any errors that are found. This is a question that must be answered, even where accountability is not the primary focus of an experiment.

The instruction phase also serves to reduce heterogeneity of the subject population. One would suppose that if the Ss were all college students, ability would be sufficiently similar that the precision of authority-expectation experiments would be fairly high. This does not appear to be the case. There is a fairly wide range of ability, and an even greater range of adaptability to conditions of an unexciting task. There is a wide variation, too, in attitudes towards organizations, in the need for a job, in the utility of a given wage per hour, and so on. Training in batches helps a little to reduce this variability, although the baseline phase is of more importance in this respect. Of particular importance is the fact that the instruction phase begins (and the baseline phase continues) to give cues about what the competence of a superior means. Being untrained and inexperienced, Ss have little idea of the difference in behavior between a competent and an incompetent supervisor. They have no frame of reference in terms of which a given behavior of the supervisor has some meaning. In the instruction phase, both the behavior of the project director and the rules he provides about how a coder should *not* perform his task, go some distance to provide S with such a frame of reference.

After training, S is required to perform a coding task under supervision of a coding supervisor. He performs this task through the baseline and expectation phases of the experiment. Each of the n trials of the experiment, in both its baseline and expectation phases has an identical structure.[6] Each requires S to classify an item of a questionnaire into one of r classes, one and only one of which is correct; S is to accomplish this task according to a set of rules, a codebook, that explains the project's system of classification and lists the r classes for each item of the questionnaire, together with their definitions and illustrations of their use. If an item falls within the scope of these rules it can be unequivocally put in the correct class, the coder classifies it, and the trial terminates. If an item does not fall within the scope of these rules, it is doubtful which of the r classes is correct. This happens because the codebook is imperfect or incomplete. At each such trial the coder is supposed to telephone his superior and obtain his opinion, although, of course, it may happen that he does not. If in fact the coder calls his superior, the superior is required to give him some instruction, and this instruction may or may not be competent. If his superior in fact gives him a competent instruction, the coder (presumably) complies with it and the trial is terminated. If instead the superior gives what the coder knows to be an incompetent instruction (e.g., that he should code the doubtful item "don't know"), the coder either complies or does not and the trial terminates.

It may help, in trying to follow this description of the basic decision-making trial of the experiment, to study the path diagram of a trial in Figure 15.3.[7] Each trial of the experiment is a four-stage decision process in which:

1. The coding rules do not determine the decision to be made (a point labeled $\bar{r}$ in the tree diagram shown in Figure 15.3), or they do (r). If they do, the coder makes the indicated decision and the trial terminates (at c on the bottom-most path of the diagram).
2. If the coding rules do not determine the decision to be made, the coder consults his superior (at $\bar{a}$), or he does not (a). If he does not, he makes

---

[6] The formulation given here of the structure of the decision-making trial and of changes in performance expectations in the context of an authority relation is based on Berger and Zelditch, 1962.

[7] This figure uses straightforward abbreviations: The letter r stands for "rules," and means that the rules cover the case; $\bar{r}$ (read "not-r") means the rules do not cover the case. An a stands for autonomy; $\bar{a}$ means that S consulted his supervisor. A k stands for knowledge (the supervisor knows what to do), $\bar{k}$ its absence. Compliance is shown by a c, noncompliance by $\bar{c}$.

his own decision and the trial terminates at $\bar{c}$, that is, in a state of non-compliance.

3. If the coder consults his superior, the superior either does not himself know what is to be done (at $\bar{k}$), or he gives a competent decision (k); if he gives what appears to be a competent decision, the coder complies and the trial terminates at c.

4. If the superior does not know what is to be done, he nevertheless gives the coder some decision, with which the coder either complies or does not, in either case terminating the trial. (All points labeled $\bar{c}$ are points at which the coder is noncompliant.)

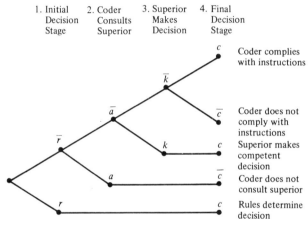

1. Initial   2. Coder   3. Superior   4. Final
   Decision   Consults   Makes   Decision
   Stage   Superior   Decision   Stage

Coder complies with instructions

Coder does not comply with instructions

Superior makes competent decision

Coder does not consult superior

Rules determine decision

Figure 15.3
Structure of a decision-making trial.

Clearly, there are two distinct kinds of trials in the experiment: one terminates after the coder has found that the rules determine a correct classification, and is a *dummy* trial; the other occurs when the rules fail to determine the decision of the coder, and is an *experimental* trial. Because the frequency of experimental trials is identical with the failure of the rules to determine decisions, the frequency of experimental trials measures the extent, or scope, of the rules. By varying this quantity the experimenter is able to vary the routinization of the task.

A good deal of pretesting is required to assure that there are no bugs in the codebook on those trials not intended as experimental trials, because it is difficult to write scripts (for the coding supervisors) for unplanned events. If all experimental trials are intended to be incompetent trials, it is a simple matter to write a script to cover even unexpected questions from the coder, and a complete list of correct answers covers the confederate who must appear competent; but any intermediate state poses problems, and it is probably best to avoid them.

In the *baseline* phase of the experiment, which follows the instruction phase, *S*s are taken to separate workrooms and given the extension of a supervisor and a set of questionnaire face-sheets to code. The face-sheet is made up of such items as occupation, income, source of income, race, sex, and religion of the respondent; and, of course, every *S* is given the identical questionnaires to code, with the identical responses and difficulties, all made from a common master set. The codebook, showing how to code occupation, occupational prestige, and so on, has the same number of imperfections as it will later have during the expectation phase (so that the routinization of the task is constant throughout a given experiment), but on every experimental trial all *S*s are given competent instruction by their supervisor, regardless of the expectation state into which they will later be put, and *S*s should complete this phase of the experiment in an $S[-+]$ state.

The purpose of the baseline phase is to increase the precision of the experiment, which it accomplishes in two ways. First, it provides a before-measure for all *S*s, permitting repeated observations on the same *S,* so that every *S* serves as his own control. This deals with the difficulties created by the fact mentioned above that *S*s vary a great deal in their abilities, attitudes toward organizations, needs for a job, perceived utilities of the wage, and so on. Second, it strengthens the frame of reference in terms of which *S*s interpret the competence of their superiors, and provides a common frame of reference for all *S*s.

The purpose of the expectation phase is to manipulate *S*'s performance expectations. The phase begins with the baseline phase supervisor calling *S* and informing him that, because the supervisor must leave, *S* is reassigned to a new supervisor (whose extension he is given). More or less conditioned to consulting his superior by the baseline experience, *S* will call the new supervisor at the next experimental trial.[8] Performance expectations are varied by manipulating the responses of the coding supervisor (or his training, if the superior is the *S*). A competent superior is created by a script in which the superior always knows the answer to the coder's questions, and, so far as the coder knows, the answer is correct. Additional resources, such as the *Dictionary of Occupational Titles,* should be used to create an impression of knowledge of the subject. A script in which the superior says he does not really know the answer to the coder's question, and instructs the coder to code the questionable item "don't know," instead of giving it a correct classification, creates an impression of incompetence. A typical incompetent response might be: "I just don't know what to do with that one. I've never run across one like it before. I think you had better code it 'don't know.' " To avoid suspicion, some variation in wording is ad-

---

[8] The interval between experimental trials should be the same in the expectation as in the baseline phase. If it is desirable to assure that all *S*s begin the expectation phase at exactly the same experimental trial, a messenger should be sent to *S*'s office with a *priority* set of questionnaires, a set that must be begun immediately, requiring *S* to put aside the set on which he had been working in the baseline phase. Simple scripts, in which the supervisor is always competent or always incompetent, do not require this; complicated scripts, in which the proportion of incompetent responses approaches .5, do.

visable, but the essential meaning of the response should always be the same. That this response is clearly wrong, the coder understands from his training. Just how often it occurs determines the degree of incompetence of the superior. The contrast is of course greatest if the superior is incompetent on every experimental trial.

Control over the personality of supervisors is obtained by rotating supervisors in the expectation phase in such a way that, not only are they counterbalanced between the baseline and expectation phases, but they are precisely balanced with treatments in the expectation phase as well. For two treatments, the design is very simple (See Figure 15.4): those Ss who had supervisor A in the baseline phase are reassigned to B, while those who had B are reassigned to A. Of those who are reassigned from A to B, ½ are given the S[—+] treatment and ½ the S[— —] treatment, and similarly for those who were reassigned from B to A. In general, if there are k treatments there must be k supervisors and $1/k^2$ subjects must be assigned to each of the $k \times k$ cells of the experimental design, in such a manner that every combination of treatment and supervisor occurs the same number of times. The purpose is to assure that not only the main effects, but also the interaction of supervisor with treatment, are easily determined.

Baseline Phase Supervisor	Expectation Phase Supervisor	Performance Expectation Treatment		
		[−+]	[−−]	
A	B	1/4 N	1/4 N	1/2 N
B	A	1/4 N	1/4 N	1/2 N
		1/2 N	1/2 N	N

Figure 15.4
Balancing of supervisors and treatments in expectation phase for two treatments.

All Ss begin the expectation phase in the expectation state $S[-+]$. If the new supervisor to whom S is reassigned knows what to do when he is consulted while the coder does not, the unit evaluation on that trial of the experiment is $(-+)$; that is, for this particular trial S believes: "I don't know what to do, but my supervisor does." Since this unit evaluation coincides with the expectation state of S, there is no reason to expect any change in that state at the next trial (See Berger & Snell, 1961; Berger & Conner, 1969). If the supervisor to whom S is reassigned does *not* know what to do, just as the coder does not, the unit evaluation on that trial of the experiment is $(-\ -)$; that is, for this particular trial S believes: "I don't know what to do, but neither does my supervisor." In this case the unit evaluation does not coincide with S's expectation state. According to the Berger-Snell expectation model, on which the present formulation is based, the effect is to make the expectation state of S unstable;

and each time that an inconsistent unit evaluation is repeated, there is a tendency for S to change his expectation state in a manner that brings it into line with his unit exaluation. A portion of this process is shown in Figure 15.5. If S encounters a competent response from his supervisor on trial i, his expectation state, $S[- +]$, is maintained; if S encounters an incompetent response, this is inconsistent with his initial expectation state, and there is some probablity, π, that he will change his expectation state to $S[- -]$. The total rate of change of expectations is equal to $e\ \pi$, where e is manipulated by the experimenter but π depends on the subject. The remaining portion of the process would show it for S in state $S[- -]$, which we omit here.

Just how often the unit evaluation $(- -)$ occurs, and how closely such events follow on each other, determines the rate at which Ss move into an expectation state that is itself inconsistent with the authority structure of the organization. Subjects will, of course, change expectations at different rates (represented by the probability π in Figure 15.5), but probably all or most of them will change expectation state before the phase terminates. If and when they do change expectation state, but only then, we are in a position to observe the effect in which we are interested. If the expectation hypothesis is correct, and if its antecedent conditions are satisfied, the authority structure itself should begin to break down. That is, in the expectation phase of the experiment those subjects in the $S[- -]$ treatment should become increasingly autonomous and decreasingly compliant.

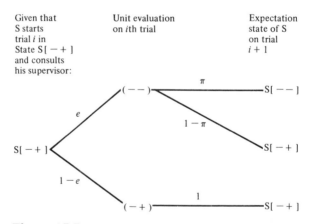

Figure 15.5
Portion of expectation process during expectation phase (from Berger & Zelditch, 1962, p. 8).

The *interview* phase of the experiment has two rather distinct purposes: (a) to assure that the manipulations of the experiment had the effects on its antecedent conditions required for a test of its hypothesis; and (b) to debrief the Ss. As for the first purpose, the conditions referred to have to do with performance expectations, task-orientations, accountability, and routinization; but routinization may safely be omitted because it does not depend on, or show itself as, a state of mind.

The interviews take place under two rather different conditions. S may be immediately informed by the interviewer (I) that he has been participating in an experiment, or the facade of the experiment may be preserved even during the interview. To preserve the experiment's facade, if desired, I informs S that *National Social Surveys, Inc.* is participating in a management survey, and I wishes to ask some questions about S's experiences in the organization. If S protests that his experience is negligible, I insists he is required to interview everyone.

The validity of the performance expectation manipulations is determined from evaluations made by S of himself and of each of the supervisors he has had in the organization. Evaluations of competence should be obtained on a 10-point scale, so as to allow for sufficient separation between, for example, the two supervisors. The difference between self and each supervisor, as well as between the two supervisors, provides a basis for inferring S's expectation states. In addition, I should probe specific unit evaluations made by S. That is, S should be asked if he ever thought that, in view of the research's objectives, his supervisor made a decision that was wrong. Further probe of unit evaluations is also informative about task-orientations; if S did think his supervisor was sometimes wrong, I should find out what he did about it and why he did it. But I should also ask directly how important it was to the research to get valid results, and what was more important to S, to get valid results or to do what he was told to do. In general, task-orientation is the most difficult variable to validate, and is the most likely to have changed during the experiment as a consequence of the same variables that change the authority structure. By contrast, accountability is rather easy to determine and fairly stable—S need only be asked whom he thought the project director would hold responsible for errors.

The second function of the interview phase is the debriefing of S. Special care should be taken in debriefing, because it is a little upsetting to Ss to discover that what they thought was a job is not. The experiment must be explained in detail, and plenty of time allowed for dealing with tension release. Above all, it is wise to have in mind other jobs of a similar nature—although real ones, of course—to which Ss who really are in need of a job can be directed. It is very helpful to the debriefing if it was explained to S before he started the job that it would be a very brief one.

Analysis and Measurement

The relevant observables of the experiment are, first, the *autonomy* of the coder, which is the frequency with which he makes decisions without consulting the opinion of his superior. (This is the event a in Figure 15.4.) Second, one is able to observe the coder's *compliance,* which includes not only his direct failure to comply with an actual instruction, but any and all events in which he makes a decision that does not accord with a decision of his superior. (This includes all events labeled $\bar{c}$ in Figure 15.4.) From the point of view of the theoretical formulation in Part I, autonomy and compliance are both aspects of autonomy in the sense of hypothesis (8); but it is useful to distinguish the two in the analysis of the experiment's results; and, of course, even the two kinds of non-compliance—failure to comply with an actual instruction, and failure to comply with an instruction which one did not in any case ever receive—could be distinguished.[9]

If experimental manipulations succeed in putting S in either a $[-\,+]$ or a $[-\,-]$ expectation state, then four theoretical quantities determine observable effects on the authority structure: first, the conditional probability that S does not consult his supervisor if he is in a $[-\,+]$ expectation state, $p(a/[-\,+])$ (this should be read: the probability of a, given that S is in state $S[-\,+]$); second, the conditional probability that S does not consult his supervisor if he is in a $[-\,-]$ expectation state, $p(a/[-\,-])$; third, the conditional probability that S complies with an instruction from his supervisor if he is in a $[-\,+]$ expectation state, $p(c/[-\,+])$; and fourth, the conditional probability that S complies with an instruction from his supervisor if he is in a $[-\,-]$ expectation state, $p(c/[-\,-])$. But these quantities are unobservable; they underlie what takes place, but are visible only in their effects. While $p(a/[-\,+])$ and $p(c/[-\,+])$ could be estimated without difficulty, $p(a/[-\,-])$ and $p(c/[-\,-])$ could not. For during the expectation phase, an S exposed to the $[-\,-]$ treatment would for part of the phase be in a $[-\,+]$ state and for only part of it be in a $[-\,-]$ state. There is even some possibility that from a $[-\,-]$ state he might change to a $[+\,-]$ state. If $p(a)$ and $p(c)$ were always 1 or 0, depending on S's expectation state, there would still be no difficulty; but there is no reason to suppose that, for example, competent supervisors are always consulted and incompetent ones never.

While methods exist by which we may overcome these difficulties, they are not really necessary; the observable quantities themselves are sufficient for testing hypotheses about the effects of expectation states on the authority structure. What we require for analysis, therefore, are only the probability of an autonomous response for the expectation phase, $p(a)_E$; the probability of an autonomous response for the baseline phase, $p(a)_B$; and the probability of compliance for the expectation phase, $p(c)_E$, and the baseline phase, $p(c)_B$. To these we may add, if desired, the conditional probability that, if S *does*

---

[9] A third observable is used if S, instead of being the coder, is put in the supervisor's role. In this case, S's problem is that the coder asks for decisions from him that he knows he is not able to make. The question is, therefore, whether he attempts to make a decision or not, and if he does whether he insists on compliance or not. Thus, *exercise of authority* is what is observed, and occurs at the third decision stage of the trial (See again Figure 15.3).

consult his superior, he does *not* comply with his instructions, $p(\bar{c}/\bar{a})$, for each of the expectation and baseline phases.[10]

These quantities are obtained in the following manner. Assume that S consults the opinion of his supervisor $n(\bar{a})_j$ (read: n not–a,j) times out of $n(T)_j$ experimental trials in the jth phase of the experiment ($j = E,B$, where E or B mean the "expectation" or "baseline" phases). On $n(c)_j$ of these trials he complies with the supervisor's instructions; on $n(\bar{a}\wedge\bar{c})_j$ (read: n not–a *and* not–c,j) of them he does not. On $n(a)_j$ trials S does *not* consult his supervisor. Although it is not strictly true, we may take it for granted that on these trials S does not comply with whatever instructions he would have received had he consulted the supervisor.

From these quantities, we obtain:

$$p(a)_j = \frac{n(a)_j}{n(T)_j} \tag{9}$$

where $n(T)_j$ is the number of trials S actually completes in the jth phase, and therefore may vary from S to S,

$$p(c)_j = \frac{n(c)_j}{n(T)_j} \tag{10}$$

and finally;

$$p(\bar{c}/\bar{a})_j = \frac{n(\bar{a}\wedge\bar{c})_j}{n(\bar{a})_j} \tag{11}$$

which is the conditional probability that S does not obey a direct instruction from his supervisor.

From (9)–(11) we obtain the change in autonomy and compliance from the baseline to the expectation phases of the experiment, $\Delta p(a)$ and $\Delta p(c)$;

$$\Delta p(a) = p(a)_E - p(a)_B \tag{12}$$

$$\Delta p(c) = p(c)_E - p(c)_B \tag{13}$$

and if desired, the change in noncompliance if S does consult his superior:

$$\Delta p(\bar{c}/\bar{a}) = p(\bar{c}/\bar{a})_E - p(\bar{c}/\bar{a})_B \tag{14}$$

The order of magnitude of these quantities is indicated by a simple numerical example based on Figure 15.6.

---

[10] One may also study effects on performance, on the theory that S cares less about how well he does after exposure to incompetent superiors, by looking at the number of dummy trials completed in each phase of the experiment and the rate at which S makes errors on these trials. Procedures are the same as for autonomy and compliance, including the use of a nonparametric analysis of variance as suggested in the last paragraph of this section.

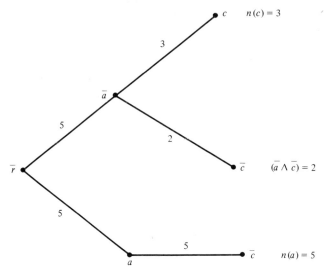

Figure 15.6

Autonomy and compliance of a hypothetical S who completed $n(T)_E = 10$ *experimental trials of the expectation phase.*

In the expectation phase, the S shown here completed 10 experimental trials (starting S at $\bar{r}$, meaning the rules did not determine the coder's decision on that trial); on only five of these did he consult the opinion of his supervisor ($\bar{a}$). On three of the five trials on which he did consult his supervisor, he complied with the instruction given him (c). On two he did not ($\bar{c}$). Furthermore, all five of the autonomous trials (a) were also trials on which S made an "error" in coding; that is, on which he did not code an item in a manner that corresponded to instructions in the script of the supervisor. Therefore, $n(c) = 3$, $n(\bar{a}\wedge\bar{c}) = 2$, and $n(a) = 5$. From these we have:

$$p(a)_E = 5/10 = .50$$
$$p(c)_E = 3/10 = .30$$
$$p(\bar{c}/\bar{a})_E = 2/5 = .40$$

In the baseline phase, suppose S was nearly "perfect" in his behavior, always consulting his supervisor and making only one error in coding on an experimental trial. Then $n(a)$ would be 0, $n(c)$ would be 9, $n(\bar{a}\wedge\bar{c})$ would be 1. Supposing that in this phase, too, $n(T) = 10$ trials, this would give $p(a)_B = 0$, $p(c)_B = .90$ and $p(\bar{c}/\bar{a})_B = .10$. Hence:

$$\Delta p(a) = .50 - 0 = +.50$$
$$\Delta p(c) = .50 - .90 = -.40$$
$$\Delta p(\bar{c}/\bar{a}) = .40 - .10 = +.30$$

which are the sort of numbers one might expect if the change in expectations did bring about some change in authority relations. What they show is that there was an increase in autonomy of five trials, a decrease in compliance of four trials, and an increase in overt noncompliance, of failure to comply with a direct instruction, of three trials.

A two-way analysis of variance, in which the expectation phase supervisors are blocks and expectation states are treatments, provides information about the magnitude of effects on the authority structure, about the degree to which control has been achieved over the personality of the supervisors, and about the interaction of the supervisor's personality with treatments. (Figure 15.4 shows the appropriate format for this analysis.) However, the distributions of $\Delta p(a)$, $\Delta p(c)$, and $\Delta p(\bar{c}/\bar{a})$ are typically not normal, and the sample sizes typically not large enough to ignore this fact. The distributions obtained by Evan and Zelditch (1961) were markedly flat, and kurtosis affects particularly the power of the analysis of variance (Srivastava, 1959). Therefore, a nonparametric analysis of variance is advisable.[11] The Mood-Brown two-way analysis of variance, which is based on a series of median tests, is easy to perform and has various advantages over other possible methods of analysis: for cell sizes greater than two it is distribution free; unequal cell sizes do not disturb the analysis; it costs fewer degrees of freedom than the more familiar Friedman analysis; and the interpretation of interaction effects is not disturbed by having more than one observation per cell, as is true of the Friedman analysis. (See Brown & Mood, 1951; Mood, 1950; and Tate & Clellands, 1957.)

III. FINDINGS AND IMPLICATIONS

There are few findings, and none very conclusive, showing the effects of performance expectations on authority structures. The main result of the Evan-Zelditch experiment (1961) was a decrease in compliance with technical commands of Ss exposed to incompetent supervision: Ss made more errors on experimental trials if they came to believe their supervisor was unable to advise them. But their failure to comply with instructions was not usually of the sort that one would call overt disobedience; on the contrary, Ss themselves did not often recall being disobedient, and their errors, instead of being efforts to classify an interview correctly, were trivial errors made in the course of trying to code

---

[11] If for any particular experiment it is found that distributions are sufficiently close to normal to permit a parametric analysis, and if for some reason such an analysis is desirable, the appropriate F ratios must use the interaction mean square, not the error mean square, as denominators. The supervisors are obviously a sample from the population of possible confederates, and therefore a random variable; and whereas the expectation states look to be fixed, even they are random, because the underlying variable is really the proportion of "don't know" responses given by the supervisor in the expectation phase, and only a small proportion of the possible values are used in any given experiment. The appropriate analysis of variance model is therefore a random-random model, the F ratios of which should use the interaction mean square for tests of main effects. (See Eisenhart, 1947; a good summary is found in Winer, 1962, pp. 155–162.)

an item "don't know" as instructed by their supervisor. For example, if the proper way to code occupational prestige "don't know" was to write 9X, followed by a blank column, in the three columns of their code sheet used for coding prestige, then Ss error might be XXX, 9XX, X9X, 999, or almost any other way of filling up the three columns than 9X followed by a blank.[12] In the case of autonomy the experiment produced much less certain results. Although Ss increased in autonomy, the results were not statistically significant, in part because Ss in the $[- +]$ treatment also increased in autonomy as they became more competent at the task. An unexpected result was that incompetent supervision produced shifts in the orientation of Ss to the mission of the organization; they became less task-oriented, that is, less oriented to obtaining valid results for their own sake. Furthermore, it is probable that as Ss shifted task-orientation, they were less likely to increase autonomy and decrease compliance as a function of performance expectations, although the *post-hoc* character of this hypothesis made analysis of results with respect to it inconclusive.

The same experiment looked also for effects on performance and legitimacy (that is, on the belief of the coders in their supervisors' right to expect compliance). Performance of the task did not deteriorate, either in speed or accuracy, as a result of incompetent supervision, and Ss continued to believe that their supervisors had a legitimate right to expect compliance with an instruction, whether wrong or not. These results may be explained in several ways. The simplest explanation may be that the experiment did not run long enough to produce results of this kind, but would have produced them had it run longer. While possible, two other explanations seem more probable. First, Ss probably believed that their performance would be evaluated by the project director who trained them and further employment might hinge on it, hence they may have responded as if they were being tested, at least until they knew whether they were to continue in the job. Unfortunately, the instruction about responsibilities was not as clear as it should have been, either on this point or another. Some Ss had the idea that it was the supervisor who was responsible for results. In this case, the supervisor would naturally have the right to control his subordinate's performance, if it were the supervisor who would be blamed for the results. But what the effect would be of different allocations of responsibility remains to be seen.

If the expectation hypothesis survives further tests, it has some interesting implications for bureaucratization and debureaucratization of complex hierarchical organizations. We will note just three of these:

1. It implies a high degree of bureaucratization in mass organizations. With mass recruitment it is difficult to screen in fine detail the competence of middle-ranking officials. They are probably in some cases of inferior competence, and as a class they are variable in competence. It would be

---

[12] No decrease in compliance with purely administrative commands was found, which is consistent with the previous literature on professional organizations. See, for example, Goss, 1961.

difficult to preserve a monocratic authority structure if they were left much discretion. A high degree of routinization would preserve a monocratic structure, and a monocratic structure would be desirable precisely because the competence of lower echelons is in doubt.

2. It implies a low degree of bureaucratization in organizations the tasks of which are seldom repeated in exactly the same way twice. What matters in these organizations is the difficulty of routinizing their tasks. Some organizations, of course, perform tasks that are often repeated in more or less the same fashion and under the same circumstances; they are easily routinized. But hospitals, universities, research teams, and similar organizations face tasks where many contingencies are difficult to predict or evaluate, and therefore decisions are difficult to prepare in advance or reduce to rules. Where this is the case, one relies instead on the training and judgment of middle- and lower-echelon officials. They must therefore be officials with a high degree of training and competence who must often exercise their judgment. The conditions of collegial authority are therefore common in such organizations.

3. It implies a low degree of bureaucratization in organizations that rely on other organizations to socialize their participants. If "schools" that are not themselves wholly controlled by the organization are the source of participants, then officials at several different levels probably hold the same certificates of competence from the same places, and are presumably of *equal* competence; furthermore, the rules to which they are subject originate outside the organization, and depend to some degree on the individual judgment of the official for their application. Both conditions favor low degrees of routinization and collegial authority.

REFERENCES

BARNARD, C. *Functions of the executive.* Cambridge, Mass.: Harvard University Press, 1938.

BERGER, J., COHEN, B. P., & ZELDITCH, M., JR. Status characteristics and expectation states. In J. Berger, M. Zelditch, Jr., & B. Anderson (Eds.), *Sociological theories in progress.* Vol. 1. Boston: Houghton Mifflin, 1966. Pp. 29–46.

BERGER, J., & CONNER, T. L. Performance expectations and behavior in small groups. *Acta Sociologica,* 1969, **12,** 186–198.

BERGER, J., CONNOR, T. L. & McKEOWN, W. L. Evaluations and the formation and maintenance of performance expectations. *Human Relations,* 1969, **22,** 186–198.

BERGER, J., & SNELL, J. L. A stochastic theory for self-other expectations. Technical Report No. 1, 1961, Stanford University, Laboratory for Social Research.

BERGER, J., & ZELDITCH, M., JR. Authority and performance expectations. Unpublished manuscript, Stanford University, Laboratory for Social Research, 1962.

BROWN, G. W., & MOOD, A. On median tests for linear hypotheses. In J. Neyman (Ed.), *Second Berkeley symposium on mathematical statistics and probability,* Berkeley, Calif.: University of California Press, 1951.

CAMILLERI, S. F., & BERGER, J. Decision-making and social influence: A model and an experimental test. *Sociometry,* 1967, **30,** 365–378.

CLARK, B. R. Faculty Authority. *Bulletin of the American Association of University Professors,* 1961, **47,** 293–302.

CLARK, P., & WILSON, J. Q. Incentive systems. *Administrative Science Quarterly,* 1961, **6,** 129–166.

COSER, R. *Life on the ward.* East Lansing, Mich.: Michigan State University Press, 1962.

DALTON, M. Conflicts between staff and line managerial officers. *Americal Sociological Review,* 1950, **15,** 342–351.

DALTON, M. *Men who manage.* New York: Wiley, 1959.

EISENHART, C. The assumptions underlying the analysis of variance. *Biometrics,* 1947, **3,** 1–21.

EVAN, W., & ZELDITCH, M., JR. A laboratory experiment on bureaucratic authority. *American Sociological Review,* 1961, **26,** 883–893.

FREIDSON, E., & RHEA, B. Processes of control in a company of equals. *Social Problems,* 1963, **11,** 119–131.

GLASER, B. G. Attraction, autonomy, and reciprocity in the scientist-supervisor relationship. *Administrative Science Quarterly,* 1963, **8,** 379–398.

GLASER, B. G. *Organizational scientists: Their professional careers.* Indianapolis, Ind.: Bobbs-Merrill, 1964.

GOODE, W. J. Community within a community: The professions. *American Sociological Review,* 1957, **22,** 194–200.

GOSS, M. E. W. Influence and authority among physicians in an out-patient clinic. *American Sociological Review,* 1961, **26,** 39–50.

HALL, R. H. Some organizational considerations in the professional-organizational relationship. *Administrative Science Quarterly,* 1967, **12,** 461–478.

HALL, R. H. Professionalization and bureaucratization. *American Sociological Review,* 1968, **33,** 92–104.

HUGHES, E. C. Mistakes at work. *The Canadian Journal of Economics and Political Science,* 1951, **17,** 320–327.

HUGHES, E. C. License and mandate. In E. C. Hughes (Ed.), *Men and their work.* Glencoe, Ill.: The Free Press, 1958. Pp. 78–87.

JANOWITZ, M. *The professional soldier.* Glencoe, Ill.: The Free Press, 1960.

KORNHAUSER, W. *Scientists in industry.* Berkeley, Calif.: University of California Press, 1960.

MARCSON, S. *The scientist in American industry.* New York: Harper & Row, 1960.

MARCSON, S. Organization and authority in industrial research. *Social Forces,* 1961, **40,** 72–80.

MOOD, A. M. *Introduction to the theory of statistics.* New York: McGraw-Hill, 1950.

MOORE, D. G., & RENCK, R. The professional employee in industry. *Journal of Business,* 1955, **28,** 58–66.

SCOTT, W. R. Reactions to supervision in a heteronomous professional organization. *Administrative Science Quarterly,* 1965, **10,** 65–81.

SCOTT, W. R., DORNBUSCH, S., BUSCHING, B., & LAING, J. Organizational evaluation and authority. *Administrative Science Quarterly,* 1967, **12,** 93–117.

SRIVASTAVA, A. B. L. The effect of nonnormality on the power of the analysis of variance test. *Biometrika,* 1959, **46,** 114–122.

STINCHECOMBE, A. Bureaucratic and craft administration of production: A comparative study. *Administrative Science Quarterly,* 1959, **4,** 168–187.

TATE, M. W., & CLELLANDS, R. C. *Nonparametric and short-cut statistics.* Danville, Ill.: Interstate Printers and Publishers, 1957.

UDY, S. "Bureaucracy" and "rationality" in Weber's organization theory. *American Sociological Review,* 1959, **24,** 791–795.

WEBER, M. *The theory of social and economic organization.* New York: Oxford University Press, 1947.

WINER, B. J. *Statistical principles in experimental design.* New York: McGraw-Hill, 1962.

ZELDITCH, M., JR. Can you really study an army in the laboratory? In A. Etzioni (Ed.), *A sociological reader on complex organizations.* (Rev. ed.) New York: Holt, 1969. Pp. 528–539.

ZELDITCH, M., JR., & EVAN, W. Simulated bureaucracies: A methodological analysis. In H. Guetzkow (Ed.), *Simulation in social science: Readings.* Englewood Cliffs, N.J.: Prentice-Hall, 1962. Pp. 48–60.

ZELDITCH, M., JR., & HOPKINS, T. Laboratory experiments with organizations. In A. Etzioni (Ed.), *Complex organizations: A sociological reader.* (1st ed.) New York: Holt, 1961. Pp. 465–478.

16

LEADERSHIP ROLE DIFFERENTIATION[1]

Peter J. Burke

INTRODUCTION

Leadership Role Differentiation Defined. If we put five strangers together in a room and provide them with a task that requires them to cooperate for achievement, something rather ordinary, but nevertheless quite remarkable happens: the social interaction among these strangers becomes patterned and a leadership structure emerges. The form this leadership structure takes depends upon a number of factors, but one of the forms, which we shall call *differentiated leadership roles*, appears to be quite common. It is with the emergence of this form of leadership structure that we are concerned in this chapter. What is leadership role differentiation? In its simplest form, leadership role differentiation involves two different persons playing two different leadership roles in a synchronized manner within a group. One role, *task leadership*, includes behaviors that are primarily oriented to the instrumental task affairs of the group (directing, summarizing, providing ideas, etc.); the other role, *social-emotional leadership*, includes behaviors primarily oriented to the expressive, interpersonal affairs of the group (alleviating frustrations, disappointments, tensions, hostilities, etc.).

From the researcher's point of view this means (a) that we can distinguish (at least) these two dimensions of leadership in the group, (b) that we can characterize each group member in terms of the extent to which he engages in behavior relevant to each dimension, and (c) that not all members are equal on either dimension. Further, it means (d) that the two dimensions are not isomorphic, that is, that the rank ordering of group members on one dimension is not identical with the rank ordering of group members on the other dimension, and especially that the top man (leader) on one dimension is not the top man on the other. Finally, it means (e) that the top man on one leadership dimension

[1] Work on this manuscript was facilitated by Research Grant GS-1696 from the Division of Social Sciences, National Science Foundation.

supports the top man on the other leadership dimension and coordinates his own behavior with that of the other. Let us look at an example.

An Illustration.   The following is a shortened and simplified version of a dialogue that transpired in a discussion group.[2] Its intent is to illustrate the roles of task and social-emotional leaders, how they differ and how they relate to one another. The members were concerned with the question of what to do about Johnny, a juvenile delinquent described in a written case study.

T: I think Johnny's problem is that he has a persecution complex. He felt every-one was against him. His teacher . . .

R: Oh, I don't think so. I don't think he was treated differently than anyone else in his neighborhood. It said the kids he hung around with were just like him —always in trouble. And he did have Mr. O'Brien for a friend.

T: That's true, but most of the people, his mother, the police, teachers, never gave him a chance. They didn't trust him. They didn't help him. Even his mother wished that he had died rather than the younger brother.

R: He had plenty of chances to prove himself if he wanted to, yet he was always getting into trouble, stealing. I think he needs a good lesson. He should be punished. The court should send him to a detention camp.

T: But that wouldn't help. If anything that would harden him beyond help.

SE: I think T has a point. We don't want to end up not being able to help Johnny. Maybe put him in a foster home where he is wanted and where authority can be exercised. Punishment makes sense only if it comes from someone you know cares for you.

T: That's right. The police didn't care for Johnny. The court didn't care, at least as far as Johnny was concerned.

R: That makes sense. I think he needs to be punished for his wrongdoings, that's the only way to teach him, but I think you're right, it has to come from someone like Mr. O'Brien who cares about him.

We can see in this little interchange that T has introduced a point into the discussion with which R does not agree. The exact nature of the point is not clear because it seems to shift from a persecution complex to the kind of relations which Johnny had with those around him, to whether or not punishment is the answer to his problems. On all of these points T and R disagree and the discussion gets nowhere until SE finds a way of resolving the conflict which supports T and allows T and R to agree and to cooperatively work out a partial answer to the question of what to do about Johnny. In this interchange both T and R have performed task functions, introducing ideas for the group to consider. SE's behavior, on the other hand, serves the social-emotional functions of soothing over a disagreement and maintaining interpersonal relationships. We can't tell from this one interchange but, if what we have observed here is part of a general pattern of T introducing ideas and guiding the discussion and

---

[2] Our purpose here is only to give some substance and feeling to the more formal defini-tion of task and social-emotional role differentiation. In the actual discussion sequence, the roles are less immediately obvious and the action is considerably more spread out in time, and contains much that is irrelevant to the illustration.

SE acting to reduce interpersonal frictions and support T, then we can say a leadership role structure exists, differentiated along the lines indicated earlier; there is task and social-emotional leadership role differentiation.

The Problems. The theoretical problem confronting us is to explain the origins and development of task and social-emotional leadership role differentiation in groups, as defined above. The empirical-experimental problem is to test the adequacy of any theory proposed, and to present the researcher with data that the theory must explain. The rest of this paper will systematically address itself to these problems. Beginning with the next section, an empirically based theory of task and social-emotional leadership role differentiation formulated by Robert F. Bales and Philip E. Slater in the 1950s is presented (Bales, 1953, 1956, 1958; Bales & Slater, 1955; Slater, 1955). Following this we discuss the techniques and procedures used by Bales and Slater to generate the data upon which their theory is based, and in later sections we present and discuss revisions of this early theory and the experimental paradigm behind it. We turn first to the theory.

THE BALES-SLATER THEORY

The theory of the genesis of role differentiation, as developed by Bales and Slater, applies to groups which have tasks that require interdependent, coordinated activity for their accomplishment. As we go through the following outline of the theory we should keep this in mind as an underlying assumption.[3]

Proposition 1. (Explaining one source of differentiation on the task leadership dimension.) As the members of the group interact with each other in performance of the task, an inequality of participation in task activity ensues. When one person engages in task acts, another is thereby denied the opportunity; in reaching decisions, some ideas are selected over other ideas; some departure from equality of participation must occur because not everyone can act at the same time. Meaningful coordination requires an inequality of participation in task actions.

Proposition 2. This inequality of task participation is commonly perceived by group members (i.e., there is consensus as to the rank ordering of members). Also greater consensus about *the* rank ordering is a concomitant of greater inequality.

Proposition 3. (Explaining one consequence of perceived differentiation on the task leadership dimension.) When there is perceived inequality, the person who is most active in the task area is perceived as the primary source of change and tension. It is his action that deprives action opportunities to others and

---

[3] These propositions are adapted from Burke (1967). It should be noted that these propositions are only the author's attempt to summarize the theory and may not correspond at all points and in all details to the ideas of Bales and Slater.

forces them to adjust their behavior and ideas to accomplish the task. Hostility, frustration, and resentment occur to the extent that there is perceived inequality in task participation.[4]

Proposition 4. (Explaining one source of differentiation on the expressive dimension.) Because the task leader (the person most active in the task area) is himself the principal source of tension and frustration, it is unlikely that he would be effective in resolving this tension and, if the tension is to be reduced, someone other than the task leader must assume a role aimed at the reduction of interpersonal hostilities and frustrations. Someone else must perform expressive leadership functions.

Proposition 5. The result is two different persons performing two different leadership functions (task and social-emotional), or, in other words, the result is task and social-emotional role differentiation.

Proposition 6. These differentiated roles are stabilized and synchronized as the task and social-emotional leaders reinforce and support one another.

It should be noted that in Propositions 4 and 6 of this skeleton "theory," the emergence of an expressive leader and the mutual reinforcement of the task and expressive leaders are not *necessary* consequences of the conditions stated. At these points, it appears that Bales and Slater make what is termed a *functional* argument: that these consequences are more stable than alternatives because they *function* to produce more satisfaction for the members. The alternatives, should they be chosen, are relatively short-lived, as they lead to the disintegration of the group.[5] Consequently, in existing stable groups one observes the above pattern.

Data upon Which the Theory Is Based

Before presenting the data, there is one point that should be made clear. The theory outlined above was not arrived at deductively prior to the gathering of data and then tested. Rather, in Bales' words, "The discovery of the differentiation of leadership was a genuine inductive-empirical discovery . . . [1968]." The theory was developed to account for the data. In this way the presentation in this chapter is backwards; the data should come first. The historical order, however, has been reversed in order that interpretation of the data be made easier. This task is simplified if we know in advance what to look for.

---

[4] Bales presents three possible explanations for this. The first is that the hostility is a transference phenomenon; that people transfer their negative attitudes toward authority to anyone who begins to achieve prominence in the discussion. The second is that the task leader, in pushing toward the goal, presents a challenge or threat to the values of some members and consequently receives some negative affect. The third possible explanation Bales presents is that substantial contributions to the discussion cannot be made without talking a great deal, and "overtalking may be resented by other members as a threat to their own status and a frustration of their own desire to talk [1956]."

[5] The nature of this functional argument and the alternatives are taken up in more detail later in the chapter.

What are we looking for? We are looking to see the evidence that task and social-emotional leadership role differentiation occurs in the manner and under the conditions spelled out in the propositions. To understand the data, the way in which the experimental groups were set up, and measures of the relevant variables taken, we look at the procedures used by Bales and Slater.

Procedures.   The subjects, paid male undergraduates recruited through the student employment office, met weekly for four weeks in groups of three to six persons. Each group was asked by the experimenter to consider itself the administrative staff of a central authority and each week they were given a five-page summary of an administrative problem. The members were asked to consider the facts and return a report giving their opinion as to why the persons in the case behaved as they did, and their recommendation about what action should be taken. Each group was given 40 minutes in which to arrive at their group decision. Since the focus of the study was on the origins of role differenti-ation, efforts were made to assure no *a priori* structure was imposed by the experimenter. For this reason subjects were put into groups such that they did not know each other, they were not introduced by name, nor was any leader appointed.

After giving the instructions and waiting until the case summaries were read, the experimenter left the room taking the written cases with him. The discussion was recorded and scored using Bales' Interaction Process Analysis (IPA) cate-gories (see below). After the 40-minute discussion, the experimenter returned and the subjects filled out a short questionnaire. Included among the questions were the following, upon which we shall focus:

1.   Who contributed the best ideas for solving problems? Please rank the mem-bers in order. *Include yourself.*
2.   Who did the most to guide the discussion and keep it moving effectively? Please rank the members in order. *Include yourself.*
3.   How well did you personally like each of the other members: Rate each mem-ber on a scale from 0 to 7, where 0 means "I feel perfectly neutral toward him," and seven means "I like him very much."
4.   Considering all the sessions, which member of the group would you say stood out most definitely as a leader in the discussion? How would you rank the others? *Include yourself* [Bales & Slater, 1955, p. 262].

The fourth question was asked only after the fourth meeting. The categories used to score the nature of the interaction are presented in Table 16.1.

The distinction of who performs the act is made by identification numbers assigned arbitrarily to the subjects. An apparatus has been constructed which pro-vides a paper tape moving horizontally, over which the vertical list of categories is placed. An action is recorded by writing down on the moving paper tape an identification number designating the person speaking, followed by a number designating the person spoken to. The score is placed on the tape in a vertical position which indicates the category of the act. The time order is provided auto-matically by the horizontal order of scores. The behavioral unit score is a single

Table 16.1

Bales' Interaction Process Analysis Categories

A. Positive reactions	1. Shows solidarity, raises others' status, jokes, gives help, reward.
	2. Shows tension release, shows satisfaction, laughs.
	3. Agrees, shows passive acceptance, understands, concurs, complies.
B. Attempted answers	4. Gives suggestion, direction, implies autonomy for other.
	5. Gives opinion, evaluation, analysis, expresses feeling, wish.
	6. Gives orientation, information, repeats, clarifies, confirms.
C. Questions	7. Asks for orientation, information, repetition, confirmation.
	8. Asks for opinion, evaluation, analysis, expression of feeling.
	9. Asks for suggestion, direction, possible ways of action.
D. Negative reactions	10. Disagrees, shows passive rejection, formality, withholds help.
	11. Shows tension increase, asks for help, withdraws "Out of Field."
	12. Shows antagonism, deflates others' status, defends or asserts self.

SOURCE. Adapted from Bales (1950), Chart 1, p. 9.

simple sentence of verbal communication or its non-verbal equivalent as understood by the observer. The scoring is continuous. Every act which occurs is thus classified as to its quality, who performed it, toward whom, and when [Bales & Slater, 1955, p. 268].[6]

These procedures were carried out for a total of 20 groups, ranging in size from 3 to 6 persons.

From the post-session questionnaires and the Interaction Process Analysis (IPA) scores, Bales and Slater rank ordered each person in each group on each of five dimensions (*roles*), according to the mean rank given him by the others in his group. These rank scores measured the relative degree to which members engaged in various types of behavior or were perceived to do so. The five dimensions were: (a) *providing ideas* (from the question pertaining to who provided the best ideas); (b) *providing guidance* (from the question pertaining to who did most to guide the discussion); (c) *being liked* (from the question pertaining to how much each person was liked); (d) *talking* (from the total

6 A full description of the Interaction Process Analysis scoring system is contained in Bales (1950). A revision of the method, with interpretive material, is now available. Bales (1970).

number of IPA acts initiated by each person); and (e) *receiving* (from the total number of IPA acts each person received). In this way Bales and Slater have accomplished the first three steps in measuring role differentiation. They have distinguished several dimensions of leadership in each group (although not necessarily distinct dimensions, as we shall see), they have characterized each member in terms of the extent to which he engages in behavior relevant to each dimension, and they have found that not all members are equal on each dimension—they can be rank ordered. We are now in a position where we can look at the data presented by Bales and Slater as they go through the remaining two steps: showing that not all the dimensions are isomorphic; and showing that the top men on each of the task and social-emotional dimensions support and reinforce one another. The analysis is based upon the data gathered in the post-session questionnaires, and upon the data gathered by observers using the IPA scoring system. As we go through the remaining steps, we shall take each of the six theoretical propositions in turn.

Data. The first proposition stated that in conditions under which these experimental groups met, there would arise an inequality among the members of participation in task activities.[7] Table 16.2 shows the average percentages of all group activity accounted for by the most active person, the next most active person, and so on. It shows that in all groups there tends to be some inequality of total activity, and that in the larger groups the most active person stands out above the others to a greater degree than in smaller groups. Now, in that these data are for *total* activity, not just *task* activity, the proposition is not yet adequately supported. It could be, for example, that there is equality in output of *task* activity, even though there is an inequality of output of *total* activity. However, the fact is that the greater the total activity of a person in the group, the greater is the proportion of his activity which is task activity[8] (Bales & Slater, 1955, p. 269), so that the amount of inequality of output of *task* activity is *greater*, on the average, than shown in Table 16.2, and the first proposition is thus supported.

[7] See above.

[8] Task activity here being defined as activity which is classified by Bales' IPA scoring system as questions or problem solving attempts (categories 4-9).

Table 16.2

Average Proportion of Activity Initiated by Members Ranked According to Output (Groups of Three to Six)

| Size of Group | Output Rank[a] | | | | | | Difference Between First and Second Output Rank |
	1	2	3	4	5	6	
3	.44	.33	.23				.11
4	.33	.27	.23	.17			.06
5	.46	.22	.16	.10	.06		.24
6	.43	.19	.14	.11	.07	.06	.24

SOURCE. Adapted from Bales, Strodtbeck, Mills, & Roseborough (1951), Chart 1, p. 467.
[a] Ranking determined for each group prior to aggregation.

Proposition 2, that the inequality is commonly perceived by the group members, is really more of a condition that must be satisfied for the remaining propositions to fully hold than it is a proposition to be tested. To implement this condition, Bales and Slater divided the groups into two sets on the basis of the amount of consensus there was among the group members as to the rank ordering of members on the dimensions of providing the best ideas and doing most to guide the discussion. Kendall's coefficient of concordance was computed for each dimension for each group.[9] This coefficient ranges from 0.00 (indicating complete lack of consensus) to 1.00 (indicating complete consensus). If the average of the two coefficients for a group was above .500 (the median value for this sample) the group was rated as having "High Status consensus." If the average value for the two coefficients was less than .500 the group was classed as having "Low Status consensus." Proposition 2 states that the remaining propositions hold primarily for High Status consensus groups. Also, since the amount of status consensus is likely a direct function of the amount of inequality of task participation, we may interpret this proposition as saying that role differentiation occurs only where inequality is great.

The third and fourth propositions state that the person most active in the task area is the source of change in achieving the goal. As a result tension and hostility are generated and a person other than the task leader emerges as one who attempts to alleviate these problems. This relates to the fourth step in measuring role differentiation (showing that the dimensions are not isomorphic). The evidence is somewhat indirect but can be inferred from Tables 16.3–16.7. We begin by looking at all the data, without distinguishing between High and Low Status consensus groups.

Table 16.3 shows that one of the five dimensions or roles, the average liking score of a person, as determined from the post-session questionnaire, does not form a perfect correspondence with his activity rank as determined by the number of IPA acts initiated by each member of the group (another of the five dimensions or roles); nor does it correspond with the ratings on providing best ideas or doing most to guide the discussion, the remaining dimensions. The most active person, the person who is rated as giving the best ideas and as doing most to guide the discussion, is not liked as well as persons who are intermediate on these dimensions. It would appear that the person who holds the top position on talking, guiding, or best ideas is not the person who holds the top position on being liked and this is consistent with the idea that the person most active in the task area is the source of some tension and hostility. It is also consistent with the idea that these dimensions are not isomorphic. Tables 16.4 and 16.5 make a similar point. In Table 16.4 it can be seen that the role of being best liked tends to be a unique role in that a person rated as being best liked is less likely to be rated tops on any of the other roles. This is not true of the roles of talking (initiating most IPA scored activity), receiving (being the recipient of most IPA acts), providing the best ideas, or guiding the discussion. The *liking* dimension thus appears to be separate and independent of the *task* dimension.

[9] A fuller discussion of this measure plus computing formulas are given in Siegel (1956).

Table 16.3

Proportion of "Total Votes Received" on each of Three Roles, Pooled for Men of Each Basic Initiating Rank

| PROPORTION VOTES ON | Basic Initiating Rank | | | | | TOTAL |
	1	2	3	4	5	
Best Ideas	.275	.218	.223	.189	.095	1.000
(Rank)	(1)	(3)	(2)	(4)	(5)	
Guidance	.255	.192	.231	.209	.113	1.000
(Rank)	(1)	(4)	(2)	(3)	(5)	
Liking	.211	.244	.240	.194	.111	1.000
(Rank)	(3)	(1)	(2)	(4)	(5)	

SOURCE. Adapted from Bales (1953), Chart 3, p. 146.

Table 16.4

Number of Sessions Out of a Possible 80 in Which a Given Person Holds Top Position in One and Only One Rank Order out of Five Possible Rank Orders[a]

Talking	11.0
Receiving	10.5
Ideas	12.0
Guidance	11.6
Liking	30.4
Total	75.5

SOURCE. Slater (1955), Table 1, p. 300.
[a] The decimals arise from ties in ranking.

Finally, in Table 16.5 we see that the task dimension becomes increasingly distinct from the liking dimension over time. In the first meeting one person is more likely than chance would predict to be rated tops on ideas *and* liking, but by the fourth meeting one person is less likely than chance would predict to be rated tops on both dimensions. The roles described by these dimensions tend over time to be played by two different people, and to the extent that being liked is coincident with performance of social-emotional activity, this is further support for Propositions 4 and 5.

Table 16.5

Percentage of Cases in Which the Same Man Holds Top Position on Like Ranking and Idea Ranking at the Same Time, by Sessions[a]

Sessions			
1	2	3	4
56.5	12.0	20.0	8.5

SOURCE. Slater (1955), Table 4, p. 303.
[a] The trends for high and low groups are identical.

As mentioned above, we have not yet distinguished between High and Low Status consensus groups. When we compare these two sets of groups, a slightly altered picture emerges as expected. In terms of the degree to which each of the five roles corresponds to (is isomorphic with) the other four, Table 16.6 shows that the bifurcated role structure that separates the task and social-emotional dimensions is apparent in groups with High Status consensus—talking, receiving, providing ideas, and guiding are highly intercorrelated, whereas liking tends to split off as a separate dimension. In the Low Status consensus groups, however, not only does liking split off as a separate factor, but talking and receiving also become distinct from either liking or from providing ideas and guiding. There are thus at least three unrelated leadership dimensions in the low groups. And, on top of this more atomistic role structure in the low groups, Bales and Slater point out that "it is difficult for a person who attains top rank in some respect in a given meeting to hold it in the next. . . . There is a high turnover of personnel in the top ranks of the various status orders [Bales and Slater, 1955, p. 299]." These facts would indicate that a *stable* differentiated status structure emerges in the groups with High Status consensus, but not in the low groups. In these latter groups there is something bordering on anarchy with a high turnover of top men on several unrelated status dimensions.

Table 16.6

Intercorrelations between Talking, Receiving, and Ratings on Ideas, Guidance, and Liking. Mean Rank Order Correlations of 64 Sessions (Size 3 excluded)

| | High Status-Consensus Groups | | | | |
	T	R	I	G	L
Talking		.88	.80	.75	.38
Receiving			.74	.74	.46
Ideas				.83	.41
Guidance					.49
Liking					

| | Low Status-Consensus Groups | | | | |
	T	R	I	G	L
Talking		.69	.48	.51	.10
Receiving			.44	.52	.16
Ideas				.71	.14
Guidance					.27
Liking					

SOURCE. Slater (1955), Table 3, p. 303.

What does this mean for the theory? First, that the most active task specialist (providing best ideas or guiding the discussion) tends not to be the best liked person in the group. He is rated as best liked less often than chance would predict and we are thus led to believe that certain factors are operating to prevent him from receiving at least an average number of best liked ratings. This of course fits with Proposition 3 that the task specialist, in his pushing toward the goal, is a source of strain in the group. Second, we note that this stabilized, differentiated role structure tends to appear only in groups with High Status consensus. Finally, we note that the person who is best liked is not the task specialist; however, we do not yet know whether he engages in behaviors designed to reduce tensions and smooth over interpersonal hostilities. We do not know, that is, whether or not the best liked man is a social-emotional specialist.

Table 16.7 provides some information on this point. In terms of the 12 categories of Bales' IPA scoring system, Table 16.7 shows the average amounts of various types of activity initiated and received by the best liked man of each group as compared with the activity of the task specialist (in this case the person rated as tops on providing the best ideas). We see there that the best liked men initiate more activity showing solidarity and tension reduction (categories 1 and 2) and they initiate less activity giving suggestion and opinion (categories 4 and 5) than do idea men. Also best liked men receive more solidarity and tension release than do idea men. In summary, the activity of the idea men is more instrumental-task oriented than is the activity of the best liked men. The activity of the best liked men is expressive-integrative by comparison. Here is evidence, then, that the best liked men do tend to play the role of the social-emotional specialist.

Table 16.7

Composite Profiles in Percentages of 44 Top Men on Idea Ranking and 44 Top Men on Like Ranking for the Same Sessions

	Initiated		Received	
	IDEA	BEST-LIKED	IDEA	BEST-LIKED
Interaction Category	MEN	MEN	MEN	MEN
1. Shows Solidarity	3.68	4.41	2.57	3.15
2. Shows Tension Release	5.15	6.98	7.95	9.20
3. Shows Agreement	14.42	16.83	23.29	18.27
4. Gives Suggestion	8.97	6.81	7.01	7.22
5. Gives Opinion	32.74	28.69	25.52	31.09
6. Gives Orientation	18.54	17.91	14.06	14.54
7. Asks Orientation	3.04	3.71	3.62	2.80
8. Asks Opinion	1.84	2.94	1.94	1.74
9. Asks Suggestion	0.93	1.33	0.85	0.84
10. Shows Disagreement	8.04	7.60	10.65	9.35
11. Shows Tension Increase	1.92	2.16	1.59	1.35
12. Shows Antagonism	0.73	0.63	0.95	0.45

SOURCE. Adapted from Slater (1955), Table 6, p. 305.

The last proposition enumerated above, Proposition 6, states that the differentiated role structure becomes stabilized as the task and social-emotional specialists reinforce and support one another. To illustrate this is to complete the fifth and last step in demonstrating the existence of task and social-emotional role differentiation. We have already seen that the pattern of differentiation is relatively stable in the High Status consensus groups, but not in the Low Status consensus groups, and we would, in accordance with Proposition 6, expect that stability to be concomitant with a mutual pattern of support between the task and social-emotional specialists. Table 16.8 reports data relevant to this question for groups where the best liked man was not also the idea man. In High Status consensus groups we note that there is a complementarity in the patterns of behavior characteristic of the idea man and the best liked man. The best liked man talks to and agrees with (supports) the idea man more than any other person, and the idea man talks to and agrees with the best liked man more so than does any other member.[10] In the Low Status consensus groups these generalizations are not supported. The stabilized complementary role structure of the high groups is not observed here.

Table 16.8

Characteristics of Interaction between Top Ranking Men on Ideas (I) and Top Ranking Men on Being Liked (L)

	Percentage of Cases in Which Characteristic Occurred	
Characteristic of Interaction Observed	HIGH GROUPS	LOW GROUPS
I *interacted* with L more than he did with any other member	57.1	52.9
I *interacted* with L more than any other member interacted with L	63.3*	50.0
I *agreed* with L more than he did with any other member	57.1	44.1
I *agreed* with L more than any other member agreed with L	75.0**	44.1
L *interacted* with I more than he did with any other member	92.9***	47.1
L *interacted* with I more than any other members interacted with I	71.4**	32.4
L *agreed* with I more than he did with any other member	85.7***	44.1
L *agreed* with I more than any other member agreed with I	46.4	29.4
Percentage expected by chance	32.1	28.8

SOURCE. Adapted from Bales and Slater (1955), Table 7, p. 283.
* $p < .05$.
** $p < .01$.
*** $p < .001$.

We have now covered most of the data upon which the theory was originally constructed. We have seen the measurement techniques which yielded five dimensions of participation in the group upon which each member could be ranked (talking, receiving, providing ideas, guiding, liking). And we saw that these five dimensions (in the case of the High Status consensus groups) reduced

[10] The idea man does not talk to or agree with the best liked man exclusively, however. He interacts with and agrees with other members at times to the same extent as with the best liked man.

to two dimensions, task leadership and social-emotional leadership, and that the top man on one of these dimensions tended not to be the top man on the other, that is, the two dimensions were not isomorphic. Finally we saw that the two persons who were tops on these two dimensions tended to interact frequently with each other and to support each other in a rather stable enduring pattern, and it was upon these results that Bales and Slater built their theory.

Basically, that's the picture. We have left out some of the details and embellishments, but those readers who are interested will want to read the original reports anyway. We now take another look at the work of Bales and Slater, this time through the eyes of some critics who offer their comments so that the "next time around" the study of role differentiation may be improved. At this point we shall present the criticisms and their implications. Tentative solutions to the problems raised in the criticisms will be presented at a later point when we discuss the methodology employed in current research.

Some Criticisms of the Bales-Slater Work

Methodological Problems.   One of the first reactions to the above work to appear in print was that of Professor D. K. Wheeler (1957) who was concerned primarily about two things: first, he criticized the use of the terms *specialist* or *top man* by Bales and Slater to designate the top man on each of the task and social-emotional dimensions. " 'Top Man,' " he writes, "has a final sound about it, but it is possible that he was *just* [barely] top man [1957, p. 147]." The second thing Wheeler was concerned about was the measurement of the social-emotional dimension—there was only one item (best liked) as opposed to at least two for the task dimension (ideas and guidance, also talking and receiving in the high groups), and this one item was not as clearly distinct from the task dimension as one would desire. This latter point was also made by Olmsted, who wrote, "the 'Liking' role of the sociometrically most popular person is closer to the [social-emotional role] than any other dimensions, though it can scarcely be said to constitute a very satisfactory operational definition of that phenomenon [Olmsted, 1959, p. 129]." Let us consider these two criticisms in order.

The first criticism, that about not being able to determine the *degree* to which the top man is tops, has several implications which need to be spelled out. In essence, what Wheeler is asking for is a technique for measuring task and social-emotional role performance in groups that is more refined than simply a rank ordering of members. Such a refined technique would allow several advantages. First, to meet Wheeler's criticism, one could specify the *degree* of inequality or differentiation on task dimension (the degree to which the top man is tops) rather than merely noting that there is always *some* inequality. Second, the concept of role differentiation (the primary dependent variable in the theory) could be measured quantitatively rather than qualitatively as either present or absent (either the top men on the two dimensions were the same person or they were not). These two advantages would allow a third, namely, the use of correlational techniques to measure the degree of association between inequality of task participation and role differentiation.

The second criticism, about the poor measurement of the social-emotional leadership role, relates to a more general problem of how to measure performance of any role. If we take Slater's definition of a role as a "more or less coherent and unified system of items of behavior [Slater, 1955, p. 300]," then a measure based upon one item is clearly inadequate. When a single item is used as in the Bales-Slater work there is no way to be certain that it is a part of a unified *system* of items or that it is an *essential* part of a unified system, or that it is not a component of each of *two or more different* systems. This is, of course, the question that is being raised by Wheeler and Olmsted. How can we be sure that being liked is not part of the task system of items, and how can we be sure that being liked is part of a social-emotional system of items? Bales and Slater do answer the first of these questions by the presentation of their data which is reproduced in Table 16.6. The second of these two questions has not adequately been answered.

The problem can be overcome, however, by using *more items* in assessing social-emotional leadership performance (or task leadership performance), and by using items that more clearly measure perceived *performance of social-emotional functions* in the group. Finally it should be shown that the items measuring each role are highly intercorrelated with each other, but that items measuring one role are not highly correlated with items measuring the other role. We shall see later that the technique of factor analysis is ideally suited to providing a resolution of this problem. In summary, our need at present, in light of the above criticisms made of the Bales-Slater work, is a technique of measuring task and social-emotional leadership role performance which (a) includes several items for each dimension that are highly correlated within dimensions, but have low correlations between dimensions, and (b) results in an ordered metric or interval scale level of measurement of performance of each dimension. These points cover the prime methodological criticisms and we turn now to some more substantive criticisms of the theory.

Substantive Problems. In 1961, Professor Sidney Verba published a book titled *Small Groups and Political Behavior* which, in part, criticized the relatively unconditional generality of the Bales-Slater role differentiation theory (Verba, 1961). Verba suggested that there were, indeed, conditions or factors that affected the likelihood of differentiation which were ignored by Bales and Slater in their work. His review of the literature yielded the following conclusions:

First, task and social-emotional role differentiation as observed by Bales and Slater seem to occur less frequently outside the experimental laboratory (e.g., in industrial work groups, conferences, etc.) than might be expected from the theory as it was set forth. Outside the laboratory a single person frequently plays both roles.

Second, investigating the possible sources for the observed differences between laboratory and nonlaboratory groups, Verba noted that in the laboratory there was no legitimate authority, outside the laboratory there was; in the laboratory task motivation was lower, outside the laboratory task motivation was higher; inside the laboratory certain values prevailed, outside the laboratory other values prevailed. These differences were seen by Verba to have the follow-ing effects:

1. The values of college students (the usual subjects in these studies) tend to make them sensitive and hostile to the exertion of direct interpersonal influence.
2. Task leadership attempts from a legitimate source differ from such at-tempts from a nonlegitimate source. The former arouses less hostility.
3. Task leadership attempts from peers are seen as a challenge, and are therefore less threatening and less likely to arouse hostility.
4. Insofar as the accomplishment of the group task is important to the group members, that is, task motivation is high, task leadership attempts will be regarded as contributing to a valued goal rather than as chal-lenges, and will be met with approval rather than hostility.

In general Verba noted that hostile responses to task actions were less likely outside the laboratory than inside; consequently, there was less impetus toward task and social-emotional role differentiation outside the laboratory than inside.

Secord and Backman, in their review of the Bales-Slater work on role differen-tiation, make some very similar points. They suggest "that the degree of role differentiation would vary directly with the extent to which task functions are unrewarding or costly. The less satisfaction experienced in working toward a goal and the more costs incurred, the more likely task and social-emotional functions are to be centered in different persons. Rewards would be low where task success is unrelated to member needs [See Verba's Point 4 above]. Costs would be higher where members disagree on both the importance of the task and how it is to be accomplished. Similarly, costs are apt to be high to the degree that influence attempts among group members must be largely personal in nature. [See Verba's Points 1, 2, and 3 above] [1964, p. 359]."

A Modified Theory

In view of these substantive criticisms, some modification of the original theory is in order. Limiting conditions, such as those enumerated above, must be added to the Bales-Slater theory in order to give it more specificity and broader scope. At this first stage of revising the theory, we have added only one specifying condition: *the legitimation of task activity*. This condition is central in both Verba's and Secord and Backman's comments, although Verba focuses on the *hostile response* to lack of legitimation, while Secord and Backman focus on *costs*.

What do we mean by legitimation of task activity? Only that it is *normatively right and proper* to engage in task activity, and consequently when one member *does* engage in task activity, he does not raise the ire of other group members and is not punished. It should be pointed out that we are here using the term legitimation in a slightly different way than Verba. He talked about *persons* having legitimation to engage in task directive actions, not about the *activity* being a legitimate activity in which to engage. What is the correspondence between these two conceptions? If the activity is legitimate for all persons, then it is legitimate for any one person and Verba's Points 2 and 4 above hold. On the other hand, it may be that task activity is legitimate for only one person in the group, in which case we have a situation that is identical to the case where legitimacy is attached to the person. This is the case of Verba's Point 3 above. Finally, if the activity itself were not legitimate for anyone, a situation like that depicted in Point 1 holds. In this way the idea of legitimation of task activity can be applied to all four of Verba's points and thus would constitute a very core addition to the theory.

Our question now is, "How is this condition of legitimacy added to the theory?" The answer is best provided by seeing the modified theory, spelled out in more detail than in the case of our earlier presentation of the Bales-Slater theory. The set of propositions that follows is, with the exception of those parts dealing with the question of legitimacy, derived from the writings of Bales and Slater. Each proposition is followed by its rationale.

Proposition 1.   The group is goal directed, but the pressures in this direction are not strong. Rationale: We need to assume some impetus on the part of the group members to engage in task activity, but not enough impetus to *legitimate* extensive task activity in the group.

Proposition 2.   Coordinated interaction of the group members in pursuance of a goal leads to an inequality of participation in task activity. Rationale: This is the first proposition in our earlier outline of the Bales-Slater theory and is incorporated here. Since a direct measure of the degree of inequality of task participation is used (see below), and since it was felt that status consensus was used as a measure of inequality, the ideas of status consensus has been omitted from the theory.

Proposition 3.   Task activity tends to create anxiety and hostility in individual group members to the extent that the level of such activity is greater than the level which is legitimate. Rationale: This is the counter-part to the earlier Proposition 3, for which Bales had three possible explanations, but these generally focused on the inequality of task participation,[11] not on the inequality where some member engages in more than a legitimate amount of task activity. The following explanation considers this aspect.[12]

Persons enter the group with an "idea" of the group in their minds: an idea of how the group should be organized and conducted (as a seminar, a discussion, a lecture, etc.). Part of this idea consists of normative expectations about the various behaviors or roles of various types of individuals (leaders-followers, males-females, students-faculty, etc.). To the extent that this idea is shared and suggested by the general culture or the experimental instructions, we may speak of a *model* of legitimate behaviors. Departures from this model produce anxiety

---

[11] See footnote 4, p. 517.

[12] The basic idea here was first put forth by the author in considering the consequences of *too little* behavior on the task dimension (Burke, 1966).

and hostility, especially in the case where there is general consensus about the model, as for example in the High Status consensus groups of Bales and Slater.[13]

Proposition 4.   The amount of excessive task activity of the task leader is, in part, a function of the intensity and balance of rewards and punishments he receives for his activity, and, in part, a function of his personality predisposition. Rationale: The first part of this proposition is an assumption of conditioning as one underlying mechanism in producing specialized activity (Bales, 1953, pp. 153ff.). Excessive task activity is rewarded because it moves the group toward the shared goal, and punished because it "upsets" the members. It is implicit here that the group members feel ambivalence toward the task leader. We might hypothesize that the intensity and balance of rewards and punishments are functions of (a) the strength of the desire for the goal, (b) the strength of the desire for maintenance of the group "model," and (c) the existence of alternative outlets for the frustration and tension than antagonism against the task leader. The second part of the proposition is included to account for the finding of Bales and Slater that under certain conditions the task and expressive specialists had higher "authoritarianism" scores (Slater, 1955).

Proposition 5.   There is some minimum amount of commitment to the group and/or goal. Rationale: Without some commitment to the group or its goal, the anxiety and tension resulting in Proposition 3 would cause the group to disband. Should that be the response of the group members to anxiety, role differentiation, of course, could not occur.

Proposition 6.   Tension and hostility are undesirable, and the group members will act to reduce or otherwise handle them. Rationale: This proposition is the expressive counterpart of Proposition 1. It shows the impetus for social-emotional activity. We have not, however, specified the nature of that activity and there is evidently some room for variability. Bales suggests three possible ways of handling the tension and hostility: (a) some person of low status is made a scapegoat and tension and hostility are drained away from the task leader through this mechanism (Bales, 1953, pp. 147–148; Burke, 1969a); (b) the person who is primarily responsible for the tension, the task leader, may be deposed as the task leader through a "status struggle" (Heinicke & Bales, 1953); or (c) someone may engage in expressive activity aimed at directly reducing frustrations, tensions, and interpersonal hostilities. Of these three, Bales suggests that only the last alternative tends to be stable and enduring. The first alternative depends upon the scapegoat remaining in the group and, unless he is a masochist, that is unlikely over a period of time. The second alternative is unlikely to last long because it prevents the group from achieving the task by deposing anyone who begins to achieve prominence in task activities.

Proposition 7.   The amount of social-emotional activity on the part of a group member is, in part, a function of the intensity and balance of rewards and punishments he receives for his activity and, in part, a function of his personality predisposition. Rationale: This is the social-emotional counter-

[13] See Festinger, et al. (1960), and Schachter (1960).

part of Proposition 4. Social-emotional activity is rewarded to the extent that it reduces tension, and is punished to the extent that is inhibits reaching the goal.

Proposition 8.   The two modes of activity—task and social-emotional—are incompatible under conditions of low legitimation of task activity, so that a specialist in task activity tends not to be a specialist in social-emotional activity. Rationale: There are two hypotheses which would lead, either separately or in combination, to this proposition. The first is a hypothesis of psychological incompatibility. High task output that meets with resistance or opposition tends to take on a negative tone, and thus precludes positive social-emotional activity. Without resistance or opposition, social-emotional activity is possible. Thus when there is anxiety and hostility due to excessive task performance on the part of one or another person in the group, task and expressive activity become relatively incompatible (Secord & Backman, 1964, p. 358). The second hypothesis is of social incompatibility; the rewards and punishments are distributed in such a way that task activity on the part of one person is reinforced, but his expressive activity is not, while expressive activity on the part of another is reinforced, but his task activity is not.

Proposition 9.   The result, from and in accordance with the above propositions, is the emergence of task and social-emotional role differentiation—two different persons being rewarded for engaging in two different modes of activity.

Proposition 10.   These differentiated roles are stabilized and synchronized as the task and social-emotional leaders reinforce and support one another.

Having now spelled out the theory with its modification to include the conditional factor of the legitimation of task activity, we are in a position to discuss some recent work on this modified theory. To do this we shall present two studies in some detail, including discussions of both advances in technique and in testing parts of the theory through the collection of data using the new techniques. Finally, we will present some directions for future research.

STUDY I

Procedures.   For this study (Burke, 1967), 21 groups composed of undergraduate students enrolled in introductory sociology courses were used. As part of a course requirement concerned with the study of social control, these groups met for a period of about one hour to discuss a human relations case study of a juvenile delinquent. The groups consisted of either four or five members and met in a "small groups laboratory" of the type described earlier.

After they had all arrived, the students were ushered into the room and asked to sit anywhere around a hexagonal table with seats on five sides. Efforts had been made to assure that students in the same group were unacquainted with each other prior to the group meeting, although this was not possible in a few cases. The nature of the room—its soundproofing, one-way mirrors, microphones, etc.—was explained to the students, and then copies of the case study were distributed.

After sufficient time to read the case, the copies were collected and the participants were instructed to analyze and discuss the case focusing on the questions: "Why were the individuals involved in the case behaving as they were?" "What, if anything, should be done about it?" The participants were told that they would have 30 minutes to discuss the case and that they should come to a "group decision" within this time. At that point, if there were no further questions, the experimenter told them to begin and then left the room. The discussions were sound recorded on tape and the interaction was recorded by an observer using the Bales method of Interaction Process Analysis.

Up to this point the procedures used followed those of Bales and Slater quite closely. The post-session questionnaire and the measures derived from it, however, differed and we shall describe in some detail the procedures used to obtain four basic measures: (a) task and social-emotional leadership performance, (b) inequality of task participation, (c) task and social-emotional role differentiation, and (d) task activity legitimation. Following each we explicitly compare these procedures with those used by Bales and Slater.

Measures of Leadership Performance. Eleven items were presented to the group participants in a post-session questionnaire, seven of which were designed to measure task leadership performance, and four of which were designed to measure social-emotional leadership performance (See Table 16.9). For each item, the participants were asked to rate each other and themselves on a 10-point scale. This technique, as opposed to providing rank orderings, allows the participants to show greater or lesser distinctions between members as they see fit. It allows someone, for example, to provide a rating of 10 to one person and 4, 3, 2, and 1 to the others, thus reflecting a big distinction between one person and the rest of the group if that is what they perceive.

The ratings provided for each person by himself and the others were averaged, giving him one average rating on each of the 11 items. These were then standardized across groups so that each person's score was taken as a deviation from the group mean. Thus, for example, if the average ratings in a group of four persons on the item providing ideas for discussion were 8.4, 6.8, 4.0, and 2.8, these scores would become respectively 2.9, 1.3, —1.5, and —2.7. The purpose of this last transformation is to eliminate idiosyncratic differences in the average level of ratings from individual to individual, and to make the groups comparable in average ratings on each item so that in the next step the focus would be on variations in ratings within groups (between individuals) rather than on variations between groups.

The next step was to systematically combine the ratings on the 11 items into a single task leadership performance score and a single social-emotional leadership performance score for each person in each group. We mentioned earlier that factor analysis was a technique ideally suited to this problem, and this is what was used. It would be impossible to elaborate the details of factor analysis in this paper for those who do not understand it, but the following is sufficient for our purposes.[14]

---

[14] For an introduction to factor analysis, the reader might consult Harmon (1968).

If we correlate each of the 11 items with every other item and look at the correlation coefficients, we find that some items are highly correlated with each other indicating that they measure roughly the same thing or *factor*.[15] We will also find that some items are relatively uncorrelated with each other, indicating that they do not measure the same factor. Factor analysis, in this sense, uses the correlations among the 11 items to find a small number of factors or underlying dimensions that are "measured" by the larger number of items, *and* it shows the correlations between each of the 11 items and the underlying hypothetical dimensions. These latter correlations are called *loadings*, and the higher the loading for an item on a factor, the better is that item a measure of the underlying factor. In our case the items were selected so as to yield two underlying factors, task and social-emotional, and the loadings may be taken to indicate how well each item represents or measures each of these factors.

Table 16.9 shows the results of this part of the analysis, and we see that there are two factors, the first of which is highly correlated with the task items and is labeled Task Leadership Performance, the second of which is highly correlated with the social-emotional items and is labeled Social-Emotional Leadership Performance.

From these results, factor scores on these two factors were generated for each and every member, thus providing the end result desired: single measures of task leadership performance and social-emotional leadership performance. These factor scores are a weighted average of the ratings provided on the 11 items. Discussion of the actual weights (standardized regression coefficient) and their method of calculation is beyond the scope of this paper. Suffice it to say that all of these procedures, the factor analysis and the computation of the leadership performance factor scores, were done automatically using the BMD General Factor Analysis computing program (Dixon, 1965).

There are several important differences between the present procedures and those used by Bales. First, we have a measure rather than a rank, and consequently, we can assess relative distances between top and next top man thus answering Wheeler's question of the *degree* to which the top man is tops. Second, the social-emotional role was measured directly in terms of its functions rather than only indirectly as being best liked. (Indeed, Table 16.9 shows that being best liked correlated only .61 with the social-emotional role as here defined.) Finally, both task and social-emotional roles were measured by several items each, rather than by one item each.

To compare the results of these procedures with those of Bales and Slater, both methods were used to identify the task and social-emotional "leaders" in each group. For the Bales-Slater procedures this amounts to finding the person

---

[15] We are presupposing here that the researcher uses items which he feels, on *a priori* grounds, do measure the same underlying dimensions, so that the above patterning of the intercorrelations is observed. Unless these patterns do exist among the intercorrelations of the items, there are no grounds for proceeding further in the analysis.

Table 16.9

Factor Analysis of Responses to Post-Session Questionnaire

	Loadings	
	I	II
		SOCIAL-
	TASK	EMOTIONAL
	LEADERSHIP	LEADERSHIP
Item	PERFORMANCE	PERFORMANCE
[a]1. Providing "fuel" for discussion by introducing ideas and opinions for the rest of the group to discuss	.87	.43
2. Standing out as the leader in the discussion	.86	.43
[b]3. Providing the best ideas for the discussion	.85	.43
[b]4. Doing most to guide the discussion and keep it moving effectively	.83	.50
5. Making most attempts to influence the group's opinion	.80	.37
6. Being the most successful in influencing the group's opinion	.79	.44
[a]7. Providing clarification, getting the discussion to the point by getting terms defined and pointing out logical difficulties	.75	.51
[a]8. Joking and kidding, finding the potentially humorous implications in the discussion	.54	.54
[b]9. Most liked	.43	.61
10. Doing most to keep relationship between members cordial and friendly	.40	.83
[a]11. Making tactful comments to heal any hurt feelings which might arise in the discussion	.37	.85

SOURCE. Adapted from Burke (1967), Figure 1, p. 384.
[a] Items adapted from Davis (1961).
[b] Items adapted from Bales and Slater (1955).

ranked first on providing best ideas and being most liked. For our own procedures, the persons with the highest task factor scores and the highest social-emotional factor scores were used.

On the task dimension, the results of the two methods are quite similar (81 percent perfect agreement). On the social-emotional dimension, the results of the two methods differ somewhat (only 57 percent perfect agreement). This latter result was to be expected, however, since the items used in the present study measured the performance of social-emotional functions more directly than did Bales', and there was only a .61 correlation overall between being liked and performing social-emotional functions (See Table 16.9).

Measures of Inequality of Task Participation. The task and social-emotional factor scores derived above were used to obtain two measures of inequality of participation on the task dimension: the variance (s^2) among the task factor scores of the members of each group (task variance), and the task factor score of the task leader (task score). The second of these measures makes sense as a measure of inequality if we remember that these scores are deviations from the mean of the group, so that to the extent that the leader's score is high, others' must be low.

The basic difference here between the present procedure and those of Bales and Slater is that we have *measured* this aspect of the group, whereas Bales and Slater only *assumed* that all groups engaged in coordinated activity in pursuit of a goal had such inequality. Since this is the primary independent variable of the theory, it is important that it be measured.

A Measure of Role Differentiation. As a measure of task and social-emotional role differentiation, a measure of dissimilarity between the roles of the task leader and the social-emotional leader was used. This measure was described in the original report as follows:

> Using the task and social-emotional factors as orthogonal axes in a Cartesian coordinate system, the locations of the task and social-emotional leaders (or of any of the group members) may be plotted. The degree of task and social-emotional role differentiation may then be defined as the linear graph-distance separating the point on the graph representing the task leader from the point on the graph representing the social-emotional leader of that group. At one extreme, if the task leader and the social-emotional leader are the same person, the distance is zero and there is no differentiation. At the other extreme the two points are on opposite sides of the graph and there is some maximum amount of differentiation . . . [Burke, 1967, p. 385].

The algebraic formula for calculating the amount of role differentiation, D, is

$$D = \sqrt{(T_t - T_{se})^2 + (SE_t - SE_{se})^2}$$

where T_t represents the task score of the task leader, SE_t his social-emotional score, T_{se} represents the task score of the social-emotional leader, and SE_{se} his social-emotional score.

Comparison with the work of Bales and Slater shows that this is another variable which was not directly measured by them except in a qualitative manner: a group had differentiated roles if the top man on ideas was not best liked, but not otherwise. With the present measure, the degree of task and social-emotional role differentiation can be indicated.

Degree of Legitimation of Task Activity. In order to ascertain the degree of legitimation of task activity, observers listened to the tape recordings of the groups blindly, that is, they had no knowledge as to what groups they were listening. They were instructed to rate the groups on items which had been designed to measure the degree to which the members displayed in their interaction acceptance of what might be termed a *task ethic*, that is, how much interest was displayed in carrying out their task of discussing the case in order to come to a group decision about why the individuals in the case were behaving the way they were and what, if anything, should be done. Two questions were asked: To what extent do the group members keep to their assigned task of discussing the case? To what extent do the group members attempt to achieve a consensus or group decision? Concern for, and acceptance of this task ethic on the part of the group members was taken as evidence of the legitimation of task activity. This, it can be seen, makes use of Proposition 1, high pressure toward the goal indicates legitimation of task activity. The groups were divided into two categories: High Task Legitimacy and Low Task Legitimacy. There was agreement on the classification of 18 (87 percent) of the cases between two independent observers, and on the three cases where there was not agreement, the author's judgment was used to classify the group.

Results. The results are presented in Table 16.10 and may be discussed in three parts corresponding to the three parts of the theory tested. The first part bears on Proposition 3 in the more extended theory—that legitimation of task activity in a group prevents inequality of task performance from leading to a disliking of the high task contributor (the task leader). Table 16.10 shows that for groups with low legitimation of task activity, there is a moderate negative correlation between inequality of task participation (using either measure) and liking of the task leader as measured by Item 8 of the post-session questionnaire (−.73 and −.43). For groups with high legitimation of task

Table 16.10

Correlations between Measures of Inequality of Task Participation and Measures of Task and Social-Emotional Role Differentiation, by Degree of Legitimation of Task Participation

	High Task Legitimation Groups (N = 10)		
	LIKING OF TASK LEADER	SE SCORE OF TASK LEADER	ROLE DIFFERENTIATION (GRAPH DISTANCE)
Task variance	.03	.11	.11
Task score	−.13	−.14	.04
	Low Task Legitimation Groups (N = 11)		
	LIKING OF TASK LEADER	SE SCORE OF TASK LEADER	ROLE DIFFERENTIATION (GRAPH DISTANCE)
Task variance	−.73**	−.78**	.64**
Task score	−.43*	−.74**	.79**

SOURCE. Burke (1967), Table 3, p. 389.
* $p < .10$.
** $p < .05$.
Correlations between task variance and task score are: for high task legitimation groups .81 ($p < .05$); for low task legitimation groups .79 ($p < .05$). Correlation between liking of the task leader and SE score of the task leader are: for high groups .51 ($p < .10$); for low groups .71 ($p < .05$).

activity, however, neither measure of inequality of task performance is correlated with liking of the task leader. These findings are consistent with Proposition 3, and we may hypothesize that task legitimation mediates the effects of inequality of task participation on the degree of liking of the task leader: only in the low groups is high inequality of task participation associated with low liking of the task leader.

The second part of the analysis bears on Proposition 8—that task and social-emotional activity are incompatible under conditions of low legitimation of task activity. Table 16.10 also presents data relevant to this hypothesis for the task leaders. We observe a negative correlation between the task and social-emotional factor scores of the task leaders ($-.74$) in the low legitimation groups, but in the high groups, there is essentially no correlation between these measures. These results are consistent with Proposition 8: concentration on task activity in the low legitimation groups apparently prevents the task leaders from engaging in social-emotional activity; the two are incompatible.

The last part of the analysis in this study bears on Proposition 9—that the outcome of inequality of task participation in groups with low legitimation of task activity is a separation of the roles of task and social-emotional leaders, that is, role differentiation as defined by our graph distance model. The results, again, are in Table 16.10. Among the groups with low legitimation of task activity, there are moderately strong positive correlations between the measures of inequality of task participation and role differentiation (.64, and .79), while among the high groups the correlations are essentially zero. Role differentiation is a concomitant of inequality only in the low groups, thus supporting the hypothesis.[16]

To summarize the findings of this study, then, we may hypothesize that the factor "legitimation of task activity" mediates between inequality of task participation and the development of task and social-emotional role differentiation, in accordance with revised propositions presented earlier. These results, however, were based upon an ex post facto labeling of groups as exhibiting high or low legitimation of task activity, and we turn now to a second study that manipulated the legitimation condition experimentally.[17] An additional step

---

[16] With respect to these last findings, one may wonder, in that the task score of the task leader is a component of both the measures of inequality of task performance and of role differentiation, whether the correlations are artifactual. To test the amount of such "built in" correlation, 10,000 pseudorandom normal-deviate numbers representing task and social-emotional scores for 1000 5-man groups were generated using a normal deviate, pseudorandom number generator on a computer. For these, the task score of the task leader was correlated with the computed role differentiation score yielding a correlation coefficient of $+.11$.

[17] The problem with the "ex post facto labeling" of the groups is that without experimental control of legitimation and the random assignment of groups to either the experimental (e.g., high legitimation) or control (e.g., low legitimation) conditions, we cannot conclude that the differences between the conditions are *due to* differences in legitimation. It may be, for example, that the differences are due to some variable which is correlated with legitimation.

forward in the following study is the introduction of a longitudinal design to investigate changes in the variables over time and the relationships between changes in one variable to changes in others.

STUDY II

Procedures. For this study 12 groups, composed of undergraduate students enrolled in introductory social psychology courses, met as part of a course requirement to discuss human relations case studies (Burke, 1968). The general procedures were the same as those of the previous study except the pressures toward task activity were introduced as experimental manipulations, rather than observed and classified ex post facto. The rationale again follows from Proposition 1. We quote from the original study:

> *High task legitimation condition.* In six of the groups, selected randomly, the students were seated around a hexagonal table and copies of the first case study were distributed. After they had read the case, the students were instructed that they would have 25 minutes to discuss the case in order to come to a unanimous agreement in answering the questions "Why were the individuals involved in the case behaving as they were?" and "What, if anything, should be done about it?" Additionally, they were instructed that the quality of their discussion and the answers they proposed would be judged and rated, and that they would be informed of their rating."[18]

At this point a prediscussion questionnaire was presented and filled out and collected. The experimenter then asked if there were any question; if not, he told them to begin and left the room.

> Following the discussion (and after filling out a post-discussion questionnaire) these groups were informed that their discussion rated only 140 points as compared with the average of 150 points achieved by groups like theirs. The groups were then given a 10-minute break, after which they were reminded of their "below average" performance, and a second case study was presented. Instructions [and procedure] were the same as for the first discussion. It should be noted that the full experimental manipulation, including the inducement to work harder—to at least do average work—was present only in the second discussion.[19]
>
> *Low task legitimation condition.* Instructions [and procedures] in this condition were identical with those in the high legitimation condition with the following two exceptions: there was no impetus to work toward consensus, in fact the members were told they need not agree with each other, and the number of points "awarded" after the first discussion was 160. When the rating was given the group members were told they were doing fine, being ten points above the 150 point

[18] This and the following paragraphs are taken from Burke (1968).

[19] The full nature of the experimental manipulations, and their rationale, were explained fully to the classes after completion of the experiment, and it was made clear that how they were rated had no bearing on their course grade.

average for groups like theirs. Again, there followed a 10-minute break, after which the members were reminded of their good score, and the second case study was passed out. Instructions for the second discussion were the same as for the first.

We might ask at this point how the experimental manipulation relates to the theoretical condition of degree of legitimation of task activity. To answer this we consider the two basic parts to the experimental procedure: (1) the instructions to achieve consensus or not, and (2) the awarding of differential points, and, for the groups that did "poorly," the admonition to work harder, i.e., to engage in *more* task activity.

The first of these provides an *explicit goal* to the high legitimation groups which is not provided to the others. There is, in addition, an implicit assumption that the members work to achieve this limited goal. Finally, there is the possibility that they can assess their progress toward the externally imposed goal and thus be aware of their "progress." That this goal was accepted is evident in the fact that results of a pre-discussion questionnaire show the high legitimation groups felt more certain, prior to discussion, that a consensus would be reached (p < .05 each discussion).[20] However, in actually achieving consensus, it was not until the second meeting that a significant difference appeared between the two sets of groups in terms of the certainty to which they felt a consensus had been reached.[21] This would indicate, perhaps, that the high legitimation groups tried harder, relative to the other groups, to achieve consensus only in the second meeting, and it is this that the differential awarding of points was designed to accomplish—to give the high legitimation groups more impetus toward task activity.

Was this aim achieved? When the two sets of groups are compared, high legitimation groups show a greater increase in their perceived task output from discussion one to discussion two than did the other groups. Their overall task ratings increased more, as did, more particularly, their rating on providing *"fuel"* for discussion, *guiding* the discussion, and *attempting to influence* the group's opinion. In summary, then, the particular experimental manipulations were designed to, and apparently succeeded in, making the members of the high legitimation groups more oriented toward task activity and more active in the task area, and this was accomplished primarily in the second discussion. Did they accept these task pressures willingly? Answers to the post-session questionnaires indicate they did to the extent that they were equally or more satisfied with the discussion than members of the low legitimation group (nonsignificant differences indicating greater satisfaction were found),[22] that they were equally or less bored,[23] and that they were no more anxious or tense than the others.[24] On these grounds, then, we would argue that the experimental manipulations were successful in producing differential degrees of legitimation of task activity by the second discussion [Burke, 1968, pp. 405–407].

---

[20] The pre-discussion questionnaire item "To what extent do you feel a consensus will be reached?" was used. This was followed by a nine-point scale ranging from "very little" through "moderate" to "very much."

[21] The post-discussion questionnaire item "To what extent do you feel a consensus was reached?" was used.

[22] Item: "To what extent were you satisfied with the discussion?"

[23] Item: "To what extent did you feel bored with what was going on?"

[24] Item: "To what extent did you feel anxious or tense in the discussion?"

Measures. The procedures used to measure the variables of task and social-emotional leadership performance, inequality of task participation, and task and social-emotional role differentiation were identical with those presented in the previous study except that the measurement of task and social-emotional leadership performance was based upon a factor analysis of 8 items, 4 task and 4 social-emotional, rather than 11 items as before (See Table 16.11).

Table 16.11

Factor Analysis of Leadership Questionnaire Items for Two Discussions

	Discussion One Loadings		*Discussion Two Loadings*	
Item:[a]	TASK FACTOR	SOCIAL-EMOTIONAL FACTOR	TASK FACTOR	SOCIAL-EMOTIONAL FACTOR
1. Fuel	.90	.33	.90	.35
2. Guide	.86	.45	.87	.45
3. Infl-A	.89	.33	.91	.31
4. Leader	.92	.34	.89	.42
5. Cordial	.28	.76	.29	.81
6. Harmonize	.48	.78	.38	.86
7. Smooth	.40	.84	.38	.87
8. Tact	.26	.87	.36	.85

SOURCE. Adapted from Burke (1968), Table 1, p. 407.

[a]1. Providing fuel for the discussion by introducing ideas and opinions for the rest of the group to discuss.
2. Guiding the discussion and keeping it moving effectively.
3. Attempting to influence the group's opinion.
4. Standing out as the leader of the discussion.
5. Acting to keep the relationship between members cordial and friendly.
6. Attempting to harmonize differences of opinion.
7. Intervening to smooth over disagreements.
8. Making tactful comments to heal any hurt feelings that might arise in the discussion.

Results. The analysis in this study focused on Propositions 8 and 9 in the extended theory, and we shall discuss data relevant to each proposition separately. The results relevant to Proposition 8 (predicting an incompatibility between task and social-emotional activity in condition of low legitimation of task activity) are presented in Table 16.12.

For the first discussion, contrary to the hypothesis, there is little difference between the two conditions in terms of the correlations between task and social-emotional activity of the task leaders. This, however, was to be expected as the full experimental manipulations had not yet taken place. For the second discussion, the hypothesis is strongly supported. In the low legitimation condition, task and social-emotional activity among the task leaders are negatively correlated and quite strongly so (−.90), whereas in the high condition the correlation is not significantly different from zero. The difference between the two conditions is significant at the .05 level.

Table 16.12

Correlations between the Task and Social-Emotional Scores of the Task Leader, by Experimental Condition and Discussion

Experimental Condition	Discussion (1)	(2)	Change from (1) to (2)
Low Legitimation	−.63*	−.90***	−.81**
High Legitimation	−.57	.34	−.96
Difference	(ns)	(p < .05)	(p < .10)

SOURCE. Burke (1968), Table 3, p. 410.
* p < .10.
** p < .05.
*** p < .01.

The last part of Table 16.12 shows the correlations between *changes* in the task leaders' task scores from Discussion 1 to Discussion 2 and *changes* in their social-emotional scores. For the low groups, in support of Proposition 8, there is a strong negative correlation (−.81), whereas in the high groups the correlation is near zero. The difference between conditions is significant at the .10 level. The results show that, for the low legitimation of task activity groups, not only are high task scores of the task leaders associated with low social-emotional scores, as in the previous study, but that if the task leader *increases* his task score from one discussion to the next, he will tend to *decrease* his social-emotional score, and vice-versa.

The results relevant to Proposition 9 (that role differentiation as a consequence of inequality of task participation occurs only in low groups) are presented in Table 16.13, and we turn to these now. Focusing on the results of the second discussion (by which time the experimental manipulation had been completed) we see that the proposition is strongly supported. The correlations between inequality of task participation and task and social-emotional role differentiation are very high for the low legitimation groups (.99 and .97), while they are not significantly different from zero for the high groups. The difference between the two conditions is significant at the .01 level.

The correlations between changes in these variables presented in Table 16.13 show further longitudinal support of the hypothesis. Changes in inequality of task participation are positively correlated with changes in role differentiation in the low legitimation groups, but not in the high groups.

Summarizing these results, the original report stated:

1. Inequality of participation in task activities leads to the emergence of separate specialized task and social-emotional roles in the low legitimation of task activities condition, but not in the high legitimation condition.
2. High task participation on the part of the task leader leads to a reduction of the amount of social-emotional activity on his part in the low legitimation of task activity condition, but not in the high legitimation condition [Burke, 1968, p. 410].

Table 16.13

Correlations between Inequality of Task Activity (Two Measures) and Role Differentiation (Graph Distance), by Experimental Condition and Discussion

Inequality Measure	Experimental Condition	Discussion (1)	Discussion (2)	Change from (1) to (2)
Task	Low Legitimation	.76**	.99***	.79**
Variance	High Legitimation	.56	—.19	.21
	Difference	(ns)	(p < .01)	(ns)
Task	Low Legitimation	.67	.97***	.79**
Score	High Legitimation	.64	—.36	—.01
	Difference	(ns)	(p < .01)	(p < .10)

SOURCE. Burke (1968), Table 2, p. 408.
* p<.10.
** p<.05.
*** p<.01.

These conclusions, it should be pointed out, do not differ from those reached in the earlier study, but are significant for three reasons: (a) they replicate the earlier findings, (b) the legitimation condition was based on experimental manipulation rather than ex post facto classification by observers, and (c) longitudinal support for the propositions was introduced.

This ends our discussion of completed work, and we can summarize our progress to this point. After describing the work of Bales and Slater, and considering some of the criticisms with which it met, we concluded that two things had to be done in future work: first, their theory had to be modified to take into account certain limiting conditions or factors, and second, the methodological procedures, especially in terms of measurement procedures, had to be improved. As a first step in accomplishing these, a modified theory was constructed that contained one limiting condition assumed from the work of Verba to be critical: that of the degree of legitimation of task activity. Improvements in the procedures of measuring task leadership performance, social-emotional leadership performance, inequality of task participation, and role differentiation were then presented in our discussion of Study I. In Study II we showed further improvements in experimental design for testing certain propositions of the modified theory, and this brings us to the question, "Where do we go from here?"

FUTURE RESEARCH

There are basically two directions in which future research on the origins of task and social-emotional leadership role differentiation should move: first, further testing and refinement of the existing propositions should be undertaken with special attention paid to those which have not yet been tested, and second, new variables and conditions to broaden the scope of the theory should be introduced. Let us consider one possibility in each of these directions.

Alternatives to Role Differentiation

An important proposition in the theory of role differentiation is Proposition 6 which states that the group members will act to reduce or otherwise handle the tension and hostility that results from excessive task activity on the part of the task leader. It is suggested in the rationale for this proposition that the performance of social-emotional activity on the part of one or more group members is the only viable manner in which the tension and hostility can be handled; however, this has not been adequately demonstrated. The argument, it will be recalled, is a functional one: the pressure of a social-emotional specialist *functions* to keep the group intact; that is, unless a social-emotional leader emerges to smooth over tensions and hostilities, the group will tend to break up.

This, of course, could be tested by studying groups in which a social-emotional specialist does not emerge, and noting whether or not they break up. If the groups do break up, then it could be argued that a social-emotional leader is necessary to the group under these circumstances. But if the groups do not break up—well, there are two alternatives. The functional hypothesis is wrong, or there are functional alternatives, that is, alternative ways of handling the tension and hostility. Bales, in fact, considers two alternatives, scapegoating[25] and the overthrowing of the task leader as the cause of the tension and hostility, but he views these as unstable (Bales, 1953).[26] If scapegoating is used as a mechanism for handling tension and hostility generated by the task leader (i.e., displacing the hostility onto a low status group member), its continuance depends upon the scapegoat remaining in the group, which is an unlikely event. The consequence is that either a different mechanism is used or slowly the group disintegrates as each new scapegoat leaves for greener pastures. If the group members use the alternative of overthrowing the task leader (and his inevitable replacements) in order to call a halt to the tension and hostility he generates, they are left without a leader and the task is unlikely to be completed. Again, the probable result is the disbanding of the group. It appears, therefore, that the only stable alternative is the emergence of a social-emotional specialist. However, there has been no adequate testing of these ideas, and this is one problem for future research.

Expanding the Theory

The second direction in which work must proceed is that of introducing and testing new variables and conditions in order to broaden the scope of the theory. Within this frame, three classes of variables should be considered: (a)

---

[25] See, for example, Burke (1969a).

[26] Another alternative which should be mentioned, although it has received little attention in the literature, is a differentiation of activity in time. It may be the case that the tensions and hostilities are not handled until a period during the last part of the meeting, or perhaps after the formal meeting is completed and the participants begin to leave.

structural and contextual variables such as group size,[27] the nature of the task,[28] and the nature of the rewards for participating in the group (Burke, 1969b); (b) *personality and individual background variables* such as attitudes toward authority (authoritarianism), social class background, and level of achievement motivation; and (c) *interpersonal or compositional variables* such as sex composition of the group, degree of familiarity of the group members with each other,[29] and compatibility or similarity of social values. So far none of these variables have been included in the theory, although there is evidence that they may be important in the genesis of role differentiation. The job, however, would not be just to include more variables under a general rubric such as "things which lead to role differentiation." The job would be to understand how and why additional factors are relevant—to understand the processes and mechanisms involved. It is quite likely that role differentiation itself depends upon a small number of "core" factors, but that these in turn depend upon a larger number of peripheral factors.

One example of such a core factor, which would fall under the interpersonal heading, might be the degree to which the interaction in the group is perceived by the members as threatening—to their status, their "ego" or self-concept, or their definition of the situation. How would this work? Let us reconsider the factor of legitimation of task activity which has already been included in the theory. Looking again at the factors Verba suggested are important conditions to the development of role differentiation, we may make the following interpretations: (a) college students are more likely than the general population to perceive task leadership attempts as challenging and threatening; (b) legitimate task leadership attempts are inherently less challenging or threatening than nonlegitimate attempts; and (c) legitimate task leadership attempts are less likely to be perceived as challenging or threatening than are nonlegitimate attempts. The result of the actual or perceived challenges or threats in the leadership attempts is a feeling of hostility toward the person making the leadership attempts, and, ultimately, role differentiation.

Other factors which might affect the core factor of perceived threat are the amount of pressure toward conformity (Festinger, 1954), the nature of the distribution of rewards or payments for participation in the group (Miller & Hamblin, 1963), and the importance of the task to the members (Verba, 1961). In this way the factor of perceived threat lies at the narrow end of a funnel, affected by a great number of factors, but being one of a possible few which affect role differentiation. The problem of testing these ideas, however, must be a concern for future research.

[27] Cf. Levinger (1964).
[28] Cf. Mann (1961).
[29] Cf. Leik (1963).

REFERENCES

BALES, R. F. *Interaction process analysis.* Reading, Mass.: Addison-Wesley, 1950.

BALES, R. F. The equilibrium problem in small groups. In T. Parsons, R. F. Bales, & E. A. Shils (Eds.), *Working papers in the theory of action.* New York: Free Press, 1953. Pp. 111–161.

BALES, R. F. Task status and likeability as a function of talking and listening in decision-making groups. In L. D. White (Ed.), *The state of the social sciences.* Chicago: University of Chicago Press, 1956. Pp. 148–161.

BALES, R. F. Task roles and social roles in problem solving groups. In E. Maccoby, T. Newcomb, & E. Hartley (Eds.), *Readings in social psychology.* New York: Holt, 1958. Pp. 437–447.

BALES, R. F. Personal communication, 1968.

BALES, R. F. *Personality and interpersonal behavior.* New York: Holt, 1970.

BALES, R. F., & SLATER, P. E. Role differentiation in small decision-making groups. In T. Parsons, R. F. Bales, et al. (Eds.), *Family, socialization and interaction process.* New York: Free Press, 1955. Pp. 259–306.

BALES, R. F., & SLATER, P. E. Notes on "role differentiation in small decision-making groups": Reply to Dr. Wheeler. *Sociometry,* 1957, **20,** 152–155.

BALES, R. F., STRODTBECK, F. L., MILLS, T. M., & ROSEBOROUGH, M. E. Channels of communication in small groups. *American Sociological Review,* 1951, **16,** 461–468.

BURKE, P. J. Authority relations and disruptive behavior in small discussion groups. *Sociometry,* 1966, **29,** 237–250.

BURKE, P. J. The development of task and social-emotional role differentiation. *Sociometry,* 1967, **30,** 379–392.

BURKE, P. J. Role differentiation and the legitimation of task activity. *Sociometry,* 1968, **31,** 404–411.

BURKE, P. J. Scapegoating: An alternative to role differentiation. *Sociometry,* 1969, **32,** 159–168. (a)

BURKE, P. J. Task and social-emotional leadership role performance. Mimeograph, 1969. (b)

DAVIS, J. A. *Great books and small groups.* New York: Free Press, 1961.

DIXON, W. J. (Ed.), *BMD biomedical computing programs.* Los Angeles, Calif.: Health Sciences Computing Facility, Department of Preventive Medicine and Public Health, School of Medicine, University of California, 1965.

FESTINGER, L. A theory of social comparison processes. *Human Relations,* 1954, **7,** 117–140.

FESTINGER, L., SCHACHTER, S., & BACK, K. The operation of group standards. In D. Cartwright & A. Zander (Eds.), *Group dynamics.* New York: Harper & Row, 1960, Pp. 241–259.

HARMON, H. *Modern factor analysis.* Chicago: University of Chicago Press, 1968.

HEINICKE, C., & BALES, R. F. Developmental trends in the structure of small groups. *Sociometry,* 1953, **16,** 7–38.

LEIK, R. Instrumentality and emotionality in family interaction. *Sociometry,* 1963, **26,** 131–145.

LEVINGER, G. Task and social behavior in marriage. *Sociometry,* 1964, **27,** 433–448.

MANN, R. Dimensions of individual performance in small groups under task and social-emotional conditions. *Journal of Abnormal and Social Psychology*, 1961, **62,** 674–682.

MILLER, L. K., & HAMBLIN, R. C. Interdependence, differential rewarding and productivity. *American Sociological Review*, 1963, **28,** 768–778.

OLMSTED, M. *The Small Group*. New York: Random House, 1959.

SCHACHTER, S. Deviation, rejection, and communication. In D. Cartwright & A. Zander (Eds.), *Group dynamics*. New York: Harper & Row, 1960. Pp. 260–285.

SECORD, P., & BACKMAN, C. *Social psychology*. New York: McGraw-Hill, 1964.

SIEGEL, S. *Nonparametric statistics*. New York: McGraw-Hill, 1956.

SLATER, P. E. Role differentiation in small groups. *American Sociological Review*, 1955, **20,** 300–310.

VERBA, S. *Small groups and political behavior*. Princeton, N.J.: Princeton University Press, 1961.

WHEELER, D. K. Notes on "Role differentiation in small decision-making groups." *Sociometry*, 1957, **20,** 145–151.

section six
CONCLUSION

In this final section, Daniel Katz, one of the most distinguished members of the discipline of social psychology, evaluates experimental social psychology from the perspective of the total field of social psychology. (For an overview of the field and its range of methodologies, see Festinger & Katz, 1953.) Katz characterizes in a succinct manner the specific virtues and limitations of the experimental approach. In doing so, he outlines both its major theoretical and methodological strengths and weaknesses emphasizing in particular the need for conceptual paradigms that consider more than one independent variable at a time without losing the theoretical and methodological rigor requisite in scientific research. It might be noted that social psychologists are indeed just beginning to recognize the necessity for developing theories and methodologies for investigating multiple causal relationships. The reader interested in such developments may wish to review the writings of Blaloch (1965), Bobbitt, Gourevitch, Miller, and Jensen, (1969), Cohen (1968), and Sonquist (1970).

Katz also emphasizes and characterizes as unfortunate the current conceptual and empirical separation between laboratory and field research. The latter is generally defined as the observation and experimental study of social behavior in "real life" situations. This separation in part reflects a historic division of labor where applied research of a descriptive and principally atheoretical nature was carried out mainly in field settings, and basic research with a stronger theoretical basis and more methodological rigor was performed within a laboratory context. It is apparent now that a more theoretical and experimental orientation is requisite to significant field research, and that simultaneously more complex, and real life situations should be investigated within the laboratory.

Furthermore, the need for communication between field and experimental research is important because in the final analysis, no matter how regularly observed or empirically validated a given relationship may be in a laboratory context, its ultimate external validity rests in its contribution to our understanding of human action and interaction in the real world. And there seems to be little doubt that social psychologists, who are increasingly confronted with the challenge to make their theories and methodologies more relevant by being more actively involved in providing theories and methods for assessing and understanding major social problems facing the society, will necessarily carry out more and more of their research in the real world.

But even granting the need for more field research, there remains the essential task of providing the field researcher with a body of principles and a set of methodologies that have been formulated and tested within the more rigorous and controlled setting of the laboratory. This indeed remains the critical task for the field of experimental social psychology. And it has been the major purpose of this volume to provide detailed examples of some of the more important conceptual and experimental paradigms in experimental social psychology, as well as to discuss some of the major theoretical and methodological problems confronting those who are working towards a scientific explanation of social behavior.

REFERENCES

BLALOCH, H., JR. Theory building and the concept of interaction. *American Sociological Review,* 1965, **30,** 374–380.

BOBBITT, R., GOUREVITCH, V., MILLER, L., & JENSEN, G. Dynamics of social interaction behavior: A computerized procedure for analyzing trends, patterns and sequences. *Psychological Bulletin,* 1969, **71,** 110–121.

COHEN, J. Multiple regression as a general data analytic system. *Psychological Bulletin,* 1968, **70,** 426–443.

FESTINGER, L., & KATZ, D. (Eds.), *Research methods in the behavioral sciences.* New York: Holt, 1953.

SONQUIST, J. *Multivariate model building: The validation of a search strategy.* Ann Arbor, Mich.: Institute for Social Research, 1970.

17

SOME FINAL CONSIDERATIONS ABOUT EXPERIMENTATION IN SOCIAL PSYCHOLOGY

Daniel Katz

The great appeal of the experimental method is its power of transcending experiential knowledge in rearranging sequences of events. In our own experience we often wish we could turn back the clock to do things differently in the hope of more propitious outcomes. When situations arise which seem similar to those previously experienced, we try to avoid past mistakes, but we are limited by two factors: (a) we lack knowledge of the comparability of the situations, and (b) we lack knowledge of the specific interaction of relevant variables with respect to given outcomes. Only scientific experimentation which defies the irreversibility of historical process can rearrange events so that we know exactly what led to what. The wisdom of individual and group experience provides useful guidelines but one never knows when such wisdom will prove fallacious because of its inexact character. The empathic insights of the artistic genius furnish a deep understanding of human nature and suggestive theories of causal processes, but again at the level of rough guidelines rather than exact laws. In history and much of social science available records are systematically explored and attempts made at deriving consistent patterns of events. Valuable as systematizing is, it can only attempt imaginary reconstruction of social reality. Only the experimental method can actually rearrange the patterns of social reality. This is why, as James Conant pointed out (1947), only experimental science can develop a cumulative body of knowledge in the form of principles and laws. The study of the humanities accumulates materials over time but does not develop tested principles of an ever-increasing level of generalization. Nor has there been any cumulative growth of artistic insight into human nature. With all the abundance of creative talent and the brilliant writing of our times, modern authors tell us no more about the human mind and heart than did Shakespeare or Homer, and often not as much. Only science has been characterized by the cumulative nature of its generalized knowledge.

The great power of experimental science in defying the dimension of time and arresting and sending back the moving finger also sets its limitations. For only within some contexts can the factor of time be ignored and by the temporal factor we mean the complex dynamic patterning of events which have their effect upon future events. Some processes are just not reversible. We cannot deal adequately with the aging process by dealing with people who have already aged. We need to take people at younger age levels and follow them over time. Here we have the advantage of the availability of such groups. But for some problems, it is as if we had to work only with the aged. We may have a temporal patterning of events leading to war or revolution where the historical process is critical. It is not so much that the present complexity of patterns makes experimentation with simulated variables difficult, as that their temporal patterning is difficult to reproduce within a laboratory setting. For example, the Arab-Israeli conflict in the Mideast reflects the cumulation of years of history, and it would be unwise to attempt a simulated model that would try to reproduce the major significant variables present in the conflict. What could be done would be to zero in on some social psychological processes involved in the conflict, such as the reactive character of threat, rather than attempt to deal with the conflict itself as part of a historical process.

TYPES OF EXPERIMENTS AND THE AMOUNT OF INFORMATION THEY PROVIDE

The experimental models used in social psychology vary greatly in their effective use of experimentation to develop cumulative and generalized knowledge. Types of experiments conceivably could be arranged on a nominal scale of the amount of information they provide from the extreme of *definitional demonstrations* to the extreme of *critical tests of theory*. At any rate, the extremes are not difficult to identify. The definitional demonstration is little more than a successful measure of experimental take. Namely, the experimenter has demonstrated that in fact the subjects are following instructions, and that he has been able to operationalize his concept. This is an important part of the experimental process in social psychology, but on occasion such demonstrations are presented as complete experiments. For example, it is not enough to show that under conformity pressures people will conform; it is necessary, as in the work of Asch, to show the relationship of conformity to other variables (1956). Nonetheless, preliminary work to establish reliable operational measures is important in a field in which theoretical concepts are often not readily translatable into clear and direct manipulations. If we do not start by developing reliable measures of our concepts, the interpretation of findings of relationship becomes difficult. If they are positive, what is it we have found significantly related; if negative, then is there truly no relationship, or did we not measure reliably what we thought we were measuring? We would probably make greater advances in our field if most social researchers could have a year or more to develop their methodology before they attempted the substantive experiments.

A second type of experiment carries us beyond the demonstrational definition in providing descriptive information. An experimental paradigm will be used for different groups and for different situations to accumulate findings rather than to establish theoretical relationships. Much of the work of the Prisoner's Dilemma games has been of this nature. The characteristic reactions of people to the gaming situation have been established, but less attention has been paid to an experimental attack upon why they behave as they do, or how such behavior relates to behavior in other settings. The early work on prestige suggestion was also of this nature. Experiments demonstrated that the prestige of the source could affect political opinions, evaluations of literary passages, aesthetic preferences for paintings, and almost any type of social judgment, but the experimental attack was not directed at the theoretical explanation of the common findings.

We have followed two approaches in accumulating descriptive information. One is exemplified by the technological advance of a clearly controlled situation as in the Prisoner's Dilemma game. There the experimenter's game is to accumulate knowledge about the reactions of varying groups of subjects in this setting. Here technology rather than theory determines the objective of the experiment. The other approach is to seize upon some common observation from everyday life and confirm it through manipulations in the laboratory as in the experiments on prestige suggestion. Both approaches have their usefulness in that descriptive knowledge suggests the nature of theoretical problems that need exploration. Especially when descriptive studies show some inconsistencies (now you see it and now you don't), the experimenter is stimulated to plan deeper investigations. The technological approach has some advantages over the transfer of the popular observation into a laboratory setting, in that it generally presents a neater and more clearly specified setting which is easier for other experimenters to replicate. Hence when it can be expanded to test theory, it starts from a more precise base. The demonstration of relationships observed in daily experience also has its advantages. Not only is the failure to confirm what seems to be the obvious a stimulus to more thinking and theorizing about the problem, but the relationships under study are less artifactual than the reactions to an unusual gaming situation.

We move further along the continuum of informative research with experiments testing propositions about the assumptions and properties of a theoretical concept. The search here is for a theoretical principle that will furnish the basis for predicting a variety of specific outcomes in a restricted area of knowledge. The properties of the concept have to be developed with respect to the psychological processes involved. With the analysis provided by this theoretical specification, it is then possible to test the validity of the assumed operations and relationships. Moreover, the theoretical analysis in terms of psychological processes allows the concept to be tied to other psychological concepts and to other theoretical formulations. Thus the Festinger theory of cognitive dissonance assumes that cognitive inconsistency has the properties of a drive. In 1967, both Cottrell and Wack, and Waterman and Katkin, in a direct experimental attack upon the issues, demonstrated that this was in fact the case. This was more than a demonstration of experimental take because the measures of energized behavior were different from the production of dissonance. Moreover, testing a basic assumption of the nature of the concept provides bridges to other theoretical knowledge; in this case dissonance now can be seen as a special case of psychological drives. Similarly, Festinger's theoretical analysis of the nature and properties of group cohesion and the experimental attack upon them was not so much a definitional demonstration of a variable as the establishment of a theoretical construct from which predictions could be made (1950).

Closely related to the testing of assumptions about a single concept is the elaboration of theory with specifications about the relationships among variables —for example, the interaction of group cohesion with patterns of leadership to produce group outcomes of various types. Most of our experimental paradigms have been weak in that they have developed around research on the properties of a single concept. This kind of experimentation is the efficient way to begin a science because it permits firm findings within a very narrow frame of reference. And the nature of experimentation calls for restricting the full play of forces as they operate in the natural world. But as science progresses, its many individual experiments and programs cumulate to broaden the scope of its knowledge and the development of more comprehensive or more general theories. And such theoretical development calls for more elaborate programs of research to test the complex relationships among variables. Thus far we have been more successful in moving from definitional demonstrations to the building up of knowledge about a single concept than we have in experimentation about processes and interactions. We know a good deal about dissonance, need achievement and other specific motives, and defense mechanisms but we do not know how these factors interact—how, for example, some of these factors affect the mode of dissonance reduction or how they may have helped to create it.

To state it in other terms, we need to move from experiments that establish construct validity to experiments which in their theoretical specifications can handle the greater share of the variance in the obtained responses. It is important to establish that an independent variable does have a statistically significant effect even though it accounts for a small fraction of the variance, but it is also important to know what patterning of variables takes account of the major share of the variance. The displacement of aggression supposedly produced by frustration is not sufficient, as Berkowitz has shown, to enable us to predict to expressions of hostility toward scapegoat groups (1962). His own experimentation has inquired into many of the related variables with interesting outcomes but we still do not have a comprehensive theory according to which we could predict safely about the specifics of displaced aggression.

Part of the problem is the stage of development of an experimental science. There has to be some technological growth and some accumulation of firm findings before we move into experimentation dealing with more complex matters. But this is only part of the story, in that much depends upon the kind and quality of theorizing which is only partly determined by the stage of technological development of a field. We shall return to this problem in the final section.

At the opposite end of the spectrum from definitional demonstration, we come to those experiments that pose critical tests of competing theories. Two theories may apply to similar sets of situations and sometimes one, sometimes another seems to account for more of the variance. The precise specification of the conditions under which one theory holds and the other does not is not only critical for the specific theories, but for the development of our science. When experiments can be devised to furnish such information, we will be over the hump in our development. Included in this type of experimentation would be the confrontation of theories that predict different outcomes. In general the problem with our theories is that in many instances, they do not lead to different predictions, nor in fact to different predictions from what the man on the street would make. Many predictions from learning and expectation theory are of this character. Whereas it is important to demonstrate the proposed relationship no matter how obvious it may seem, it is even more important to attempt experiments which will show how and why one theory is superior to another. One reason for the interest in dissonance theory was that it attempted critical experiments in which it opposed its predictions to predictions from conventional learning theory.

TECHNICAL PROBLEMS IN EXPERIMENTATION

In spite of the major advances in experimental technology there are still weaknesses in our practices which need to be remedied. Six such weaknesses are: (a) insufficient measurement of the dependent variable, (b) the neglect of sampling procedures with respect to subjects, (c) the neglect of sampling procedures with respect to stimuli and situations, (d) the confounding of replication with other purposes, (e) the use of intricate and unassessed complex manipulations, and (f) the failure to come to grips with the problems created by the deception of subjects.

Insufficient Measurement of the Dependent Variable. Many experimental studies that employ careful manipulations of conditions rely upon the scantiest measures of the dependent variable by using one or two direct questions in a limited questionnaire for subjects—questionnaires which would not be accepted as good measures in field research. The attempt to get away from paper and pencil techniques through careful arrangement of conditions is not followed through by actual behavioral observations or performance tests in measuring the dependent variable.

Another weakness in assessing changes in the dependent variable is the restriction of measurement to a single point in time—generally immediately following the experimental manipulation. Experiments are based upon the creation, or influencing, of a change process: yet experimenters are generally satisfied with a single cross-sectional slice of the process. Some of the most interesting findings in experimentation on attitude change have resulted from followups after several weeks of the tests administered at the end of the experiment. Hovland and Weiss set a good example here which has been followed by but a few researchers (1952). The rationale for not extending measurements beyond the experimental session is that the experiment is really over and that all sorts of uncontrolled factors can affect further measures. Clear as is this rationale, it is still true that the use of measures over time can add considerably to our information about effects some of which quickly wash out, others which persist, and still others which undergo modification. Moreover, the temporal dimension can be more fully exploited within the controlled experiment by repeated or continuing observations before the subjects are dismissed. And experiments can often be extended beyond the one or two hours permitted by the introductory course providing the subject pool. Another way of dealing with the change process resulting from the experimentally induced setting is to use counter instructions after the first effect has been measured.

The Neglect of Sampling Procedures with Respect to Subjects. For many types of experimental studies the random assignment of subjects to different experimental conditions obviates the need for the sampling of people. The generalization is, of course, limited, but this can easily be remedied by replicating the experiment with other groups of subjects. The closer the process under investigation is to basic psychological and biological factors, the less important is the sampling problem. College sophomores are not likely to differ in these basic respects from mature businessmen, housewives, or coal miners. The closer we are to social variables, however, the more important replication among varying groups becomes. Thus Wallach and his colleagues (1962) rightly moved toward replication of their findings on group risk taking among male business school students to liberal arts females. Similarly Milgram extended his work on obedience among student subjects to nonacademic groups (1963). The same type of replication is badly needed for investigations that can be affected by social values and social structure.

There is another type of experiment, however, that does require a sampling procedure for subjects, and this has to do with investigations calling for comparisons across groups. For example, if an investigator compares hospitalized patients with normal individuals on the effects of an experimental manipulation, the study calls for a sampling design. Without an adequate sampling design, the normal group is likely to be heavily weighted with hospital attendants. It is of interest that in dealing with group comparisons the experimentalist is much sloppier in a critical part of his methodology than the field researcher. One illustration can be found in the experiments that compare conformity responses across nations. The Asch type techniques can be faithfully reproduced, but comparing the findings of different subject groups representing no known sample of no known universe is a speculative enterprise.

The Neglect of Sampling Procedures with Respect to Stimuli and Situations. There is some recognition of the sampling problem with respect to subjects, although more noticeable in the breach than in the observance; but there is less recognition of the importance of sampling the stimulus situations created or manipulated in the laboratory. The stimulus situation may represent some particular combination of factors or it may represent just one point on a wide continuum of points with differing values. Some of the work on the effects of motivation and anxiety on accomplishment in relation to the nature of the task constitutes a notable exception. Here it has been shown that varying the degree of anxiety and utilizing different types of tasks lead to more valid and interesting generalizations about the problem. The controversy about the role of race and belief congruence in attitudes toward members of other groups requires much more of a sampling of stimulus situations than has thus far been attempted, although the work of Triandis is a step forward in this direction (1965). Admittedly what is needed here is a program of experimentation when dealing with a given problem.

An adequate sample of the variables under consideration calls for a representation of many sample points along the dimension of the strength or intensity of a given variable. The weaknesses of the use of extreme groups to give only two points on the continuum have often been pointed out. Many experimenters try to meet the difficulty by including three points. This is a considerable advance, but the generalizations about the curves of the experimental groups go much beyond what the measures of three degrees of intensity would justify. All the scaling problems familiar in attitude research apply here. Often we do not know where these three points really belong on the continuum in question. The high may really be in the intermediate range and the middle point may be in the low range.

Factor analytic techniques can be profitably combined with experimental procedures to assure more adequate sampling of stimulus properties. Traditionally, however, there has been too much reliance upon statistical manipulations for pulling out factors, and too little upon adequate sampling of relevant data. The holes in the data can never be corrected by subsequent statistical manipulation since the researcher has no knowledge of the character of the missing data.

The Confounding of Replication with Other Purposes.   Important as replication is for the development of a science, it is often defeated in social psychological experiments by the failure to carry through a clear duplication of an original experiment. Often the researcher tries both to replicate and to introduce some variations of his own and ends up with findings at variance with the original study and we are no further ahead. The reason for this obvious error is that experimenters often feel that the variation introduced does not affect the basic original manipulation. This, of course, cannot be assumed. Sometimes the variation is attempted with additional groups beyond those used in the replicated experiment. This procedure is excellent in theory in repeating the original experiment and the opportunity for providing additional information about some of the variables involved. It needs to be carried out with extreme care in that the total context may affect the different groups through informal communication not under experimental control.

The Use of Intricate and Unassessed Complex Manipulations.   Elaborate procedures can have many effects other than that of the experimental condition the researcher has in mind. The Chapanises (1964) have made this point effectively in their critique of dissonance experiments. By the time the subject is ready for the experimental task he may have been subject to such a range of influences, to establish an experimental condition, that it is not clear what the experimental condition really is. It is almost as if a premium were placed upon the ingenuity of the experimenter in devising imaginary situations to confound the subject. The attempt is often successful in confounding the subject, but the results of the experiment can also be confounded.

The Failure to Come to Grips with the Problems Created by the Deception of Subjects.   Apart from the ethical issues of deceiving and sometimes traumatizing subjects, there is the continuing problem of the effect of manipulations of this type upon experimental outcomes and their interpretations. This is especially true in that experimentation occurs in a social context and continues overtime so that natural processes of social communication, not under the control of the experimenter, can affect the perceptions and expectations of subjects as they enter and proceed through an experiment. Though the experimenter may ask the subject at the completion of his task not to talk to other students about it since there are still groups to run, not every student complies. The forces for communication among peers are often much greater than an experimenter may realize. Even though instructions not to communicate are successful within a single experimental setting, there is the larger social process of communication. Feedback after the experiment, publication and discussion of experiments both at the scientific and popular levels, accounts of personal experience, and rumors all contribute to the cultural climate of expectations at a given university or one of its subcultures. Many a student enters the experimental situation with his own hypotheses and his own expectations of why he is there and what he is supposed to do. A not uncommon reaction of the experimenter is to meet this challenge with even fancier deceptions so that a game develops between subject and experimenter.

There is no simple solution to the problem of the interpretations that subjects give to the experimental setting in which they are placed. One procedure is to try to insure that such perceptions have little or no influence in altering the effect of the experimental manipulation. This often requires a large program of experimentation with various types of subjects and with clear confirmation of predictions for a series of specific conditions. Another procedure is to leave the home campus and search for the naive subject. Herbert Kelman has suggested greater use of experimental situations in which subjects are not deceived but given information about the true nature of the experiment (1967). There are many areas of investigation in which deception is not a necessary part of the experimental approach. A related procedure is to use hypothetical situations to which the subject is asked to respond. He is asked to assume a given role and to act as if certain things were true. This is a less powerful experimental technique, but there are areas in which it is useful.

THE NEED FOR NEW THEORETICAL ORIENTATIONS
AND CONCEPTUALIZATION

The interaction between theory and findings which characterizes a science has interesting implications for the present stage of the development of social psychology. We have moved away from the global theories of the past which attempted comprehensive models of social man. Much of this theorizing was too loose in its formulation to provide an adequate framework for generating specific predictions for experimentation or clear interpretations of results. It was helpful in guiding experimenters to types of problems and in fact one could readily distinguish the school of thought represented in any specific piece of work. Behaviorists worked on problems of social facilitation, on the effects of the prestige of numbers and authority, whereas field theorists worked on group atmosphere and cognitive restructuring. Increasingly, however, the lack of fit between theory and experimental methodology led to more emphasis on the problem and less concern with theoretical orientation. The interest in recent years has been in building up a firm body of knowledge about a given concept. Whether a variable is suggested by one theory or another is less important than its ease of operational definition and manipulation and relevance to the problem. In fact, many experimenters are no longer identified with a given theoretical approach.

This is a necessary and healthy development in the early stages of an experimental science. The more global theories have to be abandoned in the interests of precise information about the operation of specific processes. There are genuine advantages in building firm knowledge around limited problem areas. Although the world is full of a related number of things, we have to start somewhere in our research, select some researchable question, and neglect others. There are, however, limits that need to be recognized in this trend. In the first place, the specific researchable question may take over to the exclusion of any theoretical concern and the results may not contribute significantly to the understanding and prediction of human behavior. Of the thousands of experimental studies published in social psychology in the past 20 years, the number that supplies new information to a cumulative body of knowledge is surprisingly small. A great deal of the experimental effort has been without impact not because of poor method, but because of the lack of ideas behind the work. The development of experimental social psychology has been costly if the energy input is compared to the significant output.

In the second place, where experimentation has had some theoretical rationale and some constructive outcome, it has been generally in the production of findings about a single concept. Although this is a necessary stage in development, we need to be concerned with the isolation of these pockets of knowledge. Our objective of a science of social psychology is an integrated body of principles and findings, and not the collection of unrelated pieces of empiricism. We have gone beyond the necessary limitation of acquiring firm information in restricting experimentation to a narrow problem area, when we have failed to relate the processes studied to similar processes under investigation in other areas or to the older body of psychological knowledge. It is not essential to put on theoretical blinders to do pioneering experimental work. The tendency toward the isolation of workers in different fields of investigation is fostered by the preference for autonomy in labeling one's own work. The concepts and variables seem more original to the investigator if he has renamed them with his own terms. Thus we have created more separation and more disorganization in the field than required in the development of a science. Some of this needless confusion is in evidence when one reads integrative and review articles in journals and handbooks. Although different authors supposedly review different materials in their separate articles, there is considerable overlap in the experiments and concepts covered. The various pieces on social influence, power, leadership, communication, and group process will deal with many of the same theoretical issues, concepts, and even the same experimental findings. Nor could it be otherwise. But if it is virtually impossible to avoid bringing together these various materials when taking supposedly different points of view toward them, why ignore these relationships when doing experimental work?

Although the more theoretically oriented experimenter rejects the general type of theories of the past, he frequently follows the same tendency of seeking a single principle of sufficient generality to cut across much of man's thinking and behavior. He is in effect creating a model of man save that it is far less comprehensive a model than that of the older theorist. Hull's behavioristic model, for example, is less simplistic than that of many of his successors. Field theory in Lewin's hand dealt with a much wider range of issues and problems than the single concept approach of some of his followers.

There is concern, then, that without some new theoretical orientations our field may stay arrested in its present stage of development for too long a period. If we merely increase the quantity of our efforts in experimental social psychology in the next 15 years without any change in direction, we will run into diminishing returns. We should not try to retrace our steps to revive old theories, but we should seek to go beyond the single concept stage of theorizing so prevalent today. In such a reorientation we need to be wary of the revival in new clothes of the old tendency to take a global theoretical approach and then move to some specific experimental manipulation without going through the intervening steps of spelling out the processes implied. Specifically this can be seen in the testing of very general concepts through a mathematical model without specification and manipulation of the psychological processes involved. In other words, we do not need a revival of the overly general theories of the past, but we do need to give more attention to theoretical issues that cut across highly restricted areas of study.

It is difficult to foretell where, how, and why new theoretical developments will arise to infuse new life into experimental social psychology. The apparent inconsistencies in findings in dealing with the same issue are often productive of new theory, and the existing pockets of knowledge provide opportunities for seeking relationships among them. In the past, psychology has benefited from the emergence of new theories in the other sciences, and our present interest in a general systems approach indicates that this is still a likely source of ideas.

We do have available for generating new conceptions a resource that has been underutilized in the past, namely research in field settings. Field research is weaker in its methodology than laboratory experimentation in the very nature of the two approaches, but it is much closer to social reality and richer in substantive content. Although the two approaches have not been divorced, they have been sufficiently isolated as to qualify for legal separation. There is no real logic in the lack of communication that does exist between them. It is true that a field researcher may be occupied with socially significant problems at one point of time that are not the theoretically significant issues for the science of psychology at the same time period. Nonetheless, the two are related and social psychological theory at some point must have a bearing on its subject matter and must stand the test of practice. Nor is the field researcher concerned only with the phenotypical aspects of social problems, since he too seeks some general principles. The reason for the separation of the approaches is in part a matter of the narrow concentration that goes with specialization and in part the defensiveness of people in an insecure period of development—the field researchers insecure in their methodology, the experimentalists insecure in their scientism.

The great contribution field research can make in supplying new ideas for the development of the field is in discovery. The strength of the laboratory experiment is in testing a hypothesis. But the hypothesis tested is often trivial or derived from some obvious common sense observation, or it grows out of the technology of the experiment. The discovery of new variables and new relationships is minimized in the laboratory. In field work, however, new issues and problems often confront the researcher. Discoveries are not assured by researchers working at the level of social reality, but they are often precluded by the conventional form of the hypothesis-testing experiment. To the extent that experimental social psychology cuts itself off from field research it will be deprived of a most important input for theoretical stimulation and growth.

It is of interest that two of the greatest contributors to social psychology as a science, Floyd H. Allport and Kurt Lewin, were both devoted to laboratory experimentation and field research. Allport's systematic laboratory experiments on social influence were the beginning of experimental social psychology, but he was also a pioneer in field investigation and sent his students into the school, factory, and church to observe behavior and to question people. Similarly Kurt Lewin developed experimentation not only on group process but in many other areas of social psychology. And again field studies and action research were among his most important contributions to psychology. In both cases the interaction of laboratory findings and field results were important in the modification and generation of theoretical concepts. As has been noted, we cannot recapture the past, but we can learn from it, and the lesson here is the importance of interrelating the work of the laboratory and the field.

One of the most impressive advances in social psychology has been in the field of social motivation through the work of McClelland and his school (1961). These investigators, starting with three widely recognized motives in our society, developed experimental measures of them within the laboratory, conducted research in field settings, and investigated the conditions and processes of these social motives in the laboratory. The vitality and breadth of this work profited from the mixture of laboratory and field approaches.

The contributions of H. Guetzkow on group process and group conflict have also been in the tradition of utilizing the strengths of both the laboratory and the field (1962). The recent work on the attitudinal effects of mere exposure of R. Zajonc (1968) is an interesting combination of correlational studies and formal experiments.

Experimentalists and field researchers should try to narrow the gap between the social psychology of the laboratory and the social psychology of field research. There is too slavish a following of experimental science by the laboratory worker without consideration of substance. But technology is a means, not an end. Many experiments may follow from its development and from the elaboration of mathematical models. Nevertheless this work is no substitute for ideas that come from our own subject matter, from observation, insights, and hunches about social behavior. It is possible to be so impressed by what is happening in other sciences and in mathematical theory that one neglects his own field of study. Social psychological theory, however, is not going to come from physics or mathematics. It will have to grow out of its own realm of phenomena. The various fields of science interchange with mutual profit forms of technology and general points of view. But no field can live very long on borrowings from its neighbors without developing some capital of its own. When there is more adequate recognition of this principle, experimental social psychology may enter a new period of progress.

REFERENCES

ASCH, S. E. Studies of independence and conformity. *Psychological Monographs,* 1956, **70**(416), 1–70.

ATKINSON, J. W. *An introduction to motivation.* New York: Van Nostrand, 1964.

BERKOWITZ, L. *Aggression: A social-psychological analysis.* New York: McGraw-Hill, 1962.

CHAPANIS, N. P., & CHAPANIS, A. Cognitive dissonance: Five years later. *Psychological Bulletin,* 1964, **61**, 1–22.

CONANT, J. B. *On understanding science: An historical approach.* New Haven, Conn.: Yale University Press, 1947.

COTTRELL, N. B., & WACK, D. L. Energizing effects of cognitive dissonance upon dominant and subordinate responses. *Journal of Personality and Social Psychology,* 1967, **6**, 132–138.

FESTINGER, L. Informal social communication. *Psychological Review,* 1950, **57**, 271–282.

GUETZKOW, H. *Simulation in social science: Readings.* Englewood Cliffs, N.J.: Prentice-Hall, 1962.

HOVLAND, C. I., & WEISS, W. The influence of source credibility on communication effectiveness. *Public Opinion Quarterly,* 1952, **15,** 635–650.

KELMAN, H. C. The human use of human subjects. *Psychological Bulletin,* 1967, **67,** 1–11.

MCCLELLAND, D. C. *The achieving society.* New York: Van Nostrand, 1961.

MILGRAM, S. Behavioral study of obedience. *Journal of Abnormal and Social Psychology,* 1963, **67,** 371–378.

TRIANDIS, H. C. Some studies of social distance. In J. D. Steiner & M. Fishbein (Eds.), *Current studies in social psychology.* New York: Holt, 1965. Pp. 207–217.

WALLACH, M. A., KOGAN, N. & BEM, D. J. Group influence on individual risk taking. *Journal of Abnormal and Social Psychology,* 1962, **65,** 75–86.

WATERMAN, C. K., & KATKIN, E. S. Energizing (dynamogenic) effect of cognitive dissonance on task performance. *Journal of Personality and Social Psychology,* 1967, **6,** 126–131.

ZAJONC, R. B. Attitudinal effects of mere exposure. *Journal of Personality and Social Psychology,* Monograph supplement. June 1968, **9**(2, Pt. 2), 1–27.

appendix

SOME STATISTICAL
TERMS AND CONCEPTS[1]

David M. Messick

It has been said that the fundamental axiom of social psychology is: "It depends." Almost any reasonable generalization regarding social behavior will be true for some people under some circumstances, but not true for others under different circumstances. Consequently, one of the major endeavors of experimental social psychology is to determine the limits of our generalizations: to whom do they apply and under what circumstances? As the limits of old generalizations are defined, new generalizations emerge which incorporate the old ones as special cases. Thus social psychological theory becomes richer and more complex.

As this occurs, research hypotheses grow correspondingly complex. The necessity of different types of control groups becomes evident. The number of independent variables needed to test hypotheses increases. Different subject populations need to be compared in similar and differing situations. As the problems become more complex, the tools required to solve them become more sophisticated.

Thus a solid working knowledge of experimental design and a functional grasp of the principles of statistical analysis are rapidly becoming indispensable to experimental social psychologists. The many imaginative experiments and statistical analyses reported in the chapters of this book clearly evidence this fact. It should be just as obvious that a brief glossary can strive to do little more than provide some definitions and explanations that may clarify some of the statistical techniques and concepts mentioned in the preceding chapters.

A GLOSSARY

Additive effects: See *Analysis of variance.*

After only design: See *Design.*

Algebraic sum: The sum of a set of scores in which the sign of a score is not neglected. The algebraic sum of *2* and *—3* is *—1.*

Alpha level: See *Significance level.*

[1] I would like to thank Francis Campos for his help in preparing this glossary.

Analysis of covariance: A type of analysis of variance in which adjustments are made in the dependent variable to account for individual differences as measured by an additional variable, which is correlated with the dependent variable.

Analysis of variance: This is the most frequently used statistical procedure in social psychological research. It is the technique used to analyze most experimental designs (see *Design*). Basically, analysis of variance provides techniques for partitioning or dividing up the variability in a set of scores into different components. The number of components and the meaning of those components will depend upon the specific design being analyzed. With most designs, however, there will be three types of components. The first is the *error variability*. This is the amount of variability that cannot be attributed to any of the independent variables or any combination of them. A *main effect* refers to the amount of variability that can be attributed to each independent variable. There will be one main effect for each variable. The final type of component is the *interaction effect*. Interaction effects measure the amount of variability associated with each combination of independent variables above and beyond the main effects for those variables. *Higher order interactions* refer to interactions of three or more variables. Interaction effects will be large to the extent that the treatment means cannot be expressed as the *sum* of effects of the independent variables. Thus, interaction effects occur when the variables combine in a *nonadditive* fashion. If they combine *additively*, interactions will be small.

Asymptotic: Refers to the limiting value a function approaches as the independent variable increases (or, sometimes, decreases).

Before-after design: See *Design*.

Binomial test: See *Sign test*.

Ceiling effect: If a base rate for a behavior is very high, it becomes difficult in many cases to increase it. For example, if one has a very positive attitude toward an issue, it may be more difficult to make his attitude more positive than it would be if he had only a moderate attitude. In the latter case there would be more room for change.

Central tendency: Some score which best typifies or summarizes a set of scores. Both the mean and the median are measures of central tendency.

χ^2 *(chi-squared):* See *Chi-squared test*.

Chi-squared test: A statistical procedure used to test the equality of two or more proportions.

Completely randomized design: See *Design*.

Conditional probability: A probability that is adjusted to account for or to incorporate the effects of known, pertinent information. The probability of randomly selecting the number 7 from the first 10 digits (0–9), for example, is 1/10. If we learn that the number to be selected is an odd number, then the conditional probability of selecting 7 becomes 1/5.

Construct validity: See *Validity*.

Contingency table: A means of displaying the results of cross-classifying a sample of subjects according to two or more variables. For example, if one classified a sample by sex and political affiliation, the table would list the number of male Republicans, female Republicans, male Democrats, and female Democrats.

Control: A control, or *control group,* is used in an experimental design to establish a base line against which the effect of an experimental treatment can be assessed.

Correlation: Refers to the degree to which two variables are "co-related" or the degree to which they vary together. A person's height and his shoe size are correlated variables. The taller one is, the larger his foot is likely to be. The correlation, in this case, is *positive:* the larger one variable, the larger the other. The correlation between intelligence and errors on a reasoning test would be *negative:* the more intelligent, the fewer errors. The *correlation coefficient, r,* is an index that measures the degree of correlation. It is *0* if the variables are uncorrelated, *+1* if they are perfectly positively correlated, and *−1* if they are perfectly negatively correlated.

Dependent variable: See *Variable.*

Design: Most generally, design, or *experimental design,* refers to the organization or structure of an experiment. The design of an experiment largely dictates the types of statistical analysis that will be employed to analyze the experiment. One important aspect of a design is whether one or more than one measurement is to be made on each subject. If a subject is to be observed and tested in more than one level of an independent variable then the design is called a *repeated measures design.* One type of repeated measure design commonly used in social pyschological research is the *before-after design,* in which the relevant variable (e.g., an attitude scale) is measured both before and after the application of the experimental manipulation (e.g., hearing a persuasive communication). In an *after only design,* the before measurement is not made and it is assumed that the groups are initially similar with respect to the relevant variable. A *completely randomized design* is one in which subjects are randomly assigned to the different experimental conditions. In a *randomized block design* subjects are divided into groups or "blocks" on the basis of a variable considered to be important to the task at hand (e.g., intelligence in a learning task). Subjects within a block are then randomly assigned to the experimental conditions. In a *factorial design* employing more than one independent variable, each level of any variable is paired with each level of all other variables. A *Latin square design* is very similar to the randomized block design. It allows the experimenter to simultaneously block two different variables.

Distribution: A distribution, or *probability distribution,* is a list, often displayed graphically, of the possible values of a variable with the probability associated with each value. The most commonly used distributions in social psychological research are the normal distribution, the t-distribution, and the F-distribution.

Error: A *Type 1 error* is made when one falsely concludes that the null or chance hypothesis is false. The probability of a Type 1 error is the significance level. A *Type 2 error* is made when one incorrectly fails to reject a false null hypothesis. *Error variance* refers to the amount of variability of the scores in an experiment that cannot be attributed to known or measured factors.

Error variability: See *Analysis of variance.*

Error variance: See *Error.*

Expected value: The expected value of a variable is the mean of the distribution of the variable.

External validity: See *Validity.*

F-statistic: See *F-test.*

F or *F-test:*   Probably the most widely used statistical test in social psychological research. This test, based on the F-distribution, tests the equality of two independent estimates of a population variance. The *F-statistic* is the ratio of these two estimates. In analysis of variance, an estimate based on a set of means is in the numerator and an estimate based on sample variances is in the denominator. If the F-statistic is unduly large, it provides evidence that the differences among the means are larger than would be expected simply by chance. The estimates are called *mean squares.*

Face validity: See *Validity.*

Factor analysis: A statistical technique for analyzing the inter-relationships among a set of different variables. It attempts to determine the extent to which different variables are measuring common traits or attributes. If the variables are measuring a common set of underlying attributes, it becomes possible to identify those attributes (which are called *factors*) and also to determine the degree to which each variable measures each of the attributes. The indices which measure the involvement of each attribute for a given variable are called the *factor loadings* for that variable.

Factor loading: See *Factor analysis.*

Factorial design: See *Design.*

Fisher exact test: A statistical test, similar to the Chi-squared test, that can be used with very small sample sizes to test the equality of two (or more) proportions.

Function: A function is a quantitative relationship between two numerical variables. One typically expresses the dependent variable in an experiment as a function of the independent variable. The form of this relationship is often of major theoretical importance. If the function is *monotonic,* the dependent variable either increases (*monotonic increasing*) or decreases (*monotonic decreasing*) as the independent variable increases. A *non-*

monotonic function changes at least once. It may first increase and then decrease, for example, as the independent variable increases. If the dependent variable is a *linear function* of the independent variable, then it makes a straight line when plotted against the independent variable. The *slope* of a linear function is the steepness of the line. A *negative* slope means that the dependent variable *decreases* as the independent variable increases. With a *positive slope,* the dependent variable increases. A *U-shaped function,* as one might imagine, first decreases, then increases. For an *inverted U-shaped function* the opposite is true. A *multimodal function* has more than one maximum. (A U-shaped function is multimodal.) A *positively accelerated function* increases (or decreases) slowly at first with the rate of change becoming greater for larger values of the independent variable. A *negatively accelerated function* increases (or decreases) rapidly at first with the rate of change becoming less as the independent variable increases.

Heterogeneity of variance: See *Homogeneity of variance.*

Higher order interaction: See *Analysis of variance.*

Homogeneity of variance: In performing an analysis of variance or a t-test one is required to assume that the scores in the different groups were drawn from populations having the same variance. If this assumption is not true, that is, if one has evidence for *heterogeneity of variance,* then certain types of corrections are required in the statistical analysis.

Hypothesis: An assertion about the value of the parameter(s) of one or more variables. A statistical hypothesis is not the same as a research or psychological hypothesis.

Independent variable: See *Variable.*

Interaction effect: See *Analysis of variance.*

Internal validity: See *Validity.*

Interval scale: See *Scales of measurement.*

Isomorphic: Having similar or identical structures or appearances.

Kendall's coefficient of concordance: A nonparametric statistic that measures the agreement among a group of judges in their rankings of a set of stimuli. If agreement is perfect, the coefficient is $+1$, if there is no agreement, the value is 0.

Kendall's Tau: A nonparametric statistic which measures the amount of agreement between two rankings of a set of stimuli. It is similar to Spearman's rank order correlation coefficient.

Kurtosis: This refers to the relative flatness or "peakedness" of a distribution.

Latin square design: See *Design.*

Main effect: See *Analysis of variance.*

Mean: The most common measure of central tendency. It is the algebraic sum of all scores divided by the number of scores.

Mean square: An estimate of a population variance. See *F-test.*

Median: A measure of central tendency. The median is any score that divides a sample into halves so that half the scores are above the median and half the scores are below it.

Median test: A nonparametric test of the equality of central tendency of two variables. The two samples of scores are combined and the number in each sample that are above (and below) the median for all scores is noted. If both samples are drawn from populations having the same median, then about half should be above and half below for each sample.

N, n: See *Sample size.*

Nominal scale: See *Scales of measurement.*

Nonadditive effects: See *Analysis of variance.*

Nonparametric tests: Statistical tests that make no assumptions about the nature of the distribution of scores in a population.

Normal distribution: Probably the most important distribution in statistics, this is the common bell-shaped distribution that closely approximates the distribution of adult heights, weights, and I.Q. scores. Most parametric tests assume that the scores in a sample have a normal distribution.

Null hypothesis: Typically the statistical hypothesis that the result of an experiment is due only to chance.

One-tailed test: See *Two-tailed test.*

Ordered metric scale: See *Scales of measurement.*

Ordinal scale: See *Scales of measurement.*

Orthogonal: Independent; uncorrelated. If two variables are orthogonal, then knowledge of one is of no help in predicting the other.

P value (or *p*):   See *Significance level.*

Parametric tests: Statistical tests that make specific assumptions about the distribution of scores in a population. Most parametric tests assume that the distribution is a normal distribution.

Population: In statistics, a population refers to a collection of elements or individuals. A population may be real or hypothetical, finite or infinite.

Probability: Probabilities are numbers between *1* and *0* that are associated with events in such a way as to indicate the likelihoods of the events. If an event has a probability of *1*, it is certain to occur. If it has a probability of *0*, it is impossible. The smaller the probability, the less likely the event.

r: The symbol designating the correlation coefficient. See *Correlation.*

Randomized block design: See *Design.*

Rank order: The arrangement of a set of scores from the largest to the smallest (or vice versa).

Ratio scale: See *Scales of measurement.*

Reactive measure: Any means of measuring a variable in which the process of measurement may bias the resulting score. Asking a vain woman her age is a reactive measure, whereas secretively peeking at her driver's license is not.

Regression: Refers to the statistical prediction of the values of one variable through the use of one or more other variables that are correlated with the one to be predicted. One might use regression techniques to predict students' college success (measured by grade point average, say) from high school grades and SAT scores.

Repeated measures design: See *Design.*

S (or s or SD): See *Standard deviation.*

S^2 (or s^2 or SD^2): See *Variance.*

Sample: A sample is a subset of elements from a population. *Statistical inference* is the science of making inferences about populations by examining samples from these populations.

Sample size: The number of scores in a sample; usually abbreviated N or n.

Scales of measurement: Measurement scales refer to the means by which one assigns numbers to objects so as to reflect some attribute or quality of the objects. If numbers are assigned only to distinguish one object from another (e.g., numbers on athletes' shirts) the scale is called a *nominal scale.* An *ordinal scale* ranks the objects on the basis of the attribute being measured. With an *ordered metric scale*, the objects are ranked and, in addition, the differences between the objects are ranked. An *interval scale*, like the Fahrenheit scale for temperature, is more informative still. One needs only to decide which object to call "*0*" and how to define a unit difference in order to assign a number to any object. The Centigrade temperature scale defines the freezing point of water as "*0*" and the boiling point of water as 100, which implicitly defines a unit (one degree of temperature equals one one-hundredth of this range). With a *ratio scale*, "*0*" has a natural definition (as with length or weight) and one merely selects the unit (feet or yards, grams or pounds).

Σ (capital Greek sigma): A mathematical symbol indicating summation. If x is the symbol for the scores in a sample, for example, then Σx denotes the *algebraic sum* of the scores.

Sign test: A nonparametric test used when the data are pairs of scores (e.g., an individual's attitude score before and after reading a persuasive communication). The numerical difference between the scores is noted for each subject and the *sign* (+ or —) of the difference is recorded. If the before and after scores are drawn from the same population, there should not be a large difference between the number of +'s and —'s recorded. If there is a large difference, one concludes that the scores were not drawn from the same population. Also known as the *binominal test.*

Significance level: The probability of falsely rejecting the hypothesis that an obtained result is due to chance. This value is traditionally set at .05 or

.01. Also known as the *alpha level.* If the chance probability of a result is less than the significance level, it is said to be *statistically significant.* The statistical significance of a result is typically indicated by an expression such as "P < .05," which means that the chance probability of the result is less than .05. Sometimes called *P* or *P value.*

Spearman's rank order correlation coefficient: A nonparametric statistic that measures the agreement between two rankings of a set of stimuli. If the rankings are identical, the coefficient is $+1$; if the rankings are in perfect disagreement it is -1; it is 0 if there is no relationship between the rankings.

Standard deviation: The positive square root of the variance of a sample of scores. It is often used as a unit of measurement. One might say, for example, that a particular score is two standard deviations above the mean of the scores. Typically abbreviated *s, S,* or *SD.*

Standardization: A procedure that allows one to convert any set of scores to a set of scores having 0 for a mean and 1 for a variance (and standard deviation). It is useful because it allows one to compare different variables having different means and variances.

Statistical inference: See *Sample.*

t or *t-test:* This test, based on the t-distribution, is a parametric test of the equality of the means of two populations. It is used when sample sizes are relatively small and when the population variances are not known.

Two-tailed test: One uses a two-tailed test when testing the hypothesis that two population means are equal, if he is interested in detecting a difference between them *no matter which is the larger.* If it would only be of interest or importance if a specific one of the two means were larger than the other, then a *one-tailed test* should be used.

Type 1 error: See *Error.*

Type 2 error: See *Error.*

Validity: The validity of a test or an experiment refers to the extent to which the test or experiment does what it claims to do. *Construct validity* refers to the extent to which a test or experiment actually taps the theoretical concept, or *construct,* it purports to measure or manipulate. The *external validity* of an experiment is the extent to which the results of the experiment may be generalized to new contexts, situations, and individuals. *Internal validity,* on the other hand, relates to the degree to which one can be sure that an experimental result was produced by some specific factor or factors and *not* other, extraneous ones. A test or experiment has *face validity* to the extent that it superficially appears to do what it claims.

Variable: A variable refers to a set of measurements (hypothetical or real) that can be made on the elements of a population or sample. Height, weight, I.Q., eye color, hair length, or frequency of belching are all variables that could be measured for individuals. In research, an *independent variable* is one that is controlled or known by the researcher. The *dependent variable* is one that the researcher hopes to predict from his knowledge of the independent variable.

Variance: A measure of the dispersion or variability of a set of scores. It is the average squared deviation of the scores from the mean of the scores. If all scores are very close to the mean, the variance of the scores will be small; if the scores vary markedly from the mean, the variance will be large. The variance of a sample of scores is usually abbreviated s^2, S^2, or SD^2, while the variance of a population is abbreviated σ^2.

X or *x:*   A symbol typically referring to a specific dependent variable or, equivalently, to the set of scores in a sample.

AUTHOR INDEX

SUBJECT INDEX